Jazz and Popular Music in America

MUL 2380

Miami Dade College

Campbell | Martin

CENGAGE
Learning™

Australia • Brazil • Japan • Korea • Mexico • Singapore • Spain • United Kingdom • United States

Jazz and Popular Music in America`: MUL 2380, Miami Dade College

Campbell | Martin

Executive Editors:
 Maureen Staudt
 Michael Stranz

Senior Project Development Manager:
 Linda DeStefano

Marketing Specialist:
 Sara Mercurio
 Lindsay Shapiro

Senior Production / Manufacturing Manager:
 Donna M. Brown

PreMedia Supervisor:
 Joel Brennecke

Rights & Permissions Specialist:
 Kalina Hintz
 Todd Osborne

Cover Image:
 Getty Images*

* Unless otherwise noted, all cover images used by Custom Solutions, a part of Cengage Learning, have been supplied courtesy of Getty Images with the exception of the Earthview cover image, which has been supplied by the National Aeronautics and Space Administration (NASA).

© 2009 Cengage Learning

ALL RIGHTS RESERVED. No part of this work covered by the copyright herein may be reproduced, transmitted, stored or used in any form or by any means graphic, electronic, or mechanical, including but not limited to photocopying, recording, scanning, digitizing, taping, Web distribution, information networks, or information storage and retrieval systems, except as permitted under Section 107 or 108 of the 1976 United States Copyright Act, without the prior written permission of the publisher.

For product information and technology assistance, contact us at
Cengage Learning Customer & Sales Support, 1-800-354-9706

For permission to use material from this text or product, submit all requests online at **cengage.com/permissions**
Further permissions questions can be emailed to
permissionrequest@cengage.com

ISBN-13: 978-1-4240-7709-0

ISBN-10: 1-4240-7709-5

Cengage Learning
5191 Natorp Boulevard
Mason, Ohio 45040
USA

Cengage Learning is a leading provider of customized learning solutions with office locations around the globe, including Singapore, the United Kingdom, Australia, Mexico, Brazil, and Japan. Locate your local office at:
international.cengage.com/region

Cengage Learning products are represented in Canada by Nelson Education, Ltd.

For your lifelong learning solutions, visit **www.cengage.com/custom**

Visit our corporate website at **www.cengage.com**

Printed in Mexico

Miami Dade College Music

Links to college and area venues

Miami Dade College-North Campus

Music, Theatre, and Dance

The Department houses the theatre, dance and music programs and has hosted quality music and theatrical productions since the 1960's. Be sure to refer to the event schedule for the Theatre Series and Concert Series Performances located on the Miami Dade College website.

http://www.mdc.edu/north/performingarts/

Miami Dade College-Kendall Campus

Music, Theatre and Dance

On Stage is the official concert series of Miami Dade College, Kendall Campus that seeks to exhibit the combined talents of students and faculty in the Music, Theatre and Dance Department. Each season On Stage will present an exciting line-up featuring performances by accomplished artists and rising stars alike that are both entertaining and culturally significant. Because On Stage encompasses each of the performing arts - from jazz and gospel music to theatrical realism and experimental dance - there is something on our calendar for everyone.

http://www.mdc.edu/KENDALL/mtd/MTD_On_Stage_performances.asp

Miami Dade College-Wolfson Campus

Music, Theatre, and Dance

Jazz at Wolfson **Presents** is the only continuously running jazz series in Miami-Dade County, offering a free, year-long jazz recital and concert series to residents, students and music lovers of all ages. The series was founded by jazz studies professor Dr. Michael Di Liddo and inspired by MDC's Lunchtime Lively Arts concert series of the 1970s. Be sure to check the news and events schedule for upcoming events.

http://www.mdc.edu/main/news/events.asp

Cultura del Lobo Performance Series

Home of the Cultura del Lobo Performance Series and the Center for Cultural Collaborations International.

http://www.mdc.edu/culture/culturadellobo/

Broward Center for Performing Arts

The Broward Center for the Performing Arts is South Florida's premier venue for arts, entertainment, and events.

http://www.browardcenter.org/

Van Dyke Café

Live jazz upstairs in the music lounge at the Historic Van Dyke Cafe

http://www.thevandykecafe.com/upstairs/UpstairsCalendar.swf

Adrienne Arsht Center
for the Performing Arts of Miami-Dade County

http://www.arshtcenter.org/

Brief Table of Contents

A Matter of Style

of

Describing Popular Music

Bill Philpot/istockphoto.com

CHAPTER

1

Sometime early in 1955, Chuck Berry (1926–) "motorvated" from St. Louis to Chicago to hear Muddy Waters perform at the Palladium Theater. For years Berry had idolized Waters, the leading electric bluesman of the postwar era. After the concert, Berry went backstage to meet him. When he asked Waters how he might find a record deal, Waters suggested that he get in touch with Leonard Chess, the owner of Chess records, the small independent label for whom Waters recorded. Two weeks later, Berry was back in Chicago, giving Leonard Chess a demo tape that contained four songs. Among them was Berry's remake of a country song called "Ida Red," which he titled "Maybellene." Chess liked the song, so Berry recorded it soon after; it was released on August 20, 1955.

"Maybellene" caught the ear of disk jockey Alan Freed, a strong and influential supporter of rhythm and blues, and the man who claimed to have given rock and roll its name. While he was a disk jockey in Cleveland, Freed had begun using "rock and roll" in 1951 as code for "rhythm and blues." The term caught on after Freed moved to New York in 1954. By the time "Maybellene" was released, rock and roll was in the air and on the charts. With Freed promoting "Maybellene" by playing it frequently on his radio show, the song quickly jumped to No. 5 on the Billboard "Best" chart.

The story of "Maybellene"—a black artist with a new sound crossing over to the mainstream, an independent label looking to break through to the big time, a disc jockey trading influence for favors (Freed received partial songwriting credit on "Maybellene," and the royalties that went with it, in return for extensive on-air promotion of the song)—is but a short chapter in a saga dating back to the emergence of popular music: the complex, often contentious, interaction among those who create the music and those who try to profit from it. From the start, this interaction has involved power, money, class, race, and gender. It will be a recurrent theme in our survey.

However, our focus in this chapter is describing popular music, what it is and how it sounds. To that end, "Maybellene" is especially useful, for three reasons. First, it is certifiably popular: it was a hit song at the time it was released, and it is still well known. As such, it serves as a point of reference for a discussion of the nature of popular music. Second, it sounds like popular music: it clearly illustrates in sound so many characteristic features of popular music. Third, it is situated at the midpoint of this survey, so it is useful as a milestone in the history of popular music from its beginnings to the present.

Toward a Definition of Popular Music

"Maybellene" sold more than 1 million units. (We don't know exactly how many copies were sold because the Chess brothers apparently kept sloppy books.) If we define *popular music* as music that appeals to a large number of people, "Maybellene" is without question popular music.

By contrast, a blues record of the 1950s by Berry's idol Muddy Waters might have sold only about 10,000 units. Yet we know that Waters was an important influence on sixties rock—a god to the Rolling Stones, Eric Clapton, and other blues-oriented British rockers. So he and his music are definitely part of the pop music world. We can reconcile this issue by taking a multilayered view of popular music.

Popular Music Appeals to a Large Percentage of the Population

Like *blues, pop, rock,* and many other words associated with popular music, the term *popular music* has acquired several different connotations. The most obvious is "music that appeals to a large percentage of the population." But if we stop here, we run into problems. Is a CD by a classical performer popular music if it goes platinum, as some have? Is punk a popular style even though such significant punk bands as the Sex Pistols and the Ramones never hit the Top 40 in the United States? Clearly, popular music embraces more than music that sells in large numbers. Popular music embraces an array of attitudes, a family of sounds, and an industry that supports it, all of which distinguish it from classical and folk music. We will consider all of these connotations from a historical perspective.

istockphoto.com

Is punk a popular style?

Popular Music Is Familiar and Widely Heard

People make choices about everything—foods, friends, homes—and it would be very surprising if they did not make choices about the music they preferred. We know that certain songs were widely known to the Greeks and the Romans. Popular songs found their way into classical compositions; Mozart, for example, wrote variations on "Twinkle, Twinkle, Little Star." Some songs became well known because they served a larger purpose. Faithful Lutherans knew Martin Luther's hymns because he set out to compose simple words and melodies that everyone could remember and sing. This is just to say, however, that a component of popular music is familiarity—still a long way from an understanding of pop music as we know it.

Popular Music Is Profitable

Popular music began to take on the trappings of business—and the component of profitability as a measuring stick—with two important developments in the eighteenth century: the growth of the middle class in Europe and America, and improvements in music publishing. The emergence of a middle class, especially in England, expanded the audience who would pay for entertainment at music halls. Publishers began to offer songs, dance music, and instrumental pieces for the amateur home performer, most often a pianist—pieces that were relatively easy to play and attractive to middle-class tastes. Profitable music tended to be appealing, simple, current, and unpretentious. Then, as now, the audience for more-sophisticated and difficult music was significantly smaller.

Almost all of the music of the eighteenth century was current, compositions written and performed for their time. The notion of "classical music"—that is, the continuing performance of music of the past—was an almost negligible part of the musical landscape for most of the century.

John Gay's *The Beggar's Opera*—a play with musical numbers woven into the plot—introduced the ballad opera, one of the most popular kinds of public entertainments. At the time the most esteemed musical genre, or stylistic category, was opera, and the most prestigious opera drew its plots from classical literature and mythology. The music of *The Beggar's Opera* came from several levels of society, from popular dances and songs to classical works and parodies of them. An "opera" about the seamy side of everyday life in London—an opera that lacked the grand themes explored in mythology—was a drastic change in 1729 and proved very popular.

These qualities—appeal, simplicity, currency, and lack of pretense—are still part of the pop music world.

In the eighteenth century, however, the musical difference between aristocratic music and more-common music was one of degree, not kind. All of the music used the same musical language at varying levels of complexity; publishers simplified aristocratic music to make it accessible to a broader, less sophisticated, middle-class audience. This held true until the vogue for blackface minstrelsy in the 1840s.

Popular Music Is a Different Sound from Classical or Folk Music

With minstrelsy in the nineteenth century, the idea of popular music as we know it begins to take shape. It is different from classical or folk music in sound, style, attitude, purpose, and audience. In the twentieth century, through the infusion of African-derived musical values and with the continued growth of the classical music industry, the differences increased. Today, although each crosses over to the other's market, classical and popular music represent two different sound worlds and two different esthetics.

Thus popular music can simply be music that appeals to a mass audience, is intended to have wide appeal, and has a sound and a style distinct from classical or folk. When a particular song or piece of music has all three of these qualities, it is easy to classify as popular music. "Maybellene" is a good example. It was measurably popular (it had wide sales); both Berry and the Chess brothers intended that it be popular (they were looking for a hit); and its sound was new, distinctly different from folk music or stylized classical music.

Positioning Popular Music. Popular music is usually positioned between classical music on the one hand and folk or ethnic music on the other. A three-tiered musical world has developed that corresponds roughly to the social standing of the respective audiences. Classical music is associated with the upper class; it helps sell Swiss watches and luxury cars. Popular music is for the middle class—the largest portion of the population—and helps sell fast food and trucks. Folk music has been associated with isolated, largely rural, working-class people—those cut off geographically and economically from mainstream culture—and doesn't help sell anything. Ethnic music is similar in this respect, although the isolation may have more to do with cultural identity and language than geography or economics.

Some of the most interesting music in the popular tradition has arisen from musicians' exploring the boundaries between popular and classical music on the one hand, and popular and folk/ethnic music on the other. Among its many virtues, classical music nurtures craft;

its greatest artists are extraordinarily skillful in manipulating musical materials. Craft, whether in composition or performance, can become an end in itself. Musicians develop skill because it interests them to do so and has become necessary to the full expression of what they have to say musically. How else does one account for the extraordinary and expressive virtuosity of guitarist Eddie Van Halen (heavy metal) and trumpeter Wynton Marsalis (jazz)? When musicians working in popular styles like heavy metal and jazz assimilate some of the values of classical music, they may deliberately forsake a larger audience to preserve their artistic vision.

The goal of folk/ethnic–popular fusions is to broaden the audience, not leave it behind. The creative concern for the folk or ethnic performer is whether to add outside elements to one's own style. Because the connection between folk musicians and their audience is more immediate and less influenced by market values, the bond between the music and its culture is typically stronger. Numerous folklike styles have come from disenfranchised, largely poor populations, some in rural, isolated areas and more recently in cities. Both punk and rap are folklike because they emerged in urban areas within underprivileged populations that were outside the mainstream and because the music expressed the attitudes and emotions of their respective subcultures.

Popular Music as Synthesis. The popular music mainstream—that is, the prevailing popular style(s)—can have either a homogenizing or an energizing effect on the creative process. An artist typically moves toward the mainstream by taking on familiar musical elements that appeal to a wider audience. This homogenization may suppress or erase altogether the artist's defining qualities. For example, in the early years of rock and roll, white artists—including Pat Boone, who sang a notoriously bland version of Little Richard's raucous "Tutti Frutti"—made numerous cover versions of rhythm-and-blues songs. Although these homogenized songs often sold better than the originals, they so diluted the music with mainstream

pop elements that they sacrificed the integrity of the new sound.

Alternatively, the mainstreaming process may create an exciting new synthesis—a new sound—as when British rockers absorbed the "deep blues" of Muddy Waters and others into their music, or when both British and American musicians integrated reggae rhythms and textures into pop music during the late 1970s and early 1980s.

The Central Fact of Popular Music. Such borrowings highlight a central fact: popular music owes its identity and its evolution to a process of creative and open-minded synthesis. From its beginnings to the present, the new sounds in popular music have emerged from the blending of different kinds of music—often so different as to be musically and culturally opposite. Popular music blurs racial, economic, geographical, cultural, and class boundaries. Ultimately, the marketplace rules, for better or worse. We encounter this synthetic process from the outset of our survey, in the music for the minstrel show. And we will encounter it again and again as we move toward the present. Popular music is an ever-expanding stream, as new styles join the mix and older styles linger. The most popular music of an era serves as our rudder as we navigate the stream, but we are also interested in what the tributaries add.

"Maybellene" illustrates this synthetic process perfectly. In creating it, Berry drew on jazz from the late 1930s and early 1940s; Muddy Waters–style electric blues; honky-tonk, a popular country music

> *Ultimately, the marketplace rules, for better or worse.*

istockphoto.com

style of the 1940s and 1950s; and up-tempo rhythm and blues. In turn, certain features of the song, such as Berry's edgy guitar sound and its strong backbeat, would profoundly influence the music of the early rock era.

To evaluate the sounds of popular music and discover what they can tell us about its meaning, its evolution, its multifarious styles, and the patterns of influence, we need to become aware of the elements of popular music and acquire a meaningful vocabulary: for example, a term like *backbeat* should call to mind a specific, easily recognizable sound. That is the focus of the discussion that follows.

• • • • • • • •

The Properties of Musical Sound

Almost every musical sound has four properties: timbre, pitch, intensity, and duration. **Timbre** (pronounced "*tam*-ber") refers to the tone color of a musical sound. It

A tuning fork vibrates at 440 cycles per second. It produces a definite pitch in the mid-range of a woman's voice; string and wind players typically use this pitch to tune their instruments.

istockphoto.com

is the term we use to describe the characteristic sound of a voice or an instrument (the characteristic that helps you distinguish a friend's voice from a stranger's). The flute, for example, has a pure timbre. When we want to describe the different sounds of the same melody played on a piano and an electric guitar, we say that they have different timbres.

Pitch describes how high or low a musical tone sounds. Our sense of low and high is a function of how fast the object creating the tone is vibrating: the faster the vibration, the higher the tone. We also distinguish between sounds with definite pitch, because they have a consistent frequency, and sounds with indefinite pitch, which do not. Many percussion sounds, including those made on a drum set, convey only a general sense of high and low. We use **intensity** to describe how loud a musical sound is. In popular music simple descriptive terms like *loud* and *soft* usually suffice. **Duration** refers to the length of a musical sound. We typically relate the length of a sound to the beat and describe the length by saying, for example, "This note has a duration of two beats."

• • • • • • • •

The Elements of Popular Music

The elements of a musical performance grow out of these four qualities of sound. **Instrumentation**, which grows out of timbre, identifies the voices and instruments heard in performance. *Performance style* describes the way the musicians sing and play. Pitches combine into *melody* and *harmony,* defined below. Intensity becomes **dynamics** on a large scale (the dynamic level of a typical heavy metal band is loud) and **inflection** on a smaller scale. Duration grows into *rhythm* as soon as more than one note is sounded.

Two other elements emerge from instrumentation, pitch, and rhythm as the music unfolds in time. **Texture** describes the relationship among the various parts—in "Maybellene," the roles played by Berry's voice and the five instruments behind him. **Form** describes the organization of music in time.

When used in a systematic and consistent manner, these **elements of popular music** enable us to describe the examples of popular music discussed in this book precisely and meaningfully.

CD 1:1

"Maybellene," Chuck Berry (1955). Berry, electric guitar and vocal; Willie Dixon, string bass; Jasper Thomas, drums; Johnnie Johnson, piano; Jerome Green, maracas.

Listen to what happens in the first fifteen seconds of "Maybellene":

- Berry begins the song alone. He plays loudly, and his guitar sound has a little distortion; the loudness and the distortion give the sound an edge.
- The rest of the musicians quickly join in; they establish a clear two-beat rhythm at a brisk tempo.
- Berry sings the chorus of the song; it begins with two complementary riffs.

In this briefest of time spans, Berry provides the three most familiar elements of popular music: its distinctive sounds, its propulsive rhythms, and its accessible melodies.

Instrumentation

This short excerpt illustrates three key features of the sound world of popular music: the diverse and heterogeneous sounds that are incorporated into the music, the cultivation of a distinctive performing style, and its core instrumental sound, the rhythm section.

Sources of Popular Music Instruments. The unparalleled variety of instrumental sounds in popular music comes from five sources:

- Instruments inherited from popular music's antecedents and contributing styles
- New ways of playing these inherited instruments
- Creation of new instruments specifically for use in popular music
- Application of electronic technology for sound modification
- Use of "found" instruments

Popular music has developed from several different kinds of music; all have added their instruments to the mix. Most nineteenth-century popular music used the same instruments as classical music. These included the piano and guitar, plus many of the instruments of the orchestra and band—especially trumpet, trombone, clarinet, tuba, violin, and drums and cymbals. African American musicians created new sounds on these instruments; many showed the influence of the blues style (the moan of a saxophone; the use of a toilet plunger as a mute for brass instruments) or emphasized the percussive component of the sound (the sharp strum of a banjo or acoustic guitar). As new styles have been incorporated into popular music, their instruments have enriched its sound world. Anglo-American folk music and country music added banjo (actually a white adaptation of an African instrument recreated by slaves in America), fiddle, and steel guitar. Latin music added an array of percussion instruments: conga drum, bongos, timbales, claves, and more. Newly created instruments like the Hammond organ and the vibraphone also found a home in popular music.

The sound of popular music has also been shaped by instruments designed expressly for use in popular music. Most of the instruments used in contemporary popular music were invented principally, even exclusively, for that purpose. These include not only the drum set, but also an almost unlimited array of electronic instruments: electric guitar, electric bass, various electronic keyboards, even synthesized drums and wind instruments.

Electronics can also drastically modify the sound of existing instruments. Sometimes amplification results in such a dramatic timbral change and leads to such significant changes in the design and setup of the instrument that it in effect becomes a new instrument. This happened with the solid-body guitar in rock and the amplified string bass in jazz. Signal processing can also reshape the basic timbre of an instrument, as guitarist Jimi Hendrix proved so convincingly.

At the opposite end of the technology spectrum are "found" instruments—instruments created from materials close at hand but intended for other uses or for no use at all. Most of these are percussion instruments that now exist in a more refined, commercial form after becoming well established. These include a handclap; a tap dancer's feet; the bones of the early minstrel show; a host of Afro-Cuban percussion instruments—claves, cowbell, gourd, and the like; the pans of calypso, originally steel drums used to store oil; and the turntable, used by rap DJs for scratching.

We hear examples of all of these sources in "Maybellene":

- The piano and string bass come from European music; so does the original version of Berry's guitar.
- Bassist Willie Dixon plucks the strings of the string bass, rather than bowing them. This technique, called *pizzicato*, is relatively rare in classical music but the norm in popular music.
- Jasper Thomas's drum set evolved from the primitive drum sets that appeared just after the turn of the twentieth century in early jazz bands and dance orchestras.
- Amplification made the guitar far more powerful, and it enabled Berry to develop an aggressive sound.
- Jerome Green's maracas are descended from a percussion instrument created by filling a hollow gourd with seeds.

The Rhythm Section. "Maybellene" offers an easily recognizable instance of the core instrumental sound of popular music, the rhythm section. The rhythm section, a fixture in popular music since the twenties, is a heterogeneous group of instruments that includes at least one chord instrument, one bass instrument, and one percussion instrument. A rhythm section can be complete unto itself, as jazz piano trios and rock power trios have

Oleg Prikhodko/istockphoto.com

demonstrated for almost half a century. The chord instruments are of two types: strummed and keyboard. Strummed instruments include banjo and guitar, both acoustic and electric. Keyboard instruments include piano, organ, electric piano, and synthesizer. Bass instruments include tuba (brass bass), string bass, electric bass, and synthesizer bass. The main percussion instrument is the drum set. Occasionally, other percussion instruments, especially the conga drum, have augmented the rhythm section or substituted for the drum set. More recently, synthesized drum sounds have replaced human drummers.

"Maybellene" brought a fresh sound to the pop charts because of Berry's edgy guitar playing and because his band was not just the foundation for the rest of the band; it *was* the band. In pre-rock pop, rhythm sections supported voices and melody instruments. In rock, the rhythm section became the nucleus of the band; other instruments, such as saxophones, were optional.

Performance Style

Instrument choice is one dimension of the sound variety in popular music; another is the varied ways in which musicians sing and play. Consider this list of singers who had or participated in No. 1 hit singles or albums in 1960:

- Elvis Presley, the king of rock and roll, the white man with the "negro feel"
- Ray Charles, who brought a unique merging of blues and gospel to pop and country music
- Marty Robbins, a popular country singer who was part of the mainstreaming of Nashville in the late fifties
- Chubby Checker, a Fats Domino fan who made a career out of one dance, the twist
- The Drifters, one of the classic black vocal groups of the fifties and early sixties
- The Kingston Trio, three pleasant-voiced young men who were part of the folk revival in the late fifties and early sixties

Most of these performers, especially the major stars, have a distinctive, easily recognizable performance style. The cultivation of a personal sound is the ultimate extension of the timbral variety of popular music; in effect, it is variety at the most local level.

Moreover, one measure of excellence in popular music is *innovation*, the ability to develop a fresh, distinctive, and personal sound. Berry's guitar style, with its frequent double notes and slight distortion, had a sharper edge than the electric guitar sounds used in jazz and country music, and a brighter sound than usually heard in electric blues.

Rhythm

Just as they do with sound, the first few seconds of "Maybellene" encapsulate key features of rhythm in popular music. **Rhythm** is the element of popular music that you connect with almost instinctively—the qualities that make you want to tap your foot or clap in time. Our goal here is to describe it, using its realizations in this song as a springboard for a more general understanding of rhythm in popular music. We begin with the beat.

In the excellent documentary *Rock and Roll: The Early Years,* there is a clip of a white preacher denouncing the evils of rock and roll. He asks rhetorically what it is about rock and roll that makes it so seductive to young people, then immediately answers his own question by shouting, "The BEAT! The BEAT! The BEAT!" pounding the pulpit in time to his words. The preacher might have been thinking of "Maybellene," which has a strong, fast beat—to keep up with the Coupe de Ville that Berry is chasing in his V8 Ford. It *was* the beat that drew teens to rock and roll during the 1950s.

This meaning of **beat**—that quality of music that makes you want to respond physically—is the most basic and familiar one. However, two other meanings of "beat" are in common use in popular music. The differences among them are exemplified in these three sentences:

- The tempo of "Maybellene" is about 140 beats per minute.
- "Maybellene" shifts between a two-beat and four-beat rhythm.
- "Maybellene" has a great beat; it makes you want to dance to the music or drive faster.

In the first sentence, "beat" refers to the regular measure of time; in the second, it refers to the fundamental rhythmic organization, to which all other rhythmic features relate; and in the third it refers to the full range of rhythmic events that interact to make the rhythm compelling. Let's consider each in turn.

Tempo. In the first instance, "beat" refers to a regular rhythm that moves at a speed to which you can comfortably respond with physical movement. If you tap your foot as you listen to "Maybellene," you will almost certainly align your foot taps with the bass notes. Except for a brief stretch during Berry's guitar solo, the bass notes mark off equal increments of time at a rate a little bit faster than two times per second. There are other regular rhythms in "Maybellene," both faster and slower than the beat, but we identify this particular regular rhythm as the beat because it lies in our physical comfort zone. You could tap your foot at the speed of the maraca rhythm, but you would most likely tire quickly,

and any slower rhythm would be contrary to the intent of the song.

We use the word **tempo** to refer to the *speed* of the beat. We generally measure tempo in beats per minute: the tempo of "Maybellene" is on the fast side at 140 beats per minute. Tempos in danceable popular music generally range between 110 and 140 beats per minute (bpm); marches and disco songs are in the midrange, around 120 beats per minute. Tempos outside this range may connect powerfully to the musical message: the frenetic tempos of punk (often around 160 to 170 bpm) reinforce the confrontational nature of the style; by contrast, the languid tempos (often between 60 and 70 bpm) of so many doo-wop songs encourage the slow dancing that accompanies the romance expressed in the lyrics.

In popular music, beats may coalesce into groups of two, three, four, or even five—Dave Brubeck's "Take Five" is a famous, if rare, example of five-beat groupings. Two and four are the most common. We call a consistent grouping of beats a **measure**, or **bar**. The measure represents a slower regular rhythm. And because it is slower, it is a more convenient form of rhythmic reference for longer time spans: for instance, we refer to the form of the chorus in "Maybellene" as a 12-bar blues rather than a 24- or 48-beat blues.

In "Maybellene," you can hear the relationship between beat and measure as soon as the other instruments enter. Berry's accompaniment sets up an oscillating pattern that repeats every two beats; as a result, we hear each measure as encompassing two beats during much of the song.

This meaning of *beat* is the most generic: it and the terms associated with it—*tempo, measure,* and *bar*—could be applied to a wide range of music: pop, jazz, classical, rock, R&B, and almost any other music with a steady pulse. By contrast, the second meaning of *beat* is specific to twentieth-century popular music.

"Style" beats. Musicians often use the term *Two-beat* to identify the rhythmic foundation of the vocal sections of songs like "Maybellene." A **two-beat rhythm** features two bass notes per measure alternating with chords played on the backbeat. In "Maybellene," Berry alternates between bass and chord underneath his vocal; the bassist reinforces the bass note, while the drummer emphasizes the backbeat with sharp raps on the snare drum.

The **backbeat** is a percussive sound on the second of a pair of beats, or—in this case—on the second half of a beat. The percussive sound can be as simple as a handclap or finger snap, or it can be a rap on the snare drum, the closing of the cymbal, or an energetic strummed chord. As heard in a two-beat rhythm, it is an African American reinterpretation of the afterbeat of a march or polka (both popular dance forms in the latter part of the nineteenth century): OOM-pah becomes OOM-chuck.

During Berry's solo in the middle of the song, the bassist shifts from two notes per measure to a "walking" bass line with four notes per measure. The backbeat remains constant: the drummer continues to rap it out on the snare drum. As a result, the tempo doubles, as if Berry and his group shifted into a higher gear right along with the narrator's V8 Ford. Typically, when the rhythmic foundation of a song features a walking bass or other steady timekeeping four times a measure, we think of it as a **four-beat rhythm**. In this context, with the breakneck tempo and two-beat frame, the matching of bass line to the beat is not as immediately apparent as it will be in subsequent examples.

We identify both the two-beat and four-beat rhythms as **style beats** because they are the most pervasive feature of the dominant (or co-dominant) style of the music of a particular era. Almost all of the songs published during the 1920s and 1930s were subtitled "a foxtrot"; beginning in the late 1930s, the newly popular four-beat rhythm most clearly differentiated swing from the more sedate "sweet" foxtrot songs. Similarly, the vast majority of rock songs from the 1960s and 1970s have a rock beat, although they differ widely in instrumentation, vocal style, and melodic approach. Although it connects to rock and roll, "Maybellene" does not have a rock beat. The lack of a rock rhythm identifies "Maybellene" as a song from the very beginning of the rock era, before Berry and others defined the essential features of rock rhythm.

So, the word *beat* in the phrase "two-beat" has a meaning distinctly different from the first meaning of "beat," which refers to the

Jeff deVries/istockphoto.com

regular rhythm to which we most easily respond. Both are relatively specific: we can say the "Maybellene" has a tempo of about 140 beats per minute and that it also has a two-beat rhythm because of the alternation of bass note and backbeat. The third meaning of beat is more subjective: what constitutes a "good beat" is a matter of taste. Still, there is close correspondence between what makes big-band swing swing, and rock bands rock.

"Good" Beat. For most people, what gives a song a "good" beat is the interplay among all the rhythms present, especially when the rhythms are syncopated. A **syncopation** is an accent that does not line up with the beat. An **accent** is a note or chord that is emphasized in some way, so that it stands out. Often, accents stand out because they are louder or longer than the notes around them. Many of the accented syllables in the chorus of "Maybellene" are syncopated:

> Maybellene, why **can't** you be true?
> **Oh** Maybell**ene,** why can't you be true?

Similarly, the last syllable in each line of the lyric in the storytelling part of the song is syncopated:

> As I was motorvatin' over the **hill**
> I saw Maybellene in a Coupe de **Ville.**

It is the interplay between the steady style beat and the syncopated accents that gives the song so much rhythmic vitality.

In popular music, as in all other kinds of music, rhythm includes more than the beat. In its fullest meaning, rhythm is the time dimension of musical sound: it encompasses any musical event heard as a function of time. Still, "beat" in all three of its meanings is central to an understanding of rhythm. Most often, it is the rhythmic point of entry into a performance and its main point of reference. Whether it's the relentless throb of a disco hit, the elegant sway of a Cole Porter foxtrot, the supercharged tempos of punk, or the sequenced syncopations of rap and hip-hop, rhythm is at the heart of our experience of popular music.

Melody

The chorus of "Maybellene" begins with two short phrases: one ("Maybellene") is three syllables, the other ("why can't you be true?") is five. Both have a lot of empty space around them. Then they are repeated immediately, with only slight variation. These four phrases are riffs that stand out sharply, both in the chorus and in the song overall, because the verse is sung mostly to a single note. By keeping the main melodic idea short and isolated, Berry makes it easy to latch onto the riff. It's one of the hooks that pulled listeners in back in 1955.

In popular music, melodies typically grow out of **riffs**. Riffs are short, easily remembered melodic ideas. When sung, riffs are typically set two to seven syllables; instrumental riffs tend to be of comparable length. Their brevity makes them easier to remember. In songs like "Maybellene," riffs are both the main melodic point of entry and the building blocks of **melody**. They can give melody a distinctive rhythm and contour (the pattern of rise and fall), which in turn makes it stand out from more generic patterns, such as repeated chords or repetitive bass lines.

In popular music, building melodies from short melodic ideas dates back to the minstrel show, but most nineteenth-century popular song employed longer, more spun-out phrases. Riffs, almost always short and often syncopated, began to appear in popular song around 1910; within a decade, the riff had become the customary starting point for popular song. In "Maybellene," Berry develops the title-phrase riff into a complete melody via a statement/response approach: "Maybellene" is answered by "why can't you be true," and the entire unit is repeated with subtle variation. On the next larger level, this statement/response phrase becomes a statement, which receives a more extended response after its repetition.

Because of their brevity and because they could be syncopated, riffs enabled songwriters to impart a conversational rhythm to the lyrics: for example, the rhythm of "Maybellene" and the rest of the chorus as Berry sings it closely approximates speech rhythm. Indeed, one of the most interesting features of "Maybellene" is the smooth continuum between speech and song: the chorus has a melody, while the verses, which focus around a single note, are more than speech but less than conventional song.

Intervals, Scales, and Blue Notes

For virtually all of the music that we will encounter, the raw material of melody is the scale, a consistent series of small intervals. The discussion that follows defines interval, scale, and blue notes, and describes an interactive way to experience the two most common kinds of scales: diatonic scales and pentatonic scales.

Intervals. Musicians use the term **interval** to describe the distance between two pitches. The most fundamental interval is the **octave**, in which the higher pitch vibrates twice as fast as the lower note. This relationship is so basic that European musicians used the same letter name to identify pitches vibrating in this 2:1 ratio. On the keyboard graphic to the right, you'll see a visual representation of the octave: it's the distance between any pitch and the nearest pitch with the same letter name. The octaves formed between Cs are marked on the graphic.

Small intervals are typically identified as **steps**; C-D, D-E, and so on are steps. Steps come in two sizes: half steps and whole steps. On a keyboard instrument, a **half step** is the interval between any pitch and the immediately adjacent pitch. E to F is a half step, but F to G is not, because there is a black key between F and G. On a keyboard, a **whole step** has one intervening pitch; F to G is a whole step. Larger intervals, such as the octave, or even C-E or D-G, are **skips**.

Scales. **Scales** are series of pitches formed exclusively from steps or from steps and small skips, a skip that's slightly larger than a step. On the keyboard graphic below, **1** to **2** and **4** to **5** are small skips.

The most common scales in popular music are the two **diatonic scales**. Both contain seven pitches per octave. The difference between them is the pattern of half and whole steps. Scales may begin on any pitch; we often call this focal pitch the **keynote**. The **major scale** beginning on C uses only the white keys on the keyboard. One form of the **minor scale** uses the white keys from A to A.

Pentatonic scales contain five pitches per octave. There are two pentatonic scales commonly used in popular music. The first occurs in folk music from the British Isles or music influenced by this folk music. We will call this scale the Anglo-American pentatonic scale. On the keyboard graphic it is identified by the green numbers. Afrocentric music in the Americas often makes use of a different pentatonic scale, which we will call the African American pentatonic scale. On the graphic it is identified by the blue numbers.

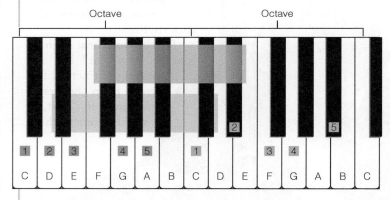

Blue notes. **Blue notes**, which we will encounter in the next several chapters, are the product of interpolating or substituting notes from the African American pentatonic scale into a melody built mainly from a major scale. As the graphic illustrates, only three of the five notes of the African American pentatonic scale match pitches in the major scale that uses the same keynote. The other two (2 and 5) are the blue notes.

If you have access to a piano or keyboard, or can locate one online (try searching on "online" + "synth" + "keyboard"), you can hear these scales. The C major diatonic scale is formed from the white keys (the keys marked in the graphic with letters). If you're inclined, play from right to left, a step at a time and beginning on C, in the rhythm of the Christmas carol "Joy to the World," to hear a familiar melody based on the major scale.

Use the keys matching the green numbers or play the black keys covered by the green rectangle to hear the Anglo-American pentatonic scale. Use the keys matching the blue numbers or the black keys covered by the blue rectangle to hear the African American pentatonic scale.

In "Maybellene," Chuck Berry draws on pentatonic and diatonic scales and blue notes to craft his melody. The guitar introduction and first phrase of the chorus uses the Anglo-American pentatonic scale. The second phrase interpolates a blue note into the Anglo-American pentatonic scale. The final phrase fleshes out the Anglo-American pentatonic scale with notes from the diatonic scale. Additionally, the verse focuses mainly on a blue note (number "2" on the keyboard diagram). The mix of pentatonic and diatonic scales is melodic evidence of "Maybellene's" mixed stylistic heritage.

Harmony

The innovative sounds, compelling rhythms, and memorable riffs heard in songs like "Maybellene" draw listeners in. Supporting these points of entry are two key background elements: harmony and texture. Harmony refers to chords; texture refers to the relationship among the parts—melody, bass line, and others. Each has a complementary relationship to melody: a melody note is typically part of the chord supporting it; the melodic line is usually the most prominent part of the texture.

In music, harmony is the study of chords: what they are, how they are formed, how long they last, and how they succeed each other. If you have ever sung or heard a four-part hymn, you are already familiar with all four of these concepts. When all four parts sing at the same time, they produce simultaneous complementary groups of pitches, or chords. The top, or soprano, part is the melody. The series of chords formed by the four parts is the harmony.

The other qualities of harmony are just as clearly evident in a hymn. Typically, chords change in a steady rhythm, once every syllable. Because chord change is usually clear and regular, the sequence of chords is easily heard. Chord sequences often become predictable, especially at the ends of phrases.

Chords are most easily recognized when all pitches sound at the same time. But there are other ways of presenting harmony, most of them more subtle. For example, accompaniments in a two-beat rhythm typically present the lowest note of the chord (the bass), followed by the rest of the chord notes. Or chord pitches may occur one after the next. We use the term arpeggio to describe a chord in which the pitches are presented in succession: the opening notes of "The Star Spangled Banner" form an arpeggio.

The most basic harmonies in popular music are a group of three chords, commonly identified as I, IV, and V. These have served as the main chords in popular song since its beginnings as a commercial music in America: many nineteenth-century songs are harmonized only with these basic chords. In the twentieth century, I, IV, and V provided the main chords in popular song, virtually the entire harmonic vocabulary of blues and early country music, and the focal chords of rock.

Chords often appear in a consistently used sequence, called a chord progression. In a chord progression there is a sense of connection between the chords. The chords are not simply following each other, but forming a larger unit that leads toward a goal chord. Certain chord progressions appear so regularly that they create a sense of expectation. When we have heard part of the progression, we have a sense of what will come next.

In "Maybellene," the supporting harmony alternates between the 12-bar blues progression in the chorus and solos, and resting on the I chord in the verses. The blues progression is outlined below, in the discussion of form.

Texture

We use the term *texture* to identify the rest of the story for sound, melody, and rhythm. For each element, it completes the picture: it goes beyond the point of entry to encompass the full range of activity. When evaluating texture in relation to sound, we consider the number of voices and instruments, the range between the highest and lowest sounds, and the areas in which sounds are concentrated. This provides an overall impression of textural density—thick or thin, dark or light. Density often has a subtle but profound impact on mood. The sound of jazz in the 1920s is often upbeat, in part because of the concentration of instruments in a higher register. By contrast, the dark, even threatening sound of electric blues, hard rock, and rap owes much to the concentration of parts in a lower register: prominent bass and low-pitched percussion sounds. In "Maybellene," the most prominent sounds come from Berry himself: his singing is in a middle range, and his guitar accompaniment is in a low-middle range.

The melodic dimension of texture is concerned mainly with the distribution of melodic interest. The melody is, by default, among the most interesting lines because it has a distinctive rhythm and melodic contour (the rise and fall in pitch of a melodic line). Using the melody as a yardstick, we observe whether other parts, if any, are of comparable melodic interest, and which parts are of lesser interest. In the vocal sections of "Maybellene," the melody—Berry's vocal line—is not sufficiently self-contained to stand alone, but it is far more distinctive than the bass line or the minimal melodic pattern formed by the chordal accompaniment. The walking bass line during the guitar solo is more interesting melodically but not comparable in interest to Berry's riff-laden line. The intermittent piano fills have a distinctive profile but do not coalesce into a continuous line.

The rhythmic texture of popular music is likely to be fuller than the melodic texture, because there are usually drums and/or other nonmelodic percussion instruments in a popular music performance. All instruments, pitched and unpitched, enrich the rhythmic texture in popular music. One aspect of rhythmic texture is its density, how many voices and instruments are contributing to the rhythmic flow.

Another aspect of rhythmic texture is the role of the various parts, whether they reinforce the beat or another regular rhythm that moves faster or slower than the beat, push against it, or float above it. The beat offers a familiar point of reference for rhythmic texture. However, those parts that confirm the beat are likely to be the least interesting parts of the texture. Strict timekeeping may produce a clear beat but little interest. A good beat, in the qualitative sense, depends on the interplay between those rhythmic layers marking or implying a regular rhythm and those that conflict with it or soar over it. In "Maybellene," bass, drums, maracas, and guitar mark the beat and backbeat during the vocal sections; the rhythmic interest comes almost exclusively from Berry's vocal line.

In observing texture, we will concentrate on general observations: impressions of density (thick/thin), register (high/low, concentrated/separated), melodic interest (concentrated in one part/diffused among several

parts), rhythmic activity (active/quiet), beat keeping (clear/implied), and rhythmic play (syncopated/unsyncopated).

The familiar points of entry in sound, melody, and rhythm may draw us into a song, but it is often the harmony and texture that sustain our interest, even through several listenings. We can easily assess the validity of this statement by this simple test: sing the melody and tap the beat and backbeat of "Maybellene" (or any other song that you like), then compare the result to the recording. The melodic and rhythmic points of entry are just a small fraction of the sound world of the song, even if they are the most prominent. That is why even "first-take" observations of harmony and texture help round out our impression of a song.

When you look at a photograph of Chuck Berry, you can take in the whole image in a glance. You can't do that with his music because it unfolds in time.

Getty Images

Form

When you look at a photograph of Chuck Berry, you can take in the whole image in a glance. You can't do that with his music because it unfolds in time. Your sense of the organization of a musical performance—its *form*—comes gradually, as you hear clues that one section has ended and a new one has begun. Eventually, the clues coalesce into a pattern, and you grasp the organization of the performance as a whole.

In most of the music that you will encounter in this text, you will observe form at two levels: the form of a section and the form of the performance as a whole. "Maybellene" uses two common formal templates. The overall form of the song is usually identified as verse/chorus form, while the chorus uses blues form.

Verse/Chorus Form. Verse/chorus form is a vocal-based form that contains two main elements, both of which are repeated. They differ in their relationship to the lyrics of the song. In the verse, the same melody sets different lyrics; in the **chorus** (also called the **refrain**), both words and music remain much the same every time. Within this general guideline is almost limitless variation. "Maybellene" begins with the chorus. This is a departure from the more typical pattern of beginning vocal sections with the verse and following it with the chorus. The graphic at the top of the next page shows the alternation of chorus and verse. ("I" refers to the short guitar intro; "T" refers to the short tag at the end of the song.)

Verse/chorus form in American popular music is as old as the first minstrel-show songs of the 1840s, and it soon became a standard feature of all popular song. During the first half of the twentieth century, the verse all but disappeared in performance, although most popular songs, and especially those written for musicals, had verses. During the rock era, the verse returned; Berry's song was among the first crossover hits to feature verse and chorus.

Each of the verses contains six lines of lyrics; they are half sung/half spoken over the I chord. Both the chorus and the guitar solo use the 12-bar blues template as the sectional form.

Blues form. The chorus of "Maybellene" uses the most characteristic version of **12-bar blues form**. This version of blues form contains three melodic phrases in each statement of the form. Each phrase and the pause that follows lasts four measures, so one statement of the complete form takes twelve measures: hence, 12-bar blues. When sung, the phrases are a rhymed couplet, with the first line repeated. A harmonic progression using only I, IV, and V supports the melody according to a well-established pattern: each phrase begins with a different chord—I, then IV, and finally V—and remains on or returns to the I chord halfway through. The graphic below shows how lyrics, melody, and harmony combine to outline the traditional 12-bar blues form.

The foundation of 12-bar blues form is its chord progression. Songs in blues form can have a different phrase structure or they may not have a predetermined melodic form at all; that is the case during Berry's guitar solo. In all cases, it is the chord progression that provides common ground. In its familiarity and adaptability, a blues progression is like a pair of old jeans: both are durable and well broken in yet extremely flexible and adaptable, and neither goes out of style. For generations, the chord progression has been familiar to musicians—who have borrowed it from the blues for use in popular song, jazz, Latin music, rock and roll, and rock—and their audiences.

Overall form of "Maybellene"

I	Chorus	Verse	Chorus	Verse	Chorus	Guitar Solo	Chorus	Verse	Chorus	T
0:00	0:05	0:17	0:29	0:41	0:53	1:05	1:29	1:42	1:54	2:06

> *A blues progression is like a pair of old jeans*

The 12-bar blues form serves as the main sectional form in "Maybellene." Here it's used as the formal template for the chorus of the song. The overall form alternates between chorus and verse, with a guitar solo serving as an interlude (and an opportunity for Berry to showcase his guitar playing) between vocal sections. Both blues form and the use of a chorus help listeners find and

Ian McDonnell/iStockphoto.com

First phrase	"Maybellene ...		true?"	
Measures 1–4	**I**		**I**	
Second phrase	"Oh, Maybellene ...		true?"	
Measures 5–8	**IV**		**I**	
Third phrase	"You done started ...		do."	
Measures 9–12	**V**		**I**	

maintain their bearings as the song unfolds. Their ease of use is one reason for their frequent use in popular music.

● ● ● ● ● ● ● ● ●
A Matter of Style

To this point, we've presented the elements of music: instrumentation, performance style, rhythm, melody, harmony, texture, and form, using "Maybellene" to exemplify their characteristic use in popular music. Now let's reverse the process, using our observations about "Maybellene" for each element to assemble a comprehensive profile of the song.

Profiles like this one enable not only those who are familiar with the song to recall its salient features, but also those who have not heard the song but have sound images for the terms used in the profile, such as *riff, blues progression,* and *12-bar blues,* to imagine the song without having heard it, or recognize it when hearing it for the first time.

The most immediate benefit of creating or studying a profile like the one below is sharper awareness of its musical features. It's a systematic way of getting more familiar with the various aspects of a song. In addition, a profile is also a useful point of departure for understanding musical style.

Musical Style

Virtually every musical feature of "Maybellene"—for example, its rhythm section–based instrumentation, rhythmic features like the backbeat and style beats, its use of riffs to build a melody, the blues progression,

verse/chorus form—occurs not only in this song but also in a wide range of popular music. They may be realized in quite different, even individual, ways, but they are commonplace features. Because they are widely used, they help define musical style.

Musical **style** is a set of characteristic musical features that typify a body of music. These features are, in essence, a statistical summary of what one expects to hear in the style: for example, most rock songs of the 1960s and 1970s have a rock beat. Musical style is comprehensive. It includes musicians' choices regarding all the elements of music, although some may play a more prominent role than others in defining the style. For example, distortion is the sound signature of heavy metal.

Style is a three-dimensional phenomenon, in that some characteristics of a style may occur in several styles, while others occur in a smaller range of music. For example, the backbeat has been a common feature in popular music from the 1920s to the present. By contrast, the two-beat rhythm through which it was introduced was wildly popular in 1920s' and 1930s' popular song and dance music. After World War II, it was widely used in country music and more conservative pop. By the time "Maybellene" hit the charts, it was an anachronism.

Because style is three-dimensional, it is possible to hear connections and patterns of influence from style to style. In "Maybellene," the instrumentation (electric guitar plus full rhythm section) comes from postwar electric blues; Berry's riff-based solo over a four-beat rhythm comes from swing via up-tempo rhythm and blues; Berry apparently adapted the two-beat rhythm from honky-tonk, a popular country music style in the post-WWII era. It is also possible to hear the innovative features present in a song, or in the work of a particular act. In "Maybellene," we hear Berry's fresh mix

Profile: "Maybellene"

Element	Description
Instrumentation	Vocals, electric guitar, bass, drums, piano (making up a full rhythm section), and maracas
Performance style	Berry sings with a gritty, yet light and good-natured, sound. In the verse, Berry finds a middle ground between song and speech by singing most of the lyric on the same note. The guitar sound has an edge plus a little country twang; bent notes in guitar solo.
Rhythm	Fast tempo; two-beat rhythm (except in guitar solo, where it shifts into a four-beat rhythm); strong backbeat; syncopation mainly in lead lines heard in vocal or guitar
Melody	Chorus melody built from short riffs; verses in long stream of notes focused around one pitch
Harmony	Blues harmony in chorus and guitar solo; one chord in verses and tag
Texture	Melody with strong OOM-pah accompaniment; piano and maracas layered in (entering separately)
Form	Overall form: Verse/chorus, with the chorus framing the verses Sectional form: Chorus is a 12-bar blues.

of blues and verse/chorus forms (framing verses with a blues-based chorus) and his more aggressive approach to blues guitar style (the occasional bent notes and the edge to his sound).

Two of the primary goals of this survey of popular music are to convey some sense of the breadth of popular music and to chart its evolutionary path over the better part of two centuries. To that end, we will discuss over 120 musical examples in some detail. Through careful and comprehensive observation of the musical features of each example, we will be able to compare and contrast styles within and between eras.

We often use one- or two-word terms to identify a style: "swing," "blues," "punk," "funk," and so on. Style labels are useful to the extent that they call to mind a specific set of musical characteristics. In this respect, "Maybellene" is an interesting case study. We label it "early rock and roll," mainly because of its creator and because of its historical position. However, it gives almost no hint of the new rhythmic direction that rock and roll would take; Berry's rock-defining songs would come later. "Maybellene" is an exception that proves the rule: most of our musical examples are more representative of the styles they exemplify. In our survey, we are interested both in the ways in which an example typifies a style and the ways in which it departs from it. To this end, consider revisiting "Maybellene" at the beginning of Chapter 9, after you have heard several different blues styles, verse/chorus songs, and western swing and honky-tonk, to hear how Berry blended and reshaped these diverse influences into a new sound, and to hear how it differs from the examples that follow.

Style and Meaning

Try putting the sound of "Maybellene" out of your mind, then read the lyrics of the song. The chorus seems to be about a failed relationship; the verses are about cars. Read as text, out of the context of the song, the verses vividly evoke the drag races that were so much a part of 1950s mythology—with the added twist that one of the drivers is a woman. The effect is almost cinematic. However, it is the music that conveys the energy and excitement of the chase. The brisk tempo, driving rhythm, shift in gears during the guitar solo, and the rapid, almost breathless, delivery of the verse all help bring the words to life.

When words and music work together in popular music to convey the meaning of a song, the words express the meaning, but the music helps listeners feel the message expressed in the words. However, with few exceptions, musical sounds are inherently abstract. Unfamiliar sounds seem meaningless to observers: the numerous comments by explorers and missionaries regarding African and Native American music are

evidence of that; so are the reactions of bluenoses to ragtime, blues and jazz in the early years of the twentieth century. The conventions of a style bridge this gap: they serve as an interface between musician and listener. As they become familiar, listeners can connect them to nonmusical experiences: the rise and fall of a melody as highly inflected speech, the energy of a fast tempo, the dark or subdued mood often implied by sounds clustered in a low register, the satisfying resolution of musical tension at the end of a chord progression. Cumulatively, imaginative handling of the musical elements can express mood and feeling with enormous power, as we will discover again and again.

• • • • • • • •

Looking Back, Looking Ahead

In this chapter, we have described many of the qualities that characterize popular music and presented characteristic musical elements. We have defined and illustrated terms that we will use frequently and demonstrated how observation of musical elements can translate the sounds on a recording into words on a page, which in turn call to mind the original sounds and others like them.

This is the foundation for the style-based discussions of virtually all of the musical examples presented in this book. For each example on the CD set, you will find in the text

1. A Listening Guide that outlines the form and identifies features and events of interest.
2. Things "…to Listen For," key observations that highlight prominent style features, to help you identify the song and its style quickly and accurately, as you might be called on to do in an exam.
3. One-sentence summaries of key points "…to Remember," which highlight noteworthy aspects of the song, connect it to other music, and offer interpretations of the expressive meaning of musical features. For example, in "Maybellene," we might observe the following:
   • A song about cars and driving, a popular teen theme in the 1950s and early 1960s
   • Strong influence of blues: conventional blues form in the chorus, electric blues band instrumentation, blues-inspired bent notes and aggressive guitar sound
   • Country influence evident in the honky-tonk-style, hard-driving, two-beat rhythm
   • Mix of blues, rhythm and blues, and country influences, anticipating important direction in rock and roll

On the web, you will find iTunes and Rhapsody playlists, as well as pdf Listening Guides, for songs *not* on the CD set (indicated by a marginal web icon in the text); downloadable Active Listening Guides; YouTube playlists; and many other resources.

Our survey of popular music ends close to the present. It begins in the next chapter with a brief overview of the sources of the first distinctively American popular music.

● ● ● ● ● ● ● ●

Terms to Know

Test your knowledge of this chapter's important terms by defining the ones listed here. If you can't recall the meaning of a certain term, refresh your memory by looking up the boldfaced term in the chapter, turning to the Glossary at the back of the book, or working with the flashcards at the Popular Music Resource Center.

genre	timbre
popular music	pitch
mainstream	intensity

duration	interval
instrumentation	octave
dynamics	step
inflection	half step
texture	whole step
form	skip
elements of popular	scale
music	diatonic scale
rhythm section	keynote
rhythm	major scale
beat	minor scale
tempo	pentatonic scale
measure (bar)	blue note
two-beat rhythm	harmony
backbeat	arpeggio
four-beat rhythm	chord progression
style beat	verse/chorus form
syncopation	chorus (refrain)
accent	12-bar blues form
riff	style
melody	

The Beginnings
of American
Popular Music

Jim Hurley/iStockPhoto.com

CHAPTER

2

We begin at the end. On the Billboard 200 chart for the week of February 23, 2008, the No. 1 album for the week is Jack Johnson's *Sleep through the Static,* which features lyrics-heavy, reggae-tinged tracks like "If I Had Eyes" and the title track. In the Top 10 are albums by a diverse group of female solo singers, from k. d. lang, who sings everything well, and gifted R&B artist Alicia Keys to teen sensation Miley Cyrus (Hannah Montana) and rising country star Taylor Swift. The Top 50 includes strange bedfellows. At No. 22, Hannah Montana's *Non-Stop Dance Party* is just above Radiohead's *In Rainbows. Symphony,* by silky-voiced Sarah Brightman, is at No. 28; pop metal band Scream Aim Fire's *Bullet for My Valentine* is next at No. 29. *Call Me Irresponsible,* which reaffirms Michael Bublé's mastery of Frank Sinatra/ Tony Bennett–style pop singing, follows at No. 30; right behind is *Still Feels Good,* by early Eagles-style country rockers Rascal Flatts. At No. 43 is the eponymous debut album of Vampire Weekend, a group that blends indie rock with Afro-pop and describes their sound as "Upper West Side Soweto." American Idol star Jordin Sparks's self-titled album is No. 44, and *Vivere: Live in Tuscany,* by blind Italian tenor Andrea Bocelli, who has crossed over from opera to pop, is next at No. 45.

The Billboard 200 measures album sales without regard to genre: if an album is selling well, it's on the charts. In 1991 Billboard began using data from Nielsen SoundScan, which tracks sales from 14,000 retailers and, more recently, online services. It was a far more accurate measure of record sales than the previous system. Because it's strictly quantitative, there is no bias in the reporting of information.

Both the diversity of the Billboard 200 and the profusion of charts—from classical crossover, country, Christian, and contemporary jazz to rock, rap, reggae, and rhythm and blues—highlight the extraordinary range of popular music at the beginning of the twenty-first century. It's truly a global industry, with music coming from and going to every part of the world. Those who create the music face no apparent social or cultural boundaries. The artists include women and men; old and young; white, black, and every shade in between; American and foreign; urban and rural; gay and straight. They draw on sounds and styles whose roots stretch across four continents—Europe, Africa, and both Americas. They blend them together according to their artistic vision, perhaps their sense of what will succeed commercially, or maybe something of both. There is no dominant style and no cultural pecking order. The top of the charts is, in principle, open to any artist.

It wasn't always that way. A century ago, the business of popular music was still a new industry. A dazzling variety of stage entertainment captivated audiences around the country, a flood of songs streamed out of publishing companies along Tin Pan Alley, and the first commercial

sound recordings found their way into the homes of the well-to-do. However, whites dominated every aspect of the business; black songwriters and entertainers had very little exposure and even less leverage. For many Americans, the most persistent images of African Americans came from the minstrel show, where blacks made themselves up with burnt cork in order to look as whites thought they should, and from the grotesque caricatures on sheet music covers. Ragtime, the first authentic black music to cross over into the pop world, was forbidden fruit for the young, provocative music for open-minded musicians, and sinful music for the "respectable."

Two centuries ago, the idea of popular music as we understand it today did not exist in America. There was music that was popular, but most of it came from Europe or imitated European music. There was commercial publishing and public performance, but there was no industry to provide and profit from mass musical entertainment.

Our account, then, begins in the early nineteenth century. In this chapter, we briefly describe the three main sources of American popular music, then highlight important nineteenth- and early twentieth-century developments, from the parlor song and minstrel show music at mid-century to the rise of Tin Pan Alley, the growth of stage entertainment, and the popularity of the concert band, all around the turn of the century.

● ● ● ● ● ● ● ● ●
Sources of Popular Music

The music of our time is fully integrated. It has deep musical and social connections to the cultures of Europe and West Africa, whose musical traditions are so contrasting as to seem almost mutually exclusive. Yet, as popular music evolved from the minstrel show to the present, it seamlessly blended musical elements from these quite different and often antagonistic cultures into new kinds of music.

> ## " The African musical tradition was the sand in the oyster. "

Popular music in America has been the product of a long evolution that began with the arrival of African slaves in the New World. The African musical tradition was the sand in the oyster—the agent of change that ultimately produced the popular music of the twentieth century, from rags to rap. The oyster was the music that European settlers had brought with them to the New World: the upper- and middle-class music of the cities and the folk traditions of the countryside and the mountains. To highlight the differences among these three traditions, we present three sets of excerpts. The first set demonstrates the close connection between African culture and the music of the African diaspora in the Americas. The second set includes excerpts of folk song and dance music. The folk song comes from the British Isles and is sung by an American; the dance tune is American but descended directly from the dance music of the British tradition. The third set demonstrates the smooth musical continuum between art music and commercial music in the early years of the nineteenth century.

African Influences

We don't know much about the music of the slaves in the United States during the early nineteenth century. We have some anecdotal evidence, written mostly by white observers who found their music baffling. But we do know that drums were largely outlawed on the southern plantations because slave owners feared that blacks were using them as a means of communication. As a result, extensive use of percussive instruments, perhaps the most crucial element of African music making, was all but eliminated. In Cuba, Brazil, and elsewhere in Latin America, African traditions were stronger, because slaves were allowed to re-create their drums, rattles, and other instruments.

Because we have virtually no hard evidence of the music made by people of African descent during the years of slavery, we must infer the nature and extent of the musical connection. The most informative path has been to compare field recordings of African folk musicians with those of musicians of African descent living in the New World. Often there are striking correspondences or retentions: we hear Cubans singing in an old Yoruba dialect as they drum and dance during a Santería ceremony and a Mississippi bluesman sounding uncannily like a man from Senegal.

From Nigeria to Cuba: *Santería.* *Santería* is the adaptation of Yoruba religious practices by Cuban descendants of African slaves, mainly from what is now Nigeria. In the traditional religions of the Yoruba people, initiates seek to establish a personal relationship with a patron spirit, called an *orisha*, who serves as an intermediary between the person on earth and God—much the same as a saint in the Catholic Church. Because of the close association of *orishas* and saints, this adaptation of Yoruba religious practice in Cuba has become known as *santería*, or "the way of the

saints." Music and dance are integral components of *santería* ceremony; it is through music and dance that initiates communicate with their personal *orisha*.

CD 1:2
"Song for Odudua," excerpt, performers and date unknown.

In the example presented here, the leader is singing in an old-fashioned Yoruba dialect: he is inviting Odudua, an *orisha*, to aid them. Soon drums, then voices, enter. The music settles into a steady rhythm, with the leader singing in alternation with the group. In this recording we hear several musical features that would be assimilated into the popular tradition:

- Prominent percussion: more specifically, drums similar to conga drums
- Complex rhythms, with constant syncopations in the percussion parts
- **Call and response**, an exchange between leader and group
- Melody built on an African pentatonic (five-note) scale.

From Senegal to Mississippi. The next recording combines the singing of Henry Ratcliff, a Mississippi prison inmate at the time of the recording, with the singing of a fieldworker in Senegal. What stands out is the remarkable similarity in vocal style between the two singers. The similarities include:

- Vocal timbre: basic sound and inflection of the voices is the same.
- Melodic shape: most phrases begin high and finish low.
- Rhythmic freedom in the delivery.
- Melody built on pentatonic (five-note) scales.
- Use of **melismas**, several notes sung to a single syllable.

CD 1:3
"Louisiana," excerpt/field song from Senegal (1977). Henry Ratcliff, vocal/ Bakasi-Badji, vocal.

These two examples demonstrate the extraordinarily faithful retention of African musical practices in the New World. The Cuban example is more richly African because slave overseers there allowed slaves to retain much more of their culture and because a significant percentage of the slaves brought from Africa during the nineteenth century came from Nigeria. Although it lacks the rhythms and percussion instruments that we associate with African music, the American example is in some ways even more remarkable. Southern slave masters vigorously suppressed such musical practices as drumming and sold slaves without regard to family

Five generations of a South Carolina slave family. The photo was taken in 1862, during the Civil War.

or tribal bonds. In effect, African Americans had to re-create the African aspects of their musical heritage from scratch. The next example shows how successful they have been.

CD 1:4

Yoruba chorus, excerpt (c. 1950)/ "Ladies Night," excerpt, George Brown (1979). Anonymous/Kool & the Gang.

Reconstructing a Heritage. During the course of the twentieth century, African-derived musical features became increasingly prominent in popular music. We can hear the close affinity between African music and recent popular music in this short excerpt, which joins a field record-ing from Nigeria with the beginning of Kool & the Gang's hit song from 1979, "Ladies Night," which reached No. 8 on the pop charts in 1979.

Some of the correspondences between the African recording and "Ladies Night" are uncanny in their simi-larity. They share:

- A dense, syncopated rhythmic texture built around what is a rock beat in "Ladies Night" and what in the African recording could be a rock beat in a more con-temporary context.
- Melismas in vocals. Note that the opening melisma in "Ladies Night" starts high and ends low.
- A layered texture made up of voices, percussion, and pitched instruments.

These two examples are an exceptional fit; not all Afri-can music matches up so well with contemporary popu-lar music. Nevertheless, the debt of popular music—of virtually all kinds—to African music is extensive and unmistakable. It includes these key features:

- An unvarying beat or other regular rhythm
- Several layers of rhythmic activity, which often create syncopations and other forms of rhythmic conflict
- Percussion instruments and percussive playing techniques
- Riff-like melodic ideas
- Layered textures

Few whites in the United States, Cuba, or elsewhere in the Americas would have heard sounds like these dur-ing the nineteenth century. Before the Civil War, the only place in the South where African Americans could revive their musical heritage was Congo Square in New Orleans. Nevertheless, despite numerous obstacles, all of these African musical features—rhythms, instru-ments, riff-based melodies, and the like—would gradu-ally reshape popular music.

Folk Music from the British Isles

The members of the lower classes who emigrated from the British Isles to North America brought their music with them: there are songs and dances that are still sung and played that date back centuries. For those people living in more isolated areas, such as the Appalachians, the traditions remained largely untouched by outside influences until well into the twentieth century. We hear excerpts from two early recordings: a British ballad recorded in 1936 by Rebecca Tarwater, a woman from Tennessee; and an American dance tune recorded in 1927 by Ben Jarrell, a fine old-time fiddler from North Carolina. The music and the performance of it represent traditions that date back decades, even centuries.

CD 1:5

"Barbara Allen," excerpt, traditional (1936). Rebecca Tarwater, vocal.

Folk Song from the British Isles. "Barbara Allen," the song presented here, is a folk ballad, one of the most common types of folksongs. A **ballad** is a simple song with a lyric that tells a story. The stories were often morbid, even grisly, and they usually had a moral. In this respect, "Barbara Allen" is typical: It intertwines love and death—two of the most enduring themes in art and life—in a most understated and succinct way, as we can learn from the lyric. It was typically sung without accompaniment.

"Barbara Allen" dates back at least to the seventeenth century. Samuel Pepys, a high-ranking British official, describes it as a "little Scotch song" in his diary entry from January 2, 1665, but it must have been popular well before that date. It almost certainly came to North America with the first colonists. The version recorded here is one of hundreds of variants found throughout the Southeast. Rebecca Tarwater came to Washington, D.C., at the urging of the folklorists John and Alan Lomax to record the song and help preserve a heritage that was rapidly disappearing.

The song is a simple four-phrase melody that forms a graceful arch: up, then down. It is constructed from the Anglo-American pentatonic scale, which is commonly heard in the folk music of Ireland and Scotland. It is **strophic**: that is, several stanzas are sung to the same melody. (We hear two in this excerpt; there are seven in this recording of the song.) Tarwater's singing is unpolished by classical standards, but her voice is pleasant and exceptionally true. There is no accompaniment. Among the features that found their way into popular music were these:

- Storytelling song, telling a "real" story, although apparently based on a long-forgotten incident
- Strophic form (this led to verse/chorus form)
- Unpolished but effective vocal style

Anglo-American Folk Dance. The most popular dances brought from the British Isles were up-tempo jigs and reels; they were typically played by a fiddler. We have no

way of knowing exactly how this music sounded in the early nineteenth century, but we do know some of the songs and can infer some of the key features of the style from the earliest country recordings and contemporary accounts. This early recording of "Old Joe Clark"—one of the first country music recordings—reveals musical features that were almost certainly present in Americanized versions of British folk music, as heard in the nineteenth century.

Ben Jarrell, who sings and plays the fiddle on this recording, lived in a rural part of North Carolina. Because Jarrell's son Tommy also played in much the same style, it is likely that Ben Jarrell's singing and playing typify a traditional approach that had been substantially unchanged for generations.

This song is somewhat unusual in that it combines song and dance. Many fiddle tunes were strictly instrumental. Here, vocal and instrumental statements of the melody alternate. Each statement of the melody includes a verse and a chorus. Their relationship is apparent from the lyric: the chorus retains the same words and melody, while the verses give unflattering snapshots of Betsy Brown. Fiddle, banjo, and voice play different versions of the melody; there is no chordal accompaniment. The song has a fast tempo and a clear, danceable beat. Among the qualities that would find their way into popular music are these:

CD 1:6

"Old Joe Clark," excerpt, traditional (1927). Ben Jarrell, vocal and fiddle; Frank Jenkins, banjo.

- Down-home, good-humored attitude
- Story told in everyday language
- Melody set to a danceable beat
- Rough, untrained singing voice
- Verse/chorus form

All of these qualities would surface in the music for the minstrel show. It's possible that the form of "Old Joe Clark" could have been influenced by minstrel show songs, because most of the stories of its origin point to events taking place after the Civil War. In other respects, however, the style seems a direct ancestor of music for the minstrel show.

Library of Congress, Prints and Photographs Division, Washington, D.C. [LC-USZ62-426]

Upper- and Middle-Class European Music

CD 1:7

"Casta Diva" from *Norma*, excerpt, Vincenzo Bellini (1831). Renata Scotto, soprano; National Philharmonic Orchestra, James Levine, conductor.

Throughout the eighteenth and nineteenth centuries, the upper and middle classes in Europe and America shared a common musical language. We know its most sophisticated statements as classical music: the music of Bach, Handel, Haydn, Mozart, Beethoven, and Schubert, among others. However, there was also a vast body of popular song and music for social dancing that used a simpler form of the same musical language, as well as patriotic music (for example, national anthems such as "God Save the King") and hymns and other church music. Through the middle of the nineteenth century, there was a smooth stylistic continuum among these different types of music. Two excerpts, from an opera aria and a popular song of the 1830s, show not only how smooth the continuum could be, but also how European musical elements were brought to America.

"Casta Diva" is an aria (a part of an opera featuring a solo singer) from *Norma,* an opera by the Italian composer Vincenzo Bellini. Bellini's music was well known in urban America as well as Europe, not only on stage, but also in numerous adaptations published as sheet music. "Woodman, Spare That Tree" is a song by Henry Russell. Russell (1812–1900) was the Elton John of the 1830s: an English songwriter, singer, and pianist who enjoyed extraordinary success in America. Russell claimed to have studied composition with Bellini before emigrating briefly to the United States; "Woodman, Spare That Tree" clearly shows the influence of Italian operatic style.

In both works, musical interest centers on a flowing melody; the simple arpeggiated accompaniment is clearly subordinate. Both have a moderately slow tempo with a clear, if lightly marked beat and use the same harmonic language. They differ mainly in their elaborateness. "Casta Diva" features an orchestral accompaniment and a florid, wide-ranging, often melismatic (recall that a melisma is a series of pitches sung on the same syllable) vocal line. "Woodman, Spare That Tree" is set for voice

CD 1:8

"Woodman, Spare That Tree," excerpt, Henry Russell (1837). Richard Lalli, vocal.

and piano. Although simpler vocally, it unfolds on much the same broad scale as "Casta Diva." Like the aria, it has a long instrumental introduction, and its phrases are of comparable length: in fact, both open with phrases based on a descending scale, like the opening of the children's song "Three Blind Mice."

"Woodman, Spare That Tree" may seem miles away in style and spirit not only from "Old Joe Clark," but also from "Maybellene" and "Ladies Night." But several of the musical features that it exemplifies became part of the sound of popular music. Among them are these:

- Chords and chord progressions
- Melody-and-accompaniment texture, with the flowing melody on top, bass on the bottom, and chords in between
- Hierarchical form, in which phrases coalesce into larger formal units
- Many of the instruments used in popular music, including piano, several wind and brass instruments, violins, and acoustic bass

Neither African music nor most of the folk music brought from the British Isles uses harmony; it is specific to urban upper- and middle-class music of Europe. So are many of the instruments of popular music, although popular musicians created new sounds from them. Classical music, and the music modeled after it, also served as the de facto standard of excellence. Aspiring to art would remain a persistent countercurrent in popular music throughout the twentieth century, from Scott Joplin's "classic" rags to the beautifully crafted albums of Radiohead.

American Popular Music: From Sources to Syntheses

If you compare the musical examples you've just heard, you can gain a clear picture of the deep contrast between musical traditions, especially between the urban European music popular during the first part of the nineteenth century and West African music. Here are some of the key differences:

	Urban European	**West African**
Instrumentation	Chord instrument (piano) is the only instrument	Several percussion instruments (including handclaps); also a plucked instrument
Harmony	Chords	No chords
Melody	Long, flowing melody	Short phrases ending in long notes
Rhythm	Gentle beat keeping	Strong beat keeping
	No syncopation	Lots of syncopation in drum parts

In short, there's virtually no common ground between the urban European and West African traditions. The extreme contrast between them makes the emergence and evolution of a distinctively American popular music even more remarkable. Popular music acquired a distinct identity only when it began to synthesize these disparate traditions into a new sound. We encounter the first such synthesis in the music of the minstrel show.

● ● ● ● ● ● ● ● ●

Popular Song in Mid-Nineteenth Century America

In a famous letter to his publisher E. P. Christy, Stephen Foster (1828–1864) reveals his ambivalent attitude about his "Ethiopian songs"—songs he wrote for the minstrel show. He wrote, "As I once intimated to you, I had the intention of omitting my name from my Ethiopian songs, owing to the prejudice against them by some, which might injure my reputation as a writer of another style of music, but I find that by my efforts I have done a great deal to build up a taste for the Ethiopian songs among refined people by making the words suitable to their taste."

Foster wrote the letter in May of 1852, almost a year after the publication of "Old Folks At Home." The published version of the song shows Christy as the composer of the song, which was already well on its way to becoming one of the most popular American songs of all time. In the wake of its success, Foster was obviously having a serious case of the druthers, as well he should. Nevertheless, the fact that Foster would have previously agreed to withhold his name from the covers of his minstrel show songs implies a deep division between "highbrow" and "lowbrow" in American cultural life during the middle of the nineteenth century.

America declared political independence from Great Britain in 1776. Cultural independence in art, theater, literature, and especially music took quite a bit longer. Virtually all of the commercially produced music one might hear in the United States during the first decades of the nineteenth century came directly or indirectly from the British Isles: orchestral and choral music in public performance; opera; music published for home performance; and hymnals for church use.

America was mostly wilderness at the beginning of the 1800s. In 1790, New York, then as now the largest city in the country, had a population of about 33,000 people. By 1840 its population had grown almost ten times, to about 312,000. The next-largest cities, Baltimore and New Orleans, had populations of just over 100,000. America remained mostly rural until well into the twentieth century, but its cities grew, and a cultural divide developed between the largely urban, literate middle and upper classes and the poorly educated, less mannered lower classes of city slums and rural counties. All forms of entertainment, including music, reflected this gulf. During the nineteenth century, the distinction was commonly expressed as *highbrow* (urban and cultivated) versus *lowbrow* (rural and vernacular).

The more respectable members of a growing middle class aligned themselves with highbrow taste in all aspects of culture. Musically, it was most evident in the songs they preferred. As they did with other aspects of culture, they looked to England for inspiration.

Stephen Foster and the Parlor Song

In the early nineteenth century, the most popular songs in England were the folk-song settings of Thomas Moore (1779–1852). Moore, an Irish poet and musician who lived in England most of his career, set his own poems to traditional Irish folk melodies. A skilled singer and pianist, he made these adaptations himself and published them in ten volumes between 1808 and 1834. According to Charles Hamm, they were, along with the songs of Stephen Foster, "the most popular, widely sung, best-loved, and durable songs in the English language of the entire nineteenth century." Not far behind were the Scottish song settings by Robert Burns, including the still familiar "Auld Lang Syne."

These folk-song settings, circulated in sheet music versions, were genteel and "correct" according to the musical standards of the day. In this form, they appealed to and circulated among musically literate members of the middle and upper classes. They helped spawn new kinds of popular music, including the most popular genre in nineteenth-century America: the parlor song.

Parlor songs resemble the art songs of classical music in their setting for voice and piano, but were more modest in their expressive range and musical requirements. They told sentimental stories, which were set to simple melodies with generally modest accompaniment. Parlor songs

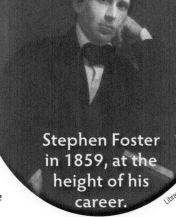

Stephen Foster in 1859, at the height of his career.

Library of Congress, Prints and Photographs Division, Washington, D.C. [LC-USZ62-22501]

derive their name from their typical setting. In the era before mass media, those who wanted music generally made it themselves. Young ladies from middle- and upper-class families often received musical instruction. After dinner, families would gather in the parlor, where they would sing and play songs like "Jeanie with the Light Brown Hair."

Stephen Foster. Stephen Foster (1826–1864) was the most important songwriter in nineteenth-century American popular music. He was versatile and skillful, and his songs were well written and often inspiring and innovative. Success came early with minstrel tunes like "Oh, Susanna!" and "Camptown Ladies." Particularly in the 1850s, at the apex of his career, Foster was a composer of real skill. His best songs far outshine the work of his contemporaries and successors. The relative simplicity of his style came about by choice, not default, as he sought to create a specifically popular style.

The parlor song was an integral part of Foster's musical world from the beginning of his career. His first published song, "Open Thy Lattice, Love" (1844), is a fine example of the genre. Among the most memorable of his parlor songs was one he composed about a decade later, after his career as a songwriter was well under way. "Jeanie with the Light Brown Hair" is a typical, and especially pretty, example of the parlor song genre. Its roots in the folk music of the British Isles are most apparent in Foster's use of an Anglo-American pentatonic scale, a feature heard in "Barbara Allen." The major musical difference is, of course, the addition of a rich if understated piano accompaniment.

CD 1:9

"Jeanie with the Light Brown Hair," Stephen Foster (1854). Richard Lalli, vocal; Michael Campbell, piano.

Library of Congress, Prints and Photographs Division, Washington, D.C. [LC-US262-5264]

LISTENING GUIDE
CD 1:9 "Jeanie with the Light Brown Hair"

STYLE	Parlor song		
FORM	The melody contains four phrases in the form AA¹BA², where A is the first melodic idea, A¹ and A² are different versions of the idea, and B is a contrasting melodic idea.		
0:00	Introduction		
	Piano alone: abbreviated		
0:13	**First statement of form**		
	A	I dream of Jeanie …	Sudden rise in the melody to "Borne, like a vapor."
		Borne, like a vapor …	
	A¹ (0:27)	I see her tripping …	Phrase begins like the first but ends differently.
		Happy as the daisies …	
	B (0:40)	Many were the wild notes …	Different melody. Notice suspension of beat at end of phrase, to spotlight singer.
		Many were the blithe birds …	
	A² (0:58)	Oh! I dream of Jeanie …	Begins like first phrase, but ends differently than both previous As, to bring song to a close.
		Floating, like a vapor …	
1:18	Interlude/fadeout		
	Piano alone		

INSTRUMENTATION
Voice and piano

RHYTHM
Subtle pulse at moderately slow tempo, with occasional suspension of timekeeping

RHYTHM
No syncopation in melody or accompaniment

MELODY
Long, flowing lines, ending in clearly punctuated phrases

TEXTURE
Melody plus simple accompaniment

SENTIMENTAL TEXT
Sentimental portrait of Jeannie in the lyrics resonated well with respectable families in nineteenth-century America.

SONG FOR HOME USE
Singers and pianists of modest skills could comfortably perform parlor songs at home.

IRISH CONNECTION
Like many folk and folk-inspired songs from the British Isles, "Jeannie" uses a pentatonic (five-note) scale.

BEAUTIFUL MELODY
Melody is the main focus and the feature that gives the song its character; accompaniment is generic; no underlying dance rhythm.

Foster was the most popular and most admired of the first generation of American songwriters. The sentimental songs that he and his contemporaries composed marked the beginning of the American popular mainstream. Quickly overshadowing them was a humbler but ultimately far more influential kind of song: a song composed (or borrowed) for the minstrel show.

The Early Minstrel Show

The first minstrel show—billed as an "Ethiopian Concert"—took place in Boston in February 1843. It featured the Virginia Minstrels, four veteran blackface performers, none of whom were from the South. These all-around entertainers sang, danced, and played fiddle, banjo, tambourine, and bones, and their first evening of entertainment was an immediate success. Following their lead—and hoping to match their success—other minstrel troupes formed almost overnight. Within a few years, troupes crisscrossed the country, and many cities had their own resident troupe. The size of the minstrel troupe also grew (and would continue to grow after the Civil War). Christy's Minstrels, formed in 1844, soon added other performers and then an orchestra.

It is difficult to give a precise description of the minstrel show because it lacked a consistent form and evolved so quickly. In the twenty years prior to the Civil War, minstrelsy developed from small-group acts to a full evening's entertainment with a large troupe and orchestral accompaniment. Audiences at the early minstrel shows were the forerunners of today's raucous rock-concert or soccer-match crowds. Rowdy patrons provoked "minstrel programs [to list] 'Rules of Hall,' which pleaded with the audience not to whistle during the performances and not to beat time with their feet."

The show by its very nature was loosely structured (and remained loose even as the size of the troupe grew). There were at least three minstrels: the interlocutor and the two endmen, Tambo and Bones, so named for the tambourine and the bones that they played. The troupe sat in a semicircle, with the interlocutor in the center and the endmen at either side. The rest of the troupe filled the gaps between the interlocutor and the endmen. There was no plot or storyline, although there were stock routines and consistent characters. The subject matter provided the continuity in a string of comic exchanges between the interlocutor, who spoke with a resonant voice, proper diction, and a rich vocabulary, and the endmen, who spoke in a caricature of African American speech. These exchanges bonded together a varied assortment of songs and dances. The interlocutor controlled the pacing of the show. According to the mood and the response of the audience, he would allow routines to continue or cut them off.

The minstrel show grew out of the blackface entertainment of the late 1820s and 1830s. The most popular performers of the era built their routines around two stock characters: the city slicker Zip Coon and the country bumpkin Jim Crow. The first blackface entertainer to portray them was George Washington Dixon, who first introduced them on-stage in New York in 1827. The names followed soon after.

In 1832, Thomas Dartmouth Rice observed (or claimed to have observed) an African American street entertainer in Cincinnati doing a song and dance with a peculiar hop step, which he called "jumping Jim Crow." He copied the man's routine and introduced it on-stage shortly thereafter with great success. Jim Crow's city counterpart acquired a name two years later, when in 1834 Bob Farrell, another blackface entertainer, introduced the song "Zip Coon" on-stage.

The first minstrel shows simply constructed a full-length show from various routines about the two most popular blackface characters: the opening section portrayed the city slicker, and the closing section portrayed the country bumpkin. Within a few years, the show had grown into three distinct parts. The opening section alternated highly ritualized minstrel material with a balladeer singing popular parlor songs. The second section, called the **olio** (an Anglicization of the Spanish word *olla* for "stew"), was the variety portion of the show and featured a wide range of acts. Many of these were novelty routines; others were **burlesques** (humorous parodies) of cultivated material—Shakespeare's plays or Italian operas, for example. The final section was an extended skit. Originally based on idealized plantation life, the skits later became topical comedy sketches. The show concluded with a **walkaround**, which featured the entire minstrel troupe in a grand finale of song and dance.

CD 1:10

"De Boatmen's Dance," Dan Emmett (1843). Ensemble directed by Robert Winans.

By the end of the nineteenth century, the walkaround had evolved into the **cakewalk**. By most accounts the cakewalk originated as a contest among slaves: couples danced for a prize, generally a cake. The winners were the "pair that pranced around with the proudest, high-kicking steps." By the 1890s it had become a dance fad, moving from the stage to the dance floor, where couples competed in contests for prizes larger than a cake. Its signature short-LONG-short rhythm was the first persistent use of syncopation in popular music; it would find its way into much turn-of-the century American song and dance music.

Dan Emmett. Dan Emmett's "De Boatmen's Dance," heard here in a 1978 performance by Robert Winans, illustrates the sound of early minstrel show music. Emmett (1815–1904) was a blackface entertainer in the 1830s and one of the founding members of the Virginia Minstrels. He also composed (or adapted from folk repertory) a number of songs for the minstrel show, including "Dixie." Among his contemporaries, only Stephen Foster surpassed him as a minstrel show songwriter. "De Boatmen's Dance" was one of the songs in the first Virginia Minstrels show in 1843.

Even a casual comparison makes clear the affinity between "De Boatmen's Dance" and Ben Jarrell's "Old Joe Clark." Both have lyrics that describe a series of "scenes" in down-home language. They share the same nucleus—voice, fiddle, and banjo—an upbeat tempo with a clear beat, alternation of singing and playing the melody, and a form that alternates verse and chorus. In this song there are two choruses: one is sung in harmony, the other in **unison**—that is, with more than one voice and/or instrument performing the same melody. The use of a chorus, in which both words and music are repeated again and again, would become more common in popular music after the Civil War, when songwriters and publishers deliberately set out to create popular songs. It is easy to imagine the song supporting action on stage as the troupe acts out the scenes described in the song or simply dances.

Perhaps the most crucial difference between "Old Joe Clark" and "De Boatmen's Dance" is the latter's use of harmony. Clearest in the chorus and implicit throughout the rest of the song, the use of harmony connects "De Boatmen's Dance" to the cultivated parlor songs of the period. This addition of urban harmony to folk content and rhythm created a mix with a different sound and attitude. So did the use of African American images and sounds.

Black Faces and Black Sounds. Without question African American music influenced the sound of early minstrel performers. Bones and tambourine formed the first "rhythm section," and the banjo developed from African instruments. But the music of the early minstrel show had little relation to authentic African

WALKING FOR DAT CAKE.

PERFORMED BY

HARRIGAN & HART.

WORDS BY
ED. HARRIGAN.   MUSIC BY
DAVE BRAHAM.

NEW YORK:
Published by WM. A. POND & CO., 25 Union Square, (Broadway, between 15th and 16th Sts.)

Sheet Music Collection, The John Hay Library, Brown University/

LISTENING GUIDE
CD 1:10 "De Boatmen's Dance"

STYLE	Minstrel show song		
FORM	Verse/chorus		
	In each statement of the form, two choruses frame the verses. Both choruses are short; the verse has four short phrases.		
0:00	**First statement of form**		
	Instrumental: classic minstrel show troupe instrumentation—fiddle, banjo, tambourine, and bones		
0:25	**Second statement of form**		
	Chorus 1	Hi row, …	Vocal, in harmony
	Verse (0:32)	1. De boatman dance … de boatman up …	Listen for the descending five notes of the
		3. And when de boatman	song's pentatonic scale in the latter part of
		4. He spends his cash …	each phrase.
	Chorus 2 (0:40)	Den dance, boatmen, dance …	Vocal, in unison
0:48	**Third statement of form**		
	Chorus 1	Hi row, …	
	Verse	Wen' on board …	
	Chorus 2	Den dance, boatmen, dance …	
1:10	**Fourth statement of form**		
	Another instrumental statement of the complete song		
1:31	**Fifth statement of form**		
	Chorus 1	Hi row, …	
	Verse	When de boatman …	
	Chorus 2	Den dance, boatmen, dance …	
1:56	**Sixth statement of form**		
	Chorus 1	Hi row, …	
	Verse	De boatman is a …	
	Chorus 2	Den dance, boatmen, dance …	
	Fade out		

American music; in fact, it had much more in common with the folk music of rural settlers, and many minstrel songs passed into the oral tradition of country music. "Zip Coon," for example, became the fiddle tune "Turkey in the Straw." The song lyrics were not authentic either, but were written in pseudo-dialect. A line from "Zip Coon" shows the inconsistency in language: "I went the udder arter noon to take a dish ob tea." Some words are in alleged dialect; others remain unchanged.

Although it is clear from drawings and accounts of the period that at least some white minstrels keenly observed the appearance, speech, and dancing of black Americans, "Jim Crow," "Zip Coon," and other minstrel songs were in fact crude parodies of the African American life that minstrels attempted to capture in song and dance. In the years before the Civil War, the majority of minstrel performers had only incidental contact with the African Americans whom they supposedly portrayed. Most minstrel troupes resided permanently in northeastern cities—New York especially—that were far from southern plantations.

There is compelling, if indirect, evidence to suggest that white minstrels did not capture the *quality* of African American music making. After the Civil War, performances by black minstrels were so much more successful than the white minstrels that the white minstrel show evolved away from traditional minstrelsy.

Routes to Popularity: Written and Oral Traditions. In the middle of the nineteenth century, the two outlets for minstrel show songs were sheet music and the stage. Publication via sheet music was the established practice. However, many minstrel show songs were simple enough, repetitious enough, and coherent enough melodically that the audience could remember

INSTRUMENTATION
Voices, fiddle, banjo, tambourine, and bones

RHYTHM
Bright, steady tempo, with a clear beat

RHYTHM
Fast rhythms in banjo and syncopated patterns in fiddle and bones

MELODY
Simple, three-phrase melody based on pentatonic (five-note) scale

TEXTURE
Some harmony in the first segment of the chorus; otherwise, voices and pitched instruments sing and play different versions of the melody.

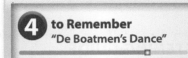

4 to Remember
"De Boatmen's Dance"

FOR STAGE ENTERTAINMENT
Song is part of an all-around show with singing, dancing, and joke-telling.

CHORUS-BASED FORM
Two choruses frame each statement of the verse.

DANCE RHYTHMS
Song uses a bright dance rhythm.

MINSTREL SHOW LYRICS
Pale imitation of black speech brings earthier element into popular song.

the melody and simply needed to be reminded of the words.

Our next musical example combines two versions of "Camptown Ladies," one of Stephen Foster's most familiar minstrel show songs. The first half of the song is a contemporary performance of the song based on the original sheet music; the second half is another contemporary recording, by the Canadian contemporary folk group the Duhks, which remakes the song with a modernized traditional instrumentation: fiddle, banjo, acoustic guitar with amplification, and percussion. The first version was designed for home use in musically literate households. By contrast, the second version sounds like a new take on an old song that was simply "out there." One can easily imagine such a song being passed on from one generation to the next, like "Barbara Allen."

Foster's songs have come down to us both ways: we can easily learn his songs by hearing them or by reading them from the music. Although created as popular songs, they have attained a folklike status; the song is simply out there. What is novel about this state of

the tune after only a few hearings. To take advantage of this accessibility, publishers put out **songsters**—books with just the lyrics to popular songs of the day—on the assumption that those who bought them already knew

LISTENING GUIDE
CD 1:11 "Camptown Ladies"

STYLE	Minstrel show song
FORM	Verse/chorus
LYRICS	The lyrics in the recordings are no longer in Foster's original pseudo-black dialect. For instance, "Gwine to run all night!" has become "Going to run all night!"

0:00	Introduction		
	Brief piano introduction: first phrase of the melody		
0:08	**First statement of form**		
	Verse 1	The Camptown ladies sing this song Doo-dah! doo-dah! ...	Melody built from pentatonic scale
	Chorus (0:21)	Going to run all night! ...	Sung without vocal harmony

Transition to second recording: Fiddle and banjo, the featured instruments, connect back to the minstrel show via bluegrass and old-time music. The percussion instruments are a modern counterpart to the tambourine and bones of the minstrel show troupe.

0:31	**Second statement of form**		
	Verse 4	Seen them flying on a ten-mile heat ...	Bass line (on "acoustic" guitar) gives Latin flavor.
	Chorus (0:48)	Going to run all night! ... (2x)	
1:05	**Third statement of form**		
	Instrumental: Banjo has the melody; fiddle plays syncopated background, then joins in on the chorus.		

4 to Listen For
"Camptown Ladies"

INSTRUMENTATION
Solo voice and piano; then voice plus fiddle, banjo, bass (on guitar), percussion

RHYTHM
Polka-like dance rhythm at a brisk tempo in first part; more active, syncopated rhythms in second part

MELODY
Melody in verse based on pentatonic scale

TEXTURE
Melody with simple accompaniment in first part; melody with active, syncopated accompaniment in second part

4 to Remember
"Camptown Ladies"

WORDS, RACIAL STEREOTYPES, AND HUMOR
A song about a horserace with multiple misadventures, originally in pseudo-black dialect

DANCE RHYTHMS
Polka-like bass/chord accompaniment gives song rhythmic energy.

THE MELODY IS THE SONG
Song is the melody, with or without accompaniment.

WRITTEN VS. ORAL TRADITION
First part based on sheet music; second part from oral tradition

CD 1:11

"Camptown Ladies," Stephen Foster (1850). Frederick Urrey, vocal; John van Buskirk, fortepiano (1994)/the Duhks (2004). At the time of this recording, the Duhks included Jessica Havey, vocals; Tania Elizabeth, fiddle and background vocals; Leonard Podolak, banjo; Jordan McConnell, acoustic guitar; and Scott Senior, percussion.

America, the more respectable members of American society looked down their noses at "the Ethiopian business." Many considered the early minstrel show and anything associated with it to be low-class entertainment, although some patronized the shows.

Nevertheless, minstrelsy and the music for it had gained a firm toehold in American life by the Civil War. Foster played a significant role in making it more palatable by creating a new genre, the "plantation song." Foster's innovative synthesis brought the sentimentality of middle-class song into the rough-and-tumble world of the minstrel show, and with it, a more human portrayal of blacks.

Approbation was not universal. John Sullivan Dwight, whose *Journal of Music* served as the semiofficial arbiter of good taste among the cultivated, admitted that "Old Folks at Home," Foster's most famous plantation song, was indeed popular but likened the song to a "morbid irritation of the skin." "Old Folks at Home" would become the best-known song in nineteenth-century America: estimates of sheet music sales of the song during the latter half of the century reach as high as 20 million, and the song remains familiar to this day.

affairs is the fact that the song existed simultaneously in a more or less official version (the sheet music) and in the multiple versions created by those who learned it by ear. However, unlike the published scores of Foster's parlor songs, the sheet music of the minstrel show songs was not an authoritative guide to performance. It was simply the best way to get the song out to the public and make some money from it.

"Camptown Ladies" would have sounded very different in the minstrel show, its real home—there would have been fiddle, banjo, tambourine, and bones supporting the vocals instead of piano, and the minstrels probably danced as they played. In terms of musical identity, this kind of popular song would occupy a middle ground between classical music, where the printed score preserved the composer's musical vision, and folk music, where there is no single authoritative source.

Social Acceptance and Synthesis

With our multicultural mindset, it is hard to imagine the kind of contempt "respectable" people felt toward the minstrel show. However, in mid-nineteenth century

> "*John Sullivan Dwight likened "Old Folks at Home" to a "morbid irritation of the skin.*"

The popularity of Foster's minstrel show songs was the clearest signal that a distinctive new musical style, one that was both popular and American, had emerged. His songs have remained part of our collective memory for more than a century and a half, while much of the more-genteel music that Dwight championed is long forgotten.

Minstrelsy and American Popular Music. American popular music—music that is distinctively and recognizably American, a commercial enterprise, and widely popular—began with minstrelsy. There had of course been music that was popular in America before minstrelsy—we still sing the revolutionary-era tune "Yankee Doodle"—but there was no popular music that sounded distinctively American until the appearance of minstrel show songs like "Camptown Ladies" and "De Boatmen's Dance."

Even in its published form, the minstrel show song introduced two innovations that would become a permanent part of popular song: use of a recurrent chorus and dance rhythms. And as performed onstage, it introduced the mixed-timbre accompaniment, complete with percussion—tambourine and bones.

Minstrelsy would give blacks their first substantial opportunity to enter the entertainment business. Black minstrel troupes took the stage right after the end of the Civil War, and they were popular from the start, drawing crowds as big as, or bigger than, the white troupes did. Promoters billed black minstrels as authentic portrayers of plantation life, although they were forced to perpetuate the stereotypes of the early minstrel show. Bert Williams, the great African American vaudeville performer of the early twentieth century, complained that he and other black performers had to appear in blackface so that they looked the way white people thought they should.

Nevertheless, in the late nineteenth century, minstrelsy was the main route to a career for black popular performers. W. C. Handy, the "father of the blues" and himself a minstrel in the 1890s, noted that "All the best [African American] talent of that generation came down the same drain. The composers, the singers, the musicians, the speakers, the stage performers—the minstrel show got them all."

The minstrel show was America's first indigenous popular music and its first musical export. It brought freshness to America's cultural life. Because of this it is doubly unfortunate that its most indelible image is its demeaning stereotypes of African Americans. Minstrelsy cultivated prejudice and ignorance in some and reinforced it in others. Still, the positive contributions of the minstrel show include four important firsts, all of which figure prominently in subsequent generations of popular music:

- It was entertainment for the masses.
- It used vernacular speech and music.
- It created a new genre by synthesizing middle-class urban song and folk music.
- It was the first instance of a phenomenon in American popular music that has continued to the present day: that of invigorating and transforming the dominant popular style through the infusion of energetic, often danceable music.

Popular Entertainment After the Civil War

The two decades before the Civil War saw the birth of popular music; the three decades after the Civil War saw the birth of the popular music industry. The minstrel show had demonstrated that stage entertainment offered an excellent way to promote songs. Brisk sales of Stephen Foster's songs had revealed a large and lucrative market for sheet music. After the war, both stage entertainment and music publishing became more commercially oriented. Stage entertainment expanded and diversified, while an increasing number of music publishers began to publish only popular songs in order to maximize profits.

By the 1890s the popular music industry was up and running. Musical comedy and vaudeville competed with the minstrel show for the stage entertainment dollar. Charles Harris's 1892 hit "After the Ball" confirmed what music publishers already suspected: the existence of a large market for popular song. And after three decades of being confined mainly to minstrelsy, blacks began to branch out into other facets of the entertainment business.

Tin Pan Alley

In the 1880s a different breed of music publisher opened for business in New York City. Whereas traditional publishers issued music of all kinds, the new publishers sold only popular songs and marketed them aggressively. They hired **song pluggers**, house pianists who could play a new song for a professional singer or a prospective customer. At first the publishers congregated in the theater district around Union Square (14th Street), but most soon moved uptown to 28th Street, still near enough to the theaters to have access to performers. Writer Monroe Rosenfeld dubbed 28th Street **"Tin Pan Alley"** because the sound of several song pluggers auditioning songs at once reminded him of crashing tin pans.

New York City became home to both popular stage entertainment and popular-music publishing. The new flood of immigrants, among them Irish, Germans, and then Jews, plus the migration of African Americans into the city, swelled New York's population. Many immigrants found work in show business, as performers or songwriters or as theater owners, agents, or publishers. New

Monroe Rosenfeld dubbed 28th Street "Tin Pan Alley" because the sound of several song pluggers auditioning songs at once reminded him of crashing tin pans.

York would be the center of popular music for decades, challenged only by Hollywood after the advent of talking movies.

African American songwriters found wider acceptance for their work. In the 1890s Gussie Davis became the first black songwriter to achieve success on Tin Pan Alley. The songwriting team of Bob Cole and the brothers J. Rosamund Johnson and James Weldon Johnson supplied music for their own shows and for interpolation into other productions. African American musicians of the time usually wore many hats. For example, the most lasting contribution of the Johnson brothers was not their popular songs but their arrangements of Negro spirituals. They would publish two sets of them, in 1925 and 1926. Will Marion Cook, musical director for the Walker-Williams Company in the 1900s, also composed songs in a style influenced by African American folksong. Later he directed one of the leading syncopated dance orchestras of the time.

"After the Ball". Charles Harris's 1892 popular song "After the Ball" was the first big Tin Pan Alley hit, eventually selling more than 5 million sheet-music copies. An early recording of "After the Ball," sung by George Gaskin, one of the Irish tenors who were so popular around the turn of the century, was a bestseller in 1893. (*Bestseller* is a relative term, however, as commercial recording was only three years old at the time, distribution was difficult, and both records and record players were expensive.) The story of its road to success tells us a lot about the growth of stage entertainment and music publishing, the way they operated, and the extent to which they intertwined.

Harris was a self-taught songwriter and performer (on the banjo). He never learned to read or write music and had to hire a trained musician to notate his songs. But he made up for his lack of training in determination, nerve, and business savvy. While living in Milwaukee, he wrote "After the Ball" for a friend. Harris then approached several popular singers whose tours with vaudeville took them through Milwaukee and asked them to perform the song in their shows. The first three, two vaudeville stars and a ballad singer in a minstrel show, unceremoniously turned him down. He finally persuaded the fourth—who was starring in a touring production of *A Trip to Chinatown*, one of the most popular musical comedies of the 1890s—to interpolate the song into the show. Reportedly, Harris convinced the star by representing himself as a correspondent for the New York *Dramatic News,* promising a glowing review and paying the star $500.

"After the Ball" was such a great success in the show that Julius Witmark, one of the new breed of Tin Pan Alley publishers, offered Harris $10,000 for the rights to the song. Instead, figuring that he could make more money publishing it himself, Harris set up his own publishing house. As it turned out, he was correct. He understood public taste and had a knack for spotting potential hits. Although he never wrote another song as successful as "After the Ball," Harris made a fortune publishing his own songs and those of other songwriters.

"After the Ball" and the Music Business. In the wake of its success, even more publishers restricted their catalogs to popular song, and by 1900 very few hit songs were published away from Tin Pan Alley. Harris's decision to go into business for himself suggests that songwriters seldom realized either fame or fortune: it was the publisher who saw most of the profits, and the singers who enjoyed the celebrity.

Part of a publisher's profits went toward recruiting singers to perform the publisher's songs. Then as now the surest route to popularity was performance by a star of the day, even when the song was intended primarily for the home market. It was standard practice to secure performances with gifts and bribes, just as record companies bribed disc jockeys sixty years later. The principle—or lack of principle—was the same; only the players and the terms of the deals differed.

Waltz Songs. By the 1890s dance rhythms, an integral feature of songs for the minstrel show, began to be used

CD 1:12

"Take Me Out to the Ball Game," Albert von Tilzer, music; Jack Norworth, lyrics (1908). Harvey Hindermeyer, vocal.

even in songs with sentimental texts. The waltz was the first dance rhythm to enjoy widespread use: many of the most memorable songs of the 1890s and 1900s had a waltz beat. In *Yesterdays,* his chronicle of popular song, Charles Hamm lists sixteen commercially successful songs (most had sales of at least 1 million copies of sheet music) from these two decades—thirteen of which have an accompaniment in waltz rhythm. Among the still familiar **waltz songs** from the turn of the century is the 1908 hit "Take Me Out to the Ball Game."

"Take Me Out to the Ball Game" is a true product of Tin Pan Alley. Its composer, Albert von Tilzer, was the younger brother of Harry von Tilzer, the most successful songwriter of the period and a partner in a very profitable music-publishing firm. The younger von Tilzer worked for his older brother's publishing house.

The lyric is fun and very much in the present, neither sentimental nor nostalgic. The language is simple, direct, and slightly slangy, and it tells of the imaginary Katie Casey's love affair with baseball. The music is as jaunty as the lyrics. The band's *OOM-pah-pah* waltz rhythm gives the song a bounce, and the rhythm of the melody swings from one strong beat to the next. Like the parlor song, "Take Me Out to the Ball Game" is all about melody; once the voice enters, everything else stays in the background. The rhythm of the melody governs the rhythm of the lyrics, which is quite different from speech rhythm.

The song uses a verse/chorus form: the verse tells us about Katie; the chorus states, then restates the song's main theme. This form was more widely used than any other from the 1860s through the 1910s. Gradually, however, perhaps because the chorus was more memorable and central to the song, performers began to ignore the verse. The verses of "Take Me Out to the Ball Game" all but disappeared from our collective memory decades ago. One rarely, if ever, hears the verses of these and other songs from the period.

> *The verses of "Take Me Out to the Ball Game" all but disappeared from our collective memory decades ago.*

In time and in topic, "Take Me Out to the Ball Game" is a long way from the minstrel songs "De Boatmen's Dance" and "Camptown Ladies." Still, we find in this song the legacy of the minstrel show and the revolution it sparked. It is apparent in the everyday language of the lyric, the dance rhythm that supports the melody, and the verse/chorus form—the most widespread influences of minstrel show songs.

Songs like "Take Me Out to the Ball Game" show the shift in popular music during the latter part of the nineteenth century. Although sentimental songs were still popular—"After the Ball" is a real tearjerker—high-spirited songs about everyday life became increasingly common. Its musical complement was the use of a dance rhythm—waltz rhythm was the most popular, but march and polka rhythms were also used.

LISTENING GUIDE
CD 1:12 "Take Me Out to the Ball Game"

STYLE	Waltz song
FORM	Verse/chorus
	Both verse and chorus are long; the chorus can (and does) stand alone. The form of the chorus is A A¹.
0:00	Introduction
	Instrumental, with wind instruments prominent

First statement of form

0:10	Verse		
	A	Katie Casey was baseball mad …	
	A¹ (0:23)	On a Saturday her young beau …	Melody begins like the first phrase, but takes a new direction toward the chorus.
0:37	Chorus		
	A	Take me out to the ball game …	Notice how the long notes in the melody line up with the bass notes.
	A¹ (0:50)	Let me root, root, root for the home team …	There is no syncopation.
1:03	Interlude		
	OOM-pah-pah bass/chord accompaniment clearly presents waltz rhythm.		

Second statement of form

1:06	Verse		
	A	Katie Casey saw all the games …	
	A¹ (1:19)	When the score was just two to two …	
1:33	Chorus		
	A	Take me out to the ball game …	As before, in the chorus, words and music are repeated.
	A¹ (1:33)	Let me root, root, root for the home team …	

5 to Listen For
"Take Me Out to the Ball Game"

INSTRUMENTATION
Solo voice with band instrument accompaniment

PERFORMANCE STYLE
Over-enunciated singing typical of early recordings; quasi-operatic voice

RHYTHM
Waltz rhythm (*OOM-pah-pah*) at a fast tempo

RHYTHM
No syncopation in the melody; rhythm of the words not speech-like

MELODY
Flowing phrases, each four measures long, with a rest at the end

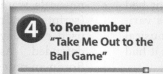

4 to Remember
"Take Me Out to the Ball Game"

ACOUSTIC RECORDING
Very early commercial acoustic recording; poor fidelity

EXPANDED VERSE/CHORUS FORM
Bigger verse/chorus form; chorus can stand alone.

WALTZ SONGS
Not for dancing, but with a clear dance rhythm in accompaniment

LIGHT-HEARTED SONG
Lyrics show shift away from nineteenth-century sentimentality.

Hindermyer's recording of the song reminds us that recordings were at best an imperfect way to get the song to its audience. If one wanted to hear a professional performance of a popular song, the best strategy was to hear it performed live. Around 1900, audiences had plenty of options.

Stage Entertainment

Stage entertainment with music exploded after the Civil War. The spark came from the minstrel show, whose appeal made it clear that there was a market for popular entertainment. Improvements in everyday life, from elevated trains in cities to electric lights in theaters and streets, made it easier to draw audiences and made the theaters safer venues. And the potential audience grew dramatically as immigrants from all over Europe poured into the United States. In just a few decades, stage entertainment with popular music went from a happy accident to a significant industry.

By 1870 three entertainment genres incorporated popular music: the minstrel show, vaudeville, and musical comedy. Vaudeville was a variety show, pure and simple. It featured a series of acts—singers, dancers, comics, acrobats, magicians, jugglers, and the like—without

In just a few decades, stage entertainment with popular music went from a happy accident to a significant industry.

any pretense of dramatic unity. Acts came on stage, did their routines, and left, not to return for the rest of the show. By contrast, musical comedies had plots, but they served more as scaffolding for a string of songs than dramatically credible stories enhanced by the music.

A fourth genre, operetta, was imported from England during the 1870s. The operettas of Gilbert and Sullivan enjoyed great success in the United States, and by the early twentieth century, European operetta composers had begun to emigrate to the United States: the Irish composer Victor Herbert was the most prominent. Operetta would remain part of mainstream musical life through the 1930s.

The slow demise of the minstrel show at the end of the nineteenth century created a void for a breezy, loosely jointed show with lots of song and dance and a skimpy plot to hold it all together. The public craved shows that were topical, upbeat, aimed at the masses, and full of comedy, song, and dance. The revue filled that void for more than twenty-five years.

Two things stand out about song on the American stage around the turn of the century: most songs had little dramatic connection to their context, and most songs did not sound particularly American. Recall that vaudeville had no plot, just a sequence. The minstrel show had songs but not much of a story. Revues used some kind of story line to hook a string of songs together with comedy and dance routines. Although it generally began with a real plot, musical comedy wasn't much better. Interpolation, in which the plot of a musical comedy was adapted to include a currently popular song, was the rule of the day; plots accommodated songs, as the history of "After the Ball" exemplifies. Only in operetta do we find a consistent connection between song and story.

Today we expect songs in musicals to serve a dramatic purpose, even though the song may become popular outside of the show. The idea of introducing a song into a show just because it is popular, or in the hope that it will become popular, seems a crude practice dramatically. However, viewed as a transitional step on the way to dramatically credible musical theater, or as a way to connect popular song and popular stage entertainment after the Civil War, interpolation is more understandable. Compared with the minstrel show, which had a deliberately loose story line (when it had one at all), and vaudeville, which was a plotless variety show, the surprise is not that the plot of a musical comedy was fair game for interpolation but that it had a plot at all.

Moreover, most songs lacked a recognizably American musical character: before 1900 very few songs evidenced musical features with a distinctively American sound. That began to change with the increasing popularity of songs by black songwriters and the production of musical comedies by George M. Cohan.

George M. Cohan: Toward an American Musical Comedy. Born into a family of vaudeville performers, George M. Cohan (1878–1942) came into prominence around 1900 with a string of successful musicals that included many still familiar songs and that were more tightly knit dramatically than their predecessors. Cohan was a one-man entertainment industry, adept at all phases of the theatrical business: songwriting, performing, directing, and producing. He was among the most important and versatile entertainers of his age.

But it is as a patriotic songwriter that Cohan's legacy endures. His **patriotic songs** have the energy of a great march, a vigorous melody, a hint of syncopation, and clever lyrics without a trace of nineteenth-century sentimentality. With the exception of Irving Berlin, no American songwriter before or since has embodied patriotic sentiment so successfully in words and music.

|||||||||||||||||||||||||||||||||||||||

"My God, what an act to follow!"
—George M. Cohan, on James Cagney's portrayal of him in *Yankee Doodle Dandy*.

In addition to their memorable songs, Cohan's musicals were also noteworthy because their books (scripts for nonmusical sections) and song lyrics used everyday speech, a practice that Cohan readily defended. As musical theater historian Gerald Bordman notes:

> A number of traditional reviewers assailed [Cohan's] excessive dependence on slang. Cohan retorted that that was the way his characters would talk could they have come to life on stage. He was not writing "literature," he was creating an entertainment about people with whom his audience could identify.

Cohan's musicals were a people's music, written for "the plumber and his lady friend in the last balcony."

We see this in the lyric of "Yankee Doodle Boy" from Cohan's musical *Little Johnny Jones* (1904). The verse contains several slang expressions that give the song an easy familiarity: "all the candy"; "ain't that a josh"; and "phony"—early twentieth-century street talk.

"Yankee Doodle Boy" is one of the most memorable of Cohan's patriotic songs. In the musical it helps establish the character of Johnny Jones, a jockey who has come to England to ride in the Derby. Jones, played by Cohan in the original production, is, in Bordman's words, "the cocky, slangy, identical twin of his creator." These qualities certainly come across in the song. It is an early example of the best kind of theater song—one that enhances the action on-stage but that has a life apart from the show as well.

CD 1:13

"Yankee Doodle Boy," George M. Cohan (1904). Richard Perry, vocal.

Cohan's musicals are seldom produced today—indeed, they might be hard to reconstruct. Still, his music has survived. Other than Stephen Foster's songs, Cohan's are the oldest still around in our time. Songs such as "Yankee Doodle Boy," "Give My Regards to Broadway," and "You're a Grand Old Flag" are still very much in the air. James Cagney's portrayal of Cohan in *Yankee Doodle Dandy* (1942), and the musical *George M.* (1968), have helped keep Cohan and his music alive and in the public eye.

The distinctly American patriotic spirit that Cohan projected in song, John Philip Sousa projected in instrumental music. We consider his music and the central role of the concert band in American musical life at the turn of the twentieth century next.

Warner Bros/ The Kobal Collection/Picture Desk

LISTENING GUIDE

CD 1:13 "Yankee Doodle Boy"

STYLE	"March" song
FORM	Verse/chorus
	Both verse and chorus are long; the chorus can (and does) stand alone. Form of the chorus is A, A¹.

| 0:00 | Introduction |
| | Instrumental: just piano and drums (added for march-like flavor) |

First statement of form

0:10	Verse		
	A	I'm the kid that's all the candy …	Cohan uses the opening of "Yankee Doodle" as the beginning of his verse.
	B (0:26)	I love to listen to the Dixie strain …	Cohan quotes three more songs: "Dixie," "The Girl I Left Behind Me," and "The Star-Spangled Banner."
0:44	Chorus		
	A	I'm a Yankee Doodle Dandy …	Notice the cakewalk rhythm on the phrase "Born … July."
	A¹ (0:59)	I've got a Yankee Doodle sweetheart …	Another quotation from "Yankee Doodle" toward the end of the phrase
1:03	Interlude		
	Like the introduction; vamp (accompaniment by itself) in march rhythm just before voice reenters		

Second statement of form

1:22	Verse		
	A	My father's name was Hezekiah …	Cohan uses the opening of "Yankee Doodle" as the beginning of his verse.
	B (1:36)	My mother's mother was a Yankee true …	Cohan quotes three more songs: "Dixie," "The Girl I Left Behind Me," and "The Star-Spangled Banner."
1:54	Chorus		
	A	I'm a Yankee Doodle Dandy …	As before
	A¹ (2:08)	I've got a Yankee Doodle sweetheart …	

5 to Listen For
"Yankee Doodle Boy"

INSTRUMENTATION
Voice, plus piano and drums (added to give march-like feel)

RHYTHM
March-like rhythm (*OOM-pah*) at a fast tempo

RHYTHM
Fast-moving rhythms in melody with occasional single syncopation

MELODY
Fairly long phrases in verse and chorus, with regular pauses

MELODY
Extensive quotation of existing songs interpolated into melody

---

4 to Remember
"Yankee Doodle Boy"

"SAMPLING," CA. 1904
Cohan quotes several patriotic tunes and a popular song of the day.

THE COMMON TOUCH
Colloquial lyrics and a bright catchy tune

PATRIOTIC CHARACTER
Patriotic tunes, plus a crisp march rhythm

CAKEWALK RHYTHM
The simple syncopation of the cakewalk is used throughout: "ain't that a josh."

The Concert Band

The most popular instrumental ensemble in late nineteenth-century America was the **concert band**. In an era without radio, TV, and other forms of mass communication, touring concert bands, as well as municipal bands found in almost every town, were a primary source of musical entertainment. They supplied their audiences with a broad range of music: classical selections arranged for band; current hit songs; and, of course, marches, which (ironically) they usually played sitting down.

Bands had been a part of American life since the Revolution. Almost every city and town, large or small, had a municipal band. They performed on most public occasions and gave concerts in season. After the Civil

John Philip Sousa in 1900.

Library of Congress, Prints and Photographs Division, Washington, D.C. [LC-US261-143]

concert band had stabilized. Bands were composed of woodwinds, brass, and percussion instruments. Trumpets, trombones, clarinets, and percussion were typically the most prominent.

From the 1890s through the 1920s, the most popular concert band in the United States was John Philip Sousa's New Marine Band. Sousa (1854–1932) was the most prominent bandleader and band composer of his era. He had established his reputation as a composer and conductor with the Marine Band, which he directed for twelve years, then formed his own band in 1892. For the remainder of his career, he led his band on annual tours throughout the United States, as well as several tours to Europe and one world tour, giving over 10,000 concerts. Sousa's band was known for its precision and musicianship and for the excellence of its soloists, several of whom subsequently led bands of their own.

A typical Sousa band concert included **marches** (music composed in regularly accented, usually duple meter, appropriate to accompany marching), original works for band, solos featuring the band's virtuoso instrumentalists, arrangements of well-known opera overtures, symphonic poems, program music, and the popular music of the day. The latter included the latest in syncopated music, such as the cakewalk "At a Georgia

War, some of the bands that had formed in major cities became professional ensembles, playing at concerts, dances, and other public occasions. By the latter part of the nineteenth century, the instrumentation of the

LISTENING GUIDE
CD 1:14 *The Stars and Stripes Forever*

STYLE	March	
FORM	Multisectional form of march; four strains in the form AABB/Trio (CDCDC)	
0:00	**March**	
	Introduction: Notice the simple syncopation in the second measure; this is the "cakewalk" syncopation.	
0:03	First strain	
	A	High woodwinds play the fast-moving melody.
	A (0:17)	The same strain repeated
0:30	Second strain	
	B	Simple melody played by brass; clarinets echo melody notes at a higher register.
	B (0:44)	Repeated
0:57	**Trio**	
	New key, sudden drop in dynamics, lyric melody, and new featured instrument mark the beginning of the trio. Melody is stated three times, with "break" between statements.	
	C	Lyric melody played by clarinets in a low register. Accompaniment changes from *OOM-pah/OOM-pah* to a single bass note at the beginning of each measure.
	D (1:25)	Break features the low brass (trombones, tubas). Accompaniment stops.
	B (1:46)	Lyric theme returns, with two countermelodies. Piccolo plays the prominent one; midrange brass countermelody is more in background.
	D (2:14)	Break is repeated.
	C (2:36)	Final statement of the trio features full band led by brass.

5 to Listen For
The Stars and Stripes Forever

INSTRUMENTATION
Full concert band, with woodwinds, brass, and percussion

RHYTHM
Duple meter, at a brisk tempo, with clear marking of the beat in accompaniment throughout, except for breaks

MELODY
Instrumental-style melodies for the most part: fast-moving notes, wide skips

MELODY
Trio has lyrical melody.

TEXTURE
Melody plus simple accompaniment, with countermelodies a striking feature of the trio when repeated; accompaniment stops during breaks.

4 to Remember
The Stars and Stripes Forever

MARCH RHYTHM
OOM-pah: bass note on the beat, chord on the afterbeat, with variants or breaks for rhythmic interest

MARCH FORM
Four strains, with a pronounced contrast in the third strain. The break is an exceptional feature.

THE CONCERT BAND
Large ensemble, with clarinets the most numerous instrument. Trumpets, trombones, clarinets, piccolo, and percussion are featured.

AMERICAN MUSIC
Sousa's marches sound musically American because of their vitality and rhythmic energy.

Although he composed other kinds of works—songs, operettas, and band suites—Sousa made his reputation as a composer of marches. Their popularity earned him the title "The March King" and made him America's best-known composer during his lifetime. He wrote 136 marches between 1876 and 1931, but most of the best known were written between 1888 and 1900: *Semper Fidelis* (1888), *Washington Post* (1889), and *Hands Across the Sea* (1899) are a few.

Sousa's most famous march, and probably the most famous American march of all time, is *The Stars and Stripes Forever*. Conceived of in 1896 and published the following year, during Sousa's peak decade as a composer, it is the quintessential Sousa march. It has stirring and lyric melodies, subtle variation in accompaniment and rhythm, and a rich texture, with several layers of activity. A typical Sousa march has a modular form, assembled from a series of melodies or "strains" that are sixteen or thirty-two measures in length. There are two main sections, the march and the trio; the trio is in a different key. Each strain is repeated at least once.

Sousa's marches are the instrumental counterpart to the songs of Foster and Cohan. They share three important qualities. First, the most famous works by all three composers were immediately popular and have remained among the best-known music from their eras. Second, they are musically significant, the best examples of their genres. Third, they are (almost indefinably) American, without extensive or obvious black influence. With ragtime, they comprise the most important legacy from American popular music before World War I.

Simply because they—and the bands that played them—were so popular, marches by Sousa and others had an impact well beyond the parade and concert venues. The two-step was a popular social dance inspired by Sousa's *The Washington Post*. The rhythm and spirit of the march animated popular song, as we discovered earlier. Most important perhaps, the march and the concert band also played a seminal role in the development of ragtime, syncopated music, and jazz.

Camp Meeting," originally published as a solo piano piece. In fact, many European listeners first gained exposure to ragtime's syncopated rhythms through Sousa's performances abroad.

The role of professional bands in American musical life around 1900 was much like that of the contemporary pops orchestra. Both feature varied programming: a mixture of popular classical music and popular music, with star soloists. And both direct their programs at a mass audience. Sousa was keenly aware of the difference in the roles of the concert band and the symphony orchestra: comparing himself to Theodore Thomas, the founder and conductor of the Chicago Symphony, he remarked that Thomas "gave Wagner, Liszt, and Tchaikowsky, in the belief that he was educating his public; I gave Wagner, Liszt, and Tchaikowsky with the hope that I was entertaining my public."

||||||||||||||||||||||||||||||||||||

"I gave Wagner, Liszt, and Tchaikowsky with the hope that I was entertaining my public."
—John Philip Sousa

CD 1:14

The Stars and Stripes Forever, John Philip Sousa (1897). Columbia All-Star Band; Gunther Schuller, conductor.

Looking Back, Looking Ahead

The American music landscape during the first few decades of the nineteenth century provides virtually no clues as to the direction popular music would soon take. Virtually all of the commercially disseminated popular music came from Europe. Only the emergence of blackface entertainment in America gave a glimpse of future developments. However, by the turn of the twentieth century, America had its own popular music, recognized as such at home and abroad, and a rapidly growing industry to promote it.

The birth of a recognizably American popular music and the growth of the popular music industry are the two most significant developments in nineteenth-century popular music. They encompass several important trends that continue through the twentieth century, including these:

- *The infusion of rhythm into popular music* Dance rhythms in support of popular song are an innovation of minstrel show music; by the end of the century, they are customary in almost all kinds of popular song.
- *Impact of "low-brow" styles* In popular music, the impetus for change comes from the more marginalized segments of American society: rural folk traditions, white and black, at mid-century, then African American elements around the turn of the twentieth century.
- *Innovation through synthesis* Innovation in popular music is mainly a matter of integrating diverse, even contradictory, musical elements into a new sound: the minstrel show song and Foster's plantation songs evidence this trend.

- *Increased role of blacks* The presence of African Americans in the popular music industry, begun in earnest after the end of the Civil War, continues during the latter part of the nineteenth century. Blacks begin to break through into genres other than minstrelsy around 1900.

The new century would bring vibrant new music, mainly through a comprehensive infusion of African American music: ragtime, syncopated dance music, blues, and jazz. We encounter these styles in the next chapter.

Terms to Know

Test your knowledge of this chapter's important terms by defining the ones listed here. If you can't recall the meaning of a certain term, refresh your memory by looking up the boldfaced term in the chapter, turning to the Glossary at the back of the book, or working with the flashcards at the Popular Music Resource Center.

call and response
melisma
ballad
strophic
parlor song
minstrel show
interlocutor
Tambo and Bones
endmen
olio
burlesque
walkaround
cakewalk

unison
songster
song plugger
Tin Pan Alley
waltz song
vaudeville
operetta
revue
interpolation
patriotic song
concert band
march
trio

The Emergence of Black Music

LIVE JAZZ

Patricia Marroquin/istockphoto.com

CHAPTER

3

Sometime in 1914, Jim Europe sat at the piano during a break between dance numbers. He was playing a song that he'd played many times before, W. C. Handy's "Memphis Blues." Irene and Vernon Castle, who had heard him play it over and over, approached him and asked him to turn it into a dance number. Europe did, and the Castles created a new dance, the foxtrot. The Castles' casual request marked the beginning of the modern era in popular music.

This new music sounded modern mainly because it incorporated unmistakable elements of black music. In the first twenty-five years of the twentieth century, black music exploded into American life. Ragtime, syncopated dance music, blues, and jazz—all found an audience among blacks and whites and eventually blended with the mainstream styles to produce a new kind of popular music.

● ● ● ● ● ● ● ●

Ragtime

Ragtime altered the sound of popular music. It was through ragtime that white Americans finally discovered the rhythmic vitality of real African American music. Whites might have encountered black performers in minstrel shows or touring jubilee choirs, but because authentic ragtime could also be performed from sheet music, whites now had a chance to study and savor it. As a result, its influence was far more extensive than that of earlier black styles. Because of this, ragtime became the catalyst for the revolutionary changes in popular music that marked the beginning of its modern era.

The history of ragtime begins in the years after the Civil War. Black musicians in the Midwest had been playing ragtime—or at least syncopated music— well before the first rags were published in the 1890s. During this same period, black pianists in bars and bordellos up and down the East Coast played what would soon be called "ragtime," according to several contemporary accounts.

During the 1893 World Columbian Exposition, ragtime pianists from all over the country migrated to Chicago. Among them were most of the St. Louis ragtime pianists, including Scott Joplin. They found employment and valuable exposure in the restaurants, saloons, and brothels in the vicinity of the exposition.

Toward the end of the century, composers and songwriters began to use the terms *rag* and *ragtime* to identify a new style. The 1896 song "All Coons Look Alike to Me," by Ernest Hogan, one of the leading black entertainers of the era, makes reference to a Negro "rag" accompaniment; the song is the first published example of a rag-like piano style. The first published rags appeared a year later. With the publication of Joplin's "Maple Leaf Rag" in 1899, *ragtime* became a household word.

Joplin's "Maple Leaf Rag" was the first commercially successful **piano rag**. It did not so much start a craze for syncopated music as give it a major push along two lines: it introduced more complex African-inspired rhythms to popular music, and it made them available in sheet-music form. The rhythms of Joplin's early rags were more intricate than the syncopated songs and dances of the 1890s. Rhythmically, they found a midpoint between the improvised style of black ragtime pianists and the cakewalks and ragtime songs of the period.

And because ragtime was the first black music that looked on paper the way it sounded in performance, any competent pianist, black or white, who was able to read music could buy the sheet music to Joplin's "Maple Leaf Rag" and perform it in a reasonably authentic manner. At a time when recordings were limited, films were silent, radio and television nonexistent, and live entertainment, especially by black performers, relatively rare outside of the big cities, sheet music was the best way to absorb new music.

Scott Joplin

GAB Archives/Redferns Music Library

Scott Joplin

The classic piano rags of Scott Joplin (1868–1917) are the most enduring music of the ragtime era. Several have remained familiar, especially since the ragtime revival of the 1970s; Joplin's piano rags remain the core of the ragtime repertoire. A professional musician from his teenage years, Joplin played in saloons and clubs along the Mississippi valley and eventually in Missouri. (The "Maple Leaf Rag" is named after the Maple Leaf Club in Sedalia, Missouri, where he worked from 1894 until the turn of the century.) He also received formal musical training in the European tradition, principally through study at George R. Smith College in

LISTENING GUIDE
CD 1:15 "Maple Leaf Rag"

STYLE	Piano rag
FORM	Multisectional form of march, four strains in the form AABBA/CCDD
0:00	First Strain
	A — Characteristic ragtime figuration: series of arpeggiated chords, timed so top-note accents are often syncopated
	A (0:22) — Notice "stop-time" effect (0:30), where *OOM-pah* stops briefly
0:43	Second Strain
	B — Relatively simple underlying melody animated by ragtime patterns
	B (1:04)
1:25	First Strain returns
	A
1:46	Third Strain
	C — New melody and shift to new key (this would be trio in a march)
	C (2:07)
2:28	Fourth Strain
	D — Fourth new melody
	D (2:49) — Strain repeats, with decisive ending

Sedalia, and was a fluent composer and arranger in the popular white styles of the day. After the turn of the century, Joplin devoted most of his professional efforts to legitimizing ragtime. In addition to a steady stream of piano compositions, mostly rags, he composed a ballet, *The Ragtime Dance,* and two operas, *Treemonisha* and the now lost *A Guest of Honor.* (Joplin received a posthumous Pulitzer Prize for *Treemonisha* in 1976 on the occasion of its revival.)

The Sound of the Piano Rag

In Joplin's own performance of "Maple Leaf Rag," we can hear virtually all the significant features of traditional

CD 1:15

"Maple Leaf Rag," Scott Joplin (1899). Joplin, piano (piano roll, 1916).

piano ragtime. The piano rag is based on the march. (At this time marches were almost as popular on the dance floor as in a parade.) Joplin and his peers

simply transformed the march into ragtime by adding idiomatic, African-inspired syncopation and adapting the style to a single instrument, the piano. The Listening Guide details both the connection with the march and the ragged syncopation that sets it apart.

5 to Listen For
"Maple Leaf Rag"

INSTRUMENTATION
Solo piano

RHYTHM
March rhythm (*OOM-pah*) in accompaniment much of the time

RHYTHM
Syncopated ragtime patterns in melody

MELODY
Instrumental-style melody: rapid arpeggiated figuration

TEXTURE
Thick texture: harmonized melody plus bass/chord accompaniment

3 to Remember
"Maple Leaf Rag"

SOUND OF PIANO RAG
Most characteristic feature is syncopated figuration.

MARCH CONNECTION
Piano rag is like a march with syncopation, played on the piano.

RAGTIME, PUBLISHING, AND SPREAD OF BLACK MUSIC
Published rags gave mainstream America its first encounter with authentic black musical style.

Ragtime Enters Popular Culture

Although initially referring to piano music, the word *ragtime* quickly came to identify almost any syncopated music and even some that was not. (For example, Irving Berlin's 1911 hit "Alexander's Ragtime Band" is a thoroughly modern song for the time, but it does not have even the modest syncopation of earlier ragtime songs.) Ragtime songs, written and performed by both blacks and whites, were often interpolated into Broadway shows. "Under the Bamboo Tree," a hit song by black musicians James Weldon Johnson, J. Rosamond Johnson, and Bob Cole, first appeared in the show *Sally in Our Alley*, sung by Marie Cahill, an Irish-American singer. (It is difficult to imagine how they worked the lyrics—about a jungle maid—into the plot and how Cahill passed herself off as an African queen.)

As it spread across the country, ragtime met with resistance from virtually every corner of the establishment. It was considered immoral, fit only for the saloons and brothels where it was played. It was deemed musically déclassé—the product of an inferior race incapable of the musical sophistication that Europeans had achieved. And it was considered a cause of moral decay. According to one writer, "the 'Ragtime Evil' should not be found in Christian homes."

> ## " ... the 'Ragtime Evil' should not be found in Christian homes. "

There were, of course, overtones of racial prejudice in virtually all of these arguments. During this low point in race relations, few whites accepted blacks as equals, so it is not surprising that many found ragtime's mix of black and white influences unacceptable.

Serious musicians stood divided on the question of ragtime's worth. Daniel Gregory Mason, one of the guardians of the cultivated tradition, sought to demean ragtime by drawing an unfavorable comparison between

C Squared Studios/Getty Images

its syncopated rhythms and those found in Beethoven's and Schumann's music. Charles Ives, the most important American classical composer of that generation and an after-hours ragtime pianist, responded that the comparison showed "how much alike they [ragtime and Schumann] are."

In retrospect, the reaction against ragtime (and the blacks who created it) was even stronger than the reaction would be against rock and roll a half century later. However, the end result was the same: ragtime, like rock and roll, won out.

The Legacy of Ragtime

Ragtime's legacy to American music includes three contributions:

- A body of music of enduring value and appeal
- A number of firsts in the history of African American music
- The catalyst for the revolution that produced the modern era in popular music

The Classic Piano Rag. The classic piano rags of Scott Joplin and other distinguished composers represent a repertoire of real artistic worth and individuality; there is no other music like it. From musical evidence in Joplin's works, we can also infer his dedication to bringing ragtime under the European classical music umbrella. The later rags are more melodious and less syncopated, and in both his tempo indications for rags and his written commentary on the correct performance of ragtime, Joplin constantly admonishes pianists against playing ragtime too fast: ragtime played at a slower tempo gains dignity.

As his later compositions showed, Joplin saw ragtime as a vehicle for serious artistic expression as well as entertainment. Accordingly, he thought of himself as a composer of art music in the tradition of the nineteenth-century nationalist composers. He believed that he had elevated a folk-dance music to concert status, in much the same way that Polish composer Frédéric Chopin had elevated the *mazurka* (Polish folk dance) and Viennese composer Franz Schubert the *ländler* (Austrian folk dance) in classical music.

Joplin's disciples approached ragtime composition with a similar seriousness of purpose, and his publisher,

John Stark, identified him as a composer of "classic" rags. In keeping with his purpose, the classic ragtime style of Joplin and his disciples was the most conservative, or European, of the ragtime piano styles current around 1900. The East Coast ragtime of Eubie Blake and the New Orleans style of Jelly Roll Morton are considerably more syncopated than Joplin's music.

Ragtime and the Preservation of African American Culture. Ragtime, or at least the classic ragtime of Joplin and his peers, enabled African Americans to become more aware of their own culture. Prior to ragtime, black folk music had been passed on through oral tradition. Each new generation of blacks would learn the songs, dances, and religious music of their culture by hearing them and singing or playing along. It is frustrating to read pre-twentieth-century descriptions of black music; attempts by interested white musicians to capture black folk music in notation fall far short of the mark, no matter how sincere they may have been.

Joplin's work marked the beginning of a movement among historically conscious black musicians to preserve their musical heritage. W. C. Handy, the "father of the blues," began collecting blues melodies and assembling them into songs, just as Joplin had done with rags. James Weldon Johnson and J. Rosamond Johnson, brothers who were also active Broadway composers, assembled and arranged spirituals, fitting them with piano accompaniments for performance at home, at church, and even in the concert hall.

Ragtime also represented the first documented instance of African Americans filtering through their own musical heritage the European music to which they had been exposed. By comparing pieces in rag style with their original versions and models, it is possible to identify the specifically African elements in the rag.

Ragtime as a Catalyst for Change. Ragtime had a widespread impact on other musical styles. It loosened up popular music (both song and dance), helped shape jazz in its early years, and aroused the interest of several of the most important classical composers in the early twentieth century. Ragtime also made popular music livelier. Its beat had more of a bounce, and its syncopated rhythms permitted a rapid yet relatively natural delivery of the words.

Even at the peak of its popularity, and despite its notoriety, however, ragtime was never the dominant popular style. Mainstream popular music remained largely unsyncopated, as we discovered in "Take Me Out to the Ball Game." But no music from its era was more influential, and no music of the period remains more popular. Even more important, it opened the doors of popular music to other, more African styles. Syncopated dance music, blues, and jazz would soon follow ragtime's path toward the popular mainstream.

• • • • • • • •

Syncopated Dance Music

In the two decades between 1905 and 1925, Americans went dance crazy. Early on, much of the music that they danced to was ragtime, but over time the music for these new dances diversified to include popular songs set to a danceable beat.

Ragtime Dance

Almost as soon as it appeared, ragtime became music for social dancing. Piano rags were scored for the dance orchestras of the period. Joplin's famous "Red Book" (so called because it had a red cover), a collection of dance-orchestra arrangements of his popular rags, is the best-known example. Original dance music in a syncopated style also appeared throughout the late 1890s and into the 1910s.

As the cakewalk fad faded away, other dances took its place, most of them adapted or borrowed from black folk dances. The most notorious of these new dances was a group of animal dances. The grizzly bear, the chicken glide, and the turkey trot all became popular in certain circles around 1910. "Respectable" citizens reacted violently to these dances, which were associated with sleazy establishments and disreputable people. As recounted in Sylvia Dannett and Frank Rachel's book, *Down Memory Lane: The Arthur Murray Picture Book of Social Dancing*:

> A Paterson, New Jersey, court imposed a fifty-day prison sentence on a young woman for dancing the turkey trot. Fifteen young women were dismissed from a well-known magazine after the editor caught them enjoying the abandoned dance at lunchtime. Turkey trotters incurred the condemnation of churches and respectable people, and in 1914 an official disapproval was issued by the Vatican.

The turkey trot was one of the most popular dances. By all accounts it was simple and awkward, but it permitted

||||||||||||||||||||||||||||||||||||||||

"A Paterson, New Jersey, court imposed a fifty-day prison sentence on a young woman for dancing the turkey trot."

—*The Arthur Murray Picture Book of Social Dancing*

Historic American Sheet Music, "Get Together," Music #542, Duke University Rare Book, Manuscript, and Special Collections Library

An early foxtrot, published in 1915: it's evidence that the dance caught on quickly.

Vernon and Irene Castle

Hulton Archive/Getty Images

"lingering close contact," a novelty at the time. Body contact between couples (presumably) delighted the dancers but scandalized the more conservative segments of American society and provoked a hostile backlash. A more refined dance, the foxtrot, soon replaced it.

James Reese Europe and the Foxtrot

James Reese Europe (1881–1919) had come to New York in 1905 from Washington, D.C., and quickly immersed himself in the popular music world. By 1910 he had organized the Clef Club, an organization for black musicians that was part union and part booking agency. In 1912 he directed the 150-piece Clef Club Orchestra in a concert at Carnegie Hall, then as now America's musical mecca. Designed to showcase the achievements of African American musicians, the concert impressed members of New York's high society, and soon Europe and his Society Orchestra were in demand for parties given by the Rockefellers and other wealthy families.

CD 1:16

"Castle House Rag," James Reese Europe (1914). Europe's Society Orchestra.

Europe's star rose even higher when Irene and Vernon Castle chose him and his orchestra to accompany them. Fresh from Europe, where they had wowed Parisian audiences with their rendition of the tango, the Castles took New York by storm, appearing in a series of Broadway productions between 1912 and 1914 and in vaudeville, starring in silent films, and opening a dance studio and a supper club.

Among the dance pieces that Europe composed for the Castles was "Castle House Rag." Europe's orchestral rag evidences the spread of ragtime and shows the evolution of the genre away from the classic piano style. In addition to Europe's multi-instrumental setting, other differences between it and a classic Joplin rag include:

- *A faster tempo.* The tempo of ragtime music gradually accelerated during this period (despite Joplin's admonition to the contrary), so the beat of this song moves considerably more quickly than "Maple Leaf Rag." It is about the same speed as up-tempo music from the early 1920s (we hear two examples in the next chapter: "Charleston" and "Fascinating Rhythm.")
- *Less syncopation and less "ragged" melodies.* Overall, there is less rhythmic conflict in this piece than in a classic rag, and the figuration is less complex—probably because it would have been challenging to perform on melody instruments at such a fast tempo. There are exceptions, most notably the transition into the trio-like third section and the drum solo at the end.

LISTENING GUIDE
CD 1:16 "Castle House Rag"

| STYLE | Syncopated dance music |
| FORM | March-inspired multisectional form, with five strains plus drum solo |

First major section

0:00	A brief introduction in the style of the first strain	
0:04	First strain	
	A	A busy melody in the style of popular piano rags (not Joplin), with a few syncopations sprinkled in. Violins and flute play the melody.
	A (0:20)	The same strain repeated. Drums keep up an active rhythm underneath the melody.
0:35	Second strain	
	B	A slower moving melody with a strong syncopation. Entire orchestra moving in much the same rhythm at the outset. Drums remain active.
	B (0:51)	Again, violins are the dominant melody instrument.
1:05	First strain returns	
	A	As before

Second major section, like trio in march

1:23	A brief transition to the next section, characterized by a tricky rhythm: the short/long pattern goes in and out of phase with the beat.	
1:27	Third strain	
	C	A slower-moving melody in a new key, with only an occasional syncopation
	C (1:58)	Both of the C strains are twice the length of the previous strains.
2:29	Fourth strain	
	D	Fourth new melody
2:45	Fifth strain	
	E	Three-note pattern repeated several times is a melodic cliché of the teens.
	E (3:00)	The band breaks away from the tight arrangement; a little improvisation by some of the melody
3:16	Drum solo	
	F	Drummer Buddy Gilmore gets a moment in the spotlight.

- *A chance to improvise.* The last two sections allow the musicians, particularly drummer Buddy Gilmore, the chance to depart from the carefully scripted arrangement used throughout most of the performance.

Jim Europe's life ended abruptly, when one of his musicians, angry about Europe's discipline of the band, attacked him and severed his jugular vein. At the time, Europe was probably the most popular and highly respected black musician in the United States. He worked tirelessly to raise the stature of African American musicians. Whether justified or not, newspapers eulogized him as the "jazz king."

Many writers have speculated that if Europe hadn't died, popular music would have been quite different. The skimpy musical evidence that survives does not lend much support to this notion. Two circumstances argue against it. One was the proliferation of dance orchestras, both black and white, beginning the year of Europe's death and continuing into the 1920s. The other was the emergence of two other black musical styles: jazz and blues.

Europe's most far-reaching contribution to popular music was his integral role in developing and popularizing the foxtrot, which would become the dominant social dance of the 1920s and 1930s. For the first time, social dancing to a clearly black beat became acceptable to a significant portion of the population. Foxtrotting caught on with all levels of society, from the Rockefellers on down. Although it may not have been condoned in all quarters, dancing to syncopated music was no longer a criminal offense. By the mid-1930s, dancing "cheek to cheek," as Fred Astaire and Ginger Rogers did so often on-screen, not only was socially acceptable, it was the epitome of elegance.

5 **to Listen For**
"Castle House Rag"

INSTRUMENTATION
Unusual instrumentation includes violins and cello, flute and clarinet, cornet and baritone horn, piano, bells, and drums.

RHYTHM
March-like rhythm at a brisk tempo

RHYTHM
Simple syncopation in melodies; syncopated accents in drum solo

MELODY
Contrasting activity in instrumental-style melodies: A, D, E are more active than B and C.

TEXTURE
Melody plus simple accompaniment (accompanying parts not always easily heard because of primitive recording equipment)

4 **to Remember**
"Castle House Rag"

SYNCOPATED RHYTHMS
Most strains have simple, rag-influenced syncopations.

DANCE ORCHESTRA IN TRANSITION
Violins connect to Europe; winds, brass and especially percussion connect to 1920s dance orchestras.

CUTTING LOOSE
Musicians break free of tight arrangement only at the end.

SPRAWLING RAG
Short strains and fast tempo = four additional strains plus drum solo

there is not one history, but two. One is familiar, the other largely unknown. Partly as a result of this experience, Handy would go on to play a leading role in the emergence of blues as a commercial music during the first quarter of the twentieth century. It was the commercial versions of the blues that would shape the sound of popular music so profoundly in the early modern era.

By contrast, like the young man at the station, a whole generation of bluesmen would remain anonymous. We have almost no anecdotal information about the early history of blues as a folk music, and no musical evidence until the mid-1920s, when a few record companies began to record folk bluesmen like Blind Lemon Jefferson. The influence of this branch of the blues on mainstream music occurred in the rock era, and only after many of its leading performers left the South for northern cities like Chicago. We consider

The success of syncopated dance music was a milestone in the mainstreaming of black popular music. Still, it was only a step toward equal opportunity, equal treatment, and dignity. During the early 1910s, Europe got dance engagements in part because white bands refused to play the new syncopated music—they considered it beneath them. Only when the foxtrot caught on did white bands hop on the syncopated-music bandwagon.

• • • • • • • •
Early Commercial Blues

In his autobiography, W. C. Handy tells of an encounter late one night in 1903. While waiting for a train, Handy heard a young black man singing and playing a guitar, using a knife on the strings—similar to the bottleneck style of other blues guitarists. He described the sound as "the weirdest I'd ever heard." That "weird sound" was almost certainly the blues; Handy's account suggests that the style was already well established by that time.

The story and its aftermath encapsulate the history of the blues in the first part of the twentieth century:

> **"** *That "weird sound" was almost certainly the blues.* **"**

George Bailey/istockphoto.com

such "folk blues" in Chapter 6. In this chapter, we focus on the commercial blues styles that emerged in the first three decades of the twentieth century.

Commercial blues entered the larger world of popular music in four stages. The first began around the turn of the century, when the first professional blues performers launched their careers. The second occurred in the early teens with the publication of blues songs. In the third stage, which began in the late teens, blues style helped shape the sound of jazz. Finally, a group of "classic" blues singers, many of whom had started their careers years before, began to record.

The First Professional Blues Musicians

By the time of Handy's encounter, blacks had begun to sing and play the blues professionally. The great blues singer Ma Rainey, who would record extensively in the 1920s, recalls that she was inspired to sing the blues after hearing a girl sing the blues at a theater in St. Louis in 1902, and several of New Orleans's first generation of jazzmen recall playing the blues before the turn of the century. Early in the century, the audience for blues—folk, semiprofessional, and professional—were blacks, mainly in the South, and those whites who had extensive contact with blacks and/or who frequented the bars and bordellos where black musicians performed. However, as blacks migrated to urban areas in both the North and the South, they took the blues with them. After the move to the cities, what had been private or small-group entertainment in the rural South became music for public performance. Blues singers, most of them women, toured on the black vaudeville circuits and performed wherever they got paid. Ma Rainey was among the first; Bessie Smith joined her in the teens. They and other blues singers remained unknown to most Americans (both white and black) until the 1920s. The blues that reached these larger audiences were filtered through other styles. In the meantime, however, white America got its first taste of the blues.

Blues in Print: The First Published Blues Songs

W. C. Handy's "Memphis Blues" was part of a wave of blues songs that appeared during the 1910s. Handy composed several more, most notably St. Louis Blues" (1914), the most frequently recorded song in the first half of the twentieth century. These published songs are a pale imitation of the blues that Ma Rainey and Bessie Smith were singing in tent shows and on the black vaudeville circuit. Still, they mark the entry of the blues into the mainstream; it was this distinction that enabled Handy to claim with some justification that he was the "father of the blues." Although he certainly didn't invent the blues, he published sheet music of his compositions, thereby disseminating many of its conventions, such as the 12-bar form, and bringing them into the world of popular music.

Blues, Jazz, and Dance Music

During the teens, a few instrumental groups recorded the published blues songs of Handy and others, but the performances had little to do with blues style as heard only a few years later in the singing of Bessie Smith. In 1917 the first jazz recording was issued; it featured the all-white Original Dixieland Jass [sic] Band. One side of the record was "Livery Stable Blues," a song in blues form replete with barnyard sounds. A host of bands, black and white, followed in their footsteps; Europe's 369th U.S. Infantry "Hellfighters Band," a military band he brought to Europe at the end of World War I, recorded several of Handy's blues songs. These recordings brought the instrumental performance of blues closer to the style of the black blues singers. However, authentic blues style in instrumental music would only appear on record when the top black jazz bands, which had been playing blues-based jazz since the turn of the century in New Orleans, began recording in the early 1920s; we hear King Oliver's Creole Jazz Band later.

Classic Blues

The blues recorded during the 1910s were strictly instrumental. That changed almost overnight with the release of Mamie Smith's "Crazy Blues" in 1920. "Crazy Blues" is not a blues song in the full sense of the term. Rather, it is a blues-influenced popular song sung in a bluesy, distinctively black singing style. The recording caused a sensation and encouraged record companies to seek out other, similar singers.

The growth of commercial radio gave the record companies added motivation to recruit black blues singers. Because people didn't want to pay for what they could get for free, record companies were forced to seek out smaller markets—blacks, southern whites, and various ethnic groups—where they would not face competition from mainstream radio.

Chief among them was the so-called race-record market. **Race records** were recordings of black performers, targeted at a black audience. The featured styles were blues and jazz. Both major labels and the 1920s equivalent of indie labels recorded black jazz and blues musicians. Columbia Records, the company that recorded Bessie Smith, was one of the top labels of the era; Paramount, which recorded the folk bluesman Blind Lemon Jefferson, was a sideline for a Wisconsin

LISTENING GUIDE
CD 1:17 "Empty Bed Blues"

STYLE	Classic blues
FORM	Blues form (strophic form with five choruses that use 12-bar blues form)

0:00	Introduction	
	Instrumental introduction: piano and trombone	
0:11	First chorus	
	[I] I woke up ... [I response]	Call and response between voice and trombone
	[IV] I woke up ... [I response]	
	[V] My new man ... [I response]	
0:44	Second chorus	
	Bought me a ...	Call and response between voice and trombone
1:18	Third chorus	
	He's a deep sea diver ...	Notice the blue notes on "can't" and "stay."
1:52	Fourth chorus	
	He knows how ...	Melody starts high and ends low.
2:26	Fifth chorus	
	Lord, he's got that sweet ...	The song continues on the other side of the 78 rpm record.

CD 1:17

"Empty Bed Blues," Bessie Smith (1928). Smith, vocal; Charlie Green, trombone; Porter Grainger, piano.

furniture manufacturer. It is on race records that we hear the sounds of classic blues.

The recordings of Bessie Smith (1894–1937) epitomize **classic blues**. They are "classic" blues because they embody the three defining aspects of the blues: its form, style, and feeling. Most of her recordings are conventional 12-bar blues with call and response between singer and an instrumentalist. Typically, the songs are personal, and she sings them with a rough, full voice, with support from jazz musicians. The accompaniment varies from recording to recording, from just a pianist to a full jazz band. We hear a famous example next, recorded in 1928 at the peak of her career.

In "Empty Bed Blues," Smith begins by singing about her man troubles. For most of

This photo, shot when Bessie Smith was about thirty, shows her looking both elegant and vulnerable. Smith was a big woman with a big voice; other publicity shots show a more rambunctious side of her personality.

the song, she describes their lovemaking, sometimes in metaphor ("coffee grinder," "deep sea diver") and sometimes directly. All of this makes his infidelity even more painful.

Particularly since the emergence of punk and rap, we are used to music being "real"—a no-nonsense, no-holds-barred representation of our lives. In popular music, classic blues is where *real* begins. Not only the subject of the lyrics but also the range of emotions they describe and the frankness with which Smith sings them were without precedent. She tells us how good it is with her man and how devastated she is when he's with someone else.

Smith sings with a rough, rich, powerful voice. Most phrases start high and end low, and cover a narrow range. She inflects key words to intensify their emotional power; her delivery is speech intensified into song.

Smith is backed by two good jazz musicians of the time, trombonist Charlie Green and pianist Porter Grainger. Green in particular tries to emulate

5 to Listen For
"Empty Bed Blues"

INSTRUMENTATION
Voice, trombone, and piano

PERFORMANCE STYLE
Smith sings with a strong, gravelly voice. Her singing is highly inflected.

RHYTHM
Four-beat feel, but with two-beat accompaniment in piano

RHYTHM
Subtle rhythmic play, moving ahead or behind beat

MELODY
In voice; medium-length phrases in a narrow range start high and finish low.

4 to Remember
"Empty Bed Blues"

BLUES FEELING
A characteristic "my man's gone now" blue mood, in the lyric and in Smith's singing

RACY LYRICS
Talking about sex through metaphors like "deep sea diver"

ESSENCE OF BLUES STYLE
Big, rough voice; high-to-low phrases; subtle timing and inflection

STANDARD BLUES FORM
Five choruses of a conventional 12-bar blues

song, jazz, and even pop-based concert music. We even find evidence of blues in musical theater. When composer Jerome Kern wanted to tell the audience of his landmark musical *Show Boat* that the character who sings "Can't Help Lovin' Dat Man" is a light-skinned mulatto passing for white, he added blues touches to the song.

> What ragtime and syncopated music did for the hips and the feet, blues did for the heart and soul.

and extend the blues vocal style: his playing is full of swoops, smears, and bent notes—all of which mimic the expressive inflection heard in great blues singing.

The earthy, direct lyrics; Smith's singing; and the use of several blues conventions—the 12-bar form, call and response between voice and instrument, and phrases that start high and end low—all of these features exemplify blues as a form, elements of blues style, and the way blues style can convey deep feeling. Through songs like this listeners could tap into the expressive power of the blues.

Smith's audience included not only black Americans but also a small, devoted group of white fans. She was admired enough to appear in a short film, an extremely unusual circumstance for a black blues singer in the late 1920s. The blues that she epitomized penetrated almost every aspect of popular music, as we will hear in the next chapter.

The Great Depression hit Americans hard—and blacks especially hard. Too few could afford to buy records or attend the theaters and clubs where these blues singers performed. As a result, the market for this kind of commercial blues singing had all but dried up by the early 1930s.

The Legacy of Blues Style

Through this multistage infusion of blues styles, both the idea and the sound of the blues entered the popular mainstream, touching social dancing (there was a popular dance in the early 1920s called "the blues"), popular

What ragtime and syncopated music did for the hips and the feet, blues did for the heart and soul. All of this filtered into popular music. The music of the 1910s and 1920s was the first generation of popular music to be shaped by the blues. It would not be the last.

Early Jazz

Legend has it that Buddy Bolden was already blowing everyone away in New Orleans before 1900. Bolden was the first of the great New Orleans cornetists. (A cornet is a close cousin of the trumpet.) But we don't know what Bolden's music sounded like, or what jazz might have sounded like around the turn of the century, because we have no recordings of him or any other jazz musician from that time.

The Roots of Jazz

We do know that New Orleans was regarded as the birthplace of jazz and that contemporary accounts date its beginnings sometime around the turn of the twentieth century. It flourished in the rich cultural mix that was New Orleans: whites of English and French descent, blacks, immigrants from the Caribbean and Europe, plus many citizens of mixed race. (New Orleans bordellos were famous for octoroon and quadroon prostitutes—those who were one-eighth and one-quarter black.) Then as now New Orleans liked to celebrate, most famously at Mardi Gras, but also for almost any occasion—for example, the trip back from the cemetery after a "jazz funeral" was usually a high-spirited affair. Music was part of this mix: brass bands for parades, and pianists and small groups for the bars, honky-tonks, and houses of prostitution, which was then legal in New Orleans. New Orleans and its visitors simply let the good times roll.

The Jim Crow laws enacted in the wake of *Plessy v. Ferguson* (the 1892 Supreme Court ruling in favor of racially segregated schools) had a profound impact on the development of jazz. Throughout much of the nineteenth century, New Orleans had been a relatively hospitable environment for blacks. During slavery, Congo Square (now Louis Armstrong Park) was the only part of the South where people of African descent could legally gather and play drums and other percussion instruments. Before the Emancipation Proclamation, there were more free blacks in New Orleans than anywhere else in the United States, and New Orleans developed a complex social structure. It assigned social status by race and ethnic heritage—not just whites and blacks but also those of mixed race. "Creoles of color," those with ancestors from both France and Africa, enjoyed a higher social standing than ex-slaves. They lived in better neighborhoods, were better educated, and had more freedom. An aspiring Creole musician received traditional classical training, whereas black musicians typically learned to play by ear. Creoles of color tended to look down on the ex-slaves. They emulated white culture rather than black.

This all changed in the wake of Jim Crow legislation. Race in New Orleans became simply "white" and "colored." Grouped together with no legal difference between them, black and Creole musicians began to work with one another. Jazz gained the spontaneity of improvisation and the feeling of the blues from the blacks, and the discipline and the traditional virtuosity of classical training from the Creoles.

In 1898 a New Orleans alderman named Sidney Story proposed that legal prostitution be restricted to a relatively small section, near the French Quarter. Story's proposal became law, and the section of the city where prostitution was legal became known, ironically, as Storyville. Most jazz musicians worked in Storyville. However, in 1917 a series of unsavory incidents involving sailors of the U.S. Navy brought Storyville to the attention of the Secretary of the Navy, who threatened to shut down the New Orleans naval base if the city fathers didn't close Storyville. They did. The closing of Storyville put many jazz musicians out of work

Jeff Griffin/istockphoto.com

and forced them to look elsewhere. Many moved out of town, and Chicago became a prime destination.

The New Orleans Jazz Band

The early history of jazz that we can document in sound begins in the early twenties, when black jazz bands began to record with some frequency. The standard New Orleans jazz band blended the instrumentation of three key popular music genres. From the marching band came the clarinet, cornet or trumpet, trombone, tuba, and drum line, now consolidated into the drum set; from the minstrel show came the banjo; and from the saloons and bordellos (and other places where one could hear professional ragtime pianists) came the piano.

The band has two parts: the front line and the rhythm section. The front line (so called because the musicians stand at the front of the bandstand) is typically three instruments: clarinet, trumpet or cornet, and trombone. The front-line instruments play melody, usually within a well-defined range and within well-defined limits, particularly when playing together.

- The cornet (trumpet) is the mid-range instrument that usually carries the melody.
- The clarinet takes the highest part, playing a fast-moving countermelody to the main part.

- The trombone carries the lowest melodic part, usually in the form of "commentary" on the melody and the clarinet part.

The standard rhythm section of the time consisted of banjo, piano, brass bass (or tuba, the lowest-pitched of the brass instruments), and drums. The rhythm section had two jobs: to mark the beat and to supply the harmony.

All three (or four, when there's an extra cornet or saxophone) melody instruments typically play at the same time, a procedure known as collective improvisation, which means that the performers simultaneously make up the music together as they play, rather than playing music that they or someone else has already written.

Collective improvisation requires teamwork: everyone has to know not only his or her own role but the others' roles as well. In this respect collective improvisation in jazz is like a fast break in basketball; the cornet or trumpet player is like the ball handler. Both are located in the center of the action—mid-range melody for the musician, center court for the basketball player. Other players flank the center and react to what the player controlling

> *Collective improvisation in jazz is like a fast break in basketball.*

CD 1:18

"Dippermouth Blues," Joe Oliver, King Oliver's Creole Jazz Band (1923). Featuring Oliver, cornet, and Johnny Dodds, clarinet.

the action does. In both cases the process is spontaneous, but it occurs within prescribed and well-understood boundaries.

King Oliver's Creole Jazz Band

Joe "King" Oliver (1885–1938) was one of the major figures of early jazz. His reputation rests on his achievements as a bandleader and a cornet player. Like many New Orleans musicians, he emigrated to Chicago in search of a better-paying job following the closing of Storyville. By 1920 he had assembled several of his New Orleans expatriates into King Oliver's Creole Jazz Band, the finest traditional New Orleans–style jazz band preserved on record.

Although in "Dippermouth Blues" Oliver and clarinetist Johnny Dodds play solos, most of the performance proceeds with all instruments playing simultaneously, with no one instrument completely dominant. This is the quintessential New Orleans jazz sound.

"Dippermouth Blues" is a blues song in form and style. Each section is twelve measures long, with the characteristic harmonic pattern of the blues. It is also a blues song in style, which is nowhere more evident than in Oliver's famous cornet solo. As a cornet player, Oliver developed an influential style deeply rooted in the blues. His solo in "Dippermouth Blues" was one of the most frequently imitated jazz solos of his generation. His playing parallels the heightened inflection, narrow range, and unconstrained rhythmic delivery of a blues singer. The manner in which he slides in and out of important notes is an instrumental counterpart to blues vocal style.

"Dippermouth Blues" shows the "deep blues" roots of early jazz. Most early jazz recordings show at least some influence of blues style, and many of them—almost half, it would seem—are based on blues form. From the beginning, jazz musicians

King Oliver's Creole Jazz Band in 1923. From left to right: Honore Dutrey, trombone; Baby Dodds, drums; King Oliver, lead cornet; Louis Armstrong, slide trumpet; Lil Hardin (Armstrong's future wife), piano; Bill Johnson, banjo; and Johnny Dodds, clarinet.

Frank Driggs Collection/Getty Images

LISTENING GUIDE

CD 1:18 "Dippermouth Blues"

STYLE	New Orleans jazz
FORM	Blues form (strophic form with nine choruses that use 12-bar blues form)
0:00	Introduction
	Instrumental introduction: piano and trombone
0:05	First chorus
	Full band; clarinet, cornet, and trombone engage in collective improvisation.
0:19	Second chorus
	Notice how each instrument stays in a particular register: clarinet, high; cornet, medium high; trombone, midrange.
0:34	Third/fourth chorus
	Clarinet solo; notice the *stop time* (rhythm section stops playing) throughout.
1:03	Fifth chorus
	Full band again, playing different material over the same blues progression; drummer can be heard marking beat, especially backbeat, here and in most of the choruses.
1:18	Sixth/seventh chorus
	Oliver's famous and widely imitated cornet solo
1:46	Eighth chorus
	Full band returns, with stop time break at the end.
	Oh, play that thing!
2:00	Ninth chorus
	Ends with tag

have liked to improvise on the blues chord progression because the chords are simple and change relatively slowly. This gives the musicians plenty of time to invent ideas—blues-like riffs (as in Oliver's solo), faster running lines, or whatever strikes their fancy.

Playing second cornet on "Dippermouth Blues" was Louis Armstrong, who had come to Chicago in 1922 at Oliver's invitation. Armstrong would leave Oliver and move to New York, where he became the most influential jazz musician of his era. His work in the late 1920s would set the standard for the two most distinctive qualities of jazz: swing and improvisation. We discuss both briefly, then hear Armstrong's realization of them.

The Essence of Jazz: Swing and Improvisation

The two qualities that most readily distinguish jazz from other popular genres are swing, its distinctive rhythmic conception, and improvisation, the spontaneous dimension of its creative process. The ability to play with time and create in the moment have been measures of artistry in jazz performance certainly since the late 1920s; both are abundantly evident in the playing of the most admired and influential jazz musicians, from Armstrong to the present.

Swing. The most essential element in jazz is swing, as Duke Ellington asserted in his 1932 song "It Don't Mean A Thing (If It Ain't Got That Swing)." Here is a succinct definition of swing: rhythmic play over a four-beat rhythm. Both the four-beat rhythm and the rhythmic play over it were paradigm-shifting innovations. They were the clearest indications that jazz—and the popular music that it influenced—had embraced an entirely new rhythmic conception. The black musicians who created jazz kept the metrical structure of European music but interpreted it through an African sensibility. Instead of accenting the first beat of each measure, jazz musicians typically stressed all beats equally—or played rhythms that used that feel as a point of departure. In the Armstrong recording we hear next, the pianist and guitarist typically play chords on each beat; each receives the same amount of emphasis.

But in isolation the undifferentiated beats of the rhythm instruments do not produce swing. Swing results from the interplay between the beat and the syncopated accents and irregular patterns that conflict with the steady timekeeping of the rhythm instruments. It is this interplay that makes the rhythm so irresistible.

Improvisation. In music, to improvise means to create new music in the moment—as one is singing or playing—rather than re-creating someone else's

5 to Listen For
"Dippermouth Blues"

INSTRUMENTATION
Front line: two cornets, clarinet, and trombone
Rhythm section: piano (barely heard), banjo, and drums/percussion

PERFORMANCE STYLE
Instrumental counterpart to blues vocal style: lots of bent notes and slides into notes, imitating the voice

RHYTHM
Four-beat rhythm (kept by banjo and felt by entire band) at fast tempo

RHYTHM
Lots of syncopation and other forms of rhythmic play, especially anticipating or lagging behind the beat in solos

TEXTURE
In most choruses, collective improvisation in the front line (three independent lines, all improvised); the rhythm section keeps time.

4 to Remember
"Dippermouth Blues"

JAZZ RHYTHM
Rhythm section chunks out steady four-beat rhythm; horns syncopate over rhythm section timekeeping.

BLUES INFLUENCE
12-bar blues harmonic progression; blues style, especially in Oliver's solo

NEW ORLEANS JAZZ INSTRUMENTATION
Standard New Orleans jazz band: front line (clarinet, cornet[s], trombone) plus rhythm section (here, banjo, piano, and drums)

COLLECTIVE IMPROVISATION
Front-line players improvise at the same time.

where Louis joined Fletcher Henderson's hot dance orchestra. In New York, Armstrong was a regular in the studio as well as the bandstand, recording with Henderson, a host of blues singers (including Bessie Smith), and the pianist Clarence Williams. Williams, who doubled as Okeh Records' A&R (artists and repertoire) man, noticed that the recordings on which he used Armstrong sold better than others. So in 1925 he offered Armstrong the chance to record as a leader rather than as a sideman. Armstrong, who had returned to Chicago, proceeded to record with what amounted to a studio band of his New Orleans friends plus Lil (and, somewhat later, pianist Earl Hines). Okeh billed them as Louis Armstrong's Hot Five or Hot Seven (depending on the number of players). Armstrong's groups made dozens of recordings over the next four years, and made jazz—and music—history in the process.

Louis Armstrong was the first great soloist in jazz. Every aspect of his playing—his beautiful sound; the bent notes, slides, shakes, and other expressive gestures; his melodic inventiveness; and above all, his incomparable sense of swing—inspired jazz and popular musicians of the era: Bing Crosby was a regular at the clubs where he worked; so were numerous jazz musicians. His playing became the standard by which other jazz musicians measured themselves.

Recordings like "Hotter Than That" captured an exuberance that is unique to early jazz, and especially the playing of Louis Armstrong. It invites a different kind of movement—foot tapping, head bobbing, lindy hopping. It comes from the particular interaction of the relentlessly pulsing beat, the ebb and flow of harmonic tension, and Armstrong's extraordinarily varied and subtle rhythmic play, with its note-to-note variation in accent, timing, and expressive gesture.

There is no known precedent for the swing heard in early jazz. No earlier music that has come down to us, not even ragtime, creates a comparably infectious rhythm. Its defining features are far too subtle to commit to notation and seem to elude precise definition. Indeed, Armstrong, when asked to explain swing, responded with something like "If you have to ask, you'll never know."

composition. **Improvisation** in music is comparable to a comedy improv troupe's creating a skit from an audience suggestion rather than performing a well-rehearsed and fully scripted routine.

The first generation of jazz musicians improvised by inventing new melodies for an existing song: a blues, a popular song, or a melody (and the accompanying harmony) created specifically as a point of departure for improvisation. In the Oliver example above, the new melodies—for example, Oliver's solo—are created over a conventional blues progression; in Armstrong's "Hotter Than That," the melody and the chord progression were composed expressly for the recording session.

Improvisation is not unique to jazz. Through the early nineteenth century, classical composers were typically also adept improvisers: Bach, Mozart, and Beethoven were renowned for their improvisational ability. However, the practice largely died out in European classical music during the nineteenth century. Only with jazz did a sophisticated form of improvisation once again become an integral component of a new genre.

Louis Armstrong: Jazz as a Soloist's Art

Early in 1924 Armstrong married Lil Hardin, the pianist with Oliver's band. Soon after, they moved to New York,

CD 1:19
"Hotter Than That," Louis Armstrong (1927). Featuring Armstrong, vocal and trumpet; Kid Ory, trombone; Johnny Dodds, clarinet; Lil Hardin Armstrong, piano; Johnny St. Cyr, banjo; Lonnie Johnson, guitar.

LISTENING GUIDE

CD 1:19 "Hotter Than That"

STYLE	1920s Jazz	
FORM	Several improvised choruses on a melody based on popular song form: AA¹	
0:00	Introduction	
	Entire band, with Armstrong in the forefront	
0:09	First chorus	
	A	Armstrong states melody, with steady timekeeping from Hardin on piano and Johnson on guitar.
	A¹ (0:27)	Instrumental-style melody, almost certainly improvised, at least in part; harmony outlines AA¹ form, but no melodic repetition
0:45	Second chorus	
	Clarinetist Johnny Dodds: arpeggio-based figuration, "bent" notes (bluesy alterations of standard pitches)	
1:19	Third chorus	
	Armstrong scat-singing over Johnson's steady guitar accompaniment	
	Second half of solo features long/short rhythm lasting three beats, repeated several times—a real rhythmic/harmonic highwire act	
1:55	Interlude	
	Armstrong and Johnson extend the vocal chorus with blues-influenced call-and-response exchanges. Hardin leads the group to the final chorus.	
2:19	Fourth chorus	
	A	Trombonist Kid Ory: improvisations are based mainly on the harmony.
	A¹ (2:31)	Collective improvisation: all of the front-line players improvising at the same time. Armstrong's repeated high notes, alternately on and off the beat, distill swing to its essence: rhythmic play over the four-beat rhythm chunking away underneath.
2:52	Tag	
	Short tag featuring Armstrong and Johnson ends performance with musical question.	

Armstrong's influence was pervasive: swing became common currency when the musicians who followed him absorbed his lessons on how to swing and audiences responded to this vital new rhythm.

Jazz in America During the 1920s

With the influx of New Orleans jazz musicians into northern cities and the recording of both white and black musicians, jazz became a truly national music in the early 1920s. Chicago and New York were the hot spots. Chicago was wide open—Al Capone and other gang leaders all but ran it—and musicians found ample employment opportunities in speakeasies and ballrooms. A generation of white musicians, among them Bix Beiderbecke and Benny Goodman, absorbed the sound of the New Orleans musicians firsthand, much as white rockers absorbed Chicago blues style in the 1960s. New York had top dance orchestras, including those led by Fletcher

Henderson and Duke Ellington. Armstrong and other top jazzmen relocated there in the latter part of the 1920s.

What blues did for the heart and soul, jazz did for the spirit. The jazz of the early 1920s was exuberant, optimistic, spontaneous, and fast paced. It suggested illicit pleasures, if only because it so often accompanied them. In these respects it captured—and often inspired—the mood of the country, which accelerated through the

> What blues did for the heart and soul, jazz did for the spirit.

5 to Listen For
"Dippermouth Blues"

INSTRUMENTATION
Front line: clarinet, trumpet/voice, and trombone
Rhythm section: just piano and banjo, switching to guitar

PERFORMANCE STYLE
Armstrong's instrumental and vocal conception much the same: musical feel is almost identical; main differences are timbre and range.

RHYTHM
Four-beat rhythm at fast tempo

RHYTHM
Abundant syncopation in fast-moving melody lines

TEXTURE
Melody with steady timekeeping and harmonic accompaniment; collective improvisation at end

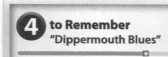

4 to Remember
"Dippermouth Blues"

SWING
Swing-producing rhythmic play especially evident in Armstrong's singing and playing

IMPROVISATION
Performance almost completely improvised, including opening chorus; underlying harmony the basis of improvisation

SOLO-ORIENTED JAZZ
Solo orientation—with collective improvisation only at end—signals shift away from collective improvisation.

EXPRESSIVENESS
Armstrong's arsenal of expressive devices includes vibrato (rapid oscillation in pitch) on long notes, slides into high notes, and rhythmic play over the four-beat rhythm.

record, on the radio, in the theaters, and even occasionally on film.

In the first three decades of the twentieth century, black music gained a secure place in American musical life. Joplin, Europe, Smith, Oliver, Armstrong, and many others left a legacy that we still value, and they helped bring a wave of black musical styles into popular music. Ragtime was first. Syncopated dance music grew out of the ragtime dances of the 1900s and became popular in the early teens. Blues (as published songs) and jazz (as performed by white musicians) caught on shortly thereafter, and both flourished in the 1920s.

Moreover, these emergent styles were the catalyst for the wholesale transformation of popular music. In large part because of their contributions, popular music entered the modern era. We encounter this revolutionary development in popular song in the next chapter.

decade until everything came crashing down in 1929. More than any other music, jazz would become the soundtrack of the decade. Small wonder that novelist F. Scott Fitzgerald and others called the 1920s the Jazz Age.

Looking Back, Looking Ahead

The publication of Joplin's "Maple Leaf Rag" in 1899, only three decades earlier, gave piano-playing Americans of all races firsthand contact with an authentic African American music. "Rag" was just beginning to be a dirty word. "Jazz" and "blues" were obscure, nameless musical styles.

By 1929 everyone was dancing the foxtrot, and *blues* and *jazz* were household words. Black music was on

Terms to Know

Test your knowledge of this chapter's important terms by defining the ones listed here. If you can't recall the meaning of a certain term, refresh your memory by looking up the boldfaced term in the chapter, turning to the Glossary at the back of the book, or working with the flashcards at the Popular Music Resource Center.

ragtime
piano rag
animal dance
foxtrot
commercial blues
race record
classic blues

jazz
New Orleans jazz
front line
collective improvisation
improvisation
swing

Popular Song *in* the Modern Era

CHAPTER 4

The setting for the big scene in *Top Hat,* a 1935 film that starred Ginger Rogers and Fred Astaire, is a posh supper club, with tables adjacent to a large dance floor, where an orchestra plays in the background. Fred walks into the club and spies Ginger, who is sitting with a woman whom she thinks is Fred's wife. Dressed formally in white tie and tails, Fred asks Ginger, in her long evening gown, to dance. Ginger reluctantly agrees. At the beginning of the number, Fred sings "Cheek to Cheek" while they're dancing. Initially, Ginger keeps her distance, but by the time Fred has finished singing and the orchestra has taken over, they've drifted off to their own private ballroom to perform a dance that's far more elaborate than the foxtrot they danced earlier in the scene. By the end of the number, Ginger is completely smitten with Fred. Shortly after, she comes to her senses, slaps him, and flounces away.

For millions of Americans, the Fred and Ginger movies were a chance to escape the misery of the depression and to dream of rubbing shoulders with the rich. They were enormously popular, mainly because of the great songs and Fred and Ginger's skillful dancing; the music and their dancing made their otherwise unlikely romantic pairing credible, if only for a few moments. "Cheek to Cheek," the most popular song from the film, was arguably the most popular song of the 1930s.

The scene encapsulates the revolutionary technological, musical, and social changes over the preceding two decades. It is a talking film—only a dream in 1915. Fred sings the song while they dance together; the song has a flowing melody far removed from the busy patterns of "Castle House Rag." In this film, dancing elegantly and cheek to cheek requires "lingering close contact." In 1935 this had become the norm. It was no longer scandalous—indeed, Ginger's dinner companion vigorously gestures for her to draw Fred closer. All of these changes confirm a new, more modern era—in popular music and in American life.

● ● ● ● ● ● ● ● ●

The Modern Era

The fifteen years between 1914 (the start of World War I) and 1929 (the start of the Great Depression) marked the beginning of the modern era, not only in popular music but also in art, literature, and American life. To be modern in America during the 1920s meant moving and living at a faster pace. It meant believing in progress, especially material progress. It meant moving out of the country and into the city. It meant taking advantage of new technologies, from automobiles and air conditioning to the zippers that were now featured on clothing, luggage, and a host of other products. It meant buying into fashionable intellectual ideas and artistic trends.

And it meant listening—and dancing—to a new kind of music.

The emergence of a distinctively American popular music expressed both the fact and the nature of America's coming of age. With its intercession in World War I, the United States had become a world power, a player on the world stage. Business, applying the assembly-line procedures used so successfully by Henry Ford and the management techniques of Frederick Winslow Taylor, grew in size and efficiency. New products, particularly electrically operated home appliances, made domestic chores significantly easier. Skilled workers had more money to spend and more time to spend it.

As a result, the entertainment industry flourished. Much of this entertainment, particularly popular music and films, projected a uniquely American cultural identity and a distinctly modern attitude. Politically, economically, and culturally, the United States relied much less on Europe for inspiration and guidance.

Sex, Booze, and All That Jazz

The teens and twenties saw enormous social change in America. Immigration and migration, Prohibition and its consequences, and a sexual revolution that dramatically redefined the place of the woman in American society all reshaped life in the modern era.

People on the Move. Immigration from abroad, especially during the teens, and internal migration within the United States, especially by African Americans, swelled cities like New York and Chicago. The biggest influx of people from abroad came in the teens. A backlash against this new wave of immigrants resulted in laws severely restricting immigration. By 1931 more people were leaving the United States than entering it, a trend that has since been reversed.

Large ethnic and minority populations in such cities as New York and Chicago helped support their resident musicians and entertainers. Most of the great songwriters of the period between the wars were Jewish or black: Irving Berlin, Jerome Kern, Richard Rodgers, Harold Arlen, George Gershwin, Duke Ellington, and Thomas "Fats" Waller. So were many vaudeville stars: Eddie Cantor, Al Jolson, Bert Williams, and Fanny Brice. Black musicians supplied dance music and entertainment for all levels of society in the 1910s and 1920s, although bands remained segregated until the late 1930s.

Prohibition. In an effort to eliminate workers' "blue Mondays" (worker absenteeism or poor performance caused by excessive weekend drinking), among other alcohol-related social problems, the Temperance movement succeeded in getting the Eighteenth

Amendment passed. Although it didn't stop Americans from drinking, Prohibition did make producing or purchasing alcohol illegal. The 1920s became the era of bathtub gin (and other kinds of homemade liquor) and **speakeasies**—clubs that required a softly spoken password for admission.

Prohibition meant work for many popular musicians. Jazz spread from New Orleans throughout the country by way of Chicago's speakeasies, as Joe "King" Oliver, Louis Armstrong, and other early jazz greats moved north in search of more and better-paying work. Benny Goodman, the "king of swing," also got his professional start in a Chicago speakeasy.

The New Woman. The passage of the Nineteenth Amendment, which gave women the right to vote, ended a long and difficult chapter in the history of women's rights. It also signaled a major shift in American attitudes toward women and their place in society. One product of this change was a new kind of young woman.

This "new woman" appeared in the 1920s. Freed from some of the drudgery of housework by a wave of new appliances and with more cash in hand, she consumed—and became a target of advertisers. Liberated from Victorian morality by trendy interpretations of Freudian ideas, she indulged in "petting" with all-too-eager young men. Inspired by Irene Castle, the queen of the foxtrot, she cut her hair and dressed in short, loose-fitting dresses. Tempted by illicit liquor, cigarettes, and other accoutrements of fast living, she partied hard. She was called a "flapper," and she danced, and danced, and danced to the new syncopated music. Her parents were, not surprisingly, horrified by this behavior. And, then as now, popular music was judged one of the causes of her

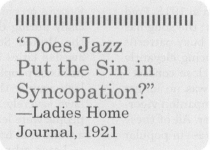

"Does Jazz Put the Sin in Syncopation?"
—Ladies Home Journal, 1921

moral degradation. To cite just one example, an article appeared in a 1921 issue of the *Ladies Home Journal* entitled "Does Jazz Put the Sin in Syncopation?"

Compared with the suffragists who had fought so hard for the right to vote and the members of the Women's Christian Temperance Union who decried the evils of alcohol, the flappers seemed frivolous and hedonistic. But what they represented—women who had the power to make choices, however misguided or silly they might seem in retrospect—was not frivolous. The battle for equal rights had a long way to go, but the flappers reaped the benefits of a significant victory and the change in attitude it symbolized.

Flappers were too-easy targets. Young men in the 1920s were certainly just as frivolous as their female counterparts. And how to label the fiscal foolishness of so many of their parents who hopped on the stock market bubble until it burst in 1929?

Jazzy, bluesy, get-up-and-dance-to-it popular music was the soundtrack to all these changes. How people heard it is the next part of our story.

The First Technological Revolution: From Radio to Talking Pictures

In 1919, if you were living in Omaha or Oklahoma City and wanted to hear a hit song, you had few choices. You could buy the sheet music and play it yourself—or get a friend to play it for you. That was a popular choice; sheet music sales peaked in the teens. Or you could buy an **acoustic recording**, like those we've heard by Jim Europe and Harvey Hindermyer. Or you could pay to see a vaudeville show passing through town, where you might hear one of the acts sing the song. Otherwise, you'd probably have to go out of town—to places like New York or Chicago.

In 1929 you had many more choices. You could still buy the sheet music and go to the theater to hear a vaudeville act. But you could also turn on the radio and find a local musician playing the song or tune in to a network broadcast of one of the top hotel bands from New York City. You could go into Woolworth's and buy a record of the song; it would sound a lot better than the recording from ten years earlier. And if a film musical featuring the song was in a local theater, you could go to the movies to hear and see the song performed onscreen.

At no time—not even our own—has the way in which popular music reached its audience changed so fundamentally. In 1919 the majority of the audience learned pop songs by looking at them—that is, by playing through the sheet-music versions. In 1929 more

Library of Congress, Prints and Photographs Division, Washington, D.C. [LC-USZC4-5780]

people learned songs by ear: on the radio, on record, at the movies, and in live performances. The advances in our own time—MP3s, streaming audio, worldwide access, and the like—don't change the way we learn the music. We listen to it through the media, just like our parents and grandparents did. The shift from eye to ear happened in the 1920s.

The new media appeared in stages: first radio, then electric recordings, followed by amplified live performances, and finally talking films. Each new medium represented another application of an innovative technology.

Radio Broadcasting. In 1920 the first commercial radio station, KDKA in Pittsburgh, began broadcasting. Within two years the number of commercial stations had grown from one to more than 200. With few exceptions each radio station, hiring local musicians and personalities to provide entertainment, generated its own programming.

Important technological advances accompanied the rapid growth of commercial radio. None was more important than the conversion from acoustic to electric broadcasting. Many of the earliest radio studios were equipped with long, conical horns similar to those used in acoustic recordings, into which performers spoke, sang, or played. These horns soon gave way to **microphones** that converted sound into electric impulses, which were then converted into the broadcast signal or transmitted to network affiliates for local broadcast. **Amplifiers** and loudspeakers were used to reconvert the electric impulses into sound. This new technology improved quickly.

In 1925 the National Broadcasting Company (NBC) began broadcasting simultaneously on twenty-five affiliates throughout the Northeast and the Midwest with a gala concert. Although American Telephone and Telegraph (AT&T) had already experimented with broadcasts over several stations from one source, it was NBC's debut that celebrated the birth of a new industry: network radio. Soon performances emanating from one location could be broadcast throughout the country and provide the nation with an unprecedented sense of unity.

Electric Recording and Amplified Live Performance. Microphones, amplifiers, and speakers found immediate application elsewhere, in recording, live performance, and instrument manufacture. In 1925 the recording

Gino Santa Maria/istockphoto.com

industry converted from acoustic to **electric recording** almost overnight. As in broadcasting, microphones replaced the cumbersome and inefficient horns used for acoustic recording. The result was a dramatic improvement in recorded sound.

The most obvious benefit of amplification was greater volume in performances both live and recorded. Amplification had an even more far-reaching effect, however, on the *sound* of popular music, first by enabling small-voiced singers to record and perform and then by boosting and transforming the sound of existing instruments and making possible an increasingly broad array of electronic instruments.

Before commercial radio, popular singers performed in theaters and auditoriums without any amplification. Many had classically trained, quasi-operatic voices suitable for the operettas fashionable in the early part of the century and for the more serious and conservative popular songs. Others, like Sophie Tucker, Bessie Smith, and Al Jolson, belted out their songs in a full voice that filled the theater.

Aided by this new technology, a new generation of singers broadened the spectrum of vocal styles heard in popular music. By 1929 listeners could choose from the intimate crooning of Bing Crosby; the jazz-inflected, conversational style of Louis Armstrong; the patter of Fats Waller; the faint sounds of "Whispering" Jack Smith; and many others who would not have succeeded in live performance or recording before the electric revolution of 1925.

Talking Films. On October 6, 1927, *The Jazz Singer*, starring Al Jolson, premiered. Although there had previously been other films with sound, this was the first talking picture. Jolson sang, talked, and acted over the soundtrack. The public loved it, and soon Hollywood was churning out talking pictures, even as theater owners were scrambling to add sound systems to the theaters.

Soon popular music was firmly entrenched on the screen. Vaudeville performers filmed their acts. Broadway stars trekked off to Hollywood, and in the 1930s songwriters would follow. By 1929 moviegoers could have seen the first film versions of *Show Boat, Rio Rita* (a spectacular adaptation of another Broadway musical), and *Broadway Melody of 1929*, the first musical and the first sound film to win an Academy Award for best picture.

The sound technology, called Vitaphone by Warner Brothers, the film studio that developed it, was good enough to make the sound realistic. Earlier attempts to merge sound and film had failed because the sound quality was so poor. The talking film was yet another adaptation of the technology that had transformed radio, recording, and live performance.

The changes in the entertainment industry during the 1920s were staggering: radio, network radio, amplification in live performance, decent recording quality, and talking pictures. All of these dreams of 1919 were reality in 1929. The closest parallel might be the Internet explosion in the 1990s; at no other time has so much world-transforming technology appeared in such a short period.

The Modern Era in Popular Music

The soundtrack for these momentous changes in American life was the new popular music created between the two World Wars. It was strikingly different from the mainstream popular music from the turn of the century, for three main reasons: (1) the application of the new technology; (2) the infusion of black musical features—riffs, rhythms, instruments, performing styles; and (3) the more open and vibrant sensibility expressed in the songs and their performance.

Despite this revolutionary transformation of the popular music mainstream, there is no umbrella term in general use that distinguishes this music from the music that came before or after. The popular song of the long period from the late nineteenth century through the early 1960s (just before the birth of rock) is typically identified as "Tin Pan Alley" song, or simply "pop," but the term *Tin Pan Alley* covers a broad range of styles and eras.

In our view, the revolutionary developments of the 1910s and 1920s in popular music marked the beginning of a new era. For ease and clarity of reference, then, we're labeling the period from the early 1910s to the early 1960s the modern era in popular music. This new popular music was modern because it became increasingly dependent on new technology for performance and dissemination; it took a leading role in improving race relations; and it introduced into popular music so many features that are still part of the sound of popular music, such as the rhythm section, the backbeat, riff-based melodies, and conversational lyrics.

In this chapter, we focus on popular song of the 1920s and 1930s, considering the changes in songwriting and performance and noting the ways in which ragtime, jazz, and blues reshaped popular song.

The New Rhythms of Popular Song

Rhythm provided the first evidence of a new kind of popular song. Around the time that Jim Europe formed his Clef Club Orchestra, songwriters like Irving Berlin were adapting the more flexible rhythms of ragtime to popular song. This became manifest mainly in two features: the isolation of a short melodic idea and a melodic rhythm that flows close to the cadence of everyday speech. Still-familiar songs like Berlin's "Alexander's Ragtime Band" (1911) and "You Made Me Love You," a big hit for Al Jolson in 1913, begin with one or more short phrases set off with silence and whose rhythm approximates that of speech: "Come on and hear"; "You made me love you." The rest of the melody mixes long and short phrases, but their rhythm also comes close to speech-like delivery of the words.

This practice contrasts sharply with the practice in turn-of-the-century songs: a simple recitation of the lyrics of "Take Me Out to the Ball Game" or "Yankee Doodle Boy" will point up the discrepancy between the lyrics as spoken and the lyrics as sung. What made the conversational rhythm possible was the division of the beat into long and short durations. This enabled songwriting teams to match the natural accentuations in the words to the flow of the melody. The difference between the two approaches to rhythm can be summarized this way: before the modern era, the rhythm of the words was adapted to the rhythm of the melody; with the modern era, the rhythm of the melody was adapted to the rhythm of the words.

Popular song and dance music were still distinct at this point: "Castle House Rag" does not have a singable melody, and popular song was typically not used for social dancing. However, there was mutual awareness, as the occasional "dance instruction" song evidences. The opening lines of the 1913 song "Ballin' the Jack," written by the black songwriting team of James Henry Burris and Chris Smith, explains how to do the dance of the same name:

> First you put your two knees / Close up tight.
>
> Then you sway it to the left / Then you sway it to the right.
>
> Step around the floor / Kind of nice and light
>
> Then you twist around and twist around / With all of your might.

Songs like this were the modern-era counterpart to Chubby Checker's early 1960s dance-instruction song, "The Twist." Still, popular song did not become dance music until after 1920. With the rise of the dance orchestra and a new generation of songwriters, popular song acquired its trademark style beat and a large dose of syncopation. New dances ushered them into the mainstream.

Dance Fads of the 1920s

The 1920s began with a second wave of dance crazes: the black bottom, the shimmy, the blues (yes, there was a social dance called "the blues"), and, above all, the Charleston. Like the ragtime dances of earlier decades, these began as African American social dances and found a new home among younger whites. Dancing to syncopated music had become commonplace and socially acceptable, but these new dances were the cutting edge, a more energetic alternative to the foxtrot.

The Charleston. The most popular and enduring of these new dances was the **Charleston**. The dance goes back to at least the early twentieth century, and there is apparently a connection to Charleston, South Carolina. It was danced in Harlem as early as 1913, but it didn't become well known until 1923, when it was introduced on-stage, most notably in an all-black musical production, *Running Wild.*

The dance was done to the song of the same name, "Charleston," written by James P. Johnson (1894–1955), who is much better known as a superb stride pianist. (**Stride piano** is a jazz piano style with deep roots in ragtime.) "Charleston" was Johnson's most memorable hit. It had lyrics by Cecil Mack, but they are seldom sung. Then and now we almost always hear it as an instrumental strictly for dancing.

Johnson's song is the textbook for the new syncopated foxtrot. The chorus presents not only the two-beat rhythm that is the rhythmic foundation of the dance but also its signature syncopation. It consists of a two-note riff over two beats, with the accent on the second note. We hear the riff all by itself at the beginning of the chorus; the words are "Charle-*ston*, Charle-*ston*." The first note

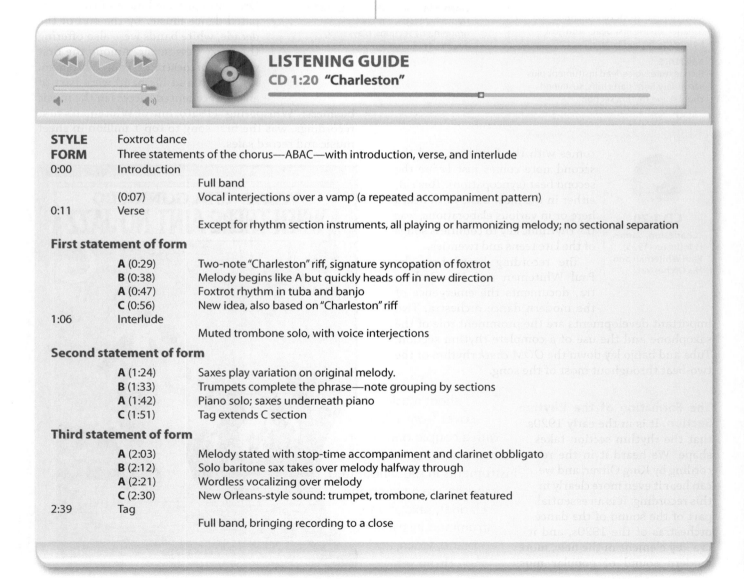

STYLE	Foxtrot dance	
FORM	Three statements of the chorus—ABAC—with introduction, verse, and interlude	
0:00	Introduction	
		Full band
	(0:07)	Vocal interjections over a vamp (a repeated accompaniment pattern)
0:11	Verse	
		Except for rhythm section instruments, all playing or harmonizing melody; no sectional separation

First statement of form

	A (0:29)	Two-note "Charleston" riff, signature syncopation of foxtrot
	B (0:38)	Melody begins like A but quickly heads off in new direction
	A (0:47)	Foxtrot rhythm in tuba and banjo
	C (0:56)	New idea, also based on "Charleston" riff
1:06	Interlude	
		Muted trombone solo, with voice interjections

Second statement of form

	A (1:24)	Saxes play variation on original melody.
	B (1:33)	Trumpets complete the phrase—note grouping by sections
	A (1:42)	Piano solo; saxes underneath piano
	C (1:51)	Tag extends C section

Third statement of form

	A (2:03)	Melody stated with stop-time accompaniment and clarinet obbligato
	B (2:12)	Solo baritone sax takes over melody halfway through
	A (2:21)	Wordless vocalizing over melody
	C (2:30)	New Orleans-style sound: trumpet, trombone, clarinet featured
2:39	Tag	
		Full band, bringing recording to a close

5 to Listen For
"Charleston"

INSTRUMENTATION
1920s rhythm section: tuba, banjo, piano, drums

INSTRUMENTATION
Melody instruments include saxes **doubling** (switching from one instrument to another) on clarinets, trumpets, and trombones; violin reinforcing melody; occasional hot vocal.

RHYTHM
Basic foxtrot rhythm (bass note and backbeat in alternation) at a fast tempo

RHYTHM
Most popular 1920s syncopation: "Charle-" on the first beat; "ston" just before the second beat

TEXTURE
Rich texture: voice/lead instrument plus secondary horn parts (riffs, sustained chords) and rhythm section

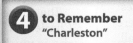

4 to Remember
"Charleston"

FOXTROT RHYTHM AND SIGNATURE SYNCOPATION
Foxtrot = bass alternating with chord on backbeat. Signature syncopation = "Charle-ston"

FORMING THE RHYTHM SECTION
Sound and beat-keeping role of rhythm section, a new sound in 1920s music

SAXOPHONE
Warmer and fuller sounding than clarinet; most enduring new instrumental sound of 1920s

DANCE MUSIC/DANCE ORCHESTRA
Dance orchestra, with occasional grouping by sections, plays song intended for dancing.

Since that time, the instrumentation of the rhythm section has changed, but its basic components have not. A complete rhythm section always has at least one chord instrument, a bass instrument, and a percussion instrument. The rhythm section's most fundamental role—to supply the beat and the harmony—also remains essentially the same.

The Dance Orchestras of the 1920s. The rhythm section was the foundation of the dance orchestras that serenaded dancers in ballrooms, hotels, and roof gardens, and eventually on record and radio. During the teens, black groups like Jim Europe's Society Orchestra provided most of the syncopated dance music. By the end of the decade, white bands were also offering this jazzy new music. Among the first was the orchestra of Paul Whiteman. Whiteman and his band were part of an unprecedented success in the music business: "Whispering" (1920), one of Whiteman's first recordings, was the first song to top 1 million in sheet music and record sales.

CD 1:20
"Charleston," James P. Johnson (1923). Paul Whiteman and His Orchestra.

comes with the first beat, and the second note comes just *before* the second beat (syncopation). This riff, either in the most basic form heard here or in various elaborations, was the rhythmic key to countless songs of the late teens and twenties.

The recording heard here, by Paul Whiteman and His Orchestra, documents the emergence of the modern dance orchestra. Two important developments are the prominent role of the saxophone and the use of a complete rhythm section. Tuba and banjo lay down the *OOM-chuck* rhythm of the two-beat throughout most of the song.

The Formation of the Rhythm Section. It is in the early 1920s that the rhythm section takes shape. We heard it in the recording by King Oliver, and we can hear it even more clearly in this recording. It is an essential part of the sound of the dance orchestras of the 1920s, and it is a key element in the new, more modern sound of popular music.

A sheet music cover from 1920 with a couple dancing in close embrace. Among the instruments in the silhouetted orchestra are a trombone, clarinet, saxophone, strummed instrument, piano, violin, and drum set.

Historic American Sheet Music, "What-cha gonna do when there aint no jazz", Music #A-6606, Duke University Rare Book, Manuscript, and Special Collections Library

By the early 1920s, Whiteman had plenty of company. Dance orchestras led by Guy Lombardo, Fred Waring, and Isham Jones (who was also a fine songwriter, e.g., "It Had to Be You") found work in hotels in resorts and major cities. Black bands also modernized: among the best was the Fletcher Henderson Orchestra, which performed at the Roseland Ballroom, one of New York's hot spots.

There were other major changes in the sound of the dance orchestra besides the consolidation of the rhythm section. Orchestras got larger, and the instruments were grouped into sections, not only rhythm but also brass (trumpets and trombones), winds (clarinets and saxophones), and strings (mostly violins). Typically, the musical spotlight would shift from one section to the next, often quickly, as if the two were talking back and forth. These changes are evident in Whiteman's recording. What's missing is the singer. Singers certainly did record, as we hear below, but not yet with dance orchestras.

The Saxophone: A New Sound of the 1920s. The saxophones that are so prominent in the recording of "Charleston" represent the most enduring new sound of the 1920s. There were other new sounds during the same time; the ukulele was an even bigger novelty when Hawaiian music was intermittently in vogue during the decade. But it was the sax that would ultimately become an integral part of the sound of popular music. James Reese Europe was the innovator; his was one of the first dance orchestras to feature the saxophone. But it did not become a staple in the dance orchestra until arrangers began to group instruments into sections. The more massive sound and the broader range of the saxophone family (most bands used three different saxes—alto, tenor, and baritone) made them a more effective counterpart to the brass instruments than the clarinets that were popular in jazz bands and early dance orchestras.

Rhythm Songs

The energy and high spirits of the modern era are evident not only in dance numbers like "Charleston" but also the aptly named rhythm songs that began to appear in the mid-1920s. As its name implies, a rhythm song is a song in which the primary interest comes from its rhythm rather than the flow and contour of its melody. Rhythm songs can be simple; the 1925 hit "Yes Sir, That's My Baby" and George Gershwin's "I Got Rhythm" (the title applies to the song as well as to the person singing) simply repeat a syncopated pattern with little variation. Or they can be more complex manipulations of a series of notes. Irving Berlin's 1929 hit "Puttin' on the Ritz" applies varying rhythms to a four-note chord; Cole Porter's "Anything Goes," the title song of his 1934 musical, does the same to a three-note pattern. In either

CD 1:21

"Fascinating Rhythm," George and Ira Gershwin (1924). Fred and Adele Astaire, vocals; George Gershwin, piano.

case, there is little or no melodic variation or development, just the tricky, syncopated rhythm.

George and Ira Gershwin's "Fascinating Rhythm" is a spectacular early example of the rhythm song. The riff that opens the song contains six syllables: "Fas-cin-a-ting rhy-thm"; together with the pause that follows, they last 3½ beats. Gershwin repeats the riff three-and-a-half times; each restatement of the riff starts a half a beat earlier than the previous one. As a result, the "fascinating" rhythm goes out of phase with the beat:

1		2		3		4	
Fas	ci	na	ting	Rhy	thm		You've
1		**2**		**3**		**4**	
got	me	on	the	go		Fas	ci
1		**2**		**3**		**4**	
na	ting	rhy	thm		I'm	all	a
1		**2**		**3**		**4**	
qui	ver						

Fred Astaire (left) with George Gershwin (center) and lyricist Ira Gershwin on the Hollywood set of the musical *Shall We Dance*, 1937.

Hulton Archive/Getty Images

LISTENING GUIDE
CD 1:21 "Fascinating Rhythm"

STYLE	Rhythm song
FORM	Verse/chorus song, verse heard only once and chorus repeated, chorus ABAB[1]
0:00	Introduction
	Piano alone

First statement of form: Verse + chorus

0:14	Verse		
		Fascinating rhythm, rhythm, rhythm ...	
0:36	Chorus		
	A	Fascinating rhythm, you've got me on the go ...	Riff lasting 3½ beats; starts earlier with each repetition
	B (0:47)	Each morning I get up ...	Two gentle arches, second higher than first
	A (0:58)	Once it didn't matter ...	
	B¹ (1:09)	Oh, how I long to be ...	Begins like B but soon takes new direction
1:19	Interlude		
	Neither melody nor harmony connects to verse or chorus.		

Second statement of form: Chorus

1:33	Chorus		
	A	Fascinating rhythm, you've got me on the go ...	Dialogue between piano and voices
	B (1:44)	Each morning I get up ...	Two gentle arches, second higher than first
	A (1:54)	Once it didn't matter ...	
	B¹ (2:05)	Oh, how I long to be ...	Begins like B but soon takes new direction
2:16	Tag		
	Piano alone; figuration borrowed from ragtime		

We hear this fascinating rhythmic trick in the song, as performed by Gershwin himself. In retrospect, it's not surprising that George Gershwin composed "Fascinating Rhythm" and several other rhythm songs, because, more than any other songwriter, Gershwin incorporated the rhythmic language of ragtime and syncopated dance music into his songs. Typically, his songs, even his ballads, grow from a riff-like figure that's short and rhythmically interesting. "I Got Rhythm" applies to the song as well as to the person singing.

"Charleston" is a syncopated song by a black musician performed by a white band; although it has lyrics, it is music for dancing. "Fascinating Rhythm" is a song for a Broadway musical by a white

3 to Remember
"Fascinating Rhythm"

FASCINATING RHYTHM
Displacement of repeated riff puts emphasis on rhythm.

SONG FORM IN TRANSITION
ABAB[1] form connects back to ca. 1900 songs; reduced role of verse anticipates common practice in modern era.

GERSHWIN'S SKILLED PIANO PLAYING
Gershwin was an excellent pianist, here supplying melody, melodic responses, and varied accompaniment.

5 to Listen For
"Fascinating Rhythm"

INSTRUMENTATION
Voices and piano

PERFORMANCE STYLE
Gershwin's aggressive piano style: heavy bass/chord or rapid chords in accompaniment; harmonized melody or figuration

RHYTHM
Foxtrot rhythm in accompanying pattern; abundant syncopation in melody in both verse and chorus

MELODY
Phrase built from repeated, rhythmically displaced riff

HARMONY
Slow-changing harmony under repeated riff, suggesting blues influence

songwriter whose composing and playing betray the obvious influence of the new black music. As performed by the Astaires and Gershwin, it is not for dancing. In the early 1920s popular songs were either music for dancing (when performed by dance orchestras) or music for listening (when sung), but not both. The electrical revolution that occurred around 1925 helped make it possible to merge song and dance.

● ● ● ● ● ● ● ●
The Integration of Popular Song

A new kind of popular song flooded the market in the late 1920s. It was upbeat and up-tempo. You could sing it *and* you could dance to it. It captured the high spirits of the age. In it you could hear jazz and blues reshape its sound, and occasionally hear a black performer, like Ethel Waters or Fats Waller, perform it, either in person or on record. And it leveraged the new technology not only to make the sound of the music more accessible but also to change how it sounded.

The Record and Recording

In referring to recordings, we commonly distinguish between "albums" and "singles." The term *album* is an anachronism; it hasn't been an accurate description of the delivery format of recordings for over half a century. The term came into use in the modern era to describe recordings bundled together. Early on, they were most often used for classical music. A 12-inch, 78 rpm (revolutions per minute) recording lasted about 4 minutes. Because most major classical compositions last longer than 4 minutes, a recording of a major classical work, such as a symphony by Beethoven or Brahms, would be spread over several discs. These discs were packaged in an *album,* with a cover, binding, and sleeves for each disc. The invention of the LP (long-playing record) made it possible to record entire pieces on one disc instead of several. Despite this, LPs were still called albums; a recording with two discs, like the Beatles' *White Album,* was a double album.

During the modern era, albums were relatively rare. Far more common were single recordings, which contained two songs, one on each side of a 10-inch disc. These records could hold about 3 minutes of music per side. Consequently, musicians had to structure their performances so that they would finish around the 3-minute mark.

In the years after the turn of the century, recordings of popular songs increasingly involved compromise. Nineteenth-century verse/chorus songs typically had several verses; a complete performance might take 6 minutes or more. To record the same song in 3 minutes, performers cut extra verses and songs got shorter and faster. The next song demonstrates how bands molded the performance of the song to optimize its impact on a 3-minute recording.

A New Kind of Popular Song

"Sunday" was a hit in 1927 for the songwriting team of Clifford Gray and J. Fred Coots. (Coots is best remembered for the Christmas evergreen "Santa Claus Is Coming to Town.") The song first appeared in the revue *The Merry World,* and when it caught on, several bands recorded it, among them the one led by Jean Goldkette.

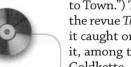

CD 1:22

"Sunday," Clifford Gray and J. Fred Coots (1927). Jean Goldkette Orchestra, with the Keller Sisters, vocals.

The song is up to date in both words and music. The lyrics are simple and tell us about the life of a young person working long hours. (Among other things, we learn that workers in the 1920s had a six-day workweek.) From the words the mood could be either up or down, depending on whether the focus is on Sunday or the rest of the week. In either event the lyrics are full of the exaggerated feelings that so often accompany infatuation.

One of the novel features of this recording of the song is the absence of a sung verse. We hear a fragment of the verse played by the band just before the voices come in, but we never hear it sung. (Compare this to Hindermyer's recording of "Take Me Out to the Ball Game" with complete verses, or "Fascinating Rhythm" with the complete verse sung.)

AABA Form. The chorus of the song resonates with the faster pace of life in the 1920s. It consists of four short sections. The first, second, and last sections are just about the same (there are minor differences between the first and the second sections); the third is different. We usually refer to this form as AABA form: A is the first section of the chorus and any repetition of it, and B is a new section. AABA form was not new to popular music, but it was not widely used before 1925. After that year, however, a decided majority of popular songs used AABA form or some variant of it until well into the rock era.

The A section consists of three phrases, two that are rather short and a third that's about twice as long. The first phrase is built from two riffs: "I'm blue" and "every Monday." The other two alter the scheme a little. The B section starts with the same rhythm as the A section but with a different melody. The music moves fast, both within and among the sections. The phrases within each

LISTENING GUIDE

CD 1:22 "Sunday"

STYLE	Foxtrot song
FORM	Four statements of the chorus (AABA), with verse as interlude

First chorus

	A (0:00)	Simple statement of the melody with the full orchestra
	A (0:09)	
	B (0:17)	
	A (0:26)	
	(0:34)	Tag

Second chorus

	A (0:38)	Violin plays variation of melody while trombone improvises
	A (0:46)	Trumpets complete the phrase—note grouping by sections
	B (0:55)	Piano solo; saxes underneath piano
	A (1:04)	Trombone returns
	(1:11)	Transition to verse
1:16	Verse	
		Full band again
	(1:35)	Guitar break—most extended and prominent of the section tags

Third chorus

	A (1:43)	I'm blue every …
	A (1:52)	It seems that I sigh …
	B (2:00)	And then comes …
	A (2:09)	But after payday …
	(2:17)	Highly syncopated tag. "Wanna see you …"

Fourth chorus

	A (2:21)	Trumpets play variation on the melody (written out, not improvised)
	A (2:30)	
	B (2:38)	Clarinet solo
	A (2:47)	A section repeats with trumpets
	(2:56)	Full band, bringing recording to a close

section are short and snappy. Performed at the brisk, Charleston-like tempo heard here, the song flies by.

Even at first hearing, we notice a big difference between this recording of "Sunday" and all the others that predate it. The song begins like a dance number, with the band playing the melody over a strong, jazz-inflected, two-beat rhythm. Midway through, however, we hear the song sung by a female trio. The band returns for a final chorus. From the late teens on, almost all new pop songs were foxtrots. (Sheet music covers and record labels make this clear.) In this sense they were for both singing and dancing. However, it wasn't until the electrical revolution that it became possible to include both instrumental statements by a full dance orchestra and a vocal on the same

recording. The practice of sandwiching a vocal between dance-oriented instrumental statements of the melody remained popular through the early 1940s.

Jean Goldkette's Orchestra. Born in France and trained as a concert pianist, Jean Goldkette (1899–1962) came to the United States in 1911 and found work in Chicago as a musician during his teens. In 1915 he heard a Dixieland jazz band and started playing in, then leading, dance orchestras. By the mid-1920s, he had put together what many considered the best jazz orchestra of the time. Among the band members were several of the top white jazz musicians in Chicago, including Bix Beiderbecke. They did well on record ("Sunday" sold very

5 to Listen For
"Sunday"

INSTRUMENTATION
1920s dance orchestra: brass, saxes, vocal, violin, over rhythm section, w/ banjo alternating w/ guitar

RHYTHM
Two-beat rhythm with a jazz feel: four-beat rhythm in vocal chorus

RHYTHM
Substantial syncopation, especially at end of vocal chorus

MELODY
Riff pairs the building blocks for A section and bridge

TEXTURE
Contrasts: full band; sections (e.g., trumpets); group vocal; solos and duets: all over steady rhythm

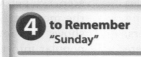

4 to Remember
"Sunday"

AABA POPULAR SONG
Newly revived AABA form the most popular song form after 1925

MAXIMIZING MEMORABLE MELODY
Form and chorus-oriented performance designed to maximize listeners' contact with opening phrase: heard 12 times in 3 minutes

JAZZY FOXTROT
Mostly two-beat rhythm throughout but with a jazz-like swing in melody; swing rhythm by guitar underneath vocal

INTEGRATION OF SONG AND DANCE
Instrumental choruses sandwich a vocal chorus = music for dancing and singing

Mainstreaming the Blues

Blues helped shape modern popular song via two paths. One was indirect and relatively unobtrusive: blues helped shape jazz, which in turn shaped popular song and its performance. The other was more direct and more obvious: blues songs and blues singing served as model and inspiration for songwriters and singers. Popular musicians drew on all three dimensions of the blues revealed in the performances of classic blues singers: feeling, style, and form.

What makes the impact of the blues on popular song stand out is the decided contrast between real blues—including the classic blues of Bessie Smith and others—and conventional pop. Of the four black styles that fed into early-twentieth-century popular music, blues is the style least influenced by European music. Recall that rags and ragtime dances were essentially black reinterpretations of the march. Jazz drew on both ragtime and blues. Its rhythms were freer than ragtime, but jazz musicians still employed many of the harmonic, melodic, and formal conventions of European-derived vernacular music, as we heard in Armstrong's "Hotter Than That."

By contrast, the blues owes relatively little to Europe. The classic blues of Bessie Smith makes use of the three basic chords of European harmony, but recontextualizes them: chords that normally imply movement to a goal chord are now stable harmonies. And harmony is not essential to the blues, as we note in Chapter 6. Further, the simple couplet-based form, the shape and pitch choices of the melody, and the use of call and response have more to do with African musical culture than with European.

It is as song that the power of the blues is fully manifest. This power is—or can be—apparent not only in the form, but also in the use of key elements of blues style and the expression of blues feeling. Even the most expressive instrumental blues use vocal style as a point of departure, as we heard in King Oliver's solo. As a result, the blues tinge in popular music evident in the 1910s, when instrumental blues were introduced, becomes a darker hue in the latter part of the 1920s.

Vocal blues influenced both the songs of the 1920s and the singing of them. Songwriters evoked the mood of blues songs, although pop song lyrics were never as direct or powerful as a blues, and they occasionally incorporated blue notes—produced by interpolating notes from a pentatonic scale into a conventional scale—usually at expressive moments.

well), but not well enough in the ballrooms. (It was probably an early example of an age-old problem among jazz musicians: playing music that's too hip for the room.) Goldkette disbanded his orchestra in 1927, and most of the top players soon joined Paul Whiteman's band.

Goldkette's band offers a jazzier version of the dance orchestra sound of Paul Whiteman. Again we hear the band grouped into sections. The first half of the last chorus has a particularly nice stretch for the trumpet section. There are also improvised solos for trombone and clarinet. The vocal trio that sings the third chorus sounds like flappers look: the nonsense syllables "vo-de-o-do" are a sound of the times, much like interjections such as "go, man, go" in early rock and roll. It is not a particularly ingratiating sound; we'll hear better examples below.

A special feature of Goldkette's band was the use of both banjo and guitar in the rhythm section. The tuba and the banjo lay down a straightforward two-beat rhythm, while guitarist Eddie Lang strums chords on every beat, which gives the song a jazzy feel. (Lang's strumming is easy to hear in the vocal chorus). This combination of rhythms is a main source of the song's bounce.

As "Sunday" evidences, the influence of jazz was pervasive in the latter half of the 1920s. Many of the top dance orchestras employed good jazz musicians, and the black dance orchestras, led by Henderson, Ellington, and others, attracted a substantial mainstream following. In recordings like "Sunday," the jazz feel is evident throughout.

Singers, black and white, brought blues style and feeling into their music, in varying degrees. Indeed, the blues helped spawn a new genre: the torch song. A **torch song** was a song about unrequited or lost love. Torch singers, like the classic blues singers, were women; most were white (Helen Morgan, heard below, was one of the most famous). They typically delivered a torch song that evoked, at least to some degree, the mood of the blues; it was a strong contrast to the generally peppy music of the time.

Ethel Waters. The singer who played the leading role in mainstreaming the blues was Ethel Waters (1896–1977). Waters survived a horrific childhood—her mother was only 13 when she gave birth to her; Waters herself married at 13 and quickly divorced—to begin her career as a vaudeville and nightclub performer. Although she sang the blues and was considered a blues singer by the audiences of the 1920s and early 1930s, she recorded mainly popular songs. Among her best known were "Am I Blue?" and "Stormy Weather," which was written for her by Harold Arlen when she was appearing at the Cotton Club. She would become even better known as an actress, on stage, in film, and briefly on television. And for fifteen years, from 1960 to 1975, she toured with evangelist Billy Graham.

The 1920s, a Breakthrough for Black Musicians. Waters was the first black performer to succeed as a mainstream popular singer—what blacks of the era called "white time." She was in the vanguard of a wave of black entertainers who gained a presence in the popular music. The 1920s saw a resurgence of musical productions by black Americans in New York, both uptown and downtown. *Shuffle Along*, a 1921 musical that featured Noble Sissle and Eubie Blake as songwriters and performers, made the first big splash. The show was notable for a romantic scene; in the minstrel show, blacks were not permitted to express their emotions honestly or realistically. Still, the conventions of minstrelsy permeated such shows;

Waller was kidnapped at gunpoint after a gig and brought to Al Capone's birthday party as the surprise guest entertainer.

many of the performers blacked up, and the plots (and scenery) perpetuated minstrel-show stereotypes, for the most part. Other shows soon followed, both book shows and revues: Lew Leslie's *Blackbirds* series was popular into the 1930s. Leslie also booked black acts at the Cotton Club, a famous Harlem night club, where Duke Ellington performed for many years. Downtown, intrepid and light-footed New Yorkers could dance to Fletcher Henderson's band at the Roseland Ballroom, or they might join Bing Crosby at a speakeasy to hear the music of Louis Armstrong. In Chicago, if you were an associate of Al Capone, you might have heard pianist/songwriter Fats Waller at his birthday party in 1926—Waller was kidnapped at gunpoint after a gig and brought to the party as the surprise guest entertainer. By the end of the decade, Waters, Smith and others had appeared in talking films. Those who knew the right record stores could find race records by Bessie Smith and Louis Armstrong; the less adventurous could still find records by Waters in their local department store.

The increased opportunities for black entertainers were a modest advance toward a truly integrated music business. Stereotypes from minstrelsy still pervaded popular culture. The white singer Al Jolson blacked up in *The Jazz Singer*, the first talking film, and Busby Berkeley's visually spectacular films from the early 1930s occasionally featured performers in blackface.

Bandstands were not integrated, and black performers had to conform to the expectations of the whites who ran the

Pictorial Press Ltd/Alamy Limited

Poster for *The Jazz Singer*, showing a scene from the film in which Al Jolson plays and sings for his adoring mom.

business. An outrageous remark by producer Lew Leslie shows the obstacles that they faced:

> They (white men) understand the colored man better than he does himself. Colored composers excel at spirituals, but their other songs are just "what" (dialect for "white") songs with Negro words.

Still, opportunities for black musicians in 1929 were far better that they had been in 1919.

Blues in Popular Song. Ethel Waters's recording of "Am I Blue?" shows the decided influence of the blues on popular song and its performance. The song is not a blues, although in this performance one chorus of a blues is interpolated between statements of the chorus. But it tells a blues-like story of a woman who's lost her man and has a tinge of blues in the melody, at the end of the A section. Waters's singing is not as gritty as Bessie Smith's, but she inflects the melody with the kind of nuance associated with blues singing, especially toward the end, when she sings responses to the instrumental statement of the melody.

CD 1:23

"Am I Blue?" Grant Clarke and Harry Akst (1929), Ethel Waters, vocal.

"Am I Blue?" effectively demonstrates, in composition and performance, the growing impact of blues style on popular song. Waters's singing helped bring a blues sensibility into popular singing.

The Modern Popular Song

With recordings like "Sunday" and "Am I Blue?" the revolution that produced the modern era in popular music is just about complete. The interaction of black music with white popular song and the integration of new technology comprehensively reshaped the mainstream popular style. Among the most significant and evident changes were these:

- *The merger of song and dance.* Popular songs before 1910 had used dance rhythms but were not sung as music for social dancing. By 1920 popular song had become dance music. By the late twenties, performances of popular songs were singable and danceable.
- *The formation of the syncopated dance orchestra.* Although dance orchestras had existed in America since colonial times, none sounded like those of Jim Europe in the teens and those of Whiteman, Goldkette, and so many others in the twenties. Two

LISTENING GUIDE
CD 1:23 "Am I Blue?"

STYLE	Blues-influenced modern-era song	
FORM	Verse/chorus song: chorus (AABA) heard twice; vocal interlude in blues form	
0:00	Introduction	
	Band introduction: first A section	

First statement of form: Verse + chorus

0:16	Verse		
		I'm just a woman …	
0:50	Chorus		
	A	Am I blue …	Phrase from a simple three-note riff
	A (1:06)	Am I blue …	As before
	B (1:21)	There was a time …	
	A (1:37)	Was I gay …	Almost identical to first two A sections
1:53	Interlude		
	A vocal chorus in blues form: dramatic shift in tempo and rhythmic feel		

Second statement of form: Chorus

2:22	Chorus	
	A	Trombone plays melody; Waters sings responses to melody: new melodic material, varied words
	A (2:36)	
	B (2:51)	Muted trumpet plays melody: as before, Waters answers with new, blues-like melody and variation
	A (3:06)	on lyrics

key differences in the instrumentation distinguished these new dance orchestras: the full rhythm section and the use of the saxophone. Violins, long the main melody voice of the dance orchestra, lost status during the twenties. In orchestras like Paul Whiteman's, they played a less prominent role. In the jazz-influenced dance bands like those of Henderson and Ellington, they disappeared altogether.

- *A foxtrot beat.* Most songs in the twenties were foxtrot songs. In performance a two-beat rhythm, played by tuba and banjo (or other bass and chord instruments) in alternation, supported the melody. The two-beat rhythm, with its crisp backbeat, was the first of the African American rhythms to reshape popular music.

- *New instrumental styles.* Popular instrumentalists, especially wind and brass players, cultivated ways of playing their instruments that distinguished them from band and orchestra performers. Brass players used mutes, plungers, and other timbre-altering devices. All wind (brass, sax, and clarinet) players used **vibrato**, a subtle alteration of the pitch of a note. Much of this came from jazz and blues.

- *Snappy, riff-based melodies.* Blues and ragtime influenced the melodies of popular song even more directly. The influence is evident in three characteristics: the use of riffs, rhythms that flow like speech, and syncopation. All three in combination created melodic rhythms that closely corresponded to the natural inflection and rhythm of American vernacular speech.

- *Conversational lyrics.* Lyrics matched the spirit and the feel of the melodies. More often than not, words were one syllable; phrases and sentences were short. Colloquial expressions replaced the more formal language of nineteenth-century song.

- *A chorus-oriented form.* Except in musical theater, verses were all but scrapped. A performance of a song consisted primarily of several statements of the chorus. A fragment of the verse might be used as an interlude, particularly in dance-band arrangements. Further, the form of the chorus was itself fast paced: four short sections, almost always in AABA form.

Any one of these changes would have been significant. Taken together they represent a comprehensive transformation of popular music. Certainly, they are

3 to Remember
"Am I Blue?"

BLUES INFLUENCE: SONGWRITING
Title and mood of lyric; nice blue note at end of A section; blues interlude specific to this recording

BLUES INFLUENCE: PERFORMANCE
Influence of blues style evident in vocal responses in second chorus, bending notes, rhythmic freedom, and intense inflection

MODERN POPULAR SONG
Typical late-1920s song in form (AABA), basic rhythm (foxtrot), and construction (built from a simple riff)

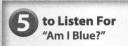

5 to Listen For
"Am I Blue?"

INSTRUMENTATION
Voice and dance orchestra, including bowed string bass in rhythm section

PERFORMANCE STYLE
Waters sings with rich, pleasant pop voice; abundant blues and jazz influence evident in rhythmic freedom and expressive nuance.

RHYTHM
Foxtrot rhythm at moderate tempo; sudden shift to slower tempo and four-beat feel in blues interlude

MELODY
A section built from short riff; B section has longer phrases.

TEXTURE
Mainly melody plus accompaniment in choruses; vocal obbligato in last chorus an appealing novelty

on a par with the changes that took place during the first fifteen years of the rock era. Add to that the advent of electric technology and its impact on how the music reached its audience, and you end up with a revolution in popular music. There was one more step: modernizing popular singing.

Popular Singing After 1930

Modern popular song emerged during the 1920s; modern popular singing emerged in the 1930s. The main reason for the gap between songwriting and performance was the limitations of technology in the early 1920s. The new technology that emerged at mid-decade opened the door for a host of new singers who would not have had professional careers previously. Among them were light-voiced singers like Gene Austin, Cliff "Ukulele Ike" Edwards, and even "Whispering" Jack Smith. However, the two most influential new singing styles were crooning and jazz singing. Among the early crooners were Rudy Vallee—who was famous for singing into a megaphone—Russ Columbo, and Bing Crosby. The more jazz-oriented singers included Louis Armstrong, whose singing would prove as influential to pop vocalists as his playing was to jazz musicians, and Fats Waller.

Bing Crosby: Quintessential Crooner

The dominant popular singer of the 1930s and 1940s was Bing Crosby (1903–1977). No singer sold more recordings, appeared in more films, or starred on more radio programs. During this period, Crosby had an impeccable public persona—affable, good-humored, easygoing; it was a perfect complement to his **crooning**, an intimate, pleasant singing style.

Crosby joined Paul Whiteman's band in 1926 as part of a vocal trio, the Rhythm Boys. During his three years with Whiteman, Crosby sang as part of the group and occasionally as a solo singer. When he wasn't singing for Whiteman, he frequented the clubs where Louis Armstrong performed. It was from Armstrong that he learned how to swing; by the late 1920s he was an excellent jazz singer, as his solo recordings with Whiteman evidence. (In the thirties, after he had become a big star, he repaid this musical debt by insisting that Armstrong be included in the 1936 film *Pennies from Heaven*.) Crosby was cool before it was cool to be cool and hip before it was hip to be hip.

Many writers have observed that Crosby was the first singer to really use the microphone well. He developed a low-key style that was as conversational as the lyrics he sang. Coming through the radio or phonograph, he sounded as though he were in the same room as his listeners. The new technology made this kind of intimacy possible; Crosby was the first to capitalize on it in a big way. He soon had many imitators.

> "*Crosby was the first singer to really use the microphone well.*"

After he left Whiteman in 1929, he diversified his repertoire and became known mainly for his comfortable crooning of ballads. "White Christmas" was the most famous of his more than 300 hits and his 4,000-plus recordings. However, in many of his recordings, his singing shows his affinity with jazz and a tinge of the blues (which came to him mainly through Armstrong). When blended with the easy delivery that the microphone made possible, it became the most influential and popular style of the era. We hear a fine example of Crosby's singing in his 1933 recording of Harold Arlen's "I've Got the World on a String."

Crosby's singing was modern because it was personal and personable. During the time that Crosby recorded

Hulton Archive/Getty Images

CD 1:24

"I've Got the World on a String," Ted Koehler and Harold Arlen (1932). Bing Crosby, vocal, with the Dorsey Brothers Orchestra.

"I've Got the World on a String," radios and record players were pieces of furniture, not portable devices, and there was no other commercial home medium—television would still be a novelty two decades later. Over the air or on record, Crosby sounded as if he were in listeners' living rooms, singing just for them. This contrasted sharply with the singing of song belters like Al Jolson, who were used to singing in theaters with no amplification, and who had been the most popular singers on stage and on record before the electrical revolution.

Crosby's sound and style complemented the words and music of the new modern-era songs. The lyrics captured the tone and cadence of everyday speech; most words were a single syllable: "I've got the world on a string..."; "...why not take all of me" (heard below). The best melodies magically matched the flow of the words while still retaining sufficient interest to stand alone.

Crosby's relaxed delivery also complemented one of the important depression-era trends in popular song performance: a greater emphasis on melody. During the early 1930s, one direction in popular music was characterized by slower tempos, less syncopation and rhythmic activity, and smoother, more subdued sonorities—the use of mutes in Crosby's song is an instance of that. By the late 1930s this direction would be called "sweet," the opposite of swing. During the course of his career, Crosby's singing moved away from the jazz-inflected

LISTENING GUIDE
CD 1:24 "I've Got the World on a String"

STYLE	Blues-influenced modern-era song
FORM	Chorus-oriented song in AABA form; verse used as introduction
0:00	Introduction and verse
	Short instrumental introduction
(0:06)	Crosby sings the verse out of tempo, to convey its introductory nature

First Chorus

A (0:36)	I've got the world on a string …	First two A sections performed out of tempo
A (1:06)	I've got the song that I sing …	Freedom from a steady pulse allows Crosby to take expressive liberties
B (1:21)	Life is a beautiful thing …	Band briefly settles into swing rhythm on bridge
A (1:37)	I've got the world on a string …	Back out of tempo

Second Chorus

A (1:57)	Muted trumpet begins, Crosby takes over at midpoint; clarinet fills; lazy swing rhythm
A (2:15)	Trombone plays melody; drummer using brushes
B (2:31)	Crosby sings bridge, with clarinet responses between riffs
A (2:48)	Crosby swings the final A section

style of his Whiteman days toward the reassuring, if sentimental, crooning that was his trademark. Still, he remained comfortable in a jazz context, as his onscreen duets with Armstrong evidenced.

Crooning helped listeners connect to the singer as a person. Another kind of singing, which we will call **song interpretation**, made listeners aware of how the singer felt. We encounter a seminal example of this approach to popular song performance in the music of Billie Holiday.

Song Interpretation

Blues and modern popular song are both first-person music. However, blues is inherently a more first-person music, because the singer often wrote the song—or could have written it—and because both song and singer can communicate deep feeling directly. As you listened to Bessie Smith describe her empty bed, you could feel that she was sharing a personal chapter in her life. Popular song is more generic, if only because those who write popular songs cannot make their songs as autobiographical as a blues. They compose knowing that someone else

 to Remember
"I've Got the World on a String"

BLUES-INFLUENCED POPULAR SONG: SONGWRITING
Arlen wrote several songs for the Cotton Club in the early 1930s; most show a blues influence, particularly in the descending melodic curve. This song shows the happy side of the blues.

CROSBY'S CROONING
Crosby's mastery of the microphone and easy delivery were the model for a subsequent generation of singers. No singer of the era was more popular and more influential.

DOMINANCE OF MELODY
Crosby sings all the way through, and timekeeping only occurs in the latter part of the song. Although the in-tempo sections have a swing rhythm, this is not a performance intended for dancing.

 to Listen For
"I've Got the World on a String"

INSTRUMENTATION
Voice and dance orchestra, with violin, and with Dorsey brothers featured (clarinet, trombone)

PERFORMANCE STYLE
Crosby's conversational crooning; use of mutes by trumpet and trombone

RHYTHM
Alternation between out-of-tempo beginning and swing rhythm in second chorus

MELODY
A section = long descending phrase from opening riff; B section = variations on repeated note

TEXTURE
Melody with rich, unobtrusive accompaniment in out-of-tempo sections. In-tempo sections feature melody plus steady timekeeping in rhythm, statement/response exchanges.

will sing them—of the important white songwriters, only Harold Arlen sang professionally. Indeed, their hope was that many singers would perform and record the song because it was a hit.

Crooning, like Waters's blues-tinged singing, made the singing of popular song a more personal statement. In the 1930s, however, there emerged another way of singing popular songs that seemed to come from even deeper inside the singer. Its two most important and influential models were Louis Armstrong and Billie Holiday, whom we hear next.

Billie Holiday. Billie Holiday claimed that her two biggest influences were Bessie Smith and Louis Armstrong. She admired Smith's power and Armstrong's style. Smith and Armstrong, along with Bing Crosby and Ethel Waters, helped chart a new path in popular singing. It was Billie Holiday, however, who took the next major step.

Born Eleanora Harris, Billie Holiday (1915–1959) led an unimaginably difficult life. Both she and her mother were born out of wedlock, and both were arrested for prostitution in 1929, when Holiday was only fourteen. Shortly after, she started her musical career singing at tables in Harlem nightclubs. These were not glamorous places like the Cotton Club, but rough bars where the girls were expected to do more than just sing. She became an alcoholic and a drug addict, and she died at age forty-four after a steady decline in her ability to perform.

We hear her ability to transmute popular song into personal statement in her 1940 recording of "All of Me." A small band led by Eddie Heywood and featuring saxophonist Lester Young provides accompaniment.

CD 1:25

"All of Me,"
Seymour Simons
and Gerald Marks
(1931). Eddie
Heywood and His
Orchestra, with
Billie Holiday, vocal,
and featuring
Lester Young, tenor
saxophone.

"All of Me," written in 1931 by Seymour Simons and Gerald Marks, is a standard; it remains one of the most popular songs of the 1930s, and over the years hundreds of artists have recorded it. Billie Holiday's version shows how she brought the deep feeling of blues and the swing of jazz into popular singing. In essence, she projects *herself* through the song. As we listen to her recording, we are less concerned with the words than with how she delivers them. Her performance transcends the sentimental lyrics to express the real and almost universal pain of lost love, with an immediacy that the song by itself can't begin to attain. As written, words and music send one message; her voice sends a second, much

Billie Holiday in a scene from *New Orleans* (1946). It was her only film appearance. In the film she plays a maid and is the girlfriend of Louis Armstrong, seen here playing a cornet (not a trumpet).

United Artists/The Kobal Collection/Picture Desk

deeper one. Hers is not a pretty sound, but it remains one of the most individual timbres ever to emerge in the popular tradition.

We notice this most clearly in the second chorus, as Holiday transforms this straightforward popular song into a blues song. The range of the melody narrows considerably, and most phrases begin high and end low. She sings this chorus in the top part of her range, giving her voice a particular urgency. The inflection of the melodic line becomes more intense, especially on the words "lips," "eyes," and "cry." The note values lengthen and the rhythm becomes freer, suggesting even more strongly than before that Holiday sings because simple speech cannot convey the emotion she wishes to express. She saves the very top note in the song for the climactic phrase, "why not take the rest"; as her voice descends, we can feel her despair. Her performance transcends the lyrics to express the real anguish of lost love.

Billie Holiday's art is not one of technical virtuosity. Nor is it a style of conventional beauty. Instead, she communicates her feelings directly, unfiltered by stylistic conventions, a conventionally pretty vocal sound, or a literal adherence to the original melodic shape of the song. Like other great performers, she is a style unto herself, instantly recognizable, broadly influential, and widely, if unsuccessfully, imitated.

Like Waters, Holiday brought blues style and blues feeling into the singing of popular songs. Her work showed how one could use a popular song as a window to a singer's heart and soul. In essence she made popular singing a more autobiographical art, bringing a

LISTENING GUIDE
CD 1:25 "All of Me"

STYLE	Pop song interpretation
FORM	Two choruses plus interlude of a song in ABAC form
0:00	Introduction
	Short instrumental introduction featuring piano

First statement of form: Chorus

A (0:18)	All of me …	Blues-derived expressive inflection (the second "All of me," "I'm no good")
B (1:06)	Take my lips …	By this time Holiday has begun to create a new melody to the song: same words, same harmony underneath, but a melody quite different from the original.
A (1:21)	Your goodbye …	
C (1:11)	You took the part …	
1:24	Interlude	
		Tenor sax solo by Basie alumnus Lester Young

Second statement of form: Chorus

A (1:47)	All of me …	Same words, but a reworked melody. Notice how Holiday compresses the melody into a narrower range.
B (1:06)	Take my lips …	The vocal inflection tells us what the lyrics are trying to say.
A (1:21)	Your goodbye …	Her continual reshaping of the original melody shows the influence of jazz practice on her singing.
C (1:11)	You took the best …	Holiday's ad-libbed lyrics are the climax of the performance.

freedom into her reshaping of a melody and the timing of her delivery. Her influence was evident on the next generation of pop singers, both women and men, and black and white, as we discover in Chapter 8.

• • • • • • • • •

Popular Song on Stage and Screen

To this point in the chapter, we've discussed six songs. Four of them, "Charleston," "Fascinating Rhythm," "Am I Blue?" and "I've Got the World on a String," were introduced on stage or film. For songwriters hoping for a hit, inclusion of a song in a show or film improved its chances considerably. Even if the show flopped, the song would get heard, often by influential people. If a song did become a hit, it quickly became decontextualized. People who might never see the show would know the song; they would not be aware of its function within the show.

In our discussion of the final two songs, we consider them as songs *and* as dramatic tools: How does each song contribute to the story? We consider this question as part of a larger discussion of popular song on stage and screen. One comes from the most influential—and one of the most beloved—musicals in the history of American musical theater. The other comes from the most popular series of movie musicals during the 1930s.

Show Boat, an American Musical Play

Show Boat, an "American musical play" created by Oscar Hammerstein II and Jerome Kern, opened at the Ziegfeld Theater in New York on December 27, 1927. Hammerstein, who wrote the libretto and the lyrics for the songs, and Kern, who conceived the idea for the musical and composed the music, came up with the phrase in order to convince Florenz Ziegfeld to produce the musical.

Kern was already a well-established songwriter by 1926, when he read Edna Ferber's best-selling novel, *Show Boat*. After reading it, he was convinced that it would make a superb musical and persuaded Oscar Hammerstein II to read it and transform it into a

5 to Listen For
"All of Me"

INSTRUMENTATION
Holiday's vocal, backed by a band
featuring trumpet, three saxophones, and
full rhythm section (guitar, piano, bass,
drums)

PERFORMANCE STYLE
Holiday's unique vocal timbre and
expressive blues-tinged inflections give
her singing a distinct personality.

RHYTHM
Moderate tempo; swing (four-beat)
rhythm marked by guitar and bass; lots of
rhythmic play in Holiday's singing

MELODY
Develops from a three-note riff;
succeeding versions of riff keep the
rhythm but assume a different melodic
shape.

MELODY
Holiday reshapes the melody in second
chorus, flattening it out to make it more
blues-like.

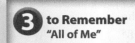

3 to Remember
"All of Me"

HOLIDAY, BLUES, JAZZ, AND POP
Holiday sings pop songs with the feeling
and style of blues and the swing and
freedom of jazz.

HOLIDAY'S VOICE
A unique, unconventional vocal sound
that set her apart

**POP SINGERS VS. SONG
INTERPRETERS**
Holiday was among the first important
song interpreters, using songs to project
her experience—and reshaping them in
the process.

libretto (a libretto is the text for a stage production with singing, from opera to musical comedy).

We can't know how clearly Kern envisioned a new, more substantial kind of musical, but we do know from his previous work that he wanted to integrate music and drama more thoroughly than was common practice at the time. To do this he would have to go against the grain.

Musical Stage Entertainment in the 1920s. The 1920s were the heyday of stage entertainment in the United States. Vaudeville was still going strong. Revues, a series of song and dance numbers held loosely together by a topical story line, were doing well. The most famous were the *Ziegfeld Follies*, presented annually from 1907 to 1927. Musical comedies, with music by American composers such as George Gershwin, Irving Berlin, and Jerome Kern, competed with operettas, composed mainly by Europeans (Herbert, Romberg, Friml) who had emigrated from Europe to the United States.

Virtually all of this was fluff. The plots for musical comedies were lighthearted, comparable in dramatic depth to an average sitcom. Operettas had fantasy plots: the long-ago-and-far-away storylines still prevailed. There was a lot of singing and a lot of dancing; shows usually opened with a string of chorus girls kicking away. And there was also a lot of comedy. These productions were fun; they were designed to entertain and

occasionally to titillate. But they didn't go much deeper than that.

All of this contrasted sharply with grand opera, which flourished in the United States during the early years of the twentieth century. New York's Metropolitan Opera company, which debuted in 1883, toured extensively throughout the United States. It featured the top singers and conductors of the day, including the tenor Enrico Caruso, arguably the most celebrated singer of the twentieth century.

Kern and Hammerstein's "musical play" would bridge the gap between grand opera and these lighter musical entertainments. It would weave elements of both into a new genre.

The Innovations of *Show Boat*. Ziegfeld, who had stopped producing revues in favor of musical comedy, was reluctant to produce a show that departed so dramatically from other kinds of stage entertainment. Only when Kern and Hammerstein convinced him to bill the production as an "American musical play" did he buy into the idea. Once committed, he threw his considerable energy and financial resources into the project. It was a lavish production in every respect.

Why was Ziegfeld so reluctant? Ferber's novel dealt with serious issues seriously, even as it portrayed a chapter in American life that had all but disappeared. *Show Boat* chronicles the life of the Hawkes family over a period of about forty years and three generations. The patriarch, Captain Andy, runs a showboat, a riverboat that cruises up and down the Mississippi, stopping at river cities to provide theatrical productions to the townsfolk. The plot centers on the marriage between Magnolia, the Hawkes's daughter, and Gaylord Ravenal, a good-looking, good-for-nothing gambler. They go through many hard times, including a separation that lasts years, before they are reunited at the end. Any happiness is certainly tempered by the heartache they have known. A key subplot involves Julie, a light-skinned mulatto, and her white husband, Steve. They are the principal actors in the production put on by Captain Andy. She is exposed as nonwhite by a jealous suitor, and because of a law against miscegenation (interracial marriage), the couple must leave the showboat. Julie returns some years later working as a cabaret singer, and obviously the worse for having become an alcoholic. Another recurrent theme is the life of the stevedores along the Mississippi. Their presence is a commentary on the hard lot of African Americans after the Civil War.

Show Boat was entertainment, not exposé, although it was entertainment with a message. And seen from our current perspective, it may seem politically incorrect.

There are reverberations of the minstrel show in the lyrics to "Can't Help Lovin' Dat Man" and other songs sung by blacks. Julie was portrayed by the white torch singer Helen Morgan rather than a light-skinned black singer. But this was the 1920s. Jim Crow laws were still on the books in the South; the Ku Klux Klan was on the rise; professional baseball was still segregated; and Al Jolson had blacked up for *The Jazz Singer*, the first full-length talking picture, which had come out less than three months earlier. Seen against this, *Show Boat* was a major statement, simply by raising such difficult issues.

Jerome Kern and the Modern Popular Song. Jerome Kern was the elder statesman among the great song-writers active in the 1920s and 1930s. He was older than Irving Berlin, Cole Porter, Gershwin, and others, and he had his first hit song in 1905, the year Harold Arlen (who composed "Over the Rainbow") was born. Moreover, Kern received traditional musical training in New York and Germany, and spent much of the 1900s and 1910s traveling between New York and London, where he sup-plied dozens of songs that were interpolated into shows.

By training, experience, and inclination, Kern, of the major songwriters, was least in touch with the sounds and rhythms of the new black-influenced popular music. Even the songs from late in his career ("The Way You Look Tonight," "All The Things You Are") favor European values: flowing melodies, surprising harmonies, and rhythms with little or no syncopation. As a songwriter, he was the anti-Gershwin.

And perhaps because of his extensive experience writing songs for the shows of others, he was the first important American songwriter to concern himself seri-ously with the integration of music and drama. Between 1915 and 1918 he collaborated with Guy Bolton on a series of musicals for the Princess Theater, a small venue in New York. These shows owed more to the operetta tra-dition that had begun in the United States with Gilbert and Sullivan and continued with other European-born composers, such as Victor Herbert, Sigmund Romberg, and Rudolf Friml.

In *Show Boat*, Kern and Hammerstein set out to integrate—or at least Americanize—operetta. The "musi-cal play" featured an American take on the typical operetta plot: long ago was the turn of the century, and the Missis-sippi River was, for 1920s New Yorkers, far enough away. To help convey this, Kern incorporated still-popular hits from the turn of the century, including "After the Ball."

Most of Kern's original songs for *Show Boat* show a closer affinity with European-inspired operetta than they do with the new music of the 1920s. The significant exceptions were the songs for black characters. To sup-port the plot musically, Kern drew on black-influenced music familiar to him and much of his audience. In the case of "Ol' Man River," Kern evoked the spiritual

CD 1:26

"Can't Help Lovin' Dat Man," Jerome Kern and Oscar Hammerstein II (1927). Helen Morgan, vocal.

to convey the dignity of the hard-working, mistreated, and under-paid black laborers. The dramatic function of "Can't Help Lovin' Dat Man" is to suggest Julie's mixed racial heritage, well before the scene where Julie and Steve, her husband, are forced to leave the showboat.

When Queenie, the black cook, hears Julie singing "Can't Help Lovin' Dat Man," she asks Julie how she knows the song, because "Ah didn't ever hear anybody but colored folks sing dat song." In 1927 the most familiar "colored-only" songs were the classic blues of Bessie Smith and others. For numerous reasons—among them the racial climate at the time, the jarring musical contrast it would have created, and Kern's own musical predilections—Kern chose instead to compose a blues-influenced popular song rather than an authentic blues.

"Can't Help Lovin' Dat Man" is an up-to-date song for 1927, in the style of its lyrics, its melodic construc-tion, its use of dance rhythms, and its form. Although the awkward imitation of black speech (downplayed in Morgan's performance) reeks of the minstrel show, the lyrics are typical of the modern era in popular song. The diction, with a preponderance of one-syllable words, is close to everyday speech, and the song is a gentrified blues lament.

A New Kind of Musical Theater. *Show Boat* was the first of the great modern musicals. It elevated the level of discourse in musical theater, dramatically and musi-cally. Through the example of *Show Boat*, musical theater became a more elite entertainment, even as vaudeville and the revue disappeared from the stage, a casualty of the onset of the Depression and the rise of talking film. Many of the top songwriters on Broadway, including Kern and Gershwin, moved to Hollywood, where they composed memorable songs for film musicals. Those who stayed behind, most notably the team of Richard Rodgers and Lorenz Hart, created musicals that fol-lowed the lead of *Show Boat* in musical sophistication and dramatic substance. However, their musicals enjoyed relatively modest success, and they are seldom revived. Only with the Rodgers and Hammerstein musicals, begin-ning with *Oklahoma!* (1943) did the musical enjoy critical acclaim and commercial success comparable to *Show Boat*.

Fred, Ginger, and the Acceptance of the Modern Popular Song

In almost all of the Fred and Ginger films, the plot fol-lowed a predictable pattern. Boy sees girl and is immedi-ately infatuated with her; girl rejects boy because of some

LISTENING GUIDE
CD 1:26 "Can't Help Lovin' Dat Man"

STYLE	Blues-influenced modern-era song
FORM	Verse/chorus song: chorus (AABA) heard 1½ times; interpolation from another song

0:00	Introduction
	An instrumental version of a fragment from a song that appears later in the show

0:14	Interpolation		
		Let me lay on my back …	This is part of another song, sung just before the point in the musical when Julie is discovered to be part black.

0:42	Chorus fragment		
	A	Fish got to swim, birds got to fly.	Black-influenced features include riff that generates melody; syncopation on "man"; "man" is also a blue note.
	A (0:59)	Tell me he's lazy, tell me he's slow …	

1:12	Interlude
	Complete instrumental statement of verse

First complete statement of form: Verse and chorus

1:35	Verse		
		Oh, listen, sister, I love my mister man …	Syncopated melody over a rhythmic background shifts back and forth between two- and four-beat rhythm.

1:58	Chorus		
	A	Fish got to swim, birds got to fly.	Modern-era popular song in a quasi-classical setting: Morgan's singing closer to opera than blues; she removes syncopations in melody. Strings and bassoon belong to classical orchestra; rhythm instruments play stiff foxtrot and four-beat rhythm (no swing).
	A (2:14)	Tell me he's lazy, tell me he's slow …	
	B (2:30)	When he goes away …	
	A (2:46)	He kin come home as late as kin be …	

5 to Listen For
"Can't Help Lovin' Dat Man"

INSTRUMENTATION
Voice plus mix of pop and orchestral instruments, including strings, bassoon, strummed guitar.

PERFORMANCE STYLE
Morgan sings with quavery, quasi-operatic voice.

RHYTHM
Foxtrot rhythm at moderate tempo in chorus; shift to heavy four-beat rhythm in verse.

MELODY
A section built from four-note riff; B section has longer phrases.

MELODY
Descending contour and blue note show blues influence.

3 to Remember
"Can't Help Lovin' Dat Man"

POSITIONING *SHOW BOAT* MUSICALLY
Mix of classical (Morgan's singing, orchestral accompaniment) and contemporary pop (blue notes, melodies growing from riffs) features imply middle ground between conventional stage entertainment and opera.

MAINSTREAMING BLUES INFLUENCE
The influence of contemporary black music—blues, jazz, dance music—is evident in the rhythm and melody, although filtered through a mainly European sensibility.

MODERN POPULAR SONG
In the form of the chorus (AABA), construction of melody from riffs, conversational rhythm of lyric, and use of two- and four-beat rhythms, "Can't Help Lovin' Dat Man" is a modern-era foxtrot song.

kind of misunderstanding; boy ardently woos girl, using song and dance; girl succumbs to boy's charm and dancing ability; the misunderstanding is cleared up, and boy and girl live happily ever after, or at least until the next film.

In *Top Hat* and their other films, Fred and Ginger are living the lifestyle of the rich, if not always famous. They wear beautiful clothes, stay in fancy hotels, drive nice cars (or have someone else drive them), and travel extensively—they are jetsetters before the jet age. Nowhere is this more evident than in the big scene from *Top Hat*.

CD 1:27

"Cheek to Cheek," Irving Berlin (1935). Fred Astaire, vocal.

The scene tells us a great deal about popular song in the 1930s, its place in society, and its role in daily life. "Cheek to Cheek" is an elegant, expansive foxtrot. Compared with the songs at the beginning of the chapter, "Cheek to Cheek" is longer, more melodious, and less syncopated. It has a more moderate tempo, and the basic foxtrot that Fred and

LISTENING GUIDE
CD 1:27 "Cheek to Cheek"

STYLE	Modern-era foxtrot
FORM	Expansive form: AABBCA, with each A section twice typical length
0:00	Introduction
	Instrumental version of fragment from song that appears later in show

First statement of form

A (0:06)	Heaven …	Clear foxtrot rhythm underneath; obbligato in violins
A (0:29)	Heaven …	Phrase "Heaven" unfolds slowly; it is 16 bars, not 8.
B (0:53)	Oh! I love to climb …	Shift to four-beat rhythm
B (1:04)	Oh! I love to go out …	Rise and fall of melody suggests mountain range.
C (1:16)	Dance with me …	
A (1:29)	Heaven …	

Second statement of form (instrumental)

A (1:53)	Strings take melody; notice shift from clear two-beat to four-beat rhythm at end.
B (2:16)	Trumpets take over melody with shift to more swinging style.
B (2:28)	Saxophones, then trumpets play more syncopated version of melody.
C (2:40)	Fanfare-like brass
A (2:52)	Solo violin

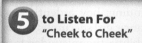

5 to Listen For
"Cheek to Cheek"

INSTRUMENTATION
Vocal, with dance orchestra featuring violins plus rhythm section (string bass and guitar stand out; piano plays fills), muted trumpet, saxophones

PERFORMANCE STYLE
Astaire has soft, reedy voice; he sings with subtle phrasing.

RHYTHM
Two-beat rhythm with discreet backbeat at moderate tempo through most of the song; B sections have four-beat rhythm.

MELODY
A section melody grows cleverly from simple two-note riff ("Hea-ven") into long arch.

MELODY
Contrast from section to section: A = long arch; B = quick rise and fall (mountains); C = dramatic skips, jagged rhythm

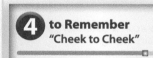

4 to Remember
"Cheek to Cheek"

CLASSY CHEEK-TO-CHEEK DANCING
Classy song and classy dancing mean that modern popular music is acceptable at almost every level of society.

LONG SONG
"Cheek to Cheek" is more than double the length of the typical popular song.

MELODIC ECONOMY
Berlin builds expansive phrase out of simple two-note riff.

WORDS AND MUSIC
Melody of all three sections reinforces meaning of lyric.

Ginger dance at the beginning is far less vigorous than the Charleston—Fred can easily sing to Ginger as they dance. That he can do both at the same time emphatically confirms the integration of song and dance. Moreover, their dancing makes clear how far up the social ladder the foxtrot song has moved.

Everything about the scene is more mature and upscale than the images of the frantic flappers of the twenties. Ginger is twenty-four and clearly a woman. Fred is thirty-six and looks as if he were never an adolescent. Their clothes must have cost a fortune, especially by thirties' standards. Elegance replaces energy; Ginger is wearing an evening gown instead of a flapper dress. The rough edges and vigorous movements of the Charleston are gone; the gliding movements of the foxtrot and the artistic dancing at the end of the scene take their place. The song offers a gentle "Heaven" instead of the syncopated "Charleston."

If you had to select one song to signal the end of the revolution that ushered in popular music's modern era, "Cheek to Cheek" would probably be a top choice. The title, the lyrics, the lush setting, the elaborate dancing, and Berlin's wonderful song—all send the same message: it's okay to dance cheek to cheek and when it's done by Fred and Ginger, it's about as classy as popular culture gets. The deep penetration of this suave and sophisticated sound into all levels of society essentially marginalized those who found popular music and its social setting objectionable. "Cheek to Cheek" demonstrates, as convincingly as any song of the era could, that the revolution that produced modern popular song was complete.

"Cheek to Cheek" and so many songs like it helped people dream, to escape the harsh reality of Depression-era America and experience vicariously the lifestyle depicted in *Top Hat*. For many people of this era, melodious popular song was the music of romance. Just like Fred and Ginger, couples often had "their" song—the song they fell in love to. Granted, it didn't pay the rent or feed the children, but it allowed people to forget about their day-to-day cares, at least for a few minutes.

Looking Back, Looking Ahead

The eight examples included in this chapter help document one of the two most eventful periods in the history of popular music; only the rock revolution of the 1950s and 1960s is comparable in significance. Compared with the music from the first part of the century, almost every aspect of this music—and the business surrounding it—had been significantly altered.

A media revolution transformed the way audiences encountered popular music: through radio, electric recording, and film, Americans learned popular music by listening to it more than they did by reading the sheet music. Moreover, it opened the door to a host of new sounds—sounds that could be preserved on recordings or broadcast over the air, but not transmitted very faithfully via sheet music. These include not only jazz and the new popular singing styles but also a variety of blues and blues-based styles and country music (which we hear in Chapter 6).

Most of the new sounds emerged through the wholesale infusion of African American elements into popular styles. Most fundamental were the rhythmic changes. First came the transformation of the march into the foxtrot, mainly by converting the afterbeat into a crisp backbeat and adding syncopation. The more active and swinging rhythms of jazz and the relaxed, free delivery of the blues penetrated popular song and its performance soon after the emergence of the foxtrot.

Song and dance, separate at the turn of the century (although songs often had a dance rhythm), came together in the 1920s, first with the performance of popular songs by dance orchestras and then by interpolating vocals between instrumental sections. Popular songs also changed, not only in rhythm and melodic style but also in form. Performances typically consisted of several statements of the chorus; the verse was ignored or used as an interlude between choruses. AABA form, which repeated the catchiest part of the melody many times, largely displaced earlier forms. The newly formed rhythm section provided the beat underneath the melody; the newly popular saxophone often played it.

The infusion of blues and jazz into mainstream music also produced a small but measurable improvement in race relations. The numerous black musicals and revues, black dance orchestras like those of Henderson and Ellington, the jazz of Armstrong and Oliver, Kern and Hammerstein's sympathetic portrait of Joe in *Show Boat*, the emergence of entertainers such as Ethel Waters and Fats Waller—all of these developments moved public perception of African Americans away from the minstrel show stereotypes and toward real people. Moreover, many acknowledged not only their person but also their genius: Crosby found in Armstrong and his music something that he could find nowhere else.

Perhaps because it is an art of the ear, music has been the most colorblind facet of the entertainment world. The majority of good musicians have been most concerned with only one thing: how well one sings or plays the music that they like. Partly because of this, racial barriers came down faster in popular music than in any other segment of American society.

The best music, black and white, helped speed this process along. There was still a long way to go in 1940, but the popular-music business had at least started down the road, with American society following along. Giving it a strong push toward a barrier-free world was a new kind of dance music: swing.

Terms to Know

Test your knowledge of this chapter's important terms by defining the ones listed here. If you can't recall the meaning of a certain term, refresh your memory by looking up the boldfaced term in the chapter, turning to the Glossary at the back of the book, or working with the flashcards at the Popular Music Resource Center.

speakeasy	stride piano
acoustic recording	torch song
microphone	vibrato
amplifier	crooning
electric recording	song interpretation
modern era	libretto
Charleston	

The *Swing* Era

Chris Schmidt/iStockphoto.com

CHAPTER

5

During the 1920s, Fletcher Henderson led one of the top hot dance orchestras in New York. Among the musicians who worked for him were Louis Armstrong and Coleman Hawkins, who would become the most influential saxophonist of the swing era. However, Henderson was a better musician than businessman. In 1934, desperate for cash, Henderson sold arrangements to Benny Goodman, whose band had just been engaged to present *Let's Dance,* a late-night radio show that was broadcast across the country.

After the contract for the radio show expired, Goodman and his band embarked on a cross-country tour, just to keep working. By the time they reached Los Angeles, they were disheartened; at almost all of their previous stops, the managers of the ballrooms had wanted sedate waltzes and foxtrots. Gun shy from the cross-county trip, Goodman began the evening playing the syrupy music they'd been forced to play on the tour. But the capacity crowd that greeted Goodman's band at the Palomar Ballroom was part of their radio audience (midnight in New York meant nine o'clock in Los Angeles) and loved their new, swinging sound. The crowd was perplexed and gave the band a lukewarm response. Sensing their indifference, Goodman and the band decided to go down in flames—they pulled out a swing tune, and the crowd went wild. This was the music that they'd come to hear, and they let the band know it. The concert at the Palomar Ballroom, which was broadcast nationwide, was a huge success. Many cite it as the event that kick-started the swing era.

> ❝*Goodman and the band decided to go down in flames—they pulled out a swing tune, and the crowd went wild.*❞

We call the years between 1935 and 1945 the swing era. Swing had bubbled outside the mainstream since the early 1930s, mainly in the music of urban black dance orchestras, most notably those of Duke Ellington and Fletcher Henderson, and Midwest bands, like Bennie Moten's, which used Kansas City as their base. (Count Basie took over Moten's band after Moten's death in 1935.) However, in the wake of Goodman's triumphant appearance in Los Angeles, it became a truly popular music. Following in Goodman's footsteps, a parade of big bands, white and black, competed for air play, ballroom engagements, and record dates. In addition to Goodman, the most notable bands were those led by both Dorsey brothers, Glenn Miller, Artie Shaw, Count Basie, and Duke Ellington.

Swing was not the dominant music of the decade. While Goodman and his band were appearing on late-night radio, Fred Astaire and Ginger Rogers were foxtrotting across silver screens in movie theaters around the country. Two camps quickly formed: those who liked swing, the energetic new dance music, and those who preferred **sweet**, the foxtrot song, now grown more melodious, less syncopated, and (usually) slower. Bands usually specialized in one or the other, although most of the top bands were capable of performing both styles. Swing and sweet were comparably popular through the end of World War II. Still, it is swing that put the musical stamp on the decade. The music seemed to capture—even create—the increasingly optimistic mood of the country as it fought off the Depression.

● ● ● ● ● ● ● ●

The Sound of Big-Band Swing

The sound of big-band swing evolved directly from the jazz-influenced dance orchestras of the 1920s. The two most important developments were the expansion and transformation of the dance orchestra, and a fundamental change in the rhythmic foundation of the music.

In 1940, the year in which he recorded "Ko-ko," Duke Ellington's orchestra included fifteen musicians, with the following instrumentation:

- Two trumpets and a cornet, a close relative of the trumpet
- Three trombones (two slide trombones and one valve trombone)
- Five saxophones (two alto saxophones, two tenor saxophones, and one baritone saxophone; Barney Bigard, one of the tenor saxophonists, doubled [alternated] on clarinet)
- Four rhythm instruments: guitar, piano (Ellington), bass, and drums

This was the minimum size for a swing-era big band. It represented an expansion in the size of the horn sections of many of the hot 1920s dance orchestras. These bands typically contained three saxophonists (who also played clarinets at times) and three or four brass instruments.

The expansion of the dance orchestra coincided with an increase in the use of riffs. From the early 1910s, riffs had been the seeds from which so many popular songs grew. In big-band swing, riffs became more repetitive (reflecting the influence of blues) and more pervasive. "Melodies" often consisted of a conversation among the sections, which traded riffs back and forth, rather than a single dominant line. This was an adaptation of the long-standing African practice of call and response, heard in a wide range of black vernacular music. In addition, one or more sections typically supported solos with riffs. Often a horn player in Count Basie's orchestra, which featured several strong soloists, would invent a riff during another musician's solo; the other members of the section would harmonize it.

William Gottlieb/Redferns Music Library

The foundation for the stacks of riffs generated by the horn section was the steady pulse laid down by the rhythm section. Between 1930 and 1940, the rhythm section went through a wholesale transformation. Acoustic guitar replaced banjo; string bass replaced tuba; and the drum set gained an important new component, the hi-hat cymbal. The changes reflected the shift in underlying rhythm from the two-beat of the foxtrot to the four-beat rhythm of swing. Instead of tuba and banjo alternating on the beat and backbeat, both string bass and guitar marked each beat: the bassist with a walking line—one note on each beat—and the guitarist by strumming chords. Often the drummer also thumped out the beat on the bass drum. The backbeat was present, but more subtly; the drummer closed the hi-hat on the backbeat, and the guitarist strummed more vigorously on the second and fourth beats. (Films of swing-era guitarists often show them strumming up on the first and third beats and strumming down on the second and fourth beats.)

The novel element in swing rhythm was not the four-beat feel; that is present in classic jazz and blues recordings of the 1920s, such as "Hotter Than That" and "Empty Bed Blues," and became a common alternative to the two-beat rhythm by the end of the decade. Rather, it is the persistent timekeeping by a full rhythm section—guitar, bass, and drums—supporting the extensive syncopation in the riffs and call-and-response exchanges between sections. Swing *swings* because of the interplay between the timekeeping of the rhythm section and the syncopations everywhere else.

Fletcher Henderson and the Roots of Big-Band Swing

The early 1930s were the worst years of the Great Depression. Times were very tough: one person in four was out of work. The devastation of the Dust Bowl—severe droughts that paralyzed agriculture and uprooted families—reached its peak. The adversity affected

African Americans disproportionately because so many doors were already closed to them. In spite of this, a few black bands managed to find enough work to live on. Their music was the main source of big-band swing.

The man most responsible for shaping the sound of big-band swing was Fletcher Henderson (1897–1952). Henderson is one of the shadow figures of popular music. We know that he came from a black middle-class family in Georgia and got his musical training from his mother, a piano teacher. He came north in 1920 to study chemistry but soon found work with the Pace-Handy music company, first as a song plugger in its publishing business, then as a jack-of-all-trades for Harry Pace's Black Swan Records. We know that during the 1920s he led one of the top bands in New York; they performed at the Roseland Ballroom and made it *the* place to go for great dancing. But hard times and Henderson's lack of business and leadership skills made it difficult to keep his band together. Still, he continued to find work for the band through the early years of the depression.

We have conflicting accounts of Henderson the person and Henderson the musician. Most agree that he was far from a dynamic leader. Some accuse him of laziness; more claim that he was a terrible businessman. He owes his fame to his skill as an arranger, but even his musical contributions have been subject to doubt. Some scholars deflect credit to other musicians, notably Don Redman, who arranged for Henderson's band in the late 1920s, and Benny Carter, who did the same in the early thirties. We will probably never know the truth.

CD 1:28

"Wrappin' It Up," Fletcher Henderson (1934). Fletcher Henderson and His Orchestra.

Nevertheless, Henderson was a major player behind the scenes for more than twenty years. He attracted to his band some of the best black jazzmen of the time, from Louis Armstrong to Coleman Hawkins, to Lester Young. And, most important, it was his arrangements that Goodman used to popularize swing. We hear a example of his approach in his 1934 recording "Wrappin' It Up."

This 1934 recording conveys the essence of how to compose and play big-band swing. The first few seconds describe swing: syncopation over a steady four-beat rhythm. The rhythm section lays down the beat. The horns (brass and saxophones) play a simple riff that is

LISTENING GUIDE
CD 1:28 "Wrappin' It Up"

STYLE	Big-band swing
FORM	Several choruses, some arranged and some improved; chorus form = ABAC
0:00	Introduction
	The essence of swing: syncopated chords by the horns over a steady four-beat rhythm from the rhythm section
0:09	First chorus
A	Repeated riff in saxes with response in brass
B (0:19)	New riff in saxes
A (0:28)	Full band
C (0:37)	More elaborate than a riff
0:48	Second chorus
	Alto sax solo, with sustained brass chords
1:25	Third chorus
A	Trumpet solo with sax riff behind
B (1:34)	Full band playing new riff
A (1:44)	Trumpet solo resumes.
C (1:53)	Trumpet solo continues.
2:02	Fourth chorus
A	New brass riff; answer by clarinets (sax players switched instruments)
B (2:12)	Clarinet solo, with low brass chords
A (2:22)	Written out "solo" for sax section (melody is like improvised solo)
C (2:32)	Full band

out of phase with the beat. The swing results from the conflict between the beat and the syncopated riff.

The melody of the song grows out of another simple riff. In this respect it's like so many of the songs from the twenties. What's different is the way it proceeds. Instead of developing the melody by varying the riff, Henderson simply repeats it one or more times, then shifts to another riff. Creating a melody by repeating a riff, rather than developing it, is one of the trademarks of big-band swing.

Another common feature is the call and response among the sections. Henderson's band features a four-man saxophone section, plus three trumpets and two trombones. Often saxes and brass exchange riffs; in the opening the brass "comment on" or "respond to" the sax riff, as if they were saying, "Yeah!" With arrangements like this one, Henderson laid the groundwork for **big-band swing**: saxes and brass exchanging riffs over a propulsive four-beat rhythm.

5 to Listen For
"Wrappin' It Up"

INSTRUMENTATION
Small-scale swing band: three trumpets, two trombones, four saxophones (doubling on clarinet), plus full rhythm section (acoustic guitar, piano, string bass, and drums)

RHYTHM
Clear four-beat rhythm at a bright tempo laid down by the rhythm section

RHYTHM
Lots of syncopation in the horn parts, especially introduction and first chorus

MELODY
Melody constructed from a series of short, repeated riffs, especially A and B phrases

TEXTURE
Strong contrasts: Extensive use of call and response; in ensemble sections, harmonized riffs over rhythm; in solo sections, background chords or riffs, all over rhythm

Henderson and his orchestra never hit it big, as Goodman and Glenn Miller did, or even like other top bandleaders, such as Count Basie, Jimmie Lunceford, or Duke Ellington. But his arranging style became the default sound of big-band swing.

3 to Remember
"Wrappin' It Up"

SWING RHYTHM
Syncopation over four-beat rhythm

SWING BAND
Four sections: rhythm (guitar, piano, bass, and drums), trumpets, trombones, and saxes

SWING TUNE
Riffs and responses: frequent call and response between horn sections

Small-Group Jazz in the Swing Era

Benny Goodman (1909–1986) earned his reputation as the King of Swing mainly from his work as leader of the first popular swing-era big band. However, his small-group recordings during the swing era, both live and in the studio, are, if anything, an even more valuable component of his legacy. One gets the impression in these recordings that he is working happily among peers, playing the music that he most wants to play, and enjoying the challenge of matching musical wits with like-minded musicians of comparable ability.

A former colleague of mine who attended Washington and Lee University around 1940 told me about Benny Goodman's big band's visit to the campus for a dance when he was an undergraduate. At the time, black guitarist Charlie Christian was traveling with the band. However, Washington and Lee is in Lexington, Virginia, and black musicians weren't allowed to perform with whites in the South. So Christian sat over in the corner, away from the bandstand, playing by himself during the intermissions, with my colleague and a few other undergraduates grouped around him. Christian would die of tuberculosis at age twenty-five shortly after the engagement.

This anecdote gives us yet another reason to deplore the institutionalized racism that has pervaded American history. But the story is more about the musicians and their audience: about Christian's acceptance of the situation (he still played for the few who were interested); about the larger loss (how many people didn't hear one of the most innovative jazz musicians of all time during his far-too-brief career); and, above all, about Goodman's courage and single-mindedness, and its consequences for popular music.

Goodman lived for music. He was passionate about playing with the best, and this passion trumped every other consideration, including race. In a potentially career-damaging move, he hired black pianist Teddy Wilson in 1935, not long after the band's big success in Los Angeles; he, Wilson, and drummer Gene Krupa would perform as a trio, separate from the rest of the band. The following year, he expanded the trio to a quartet by hiring black vibraphonist Lionel Hampton. At his landmark Carnegie Hall concert in January 1938, he featured not only the quartet with Wilson and Hampton but also members of the Count Basie and Duke Ellington orchestras, who joined him for a jam session. He hired Christian in 1939. Goodman integrated the bandstand and did more than any other white musician before him to break down the color barrier in music and, through music, American life.

Getty Images

"Goodman lived for music."

Benny Goodman's Small Groups

Although big-band swing was more commercially successful and better known, small-group jazz remained a vital part of the jazz scene through the thirties and early forties. Many of the important bandleaders of the swing era—not only Goodman, but also Duke Ellington, Count Basie, Artie Shaw, and Lionel Hampton—also performed or recorded with small groups, either from their own band or assembled specifically for a recording session. "I Found a New Baby," the recording discussed below, brings together two of these bandleaders, Goodman and Basie.

CD 1:29

"I Found a New Baby," Jack Palmer and Spencer Williams (1934). The Benny Goodman Sextet.

The track includes Charlie Christian (1916–1942), one of the true innovators of the swing era. Christian was the first important jazz musician to perform on electric guitar; amplification turned the guitar into a melodic solo instrument. Christian, who wanted to play saxophone, plays as fluently as any horn player. Moreover, Christian's improvising style is, in the opinion of many jazz historians, the bridge between swing and bebop, the revolutionary jazz style that emerged after 1945.

Goodman's "I Found a New Baby" is particularly instructive in three ways. It gives us our first example of a jazz performance of a popular song; it presents, even more clearly than the big-band recordings, the timekeeping in the rhythm section that was the foundation of swing style; and it illustrates several improvisational

LISTENING GUIDE
CD 1:29 "I Found a New Baby"

STYLE	Small-group swing
FORM	Several improvised choruses on pop song; chorus form = AABA

0:00	Introduction	
	Riff-based introduction. Jones's timekeeping at outset is classic swing drum style that he invented: long/long-short ride pattern on hi-hat	
0:06	First chorus	
	A	Goodman paraphrases melody of song in first two A sections.
	A (0:16)	
	B (0:26)	Bridge and final section are thorough departure from the song.
	A (0:35)	More elaborate than a riff
0:44	Second chorus (electric guitar solo)	
	Charlie Christian, in one of the first solos on electric guitar, creates a new, fast-moving melody over chord progression of song.	
1:21	Third chorus (piano solo)	
	A	Count Basie plays piano responses to a riff derived from the melody.
	A	
	B	Showcasing the rhythm section: four-beat timekeeping by guitar and bass are foundation of swing
	A	Back to Basie
1:58	Fourth chorus	
	A	Trumpeter Cootie Williams's solo is a more melody-like new melody.
	A	
	B (2:16)	Saxophonist Georgie Auld integrates arpeggios based on the underlying harmony into his solo.
	A	
2:35	Fifth chorus	
	A	Drummer fills between statements of a short riff.
	A (2:45)	Recalling New Orleans–style collective improvisation: clarinet on top, trumpet playing melody, saxophone (substituting for trombone) playing countermelody

strategies, including melodic paraphrase, harmonically based running notes, and repeated riffs.

In this performance, both connotations of "swing" are apparent: swing as a rhythmic feel and swing as a style. The performance swings because of the rhythmic interplay of the soloists with the rhythm section. This interplay takes several forms: the marked syncopations of the opening riff, Goodman's bent notes that glide over the beat, and, in Christian's solo, phrases that end abruptly off the beat and the on again/off again accents at the end. The most recognizable elements of swing style are the explicit beat keeping of the rhythm section and the call-and-response exchange of riffs in the second chorus.

The Goodman group's "I Found a New Baby" is swing, not as a popular style, but as jazz, closely related to a popular style. It is not music for dancing, although the tempo is steady and not impossibly fast. It demonstrates the central place of improvisation in typical jazz performance and presents an inventory of common improvisational strategies. The next selection is its

opposite: a composition for big band that includes no improvisation. It also swings.

• • • • • • • •

Duke Ellington, Painter in Sound

The most distinctive big band of the swing era was the one led by Edward "Duke" Ellington (1899–1974). The quality that most distinguishes Ellington's music from that of all other bands was sound color. His masterpieces, like "Ko-ko," offer a dazzling variety of timbres unmatched by any other band of the era. The difference might be described in this way. Imagine the three basic timbres—trumpets, trombones, and saxophones—as primary colors. Arrangers of the era typically used these timbres as one might use crayons. By contrast, Ellington used timbres as an artist might use oils on a palette,

5 to Listen For
"I Found a New Baby"

INSTRUMENTATION
Clarinet, trumpet, tenor saxophone; rhythm section of guitar (alternating between electric and acoustic), string bass, piano, and drums

PERFORMANCE STYLE
All soloists play with considerable blues-tinged inflection; Williams uses a mute.

RHYTHM
Swing comes from frequent syncopations against rhythm.

RHYTHM
Varied rhythmic activity—riffs, running lines, melodic phrases with rhythmic contrast

MELODY
The song is based on a short riff. The solos are instrumentally conceived: fast-moving and wide-ranging lines or riffs.

3 to Remember
"I Found a New Baby"

JAZZ REPERTOIRE
Jazz musicians began improvising on popular songs in the late 1920s; by the late 1930s, many jazz recordings used a familiar song or a blues as a point of departure.

IMPROVISATIONAL STYLES
Several different improvisational styles, from simple riff exchanges to complex streams of notes

CONVENTIONS OF JAZZ IMPROVISATION
Jazz musicians rely on harmony, rather than melody, as framework for improvisation; they typically create new or substantially modified melodies over the chord progressions of the song.

recordings made him a national celebrity by the early 1930s. At the Cotton Club, Ellington had to provide what his manager Irving Mills called "jungle music." Although Ellington's music bore virtually no resemblance to sub-Saharan African music, it did encourage his musicians to develop novel effects, and Ellington to call on them as needed.

From the late 1920s to 1943, when he and his orchestra made their Carnegie Hall debut, the membership of the band remained remarkably stable. He gradually added musicians over the years, from ten musicians around the time he started at the Cotton Club to the fifteen heard on "Ko-ko." Few musicians left Ellington's band during this period; some had been with him since the Washingtonians days.

What made Ellington's musicians special was their individuality. Most of the horn players had a special sound. Some derived their sound from the choice of instrument, for instance, the cornet, a slightly darker sound than the trumpet, or the valve trombone instead of the more conventional slide trombone. Others, like baritone saxophonist Harry Carney, had a distinctive tone. Still others cultivated special effects; Ellington always had brass players who could produce growls and other effects through the use of mutes. Ellington and his musicians seemed to enjoy a symbiotic relationship: their unique abilities stimulated his imagination; he produced music that was successful enough to make them one of the most popular bands of the era and provide them with steady employment. For Ellington, the band was a laboratory for constant experimentation. We hear the fruits of this association in "Ko-ko," a masterpiece recorded in 1940.

At first glance, the phrase "jazz composer" sounds like an oxymoron because, throughout its early history, jazz was largely an improviser's music—to the extent that it was hard to conceive of jazz without improvisation. The Goodman recording is far more typical of jazz

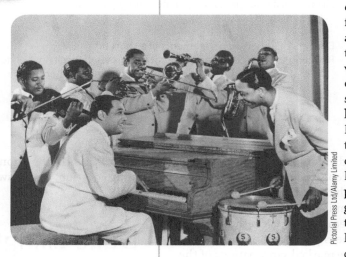

Pictorial Press Ltd/Alamy Limited

blending them to produce a far greater range of shades and hues.

Ellington's unique sound has three principal sources: his own musical imagination, a long apprenticeship in New York nightclubs, and a core of musicians, some of whom remained in his band for their entire career. Ellington's creativity was evident almost from the start of his professional career, when he led a band called the Washingtonians—Ellington had been born and raised in Washington, D.C. The high point of his tenure in New York was his extended run at the Cotton Club, a Harlem nightclub. He and his orchestra performed there from 1927 to 1931; radio broadcasts from the club and

> *Ellington used timbres as an artist might use oils on a palette.*

LISTENING GUIDE
CD 1:30 "Ko-ko"

STYLE	Big-band swing
FORM	Several arranged choruses over 12-bar blues, with introduction that returns at the end
0:00	Introduction
	Call and response between baritone sax and trombones
0:12	First chorus
	Call-and-response riffs between valve trombone (low) and saxophones (high)
0:31	Second chorus
	Riff in high trombone (with plunger mute), with offbeat figure in lower brass underneath
0:50	Third chorus
	Another high trombone sound, with offbeat answers continuing
1:09	Fourth chorus
	Repeated riff in the saxes, jagged responses in brass, piano fills. Note the quicker riff rhythm, repeated every four beats instead of eight.
1:27	Fifth chorus
	After riff, in trumpets, with two responses: high saxes/clarinets and trombones
1:45	Sixth chorus
	Short four-note riff, handed from saxes to trombones to trumpets to clarinets, followed by walking bass all alone; instrument order varied with each repetition
2:04	Seventh chorus
	Massive brass chord, followed by sax riff
2:23	Introduction = Ending
	The introduction returns, but leads this time to a climactic ending.

CD 1:30

"Ko-ko," Edward "Duke" Ellington (1940). Duke Ellington and His Orchestra.

performance than "Ko-ko" is. By contrast, Ellington, who was certainly an able improviser at the piano, is remembered as the greatest composer in the history of jazz.

Almost any music by Ellington in the 1930s and 1940s demonstrates his special sound world: vibrant and varied timbres, exotic harmonies, careful use of register and dynamics, and a clear sense of pacing. They also shed light on Ellington's solution to a major issue in jazz composition: imparting a sense of structure.

In creating compositions that were formally analogous to classical compositions, Ellington had to resolve an issue created by the fundamental rhythmic difference between European concert music and African-inspired jazz. In the music of Bach, Beethoven, and Brahms, differences in accentuation—downbeats versus upbeats, notes on the beat versus notes off the beat—help imply movement toward a goal, even if the goal is simply the beginning of the next beat or the next measure. Through the skillful manipulation of accentuation on a small and large scale, composers could outline the structure of a work as it unfolds through time—the beginning and end, as well as hierarchically arranged intermediate goals. By contrast, the African-influenced rhythm of jazz gives equal emphasis to each beat, as we hear in Jimmy Blanton's walking bass line in "Ko-ko." Only the changes in pitch imply a larger grouping and movement toward a point of arrival.

Ellington's inspired work-around was to regulate the "exchange rhythm," the alternation of material between sections. In the first part of "Ko-ko" it is relatively slow. By the time of the bass solo, it is much quicker; horn sections are tumbling over each other. The bass solo is a deep breath before the final push. By continuing to compress the exchange rhythm, Ellington conveys movement toward the final chord and, as a result, imparts a sense of direction that transcends a simple string of 12-bar blues choruses.

Such features as his inventive use of timbre, his colorful harmonies, and his handling of rhythm put Ellington's music "beyond category." No other jazz composer of his era brought his combination of craft and imagination to the work.

A final note: "Ko-ko" provides a useful perspective on the connection between swing, improvisation, and the essence of jazz. "Ko-ko" is jazz most fundamentally

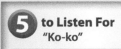

5 to Listen For
"Ko-ko"

INSTRUMENTATION
Full big band: two trumpets and cornet, two slide trombones and valve trombone, five saxophones, and rhythm section (guitar, bass, drums and piano)

PERFORMANCE STYLE
Several band members cultivated distinctive sounds (trombonist Sam Nanton's use of a plunger mute).

RHYTHM
Four-beat swing rhythm in rhythm section, with syncopated riffs pushing against the beat

RHYTHM
"Exchange" rhythm, that is, the rhythm created by the call and response between sections; initially eight beats per call/response pair, but altered at middle and end

TEXTURE
Multilayered texture over steady rhythm section Considerable variation in density—the number and spacing of parts—and register: effective use of extremes in both variables

3 to Remember
"Ko-ko"

ELLINGTON = SOUND PAINTER
For Ellington, timbral variety is like paints on a palette: "Ko-ko" spotlights trombones, first as a section, then individually. Timbre and register change from chorus to chorus.

USE OF REGISTER
Registral placement contributes to pacing of piece; on largest scale, it goes from low to high: the very low repeated note by baritone sax to final flourishes at end.

BEYOND BIG-BAND SWING
Ellington starts from big-band swing conventions, but his treatment of them is more imaginative, more sophisticated, and more individual—and because of this, closer to art.

---

because it swings. A skilled improviser can play with time in a way that is virtually impossible to notate comprehensibly. In "Ko-ko," this subtlety is not present; in its place is a collective understanding of how to push against the beat. The sax riffs in the first chorus amply demonstrate this.

• • • • • • • •

Swing as Popular Music

In the now obscure and otherwise forgettable 1941 film *Sun Valley Serenade*, there is a scene where Glenn Miller's band performs a number entitled "Chattanooga Choo Choo." The movie tanked, but the song became one of Miller's biggest hits, selling more than a million copies in less than three months. As a publicity stunt, RCA (Glenn Miller's record label) coated one of its records with gold lacquer and presented it to him on a radio broadcast in February 1942. Because of this, "Chattanooga

CD 1:31
"Chattanooga Choo Choo," Glenn Miller (1941). Glenn Miller and His Band, with Tex Beneke and the Modernaires, vocals.

As a publicity stunt, RCA coated one of its records with gold lacquer.

Choo Choo" was the first certified "gold" record. (Later, the Recording Industry Association of America [RIAA], the trade group that represents U.S. recording interests, would set the benchmark for a gold record at 500,000 units.)

Glenn Miller: Singing, Swing, and Popular Success

Swing as jazz was usually an instrumental music. Swing as popular music was usually a vocal music. There were a few big hits that were strictly instrumental: Glenn Miller's "In the Mood" and Count Basie's "One O'Clock Jump" stand out. However, most of the hit songs recorded by swing bands were popular songs sung and played in a swing style. Also popular were swing-based novelty numbers—vocals where the melody resembles a riff-type swing melody. We hear a famous example of this style next.

Glenn Miller (1904–1944) led the most popular band of the era. Goodman was the "King of Swing," and Count Basie and Duke Ellington were among its royalty, but no band was more popular than Miller's. One reason was his ability to move effortlessly between swing and sweet. For every "In the Mood" hit (swing), he had a "Moonlight Serenade" (sweet). Among the band's biggest hits was "Chattanooga Choo Choo."

The recording is a real period piece; it can belong only to the swing era. The song sounds like an instrumental riff-based song ("Pardon me, boy") that acquired words along the way. In particular, the melody of the B sections moves quickly and skips around (it's easier to play than it is to sing). Although there's the obligatory sweetheart at the end, the song is about a train ride, much like Berry's "Maybellene" is about a car chase.

Tex Beneke, one of the saxophone players in Miller's band, sings the lead vocal. The Modernaires, a close-harmony vocal group that had joined Miller in 1939, back up Beneke and occasionally step into the spotlight. Close-harmony groups like the Modernaires and the

LISTENING GUIDE

CD 1:31 "Chattanooga Choo Choo"

STYLE	Big-band swing
FORM	Expanded popular song form (AABBAA¹) vocal chorus surrounded by verse, introduction, plus fragmentary statements of form

0:00 Introduction
Instrumental introduction. Notice the mix of real and imitation train sounds.

(0:22) Introduction continues; final A section. An unusual beginning (perhaps because of 3-minute time limit): we hear only last A section. Melody leaves room for two responses per riff: clarinets high and trombones low.

Full statement of form (vocal)

0:48	Verse		
	Hi there, Tex …		
1:08	First chorus		
	A	Pardon me, boy …	Tex and the vocal group in effect function like a fourth
	A (1:21)	Can you afford …	section; answering riffs in saxes and occasionally brass
	B (1:34)	You leave the Pennsylvania …	Note shift to strong two-beat rhythm with clear backbeat
	B (1:47)	When you hear …	(still with a swing feel) at beginning of bridge, then shift back to four-beat rhythm.
	A (2:04)	There's gonna be …	
	A¹ (2:17)	She's gonna cry …	Fade-out seems to signal end of song, but …
2:46	Ending		

New instrumental melody enters, based on chords of A section.

(2:59) Another new melody, this time expanded into a tag

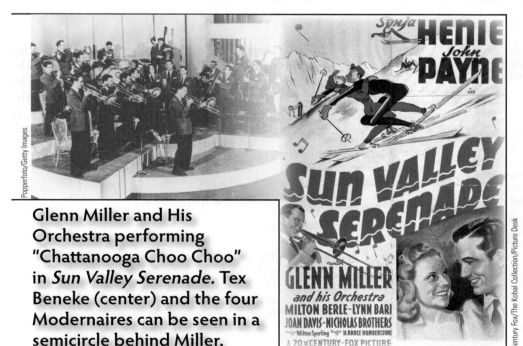

Popperfoto/Getty Images

Glenn Miller and His Orchestra performing "Chattanooga Choo Choo" in *Sun Valley Serenade*. Tex Beneke (center) and the four Modernaires can be seen in a semicircle behind Miller.

20th Century Fox/The Kobal Collection/Picture Desk

Andrews Sisters were also part of the sound of swing-based popular music.

With its vocal, special effects, riffs, syncopation, and growled/smeared/bent notes in the horns—all sounding over a firm four-beat rhythm at a brisk tempo—"Chattanooga Choo Choo" epitomizes swing as a popular style. The music is exuberant. It's fun in both words and sounds—the kind of sound that put smiles on peoples' faces and got them out on the dance floor.

In the fall of 1942, Glenn Miller joined the army, to lift the spirits of the soldiers at war. Two years later, his plane disappeared en route to France, and his body was never recovered. Miller's death seemed to signal the end of the swing era. After the end of World War II, a few bands kept going, but most disbanded. Goodman's appearance at the Palomar Ballroom and Miller's death frame the swing era. These events, and the memorable events in between, sharply define a time, place, and mood. Only the rock and roll of the 1950s evokes such strong associations in image and sound.

Looking Back, Looking Ahead

Swing brought a new and welcome energy to popular music: it lifted people's spirits as America lifted itself out of the depression. Among the enduring images of the swing era are dancers frenetically jitterbugging and Lindy-hopping around ballroom dance floors. They are a strong contrast to the sedate foxtrot with which Fred and

> Miller's death seemed to signal the end of the swing era.

Ginger begin "Cheek to Cheek." Interestingly, the energy of swing is not so much a function of tempo as it is of rhythmic activity. "Cheek to Cheek" actually moves at a faster tempo, in relation to the backbeat, than any of the four examples presented in this chapter. But the bass moves more slowly, which prompts slower movement, and there is little syncopation in "Cheek to Cheek." In swing, the strong four-beat rhythmic foundation plus lots of syncopation invest the performance with more drive despite its slower tempo. This pattern will repeat itself when rock and roll surfaces in the 1950s and shifts popular music to an even more active eight-beat rhythm.

By the end of World War II, the swing era was over, but the sound of swing did not disappear. Many swing-era musicians found steady employment in recording studios, where they played behind many of the top pop singers of the postwar era. This kind of singing was the most popular continuation of swing—but it was not the only one.

In the postwar years, swing split off in three directions; jazz-influenced popular singing, bebop (a daring new jazz style just for listening), and an upbeat brand of rhythm and blues. We hear good examples of all three trends in Chapter 8.

Terms to Know

Test your knowledge of this chapter's important terms by defining the ones listed here. If you can't recall the meaning of a certain term, refresh your memory by looking up the boldfaced term in the chapter, turning to the Glossary at the back of the book, or working with the flashcards at the Popular Music Resource Center.

sweet
big-band swing

5 to Listen For
"Chattanooga Choo Choo"

INSTRUMENTATION
Lead singer and close-harmony vocal group plus full big band: saxes/clarinets, trumpets, trombones, and rhythm; plus train noises at beginning

PERFORMANCE STYLE
Beneke's vocal style neither personal nor suave; his "stepped-out-of-the-band" sound works well here.

RHYTHM
Strong swing rhythm except for bridge; lots of syncopation—in melody, where phrases end on an offbeat, and in many of the answering riffs

MELODY
A section: from simple riff to instrumental-type melody; B section: instrumental-type melody, but sung

TEXTURE
Layers of riffs, generally in call-and-response arrangement, with rhythm section underneath

3 to Remember
"Chattanooga Choo Choo"

NOVELTY SONG
A swing tune about a train ride, not love

INSTRUMENTAL SONG
Instrumental-style swing tune with lyrics added.

IMAGINATIVE DESIGN
Bigger than usual form (two statements of bridge, B), train sounds, pause before end—all distinctive touches

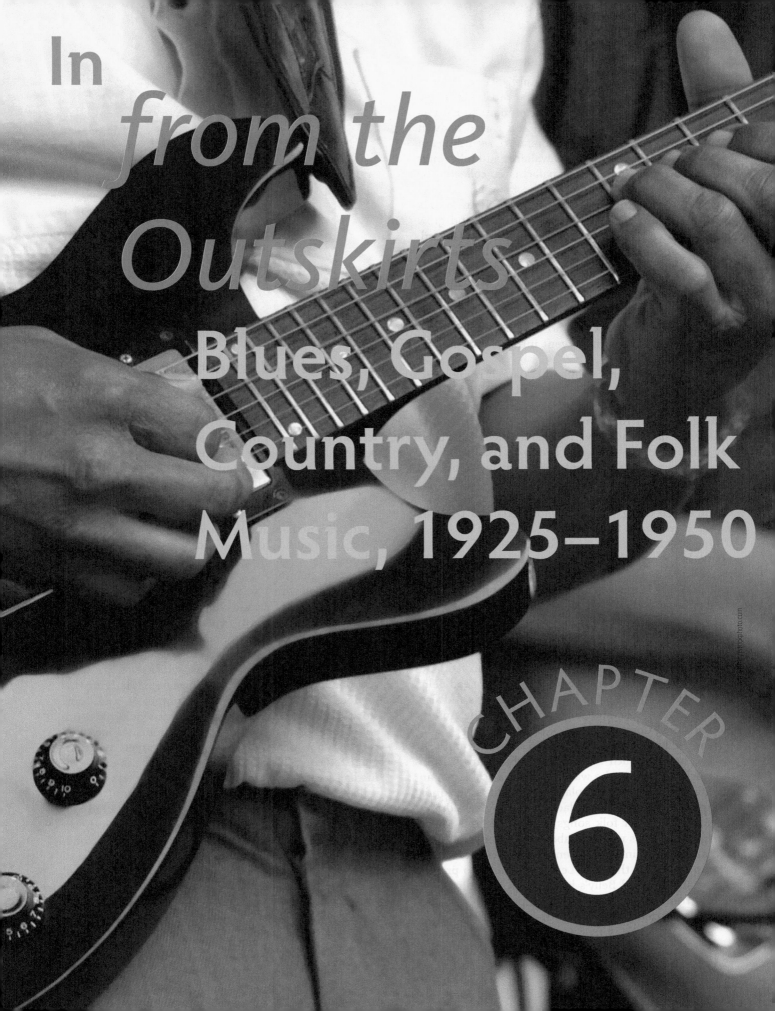

In *from the Outskirts*

Blues, Gospel, Country, and Folk Music, 1925–1950

CHAPTER

6

In 1928 the Library of Congress established an Archive of American Folk Song within its Music Division. Through the efforts of Robert W. Gordon, its first director, it soon amassed a substantial and varied body of music. Among its early acquisitions were recordings of Native Americans, ex-slaves, Hawaiians, and folk songs and fiddle music from the Appalachians, collected by Gordon himself.

The first curator of the Archive was John Lomax (1867–1948), who was born in Mississippi and grew up in Texas. While a graduate student at Harvard, he met George Kittredge, an eminent folklorist who encouraged Lomax's longstanding interest in cowboy songs. Lomax returned to teaching but was fired in 1917, when he came out on the wrong end of a tug of war between the president of the University of Texas and the governor of Texas (who was later impeached). Moving to Chicago, Lomax went into banking for the next fifteen years.

About the time most people think about retirement, Lomax returned to the music that had been his passion since childhood. In 1932 he secured a contract from a leading publisher for a wide-ranging anthology of folk ballads. He had previously prepared a collection of cowboy songs in 1910, which had been well received. After signing the contract, he went to the newly established Archive of American Folk Song to examine its holdings. In 1933 he made the first of his field trips through the South, where, using equipment mounted in the trunk of his car, he recorded folksingers.

One of his stops was Angola Prison in Louisiana, where he recorded Huddie Ledbetter (1888–1949), better known as Lead Belly. Lead Belly grew up in Louisiana and spent time in Dallas working with Blind Lemon Jefferson. He was sent to prison for murder in 1918 and won a reprieve in 1925 on the strength of his good behavior, which included entertaining prisoners and staff. By 1930 he was back in prison. Lomax recorded him for the Library of Congress, got him paroled, and brought him to New York the following year. Lead Belly continued to record for the Library of Congress and also began recording commercially, initially for the American Recording Company.

Lead Belly sang the blues often and with authority, but he was much more than a bluesman. Within the black community he was known as a **songster**, an entertainer who sang and played many different kinds of music, including blues, ballads, work songs, children's songs, and familiar folk songs, both black and white. The first songsters we know about appeared in the latter part of the nineteenth century; the tradition was dying out around the time Lead Belly came to prominence. Among Lead Belly's best-known recordings are the old frontier/children's song "Skip to My Lou" and "Goodnight, Irene," a nineteenth-century parlor song

Library of Congress Prints and Photographs Division Washington, D.C. [ppmsc 00348]

A prisoner and his guitar at Angola prison in Louisiana, where Lead Belly served time.

written by a black Cincinnati songwriter, which would become a hit song for the Weavers and then for pop singer Jo Stafford and country singer Ernest Tubb. Lead Belly performed both songs without any trace of blues style beyond the inherent huskiness of his voice, and his guitar accompaniment is simple and straightforward, with no bent notes or syncopation. It is as if Lead Belly assumed a different musical persona when singing white songs.

In this chapter, we present four different kinds of music, all of which were recorded between 1925 and 1950: an array of folk and commercial blues styles, early black gospel, early country music, and topical folk music. The first two styles feature black performers; the latter two feature white performers. There is an obvious racial divide between the two groups, which was far more consequential then than now. However, underlying this obvious divide is much common ground. All were "outsider" styles, and much of their music would influence subsequent generations of popular music. Blues and country first appeared on recordings targeted at marginalized constituencies not served by the mainstream media: race records for blacks and what was initially called "old time" or "hillbilly" music for rural whites. Similarly, recordings of black gospel were directed at a niche market; Woody Guthrie recorded extensively for the Library of Congress. All began as, or had deep roots in, folk traditions, and all became commercial musical styles, at least to the extent that musicians performed and recorded for profit.

And, most important, they often listened to each other, as Lead Belly's repertoire makes clear. All of the musicians came from the South or Southwest, where whites and blacks rubbed shoulders despite persistent and pernicious segregation. The depth of musical exchange becomes clear when we hear Jimmie Rodgers sing a blues more authentically than any white pop singer of his time; the Hokum Brothers reshape blues form to include a chorus; or Bob Wills plays countrified swing. We divide the chapter into two distinct halves to reflect the obvious division by race, yet include all of this music in one chapter to underscore the numerous connections between these styles.

Farm Security Administration - Office of War Information Collection 11671-7. Library of Congress Prints and Photographs Division Washington, D.C. [LC-USF35-135]

Blues and Black Gospel Music, 1925–1950

In 1955 Ray Charles would scandalize the black church community by giving the gospel hymn "Jesus Is All the World to Me" new words and a new beat: the new song, "I Got a Woman," was his first big hit. Blues singer Big Bill Broonzy summed up what Charles had done and why it outraged so many when he said, "He's crying, sanctified. He's mixing the blues with the spirituals. He should be singing in a church."

If Broonzy had reflected a little on the history of black gospel, he might not have judged Charles so harshly. Early in his career, Thomas A. Dorsey, the father of black gospel music, was a blues pianist known professionally as Georgia Tom. He played behind Ma Rainey and with guitarist Tampa Red; we hear their big hit below. In reminiscing about his music, Dorsey acknowledged the influence of the blues on gospel music: "You see, when a thing becomes a part of you, you don't know when it's gonna manifest itself. And it's not your business to know or my business to know."

In this section, we survey three developments in black music between 1925 and 1950: the recording of what is usually called country blues; the emergence of up-tempo, piano-based blues styles; and the beginnings of black gospel music. There is a clear difference in intent and result between the blues and black gospel: one is for Saturday night and the other is for Sunday morning. Yet there is also common ground, as Charles demonstrated and as we discover below.

" … when a thing becomes a part of you, you don't know when it's gonna manifest itself. And it's not your business to know or my business to know."
—Georgia Tom, on the influence of the blues

Country Blues

In the latter part of the twenties, Paramount Records advertised the music of Blind Lemon Jefferson as "real old-fashioned blues by a real old-fashioned blues singer." As Paramount's ad intimates, Jefferson's blues was an old style that was new to records. Jefferson was the first major country blues singer to record. From 1926, the year of Jefferson's first recording, until about 1940, country blues—so called because it flourished in rural settings throughout the South—carved out a small but viable niche in the record industry.

The Origins of the Blues. Country blues flourished in isolated regions of the rural South from the Carolinas and Virginia to Texas and Oklahoma. If blues had a home, it was the Mississippi Delta, in the northwest part of the state. Many important bluesmen, including Robert Johnson and Muddy Waters, called the Delta home.

In the first half of the century, the Mississippi Delta was mostly black. Jim Crow laws enforcing rigid segregation throughout the South had particular force there because so few African Americans had any economic, legal, or political leverage. Sharecropping, with its poor wages, few rights,

If blues had a home, it was the Mississippi Delta.

and high prices at the company store, kept many blacks almost as dependent as they had been during slavery. Some men—roustabouts and stevedores—worked on the river, building up the levees or moving cargo on and off the riverboats. Pay for this work was marginally better than for sharecropping—although it would make today's minimum wage seem like a fortune—but working conditions were harsher. White overseers carried guns to enforce discipline, and men labored long hours and lived in squalid work camps.

Most rural black Americans had little direct contact with white society, and none of it was on an equal footing. Moreover, in these days before television, few had much awareness of the outside world. Perhaps because they were so isolated in every way, rural blacks rediscovered, or perhaps reinvented, many aspects of the cultures their ancestors had left behind in Africa. We sense this when Muddy Waters, a Delta native, sings about "mojo" or when we discover that Bo Diddley's stage name mirrors that of the diddley bow (which he claims never to have heard of), an instrument similar to those found in West Africa, or when we hear a group of laborers singing a work song. It is in the South that we find what Robert Palmer called "deep blues"—the starkest, most powerful expression of blues feeling.

The Blues and African Culture. The blues is the most African of the African American musical traditions that emerged during the early years of the twentieth century, as Chapter 2's recording of Henry Ratcliff and the Senegalese worker demonstrated. West African cultures most often create music communally. However, within these cultures there is a direct precedent for the bluesman, the *griot*.

In West African culture, the *griot* fulfills many roles. He is the healer (the witch doctor), the tribe historian (he preserves its history in his songs), and, along with the master drummer, its most important musician. Although the *griot* is respected for his abilities, he is sometimes feared, or at least distrusted. As a result, he often stands outside of tribal life.

The *griot*'s incarnation in African American culture has been the bluesman. Like the *griot*, he told stories through songs and earned admiration and respect for this ability, but he also lived on the fringes of society. Many bluesmen traveled around in search of work and company. The bluesman led a life much different from that of the sharecropper or the roustabout—working when others played, and playing around when others worked.

> *The griot's incarnation in African American culture has been the bluesman.*

The bluesman was a part of life in the Delta, yet apart from it. He entertained on street corners and at almost any social occasion—fish fries, parties, picnics, and the like—to make money, if only enough for his next drink. The majority of his songs were takes on the universal "my baby done left me" theme. The solitary aspect of folk blues differentiates it from most other African American folk styles, including work songs and spirituals, which are based on collective music making.

Traveling from town to town, the bluesman would stay long enough to earn some money and entertain the ladies, especially when their men were off working on the river. For roustabouts, the bluesman was often the notorious "backdoor man," sneaking out the rear of the house as the man came home. Many viewed the bluesman's arrival in town as a mixed blessing.

The Sound of Country Blues: Blind Lemon Jefferson. "Country blues star" sounds like a contradiction in terms. Compared to the pop market, or even the market for classic blues singers, the market for "old-fashioned blues" was exceedingly modest. But there was a market, and Blind Lemon Jefferson (1894–1929) was the first to

Hulton Archive/Getty Images

capture it. Jefferson was born near Wortham, Texas, a small town about 80 miles south of Dallas. Early in his career, he was an itinerant street musician, like many bluesmen; by 1917 he had settled in Dallas, where he developed a following in the black community. His reputation grew sufficiently that "Ink" Williams, a talent scout for Paramount records, brought him to Chicago at the end of 1925 to record for the label. Jefferson recorded frequently until his death in 1929, and his records sold well enough that he was reportedly given a car and a chauffeur by Paramount in lieu of cash payment of his record royalties.

CD 2:1

"That Black Snake Moan," Blind Lemon Jefferson (1927). Jefferson, vocal and guitar.

For many serious students of the blues, the purest blues has been the country blues of artists like Jefferson. Its "purity" lies in its freedom from commercial influences. We hear no pop, no jazz, no horns in country blues—just a man and his guitar. In "That Black Snake Moan" (1927), one of Blind Lemon Jefferson's first recordings, the distance from European practice is striking. Jefferson even eschews the standard blues progression. He strums a I chord, but only as a tag to the intricate running figure that serves as the instrumental response; he does not accompany himself with the conventional blues chord progression. Although lyrics are a series of rhymed couplets with the first line repeated, there is no steady pulse underneath his vocal line. As a result, the predictable regularity of conventional blues form is not present.

His lyrics are rich in metaphor and graphic in subject—it's not difficult to imagine what his "black snake" is, even out of context. His singing is more moan than anything else; phrases start high and end low. The most striking feature of his guitar playing is the elaborate response figure, which briefly establishes a steady beat.

The market for country blues would remain small but stable, despite the onset of the Depression; most of the recordings of country bluesmen before the blues revival of the early rock era date from the 1930s. Among the most outstanding are those of Robert Johnson.

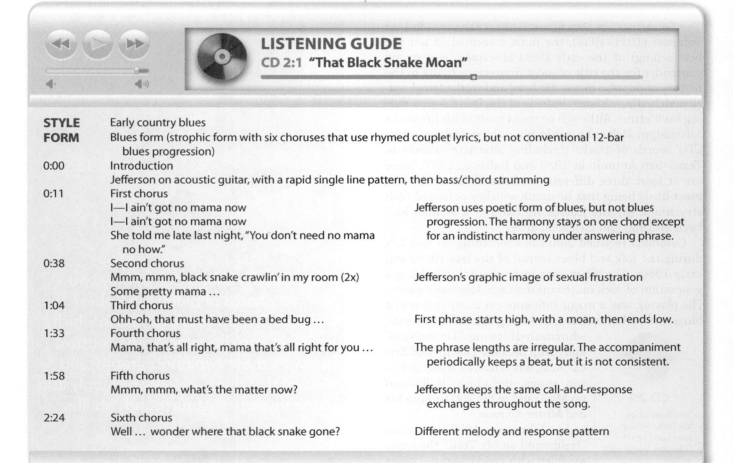

LISTENING GUIDE

CD 2:1 "That Black Snake Moan"

STYLE	Early country blues
FORM	Blues form (strophic form with six choruses that use rhymed couplet lyrics, but not conventional 12-bar blues progression)
0:00	Introduction
	Jefferson on acoustic guitar, with a rapid single line pattern, then bass/chord strumming

0:11	First chorus I—I ain't got no mama now I—I ain't got no mama now She told me late last night, "You don't need no mama no how."	Jefferson uses poetic form of blues, but not blues progression. The harmony stays on one chord except for an indistinct harmony under answering phrase.
0:38	Second chorus Mmm, mmm, black snake crawlin' in my room (2x) Some pretty mama …	Jefferson's graphic image of sexual frustration
1:04	Third chorus Ohh-oh, that must have been a bed bug …	First phrase starts high, with a moan, then ends low.
1:33	Fourth chorus Mama, that's all right, mama that's all right for you …	The phrase lengths are irregular. The accompaniment periodically keeps a beat, but it is not consistent.
1:58	Fifth chorus Mmm, mmm, what's the matter now?	Jefferson keeps the same call-and-response exchanges throughout the song.
2:24	Sixth chorus Well … wonder where that black snake gone?	Different melody and response pattern

5 to Listen For
"That Black Snake Moan"

INSTRUMENTATION
Voice and acoustic guitar

PERFORMANCE STYLE
Jefferson's moaning, rough-edged voice, half-talking, half-singing style typifies country blues.

RHYTHM
No steady tempo; alternates between out-of-tempo vocal and occasional steady tempo in response figures

MELODY
First line phrases start high, finish low; answering phrase has flatter contour.

HARMONY
Mostly one chord; chord under answering phrase indistinct—not V

3 to Remember
"That Black Snake Moan"

SEXUAL METAPHOR
Like many blues lyrics, song uses metaphor to describe sexual matters.

BLUES VOCAL STYLE
Moaning; starting high, ending low; half singing, half talking, rough voice all characteristic of blues style

BLUES FORM
Lyric is regular; music has irregular phrase lengths, static harmony, varying tempo.

on my trail"—and he delivers them straight. We listen to what the words have to say and how Johnson delivers them. His guitar playing is extraordinary. Johnson can make his guitar mimic his voice, provide strong accompaniment, or serve as another voice. We hear all of these qualities in this important recording.

By the time Johnson made his last recordings in 1937, country blues had peaked as a commercial style, at least in the eyes of the record executives. It went into decline for about two decades, resurfacing only as part of the folk revival around 1960. Johnson's recordings were among those reissued on LP about this time.

Country blues, and especially Johnson's music, hit British blues-based rock bands like a heavyweight's right hand, partly because it leapfrogged a generation and partly because it defined the essence of the blues. Its impact on rock was sudden and dramatic: Johnson inspired rock musicians to get real.

The Sound of Country Blues: Robert Johnson. Robert Johnson (1911–1938), the most esteemed (if not the best selling) of the early Delta bluesmen, is a strong contender for the title of most mysterious figure in the history of popular music. He lived and worked in obscurity, virtually unknown outside of the Delta region during his lifetime. Although he spent most of his life in the Mississippi Delta, he made his only recordings—two CDs' worth of tracks (including alternate takes)—in Texas: San Antonio in 1936 and Dallas in 1937. There are at least three different versions of his death, the most likely being that he drank whiskey poisoned with strychnine (by the jealous husband of a woman he'd been visiting) and died soon after.

Columbia reissued Johnson's recording on two LPs during the folk and blues revival of the late 1950s and early 1960s. The album was instrumental in helping a generation of rock musicians discover Johnson's music. His playing was a major influence on many important blues and rock musicians, including the Rolling Stones, who covered his songs "Love in Vain" and "Stop Breakin' Down," and Eric Clapton, who covered many Johnson songs, including "Hellhound on My Trail," in his 2004 album *Me and Mister Johnson.*

In Johnson's 1937 recording "Hellhound on My Trail," the lyrics are filled with vivid images—"blues fallin' down like hail, ... hellhound

CD 2:2

"Hellhound on My Trail," Robert Johnson (1937). Johnson, vocal and guitar.

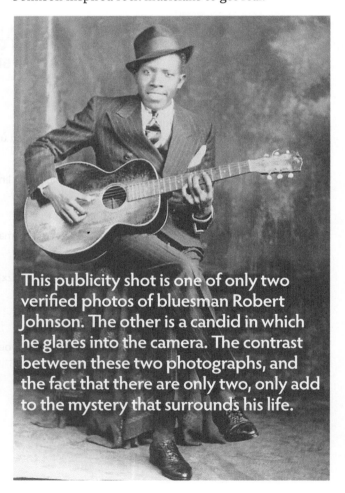

This publicity shot is one of only two verified photos of bluesman Robert Johnson. The other is a candid in which he glares into the camera. The contrast between these two photographs, and the fact that there are only two, only add to the mystery that surrounds his life.

LISTENING GUIDE
CD 2:2 "Hellhound on My Trail"

STYLE	Country blues
FORM	Blues form, but with varying bar lengths, phrase lengths; more static harmony

0:00	Introduction	
	Johnson sets tempo, rhythm, and mood in the introduction.	
0:08	First chorus	
	I got to keep movin'…	Vocal starts high, ends low; guitar mimics, accompanies voice, then answers.
	(0:24) Mmmmmmmmm, blues fallin' down …	
	(0:36) And the days keep …	Rhyming phrase, with guitar response
0:51	Second chorus	
	If today was Christmas …	Two quite different guitar sounds here: high chords behind the voice and two-part response figure (bass sounds plus riff on higher strings)
1:25	Third chorus	
	You sprinkled hot …	Harmony more static than conventional blues progression: no change on second phrase; move to V on third phrase
1:58	Fourth chorus	
	I can tell the wind …	Vocal phrases start high and end low

5 to Listen For
"Hellhound on My Trail"

INSTRUMENTATION
Voice and acoustic guitar

PERFORMANCE STYLE
Guitar part often contains both strummed chords and melodic answer to the vocal phrase.

RHYTHM
Lazy tempo; guitar keeps intermittent shuffle rhythm (a **shuffle rhythm** divides each beat into two unequal parts; long/short).

MELODY
First line phrases start high, finish low; answering phrase has flatter contour.

HARMONY
Not quite blues progression (second phrase uses same harmony; third phrase goes to V, then back to I)

3 to Remember
"Hellhound on My Trail"

DARK IMAGES
("hellhound …") evoke the world of the Delta bluesman

BLUES VOCAL STYLE
Strong, unfiltered, raw, powerful, acrid quality; phrases starting high, ending low; half singing, half talking style

GUITAR ROLES
Accompanist, responder, reinforcer: sometimes two at a time

Good-Time Blues

Blues is a bipolar music. The most characteristic forms of the blues are songs that convey a "blue" mood: sadness, heartache, and longing. The blues of Smith, Jefferson, and Johnson project these moods powerfully; Waters's "Am I Blue?" is a pop reflection of this sensibility. But blues can also accompany good times. There are blues songs that are fun—even funny at times—and upbeat in mood and tempo. We heard this kind of exuberance in King Oliver's "Dippermouth Blues" and encounter it in songs that illustrate two important blues styles of the late 1920s and 1930s, hokum and boogie-woogie.

Hokum. New, more urban blues styles began to appear on record in the late twenties. They featured singers who sounded bluesier than pop or jazz singers but not as emotionally charged as Bessie Smith or as raw as the country bluesmen. The accompaniment, typically piano and guitar, gave the music a stronger, more consistent beat than country blues, but it was not as elaborate as the jazz accompaniments of the classic blues singers.

Among these new blues styles was **hokum**, a blues novelty style that was popular between the two world wars. Hokum songs showed an entirely different side of the blues: upbeat, salacious, good-humored, and light-hearted. They were miles away from the elemental power of Johnson's blues.

Perhaps the most famous hokum blues is "It's Tight Like That," a 1928 recording featuring pianist Georgia Tom (1899–1993) and guitarist Tampa Red (1904–1981), who advertised themselves as the Hokum Brothers. Georgia Tom was the Thomas A. Dorsey from the beginning of this chapter, who turned his back on the blues shortly after this recording to devote himself to black gospel.

CD 2:3

"It's Tight Like That," Tampa Red and Georgia Tom (1928). The Hokum Brothers.

"It's Tight Like That" is also an early example of a verse/chorus-type blues form. The harmonic form of the song is a 12-bar blues, but lyrics replace the conventional rhymed couplet with a verse/chorus scheme. The first four bars describe a scene; the last eight repeat the same words and melody. Verse/chorus blues forms resurfaced in the jump-band rhythm and blues of Louis Jordan and others and in many of Chuck Berry's breakthrough hits; "Maybellene" was Berry's first of many. Other elements of the song—most notably the bright tempo and the humorous lyric with sexual overtones—were also common in post-WWII rhythm and blues.

In "It's Tight Like That," Tampa Red's guitar playing dominates the accompanying; Dorsey's piano playing is very much in the background. In the next example, the piano is the only accompanying instrument; it was the only one needed.

Boogie-Woogie. Boogie-woogie is a blues piano style that chases the blues away. It is typically exuberant, even boisterous, loud, and strong. Originating in the rural South during the early years of the century, boogie-woogie was born of necessity. Its creators were pianists who performed in noisy working-class bars and clubs, variously called juke joints, barrelhouses, and honky-tonks. To be heard over the crowd, pianists created a powerful two-handed style in which they played an active left-hand pattern in the lower part of the instrument

---

LISTENING GUIDE
CD 2:3 "It's Tight Like That"

STYLE	Hokum (salacious, up-tempo blues style)	
FORM	Early verse/chorus blues form. First four bars briefly describe a scene; the last eight repeat a chorus based on title phrase.	
0:00	Introduction	
	A brief instrumental introduction sets the tempo and the mood of the song.	
0:09	First chorus	
	Listen here folks, want to sing a little song …	An "apology" in advance
	It's tight like that …	
0:24	Second chorus	
	There was a little black rooster …	Each of the verse sections describes a short scene; this one is innocent enough.
0:38	Third chorus	
	Went to see my gal over across the hall …	A two-timing partner …
0:52	Fourth chorus	
	The gal I love she's long and slim …	The musicians use stop time in verse to highlight words; timekeeping resumes in the chorus.
1:07	Fifth chorus	
	The rooster crowed …	The return of the rooster …
1:20	Sixth chorus	
	Mamma had a little dog his name was Ball	
1:35	Seventh chorus	
	Instrumental, with spoken asides	
1:49	Eighth-twelfth choruses	
	Uncle Bud and Aunt Jane went to …	

4 to Remember
"It's Tight Like That"

UP-TEMPO BLUES
This is a happy blues. It moves at a bright tempo with a strong beat.

GOOD-HUMORED LYRIC WITH SEXUAL INNUENDO
This is literally barnyard humor. Sexual matters are described via animal metaphors: for example, "another mule kicking in my stall." It's another way of getting the message across without being explicit. Toward the end of the song, lyrics move away from the barnyard to other ways of describing sex (or the lack of it).

INSTRUMENTATION AND REGULAR BLUES PROGRESSION
Two accompanying instruments require coordination of harmony; conventional blues progression used throughout.

VERSE/CHORUS BLUES FORM
In its approach to blues form, there is a direct line from songs like this to many of the Chuck Berry hits of the 1950s.

5 to Listen For
"It's Tight Like That"

INSTRUMENTATION
Voices plus acoustic guitar and piano

PERFORMANCE STYLE
Bent notes in guitar solo

RHYTHM
Bright tempo, syncopation in melody

MELODY
Narrow range throughout; riffs in chorus

HARMONY
Conventional blues progression

Among the most famous boogie-woogie performances is the 1936 recording of "Roll 'Em, Pete," featuring blues shouter Joe Turner (1911–1985) and pianist Pete Johnson (1904–1967), one of the kings of boogie-woogie piano. Turner grew up in Kansas City and started his career by singing while tending bar. After teaming up with Johnson through the early 1940s, Turner became a prominent figure in the postwar rhythm-and-blues scene.

"Roll 'Em, Pete" is a straightforward blues in form, the kind that Turner could have made up on the spot. (The title of the song apparently came from the patrons of the club where Turner and Johnson worked. They would shout, "Roll 'Em, Pete," as Johnson played chorus after chorus.) In its power Turner's singing is reminiscent of Bessie Smith's classic blues ("Empty Bed Blues," Chapter 3), but "Roll 'Em, Pete" is good-time music. There's a smile in Turner's voice that matches the exuberance of Johnson's playing.

CD 2:4
"Roll 'Em, Pete," Joe Turner and Peter Johnson (1936). Turner, vocal; Johnson, piano.

In this recording Pete Johnson sets up a steady rhythm in the left hand that divides each beat into two parts and builds piles of riffs on top of the left-hand pattern. In a medium-tempo boogie-woogie song, the division of the beat is uneven: a long/short pattern. At really fast tempos, however, it is difficult if not impossible to sustain the long/short rhythm in the left hand. So, in "Roll 'Em, Pete," the rhythm tends to even out so that each beat is divided in two halves of equal length.

Boogie-woogie's flirtation with the mainstream was brief. After World War II, boogie-woogie piano playing was heard mainly in rhythm and blues. The driving left-hand rhythm heard in "Roll 'Em, Pete" would resurface in the music of Chuck Berry and become the rhythmic foundation of rock 'n' roll, then rock.

and repeated riffs on the upper part. By the late 1920s, pianists were playing boogie-woogie in such urban centers as Chicago, New York, and Kansas City. It flourished in the 1930s and '40s, spreading beyond black neighborhoods into mainstream America. The Andrews Sisters scored a hit with "Boogie Woogie Bugle Boy." Tommy Dorsey's "Boogie Woogie" (an arrangement of Pine Top Smith's 1929 recording "Pine Top's Boogie Woogie") was his biggest instrumental hit.

Library of Congress, Prints and Photographs Division, Washington, D.C. [LC-USF351-113]

All-purpose destination in Louisiana, ca. 1940: Crossroads store, bar, juke joint, and gas station. Inside the juke joint might be a beat-up piano where someone would play boogie-woogie.

Black Gospel Music

Black gospel blends white Protestant hymnody, the black spiritual, and more fervent religious music with a touch of the blues. It emerged as a new style around 1930 and flourished over the next several decades.

Gospel came by its blues tinge naturally. Recall that Thomas A. Dorsey, the father of gospel music, had begun his musical career as the blues pianist Georgia Tom. However, the message of gospel was quite different from that of the blues. Blues comments on everyday

LISTENING GUIDE

CD 2:4 "Roll 'Em, Pete"

STYLE	Boogie-woogie	
FORM	Conventional 12-bar blues form	
0:00	First chorus: instrumental	
	After playing some high chords, Johnson settles into his rock-solid boogie pattern.	
0:15	Second chorus	Typical blues melody: starts high, ends low; in a narrow range; made up of riffs
	Well, I got a gal, she lives up on the hill = (2x)	
	Well, this woman's tryin' to quit me, Lord, but I love her still.	
0:30	Third chorus	Three layers: vocal, piano riffs behind the vocal, and boogie-woogie pattern supporting everything
	She's got eyes like diamonds, they shine like Klondike gold …	
0:46	Fourth chorus	New melody, and new riff behind the melody
	Well, you're so beautiful, you've got to die someday …	
1:01	Fifth chorus	Creating a stop-time effect by interrupting the boogie-woogie pattern in the lower part
	Roll it, boys, let 'em jump for joy …	
1:16	Sixth/seventh choruses	
	Classic boogie-woogie piano playing	
1:46	Eighth chorus	
	Well babe …	
2:01	Ninth chorus	
	Yes, yes [five times]	Sung at two-measure intervals
2:16	Tenth chorus	
	Well, all right then …	Also sung every two bars; made up on the spot?
2:31	Eleventh chorus	
	Bye-bye	Classic blues singing: moaning sound, narrow range, high to low

life—good times and bad. Gospel, by contrast, is strictly good news. Again in Dorsey's words:

This music lifted people out of the muck and mire of poverty and loneliness, of being broke, and gave them

Gerri Hernández/istockphoto.com

some kind of hope anyway. Make it anything [other] than good news, it ceases to be gospel.

Dorsey gave the new music its name:

In the early 1920s I coined the words "gospel songs" after listening to a group of five people one Sunday morning on the far south side of Chicago. This was the first I heard of a gospel choir. There were no gospel songs then, we called them evangelistic songs.

Although Dorsey considered C. A. Tindley the first gospel songwriter, he himself was the person most responsible for creating both the music and the environment in which it flourished. His first gospel hit "If You See My Savior, Tell Him That You Saw Me," written in 1926, was a sensation at the 1930 Baptist Jubilee convention. After it caught on, Dorsey devoted himself full time to gospel.

100   CHAPTER 6   In from the Outskirts: Blues, Gospel, Country, and Folk Music, 1925–1950

In its first two decades, gospel was a world unto itself. Performers traveled from stop to stop along the "Gospel Highway," churches and conventions where black believers congregated. Through the first decade, the music remained virtually unknown outside the black community; it gained a wider audience after World War II.

Gospel represented both a repertoire and a way of performing. Gospel songs included traditional hymns such as "Amazing Grace" and newer compositions by Tindley, Dorsey (such as "Precious Lord"), and W. Herbert Brewster ("How I Got Over"). There were two distinct performing traditions in early gospel music: male quartets and female solo singers. Mixed-gender groups were largely unheard of, even in the forties and fifties.

One reason why male gospel singers formed into groups while females generally sang solo in the early days of gospel is that a male quartet can present complete harmonies in low and middle registers, which eliminates the need for accompanying instruments—as we hear in the Golden Gate Jubilee Quartet's recording. By contrast, a female group would not have a voice in the lower ranges, so that a performance would virtually demand some kind of instrumental accompaniment.

Male Quartets. Black male quartets were not unique to black gospel music. The Dinwiddie Colored Quartet had recorded in 1902, and the Mills Brothers, a popular modern-era vocal group, began their career in the early thirties, about the time gospel was getting off the ground. However, gospel quartets, who often sang *a cappella*—without instrumental accompaniment—developed their own approach, which would often add rhythm section-like support to the lead vocal: not only harmony, but also a strong beat.

We hear this in "The Golden Gate Gospel Train," a song recorded by the Golden Gate Jubilee Quartet in 1937. The recording shows how resourceful such groups could be in depicting images in sound. The

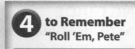

4 **to Remember**
"Roll 'Em, Pete"

BOOGIE-WOOGIE = SOURCE OF ROCK RHYTHM
At a faster tempo, shuffle rhythm evens out. Berry would adapt patterns like this to his rhythm guitar playing; they would become foundation for rock rhythm.

MELODIES CONSTRUCTED FROM REPEATED RIFFS
Both the vocal line and the melody lines in the instrumental choruses typically begin with a repeated riff, then break off into a more elaborate line toward the end of the chorus.

CONVENTIONAL BLUES FORM AND HARMONY
Like Bessie Smith's blues, this is a straightforward blues in lyrics, harmony, and form. This would remain the most widely used version of blues form in the early rock era.

STRONG PIANO PLAYING
Boogie-woogie is a piano style designed to be heard over a crowd; strong, active, steady left hand, lots of double notes in right hand.

||||||||||||||||||||||||||||||||||

"This music lifted people out of the muck and mire of poverty and loneliness."
—Thomas A. "Georgia Tom" Dorsey

5 **to Listen For**
"Roll 'Em, Pete"

INSTRUMENTATION
Voice and piano

PERFORMANCE STYLE
Blues "shouting": big, rough-voiced singing

RHYTHM
Bright tempo with active, steady rhythms

MELODY
Narrow range throughout

HARMONY
Conventional blues progression

group replicates the sound of the train whistle and bell, as well as the chug of the engine. More important, the singers back up the lead vocalist with an accompaniment that supplies more rhythm than harmony. Both the static harmony and the percussive vocal sounds anticipate rock-era music, especially funk and rap. Other prominent African-derived elements include a melody of mostly descending phrases constructed from a pentatonic scale, blues-like inflection, and an active rhythmic texture.

Female Soloists. Women were the brightest stars on the gospel circuit. Female vocalists such as Mahalia Jackson, Clara Ward, and Shirley Caesar sang alone, or at least in the forefront. Their accompaniment often included both piano and Hammond organ, both popular instruments in black churches; backup vocalists were optional.

The best gospel solo singers of the era sang with rich, resonant voices. They occasionally colored their singing with blues-like inflection and, more distinctively, expressive melismas (recall that a melisma is a group of pitches sung on a single syllable). During the thirties and forties, it was a sound distinct from every other kind of singing related to popular music: pop, jazz, country, blues,

CD 2:5

"Golden Gate Gospel Train," traditional (1937). The Golden Gate Jubilee Quartet.

CD 2:6

"Move On Up a Little Higher," W. Herbert Brewster and Virginia Davis (1947). Mahalia Jackson, vocal.

STYLE	Black gospel	
FORM	Strophic, with last line of each verse serving as the chorus	
0:00	Introduction	
	My lord, she blow, Get on board, better get your ticket now	An impressive display of train noises, including the whistle
	My lord, she blow	
0:19	Verse 1	
	Faster the train is coming,	Each chorus contains four lines; last line serves as a
	Better get your business right	chorus. The melody contains short phrases that
	You better set your house in order, friends	start high and end low; other vocalists sing same
	Chorus: You know the train gonna be here tonight	chord over and over in syncopated rhythm.
0:34	Verse 2	
	Don't you hear the whistle blowing,	Occasionally, one of the accompanying vocalists
	hear the bells ring …	breaks away to imitate more train sounds.
0:50	Verse 3	
	Now she pullin' in the pearly gates of heaven …	As before
1:06	Verses 4/5	
	The train gonna be here tonight (Ahh lord)	An "instrumental" vocal sound—like an improvised solo in a jazz performance
1:36	Verse 6	
	Ah … sinner man …	As before
2:06	Verse 7	
		More vocalized solo with train whistle tag; reprise of introduction sound

and others. Only with the migration of singers from gospel into R&B did this vocal style enter the popular mainstream.

Mahalia Jackson's 1947 recording of "Move On Up a Little Higher" showcases her rich, blues-inflected voice. Dorsey may have brought the blues into gospel, but it was Mahalia Jackson (1911–1972) who adapted the feeling and style of her idol, Bessie Smith, to gospel singing. She would in turn influence Aretha Franklin, the queen of soul, who heard her sing at her father's church.

Black gospel, especially when sung by women, gave the Hammond organ an early toehold in a style related to popular music. The Hammond organ was invented in the thirties and immediately found a home in churches, white and black, that could not afford a pipe organ. By contrast, it was a novelty instrument in popular music and

5 to Listen For
"The Golden Gate Gospel Train"

INSTRUMENTATION
Four male voices

PERFORMANCE STYLE
Percussive vocal effects; train noises: sound imagination

RHYTHM
Syncopated accompaniment patterns under lead vocal

MELODY
Phrases start high, end low; built on pentatonic scale

HARMONY
Static: only one chord

5 to Remember
"The Golden Gate Gospel Train"

PERCUSSIVE VOCAL SOUNDS
Backup singers create percussive vocal sounds instead of using words.

PENTATONIC SCALE
Another example of black pentatonic scale, in a setting quite different from the blues

SYNCOPATED RHYTHMS IN ACCOMPANIMENT
Rhythms underneath lead vocal are much like the rhythms of a horn section in a big band behind a soloist.

RIFF-BASED MELODY
As in blues songs, melody grows out of repeated riffs, most of which start high and finish low.

STATIC HARMONY
Only one chord; anticipates more rhythmic forms of soul and—later—funk

| STYLE | Black gospel |
| FORM | Strophic, with verses of varying length |

0:00 **Verse 1**
Move on up a little higher
Meet with old man Daniel …
It will be always howdy, howdy (3x)
It will be always howdy, howdy, lord
　　and never goodbye.

Jackson's rich voice dominates. Blues influence is evident in the timbre, use of melisma, choice of notes (occasional blue notes), and shape of the melody—phrases start high and finish low.

1:01 **Verse 2**
Oh, will you be there …
Will you be there early Monday morning
Will you be there, yes,
　　when the angels shall call the roll

Underlying rhythm is a "swinging" two-beat, specific to black gospel. Organ responses to Jackson's singing are similar in style to answering riffs in big-band swing.

1:25 **Verse 3**
Oh children, I'll be waiting
Yes, I'll be watching early Monday morning
Yes, I'll be waiting at the beautiful, yes golden gate …

Accompaniment of piano *and* organ was a distinctive element of black gospel, in part because it was so unusual. However, many black churches along the gospel highway had both instruments on hand; keyboard players found ways to work together.

1:47 **Verse 4**
Soon as my feet strike Zion
Lay down my heavy burden …

Jackson ends the song with a wonderfully expressive, out-of-tempo melisma.

5 to Listen For
"Move on Up a Little Higher"

INSTRUMENTATION
Vocal, piano, and organ

PERFORMANCE STYLE
Jackson's rich voice, with occasional melisma

RHYTHM
Slow tempo with "swinging" two-beat rhythm

MELODY
Mix between major scale and pentatonic scale (source of "blue notes"

HARMONY
Mostly static: only one chord, until the end of each verse; then progression away from and back to tonic

3 to Remember
"Move on Up a Little Higher"

VOCAL STYLE
Jackson's rich, blues-tinged voice and use of melisma would influence numerous black vocalists in the early years of the rock era.

USE OF HAMMOND ORGAN
Hammond organ, first sold in 1930s, would become a popular keyboard instrument in sixties rock. This is an early use of it in a non-pop setting.

RICH, BLUES-TINGED HARMONY
The static harmony and chord choices in the opening part of each verse show the influence of the blues. The quick progression at the end mixes blues notes into a conventional progression.

jazz; one heard it playing background music on radio soap operas and in cocktail lounges. It became a viable jazz instrument around 1960 and in rock and soul toward the end of the sixties.

Gospel Harmony. As it developed during the thirties and forties, gospel took its harmonic language from nineteenth-century European hymns and colored it with blues harmony. This produced a distinctive harmonic vocabulary, richer than blues, country, and rhythm and blues, yet distinct from the pop music of the same era.

Implicit in this distinctive harmonic approach is a message of hope. Even in "Move On Up a Little Higher," which has relatively static harmony throughout much of the song, there is a slight harmonic digression just before the end and a quick, straightforward return to the home key. This seems to suggest that no matter how stuck we are—harmonically or in life—we will find happiness when we go home—to the Lord, to heaven, and to the tonic. This kind of harmonic tension and release—drift away from the tonic chord, then return to it—is not present in conventional blues harmony in the same way; indeed, in one-chord songs like "That Black Snake Moan," there is no possibility of harmonic tension.

The harmonic tension and release found in many gospel songs parallels the tension and release used in pre-rock pop. It has survived in rock-era music mainly in songs about love and happiness, most notably mainstream pop, by black and white acts.

Gospel's legacy to rock-era popular music is substantial. Doo-wop, 1960s girl groups, Motown, and soul are inconceivable without gospel. Singing—the presence of both lead and backup singers, the vocal sounds and styles of the lead singers, call and response between lead and choir—is its most obvious contribution. In addition, its distinctive rhythms (especially the heavy backbeat), the Hammond organ, and rich harmony also filtered into rock-era music, both black and white. It is an impressive contribution.

All of this music—the numerous blues styles and black gospel—existed on the fringes of the popular music industry. The music was recorded commercially, but its target audience was narrowly circumscribed. Only boogie-woogie had a noticeable impact on swing-era pop, and that was filtered through whites who adapted black versions. Mahalia Jackson's "Move On Up a Little Higher" actually made the charts, and she would soon gain international celebrity. But black gospel as a genre would, like the blues styles, largely remain under the radar.

• • • • • • • • •

Country and Folk Music, 1925–1950

Before there were country music and folk music, there was folk music from the country—that is, the southern Appalachians. The music that spawned both country and folk came originally from the British Isles: England, Scotland, Wales, and Ireland. America's first Anglo-American settlers brought their music with them. Some found their way into the mountains of Virginia and the Carolinas, where they preserved many of the songs and dances from their home countries and created new ones like "Old Joe Clark," which we heard in Chapter 2.

There was—and is—a timelessness to this music. When we listen to a recording like "Old Joe Clark," we sense that the style would have sounded much the same

in 1875. The fieldwork of English folklorist Cecil Sharp confirms this impression. In trips through the southern Appalachians between 1916 and 1918, he discovered songs that went back centuries (and which were no longer sung in England).

When Sharp visited the United States, there was no such thing as country music or folk music. The music that he heard and transcribed for posterity was a real folk music; that is, it was music made by members of a group for their own entertainment and passed down—and around—by ear. The musicians were not professional, and there was no industry to support and promote this music. It just was. That would all change within a decade.

Look at a current map of the southeastern United States and you'll find a web of interstate highways crisscrossing Virginia and West Virginia, the Carolinas, Tennessee, Alabama, Mississippi, Kentucky, and Louisiana. Were you to drive down one of these interstates and pull off, chances are you would find modern gas stations with minimarkets, chain motels, and a belt-stretching array of fast-food restaurants. There would be cable or satellite TV in the motel rooms and probably phone service to anywhere as well as a modem hookup for your laptop. This is the twenty-first-century American South.

So it may be difficult to imagine a time when there were only dirt roads, few cars, no phones, no electricity, no running water, no indoor plumbing, no television or radio, no CD players, and no Internet. Whole regions lacked most if not all of the conveniences that we associate with modern life. People who lived in the southern Appalachians had little knowledge of the outside world. A trip to the nearest large city produced severe culture shock.

Technology Creates Country Music from Folk

Given these circumstances, it is a sweet irony that country music, which reflects the traditional values of southern culture, is the product of a modern technology. The folk music of white southerners became country music when commercial radio came on the air and commercial records arrived in stores. Before long, clear-channel AM radio—50,000-watt stations like WSM in Nashville, which began broadcasting in 1925—covered most of the country when the sun went down. WSM became the radio home to the *Grand Ole Opry* in 1928. Radio's impact on what would become known as country music was enormous, not only through broadcasting but also because of its impact on the recording industry: artists' live appearances on WLS's Barn Dance or Grand Ole Opry boosted their record sales.

The new technology helped create a class of professional, or at least semi-professional, musicians. Appearances on radio and records led to opportunities for live performances. Bands or solo acts with a weekly radio show would fill in the days between broadcasts with engagements in cities and towns within the listening area of their radio station.

Records helped spread the sound of "old-time music" beyond the South. By 1930 a guitar player in Oklahoma could learn Virginian Maybelle Carter's distinctive accompanying style simply by buying a record and copying it. Just as important, this new technology helped connect rural southerners to the outside world. They could share their own music and discover other kinds. This contact with one another and the outside would become the main impetus for the evolution of country music.

In little more than a decade, what had been simply a folk music transplanted from the British Isles had split into country and folk, two worlds that were almost mutually exclusive. (It took Bob Dylan to bring them together again.) And each world divided further into several streams, some creating paths to the mainstream, others running counter to the trend. At the heart of it all were the central tensions of this music: between commerce and culture, between innovation and preservation, between old and new, between inside and outside, and between staying home and roaming far and wide.

Ralph Peer and the Business of Country Music

At the center of early country music, yet behind the scenes, was a man named Ralph Peer (1892–1960). Peer was arguably the most influential man in country music during its first three decades. He played an instrumental role in finding it, disseminating it, and making money for those who created it.

Peer grew up in Missouri and as a young man helped his father sell sewing machines and phonographs. He went to work for Columbia Records, moved to Okeh Records in 1920, and moved again in 1925 to Victor. As a talent scout and producer, Peer would go from town to town, setting up temporary recording studios wherever he could. Word would spread that he was coming, and musicians would come down from the hills to record for him.

Peer always seemed to be at the right place at the right time. He was responsible for the first on-location recording and the first country recording to be released, "Fiddlin'" John Carson's "The Little Log Cabin in the Lane" (1923). A few years later, he helped give old-time music a new name: hillbilly music. The term *hillbilly* had been in use since the turn of the century to identify rural white southerners, but its musical association dates from a 1925 recording session with Al Hopkins, leader of a four-man string band (a small group consisting mainly of string instruments of various types). Peer, who was running the session, asked Hopkins to give his band a name. Hopkins replied, "Call the band anything you want. We are nothing but a bunch of hillbillies from North Carolina and Virginia anyway"; they became Al Hopkins and His Hillbillies. Peer's biggest coup, however, came in August 1927, when he recorded the Carter Family and Jimmie Rodgers, the two biggest acts of early country music, in Bristol, Tennessee.

Peer was an astute businessman. He negotiated a split of the publishing rights to the songs he recorded for Victor and created his own publishing firm, Southern Music, in 1928. Southern Music grew into one of the leading publishers of country music and made Peer a rich and powerful man.

Peer also played a key role in establishing BMI (Broadcast Music Incorporated), a music licensing organization sponsored by the radio industry. Music licensing was the mechanism by which those who created the music received payment from those who made money from it. ASCAP, the American Society of Composers, Authors, and Publishers, the dominant licensing organization since its formation in 1914, required five hit songs for membership—in effect excluding almost everyone who was not part of the pop-music inner circle. In particular, country music songwriters and black musicians were on the outside, looking in. So were most of those just starting their careers.

> *By 1930 a guitar player in Oklahoma could learn Virginian Maybelle Carter's distinctive accompanying style simply by buying a record and copying it.*

Library of Congress, Prints and Photographs Division, Washington, D.C. (LC-USZ61-312)

When ASCAP proposed a massive increase in royalties from the agreement they had signed in 1932, broadcasters formed their own organization. They chartered Broadcast Music Incorporated in 1939; BMI opened its doors early the next year. Unlike ASCAP, BMI accepted all aspiring songwriters. Overnight, all musicians had a potential stake in the music industry. That was good news for those who had been on the outside, looking in, especially jazz, country, and blues musicians. Many joined BMI, which gave the organization some much-needed leverage. Peer's support played a big role in getting BMI off the ground.

Peer's musical and business interests went well beyond country music. Almost as soon as he began working for Okeh Records, he set up the first race record recording session, which produced Mamie Smith's "Crazy Blues," and he negotiated the rights to Victor's race records along with the hillbilly music he had been recording. By the early 1930s, he had branched into popular music; and after a trip to Mexico, he secured the rights to several Latin hits. He continued to diversify his catalog after World War II by signing up rockabilly and rhythm-and-blues artists.

As his pragmatic, entrepreneurial, and open-minded stance toward music suggests, Peer represented the progressive direction in country music. He helped transform a folk music into a powerful segment of the music business. At the opposite pole philosophically were Lomax and the preservationists, and George Hay, the founder of the Grand Ole Opry radio program, who looked to retain and preserve traditional values. Their positions represent the central tension in country and folk, the clash between tradition and innovation.

Country and Folk: Tradition versus Innovation

With few exceptions, country changed over time not by charting a different path, but by absorbing and transforming elements from black music and pop. This process was evident almost from the start. The first country music hits were two songs recorded by Vernon Dalhart. Unlike most of the great country performers, Dalhart, although born in Texas, aspired to be an opera singer, and worked and recorded professionally in New York as a popular and light-opera singer under several pseudonyms, one of which was Vernon Dalhart, taken from two adjacent cities on a map of Texas. His first two hits, "The Prisoner's Song" and "Wreck of the Old 97," were country-type songs in that they dealt with common themes in country music and were similar melodically to other traditional songs. But Dalhart's singing, not surprisingly, has little affinity with vocal styles of folk performers recorded during the same period, and the viola obbligato on "The Prisoner's Song" has nothing to do with country fiddle playing.

In country music, tradition is relative, not absolute. A traditional sound is what the last generation did; only bluegrass tried to turn back the clock completely, and even in that style outside influences are evident. Even more conservative musicians were not immune to change. Roy Acuff, widely recognized as a champion of traditional values in country music, recorded the "Wabash Cannon Ball" with a band featuring amplified guitar and dobro (a steel guitar with a metal resonator instead of amplification) as the major solo instruments instead of the traditional fiddle, and both the guitarist and dobro player had clearly been listening to blues guitarists. Even bluegrass, the neo-traditional country style of the post-war era, shows the influence of ragtime and early jazz.

The gradually shifting core of country music is defined by the way in which newly assimilated elements are transformed by country musicians and blended with existing musical practices. The mix gives the final result a distinctly country identity. Both banjo and steel guitar, for example, were "borrowed" instruments. (The banjo, of course, belongs to the prehistory of country music; the steel guitar was introduced into country music in the late twenties.) Earl Scruggs's three-finger banjo playing updates the banjo style of the early string band; it is unquestionably country despite its obvious debt to ragtime and blues guitar. Similarly, Leon McAuliffe, the musician who put the steel guitar in the country-music limelight, removed the Hawaiian associations from the instrument by creating a jazz-influenced style.

Another mix of old and new emerged around the time that country music began to gain a national audience; Woody Guthrie recorded topical songs using a newly established style based on old practices. His work in the 1930s and '40s springs from the same source as country music but followed a markedly different path.

Country Music

At the tail end of July 1927, Ralph Peer got off the train with his recording equipment and set up a temporary studio in a hotel on State Street in Bristol, Tennessee, for an open call for musicians. Over the next four days, he recorded two of country music's most important and influential acts: the Carter Family on August 1 and 2, and Jimmie Rodgers on August 4. Country music historian Bill Malone contrasted them in this way:

> Rodgers brought into clear focus the tradition of the rambling man which had been so attractive to country music's folk ancestors and which ever since fascinated much of the country music audience. This ex-railroad man conveyed the impression that he had been everywhere and had experienced life to the fullest. His music suggested a similar openness of spirit, a willingness to experiment, and a receptivity to alternative styles. The Carter Family, in contrast, represented the impulse

toward home and stability, a theme as perennially attractive as that of the rambler. When the Carters sang, they evoked images of the country church, Mama and Daddy, [and] the family fireside. … Theirs was a music that might borrow from other forms, but would move away from its roots only reluctantly.

The Carter Family and "Wildwood Flower." The Carter Family, one of the most influential groups in the history of country music, consisted of Alvin Pleasant "A. P." Carter (1891–1960); his wife, Sara (1898–1979; after 1933, his ex-wife); and his sister-in-law, Maybelle (1909–1978). All three sang, Sara played guitar and autoharp, and Maybelle developed one of the most widely imitated guitar styles in the history of country music. A. P. had grown up playing the fiddle and learning ballads and other songs from his mother, and he never lost his love for this music. The Carter Family performed and recorded traditional songs that A. P. had collected and arranged, often in an unpaid partnership with his black chauffeur. Among the best known was their 1928 recording of a song they called "Wildwood Flower." It had started out as a commercially published parlor song, composed in 1860 by Maud Irving and J. D. Webster, entitled "I'll Twine 'Mid the Ringlets"; but like so many nineteenth-century commercial songs, it had found its way into oral tradition.

CD 2:7

"Wildwood Flower," traditional (1928). The Carter Family.

The sound of the Carter Family was an intriguing mix of old and new. Certainly the song was old, although not nearly as old as those Cecil Sharp had heard in 1918. Maybelle's singing exemplifies one **traditional country vocal sound**—flat, nasal, and without much inflection.

It is the accompaniment that begins the break with the past. There is no fiddle, just guitar. The clear separation of melody and accompaniment is more like Dalhart's "The Prisoner's Song" than it is like "Old Joe Clark." The most important and influential feature of the accompaniment is Maybelle's **thumb-brush style**. She plays the melody on the lower strings and, between melody notes, brushes the chords on the upper strings. We will hear this style in a Woody Guthrie song later in this chapter.

The Carters' professional career lasted from their discovery by Ralph Peer in 1927 until 1943. After World War II, Maybelle and her daughters continued to tour as the Carter Family, and subsequent incarnations of the group performed through the 1960s.

LISTENING GUIDE
CD 2:7 "Wildwood Flower"

STYLE	Country ballad
FORM	Strophic: 4-line stanzas for each verse

Instrumental Statement
Maybelle plays the melody in the lower register of the guitar, with the chords inserted in between melody notes. This is her famous "thumb-brush" style.

0:22	Verse 1	
	Oh, I'll twine with my mingles and waving black hair	Instrumental statements of melody interpolated
	With the roses so red and the lilies so fair	between verses
	And the myrtle so bright with the emerald hue	
	The pale and the leader and eyes look like blue.	
1:05	Verse 2	
	Oh, I'll dance, I will sing and my laugh shall be gay	Unadorned singing; straight delivery
	I will charm every heart, in his crown I will sway …	
1:46	Verse 3	
	Oh, he taught me to love him and promised to love	
	And to cherish me over all others above …	
2:28	Verse 4	
	Oh, he taught me to love him and called me his flow'r	
	That was blooming …	

5 to Listen For
"Wildwood Flower"

INSTRUMENTATION
Voice and guitar

PERFORMANCE STYLE
Pure, plain vocal sound

PERFORMANCE STYLE
Innovative "thumb-brush" guitar style

MELODY
Four short phrases form an arch: rise, then fall

HARMONY
Three chords (I, IV, V); mostly I

3 to Remember
"Wildwood Flower"

SAD STORY
Ballads often tell sad stories; this is one. Absence of overt emotion in singing belies pain of love lost.

PURE COUNTRY VOCAL STYLE
Strong, nasal sound, with no vibrato

GUITAR STYLE
Thumb-brush guitar style (melody on bottom, chords on top) borrowed by Woody Guthrie, then folk revivalists of 1960s

CD 2:8
"Blue Yodel No. 11," Jimmie Rodgers (1929). Rodgers, vocal and guitar.

lyrics, melodic style, harmony, and form. More significantly, it is a blues in style. Rodgers sounds natural and very much at ease singing a blues. He has captured essential elements of the blues singing style: a rhythmically free and unstilted delivery of the text, a highly inflected phrasing (listen to the extra emphasis on the word "presents" in the third phrase of the first section), and a vocal style more expressive than pretty.

The differences between the Carter Family and Jimmie Rodgers are manifest in the songs. The Carters recorded traditional songs or songs written by A. P. Carter in the traditional style. Rodgers, drawing on the blues, pop, jazz, and country music of the time, wrote his own songs. The Carters preserved the past; Rodgers showed the way to the future of country music.

New Directions in the 1930s

Important new sounds of the 1930s in both country and folk music came from the Southwest in an almost vertical line that connects Kosse, Texas; Tioga, Texas; and Okemah, Oklahoma. Tioga, a small town due north of Dallas, was the birthplace of Gene Autry, the first of the singing cowboy movie stars. Bob Wills, the man most responsible for western swing, the hottest country sound of the 1930s, came from Kosse, a small town almost directly south of Dallas. Woody Guthrie, the man who made folk a contemporary music, was born in Okemah, mostly north and a little east of Dallas (and Tioga).

Gene Autry: Putting the "Western" in "Country and Western". It was inevitable that there would be musical westerns. America had long had a love affair with cowboys and the Wild West. Kids idolized not only the good guys like Wyatt Earp and William "Buffalo Bill" Cody (at least we *thought* he was a good guy), but also bad guys like outlaws Jesse James and William "Billy the Kid" Bonney. Cowboy songs like "Home on the Range" and "Git Along, Little Dogies" were as much a part of everyday life as Foster's minstrel songs, patriotic anthems, and current hits. It simply remained for Hollywood to put everything together. Beginning in 1935, it did.

The first singing cowboy on screen was Gene Autry (1907–1998). As a young man, he got a job as a telegraph

Jimmie Rodgers's "Blue Yodel No. 11." Jimmie Rodgers (1897–1933) had a brief but extraordinarily influential career. His musical legacy, preserved primarily through recordings, inspired an entire generation. According to Bill Malone, "Ernest Tubb estimated that perhaps 75 percent of modern country music performers were directly or indirectly influenced to become entertainers either through hearing Rodgers in person or through his recordings."

Born in Mississippi, Rodgers spent much of his childhood and early adult life around the railroad, at first accompanying his father, a gang foreman, and then working off and on as a railroad man, before contracting the tuberculosis that was to end his life so prematurely at age thirty-six.

Rodgers's first recordings for Peer, in Bristol, Tennessee, and later that year in Camden, New Jersey, made him one of country music's first stars. Almost immediately he was making $2,000 a month in record royalties alone. For the rest of his life, he enjoyed great popularity throughout the South in personal appearances, radio broadcasts, and frequent recordings.

Forced to move to Texas because of his illness, he gained an especially strong following in the Southwest. The greater receptiveness of southwestern country music to outside influences is surely due in part to Rodgers.

The image of the rambling man roaming far and wide that Rodgers carefully cultivated in his songs had great appeal for his fans. Musically, Rodgers borrowed liberally from all the styles with which he came into contact; there are elements of Tin Pan Alley song, blues, and jazz in many of his recordings.

"Blue Yodel No. 11," one of thirteen blue yodels that Rodgers recorded, is a blues, pure and simple—in its

LISTENING GUIDE
CD 2:8 "Blue Yodel No. 11"

STYLE	Blues sung by country singer
FORM	Blues form, but with irregular timing and extension for yodel at end of each phrase

0:00 Introduction
A short guitar introduction with Rodgers and Billy Burke on guitars.

0:09 First chorus
I've got a gal, I give her presents by the score. (2x)
No matter how many presents I give her, she always
    asks for more.

Rodgers is completely at home singing the blues. The vocal style is idiomatic, and the delivery of the lyric evidences the kind of rhythmic freedom associated with blues singing. The trademark yodels come at the end of the chorus.

0:39 Second chorus
Look here, sweet baby …

Like so many blues songs, this one is about man/woman problems: Rodgers has a litany of complaints.

1:07 Third chorus
You want pearls and diamonds …

1:33 Fourth chorus
I believe to my soul …

Again, a familiar metaphor for a partner two-timing the singer

2:00 Fifth chorus
You may call yourself the meanest gal …

Like so many blues songs, this one is about man/woman problems: Rodgers has a litany of complaints.

2:28 Sixth chorus
Listen here, sweet mama …

operator. In one of those happy coincidences that never seem to happen any more, Autry was passing the time singing and playing the guitar one day in 1926 when a man walked in to send a telegram. The man was Will Rogers, the most popular humorist of the twenties and thirties. Rogers asked Autry to keep singing, then suggested that he get a job in radio. After an unsuccessful audition for Victor in 1927, Autry landed a radio show in 1929. This led to a recording contract later that year. After much success on radio and record—he was featured on the *Grand Ole Opry* and *National Barn Dance*; Sears, Roebuck sponsored his radio show and promoted his records—Autry made his way to Hollywood in 1934.

The next year he starred in the film *Tumbling Tumbleweeds*. The film is generally considered to be the first musical western (or horse opera) because the plot depends on the singing ability of Autry's character. The success of the

film created a demand for singing cowboys. Autry became one of the most popular Hollywood stars, and other singing cowboys, like Roy Rogers and Tex Ritter, were not far behind. For many Americans in the 1930s and '40s—especially those who went to the movies but didn't listen to the *Grand Ole Opry*—this was country music.

Michael Ochs Archives/Getty Images

A meeting of country music legends Jimmie Rodgers and the Carter family in Louisville, Kentucky.

5 to Listen For
"Blue Yodel No. 11"

INSTRUMENTATION
Voice and two guitars (Rodgers and Burke)

PERFORMANCE STYLE
Blues inflections-stressed syllables, sliding into notes, and conversational pacing. The yodeling at the ends of sections is a Rodgers trademark.

RHYTHM
Lazy four-beat rhythm. Rodgers's singing plays off the beat, as is common in blues singing. Occasional confusion about timing.

MELODY
Short phrases that start high and finish low; most are derived from pentatonic scale.

HARMONY
Basic blues progression, with occasional modification of the timing

3 to Remember
"Blue Yodel No. 11"

COMMON BLUES SUBJECT
Like many songs, "Blue Yodel No. 11" is about man/woman problems.

RODGERS'S INFLUENCE
Rodgers was the most influential of the early country musicians. His assimilation of non-country styles—and especially black styles like blues and jazz—becomes the primary source of change in country music. The road to rockabilly began with his blue yodels.

FIRST "WHITE MAN WITH A NEGRO FEEL"
Rodgers sings the blues idiomatically a quarter century before Elvis becomes a star.

Much as "The Prisoner's Song" did, western songs followed the formula for country crossover success:

- Begin with a vocal sound that is recognizably country but not intensely so.
- Sing a simple melody with a simple accompaniment based mainly on three chords.
- Add in some country instrumental sounds, then mix in a little pop sophistication: more complex chords, melodic lines, and forms.
- Package it with an appealing personality.

The formula worked for Autry, and for generations to come it would work for many more country and western singers. It still works today.

CD 2:9

"Steel Guitar Rag," Leon McAuliffe (1936). Bob Wills and the Texas Playboys, featuring Leon McAuliffe, electric steel guitar.

Bob Wills: Putting the Swing in Country. Bob Wills (1905–1975) was a maverick. In a genre that valued tradition and respected success, Wills took the bold step of blending the country string-band sound with pop, blues, and jazz into a new style called **western swing**. The blues and jazz influence was most often evident in the heavier beat, the fuller instrumentation, and the

styles of many of the soloists in Wills's band, the Texas Playboys. Wills, a fiddle player as well as a bandleader and all-around entertainer, surrounded himself with good musicians.

"Steel Guitar Rag," a 1936 recording, features Leon McAuliffe playing the then-novel electric steel guitar. The **electric steel guitar** stands alone among contemporary popular instruments as the signature instrument for two—and only two—kinds of music: Hawaiian and country. These are two different musical worlds, yet the instrument sounds equally at home in both.

During the 1920s there was a tremendous vogue for Hawaiian music. Hawaiian guitarists, playing the lap steel guitar, were a vaudeville staple, and most of the bigger music publishers published learn-at-home methods for the instrument. In search of a more powerful sound, instrument makers created the dobro, a guitar with a built-in steel resonator, also played on the lap. (The term *dobro* reportedly comes from *Dopyera Brothers*, a family of Czech immigrants who created the first dobros in 1928; *dobro* also means "good" in Czech). The electric steel guitar, invented in the early thirties, soon replaced the dobro as the instrument of choice for lap guitarists. As with the steel guitar, the origins of the electric steel guitar are cloudy, but it seems safe to say that the steel guitar was the first electric guitar.

A strictly instrumental song featuring an almost brand-new instrument is innovative enough, but Wills's "Steel Guitar Rag" featured a host of country music innovations, most of which were borrowed from other genres. Wills and the Texas Playboys were not responsible for all of them, but, as the most popular band in the Southwest during the late 1930s and '40s, they did more than anyone else to popularize them.

Most of these novel features eventually wove their way into the fabric of country music. For example, the sound of a country rhythm section playing a honky-tonk two-beat (or a **country rock beat**, which merges the honky-tonk beat with a rock rhythm) is the traditional country rhythm these days.

In his receptiveness to other styles, Wills certainly drew on Jimmie Rodgers's legacy. His stage demeanor, with his frequent words of encouragement to his musicians and his yodeled expressions of pleasure, also recalls Rodgers's occasional spoken asides. In turn Wills too left an enduring legacy of stylistic innovation. No one did more to popularize the sound of western swing than Bob Wills.

LISTENING GUIDE

CD 2:9 "Steel Guitar Rag"

STYLE	Western swing
FORM	ABC for the melody; solos only on A (A and C share same chord progression)
0:00	Introduction
	"Take it away, Leon …" (Leon = Leon McAuliffe, the steel guitar player)
0:07	**First chorus**
A	Leon's bent notes = country take on blues style
B (0:25)	A clear two-beat rhythm underneath McAuliffe's solo
C (0:43)	Rag-like figuration at slow speed
1:00	**Solos**
A	Piano solo: not very country sounding
A (1:17)	Return of A serves as interlude
A (1:34)	Honking saxophone solo
1:52	**First chorus reprise**
A	Steel guitar, with Wills's voice-over
B (2:09)	As before
C (0:4)	As before, but with tag

Woody Guthrie and Contemporary Folk Music. Whether it's riding a horse on the range, hopping a train, or driving an eighteen-wheeler down the interstate, one of the enduring images in country music is the traveling man. But you wouldn't find America's greatest musical wanderer on the stage of the Grand Ole Opry, even though he was born in a small town in Oklahoma and borrowed his guitar style directly from Maybelle Carter. Instead, he forged a new path—one that created the contemporary folk movement.

> ❝*Whether it's riding a horse on the range, hopping a train, or driving an eighteen-wheeler down the interstate, one of the enduring images in country music is the traveling man.*❞

Julie Fisher/istockphoto.com

For Woody Guthrie (1912–1967), growing up was hard. His parents were pioneers. His sister died when a stove exploded; his father rode the oil boom, then went bust; and his mother ended up in a mental institution with an undiagnosed case of Huntington's chorea, a congenital disease that would curtail Guthrie's career and claim his life. He left home at age sixteen, just before the stock market crash and a few years before the Dust Bowl drove so many Oklahomans west in search of a better life.

His first stop was Pampas, Texas, where his uncle, Jack Guthrie, nurtured his interest in country music. Before long he had assembled the Corncob Trio and was doing what so many other country bands were doing. But his music soon went in a different direction, and in the early thirties he started writing songs. Here is how he described them in *Bound for Glory*, his novel-like autobiography of the early years of his life:

Some people liked me, hated me, walked with me, walked over me, jeered me, cheered me, rooted me and hooted me, and before long I was invited in and booted out of every public place of entertainment. But I decided that songs was a music and a language of all tongues.

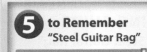
INSTRUMENTATION
Steel guitar in the spotlight, plus small horn section (trumpets and saxophones stand out) and rhythm section (including piano, bass, and drums)

PERFORMANCE STYLE
Occasional blues-influenced bent notes in steel guitar line

RHYTHM
Fast tempo; two-beat rhythm with a strong backbeat

MELODY
Riffs in A and B; rag-like figuration in B and C

HARMONY
I, IV, V most of the time, with long stretches on I

BLUES INFLUENCE
A few blue notes in the melody and a few bent notes in McAuliffe's playing

JAZZ INFLUENCE
Improvising style in piano and sax solos; expanded instrumentation—Wills augments the traditional country band with a full rhythm section and a small horn section, plus the steel guitar; use of drums—Wills was the first important country bandleader to use drums.

HONKY-TONK BEAT
Countrified two-beat: clear OOM-pah rhythm with a crisp backbeat

COUNTRIFYING
Rhythm (two-beat), melody (blues/rag inspiration), and sound (steel guitar) all demonstrate country adaptation of outside influences.

BOB WILLS = COUNTRY PROGRESSIVE
Western swing would influence honky-tonk, rockabilly, and country rock.

I never did make up many songs about the cow trails or the moon skipping through the sky, but at first it was funny songs of what all's wrong, and how it turned out good or bad. Then I got a little braver and made up songs telling what I thought was wrong and how to make it right, songs that said what everybody in that country was thinking. And this has held me ever since.

Guthrie makes clear that he is the champion of the working class. In the course of his career, he wrote songs—more than a thousand of them—told stories, and authored articles (for a Communist Party newspaper) that commented on social injustice, the lives of the poor and the unknown, and anything else that caught his sharp eye. He spent most of the 1930s crisscrossing the United States, sometimes hopping trains to get from one place to the next.

In 1940 he made his way to New York, where Alan Lomax (John's son, also a Library of Congress folklorist) discovered him singing at a "Grapes of Wrath" rally for farm workers. Within a year Lomax recorded him at the Library of Congress and featured him on his radio show. Pete Seeger was also part of the liberal/radical circle in which Lomax moved, and Guthrie joined Seeger and two others in 1941 to form the Almanac Singers.

In "Do-Re-Mi," a song Guthrie wrote in 1937, we can hear what drew Lomax, Seeger, and working-class folk to his music. We don't listen to Guthrie's songs for

CD 2:10

"Do-Re-Mi," Woody Guthrie (1937). Guthrie, vocal and guitar.

the beauty of his singing; what Robert Christgau calls his "vocal deadpan" was the opposite of the crooning of Bing Crosby, whom Guthrie openly despised. And we don't listen for the sophistication of the accompaniment; Guthrie was fond of saying that three chords were one too many. We listen for the words.

With no sugarcoating, Guthrie tells the tough-times story of the desperate people who migrated west in search of a decent life. He gets his point across with a wry humor that, if anything, intensifies the grim circumstances that he describes. This is a funny song that isn't funny at all.

Guthrie's music is centuries old and brand new at the same time. In his music are echoes of British broadside ballads, a tradition that dates back to the sixteenth century. (A **broadside** is a topical text sung to a well-known tune. Broadsides were, in effect, an urban folk music with printed words.) In fact, Guthrie occasionally fashioned new words to familiar songs, in true broadside and folk tradition. But in the musical context of the 1930s—the world of silver-screen pop, swinging big-band jazz, singing cowboys, and crooners—Guthrie's songs stood apart. From the late 1930s through the end of World War II, there was no sharper musical commentator on the inequities of life in America, no more persistent musical voice for social justice, and no more prolific musical advocate for the cause of the working class than Woody Guthrie.

He wrote and delivered his songs in a folk style, sometimes fitting old melodies with new words, but the songs were new. In so doing he made folk a commercial music—even if much of the time his songs had an anticommercial message. He also made folk a living music. Others, most notably the Weavers, would follow in his footsteps.

Autry died in Los Angeles, home of the motion picture industry. His music and the music of the other singing cowboys was the most visible segment of country music; it was the interface between country music and pop. Wills died in Tulsa; although his group traveled to California and even appeared in films, his music remained familiar mainly to that slice of country music's core audience that was open to outside influences.

LISTENING GUIDE

CD 2:10 "Do-Re-Mi"

STYLE	Topical folk song
FORM	Verse/chorus

0:00   **Introduction**
A short introduction that shows Guthrie's mastery of Maybelle Carter's thumb-brush style

0:18   **Verse 1**
Lots of folks back East, they say, is leavin' home every day ...
| The simple setting—straightforward melody, plain singing style, unobtrusive accompaniment—brings the lyrics to the fore.

0:43   **Chorus**
Oh, if you ain't got the do re mi, folks ...
| This song uses a verse/chorus form to emphasize the main point and to make the point more memorable.

1:15   **Interlude**
Instrumental interlude, a repetition of the introduction

1:31   **Verse 2**
You want to buy you a home or a farm ...

1:55   **Chorus**
Oh, if you ain't got the do re mi ...
| As before

5 to Listen For
"Do-Re-Mi"

INSTRUMENTATION
Voice and guitar

PERFORMANCE STYLE
Twangy singing style; easy delivery of words; the Carter thumb-brush guitar style

RHYTHM
Moderate tempo; light beat keeping in regular accompaniment rhythm (no syncopation or rhythmic play)

MELODY
Long phrases at quick pace; narrow melodic range

HARMONY
Simple three-chord song

3 to Remember
"Do-Re-Mi"

TOPICAL SONG
Guthrie brought topical songs into Depression-era American life. Social commentary rare in any kind of song before World War II.

FOLK-STYLE ACCOMPANIMENT
Guthrie adapted Maybelle Carter's thumb-brush accompanying style; link between traditional country and folk revival

ANTI-POP/INSPIRATION FOR ROCK
Guthrie embraces reality instead of escaping it (as pop songs did); important influence on rock's "realness."

Guthrie died in New York. He had essentially left country music behind, or at least a country music audience, to forge a new direction. The difference between Guthrie's folk music and country music had more to do with politics and social issues than with the music itself. Folk music found a new home in New York's Greenwich Village and a new, politically liberal, and largely urban audience. Country music kept its home base, in the South and southern California, and retained its conservative values. Country and folk were like two brothers who grew up together but followed paths so different that they became estranged. Their reconciliation came only in the 1960s, through the music of Bob Dylan.

Bluegrass: A Neo-Traditional Style

Country music prizes its roots more than any other major genre. It let the world come to Nashville, rather than relocating to the main media centers. Its institutions honor and preserve its past. It holds on to its core values rather than searching for the next new thing. So it was fitting that one of the most distinctive sounds in postwar country music was a new take on its oldest tradition.

Bill Monroe and the Birth of Bluegrass. Bill Monroe (1911–1996), a singer and mandolin player, is known as the "father of bluegrass." He was responsible not only for the sound but also the name: Kentucky, where he was born, is the bluegrass state. Monroe grew up surrounded by skilled folk musicians, including his uncle Pendleton Vandiver (whom he would remember in the song "Uncle Pen"). He took up the mandolin because no one else in the family played it.

Monroe began to build his career in the 1930s and arrived on the stage of the Grand Ole Opry in 1939. By that time he was well on his way to assembling the sound of bluegrass. It would come together in 1945, when virtuoso banjo player Earl Scruggs joined Monroe's group.

Monroe's **bluegrass** music descends directly from the early string bands. The acoustic instrumentation (no electric instruments or amplification) and the mountain vocal style (the "high lonesome" sound) preserve important country music traditions. But there are some important differences as well:

- *Expanded instrumentation.* Monroe and the Blue Grass Boys offered a complete array of acoustic string instruments: fiddle, guitar, banjo, mandolin, and string bass.
- *Chop-chord mandolin style.* Bill Malone calls Bill Monroe's mandolin style "chop-chord." The chop-chord style, a percussive sound occurring in alternation with the bass, is the bluegrass answer to the honky-tonk backbeat.
- *Earl Scruggs's virtuoso banjo playing.* Scruggs updated the Appalachian three-finger banjo style. It combined the continuous stream of notes found in earlier banjo styles with the syncopated groupings of ragtime and the occasional blues lick—all at breakneck tempos.
- *Collective improvisation.* The texture and the form of a bluegrass recording have close parallels with New Orleans jazz. In both there is a dense, active texture resulting from simultaneous improvisation on several melody instruments over a timekeeping rhythm section, with occasional interruptions for a featured soloist. This collective improvisation harks back to the thoroughly blended texture of the string band, but there are more parts and their roles are more varied.
- *Exceedingly fast tempos.* String-band music was often dance music, but the tempos in many bluegrass songs are much too fast for all but the most agile dancers. This is listening music, although it invites a physical response. Part of the excitement of bluegrass is the skill with which its best performers reel off streams of notes at very fast speeds.

CD 2:11

"It's Mighty Dark to Travel," Bill Monroe (1947). Bill Monroe and the Blue Grass Boys: Monroe, mandolin and vocal; Earl Scruggs, banjo; Lester Flatt, guitar and vocal; Chubby Wise, fiddle; and Howard Watts, bass.

We hear all of these features in "It's Mighty Dark to Travel," a 1947 recording by Bill Monroe and the Blue Grass Boys. The recording features Earl Scruggs on banjo, Lester Flatt on guitar, and Bill Monroe on mandolin. Flatt and Scruggs would leave the following year to form their own group. By the end of the 1940s, other musicians were copying features of Monroe's music, and it remains the standard by which bluegrass groups are measured.

In the postwar World War II, bluegrass was the country music style closest to the old-time music of country fiddlers like Ben Jarrell. As such, it represented a countercurrent in country music. It would remain on the periphery of country music, although its stars remained widely admired. The sound of bluegrass charted in 1962, when Flatt and Scruggs's "The Ballad of Jed Clampett" served as the theme music for the television show *The Beverly Hillbillies.*

● ● ● ● ● ● ● ●

Looking Back, Looking Ahead

In 1920 the musical styles that we now identify as country music did not exist, and there was no industry in place to support what would become country. Three decades later, country music had acquired a name: country and western, not folk. It had also acquired an array of styles—honky-tonk, western swing, bluegrass—and a sizeable share of the popular music marketplace, not only within the loyal country music market but also with country songs and singers crossing over to the pop charts. Country mutated from the folk music that was its primary source mainly by absorbing elements of other traditions: pop, blues, and even jazz.

Country blues did exist in 1920, but its audience was limited almost exclusively to blacks and those southern whites who stopped to listen to street singers like Jefferson. Jefferson's recordings were the beginning of a second wave of blues on disc in the late 1920s and 1930s. It included not only country bluesmen from all over the south but also more urban blues, often with piano as an accompanying instrument. These largely replaced classic blues in race-record catalogs.

LISTENING GUIDE

CD 2:11 "It's Mighty Dark to Travel"

STYLE	Bluegrass	
FORM	Verse/chorus	
0:00	First chorus	
	Instrumental statement of the melody	
0:07	Chorus	
	It's mighty dark ...	The vocal harmony has a traditional sound because the intervals between the two voices are different from pop vocal harmony; they have a more open sound.
0:26	Instrumental chorus	
	Fiddle plays the melody.	
0:40	Verse 1	
	To me she was ...	Notice the fast mandolin chords behind the vocal.
0:53	Chorus	
	It's mighty dark ...	
1:05	Instrumental chorus	
	Banjo solo. Notice the syncopation produced by the accents in Scruggs's line and the blue notes. We hear echoes of ragtime in some of the figuration.	
1:18	Verse 3	
	Many a night	There is a lot going on underneath the vocal: Flatt's guitar runs, Monroe's busy mandolin part, Wise's sustained fiddle harmonies, and Scruggs's picking.
1:31	Chorus	
	It's mighty dark ...	
1:44	Instrumental chorus	
	Mandolin solo. Monroe embeds the melody into the fast chords he's playing.	
1:56	Verse 3	
	Traveling down ...	
2:08	Chorus	
	It's mighty dark ...	
2:22	Instrumental chorus	
	Violin solo. Notice how Wise decorates the melody with harmony notes (like the vocal) and the occasional quick run.	
1:13	Chorus	
	It's mighty dark ...	Abrupt ending = finish song neatly

Black gospel and urban folk music did not exist in 1920. Black sacred music had a long history, and spirituals were familiar to blacks and white, but the mix of spiritual and blues that gave gospel its distinctive sound awaited Dorsey's conversion. Guthrie was in effect a one-man genre through the 1930s. His mordantly humorous topical songs were a new style, but one with roots in the centuries-old British broadside, folk song, and Maybelle Carter's guitar style.

Country music was by far the most popular of these four styles, in large part because it had access to the media. Broadcasts of the Grand Ole Opry reached most of the eastern United States, and up into Canada;

singing cowboys always found a few minutes every film to sing a song or two. However, except for the occasional crossover hit and the singular exception of the singing cowboys, country remained a regional music until after World War II. The other three styles were known mainly to the adventurous, although boogie-woogie was a fad during the Swing Era.

We might summarize the relationship between white and black outsider styles to each other and to more mainstream music in the generation before World War II like this: if popular music were a freight train, blues would be the locomotive, pop would be the boxcars, and country would be the caboose. As a description of the

5 to Listen For
"It's Mighty Dark to Travel"

INSTRUMENTATION
Vocals, banjo, fiddle, guitar, bass, and mandolin.

PERFORMANCE STYLE
"High lonesome" mountain vocal sound

RHYTHM
Very fast tempo. Strong two-beat rhythm with crisp offbeat chords.

RHYTHM
Very active banjo and mandolin rhythms

MELODY
Vocal line consists of short phrases. Instrumental solos generally move at faster pace and with more skips.

3 to Remember
"It's Mighty Dark to Travel"

BLUEGRASS INSTRUMENTATION
The core bluegrass instrumentation: all strings, no drums or horns

BLACK MUSIC INFLUENCE: RAGTIME, BLUES, JAZZ
Banjo lines have rag-like figuration and a few blue notes; interaction among instruments recalls New Orleans jazz.

TEMPO AND TEXT
Very fast tempo versus mournful lyric

the emergence of new styles that were closer to mainstream pop, such as jump-band rhythm and blues, doo-wop, honky-tonk, and rockabilly. We consider these developments in Chapter 8. The long-term impact of all four styles—country, folk, blues, and black gospel—would not become manifest until the rock revolution of the 1960s.

In the next chapter we encounter another family of musical styles that began as exotic alternatives. These developed beyond the borders of the United States, mainly in Cuba and Brazil, but found a home, and distinctive new sounds, in North America. We consider Latin music in the United States next.

dominant patterns of influence, it is largely accurate. Blues styles were helping to reshape the mainstream as well as country music, while the new directions in country music came from musicians like Jimmie Rodgers and Bob Wills, who listened to blues and jazz and brought it into their music, or those who mixed country, western and pop. However, this generalization obscures a more complex relationship: the most progressive country styles in the second quarter of the twentieth century are in many ways more attuned to a blues and jazz sensibility than they are to pop; concurrently, blues styles show the influence of pop and country in varying degrees.

After World War II, both blues and country would gravitate toward the mainstream. The increased awareness of both was a product of changing tastes of the larger public, especially among younger listeners, and

Terms to Know

Test your knowledge of this chapter's important terms by defining the ones listed here. If you can't recall the meaning of a certain term, refresh your memory by looking up the boldfaced term in the chapter, turning to the Glossary at the back of the book, or working with the flashcards at the Popular Music Resource Center.

songster
country blues
griot
hokum
boogie-woogie
gospel
folk music
country music

traditional country vocal
   sound
thumb-brush style
western swing
electric steel guitar
country rock beat
broadside
bluegrass

Latin Music in the United States

istockphoto.com

In the late 1850s, Louis Moreau Gottschalk (1829–1869), a composer and pianist who was America's first classical music star, toured South America and the Caribbean. On his return, Gottschalk, a native of New Orleans, composed several piano pieces—the first noteworthy American music to show Latin influence. Native Latin music was not widely known in the United States, and Gottschalk's pieces were exotic novelties. But no one of importance followed Gottschalk's lead; other American musicians stayed home or turned to Europe for inspiration.

A century later, the biggest break a pop star could get was an appearance on *The Ed Sullivan Show*—the television show now most remembered for introducing Elvis and the Beatles to the huge American audience. When rhythm-and-blues artist Bo Diddley got the chance to appear on the show in 1955, he agreed to perform "Sixteen Tons," a big hit at the time for popular country singer Tennessee Ernie Ford. But when the curtain opened, Diddley and his band played their hit song "Bo Diddley." It had been a Number 1 R&B hit for them in 1955, they felt most comfortable with it, so they played it, even if it cost them a return engagement on the show.

The most distinctive musical feature of "Bo Diddley" (which we hear in Chapter 9) is the "shave and a haircut, two bits" rhythm in the guitar's response to each phrase of the lyric. This rhythm had been around for a while before Bo Diddley built his song around it. Some called it the "hambone rhythm"; others have connected it to **patting juba**, a slave practice in which they tapped out tricky rhythms on their thighs, chest, and almost any other part of their body that they could slap. But the rhythm is much more familiar to Cubans than it is to Americans.

Also familiar to Latin listeners is the sound of **maracas**, a percussion instrument made by putting handles on dried, seed-filled gourds; the shaking of seeds against the interior walls of the gourd makes the distinctive sound. Jerome Green, a longtime associate of Bo Diddley, played maracas in his band. One can find homemade percussion instruments throughout the Delta, but maracas are not one of them. They are, however, a staple in Latin bands, such as those led by bandleader Ricky Ricardo.

Ricardo was a main character in another extremely popular CBS show, *I Love Lucy*. The show featured the real-life husband-and-wife team Desi Arnaz and Lucille Ball, portraying husband and wife Ricky and Lucy

Ricardo. Ricky led a Latin band at the Tropicana nightclub; Lucy was a show-business wannabe. The commercial viability of a white woman married to a Latin musician was a hard sell to CBS executives, so Lucy and Desi spent $5,000 of their own money to make a pilot showing that the couple would be believable. CBS finally bought the idea, the show went on the air in 1951, and the result was the popular, now classic, sitcom of the 1950s (still showing on cable stations).

> " *Lucy and Desi spent $5,000 of their own money to make a pilot showing that the couple would be believable.* "

What *I Love Lucy* and Bo Diddley's appearance on *The Ed Sullivan Show* have in common is the blending of Latin music and Latin musicians into American life. There was little sense of the exotic in *I Love Lucy*, and the Latin influence in Bo Diddley's song is seldom acknowledged. Yet the Bo Diddley beat is his (seemingly unintentional) take on the **clave** (pronounced "*clah*-vay") **rhythm**, the defining rhythm of Afro-Cuban music.

He may have learned the rhythm from Latin bands that played black neighborhoods as novelty acts, and it was explicitly a part of New Orleans rhythm and blues from the late 1940s. Similarly, the maracas are one of many Afro-Cuban instruments that have become commonplace in popular music. Think of the cowbell sound

Desi Arnaz and his band in the Universal movie *Holiday in Havana*.

Markfgd/Dreamstime LLC

The Everett Collection/Everett Collection

that starts the Rolling Stones' "Honky Tonk Women" and appears in so many other popular songs, or the conga drums that can be heard on so many Motown recordings, such as Marvin Gaye's version of "I Heard It Through the Grapevine." By 1955 Latin music had become a subtle seasoning in popular music, jazz, and rhythm and blues, and it had become an acceptable alternative to more conventional American music. In fact, the biggest hit of 1955 was a Latin song, Perez Prado's "Cherry Pink and Apple Blossom White." In about a century, the place of Latin music in the United States had changed dramatically from exceptional oddity to part of the mix. In this chapter, we briefly survey Latin music in the United States from the turn of the twentieth century through the early years of the rock era, with a particular focus on Cuban music.

Claves.

C Squared Studios/Photodisc/Getty Images

Jeannette Schwager/istockphoto.com

Cowbell.

Americans without a Latin heritage who adapted Latin elements—particularly the rhythms—into their popular songs, dance music, and jazz. Like popular music styles in the United States, Latin styles grew out of the interaction between African and European musical traditions. However, the richer rhythmic textures of Cuban and Brazilian music were a product of the more relaxed oversight of slaves in those regions.

The Roots of Latin Music

The slave trade that brought Africans to the United States also brought them to other parts of the New World, particularly the Caribbean islands and Brazil. Unlike their counterparts in the American South, however, slaves in Latin America and the Caribbean kept much of their culture. They merged their tribal religions with the various forms of Christianity introduced by European colonialists. They created Creole dialects—hybrid languages that were part European, part African. And because drums (banned in the slave-holding American South) were permitted in most other parts of the New World, folk music from these regions remained much closer to its African roots than almost all African American music. Afro-centric folk music from Latin America typically features more percussion instruments and a denser, more complex rhythmic texture, as we heard in "Song for Odudua."

> *The biggest hit of 1955 was a Latin song: Perez Prado's "Cherry Pink and Apple Blossom White."*

Rolhat/Dreamstime LLC

Conga drums.

Latin Music in the United States

In the first half of the twentieth century, *Latin music* was the American umbrella term for music that originated in countries in the New World where Spanish or Portuguese was the native language, music created in the United States by Latin musicians, and music by

The Assimilation of Latin Music

The assimilation of Latin elements into popular music took place in three stages. They followed a roughly chronological progression, with considerable overlap.

- In the first stage, lasting until the early 1940s, Latin styles emerged as exotic novelties, usually dance fads that departed from mainstream fare. As they became popular in America, they moved away from their native forms, especially when played by the most popular bands.

- The second stage, lasting from the 1930s through the 1950s, saw the emergence of hybrid or transformed styles. These grew out of the interpretations of Latin music by American musicians—and, more significant—the incorporation of American music into Latin styles. Because of their different rhythms and instrumentations, these Latin-influenced or Latin-derived styles remained distinct from mainstream pop music until well into the rock era.

- The third stage coincided with the emergence of rhythm and blues and rock and roll, as elements of Latin music became part of the fabric of dominant styles. Latin rhythms helped shape the rhythms of rock-era popular music, and Latin instruments now appeared routinely in a broad range of musical styles. Latin music still stood apart from American popular styles, but the line distinguishing Latin from mainstream was, and is, not nearly so clear as it had been before rock.

The Habanera and Tango

The story of Latin dance music in the United States begins more than a century ago with the emergence of the Cuban **habanera**. Its name is probably an abbreviated form of *contradanza habanera*—that is, a *contredanse* (a European ballroom dance) from Havana. Its characteristic rhythm is one of the first recorded instances of African influence on European music. Developing during the early part of the nineteenth century, the habanera spread beyond Cuba after 1850, traveling to Europe, the United States, and South America. In Europe the habanera caught on not only in Spain but also in France. The French composer Georges Bizet composed a habanera for his immensely popular opera *Carmen* (1875).

The habanera entered the United States by way of Mexico, where it had become popular in the 1870s. A Mexican military band performed the dance at an international exposition held in New Orleans in 1884–1885. The band was the musical hit of the event, and its popularity led to the publication of several of the most popular pieces in its repertoire. By the end of the century, the influence of the habanera was evident in more mainstream American popular music. The rhythmic signature of cakewalks and many ragtime songs is virtually identical to that of the habanera.

Musical evidence suggests that the *habanera* also went south to Argentina, where it became the rhythmic basis of the tango. The tango arrived in America in 1913 from Argentina by way of Paris, where Irene and Vernon Castle had captivated audiences with their dancing of the tango. Upon their return to the United States, they introduced it in a Broadway show, *The Sunshine Girl*, where it was a sensation. Almost overnight, the tango became the first of the twentieth-century Latin dance fads in the United States, then became a fixture in popular culture, especially in musicals and films. However, for most Americans, authentic Argentine tangos remained an exotic and relatively unfamiliar sound throughout the first half of the twentieth century.

The Rumba

The surprising success of Don Azpiazú's 1930 recording of "El Manisero" ("The Peanut Vendor") triggered the second of the Latin dance crazes in the United States—the **rumba** (also spelled *rhumba*). Its success touched off widespread enthusiasm for Latin music, sending publishers back to their catalogs for Latin numbers and inspiring a number of Latin songs by American songwriters. When performed by Latins, the rumba was a spectacular exhibition dance, but simplified rumbas were also widely used for social dancing. It remains the most popular of the Latin ballroom dances.

The rumba grew out of the *son*, an Afro-Cuban dance. The *son* apparently originated in eastern Cuba. Brought to Havana around the turn of the century, it flourished in the 1920s among all classes with the growth of Cuban commercial radio. Many Cuban radio shows featured live performers; and because they were heard but not seen, Cubans of African descent gained access to audiences who would not normally have heard them perform.

The Cuban influence in Don Azpiazú's recording of the rumba "El Manisero" is most evident in the vocal, the prominent Latin percussion, and the reverse clave

CD 2:12

"El Manisero" ("The Peanut Vendor"), Sunshine Marion, Gilbert Wolfe, and Simons Moises (1930). Don Azpiazú and His Havana Casino Orchestra.

The rumba was a spectacular exhibition dance.

rhythm. (Clave rhythm, so called because it is played on **claves**, a pair of cylindrical wooden sticks that are tapped together, is to Cuban popular music what the backbeat is to American popular styles: a consistent point of rhythmic reference. The clave rhythm consists of five irregularly spaced taps, spread over two four-beat measures. In **reverse clave rhythm**, the second half of the pattern comes first.) In other respects, the recording is comparable to American pop styles of the period. The trumpet is muted, and the piano style is halfway between Cuban and cocktail piano.

Still, "El Manisero" is a milestone in Latin music in the United States. It brought authentic Cuban music to a broad American audience: "El Manisero" was a Cuban song, Don Azpiazú was Cuban, and His Havana Casino Orchestra recorded it with a complete Cuban rhythm section. And it triggered a wave of Latin music, both by American musicians intrigued by the new sounds and rhythms, and by Hispanic musicians living in the United States.

LISTENING GUIDE
CD 2:12 "El Manisero"

STYLE	Rumba	
FORM	Open form: alternation of two sets of phrases, with variation in pitches and phrase length	
0:00	Introduction	
	First piano, then maracas, then clarinets (layers); the longer notes in the clarinet riff match up with the reverse clave rhythm.	
	0:06	Muted trumpet plays fragments from vocal line.
0:19	A section	
	Maní, maní …	Three phrases—two calls and a spun-out melody
	(0:41)	Instrumental interlude
0:52	B section	
	Qué calentico y rico está …	Two parts; short, active phrases
	(1:11)	Instrumental interlude
1:18	A section (varied)	
	Dame de tu maní …	Harmony consists of two chords in alternation = no long-range harmonic goal
1:43	B section (varied)	
	Cuando la calle sola está …	Vocal line also in clave in fast-moving parts
2:10	A section (varied)	
	Dame de tu maní …	
2:43	Ending	
	Calls from A; fadeout ending	

5 to Listen For
"El Manisero"

INSTRUMENTATION
Voice, piano, bass, guitar, clarinets, trumpet (muted), and a battery of percussion instruments

INSTRUMENTATION
Most prominent percussion: maracas, claves, and timbales (shallow, single-headed drums tuned to different pitches)

RHYTHM
Reverse clave rhythm; other rhythms line up with clave pattern; steady activity in accompaniment

MELODY
Two melodic phrases, with either long notes or active lines whose accents line up with clave rhythm

TEXTURE
Melody with rich, percussion-heavy accompaniment

4 to Remember
"El Manisero"

REVERSE CLAVE RHYTHM
Played on claves; amplified by "in clave" clarinet riff that runs through song

LATIN PERCUSSION INSTRUMENTS
Claves, maracas, and timbales introduced to American ears

OSCILLATING HARMONY
Simple alternation between two chords; not a progression, thus making open-ended form possible

OPEN FORM
Extensible form—both vocalist and trumpeter can expand phrases—plus layered opening and fadeout ending show African roots, anticipate rock-era music.

Cole Porter

Among Cugat's biggest fans was Cole Porter (1891–1964), then living at New York's Waldorf Hotel. Of the great Tin Pan Alley songwriters, Porter was the most open to the sound of Latin music, or at least the commercial Latin music that Cugat played. Porter wrote several Latin songs, beginning in the 1930s, identifying the rhythm variously as "rhumba" or **beguine** ("beh-*geen*"). What is noteworthy about most of Porter's Latin songs is that their lyrics have nothing to do with Latin culture. Apparently, he simply liked the feel of the rhythm. A spectacular exception is his most famous Latin song, "Begin the Beguine" (1935): the lyrics would make great ad copy for a Caribbean getaway.

CD 2:13

"Begin the Beguine," Cole Porter (1935). Xavier Cugat and His Orchestra.

• • • • • • • •
Americanized Latin Music: Porter, Cugat, and the Latin Song

With the success of "El Manisero," Latin music gained a toehold in the pop world. American songwriters showed a greater sensitivity to Latin style—Irving Berlin's "Heat Wave" (1933) is a well-known example—and songs by Latin composers, such as Cuban Nilo Melendez's "Green Eyes," were on their way to becoming pop standards. Both stage and film musicals featured Latin music more prominently. Bandleader Xavier Cugat popularized Latin music in a hybrid style—rhythmically simplified and commercially acceptable to white audiences. They gave the most visible evidence of a growing Latin musical presence in the United States, especially in New York.

Cole Porter

Washington, D.C. [200033557]
Library of Congress Prints and Photographs Division.

Xavier Cugat

Xavier Cugat's orchestra was among the first to record "Begin the Beguine." Cugat (1900–1990), a Spanish-born violinist raised in Cuba, came to the United States in 1921 and worked as a violinist before forming his own bands. Cugat helped establish a commercial Latin style, initially through long-term engagements at the Waldorf Hotels in New York and Los Angeles and performances on the network radio show *Let's Dance,* then as the most filmed bandleader in Hollywood. Cugat was Latin music's Paul Whiteman. Both wore moustaches and were rotund. Both were string players who became bandleaders. Both hired the best musicians. Whiteman's band included top jazzmen of the 1920s; Cugat's bands included top Cuban musicians. Both were showmen, but Cugat put more emphasis on the show—and on showing off. The band wore ridiculous uniforms, played corny arrangements, and did campy routines. Still, each bandleader was responsible for bringing his music into the mainstream. Whiteman was instrumental in making jazz

MGM/The Kobal Collection/Picture Desk

and the dance orchestra popular during the twenties, whereas Cugat was making Latin music for the masses in the thirties, forties, and fifties.

Cugat's recording of "Begin the Beguine" was a hit—one of three for him that year. Although the song has a lyric, Cugat's orchestra performs it as an instrumental. Only two short vocal sections frame an instrumental statement of the melody. It is elegantly done. Violins play the opening phrase of the melody, while the rest of the orchestra supports the melody with the American-ized Latin rhythm and Porter's original offbeat accents. The rich overlay of percussion instruments gives the

Cugat was Latin music's Paul Whiteman. Both wore moustaches and were rotund. Both were string players who became bandleaders. Both hired the best musicians. Whiteman's band included top jazzmen of the 1920s; Cugat's bands included top Cuban musicians.

performance a more authentic Latin sound; among these instruments are the claves.

American versus Latin Rhythms

For songwriters like Porter, "Latin" meant mostly a change in the rhythm, from an uneven division of the beat to an even division. In a typical foxtrot, like "I've

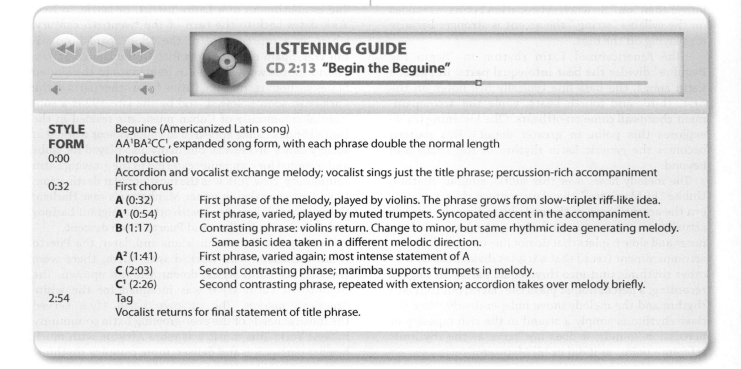

LISTENING GUIDE
CD 2:13 "Begin the Beguine"

STYLE	Beguine (Americanized Latin song)	
FORM	AA¹BA²CC¹, expanded song form, with each phrase double the normal length	
0:00	Introduction	
	Accordion and vocalist exchange melody; vocalist sings just the title phrase; percussion-rich accompaniment	
0:32	First chorus	
	A (0:32)	First phrase of the melody, played by violins. The phrase grows from slow-triplet riff-like idea.
	A¹ (0:54)	First phrase, varied, played by muted trumpets. Syncopated accent in the accompaniment.
	B (1:17)	Contrasting phrase: violins return. Change to minor, but same rhythmic idea generating melody. Same basic idea taken in a different melodic direction.
	A² (1:41)	First phrase, varied again; most intense statement of A
	C (2:03)	Second contrasting phrase; marimba supports trumpets in melody.
	C¹ (2:26)	Second contrasting phrase, repeated with extension; accordion takes over melody briefly.
2:54	Tag	
	Vocalist returns for final statement of title phrase.	

INSTRUMENTATION
Full downtown Latin orchestra, with the most audible being vocal, strings, rhythm section with piano, bass, and many Latin percussion instruments (bongos, maracas, and claves), trumpets, accordion, and marimba

RHYTHM
Beguine rhythm: bass on beats 1, 3, and 4; chords on every afterbeat

RHYTHM
Two kinds of rhythmic play: slow triplets float over accompaniment; offbeat accents in accompaniment

MELODY
Unfolds slowly from riff-like ideas that float over the beat rather than bounce off it; builds gradually toward the final climactic phrases

TEXTURE
Melody with rich, percussion-heavy accompaniment

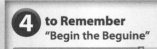

PORTER'S LONG SONG
A very long, well-integrated song, three times the length of a typical pop song

LATINESQUE SONG
Porter's take on Latin rhythms, delivered in Cugat's commercial Latin style. Music sounds Latin, but is not in clave.

LATIN ORCHESTRA
A sweet band (note the violins) with Latin percussion instruments, plus accordion and marimba

UPSCALE MUSIC
Porter's song = significant step up in sophistication from late 1920s songs. Cugat's rendition, with strings, rich percussion, floating rhythms = comparably high-class

Cugat's recording shows one important way in which Latin elements filtered into American popular music. American composers borrowed from the Latin music that they heard and interpreted it through their own musical understanding. Latin bandleaders like Cugat accommodated the American composer and played to the American public. Most American musicians ignored the clave rhythm because it was so foreign to their musical experience, but they found the rippling beguine accompaniment, with patterns similar to more familiar music, easy to adapt.

While Cugat was performing downtown at the Waldorf, a group of Latin musicians were creating a new kind of Latin music uptown. From their efforts would come the third Latin dance fad, the mambo.

The Mambo: An American Afro-Cuban Music

The establishment of a Latin district, or *barrio,* in New York dates back to the turn of the twentieth century, when, as a consequence of the 1898 Spanish-American War, Spain ceded Puerto Rico to the United States. Puerto Ricans were allowed to immigrate to the United States without restriction. Latins from other parts of the Caribbean soon followed, and by the late 1920s a substantial community of Cuban musicians resided in the United States. Some appeared in vaudeville or worked in society dance orchestras, but many also played for clubs and recorded for companies catering to the growing Latin community. New York was the most popular destination. Most Latins settled in upper Manhattan's east Harlem; Cubans shared their music with other immigrant Latinos and Americans of Cuban and Puerto Rican descent.

Among the Cuban musicians and, later, the Puerto Rican musicians who worked with them, there were two distinct Latin styles, downtown and uptown. The **downtown Latin style** was intended for the white American market. The **uptown Latin style** served the musical needs of the ever-growing Latin community in New York. This music was more African, with much heavier percussion and denser, more complex rhythmic

Got the World on a String," the beat is divided into a long/short rhythm: "got" is longer than "the," "world" is longer than "on." So when syncopation occurs, as it does on the syllable "string," the accent is stronger because it's playing off the beat.

The Americanized Latin rhythm in "Begin the Beguine" divides the beat into equal parts. In Porter's Latin songs, the bass line typically has notes on the first, third, and fourth beats, while the accompaniment chords all come on offbeats. (The Listening Guide explores this point in greater detail.) This pattern becomes the generic Latin rhythm of the 1930s and beyond.

The melody flows over this subtle, sinuous rhythm. Unlike "El Manisero," the clave pattern does not govern the accentuation of the melody; in fact, the melody actually soars over the underlying rhythm with long notes and slow triplets that do not line up with the Latin accompaniment (recall that a **triplet** divides the beat or other rhythmic unit into three equal parts). In Cugat's recording, a percussionist plays the claves, but the clave rhythm and the melody move independently. Here the clave rhythm is simply a strand in the rich tapestry of percussion sounds; it does not serve as the rhythmic reference point, as it did in "El Manisero."

textures. In the 1940s uptown Manhattan would be home to the mambo and cubop, the first sustained experiment in Latin jazz.

The Mambo

The **mambo** was the third of the twentieth-century Latin dance fads, after the tango and the rumba, but the first to develop on American soil. It merged authentic Afro-Cuban *son,* as performed in New York by musicians like Arsenio Rodriguez, with big-band horns and riffs. The style was born in 1940, when Machito (Frank Grillo), New York's first important *sonero* (lead singer in a *son* band), formed his own band, Machito's Afro-Cubans, and hired fellow Cuban Mario Bauza as musical director. Bauza had worked in the African American swing bands of Cab Calloway and Chick Webb and wanted to combine Cuban rhythms with the horn sound of swing. Their new style provided an uptown alternative to the commercial Cugat sound.

By the late 1940s, the mambo had begun to attract notice outside of uptown New York. Downtown ballrooms like New York's Palladium Dance Hall served as venues for this new dance fad. The mambo caught on with the non-Latin audience, although Americanized mambos enjoyed greater mainstream success. The dilution of the mambo as it entered the mainstream paralleled the watering down of the rumba in the early 1930s or, for that matter, almost any outsider style in the first half of the century. What differentiated the fate of the mambo from that of the rumba was the presence of a stable, enthusiastic U.S. audience for Afro-Cuban–inspired music. In the 1930s the audience for authentic Cuban music had been too small to support expatriate Cuban musicians. Twenty years later that audience had grown large enough to support the undiluted Afro-Cuban sounds of the mambo.

Courtesy, Everett Collection

Tito Puente performing at a Hispanic gala in Miami, 1996. Note the expanded timbales setup: several drums, all about the same size.

The presence of two "mambo kings" in the 1950s brings to light the division between commercial and Afro-Cuban Latin music. For white audiences pianist/bandleader Perez Prado was king. His recordings, many of them called simply Mambo No. 1, 2, and so on, offered the commercial sound of the mambo for the masses. The extent of his entry into the mainstream market can be gauged by the success of his biggest hit, "Cherry Pink and Apple Blossom White." But his style often had little to do with authentic Afro-Cuban music. In many of his recordings, Afro-Cuban rhythms and instrumentation are severely diluted or completely absent.

For Latins the "king of the mambo" during the 1950s was Tito Puente (1923–2000). Born in New York of Puerto Rican parents, Puente was an alumnus of Machito's band, in which he played timbales. By the early 1950s, he had formed his own band, for which he also composed and arranged. His style, with its heavy brass and full Cuban rhythm section, appealed much more strongly to Latin audiences than Prado's music did.

CD 2:14
"Complicacion," Francisco Aguabella (1958). Tito Puente and His Band.

"Complicacion," which Puente recorded in 1958, shows a successful blend of American and Afro-Cuban elements. The instrumental accompaniment mixes big-band–style horns (brass and saxes playing riffs and sustained chords) with a full Latin percussion section.

Particularly in the second section, it is possible to hear key elements of Afro-Cuban rhythm. The repeated riff conforms to the clave rhythm, and several layers of percussion produce a dense texture with considerable rhythmic conflict. The bass plays the offbeat *tumbao* pattern, while the piano plays an active pattern, called a *montuno,* that recalls ragtime figurations but is even more syncopated.

The other Cuban-inspired dance fad in the 1950s was the cha-cha-cha. It became popular among white Cubans in the early 1950s, and its popularity quickly spread to the United States, at least in part because Havana was a popular and inexpensive vacation destination at the time. Both the rhythm and the dance step of the cha-cha-cha were simpler than the mambo, and its tempo was slower. As a result, it replaced the mambo as the Latin dance of choice in the United States.

Mainstreaming Latin Music

Like the rumba, the mambo spawned a host of imitations and adaptations. Top pop singing stars occasionally dabbled in it. Both Perry Como and Nat "King" Cole recorded a song called "Papa Loves Mambo"; it was a million-seller for Como in 1954. Dean Martin and Rosemary Clooney both scored with "Mambo Italiano,"

LISTENING GUIDE
CD 2:14 "Complicacion"

STYLE	Mambo	
FORM	Multisectional form with two similar chorus-like sections	
0:00	Introduction	
	Big-band brass riffs over Latin rhythm	
0:14	First verse	
	Yo no quiero complicacion…	
0:28	Chorus	
	Yo la queria…	The rhythm of this phrase lines up with the clave rhythm.
0:37	Second verse	
	Singer returns.	Sustained sax chords underneath the vocal
0:51	Instrumental interlude	
	Brass and sax riffs	
1:12	Chorus	
	Yo la queria …	As before
1:22	Third verse	
	Solo singer	
	Instrumental tag signals end of first big section.	
1:35	Chorus (varied)	
	Yo no quiero complicacion …	This chorus is a variant of the first chorus, different mainly because of the words.
1:58	Inspiracion	
	Repeated riff over two chords: percussionists jam over sax and brass riffs.	
2:21	Chorus (varied)	
	Yo la queria …	Notice tumbao bass and piano montuno.
2:43	Instrumental ending	
	Two chords: riff based on chorus. With vocal, a series of similar riffs.	

a novelty song. Tommy Dorsey's big band, a holdover from the swing era, scored a surprise top-ten hit in 1958 with the pop standard "Tea for Two," redone as a cha-cha-cha.

Latin Music and Jazz. Latin/jazz fusions flourished in the 1950s. Although the impact of Latin music on jazz dates from the time of its origins—Jelly Roll Morton, the self-styled inventor of jazz and one of its early greats, claimed that it was a "Spanish tinge" that differentiated jazz from ragtime—Latin music had little impact on jazz before 1945. Duke Ellington's extensive use of Latin rhythms and percussion in compositions like "Caravan" was an almost singular exception.

However, when bebop jazz musician Dizzy Gillespie formed a big band in the late 1940s, he hired Chano Pozo, a Latin percussionist. This sparked the development of cubop, a true Latin jazz style. At about the same time, Stan Kenton, who composed for and directed an innovative postwar big band, also incorporated Latin rhythms and instruments into extended jazz compositions.

Throughout the 1950s Latin-influenced jazz maintained a consistent if modest presence. Gillespie continued to experiment with Latin/jazz fusions, as did the popular British jazz pianist George Shearing. In the early fifties, Shearing formed a combo that included three Latin percussionists as well as vibraphonist Cal Tjader. Cuban Mongo Santamaria, who played conga with Shearing, would play an important role in bringing jazz, rock, and Latin music together in the sixties. Other prominent jazz musicians, among them Sonny Rollins, Clifford Brown, and Horace Silver, also explored Latin-influenced rhythms.

Typically, the rhythms of Latin jazz were richer and more complex than those used in mainstream pop, but they were not authentically Afro-Cuban. Jazz musicians evened out the rhythmic flow, but did not build their rhythmic play around the clave pattern.

5 to Listen For
"Complicacion"

INSTRUMENTATION
Big-band horn section (full trumpet and sax sections) plus piano, bass, and full Afro-Cuban percussion section: conga drums, claves, cowbell, and timbales, among others

RHYTHM
Fast-moving rhythms in percussion parts, with no instrument consistently marking the beat

RHYTHM
Lots of syncopation: in percussion, vocal lines, tumbao (offbeat bass rhythm) and montuno (completely syncopated piano figures) patterns, and horn riffs

MELODY
A series of short riffs, usually repeated, in the instrument and group vocal lines. Solo vocal part has longer phrases.

TEXTURE
Thick, with several layers: lots of rhythmic activity in percussion parts, plus chords in horns

4 to Remember
"Complicacion"

MAMBO
Afro-Cuban rhythm (full percussion section and complex rhythms) plus big-band swing (horn sections playing riffs)

CLAVE RHYTHM
Hear it clearly at 0:28—**Yo la que**-ri-**a** (**x**) (bold syllables = clave rhythm)

RHYTHMIC FLOATING
Piano and bass often play against time rather than marking the beat; other instruments play fast patterns.

INSPIRACION
Inspiracion = Latin jamming; in big band jazz, horns solo; in mambo, percussionists improvise together

Latin music formed an even stronger kinship with rhythm and blues. R&B/Latin fusions ranged from the mainly cosmetic—Ruth Brown's "Mambo Baby," a No. 1 R&B hit in 1954 is a prominent example—to the smooth integration of Latin and blues elements heard in New Orleans rhythm and blues and the music of Bo Diddley. Especially as the more active rhythms of rock and roll replaced the swing-based shuffle rhythm used in so much post-war rhythm and blues, Latin rhythms and instruments blended smoothly—even imperceptibly—into the musical fabric, because adding Latin elements no longer required adjusting the rhythmic foundation.

• • • • • • • •

Looking Back, Looking Ahead

At the beginning of the twentieth century, the influence of Latin music was evident but unacknowledged. The cakewalk rhythm that introduced syncopation into American popular dance and song derived from the habanera, but songwriters seldom credited the source of the rhythm. (Scott Joplin's "Solace," which he subtitled "A Mexican Serenade," is a rare exception.)

The tango craze of the teens marked the entry of Latin music into American popular culture. The Cuban rumba, an even more popular Latin dance fad, introduced Cuban rhythms and instruments into American popular music. It led to American takes on Latin music and to new American-influenced Latin styles, most notably the mambo. Especially after World War II, these new Latin sounds gained greater prominence, in both commercial and Afro-Cuban versions, and insinuated themselves into popular music, especially rhythm and blues.

Musical exchange with Cuban musicians effectively ended in 1959 as a result of the Cuban revolution, Castro's ascent to power, and the severing of diplomatic relations. Almost immediately, the Brazilian bossa nova found an enthusiastic American audience. Both Brazilian- and Cuban-inspired music from the United States would find a growing audience and flavor the sounds of rock-era music, from Latin rock to pop and jazz, as we note in subsequent chapters.

• • • • • • • •

Terms to Know

Test your knowledge of this chapter's important terms by defining the ones listed here. If you can't recall the meaning of a certain term, refresh your memory by looking up the boldfaced term in the chapter, turning to the Glossary at the back of the book, or working with the flashcards at the Popular Music Resource Center.

patting juba	triplet
maracas	downtown Latin style
clave rhythm	uptown Latin style
habanera	cubop
rumba	mambo
son	*tumbao*
claves	*montuno*
reverse clave rhythm	cha-cha-cha
beguine	

On the *Charts,*

1945–1954

CHAPTER

8

Billboard, the "bible" of the music industry, had begun publication in 1894 as *Billboard Advertising*, a monthly trade magazine for the billposting business. By 1897 it had become simply *The Billboard*, a name it would retain until 1961, when it became simply *Billboard*. The magazine had began to include advertising for fairs and outdoor attractions (events that frequently used bills [i.e., posters] for promotion). By 1900 it had become "The Official Organ of the Great Out-Door Amusement World." *Billboard* continued to broaden its coverage of—and advertising from—other entertainment media, including silent films, stage entertainment, and music publishing. By the 1920s, *Billboard* was covering radio and recording.

In 1936, in response to advertising from jukebox manufacturers, *Billboard* introduced "Chart Line," a listing of the most popular songs on network radio. In 1940 the magazine offered its first record chart, labeled the "Best Selling Retail Records." In 1942 it began publishing "Harlem Hit Parade," a list of top-selling records within the black community, compiled unscientifically through a survey of five Harlem record stores. The chart was renamed "Best Selling Retail Race Records" in 1948, and a year later it became "Best Selling Retail Rhythm and Blues Records." (Jerry Wexler, who was working for *Billboard* at the time, coined the term "rhythm and blues" as a more musically accurate and less offensive substitute for "race"; he would soon leave to found Atlantic Records.) In 1944 *Billboard* published its first "Folk Records" chart. The name was changed to "Hillbilly Records" in 1947 and "Country and Western" in 1949. By 1950 *Billboard* had charts covering pop, R&B, and country and western, plus a sporadically released album chart. By 1963 its focus was strictly on the music business. It was finally "a weekly business journal for the professional user of music, with the emphasis on recordings, and of music playback equipment."

The proliferation of *Billboard* charts during the 1940s points to the rapid growth of the record industry; it would continue to grow in the 1950s in part because of the emergence of commercial television and the development of new record formats. More significantly, it also underscores the rapidly expanding horizons of popular music in the decade after World War II. By the early 1950s, popular music—and less popular music connected to the mainstream popular styles—covered an enormous amount of musical territory. Consider that in New York alone, one could hear:

- Mambos and other Afro-Cuban music in ballrooms uptown and downtown
- Bebop in many of the several jazz clubs on 52nd Street
- Song interpreters singing standards in swanky cabarets
- Folk groups like the Weavers in Greenwich Village clubs
- Aspiring doo-wop groups on street corners throughout the city
- Musicals on Broadway
- Black gospel in Harlem churches

This burgeoning variety was replicated on a smaller scale throughout the United States, often with a regional accent: electric blues in Chicago, Latin-tinged rhythm and blues in New Orleans, cool/West Coast jazz in southern California. To highlight this diversity, we sample a broad cross-section of music recorded (with one exception) between 1945 and 1954.

We tend to filter our understanding of an earlier time and place through more recent developments and the current state of affairs. In this domain, the rise of rock, beginning in the latter half of the 1950s, has skewed our perspective on musical life at mid-century. The playlist for this chapter bears this point out: for rock fans, the most influential song on the list is arguably Muddy Waters's "(I'm Your) Hoochie Coochie Man," because of Waters's seminal role in shaping the sound of rock. Yet, at the time of its release (1954), it was almost certainly the least popular track on the playlist. The world of popular music as understood by the audiences of that time is far different from our rock-skewed perception.

To convey not only the relative popularity of the music discussed in this chapter but also its relative cultural prestige, we use the charts that surfaced in the 1940s and 1950s. The most admired music was, in a way, above the charts: musical theater and jazz were, with classical music, among the first genres to appear on long-playing records. Pop was by far the most commercially important singles chart; this was the music that dominated the media. By contrast, the audiences for R&B and country were more narrowly focused. Even the top hits on the rhythm and blues and country and western charts seldom crossed over to the pop charts. We begin with a brief summary of the mid-century media revolution that would transform the music industry, then survey a range of "classic" styles, from bebop and Broadway to electric blues and honky-tonk.

• • • • • • • •

The Media Revolution

The first decade after World War II saw two major developments that would have a heavy impact on the popular music industry. One was the emergence of commercial television; the other was the introduction of two new record formats.

abandoned the rhythmic innovations of the modern era; syncopation all but disappeared, and swing was in another musical world entirely.

In a genre in which so much of the music is tuneful melody, it is challenging to make the music dramatically evocative. Kern could allude to black characters in *Show Boat* because the spiritual and blues were familiar genres with strong associations, but that was a special circumstance. More often, Rodgers and his peers made little effort to adapt their style to the story. The music from *Oklahoma!* bears almost no resemblance to country or western music, nor does the music for *South Pacific* have much relation to Polynesian music or even popular music during World War II. Instead, Rodgers made his music more dramatically compelling mainly by bringing to his songs some of the breadth and sophistication of classical music. He uses popular song conventions as a point of departure but expands and modifies them; their orchestration and performance complement these changes. We hear these developments in a performance of "Some Enchanted Evening," a love song from *South Pacific*.

CD 2:15

"Some Enchanted Evening," Richard Rodgers and Oscar Hammerstein II (1949). Ezio Pinza, vocal.

> *If Broadway were in the South, the marriage of Liat and Joe would have been so controversial that the show would likely not have made it to the stage.*

South Pacific. *South Pacific* is a musical based on two short stories from a book by James Michener entitled *Tales of the South Pacific*. The plot takes place far away but not long ago; the action occurs during World War II. The story centers around the war and around love. There are two relationships, both of them with an interracial component. One involves Emile de Becque, a French plantation owner on a Polynesian island, and Nellie Forbush, a Navy nurse from Arkansas. The other involves Joe Cable, a Marine lieutenant, who falls in love with Liat, a beautiful local girl. Both couples talk about marriage, but neither of the Americans is willing to commit to a permanent relationship because of race: Liat is Polynesian, and Emile, a widower, has two biracial children from his first marriage. When Nellie rejects Emile's proposal, Emile and Joe lead an expedition behind Japanese lines. In a bittersweet ending that is a reflection of the times, Joe is killed in combat and Emile returns home. Nellie overcomes her prejudice, and they marry. There was a hostile reaction, especially in the South, to the song "You've Got to Be Carefully Taught," in which the lyric, sung by Joe, asserts that racism is learned, not inherited. If Broadway were in the South, the marriage of Liat and Joe would have been so controversial that the show would likely not have made it to the stage.

Emile sings "Some Enchanted Evening" when he first meets Nellie; the song expresses his immediate infatuation with her, although he does so in the second person. Its lush orchestration, expansive form, and above all its soaring melody, sung with great dignity by opera star Ezio Pinza, enable Ezio/Emile to linger in the moment.

Evolution and Devolution in Musical Theater. The most succinct way to describe the difference between musicals produced before *Oklahoma!* and musicals produced since is this: before *Oklahoma!* we remember mainly the songs; beginning with *Oklahoma!* we remember mainly the shows. Few pre-1943 musicals are revived with any frequency; *Show Boat* and Cole Porter's lighthearted *Anything Goes* are the almost singular exceptions. By contrast, the musicals of Rodgers and Hammerstein, Lerner and Loewe (*My Fair Lady*), Frank Loesser (*Guys and Dolls*), and Leonard Bernstein (*West Side Story*) are performed regularly at all levels, from high school,

> *Before* Oklahoma! *we remember the songs; beginning with* Oklahoma! *we remember the shows.*

Copyright @ 20th Century Fox Film Corp./Everett Collection

RODGERS & HAMMERSTEIN'S
SOUTH PACIFIC
COLOR by DE LUXE

ROSSANO BRAZZI · MITZI GAYNOR · JOHN KERR · FRANCE NUYEN
PRODUCED BY BUDDY ADLER   DIRECTED BY JOSHUA LOGAN

LISTENING GUIDE
CD 2:15 "Some Enchanted Evening"

STYLE	Musical theater song
FORM	Individualized popular song form: three long phrases (A, A¹, A²) with an interlude (comparable to the bridge, but shorter) that also serves as the closing section
0:00	Introduction
	Orchestra, with violins prominent

One complete statement of form

A (0:25)	Some enchanted evening You may see a stranger …	Melody built from two short melodic ideas, one at beginning, other at midpoint
A¹ (1:03)	Some enchanted evening Someone may be laughin' …	Note the way slight melodic variations highlight repetition in lyric
Interlude (1:41)	Who can explain it? Who can tell you why? …	Like the bridge in an AABA form song, but shorter
A² (1:59)	Some enchanted evening When you find your true love …	Climactic version of the main melody
Postlude (2:37)	Once you have found her, Never let her go …	Different mood, as if different character is singing

college, and community theater productions to revivals on Broadway and London's West End.

A primary reason for the frequent production of the golden-age musicals is their success as dramas. They tell good stories well. Recall that the majority of the plots are based on existing literature, from Shakespeare to top contemporary writers. Moreover, song and dance are in the service of the story. As "Some Enchanted Evening" suggests, Rodgers tweaked popular song conventions to create songs that were distinctive and dramatically appropriate. The combination of compelling stories and appealing, artful music helps account for the frequent production of these musicals.

At the same time, however, Rodgers's music "devolved." In other words, songs like "Some Enchanted Evening" show virtually no evidence of the evolutionary developments that took place in popular music during the first half of the twentieth century. There is a light two-beat rhythm supporting the melody (but not really danceable), only a hint of ca. 1900 syncopation, operatic singing, and classical accompaniment.

5 to Listen For
"Some Enchanted Evening"

INSTRUMENTATION
Voice plus full orchestra, with violins and orchestral winds most prominent

PERFORMANCE STYLE
Pinza sings in operatic vocal style.

RHYTHM
Moderately slow two-beat rhythm, but not for dancing

RHYTHM/MELODY
Main melodic idea = "riff-inspired" six-note pattern, but with no syncopation

MELODY
A sections comprised of two long-arching phrases

4 to Remember
"Some Enchanted Evening"

LOVE SONG
Soaring, expansive melody supports "love-at-first-sight" lyric.

CLASSICAL INFLUENCE = UPSCALE POP
Song and performance invest popular song with classical trappings: melody with almost no syncopation, rich harmony, operatic singing, orchestral accompaniment; all suggest alignment with classical music, the most prestigious musical tradition at mid-century.

BIG SONG
Long phrases, individual form, and slow tempo = one statement of form in three + minutes

TURNING BACK THE CLOCK
Musical theater looks back to the musical past (melody-oriented song; classical music) rather than connecting with present to look to future.

As such, it is completely out of step with the more progressive musical developments of the era, such as jazz-influenced pop singing, rhythm and blues, country music, and the mambo. By contrast, Cohan's "Yankee Doodle Boy" was up to date stylistically when it was written. Kern's song "Can't Help Lovin' Dat Man" was not a blues (which would have been more appropriate dramatically but inconceivable in the context of the musical), but it was a bluesy pop song. With Rodgers and Hammerstein, musical theater turned back the clock stylistically, even as most other styles continued along the evolutionary path of the 1920s and '30s. Among the latter was modern jazz.

Modern Jazz

In the first verse of his 1957 hit "Rock and Roll Music," Chuck Berry sings, "I've got no kick against modern jazz/Unless they try to play it too darn fast/And change the beauty of the melody." In these three lines, Berry highlights the salient features of the new jazz style of the late 1940s and 1950s and its reception. Bop, the trend-setting style of the 1940s, often featured performances at breakneck speed ("too darn fast"), with new melodies set

|||||||||||||||||||||||||||||||||||||
"I've got no kick against modern jazz / Unless they try to play it too darn fast / And change the beauty of the melody."
—Chuck Berry, "Rock and Roll Music"

to familiar chord progressions. "Salt Peanuts," the performance discussed in this chapter, moves at a tempo of about 300 beats per minute and features an acrobatic, angular melody that replaces the much simpler Gershwin song "I Got Rhythm" ("change the beauty of the melody"). And, like Berry, many listeners found the modern jazz that emerged after bop to be more accessible when the tempos dropped and the melodies became more tuneful.

Bop: A Music of Liberation. Bop (or bebop) was a radically new jazz style that seemed to appear out of nowhere. It took shape during the early 1940s at Minton's Playhouse, a Harlem jazz club, while a ban on instrumental recording was in effect. When bop musicians finally began recording in 1945, their music touched off a revolution in jazz.

Bop conveyed a new message: liberation. It permeated every aspect of the music and the milieu in which it thrived. The freeing of jazz began with the music itself: the innovations of bebop gave the music and those who played it unprecedented freedom. Its emergence as a commercial music—music played not only for fun but also for enough funds to live on—would play a major role in freeing American culture from the idea that art in music was more or less the exclusive province of European white males. Bebop musicians would comprise the first counterculture, planting the seed for the revolution in mass culture for which rock was the soundtrack.

The musical changes affected virtually every parameter of the music: rhythm, melody, harmony, sound, and texture. Among the most significant innovations were these five:

1. *The emancipation of the rhythm section.* In pre-bop jazz, the almost exclusive rhythmic role of the rhythm section was beatkeeping. In bop, only the bassist consistently marked the beat, with a walking

Jeff DeVries/fstockphoto.com

" *Bebop musicians would comprise the first counterculture, planting the seed for the revolution in mass culture for which rock was the soundtrack.* "

bass line. Pianists "comped." That is, they played chords intermittently to provide accents; these often fell on the offbeats. Drummers transferred the ride pattern from the hi-hat to the ride cymbal, which gave a more continuous sound, and played intermittent, syncopated accents. As a result, both drums and piano (or guitar) were almost completely liberated from the steady timekeeping of swing-era jazz.

2. *Rapid tempos.* Tempo took a quantum leap in bop. One reason for this dramatic jump was simply the exhilaration the musicians felt improvising fluently at such daredevil speeds—bop was the downhill skiing of music. In addition, the brisk tempos were one way of separating musical wheat from the chaff during the after-hours jam sessions: it was bop musicians' most obvious method of excluding those who had not spent enough time in the woodshed to develop their skill.

3. *Asymmetrical, irregular melodic lines.* Much of the repertory of bop musicians consisted of newly composed melodies set to the chord progressions of familiar popular songs and blues. "Salt Peanuts," the example presented in this chapter, is one of countless jazz remakes of George Gershwin's 1930 hit "I Got Rhythm." In bop, the melodies matched the improvisational style of the musicians: bop-style melodic lines typically consist of a stream of fast-moving notes ending on an offbeat accent (be-BOP).

4. *Complex harmony.* Bop musicians enriched the harmonic vocabulary of jazz, interpolating new, more complex chords to the relatively simple harmony of blues and popular song.

5. *An aggressive sonority.* Bop horn players, especially Charlie Parker and Dizzy Gillespie, turned their back on the warm, mellow timbres of swing-era horn players. Parker, in particular, opted for a full but penetrating sound, usually produced with little or no vibrato.

These innovations were the product of a small circle of musicians, including drummers Kenny Clarke and Max Roach, pianists Bud Powell and Thelonius Monk, and trumpeter Dizzy Gillespie. However, the dominant figure in the formation of bop style was a saxophonist named Charlie Parker.

Bird. Charlie Parker (1920–1955), known familiarly as "Bird" (a shortened form of "Yardbird," a nickname he acquired early on) came of age in Kansas City, Missouri, a jazz hotbed in the 1930s. By 1940 he was in New York and had joined with the handful of musicians who would create bebop. By 1945 the small circle of bop musicians were on disc, and Parker would be bop's guiding force for most of his too-short life; he died at an early age from severe substance abuse problems. Heroin was the

CD 2:16

"Salt Peanuts," Dizzy Gillespie (1945). Gillespie, trumpet and vocal; Charlie Parker, alto saxophone; Al Haig, piano; Curly Russell, bass; and Sidney Catlett, drums.

drug of choice for too many jazz musicians; Parker was the most conspicuous casualty.

We hear all of the key features of bop style in a 1945 recording of "Salt Peanuts," a tune written by trumpeter Dizzy Gillespie. It features Gillespie on trumpet and singing the signature riff, plus Parker on alto saxophone, and a rhythm section of piano, bass, and drums.

Bop was a hot music: aggressive sounds and high energy. The first post-bop style to emerge was "cool," which kept the intricacy of bop but took the edge off. One offshoot of cool was "West Coast" jazz, so called because so many of its players were based in Los Angeles or San Francisco. The keepers of the flame were the hard bop musicians of the 1950s, most of them black and based on the East Coast. More than any other, they built on the legacy of Charlie Parker, even as he was wasting away. Bop spawned a broad range of progressive jazz styles, collectively identified as "modern jazz." Most retreated from the high intensity of bop or veered off in another direction. Still, its imprint was evident on virtually all of the new jazz of the early 1950s.

Jazz as Art: The Modern Jazz Quartet. The currently fashionable—and largely accurate—description for jazz is "America's art music," but the definition of jazz as an American art came well after the fact. Armstrong's playing in recordings like "Hotter Than That" evidences the classic measures of artistry: mastery, expressiveness, inspiration, individuality. But it was not regarded as art because it was not like classical music, the one widely accepted art music, and it was heard in speakeasies, not concert halls. Benny Goodman's appearances at Carnegie Hall, with his own bands and as part of the "Spirituals to Swing" series, showcased the artistry of top swing musicians. However, swing as a style was still mainly dance music, despite the work of Goodman, Ellington, and others.

By contrast, bop was an art music from the start. Its originators created a style so novel, so complex, and so technically demanding that when it first became known, only a very few musicians—jazz, popular, or classical—were capable of performing it capably. Its original venues were dingy nightclubs in Harlem and along 52nd Street in New York, a short distance from Carnegie Hall geographically but far away socially and culturally. However, around the time that bop emerged, promoters such as Norman Granz began booking jazz concerts. His "Jazz at the Philharmonic" tours began in 1944 and remained a part of the jazz scene through 1957. In the summers, jazz became outdoor concert music with the creation of

LISTENING GUIDE
CD 2:16 "Salt Peanuts"

STYLE	Bebop	
FORM	Several improvised choruses on a melody based on AABA popular song, with periodic interludes	
0:00	Introduction	
	Drummer plays ride pattern on hi-hat, then other instruments with an introductory figure, plus "Salt Peanuts" three-note riff.	
0:09	Head	
	A	Simple riff, plus "Salt Peanuts" riff
	A (0:19)	Repeated
	B (0:25)	Bridge
	A (0:32)	Back to A
0:38	Interlude	Bop-like melodic line: several fast-moving streams of notes
0:44	Head, repeated with vocal	
	Restatement of the head, with vocal "Salt Peanuts," improvised bridge	
1:11	Interlude 1	A section of head, with just walking bass
1:17	Interlude 2	Angular line with dissonant chords
1:22	Third chorus	
	Piano solo; mainly streams of fast-moving notes; sparse "comping" in lower register.	
1:49	Fourth chorus	
	Parker's solo: note aggressive sax sound, typical bop texture—bass walking, ride pattern on hi-hat plus offbeat accents, piano comping.	
2:16	Interlude	Another interlude, this time with a fast-moving line over a low note on the backbeat
2:22	Fifth chorus	
	Gillespie's trumpet solo, in characteristic bebop style	
2:50	Ending	
	Extended drum solo, followed by introducy horn figure, which now serves as the ending	

jazz festivals. The festival provided a concert-like setting: the focus squarely on the musicians, usually with a large audience in attendance; the outdoor location made it less formal and more relaxed than a traditional concert hall. There were festivals as early as the mid-1940s, but the first annually recurring festival was the Newport (Rhode Island) Jazz Festival, which began in 1954.

The most consciously art-oriented developments in modern jazz were jazz/classical syntheses. These took many forms. Among the most noteworthy were collaborations between Dave Brubeck, Leonard Bernstein, and the New York Philharmonic; a series of albums by Miles Davis and Gil Evans, who had first worked together to create cool jazz; and **third-stream music**,

4 **to Remember**
"Salt Peanuts"

EMANCIPATED RHYTHM SECTION
Liberation of drummer and pianist (chord instrument) from steady timekeeping

AGGRESSIVE SOUND
Both horns have edgy sound; not warm, like swing-era saxophone

VIRTUOSITY
Improvisation at extremely fast tempos a supreme technical challenge

MUSIC FOR LISTENING
Bebop divorces modern jazz from any connection with dance because of fast tempos and prominent syncopation.

5 **to Listen For**
"Salt Peanuts"

INSTRUMENTATION
Alto saxophone, trumpet, piano, string bass, drums

RHYTHM
Walking bass keeps four-beat rhythm at very fast tempo.

RHYTHM
Fast streams of notes with offbeat accents (be-BOP) in improvised solos

MELODY
Bop-style lines in solos and interludes: fast-moving, angular lines

HARMONY
Complex, clashing harmonies in introduction, interludes

Michael Ochs Archives/Getty Images

From the start, the Modern Jazz Quartet presented themselves elegantly. In their publicity photographs, they are dressed in matching suits or formal wear, as befits the elegance of their music.

a concerted effort by the Modern Jazz Quartet, Gunther Schuller, and the Beaux Arts String Quartet to fuse jazz and classical music.

The third-stream experiment was the most extreme expression of the classicizing-jazz approach of the Modern Jazz Quartet (Milt Jackson, vibraphone; John Lewis, piano; Percy Heath, bass; Connie Kay, drums). The original members had worked with Gillespie in the late 1940s. The group came together in 1952; Connie Kay replaced Kenny Clarke, the group's first drummer, in 1955. Beginning with their first recordings, the quartet projected a sound that showed the influence of classical chamber music: more restrained dynamics and more transparent textures, less frenetic tempos, and—above all—the structure provided by John Lewis's compositions.

Lewis's compositions describe a middle ground between a fully composed work like Ellington's "Ko-ko" and Gillespie's approach, which was to supply a new melody for the chord progressions of a familiar song. Lewis not only provides melodic and harmonic material for improvisation, but also controls the environment in which the improvisation takes place by specifying the activities of the supporting musicians. We hear a noteworthy example of this in "Django," one of Lewis's first compositions for the MJQ.

"Django," composed in 1954 and dedicated to the famous Belgian jazz guitarist Django Reinhardt, transcends conventional jazz tunecrafting in three ways: by providing a richer and less predictable chord progression for the improvised

CD 2:17

"Django," John Lewis (1954). The Modern Jazz Quartet.

solos; by creating an arch-like structure around the solos; and by controlling the activity behind the soloists to flesh out the arch. (Although the Modern Jazz Quartet originally recorded the work in 1954, we use a later recording, from a 1960 European concert, because the original recording would not fit on the CD set.)

Modern Jazz = Jazz. Bop was an exclusive music; it required considerable skill of those who played it and commitment from those who listened to it. By 1950 it had given way to a host of jazz styles: west coast, east coast, hard bop, cool—all branches of what was called modern jazz. With the ascent of rock, "modern jazz" was no longer modern. But so many of the innovations of bop—the interplay within the rhythm section, the increased harmonic complexity, an improvisational approach based on flowing streams of notes, performances based on newly composed jazz-oriented melodies or significant adaptation of existing songs—became standard practice and have remained the default jazz style to the present.

Bop and the array of post-bop styles also confirmed jazz as a listening-only music. It was music completely divorced from social dancing, at times because of its tempos, and almost always because of the emancipation of the rhythm section from routine timekeeping and the emphasis on improvisational brilliance rather than tuneful melody.

Pop

World War II was a time of transition in popular song as well as in musical theater. The paradigm is similar: before 1945, we remember the songs; after 1945, we remember the singers. This is not a universal. There are singers active before 1945 whose work we value: Ethel Waters, Astaire, Armstrong, Crosby, Holiday. And there are memorable songs written after 1945. We hear Nat Cole's version of the 1951 song "Unforgettable" very shortly. However, the majority of memorable modern-era songs were composed before 1945, and the majority

Before 1945, we remember the songs; after 1945, we remember the singers.

LISTENING GUIDE
CD 2:17 "Django"

STYLE	Modern jazz	
FORM	Large-scale arch form, with high point in middle; improvisation on an unusually structured four-section chord progression. There is no head, just solos over the progression.	
0:00	Introduction	
	A	Out of tempo
	B (0:13)	In time, but with only the first beat of every four marked
	C (0:25)	The high point of the introduction, and, later, of the composition
0:36	Vibes solo	
	A	Behind vibraphonist Jackson: light comping, bass on only first and third beats, drummer using brushes
	B (0:53)	Bass plays a **pedal point**: a low note repeated on every beat.
	C (1:04)	Bass back to playing on alternate beats
	D (1:09)	New key, riff replaces walking bass line, drummer switches to sticks, plays a shuffle rhythm.
1:20	Vibes solo continues for two more choruses	
		Now typical "modern jazz" rhythm section: bass walking, drummer keeping time on ride cymbal and playing offbeat accents, pianist comping
	(2:04)	Continued increase in activity behind Jackson
2:48	Keystone of the arch	
	The **C** part of the introduction, played twice as fast, is the highpoint of the composition and the bridge between the two solos.	
2:53	Piano solo	
		First statement of the form
	(3:38)	Second statement of the form: gradual slowing down at the end (D section), to return to the tempo of the introduction
4:30	Introduction restated	
	Identical to the opening until the very end	

of memorable modern-era performances of popular songs were recorded after 1945.

Several postwar developments confirm this shift in emphasis. One was the choice of songs to sing. Increasingly pop singers balanced more recent songs with **standards**, the songs of the modern era that have remained popular with singers and their audiences. These are the songs that continue to live on in recordings, films, and live performances. By way of example, Frank Sinatra's recordings for Columbia between 1943 and 1952, which documented the first stage of his career as a solo singer, divide into two comparably sized groups: songs written before 1943 and songs written after 1943.

Another shift was a new generation of singers. Of the top recording artists in the first half of the 1950s, all were singers. Several had begun as band vocalists during the swing era, but only Bing Crosby had a significant career before 1940. Among them were once-popular stars (Kay

Starr and Eddie Fisher—probably best remembered as one of Elizabeth Taylor's many husbands); those who used singing as a stepping stone to careers in television and film (Dinah Shore and Perry Como hosted television shows, Doris Day starred in films); Patti Page, the first country crossover singer; and Dinah Washington, who crossed over from the R&B charts.

A third change was the increased prominence of the singer in recording. Recall that in the late 1920s and 1930s, the majority of pop recordings sandwiched the vocal between instrumental statements of the melody. This practice was turned on its head after World War II. It became far more common to feature the singer exclusively or to use instrumental statements of the melody as an interlude between vocal choruses. Moreover, popular song no longer had to be danceable.

Many of the singers of the postwar era are known mainly by those who grew up during that time or by nostalgia buffs. Others have remained popular to the

5 to Listen For
"Django"

INSTRUMENTATION
Vibraphone, piano, string bass, drums

RHYTHM
Varied timekeeping: from no steady pulse to steady walking bass

RHYTHM
Delicate swing: solos, comping and drum accents create rhythmic play over bass timekeeping.

HARMONY
Long, irregularly patterned progression in multiple keys

TEXTURE
Airy variant of postwar rhythm section interplay: timekeeping in bass and ride pattern; rhythmic play from chord instrument and drums

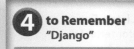

4 to Remember
"Django"

MODERNIZING SWING
Rhythm section = less emphasis on timekeeping, more on rhythmic play (comping, offbeat drum accents)

IMPROVISATION WITHIN COMPOSITION
Arch form, control of activity behind soloists gives performance structure

CONCERT JAZZ
MJQ present themselves as concert performers in appearance, manner, and sound.

TIMELESS JAZZ STYLE
The core features of "Django"—approach to swing rhythm, interplay within rhythm, improvisational approach—become the standard for "straight-ahead" jazz after 1955.

present. Among the most prominent are those we identify as song interpreters.

Song Interpretation

The practice of personalizing a song performance, begun in the 1930s by singers such as Armstrong, Waters, Holiday, and Crosby, became the most enduring approach to popular singing after 1945. Singers like Ella Fitzgerald, Frank Sinatra, and Sarah Vaughan, all of whom had begun their careers as band singers, and Nat Cole, who began his career as a jazz-oriented lounge pianist in the early 1940s, became popular solo artists during the late 1940s and 1950s. A new generation of singing stars, including Tony Bennett and Dinah Washington, joined them. Their recordings remain some of the most treasured pop recordings of the era.

One distinguishing feature of all of these singers is the way in which they put their personal stamp on a song performance: within seconds, we recognize their sound and style. Moreover, they and the arrangers with whom they worked often reconceived the song by changing its underlying rhythm, performing it at a different tempo, or introducing new instrumental colors. As a result, new versions of standards were distinctively different from earlier recordings, and songs introduced by singers like Cole and Sinatra became identified more with the singer than with the songwriter.

Song interpretation begins with a distinctive vocal style. None of the song interpreters has a conventionally pretty voice. For example, Sinatra's voice at the beginning of his career, when he sang with Tommy Dorsey's orchestra, was silkier; he was a real crooner. Years of fast living, cigarettes, and alcohol took away the sweetness and added a heavy dose of grit. Cole's voice was warm and husky from the start.

All are masters of pacing; they are not bound by the beat. Typically, they will, at the very least, mold the song to their style. This often involves reshaping the melody, perhaps with subtle changes in timing to make the delivery of the lyric more speech-like, or even with significant alteration of the contour. Especially with standards, they may reconceive the song completely: an up-tempo song becomes a ballad; a Latin song swings.

All of this transforms the relationship between song and singer. When

> 66 *Their version of a song stands out; it may come to be regarded as the definitive interpretation of the song.* 99

Nat Cole and Frank Sinatra in the late 1940s

Michael Ochs Archives/Getty Images

we listened to Astaire sing "Cheek to Cheek," the focus was on the song. He delivered it impeccably, in a way perfectly suited to his film character, but he did not open a window to his soul. The new generation of popular singers reversed this dynamic. When they sing a song, we sense that they are using the song to share their feelings and life experiences. In so doing they make what is essentially an impersonal song—a song anyone can choose to perform—more personal. Their version of a song stands out; it may come to be regarded as the definitive interpretation of the song.

Two recordings, Nat Cole's recording of "Unforgettable" and Frank Sinatra's version of Cole Porter's 1929 hit "You Do Something to Me," hint at the range of interpretive possibilities. "Unforgettable" was a new song when Cole recorded it. It is more complex and expansive than most pre–World War II songs. Cole's version was so popular that "Unforgettable" in effect became *his* song. Sinatra's rendition jazzes up Porter's song; it is considerably brighter than Marlene Dietrich's sultry version, recorded several years earlier.

The two recordings also demonstrate popular options among song interpreters: lush and lively. Cole performs "Unforgettable" as a **ballad**, a song with a slow, barely danceable tempo. Strings, playing sustained chords, countermelodies, and pizzicato figuration, dominate the accompaniment. By contrast, Sinatra's recording makes clear that swing did not die; it simply moved to the recording studio. It is slightly modernized big-band swing, with the vocal in the forefront.

Nat Cole. Nat "King" Cole (Nathaniel Coles, 1917–1965) parlayed his superb piano-based jazz conception, smoke-filtered voice, and winning personality into a major career. He was the most popular and important black pop artist of the postwar era. Cole formed a piano-guitar-bass jazz trio in 1937, which he continued to lead through 1951. He gradually incorporated vocals into the group's performances. Backed by the trio, he scored his first big hit in 1943 with "Straighten Up and Fly Right," a bouncy song with a cautionary lyric. After the war, he gravitated to the pop marketplace. Recording mainly with a large studio orchestra and supported by lush

"Unforgettable," Irving Gordon (1951). Nat Cole, vocal.

5 to Listen For
"Unforgettable"

INSTRUMENTATION
Voice, plus rhythm section, vibraphone, violins and other strings

PERFORMANCE STYLE
Cole's husky singing; violin pizzicato in instrumental section

RHYTHM
Two-beat rhythm, but with jazz feel

HARMONY
Unusually, song starts and ends in different keys

TEXTURE
Voice, sustained strings, string countermelodies, rhythm section, including piano tinkling

4 to Remember
"Unforgettable"

BALLAD TEMPO
Slow tempo, two-beat rhythm = ideal for romantic dancing

COMPLEX, EXPANSIVE SONG
Melody consists of two long arches (AB, AB[1])

LUSH SETTING
Rich texture, with warm sounds: Cole's singing, violins, plus rhythm and vibraphone occasionally

COLE'S SINGING
Cole's warm, husky voice one of the distinctive vocal styles of the era

arrangements, he produced an almost unbroken string of pop hits, beginning with "(I Love You) For Sentimental Reasons" and "The Christmas Song" (both 1946). A long string of hit songs followed, including "Unforgettable" (1951), the song presented here. The majority were smooth ballads with little obvious jazz influence. However, Cole's singing always evidenced two qualities that betrayed his jazz background: a distinctive sound—one of the most distinctive of the era—and exquisitely subtle timing. We hear both in his recording of "Unforgettable."

During the 1950s, Cole was a frequent guest on the Ed Sullivan show, and became the first black star to host a network television show: his *Nat King Cole Show* ran for a year in 1956 and 1957 before being canceled because of the lack of national sponsors. Cole would die of lung cancer in 1965.

CD 2:18
"You Do Something to Me," Cole Porter (1929). Frank Sinatra, vocal (1950).

Frank Sinatra. Frank Sinatra (1915–1998) was the dominant pop singer of the postwar era. He got his first major break in 1939, when Harry James hired him. Within a few months, he left James for Tommy Dorsey's band, where he recorded the first of his big hits "I'll Never Smile Again" (1940). By 1942 he had become the first of the teen idols—anticipating Elvis by almost

LISTENING GUIDE
CD 2:18 "You Do Something to Me"

STYLE	Jazz-influenced song interpretation
FORM	Three statements of the form: A, A¹, B, A²
0:00	Introduction
	Baritone sax and high brass featured

First statement of form

A (0:09)	You do something to me …	Sinatra's distinctive singing style, supported by
A¹ (0:21)	Tell me, why should …	rhythm section (guitar, bass, drums keep time) plus
B (0:32)	Let me live …	riffs and sustained harmonies from brass and saxes
A² (0:43)	You do something to me …	

Second statement of form

A (0:54)	Muted trumpets play arranged variant of the melody
A¹ (1:05)	
B (1:17)	Improvised saxophone solo
A² (1:28)	Back to brass

Third statement of form

A (1:39)	You do something to me …	Sinatra's second statement of the melody
A¹ (1:51)	Tell me	substantially reworked: more speech-like rhythm,
B (2:03)	Let me live …	more inflection, more deviation from original
A² (2:14)	You do something to me …	melody

fifteen years. During the 1950s, he became one of the biggest stars in the entertainment industry—as a singer, actor, and all-around celebrity. By 1960 he was secure enough in his status to form his own record company, Reprise. Beginning in 1961, he flooded the market with his own albums, all of which charted.

Sinatra did not have Cole's jazz background but, like Crosby, listened carefully to jazz and was comfortable in a jazz setting. His ease is evident in his version of Cole Porter's "You Do Something To Me," which was included on a 1950 album; Sinatra's version swings Porter's sedately sultry foxtrot.

Sinatra would leave Columbia records, for which he had been recording since 1943, shortly after making

5 to Listen For
"You Do Something to Me"

INSTRUMENTATION
Voice plus swing-era-style big band: saxes, trumpets, trombones, plus full rhythm

PERFORMANCE STYLE
Sinatra's gritty crooning, like talking in song

RHYTHM
Bright swing (four-beat) rhythm, clearly marked in rhythm section

RHYTHM
Several kinds of rhythmic play, including strong syncopations in horns and Sinatra's subtle beat-defying timing

TEXTURE
Rich texture: voice/lead instrument plus secondary horn parts (riffs, sustained chords) and rhythm section

4 to Remember
"You Do Something to Me"

SINATRA'S STYLE
Sinatra personalizes songs through distinctive, slightly edgy sound and reshaping of melody

NEW TAKE ON OLD SONG
Porter's sedate fox trot redone as swing-style song

VOCALS IN FOREFRONT
Two vocals frame instrumental chorus.

SWING LIVES ON
Almost every feature of this recording comes from swing era; biggest difference is Sinatra's jazzier singing style.

this recording. He moved to Capitol records, where he joined Nat Cole as a top star. They and a handful of other top singers, most notably Ella Fitzgerald, would set a new standard for pop singing. Their work from this period remains the reference point for the interpretation of modern-era popular song.

From Folk to Pop

Among the most unlikely pop successes of the postwar era were the Weavers. The Weavers grew out of the Almanac Singers, a folk-singing group that included Woody Guthrie, Pete Seeger, Millard Lampell, and Lee Hays. The Almanac Singers were the spiritual forebears of the protest singers of the early 1960s. Politically, they leaned well to the left and advocated isolationism, a path that was rendered moot after Pearl Harbor.

After Woody Guthrie left the Almanac Singers to join the merchant marine in 1943, Seeger and Hays continued to sing together. In 1949, joined by Veronica "Ronnie" Gilbert and Fred Hellerman, they formed the Weavers. They all sang, and the three men played the accompanying instruments, Seeger on the banjo, Kellerman on guitar, and Hays on bass.

The Weavers' breakthrough as a pop act came at the end of 1949 during an engagement at the Village Vanguard, a nightclub in New York. Booked for two weeks, they stayed for six months. They had begun recording for a small independent company, but their success caught the attention of the major record labels. The Weavers eventually signed with Decca Records, where Gordon Jenkins, one of the top pop arrangers of the day, provided lush string backgrounds.

Their first and biggest recording coupled a folklike Israeli song, "Tzena, Tzena," with "Goodnight Irene," a folklike song associated with Lead Belly (see Chapter 6). The song may have been written by the black songwriter Gussie Davis in the late nineteenth century, but Lead Belly learned it from his uncle. "Goodnight Irene" is in the style of a folk ballad, in spirit very much like "Barbara Allen." It is a depressing story of a failed marriage; in one of the verses in Lead Belly's version, Irene seems to be underage when she marries. The story is told in plain language and is sung by Lead Belly in a matter-of-fact manner, with a simple accompaniment on the guitar. The emotional neutrality is in stark contrast with the powerful events in the story.

In this track, we compare Lead Belly's version with the Weavers'. Lead

CD 2:19

"Goodnight Irene," Gussie Davis? Lead Belly, vocal (1936); The Weavers (1950).

Belly's is consistent with traditional folk singing. The guitar accompaniment is simple; the chorus and the verse use just I, IV, V, the three basic chords, in a well-trodden progression. By contrast, the Weavers' version is like dressing a farmer in a tuxedo. Jenkins's syrupy setting, with strings and choir behind the Weavers, clashes with the lyric of the song. The Weavers are somewhat closer in spirit to the folk tradition. Their singing is warm and hearty. It exudes an optimistic, "everything's all right with the world" spirit, which is one source of their appeal. But the close harmony in the chorus and supporting vocals in the verses have more to do with mainstream practice than traditional folk music. (In close harmony singing, the other notes of the chords are near in pitch to the melody note; all parts typically move in the same rhythm.)

The Weavers were the first ambassadors of folk music and the first prominent musical advocates of leftist politics and causes, which made them a target of the McCarthy-era witch-hunts. Although they continued to work through the fifties—a 1955 Carnegie Hall concert was the highpoint—they never recaptured their early success.

The Weavers' importance lies more in their influence than in their music. The folk revival of the late 1950s and early '60s was a revival in two senses. The more obvious was the recapturing and updating of traditional folk music. But it was also a reenergizing of the Weavers' attempt to use the accessibility of folklike music to advance their political and social agenda—to address the inequities of American life and the need for social justice—by taking it to a broader audience. Guthrie was the first to bring folk-style singing into the present; the Weavers were the first to take it to a big audience.

They had another, more long-range impact on popular music, one that would not be fully evident for several decades. Their versions of international folksongs, which find a middle ground between conventional singing and the authentic style of the song, planted the seed that would grow into the world music movement of the latter part of the twentieth century. The Weavers and their music served as a bridge not only between folk traditions and the pop mainstream but also between the social commentaries of Guthrie and important rock-era artists like Bob Dylan and Phil Ochs.

The Weavers' version of "Goodnight Irene" is like dressing a farmer in a tuxedo.

STYLE	Folk ballad/pop version of folk song		
FORM	Verse/chorus		
0:00	First statement of form		
	Chorus	Irene Goodnight (2x) …	Simple lyric asks difficult questions: Who is Irene and where is she?
	Verse (0:25)	Sometimes I live in the country …	Common ballad narrative style: extremely condensed, matter-of-fact style, radical action.
0:48	Second statement of form		
	Chorus	Irene Goodnight (2x) …	As before: simple OOM-pah-pah guitar accompaniment
	Verse (1:08)	Stop rambling, stop your gambling …	Narrator in this verse is unclear: first person or third person?
1:32	Transition to second recording: a pop setting of this folk song. Introduction on Weavers' recording features solo violin playing last part of chorus, then a steady waltz accompaniment.		
1:48	First statement of form		
	Chorus	Irene Goodnight (2x) …	Weavers sing melody and harmony; orchestra replaces guitar accompaniment.
	Chorus (2:08)	Instrumental repetition of chorus	Sumptuous strings and choir, in close harmony
	2:28	Last Saturday night, I got married …	Solo voice, plus vocal harmony and simple accompaniment
2:48	Second statement of form		
	Chorus	Irene Goodnight (2x) …	Choir behind the Weavers
	(3:09)	Sometimes I live in the country …	As in previous verse, but with Ronnie Gilbert (female voice) singing lead

• • • • • • • •

The Sounds of Rhythm and Blues, 1945–1954

Jerry Wexler pretty much got it right. *Rhythm and blues,* the term that he coined to replace "race records," highlights the most significant change in blues-based music after World War II: more rhythm. **Rhythm and blues (R&B)** was not one style but several, most of which had strong beats and made extensive use of blues style and form. The differences among them were, for the most part, more a matter of emphasis and provenance. The roots of electric blues are in the country blues of Robert Johnson and others; much of the "big-beat" music of the postwar era built on the rhythms, riffs, and sounds of big-band swing. The singular important exception was

❸ to Remember
"Goodnight Irene"

BALLAD
A grim story, told succinctly and in fragments

SIMPLE SONG
Both melody and harmony are easy to learn and remember.

FOLK VS. POP
Lead Belly's simple, plain folk style vs. Weavers' hearty harmony + arranger Jenkins's pop sophistication

❺ to Listen For
"Goodnight Irene"

INSTRUMENTATION
Solo voice and guitar; then voices plus plus guitar, bass, violin(s) and choir

RHYTHM
Simple waltz-like accompaniment rhythm, with no syncopation in melody

MELODY
Simple three-phrase melody (short, short, long) in both verse and chorus

HARMONY
Basic chords: I, IV, V

TEXTURE
Simple melody plus accompaniment vs. rich harmonies in voices and/or strings, plus bass/chord instrumental accompaniment

slow doo-wop, which mixed black gospel and pop. We consider three trends in rhythm and blues below and discuss doo-wop in Chapter 9.

Jump Bands

Jump bands stripped down and souped up the sound of big-band swing. They kept the rhythm section but reduced the horn sections drastically, paring down three full sections to a couple of saxophones and a trumpet. Often, they strengthened the beat by converting the four-beat swing rhythm to a shuffle. They built songs on repeated riffs, usually over a blues or blues-based form. The songs typically took a medium tempo because shuffle rhythm put the more frenetic swing tempos out of reach. Jump bands also emphasized singing more

CD 2:20

"Choo Choo Ch'Boogie," Louis Jordan (1946). Louis Jordan and His Tympany Five.

than swing had. The vocalist was the key figure in the group, and the lyrics typically told a funny story or allowed the singer to brag a little, or both. A blend of hokum, boogie-woogie, and big-band swing, jump-band music was different from all of them.

"Choo Choo Ch'Boogie," was a big hit in 1946 for Louis Jordan and His Tympany Five. Louis Jordan (1908–1975) first made his mark as a saxophonist in Chick Webb's fine swing band. He played for Webb from 1936 through 1938, then formed his own smaller group a year later. Unlike many later rhythm-and-blues artists, Jordan got a record deal with a major label, Decca, with

LISTENING GUIDE
CD 2:20 "Choo Choo Ch'Boogie"

STYLE	Jump-band song
FORM	Blues-based verse/chorus form. Verse contains six two-bar phrases over blues progression; chorus is last eight bars of blues progression.
0:00	Intro
	Mixed horns (trumpets and saxophones) act as a single section. Riffs over blues harmonic progression.

First statement of form

0:17	Verse	
	Headin' for the station …	Uses 12-bar blues progression but has six lines of text instead of three
0:34	Chorus	
	Choo choo …	Last eight bars of blues progression
0:45	Instrumental interlude	
	Piano solo, boogie-woogie style, based on 12-bar blues progression; shuffle rhythm in the left hand	

Second statement of form

1:02	Verse	
	You reach your destination …	As before
1:19	Chorus	
	Choo choo …	As before

Third statement of form

1:30	Verse and Chorus 1
	Jordan's sax solo (verse and chorus). Jordan builds his solo out of a series of riffs. Background riffs by the horns.

Fourth statement of form

1:59	Verse
	I'm gonna settle down …
2:14	Chorus 1
	Choo choo …
	Tag (2:26)

5 to Listen For
"Choo Choo Ch'Boogie"

INSTRUMENTATION
Vocal, rhythm section (piano, bass, drums—using brushes—and guitar), and small horn section

RHYTHM
Shuffle rhythm (intensified four-beat rhythm),with a light backbeat

RHYTHM
Vocal and horn parts move in tandem with shuffle rhythm, with occasional strong syncopation

HARMONY
Blues progression in verse; chorus = last two-thirds of a blues chorus (IV-I-V-I)

TEXTURE
Melody plus background riffs and rhythmic accompaniment during vocals

5 to Remember
"Choo Choo Ch'Boogie"

JUMP BAND
Essentially a streamlined swing band: a full rhythm section plus a mixed horn section—trumpet(s) and saxophones.

SHUFFLE RHYTHM
Long/short division of each beat intensifies swing rhythm.

RIFF-HEAVY MELODY:
Both vocal line and solos are built mainly from riffs.

FLEXIBILITY OF BLUES FORM
Another verse/chorus blues: blues progression in verse; last two-thirds of progression in chorus

TRAINS
Popularity of trains in black music reflects not only the useful sounds but also their importance to transportation at mid-century.

of fellow. (The wanderer has pretty much disappeared from our twenty-first-century lives, but even a half century ago, hoboes—men who "rode the rails" from place to place [stowed away on trains], working odd jobs in exchange for food, a roof, and maybe a little cash, or simply begging—were more common. Their mystique, a hold-over from the Great Depression, was still powerful.) The music—with its bouncy shuffle beat, catchy riffs (not only in the vocal parts but also in both the piano and the sax solos), and pleasant vocal style—helps capture the mood of the lyric.

This became the formula for Jordan and many of the jump bands that followed him. One reason for the increasing appeal of these songs, to black Americans and gradually to whites as well, was the easy points of entry: upbeat lyrics; repeated riffs, either sung or played on a honking saxophone; a clear beat, usually in a shuffle rhythm; and a chorus-based form. Among the first artists to capitalize on R&B's newly gained accessibility was Ruth Brown.

Ruth Brown

Ruth Brown (1928–2006) was arguably the top female R&B performer of the early 1950s: between 1950 and 1954, she had five No. 1 hits on the R&B charts. Only Dinah Washington, a more pop-oriented singer, was a serious competitor. More than any other artist on their roster, Brown helped Atlantic Records, who had signed her in 1948, grow from a struggling indie startup to a major player in the rhythm and blues market.

Brown earned the label "Miss Rhythm" on the strength of her medium and uptempo hits. She sang with a hoarse voice, occasionally interjecting squeaks and moans at the ends of phrases, and delivered the lyrics either with emphasis on the beat as a prelude to a strong syncopation, or with the rhythmically free, speech-like phrasing of good blues singers. Her singing was an ideal complement to the propulsive rhythms and aggressive, bluesy horn sounds of the instrumental accompaniment.

CD 2:21

"Mama, He Treats Your Daughter Mean," Herbert Lance, Charles Singleton and Johnny Wallace (1953). Ruth Brown, vocal.

whom he signed a contract in 1939. This undoubtedly helped build his audience.

The song begins with the pianist laying down a boogie-woogie bass while the horns play a simple riff. The first part of Jordan's vocal is a series of six short phrases, all of which rhyme and all of which develop from a simple repeated riff. Although the words happen over a blues harmonic progression, they do not follow the standard form of the blues lyric. Instead, they serve as a storytelling verse to the catchy chorus that follows. The theme, of course, is life on the railroad—certainly a common topic for songs of that era. (Note the reference to "ballin' the jack," that is, getting the train moving.) As with "Maybellene" (Chapter 1), "Choo Choo Ch'Boogie" adapts the conventional blues form to a verse/chorus pattern; the hook of the chorus provides an easy point of entry into the song.

In a jump band like Louis Jordan and His Tympany Five, the roles of the musicians are clearly defined: the bass walks; the drummer plays a shuffle beat; the guitar and/or the piano also helps keep the beat—the pianist may also play fills and solo; the saxophone honks riffs, either behind the vocalist, in response to him, or in a solo; and the other horns join the sax in creating harmonized response riffs. There is a clear hierarchy.

The tone of the lyric is humorous and self-deprecating; we sense that the "I" in the song is a happy-go-lucky kind

Her third No. 1 R&B hit, "Mama, He Treats Your Daughter Mean" (1953), was the first to cross over to

LISTENING GUIDE
CD 2:21 "Mama, He Treats Your Daughter Mean"

STYLE	1950s rhythm and blues
FORM	Blues-based verse/chorus form. The chorus expands 12-bar blues form by repeating the first phrase: A A¹ A B. The verse consists of short phrase.

0:00	Introduction			
	Swing ride pattern tapped out on the tambourine, with emphasis on the backbeat			
0:11	Chorus			
	A	Mama he treats your daughter mean	First line	
	A¹	Mama he treats …	First line repeated, with different harmony	
	A	Mama he treats …	Surprise! First line restated.	
	B	He's the meanest man …	Answering phrase in typical 12-bar blues	
0:43	Verse 1			
		Mama he treats me badly …	Brown tells her tale of woe over simple alternation of I and IV.	
	(0:58)	Mama he can't be trusted …	The story continues, breaking only at the end to lead back to the chorus.	
1:14	Chorus			
		Mama he treats your daughter mean …	Horn riffs respond to vocal; intermittent triplets in guitar and piano underneath	
1:45	Verse 2			
		Mama this man is lazy …	As before	
2:16	Chorus			
	Chorus	Mama he treats your daughter mean …	A different response riff in the horns	

the pop charts (it would reach No. 23). Its success can be explained in part by a lyric that gives a good account of a no-account man. It was a woman's response to the male posturing found in so many R&B songs of the era.

The rhythmic texture shows a different aspect of rhythmic rhythm and blues. The point of departure of the rhythms of post rhythm and blues was the four-beat rhythm of swing. To make the rhythm stronger and more active, R&B musicians used one or more of the following strategies: more emphasis on the backbeat; a shuffle rhythm in place of a regular swing rhythm; and triplets, rhythmic activity that divides each beat into three equal parts. "Choo Choo Ch'Boogie" featured a shuffle rhythm; "Mama, He Treats Your Daughter Mean" features a strong backbeat, emphasized on the tambourine and drums, and triplets, played intermittently by both electric guitar and piano.

 3 to Remember
"Mama, He Treats Your Daughter Mean"

INFLUENTIAL VOCAL STYLE
Brown's singing, with its rough timbre and occasional squeaks, would influence Little Richard, and through him, rock and soul.

FLEXIBILITY OF BLUES FORM
A verse/chorus blues, with chorus using expanded blues form and verses building section from repeated riff in vocal

RHYTHM IN FOREFRONT
Strong backbeat and beat, frequent triplets, and Brown's occasional heavy accents, put beat and syncopations in forefront.

 5 to Listen For
"Mama, He Treats Your Daughter Mean"

INSTRUMENTATION
Standard R&B instrumentation: vocal, plus full rhythm section, including electric guitar, plus small horn section

PERFORMANCE STYLE
Brown's hoarse vocal style, with bent notes, squeaks, and other effects

RHYTHM
Strong, active rhythms, including occasional triplets, at a moderate tempo

HARMONY
Modified blues progression in chorus; mainly I/IV alternation in verse

TEXTURE
Frequent call and response, especially in the last two choruses

Brown would have more crossover hits in the latter part of the 1950s; her success was one of several signs of more widespread enthusiasm for black music. She retired briefly in the 1960s, then made a comeback in the 1970s not only as a singer but also as an actress in film, television, and on Broadway.

Electric Blues

Attend any of the many blues festivals throughout North America and you will hear band after band take the stage. Most will feature a full rhythm section with one or more electric guitars; horns are optional. For most contemporary listeners, this is the sound of the blues, the classic blues style that has remained largely unchanged for half a century. The basic sound of these bands is unlike the blues of the twenties and thirties, and it's different from the rhythm and blues that we've just heard. It came together in the early fifties, when deep blues moved north from Mississippi to Chicago and went electric.

Electrifying the Blues. The electric guitar, already a staple in country music and jazz by the early forties, soon began to find its way into the blues. Muddy Waters began playing electric guitar in 1944 so that he could be heard over the crowd noise in the bars where he performed; others followed suit. At the same time, bluesmen like Waters surrounded themselves with other instrumentalists—another guitarist, a drummer, a bass player, and in Waters's case, Little Walter, the soulful master of the harmonica. This new sound has been called electric blues; now it is just the blues.

Electric blues came of age in the fifties. It completed its transformation from a rural to an urban music and its migration from the juke joints and street corners of Mississippi to the bars of Chicago's South Side. Blues kept its soul through the journey, most notably in the music of Muddy Waters.

Muddy Waters. Muddy Waters (1915–1983), born McKinley Morganfield, grew up in Clarksdale, Mississippi, the northwest part of the state in the heart of what is called the Delta region. The population was mostly black, and for the vast majority, life was brutal. Both males and females worked as sharecroppers, often from childhood; Waters was a farm laborer as a boy. Some men made a little more money working as stevedores loading riverboats along the Mississippi, but there too the days were long, the work hard, and the pay meager. Most lived at subsistence level, trapped in an unending cycle of economic dependence. From this harsh and isolated environment came what Robert Palmer called deep blues, a powerful music that gave expression to, and release from, the brutal conditions of the Delta.

Waters heard this music while he was growing up and began to play it in his teens. He started on the harmonica, then took up the guitar, because, "You see, I was digging Son House and Robert Johnson." By his late twenties, Waters had become a popular performer in the region.

Like many other southern blacks, Waters moved north during World War II, settling on Chicago's South Side. He continued to play, first at house parties, then in small bars, and recorded for Columbia in 1946. (The recordings were not released until many years later.) Still, it was not enough to pay the rent, and Waters was working as a truck driver when he approached Aristocrat Records about recording for them.

The Sound of Electric Blues. Muddy Waters's singing and playing retained its earthiness and passion after he moved north; he added the power of amplification and a full rhythm section during his first years in Chicago. Both voice and guitar gained a presence not possible with the "man and his guitar" setup of country blues.

In the music of Waters and other like-minded Chicago bluesmen, electric blues found its groove during the fifties. By the end of the decade, it had evolved into its classic sound, which it has retained to this day. Its most consistent features include:

- Regular blues form (or an easily recognized variant of it)
- Rough-edged vocals
- Vocal-like responses and solos from the lead guitar or harmonica
- A dense texture, with several instruments playing melody-like lines behind the singer

IIIIIIIIIIIIIIIIIIIIIIIIIIIIIIIIIIIIIII

"It's real. Muddy's real. See the way he plays guitar? Mississippi style, not the city way."
—Big Bill Broonzy

John Cohen/Getty Images

- A rhythm section laying down a strong beat, usually some form of the shuffle rhythm popularized in forties rhythm and blues

CD 2:22

"(I'm Your) Hoochie Coochie Man," Willie Dixon (1954). Muddy Waters, guitar and vocal; Little Walter, harmonica; Willie Dixon, bass; Jimmy Rogers, guitar; Otis Spann, piano; and Fred Below, drums.

Its stars attracted a loyal following, mostly in the black community. Records by Muddy Waters, B. B. King, Howlin' Wolf, Lowell Fulson, Elmore James, and Bobby Bland consistently found their way onto the R&B charts. They were not as well known as the pop-oriented groups, but far better known—within and outside the black community—than their country kin from previous generations. We hear a famous example of this sound next.

"(I'm Your) Hoochie Coochie Man," the 1954 recording that was Muddy Waters's biggest hit, epitomizes the fully transformed electric blues style. It retains the essence of country blues in Waters's singing and playing yet creates a far richer and more powerful sound than we heard in Robert Johnson's blues. Blues singer Big Bill Broonzy described Waters's appeal in this way:

It's real. Muddy's real. See the way he plays guitar? Mississippi style, not the city way. He don't play chords, he don't follow what's written down in the book. He plays notes, all blue notes. Making what he's thinking.

Willie Dixon's lyrics makes references to love potions and voodoo charms, sexual prowess and special status; Waters's singing makes them credible. It is easy to conjure up such a world and envision him as the hoochie-coochie man. That much remained virtually unchanged from the rawest country blues of the twenties and thirties. Plugging in and adding a rhythm section simply amplified the impact of the message.

The song alternates between two textures: the stop time of the opening (an enormous expansion of the first four bars of the standard 12-bar blues form), where an instrumental riff periodically punctuates Waters's vocal line, and the free-for-all of the refrain-like finish of each chorus. The stop-time opening contains two competing riffs—one played by the harmonica, the other by the electric guitar. In the chorus, everybody plays—harmonica trills; guitar riffs; piano chords, either lazy Fats Domino– style triplets or on speed; thumping bass; shuffle pattern on the drums—all are woven together with Muddy's singing.

LISTENING GUIDE
CD 2:22 "(I'm Your) Hoochie Coochie Man"

STYLE	Electric blues		
FORM	Modified blues form: first phrase is doubled in length; it serves as a verse; last two phrases are the refrain.		
0:00	Introduction		
	The stop-time riff, with harmonica the lead instrument		
0:08	First Chorus		
	Verse	The gypsy woman told my mother …	All of this happens over repeated riff built on pentatonic scale associated with I chord.
	Refrain (0:35)	But you know I'm him …	Move to IV chord signals shift to the refrain part of form.
	(0:48)	Well, you know I'm the hoochie coochie man …	Punch line of refrain coincides with move to V chord.
1:01	Second Chorus		
	Verse	I got a black cat bone, I got a mojo too I got the John, the Conqueroo …	Band uses stop time to highlight vocal during the verse segment; the refrain is a free-for-all, with harmonica, piano (in a high register), and guitars all playing active parts behind the vocal. Steady shuffle rhythm underneath Waters, piano triplets.
	Refrain (1:28)	But you know I'm him …	
1:55	Third Chorus		
	Verse	On the seventh hour on the seventh day …	As before

5 **to Listen For**
"(I'm Your) Hoochie Coochie Man"

INSTRUMENTATION
Vocal, electric guitars, harmonica, piano, bass, and drums

PERFORMANCE STYLE
Waters sings passionately, with great rhythmic freedom, over both the stop time and strong, active rhythm.

RHYTHM
Strong contrast between stop time in verse section and shuffle + triplet rhythm in the refrain segment, all at slow tempo

HARMONY
Blues progression with first phrase expanded to eight bars on I chord

TEXTURE
Dense, dark sound, from several instruments active in low and mid register

4 **to Remember**
"(I'm Your) Hoochie Coochie Man"

EXPANDED BLUES FORM
The first phrase is twice as long as in a conventional blues; the last two phrases serve as a refrain.

VOCAL-LIKE RESPONSES AND SOLOS FROM LEAD GUITAR AND HARMONICA
In particular, harmonica player Little Walter almost sings through his instrument.

RHYTHMIC CONTRASTS
Stop-time at beginning of each chorus; rhythm guitar and drums lay down a strong shuffle rhythm, piano adds triplets, over which Waters's vocal and Walter's harmonica soar freely.

BLUES AS "REAL" MUSIC
Waters's singing is especially passionate in the refrain-like part of the song; Little Walter's harmonica mimics vocal style; rhythm instruments add to impact.

Country Music After 1945

The proliferation of *Billboard* "folk" charts during the late 1940s and early 1950s—one each for radio airplay, jukeboxes, and record sales—indicated the growing and broadening audience for country music. Other clues include the offer of a movie contract to Hank Williams (who died before he could fulfill it) and cover versions (recordings of a song by acts other than the first to record it) of country hits by pop artists. Patti Page's 1950 version of Pee Wee King's "Tennessee Waltz" was a huge hit, with sales of more than 6 million records; it was the most popular of several pop makeovers of country songs.

Among the reasons for the growth of country music was the continuing migration of people from the South and Southwest to other parts of the country. This had begun in the 1930s, particularly in the Southwest, during the Dust Bowl, and continued when those in the military returned home from the war. Another was the change in the music itself. The dominant new sound in country music after 1945 was honky-tonk. It borrowed from pop and black music, which moved the sound closer to mainstream music, and redefined country music in the process.

The electric blues of the fifties brought nastier guitar sounds into popular music.

These different melodic and rhythmic strands are an important part of the mix, but none is capable of standing alone. This kind of dense texture, with independent but interdependent lines, was almost unprecedented in small-group music before rock. The closest parallel would be early New Orleans jazz band recordings, such as those by King Oliver. And it works. No one gets in anyone else's way. There is no stylistic inconsistency, as is so often the case when country blues singing is mixed with horns or strings.

The electric blues of the fifties brought nastier guitar sounds into popular music. The overdriven guitar sounds that jumped off numerous blues records were intentional. Almost as soon as they went electric, blues guitarists began to experiment with distortion in order to get a guitar sound that paralleled the rawness of singers like Muddy Waters and Howlin' Wolf. Among the leaders in this direction were Buddy Guy and Elmore James, both based in Chicago through much of the fifties.

Hank Williams and the Redefinition of Country Music

A *honky-tonk* is a working-class bar. Honky-tonks catering to white audiences typically featured country music, often performed by a live band. After the repeal of Prohibition in 1933, bars and dance halls catering to a working-class clientele sprang up all over the South and the Southwest, but particularly in Texas and Oklahoma. These bars were usually rough, noisy establishments, and musicians who performed in them needed a musical style that could be heard above the din. At the same time, their songs needed to articulate the problems and pleasures of the audience. Most of the traditional country repertoire, particularly sentimental or religious

Allison Murray/istockphoto.com

songs, would have been wildly inappropriate for a honky-tonk. Out of this environment came a new kind of country music, called (appropriately enough) **honky-tonk**. By the early 1940s, it had taken shape, and by the end of the decade it had become the most popular style in country music.

One big reason for its success was Hank Williams (1923–1953), the quintessential country singer. Williams was born into a poor family in rural Alabama. While still in his teens, he performed in rough honky-tonks near his home and later in southern Alabama. His career received a boost from Fred Rose, a Nashville-based pianist, songwriter, and music publisher and one of the most successful promoters in the history of country music. Williams gained widespread exposure throughout the South and the Southwest through appearances on the *Louisiana Hayride* and the *Grand Ole Opry.*

Williams suffered from spina bifida, a birth defect affecting his back. Throughout his life he was in constant pain, which may have contributed to his alcoholism and which cost him his life before his thirtieth birthday. At the time of his death, he was the dominant figure in country music and the standard-bearer for the new sound of country music. A song that provided a major stepping-stone in his rise to the top was "Lovesick Blues," his first big hit.

Williams recorded "Lovesick Blues" late in 1948 over the strong objections

CD 2:23

"Lovesick Blues," Irving Mills and Cliff Friend (1948). Hank Williams, vocal.

Williams referred to his own singing as "moanin' the blues."

Michael Ochs Archives/Getty Images

of Fred Rose and the backup musicians. "Lovesick Blues" was a curious choice for Williams, who typically recorded his own songs. It was a pop song from the early 1920s that had been recorded by Emmett Miller, one of the last blackface minstrels. Miller's 1929 recording of the song, on which he was backed by some of the top white jazz musicians of the day, was familiar to country audiences. Williams essentially copied Miller's version, including his yodels and occasional dropped beats; his instrumental accompaniment was a modern country band, with full rhythm and steel guitar, instead of a jazz band.

Williams's remake of "Lovesick Blues" is a more modern version of an established country practice: redoing an old pop song in a country style. Recall that the Carter family's "Wildwood Flower" was a reworking of a nineteenth century parlor song; Williams simply takes advantage of recording technology to revive "Lovesick Blues," giving it a country sound and feel that the original did not have.

The song was Williams's ticket to an appearance on *Grand Ole Opry.* As Bob Wills discovered, the Opry management resisted non-country elements like drums. Williams's electrifying performance of "Lovesick Blues" earned him six encores and effectively washed away any significant resistance to the modern sound of honky-tonk.

In "Lovesick Blues" (1949), we hear many of the elements that define the new sound in country music. The band behind Williams includes a full rhythm section, including drums, plus the "newly traditional" country instrument, the steel guitar. They lay down a two-beat rhythm with a crisp backbeat; it is in essence a country take on the foxtrot. (We heard this rhythm previously in Bob Wills's "Steel Guitar Rag.")

Williams's singing also blends old and new. It has a uniquely country timbre. It is thin, nasal, and flat yet intensely expressive, as plaintive or high-spirited as the song demands. It is also tinged by the blues that Williams heard from street-corner blues singers when he was growing up. In particular, he credited Rufus Payne, a local blues singer whom he

LISTENING GUIDE
CD 2:23 *"Lovesick Blues"*

STYLE	Honky-tonk		
FORM	Verse/chorus song, verse heard only once and chorus repeated, chorus ABAC		
0:00	Introduction		
	Country-style rhythm section: bass, guitar, mandolin, drums (using brushes)—lay down a country-style two-beat rhythm behind the lead guitar and steel guitar.		
0:08	Chorus		
	A	I got a feelin' called the blu-ues, oh, Lawd	Williams's distinctive vocal sound: no vibrato, lots of inflection, an occasional yodel
	B (0:23)	That last long day she said goodbye …	
	A (0:58)	Sweet dad-ad-ad-dy, such a beautiful dream …	Responses from steel guitar shows influence of blues and swing
	C (0:52)	I've grown so used to you somehow.	
1:08	Verse		
		Well, I'm in love, I'm in love, with a beautiful gal …	This is a verse-like section. It is interpolated between choruses, as was the practice in 1920s pop.
	1:23	Lawd, I tried and I tried, to keep her satisfied …	
1:39	Chorus		
	A	I got a feelin' called the blu-ues, oh, Lawd …	On several occasions, Williams shortens the measures from two beats to one (like Rodgers in "Blue Yodel").
	B	That last long day she said goodbye….	
	A	Sweet dad-ad-ad-dy, such a beautiful dream …	Williams sings with an easy swing, showing influence of western swing and blues.
	C	I've grown so used to you somehow.	

befriended, with giving him "all the music training I ever had." Indeed, Williams referred to his own singing as "moanin' the blues." This fusion of country and blues was Williams's own synthesis, one that made him perhaps the most easily recognized singer in country music.

Even more important, Williams unlocked the expressive potential of country music. Like Billie Holiday and Frank Sinatra, he is one of the great song interpreters. The intensity of Williams's rendition invests this rather humdrum song with real feeling. He conveys it with the inherent fragility of his vocal sound—it comes close to breaking several times—emphatic inflection of the lyric, and the plaintive quality with which he sings the longer notes in the melody.

In large part because of Williams, honky-tonk quickly became an important country style after World War II.

5 to Listen For
"Lovesick Blues"

INSTRUMENTATION
Voice, plus electric guitar, steel guitar, mandolin, string bass, and drums

PERFORMANCE STYLE
Williams's patented "moanin' the blues": blues-tinged country vocal style, with occasional yodel via Jimmie Rodgers

RHYTHM
Honky-tonk beat = countrified two-beat rhythm

HARMONY
Harmony closer to early twentieth-century songs (like "Take Me Out to the Ball Game") than to typical three-chord country song

TEXTURE
Melody with simple accompaniment, plus responses from steel guitar

3 to Remember
"Lovesick Blues"

MOANIN' THE BLUES
Williams sings with a characteristic country twang, but with a grittiness that shows blues influence.

HONKY-TONK SOUND
Full, discreet rhythm section laying down a two-beat rhythm, plus steel guitar and electric guitar lead

COUNTRIFYING POP AND BLUES
Williams's first big hit was a cover of a 1920s pop song, not an original composition.

A host of new singing stars emerged: Lefty Frizzell, Hank Thompson, Patsy Cline, Ray Price, and more. Most remain well known and well loved. Among the brightest new stars was a reluctant feminist, Kitty Wells.

Kitty Wells and the Heart of Country Music

Kitty Wells (b. Muriel Deason, 1919) had been on the fringes of country music for almost two decades when she was persuaded to record an "answer" song to Hank Thompson's "The Wild Side of Life," a No. 1 country hit for him in 1952. In the song, Thompson proclaimed his true love to a "honky-tonk angel," a woman who rejected him so that she could return to the "glamor of the gay night life." The song all but demanded a rebuttal, which was written by J. D. Miller; Miller took the title "It Wasn't God

CD 2:24

"It Wasn't God Who Made Honky Tonk Angels," J. D. Miller (1952). Kitty Wells, vocal.

Who Made Honky Tonk Angels" from a line in the lyric of Thompson's song.

By 1952 Wells's career had been stuck in neutral for more than a decade. She was married to Johnnie Wright, a popular country singer, but had not made much of an impact on her own; a four-year tenure at RCA had produced nothing of note. She had just signed on with Decca records in 1952 when Paul Cohen, a Decca executive, approached her about recording the song. Perhaps enticed by the $125 she would receive for the recording, she overcame her initial reservations and made history in the process. The recording sold 800,000 copies, topped the *Billboard* country chart, and crossed over to the pop charts, which made her the first female solo country artist to do so and made her one of the top stars of country music.

Several features of the song stand out: the primacy of the lyric and the role of music in supporting it, the sincerity and lack of artifice in Wells's singing, and the newly traditional sound of the accompanying instruments.

LISTENING GUIDE
CD 2:24 "It Wasn't God Who Made Honky Tonk Angels"

STYLE	Honky-tonk		
FORM	Verse/chorus song: both verse and chorus use same melody; words remain same in chorus, differ in verse. Form of melody = A A¹		
0:00	Introduction		
	Steel guitar featured instrument		
0:07	Verse		
	A	As I sit here tonight the jukebox playin'…	Simple, familiar song puts focus on the words. Wells delivers lyric plainly and comprehensibly
	A¹	As I listen to the words you are sayin'…	
0:34	Chorus		
	A	It wasn't God who made Honky Tonk Angels…	Same melody as verse; it becomes chorus because lyrics are repeated
	A¹	Too many times married men think they're still single…	
1:08	Instrumental interlude		
	1:23	Fiddle plays varied version of melody: occasional elaborations, harmonized alternately above and below; characteristic country fiddle style, ca. 1950 (compare to Ben Jarrell).	
1:31	Verse		
		It's a shame that all the blame is on us women…	A strong statement in 1952
		From the start most every heart that's ever broken…	
1:59	Chorus		
	A	It wasn't God who made Honky Tonk Angels…	As before
	A¹	Too many times married men think they're still single….	

5 to Listen For
"It Wasn't God Who Made
Honky Tonk Angels"

INSTRUMENTATION
Voice, plus fiddle, steel guitar, and guitar/
bass/drums rhythm section

PERFORMANCE STYLE
Typical country sounds: flat, clear vocal;
flat, clear fiddle playing—no vibrato
or special sounds, but with double
notes

RHYTHM
Steady two-beat rhythm with crisp
backbeat on guitar and drums

MELODY
Four phrases of moderate length

HARMONY
Simple progression over and over:
I-IV-V-I

4 to Remember
"It Wasn't God Who Made
Honky Tonk Angels"

WORDS IN FOREFRONT
Wells sings with a plain, sincere sound:
no vibrato, no inflection, no affectation
or special effects; it makes words easy to
understand.

HONKY-TONK SOUND
The now-traditional sound of honky-tonk:
full rhythm playing a two-beat rhythm
with a crisp backbeat; steel guitar and
fiddle as dominant instrumental sounds

SONG RECYCLING
Wells's answer song fits new words to
Thompson's song, which is in turn based
on sacred song "Great Speckled Bird"
sung by Acuff.

COMMONSENSE FEMINISM
Pointing out the obvious—a courageous
stance for Wells in male-dominated
country music

The song is a modern (for 1952) version of a long-established practice in British and American music: fitting new words to old songs. Thomas Moore had gentrified the practice with his *Irish Melodies*. In 1831 Samuel Francis Smith had given "God Save the King," the British national anthem, new words; Americans know the song as "My Country 'Tis of Thee." Woody Guthrie had given several old songs new lyrics. Thompson continued this practice by using the melody of "Great Speckled Bird," a white gospel song recorded by Roy Acuff in 1936. Miller's reuse of Thompson's melody was an obvious way of highlighting the fact that "It Wasn't God Who Made Honky Tonk Angels" was an answer song.

The use of a familiar melody shifts the spotlight to the words, which asserts that men are far more likely to be unfaithful than women. Wells's singing, with its plain, honest timbre and straightforward delivery of the words, underscores the message. It resonated with everyone: audiences, industry executives and producers, and musicians and songwriters: Wells had opened the door for a generation of female country singing stars.

The frankness of the song and Wells's singing of it is in sharp contrast to the popular music of the era. There is no stardust in her eyes. Rather, it is as if she's sitting with you at the kitchen table, pouring her heart out. In this respect, it's like the blues. However, because there is comparatively little musical interest—the melody is short and repetitive, its harmony is similarly simple, and the accompaniment is unobtrusive—there is even more focus on lyric; the music enhances the storytelling, rather than deflecting attention from it.

The Sound of Honky-Tonk

In 1950 honky-tonk was the avant-garde of country music. Almost overnight, it became the country music's traditional, almost timeless style. Its chief musical features remain the key qualities of country music today, the ones that preserve its identity:

- Song texts that speak plainly and personally about everyday life: love, alcohol, hard times, loneliness, work, or life on the road
- A nasal, often twangy vocal style
- Straightforward melodies, delivered plainly and directly with simple accompaniments, usually built from the three basic chords: I, IV, and V
- The old and new country instruments: fiddle and steel guitar
- A full rhythm section playing a countrified version of a popular dance beat

With honky-tonk, country music redefined itself. For the most part, it abandoned the old-time roots of its prerecording past. The two clearest links to its heritage were the singing and the fiddle playing. Still, the expressive intent in the singing was more personal, its vocal sound showing influences of blues and pop. And the fiddle playing lost its rough edges. Everything else about honky-tonk was new: the full rhythm section, the honky-tonk beat, and the steel guitar. Country songs were freshly written and had contemporary themes. The music's more distant past became a much dimmer, almost forgotten memory.

Wells's recording obliquely shows country music gravitating toward the mainstream. Her singing is pure country; it resembles the singing of Rebecca Tarwater (who sang "Barbara Allen") and Maybelle Carter far more than it does any other female vocalist heard in this survey. But she is backed by a band with a full rhythm section, rather than just guitar—or singing without accompaniment. As a result, even listeners unfamiliar with pure country singing would be able to relate to the dance rhythm supporting it.

Honky-tonk was part of a larger movement within country music to shift toward the mainstream. Other trends included the "Nashville sound," which featured a wholesale infusion of pop elements—strings, choirs, smooth-voiced singers; and rockabilly, a country take on rhythm and blues.

● ● ● ● ● ● ● ●
Looking Back, Looking Ahead

This chapter, the midpoint in our survey, complements the previous chapters in that it presents a wide range of music within a narrow time span rather than focusing on particular genres over a longer period of time. It lets us immerse ourselves in a musical world much like our own in several respects.

Among the outstanding features of American musical life in the decade after World War II was its unprecedented diversity. Never before had such a broad range of music been so accessible, as the following list evidences.

Add to that list uptown and commercial Latin music—most notably the mambo style heard in Puente's music, many more pop singing styles, doo-wop, cool and West Coast jazz, plus still popular legacy styles, like swing and sweet—and listeners around 1950 had much to choose from. The patchwork quilt that is our current popular music landscape represents an expansion of this diversity on a global scale.

As we look back on this music a half-century later, what stands out is the timelessness of so much of it. It was in this postwar era that the "classic" styles in each tradition were established: song interpretation, electric blues, modern jazz, honky-tonk, bluegrass, and mambo, which became salsa. Moreover, the musicals from this time are classics, the heart of the musical theater repertory. All of this has remained substantially unchanged to the present. There have been new generations of artists working in these established styles—oftentimes alongside established artists—but there have not been substantive changes within the styles themselves.

At the same time, we sense the emergence of a new kind of music: "outsider" styles—blues, R&B, country, and Latin music—were already laying the foundation for the rock revolution. What stands out about all these styles is the fact that so much of their essence was maintained in the music that gained a toehold in the pop market. Granted, there were pop covers of much of this music, and most were more popular than the authentic

Year	Track	Artist	Style
1945	"Salt Peanuts"	Charlie Parker	Bebop
1946	"Choo Choo Ch'Boogie"	Louis Jordan	Jump-band song
1947	"Move On Up a Little Higher"	Mahalia Jackson	Black gospel
	"It's Mighty Dark to Travel"	Bill Monroe	Bluegrass
1949	"Some Enchanted Evening"	Ezio Pinza	Musical theater song
	"Lovesick Blues"	Hank Williams	Honky-tonk
1950	You Do Something to Me	Frank Sinatra	Swinging version of fox-trot standard
	"Goodnight Irene"	The Weavers	Folk/pop fusion
1951	"Unforgettable"	Nat Cole	Distinctive interpretation of pop ballad
1952	"It Wasn't God Who Made Honky Tonk Angels"	Kitty Wells	Honky-tonk
1953	"Mama, He Treats Your Daughter Mean"	Ruth Brown	1950s rhythm and blues
1954	"Hoochie Coochie Man"	Muddy Waters	Electric blues
	"Django"	Modern Jazz Quartet	Modern jazz

styles. We cited Patti Page's cover of "Tennessee Waltz" as a spectacular example of this; there were many more. But unlike the "western" music heard in horse operas, or bluesy or Latin popular songs, this music did not mask its identity with a pop overlay.

The decade was a time of transition, between the modern era of the 1920s, '30s, and '40s, and the rock era. Even as most modern-era styles assumed their "classic" form, a new and revolutionary kind of music was taking shape. In this respect, it is worth remembering that winners write history. Rock historians have written much more extensively about the postwar years than have historians of other genres, to the point that one might have the impression that rock and roll was a dominant music from the outset, or at least the most valuable. However, the music that fomented the rock revolution was only a small if rapidly expanding corner of the popular music industry, even toward the end of the 1950s. Throughout the 1950s, pop and musical theater dominated the media and, with jazz, enjoyed far greater prestige than rock. That would change within a decade.

Terms to Know

Test your knowledge of this chapter's important terms by defining the ones listed here. If you can't recall the meaning of a certain term, refresh your memory by looking up the boldfaced term in the chapter, turning to the Glossary at the back of the book, or working with the flashcards at the Popular Music Resource Center.

disc jockey (DJ)
78 rpm recording
long-playing (LP or
  33 rpm) record
45 rpm single
bop (bebop)
comped
third-stream music

standard
ballad
rhythm and blues (R&B)
jump band
electric blues
deep blues
cover version
honky-tonk

Rock 'n' Roll,
1954–1964

CHAPTER

9

Valerie Loiseleux/istockphoto.com

By the time "Maybellene" hit the charts late in the summer of 1955, DJ Alan Freed was in New York, and the famous phrase to which he claimed ownership, "rock 'n' roll," was on everyone's lips. Freed had moved to New York the previous year in order to offer his rock-and-roll radio show on WINS, just as rock and roll took its first steps toward an identity distinct from rhythm and blues; the differences would become more pronounced over the next decade. In this chapter, we survey the first decade of the rock era. After a brief overview of key economic and social developments during the 1950s, we'll begin the hunt for the first rock and roll record.

American Society in the Postwar Years

Through the 1930s, America suffered from one of the greatest economic downturns in its history. The Great Depression put millions of people out of work. It crippled the recording industry and other entertainment media. World War II helped put an end to the Depression, through heavy investment in the industries that produced the armaments needed to win the war.

After the war, the economy continued to boom. Economic growth meant more disposable income, some of which was spent on entertainment. During the 1950s, the television went from luxury item to essential household furniture, and record sales grew at the astounding rate of 20 to 25 percent per year.

America's newfound prosperity trickled down to a newly enfranchised segment of society, the teenager. No longer burdened by farm chores or the work-to-survive demands of the Depression, teenagers had far more leisure time than their predecessors. They were also better off: parents gave them allowances, and many found after-school jobs. More time and more money inevitably led to the emergence of the new teen subculture.

Image courtesy of The Advertising Archives

> All of it—the music, the lyrics, the look— horrified teens' parents; that was part of the appeal.

Teens defined themselves socially, economically, and musically. "Generation gap" became part of everyday speech; so, unfortunately, did "juvenile delinquent." Teens put their money where *their* tastes were, and many had a taste for rock and roll. They rebelled, by putting down high school; by idolizing Marlon Brando, James Dean, and other "rebels without a cause"; and by souping up cars (celebrated in the rock and roll of this era, from Chuck Berry's "Maybellene" to the Beach Boys' "Little Deuce Coupe" and "409"). However, the most obvious symbol of their revolt against the status quo was their music.

Rock and roll and rhythm and blues epitomized this new rebellious attitude. Although most of it seems tame to us now, the music was, by contemporary pop standards, "crude" and obviously black or black inspired. Some songs were blatantly sexual: Jerry Lee Lewis's "Great Balls of Fire" was a prime offender. Elvis and his fellow rock and rollers talked differently, wore their hair differently, dressed differently, danced and walked differently. All of it— the music, the lyrics, the look— horrified teens' parents; that was part of the appeal.

The First Rock and Roll Records

Among the most persistent subjects of debate among rock historians is the identity of the very first rock and roll record. Some have sought to identify the first instance of a musical feature that would later become commonplace in rhythm and blues or rock and roll: the honking saxophone, first popularized by Illinois Jacquet in the mid-1940s, or the accidentally distorted guitar of Willie Kizart in Jackie Brenston's 1951 R&B No. 1 hit, "Rocket 88." Others cite technology: Arthur Crudup's "That's All Right" (1946), the first R&B record released (in 1949) on a 45 rpm disc; Les Paul and Mary Ford's "How High the Moon" (1951), the first recording to feature extensive overdubbing, an increasingly common practice in the 1950s. Still others went no further than the title, such as Wynonie Harris's "Good Rockin' Tonight" (1948). Many focused on the pop charts, looking for songs with an unequivocal black orientation. Among the prime candidates in this last group were the Chords' "Sh Boom" and Bill Haley's "Rock Around the Clock," both released in 1954. A cover version of "Sh Boom" by the Crew Cuts reached No. 1 on the pop charts in 1954; "Rock Around the Clock" topped the charts in 1955. "Sh Boom" is doo-wop; "Rock Around the Clock" is rockabilly. Both styles were among the first to find a pop audience.

Doo Wop, Covers, and "Sh Boom"

After World War II, pop, gospel, and rhythm and blues came together in a new family of styles that featured male or mostly male singing groups. The styles ranged from gospel-tinged pop ideally suited for slow dancing to up-tempo numbers and novelty songs. The common threads seem to be the gospel and pop influences (the male gospel quartets and pop vocal groups like the Mills Brothers) and the names, which identify the groups as a unit: the Platters, the Penguins, the Cadillacs, the Drifters, and countless others. The first recordings of these new sounds appeared in the late forties, many by "bird" groups such as the Ravens and the Orioles.

From the mid-fifties to the early sixties, doo-wop crossed over to the pop market more consistently and with greater success than any other rhythm-and-blues style. The Orioles' 1953 hit, "Crying in the Chapel," blazed the trail. Its history highlights the blurred genre boundaries in the early rock era: "Crying in the Chapel" was a country song that crossed over to the pop charts, which was then covered by an R&B group whose version also made the pop charts!

The breakthrough hit "Sh Boom" came the following year. The original R&B version by the Chords hit both pop and rhythm-and-blues charts the same week: July 3, 1954. A cover version by the Crew Cuts, a white singing group, hit No. 1 on the pop charts a week later. Other doo-wop hits consistently crossed over: from the Penguins' "Earth Angel" and the Moonglows' "Sincerely" to the appropriately titled 1961 hit "Beat of My Heart," the first big hit for the Pips.

For whites, doo-wop put a fresh coat of paint on familiar-sounding material. For the majority of white teens who had heard their parents' Tin Pan Alley pop growing up, the familiar elements must have made the music more accessible. They also made it easier for white singers to copy. The success of these black vocal groups and the even greater success of white groups like the Crew Cuts spawned countless other white imitators, like Danny and the Juniors.

The sound and the style died out in the early sixties with the rise of the girl groups, Motown, and other fresh black pop sounds.

Doo-Wop: Voices as Instruments. "Life could be a dream, life could be a dream"; "doo, doo, doo, doo, Sh Boom." The first part of the lyric is typical of the romantic pop of the era, the second is the signature of **doo-wop**, the most popular kind of fifties rhythm and blues. As the song unfolds, the lyric alternates between explaining why life could be a dream and nonsense syllables like "hey, nonny ding dong, shalang alang alang." "Sh Boom" returns regularly between phrases of the lyric; it is like a gentle prod that keeps the rhythmic momentum going. Periodically, an entire phrase of nonverbal sounds interrupts the romantic scene unfolding in the rest of the lyric, and the nonverbal sounds from the introduction also serve as the vocal part behind the saxophone solo. Significantly, the title of the song comes from one of these nonsense syllables, not from the first phrase of the lyric.

The function of the nonsense syllables is to inject rhythmic energy into the song. The syllables are typically rich in consonant sounds that explode (*b*) or sustain (*sh* or *m*). In the "Sh Boom"–like parts of the song, the voices become instruments. They are not percussive instruments per se, because they have pitch, but the vocal sounds have a percussive quality, like the plucking of a string bass or the slapping of an electric bass.

The practice of using the voice to imitate instruments, especially percussive-sounding instruments, is a distinctively black practice. In jazz, the practice is called **scat singing**. The first familiar examples come from Louis Armstrong's late twenties recordings; there is no difference in conception between Armstrong the trumpeter and Armstrong the vocalist. Armstrong's

> *Doo-wop put a fresh coat of paint on familiar-sounding material.*

The Platters

Michael Ochs/Getty Images

vocalizations influenced black performers like Cab Calloway, famous as the "hi-de-ho" man. ("Hi-de-ho" were nonsense syllables woven into his account of "Minnie the Moocher," a big hit for him in 1931; the parallel with "Sh Boom" should be clear.) Scat singing gave **bebop** (later shortened to **bop**), the new jazz sound of the forties, its name: "be-bop" are the syllables that end a scatted stream of notes. Male gospel quartets were a more direct influence. Most sang *a cappella* (that is, without instrumental accompaniment), so backup vocal parts often assumed a rhythmic as well as a harmonic role.

The practice became part of the sound of rhythm and blues in the forties, in such hit songs as Lionel Hampton's "Hey! Ba-Ba-Re-Bop" and "Stick" McGhee's "Drinking Wine Spo-Dee-O-Dee." With doo-wop the practice became so integral to the music that it gave the style its name. The term *doo-wop*—borrowed from songs that used the phrase—was applied retrospectively to this music to acknowledge its most salient feature.

Cover Versions and Commercial Success. The notion of a cover version is a rock-era concept; it depends on a recording being understood as *the* song and not simply a *version* of the song. The record—whether bought outright or heard on the air—was becoming the primary document. By contrast, pop songs from the prewar era usually existed independently of any particular version of them.

Many doo-wop songs were, in effect, cover versions—that is, remakes of existing songs—before the idea of covers surfaced. Many of the songs reconceived by the early doo-wop groups were standards that had been around for a while. The repertoire that doo-wop groups recorded clearly suggests that they were trying to locate the pop middle ground.

White covers of black songs occurred frequently in the early years of rock and roll. The Crew Cuts' cover of "Sh Boom" is a familiar instance; Pat Boone's covers of Little Richard's "Tutti Frutti" and Fats Domino's "Ain't That a Shame," both of which outsold the originals, are particularly notorious examples. Because of these and other similar instances, cover versions have acquired racial baggage; some commentators have viewed them as white acts' riding on the coattails of black acts and enjoying the success that should have gone to the black acts.

The injustice of covers is not so much a musical issue. The blacks who sang doo-wop were borrowing liberally from white pop. The greatest *musical* injustice in white covers of black recordings is bad taste: the pop music establishment superimposing their conception of a sound with mass appeal, and enervating the music as a result. Instead, it's a financial and racial issue: that blacks did not have easy access to the

Some commentators have viewed covers as white acts' riding on the coattails of black acts and enjoying the success that should have gone to the black acts.

The 2006 Academy Award–winning musical film *Dream Girls*, set during the years of early doo-wop and R&B, was in part the story of a "stolen" cover, in which James "Thunder" Early's (Eddie Murphy) first single flops after being covered successfully by a white pop group.

pop market, that many were naive about the music business and never saw the money that their records made, that the labels that signed and recorded them could not compete with the majors, and that white versions sold better than the black originals. Covers became less common as white audiences opened up to black music of all kinds. Perhaps the best evidence for this shift in consciousness would be the Marcels' raucous version of the standard "Blue Moon," which topped the pop charts in 1961. It was a sound that no white group could imitate.

The Sound of Upbeat Doo-Wop. In any event, the Chords' eye toward the pop charts is clearly evident in "Sh Boom," which we might describe as "jump-band lite." Because many of these groups developed their songs a capella and were given backup studio musicians—many of them jump-band performers—they took on

| STYLE | Doo-wop |
| FORM | One statement of AABA form, plus introduction, interlude, and ending |

0:00	Introduction		
	Oh, life could be a dream (*doo-doo-doo-doo-sh-boom*) …		
0:09	Chorus 1		
	A	Oh, life could be a dream (sh-boom) …	The first and last phrases are extended with nonsense syllables; the last A section also features close harmony.
	A (0:29)	Oh, life could be a dream (sh-boom) …	
	B (0:43)	Now every time I look at you …	
	A (0:57)	Oh, life could be a dream (sh-boom) …	
1:23	Instrumental Interlude		
	Sax solo over the "Heart and Soul" progression; singers sing a response-like riff, as if a big-band horn section.		
1:52	Chorus 2 (partial)		
	A	Oh, life could be a dream (sh-boom) …	The second chorus includes only the last A section plus the introduction, which is modified to work as the ending.

CD 3:1

"Sh Boom,"
Edwards, Feaster,
Feaster, Keyes,
McRae, the Chords
(1954).

the jump band's shuffle rhythm and instrumentation: rhythm section plus saxophone. But the beat is discreet—very much in the background—and the good saxophone solo straddles the boundary between jazz and honking R&B. Moreover, the song is not a blues; its form and underlying harmony use "Heart and Soul," a familiar pop standard, as a model.

The song focuses on the voices; the instrumental accompaniment is very much in the background. The Chords' sound is typical: a lead singer (Carl Feaster) with a pleasant but untrained voice, plus four backup singers, including the requisite bass voice (William "Ricky" Edwards), who steps into the spotlight briefly. When singing behind Feaster, the backup singers alternate between sustained chords and the occasional rhythmic interjection— "Sh Boom." During the saxophone solo, the voices mimic a big-band horn section playing a riff underneath a soloist.

The Crew Cuts' version of "Sh Boom" was a white take on a black song (inspired in part by white pop). Rockabilly, another music that soon crossed over to the pop charts, was a white take on a black style.

5 to Listen For
"Sh Boom"

INSTRUMENTATION
Male vocal group plus full rhythm section (electric guitar, bass, piano, drums) and saxophone

PERFORMANCE STYLE
Pleasant but untrained voices; honking saxophone style

RHYTHM
Shuffle rhythm at moderate tempo

HARMONY
Use of "Heart and Soul" progression

TEXTURE
Either call and response between lead and backup singers or close harmony (sung chords in a narrow range)

3 to Remember
"Sh Boom"

JUMP-BAND LITE
The Chords backed by a standard R&B band: horns + rhythm instruments; song has shuffle rhythm, like most 1950s R&B songs. But moderate tempo and less aggressive sound.

DOO-WOP VOCAL SOUND
Pleasant but not sweet vocal timbre, with lead singer, bass soloist (in the bridge) and close harmony behind the lead

NONSENSE SYLLABLES FOR RHYTHM
The use of "nonsense" syllables to inject energy into performance harks back to the gospel quartets (e.g., Golden Gate Gospel Quartet) and big-band horn sections, which backup vocalists emulate.

Rockabilly

Carl Perkins, perhaps the truest of the rockabilly stars, once explained his music this way: "To begin with ... rockabilly music, or rock and roll ... was a country man's song with a black man's rhythm. I just put a little speed into some of the slow blues licks." Rockabilly was the latest in a long line of country takes on black music. You've already heard Jimmie Rodgers's blue yodels, Bob Wills's western swing, and Hank Williams's honky-tonk. Rockabilly simply continues that trend.

Rockabilly began as a white southern music. Its home was Memphis, more specifically Sam Phillips's Sun Records. Perkins and Jerry Lee Lewis recorded there; so did Elvis. Even today the style retains this strong southern identity. The sound of rockabilly, however, was not confined to Memphis or even the South. Just as earlier country styles had spread throughout North America, so did the idea of countrifying rhythm and blues.

Bill Haley's "Rock Around the Clock." The first big rockabilly hit came from an unlikely source, by way of an unlikely place, and took an unlikely path to pop success. Bill Haley (1925–1981), who recorded it, grew up

> "To begin with, ... rockabilly music, or rock and roll ... was a country man's song with a black man's rhythm. I just put a little speed into some of the slow blues licks."
>
> –Carl Perkins

CD 3:2

"Rock Around the Clock," Max Friedman and James Myers (1954). Bill Haley and His Comets.

in Pennsylvania listening to the *Grand Ole Opry* and dreaming of country music stardom. By the late 1940s, he had begun fronting small bands—one was called the "Four Aces of Western Swing"—and enjoyed some local success. Over the next few years, he began to give his music a bluesier sound and chose—or wrote—songs with teen appeal. "Crazy, Man, Crazy" (1953) was his first hit. In 1954 he had some success with a song called "Rock Around the Clock." (This was not the first time he had sung a song with *rock* in a lyric; an earlier song entitled "Rock-a-Beatin' Boogie" talked about rocking and rolling.)

A year later "Rock Around the Clock" resurfaced in the soundtrack to the film *The Blackboard Jungle.* The connections among film, song, and performer were tenuous. The film portrays juvenile delinquents in a slum high school, but "Rock Around the Clock" is exuberant rather than angry, and Haley, at almost thirty, looks nothing like a teenaged rebel. But it was music for and about teens (parents weren't likely to rock around the clock), and that was enough for the producers. With the release of the film, the song skyrocketed to No. 1. It was Haley's big moment. He had a few other minor hits, but he never repeated his chart-topping success.

Was "Rock Around the Clock" the first rock-and-roll record? It depends on your point of reference. It certainly was the first big hit clearly associated with rock and roll. And it was a different sound—at least for pop. But it connects more to the past than to the future. As with "Sh Boom," the sound is a light version of jump-band rhythm and blues. Haley's voice is bright, but it has little of the inflection that we associate with blues singing. The band supports Haley's voice with a small rhythm section that includes a guitar played in a high register (compare this with the Muddy Waters recording in the previous chapter) and drumsticks tapping out a brisk shuffle rhythm. The band plays riffs underneath Haley, then alone. This is much closer to rockabilly than it is to the rock and roll that came later in the decade.

Even as Haley's record zoomed to the top of the charts, Elvis Presley was recording a grittier kind of rockabilly at Sam Phillips's Sun records.

LISTENING GUIDE
CD 3:2 "Rock Around the Clock"

STYLE	Rockabilly
FORM	Verse-chorus blues form

0:00 Introduction
One two three o'clock …

0:12 First chorus
[I] Put your glad rags on …
[IV] We're gonna rock, rock …
[V] We're gonna rock, gonna rock …

The verse part of the form covers the first four measures. The last eight measures of the form make up the refrain part of the chorus.

0:28 Second chorus
When the clock strikes two, three, and four,
If the band slows down we'll yell for more …

The walking bass and the shuffle rhythm tapped out by the drummer give the beat a buoyancy that is characteristic of rockabilly.

0:44 Third chorus: instrumental
The guitar solo begins with a double-time burst; the technique would soon become a trademark of surf guitarists.

1:00 Fourth choruses: vocal
When the chimes ring five, six, and seven,
We'll be right in seventh heaven …

The guitar and sax play a swing-style riff behind Haley's vocal. It is more evidence that this song is more connected to the past than previewing the future.

1:16 Fifth chorus: vocal
When it's eight, nine, ten, eleven too,
I'll be goin' strong and so will you …

1:32 Sixth chorus: instrumental
A swing-era style riff played by the saxophone and guitar: note that it's a single note; the energy comes from the syncopated rhythm.

1:48 Seventh chorus: vocal
When the clock strikes twelve, we'll cool off then,
Start a rockin' round the clock again.

The song ends with an instrumental tag that was popular during the 1950s.

Elvis Presley

In the summer of 1953, a young truck driver named Elvis Presley walked into the Sam Phillips Recording Service in Memphis to make a demo record. Phillips wasn't in, so his assistant, Marion Keisker, handled the session. Perhaps to make him feel at ease, she asked him about himself. The conversation went something like this:

Marion: "What kind of singer are you?"

Elvis: "I sing all kinds."

Marion: "Who do you sound like?"

Elvis: "I don't sound like nobody."

Marion: "Hillbilly?"

Elvis: "Yeah, I sing hillbilly."

istockphoto.com

5 to Listen For
"Rock Around the Clock"

INSTRUMENTATION
Voice, electric guitar, acoustic bass, drums, and saxophone (accordion)

PERFORMANCE STYLE
Haley's voice is light and friendly but not bluesy or country—and not pop crooning either.

RHYTHM
Shuffle rhythm at a fast tempo

RHYTHM
Syncopation in vocal line, guitar riff, and instrumental riff in sixth chorus

TEXTURE
Light, layered texture with most instruments and voice in a high midrange contribute to bright sound.

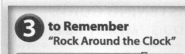

3 to Remember
"Rock Around the Clock"

LIGHT-HEARTED LYRIC
"Rocking" here is simply about dancing the night away; nothing suggests a more intimate involvement between partners.

LIGHT-HEARTED MUSIC
The brisk tempo, discreet shuffle beat, and generally high register of Haley's voice and the guitar give the song a bright feel.

SOUND OF ROCKABILLY
A "lite" version of rhythmic R&B: faster tempo, higher register, less rough-edged vocal

Marion: "Who do you sound like in hillbilly?"

Elvis: "I don't sound like nobody."

This now-legendary encounter gives us some insight into Elvis's success. Imagine yourself—barely out of high school and with no professional experience—having such a clear sense of who you are and what you can do. Elvis truly didn't sound like anyone else; he was the "white man with the Negro feel" that Sam Phillips had been seeking for several years.

Elvis at Sun

Elvis Presley (1935–1977) recorded his first local hit for Phillips's Sun Records in 1954. The record, a cover of bluesman Arthur Crudup's "That's All Right," sparked interest on country-western radio (although some stations wouldn't play it because Elvis sounded too black). Within a year he had reached No. 1 nationally on the country-western charts with "Mystery Train"—one of Elvis's most enduring early hits.

CD 3:3

"Mystery Train," Elvis Presley (1955).

> *Elvis was rock and roll's lightning rod.*

Like many of Elvis's Sun recordings, "Mystery Train" was a cover. The original version was a 1953 recording by bluesman Junior Parker, also recorded for Sun. Parker's version moves at a stodgier pace; its underlying rhythm emulates the sound of a locomotive and provides a preview of rock rhythm. Elvis's version has a much brighter tempo. Like Carl Perkins, Elvis "put a little speed in those slow blues licks."

Elvis's Sun sessions are quintessential rockabilly, in large part because of his singing. In both its basic timbre and its variety, his sound is utterly unique. Equally remarkable is his ability to adapt his sound to suit the material. He could emulate almost any style—pop, country, gospel, R&B—and still sound like himself. And like other great country singers, especially Jimmie Rodgers and Hank Williams, he was very much at home with black music. Although he didn't play much guitar, he played the radio really well. He was an equal-opportunity listener with an insatiable appetite for music. And what he heard, he used.

Elvis in Hollywood

Elvis's sound brought him radio attention, but it was his looks and his moves that propelled him to stardom.

In late 1955 he signed a personal management contract with Colonel Tom Parker (actually Andreas van Kuijk, an illegal immigrant from Holland), who arranged a record contract with RCA. Within a year Elvis had become a national phenomenon. Within two years he had recorded several No. 1 hits and appeared on TV's *The Ed Sullivan Show* as well as many others. He had become the symbol of rock and roll for millions, for both those who idolized him and those who despised him. With his totally uninhibited stage manner, tough-teen dress, greased pompadour, and energetic singing style, Elvis projected a rebellious attitude that many teens found overwhelmingly attractive.

To the audiences of today, Elvis may seem almost wholesome. However, his seeming lack of inhibition when performing contrasted sharply with white pop singers who stood in front of microphones and crooned. In his day, this was

LISTENING GUIDE

CD 3:3 "Mystery Train"

STYLE	Rockabilly
FORM	Blues form with modified harmony (both first and second phrases start on IV) and phrases of variable length

0:00	**Introduction**	
	Backup band of guitar, bass, and drums set the tempo and establish the basic rhythmic feel.	
0:07	**First chorus:** vocal	
	Train I ride, sixteen coaches long … (2x) Well that long black train got my baby and gone …	The underlying rhythm is a two beat: the honky-tonk influence.
0:34	**Second chorus:** vocal	
	Train train, comin round, round the bend …	In this chorus, the first and second phrases contain five measures, which undermines the predictability of the form.
1:03	**Third chorus:** vocal	
	Train train, comin down, down the line …	Elvis uses some of his trademark vocal devices in the asides ("she's mine," etc. …)
1:30	**Interlude:** instrumental	
	A brief guitar solo by Scottie Moore is based on the last eight bars of 12-bar blues form.	
1:46	**Fourth chorus:** vocal	
	Train train, comin' round, round the bend again (no, not again) …	The song ends with a nice fadeout.

CD 3:4

"Jailhouse Rock,"
Jerry Leiber and
Mike Stoller (1957).
Elvis Presley, vocal.

bold stuff, and he took a lot of heat for it. We can also admire Elvis's courage: he refused to tone down his style despite the criticism. In sticking to his guns, he gave rock and roll a sound and a look—both of which immediately set the style apart from anything that had come before. Elvis was rock and roll's lightning rod. For teens he was all that was right with this new music; for their parents he symbolized all that was wrong with it. And for all intents and purposes, he stood alone.

This is evident in *Jailhouse Rock*, one of the films he made before he went into the army, and especially in "Jailhouse Rock," the title song of the film. The song was written for Elvis by Jerry Leiber and Mike Stoller. Released in conjunction with the film, it went to No. 1 in the fall of 1957. In the film, it serves as a sound-track to an extended dance number.

5 to Listen For
"Mystery Train"

INSTRUMENTATION
Voice, electric guitar, acoustic bass, drums

PERFORMANCE STYLE
Elvis's high lonesome sound, plus occasional special effects in vocal asides

RHYTHM
Two-beat rhythm with "rebound" backbeat at fast tempo

HARMONY
Different take on blues harmony: start on IV chord

TEXTURE
Open sound, with light bass and drums, guitar just under Elvis's voice

3 to Remember
"Mystery Train"

FAST TEMPO WITH A MODIFIED TWO-BEAT RHYTHM
Drums maintain a light, fast rhythm very much in the background; the distinctive feature is the "rebound" backbeat in the guitar, which comes with, then ahead of the backbeat

ELVIS'S SOULFUL SINGING AND UNIQUE SOUND
Elvis's singing is bluesier than traditional country singing, and without a twang. At the same time, it is distinct from the timbres of 1950s R&B singers.

MODIFIED FORM OF THE BLUES PROGRESSION
Each chorus starts on a IV chord instead of a I chord; in the vocal sections, the first two phrases are of variable length, instead of the customary four bars.

LISTENING GUIDE
CD 3:4 "Jailhouse Rock"

STYLE	Rock 'n' roll	
FORM	Verse/chorus blues form in which the first phrase is doubled in length	
0:00	Introduction	
	Two-chord guitar riff over syncopated drum tap	
0:06	First chorus: vocal	
	(Verse 1) The warden threw a party ...	Stop time accompaniment under Elvis's vocal during the verse; the
	The prison band was there ...	band keeps time in the refrain with a rudimentary rock beat. The
	The band was jumpin'...	drummer also marks a rock beat, while the bass plays a walking
	You should've heard....	line.
	(0:17) (Refrain part) Let's rock ...	
0:29	Second chorus: vocal	
	(Verse 2) Spider Murphy played the tenor saxophone ...	As before
	(0:40) (Refrain part) Let's rock ...	
0:51	Third chorus: vocal	
	(Verse 3) Number forty-seven said to number three...	As before
	(1:02) (Refrain part) Let's rock ...	
1:14	Instrumental break	
	The band shifts back to a swing (four-beat) rhythm for the break, which is simply an instrumental version of the refrain (last eight bars of the blues progression).	
1:25	Fourth chorus: vocal	
	(Verse 4) The sad sack was a sittin' on a block of stone	
	(1:36) (Refrain part) Let's rock ...	
1:48	Fifth chorus: vocal	
	(Verse 5) Shifty henry said to bugs, for heavens sake...	Fadeout ending to the last line of the refrain
	(1:59) (Refrain part) Let's rock ...	

Elvis and the Popularity of Rock and Roll

The *Billboard* charts reflect Elvis's singular status. Except for Elvis hits, rock and roll represented only a modest segment of the popular music market. The top-selling albums during this time were mostly soundtracks from Broadway shows and film musicals. Even sales of singles, which teens bought, show that rock and roll did not enjoy the unconditional support of America's youth. Besides Elvis, the top singles artists during the same period were either pre–rock stars like Frank Sinatra and Perry Como; younger artists singing in a pre-rock style (Andy Williams and Johnny Mathis); teen stars like Pat Boone, who covered early rock and roll songs; or vocal groups like the Platters, whose repertoire included a large

number of reworked Tin Pan Alley standards. Among the lesser figures—from a commercial perspective—are such important and influential artists as Buddy Holly, Chuck Berry, Little Richard, and Ray Charles. Elvis was by far the most important commercial presence in rock and roll; no one else came close.

The musically significant part of Elvis's career lasted only three years. It ended in 1958, when he was inducted into the U.S. Army. Although still a major public figure in the sixties and seventies, he seldom recaptured the freshness of his earlier years. His fans still call him the "king of rock and roll," but to what extent was it the image and to what extent was it the music? Certainly, he brought a new vocal sound into popular music. In his various blends of blues, R&B, country, gospel, and pop, Elvis summarized the musical influences—and

ELVIS'S SINGING
It's exuberant and uninhibited, influenced by blues and country, but a completely new vocal style.

FULL RHYTHM SECTION WITH PROMINENT ELECTRIC GUITAR
The rhythm section includes drums, bass, piano, and electric guitar; the guitar stands out in both its accompanying and solo roles.

EXPANDED VERSE/CHORUS BLUES FORM
The verse-like section is extended to eight measures; the chorus remains eight measures in length.

RHYTHMIC VARIETY
Stop time in the verse versus consistent timekeeping in the chorus.

MULTIPLE RHYTHMIC CONCEPTIONS
Rock rhythm in the band during the chorus, swing during the instrumental interlude (one can almost hear the band relax back into a rhythm they're familiar with), and Elvis somewhere in between: not really swing or the even beat division of rock.

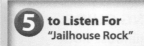

INSTRUMENTATION
Voice, electric guitar, piano, bass, and drums

RHYTHM
Primitive rock rhythm, kept mainly in guitar during refrain; Elvis and band not sure whether to rock or swing

RHYTHM
Nice contrast between syncopated stop time in verse and rocking/walking in refrain

MELODY
"Talking blues" in verse; simple riff in refrain

TEXTURE
Wide spacing: guitar low, just above bass, Elvis in the middle, piano high

and rock and roll songs heard to this point, only Elvis's "Jailhouse Rock," released late in 1957, uses a rock beat, and even there not everyone, including Elvis, is on the same page.

The first intimations of a new kind of rhythm surfaced in the early 1950s in the Latin rhythms heard in some New Orleans rhythm and blues. The Latin influence became more obvious in Bo Diddley's eponymous hit, "Bo Diddley."

The Latin Tinge

The connection between Latin music and R&B goes back to the beginning of rhythm and blues. To cite just one obscure but noteworthy example, "Longhair's Blues Rhumba," a 1949 recording by the New Orleans pianist Professor Longhair (whose real name was Roy Byrd), layered a clave rhythm—played on claves, cylindrical sticks about one inch in diameter used to tap out the rhythm—over a boogie-woogie-style piano blues. By the early 1950s, Professor Longhair and those New Orleans rhythm and blues artists who followed his lead (such as Fats Domino) were creating Latin-flavored rhythm and blues songs. During the fifties several R&B artists began to include Latin-influenced songs in their shows. Later in the decade, after the emergence of rock and roll, some artists began using Latin rhythms as an alternative to the eight-beat rhythm of rock and roll. Perhaps the most familiar example of this trend is Ray Charles's classic 1959 recording, "What'd I Say." However, the most overt, and distinctive, link between Latin music and rhythm and blues was heard in Bo Diddley's first hit.

Bo Diddley. The enigma of Bo Diddley (1928–2008) begins with his name. He was born in McComb, Mississippi, in 1928. His father's name was Bates, but he was adopted by a relative, Gussie McDaniel; by most accounts his real name is Elias McDaniel. In the mid-thirties the McDaniels moved to Chicago and settled on the South Side. He acquired his stage name from his schoolmates in his teens. As he tells it, students started calling him "Bo Diddley" and it stuck. (How it connects to the diddley bow, a homemade, guitar-like instrument popular in Mississippi, remains unknown.)

The enigma persists when we consider the extent of his influence compared with his lack of

epitomized the musical direction—of this new music. But his musical significance stops there. He neither wrote his own songs nor consistently used the rock-and-roll beat copied by so many late-fifties and early-sixties bands. The road from rock and roll to rock would follow a different path.

● ● ● ● ● ● ● ●
The New Rhythms of Rock and Roll

Much of the rhythm and blues of the early and mid-1950s featured rhythms that were more active and aggressive than those heard in pop or country. However, almost all of them were based on existing style beats: recall the honky-tonk two beat with a heavy backbeat in "Maybellene," the shuffle rhythm in "Sh Boom" and "Rock Around the Clock," or the occasional triplets in "Mama, He Treats Your Daughter Mean." Of the R&B

CD 3:5
"Bo Diddley," Bo Diddley (1955).

LISTENING GUIDE
CD 3:5 "Bo Diddley"

STYLE	Latin-tinged rhythm and blues
FORM	Strophic form, with sections of variable length
0:00	Introduction
	The Bo Diddley beat groove on one chord
0:09	**Verse 1**
	Bo Diddley bought his babe a diamond ring …
0:48	**Verse 2**
	Bo Diddley caught a nanny goat …
1:42	**Verse 3**
	Mojo come to my house, ya black cat bone …
2:12	**Fadeout ending**
	The song ends like it begins, with a compelling rhythm animating a single chord. It's as if the song has neither a beginning nor an end.

Melody consists of series of short riffs sung over churning, relentless rhythm. A simple three-chord guitar riff follows the vocal.

The same basic feel, but with slight changes in the melody and a more expansive guitar interlude

Guitar and percussion create dense rhythmic texture. Maracas move at rock-beat speed; drum layer is more active and complex. By repeating single chord, Bo Diddley effectively turns his guitar into another percussion instrument.

commercial success. In his fifty-year career, he has had only one Top 40 hit—his 1959 recording "Say Man." Yet he is without question a rock icon; among his many distinctions, he was a second-year inductee into the Rock and Roll Hall of Fame (1987).

Bo Diddley was fascinated by rhythms and percussion. (The story goes that he added maracas to his street-corner band because he wanted a percussive sound but didn't want to lug a drum set around town. Still, he kept the maracas when he added drums.) Not surprisingly, his most important and memorable contribution to popular music is not a song but a beat—the Bo Diddley beat—which appears in the aptly titled 1955 song "Bo Diddley," the first of his R&B hits. The Bo Diddley beat is a distinctive rhythm that is virtually identical to the clave rhythm we encountered in the rumba example ("El Manisero") in Chapter 7.

The song "Bo Diddley" is all about rhythm. It consists mainly of riff-like vocal fragments alternating with the Bo Diddley rhythm, played (more or

 **to Listen For**
"Bo Diddley"

INSTRUMENTATION
Vocal, electric guitar, drums, maracas, and perhaps bass

PERFORMANCE STYLE
Hawaiian guitar–like effects on the guitar. The drummer plays on low-tuned drums; no cymbals.

RHYTHM
Three insistent rhythms dominate song: the maracas rhythm (2x beat speed), the drums rhythm (4x beat speed), and the famous Bo Diddley beat (a rhythmic pattern close to the clave rhythm).

HARMONY
Most of the song just one chord; simple shift between chords in instrumental interludes.

TEXTURE
Three layers around voice: low-sounding drums, midrange guitar, and high-pitched maracas

 to Remember
"Bo Diddley"

"BO DIDDLEY BEAT"
As heard here, the "Bo Diddley" beat is a slightly altered version of the clave rhythm (in this recording; in a television performance, Bo Diddley and his band play the clave pattern.) This song shows the relationship between Afro-Cuban music, Americanized Latin rhythms, and rock rhythm. The rhythms of this song map onto a basic rock beat. They are more active and complicated than a simple rock rhythm, but less complex than a real Afro-Cuban rhythm.

USE OF MARACAS
Bo Diddley adds maracas to conventional blues band instrumentation.

ALMOST EXCLUSIVE EMPHASIS ON RHYTHM
The vocal melody is a simple riff, the instrumental breaks are even simpler. The main thing is the beat.

less) on guitar and drums. All of this happens over one chord. The lyric is based on a nursery rhyme with British antecedents; there is no real "story." Bo Diddley's self-titled song was the first big R&B hit to feature Latin-inspired rhythms and instruments so prominently. Rock musicians would borrow the beat; we encounter Buddy Holly's remarkable take on it later in the chapter.

The Bo Diddley beat became part of the fabric of rock and roll. But the rhythm that ultimately defined rock and roll and led to rock was mainly the work of two musicians, Little Richard and Chuck Berry.

Little Richard and Chuck Berry: the Architects of Rock and Roll

Assemble a mix of up-tempo recordings by 1950s rhythm and blues artists, from Jackie Brenston (of "Rocket 88" fame) to Wilbert Harrison, whose recording of "Kansas City" topped the pop and R&B charts in 1959. If you also include tracks by Little Richard and Chuck Berry, chances are they will stand out because of their beat.

Throughout the 1950s, most rhythm and blues acts continued to use the shuffle and swing rhythms of the 1940s. By contrast, both Little Richard and Chuck Berry built their songs on a rhythmic foundation that moved twice the speed of the beat. This new rhythm, with clear roots in up-tempo boogie-woogie, first surfaced in early recordings by Little Richard, released in late 1955 and early 1956.

Little Richard. Born Richard Penniman (1932) in Macon, Georgia, Little Richard was on the road in black vaudeville shows by the time he was fourteen. He made a few records in the early fifties, but none of them did much. In 1955 Lloyd Price (of "Lawdy Miss Clawdy" fame) suggested that Little Richard send a demo to Art Rupe, who ran Specialty Records, one of the many independent labels recording rhythm and blues. He did, and a few months later Bumps Blackwell set up a recording session at Cosimo Matassa's J&M studio in New Orleans. The house band included some of the legends of New Orleans rhythm and blues, including drummer Earl Palmer and saxophonist Lee Allen. The session got off to a slow start because Little Richard sang mostly slow blues songs, which were not his strength. During a break in the recording session,

they went to a local club, where Little Richard began to sing a "blue" song, a naughty novelty number that he'd featured in his act. Blackwell realized that that was the sound they wanted, so on the spur of the moment they recruited local songwriter Dorothy LaBostrie to clean up the words. At the time, her new lyrics didn't make any more sense than they do now, but they were enough to get Little Richard his first hit, "Tutti Frutti."

Especially in his post-1956 hits, we hear Little Richard's biggest contribution to the sound of rock and roll: a clear, locked-in rock rhythm. For example, "Lucille," which topped the R&B charts and almost reached the Top 20 on the pop charts in 1957, begins with bass and guitar playing a boogie bass line, the most prominent sound until Little Richard starts singing. Drummer Earl Palmer keeps an absolutely pure rock rhythm—a steady rhythm moving twice as fast as the beat with a strong backbeat-perfectly in sync with the rest of the band. As the song unfolds, the piano line reinforces the rock rhythm with repeated chords. All this is the backdrop to Little Richard's vocals.

In his sound and persona, Little Richard officially put rock and roll over the top. He was flagrantly gay in an era when gay meant only "happy" and the vast majority of homosexual men were firmly in the closet. And he was black. When Little Richard performed, he made the outrageous seem routine. In a favorite pose—one leg up on the lid of the piano, hands beating out a boogie beat, and a smirk on his face—there was no way you could avoid noticing him. Generations of rockers—gay, straight, androgynous, and cross-dressing—have followed his example. Mick Jagger, Jimi Hendrix, Elton John, David Bowie, and Prince are just a few of the artists for whom performance is—or can be—a spectacle.

Little Richard has claimed that he was responsible for the new beat of rock and roll. He was right, up to a point. However, it didn't become a rock-defining sound until Chuck Berry showed how it could be played on the guitar.

> Chuck Berry was the ultimate architect of rock and roll.

Chuck Berry. Chuck Berry (b. 1926) was the ultimate architect of rock and roll. More than any other musician of the 1950s, he crafted the style that would soon lead to rock: up-and-coming rock bands in the early 1960s, like the Beach Boys and the Beatles, covered his songs more frequently than any other artist from the 1950s.

Berry spoke to its audience and defined its sound. The lyrics of his songs captured the newly emerging teen spirit. He talks about them ("School Days" and "Sweet Little Sixteen"), to them ("Rock and Roll Music"), and for them ("Roll Over, Beethoven"). His music enunciates the core elements that make rock and roll stand apart not only from pop and country, but also rhythm and blues.

CD 3:6

"Johnny B. Goode," Chuck Berry (1958).

"Maybellene," Berry's first big hit, gave little rhythmic hint of the direction in which his music would evolve. However, over the next thirty months, Berry assembled the sound of rock and roll, step by step. Finally, in "Johnny B. Goode" (1958), he put all the pieces together.

In this song we can hear how Berry forged this revolutionary new style. Berry's voice is neither bluesy nor sweet, but it's well suited to deliver the rapid-fire lyrics that are a trademark of his songs.

The basic instrumentation of "Johnny B. Goode" is conventional enough. It is Berry's **overdubbing**—recording an additional part onto an existing recording—that is the breakthrough and the key to the sound of rock and roll. (We can assume that one of the guitar parts was overdubbed because both lead and rhythm guitar styles are Berry's and no other guitarist is credited in the album notes.) The two guitar lines, the

---

LISTENING GUIDE
CD 3:6 "Johnny B. Goode"

STYLE	Rock 'n' roll
FORM	Large scale form: verse/chorus; both verse and chorus use blues progression
0:00	Introduction
	The famous opening to the song, played over one chorus of a blues progression. Notice the double notes at the beginning and the syncopated pattern toward the middle, and the combination of lead and rhythm guitar.
0:17	First verse

	Deep down in Louisiana close to New Orleans;	"Johnny B. Goode" features a word-packed six-line verse (2 bars per line) instead of the simpler rhymed couplet of a conventional blues lyric.
	Way back up in the woods among the evergreens …	
0:34	Chorus	
	Go go, Go Johnny go;	Call and response between Berry's voice and guitar
	Go, Go Johnny go …	
0:51	Second verse	
	He used to carry his guitar in a gunny sack …	Berry only one playing rock rhythm: bass walks, drummer plays swing rhythm with heavy backbeat, pianist plays triplets
1:08	Chorus	
	Go go, Go Johnny go …	Berry playing lead guitar answers plus rhythm guitar (overdubbing)
1:25	Guitar solo	
	Guitar solo over two choruses of a blues progression. Stop time in the other instruments at the beginning of each chorus.	
2:00	Third verse	
	His mother told him some day you will be a man …	As before
1:42	Chorus	
	Go go, Go Johnny go …	As before

5 to Listen For
"Johnny B. Goode"

INSTRUMENTATION
Vocals, plus two guitars (overdubbed), piano, bass, drums

PERFORMANCE STYLE
Berry's singing neither pop-pretty nor bluesy—it is too light and friendly; his guitar playing has an edge—in its basic sound, his use of double notes in solo and rhythm lines, and the occasional bent notes.

RHYTHM
Steady eight-beat rhythm in vocals, lead and rhythm guitar; rest of band in four

HARMONY
Blues progression used in verse and chorus

TEXTURE
Strong rhythmic layer, with rhythm guitar, bass, and drums, underpins vocal lines and solos.

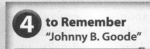

4 to Remember
"Johnny B. Goode"

ROCK RHYTHM GUITAR PATTERNS
Berry adapts the boogie-woogie left-hand patterns to the guitar; they become the foundation for rock rhythm guitar.

ROCK LEAD GUITAR PATTERNS
The double notes, bent notes, and syncopated patterns were features of the first important rock lead guitar style.

VERSE/CHORUS BLUES FORM
Verse and chorus (both over the 12-bar blues progression) alternate throughout the song.

BERRY AND ROCK RHYTHM
Berry clearly projects rock rhythm through the patter-style vocal and the lead and rhythm guitars lines, which are heard simultaneously. The rest of the band does little to support his conception of rock rhythm.

and up-tempo R&B styles, he took the blues-based verse/chorus form and the heavy backbeat.

At the same time, it's clear that the song is more than just the blending of these influences. The guitar work, Berry's voice, the content and style of the lyrics—all of these features were new elements, and all would prove extraordinarily influential. Berry's guitar breaks and solos are on the must-learn list of every serious rock guitarist. His lyrics, among the first to discuss teen life, are humorous, irreverent, and skillful.

Both the content and the style of his songs were widely copied. The surfing songs of the late fifties and early sixties are an especially good example of Berry's influence on song lyrics and musical style. No rock-and-roll artist was more covered by the creators of rock—the Beach Boys, the Rolling Stones, and the Beatles—than Chuck Berry.

rhythm section—a walking bass, drums (here adding a heavy backbeat), and a steady rhythm guitar—and an active piano **obbligato** (second melody playing under the main melody) create a dense texture. Lead guitar plays solo choruses and the response line in dialogue with the vocal.

To create the rhythm guitar line, Berry took the patterns he learned from working with pianist Johnnie Johnson and made two innovations. He adapted the standard boogie-woogie left-hand pattern to the guitar (moving it up into a slightly higher register), and he evened out the rhythm so that each beat is divided into two equal parts.

The lead guitar lines were radically new. He borrowed the double notes from the boogie-based rhythm lines and blends them with repeated notes and running lines—all played with the twang heard in "Maybellene." The lead guitar sound is forceful and compelling.

In "Johnny B. Goode" we hear the three main influences on rock and roll come together. From electric blues Berry took the instrumentation, the thick texture, and the prominent place of the guitar. From boogie-woogie he took the eight-beat rhythm. From more rhythmic

Rock and Roll's Second Generation

A second wave of rock-and-roll stars emerged in Elvis's wake: Eddie Cochran, Gene Vincent, the Everly Brothers, and many more. Standing above all of these was Buddy Holly, the most creative mind in rock and roll's second generation.

Buddy Holly

Born Charles Hardin Holly in Lubbock, Texas, Buddy Holly (1936–1959) grew up in a musical family. To hear the rock and roll he loved, he would drive with his friends to locations where he could pick up clear-channel broadcasts of rock-and-roll radio shows at night. After graduating from high school, Holly formed the Crickets. They were a big enough hit locally that they opened a show for Elvis when he came through Lubbock in 1955, but their first records went nowhere. Holly scored his first hit late in 1957 with "That'll Be the Day." It would be his biggest hit but not his most interesting.

When Holly began to play around with the still-brand-new elements of rock and roll, he found a helpful collaborator in an unlikely place. Norman Petty ran a recording studio in Clovis, New Mexico, a small town about 100 miles from Lubbock. Petty encouraged Holly and the Crickets to go for new sounds, some of which Petty created himself (he was a master of echo and reverb). Still, it was Holly's imagination that took rock and roll to a new level. We can hear this on one of his less popular but more enduring songs from 1957, "Not Fade Away."

Like the foxtrot and swing, rock and roll entered popular music as a dance music. If we keep that in mind, we realize how

> Buddy Holly was rock and roll's first everyman.

extraordinary the beginning of "Not Fade Away" is. Most rock-and-roll songs, including the ones that we have heard, begin by laying down a clear, steady beat. Even Bo Diddley's "Bo Diddley" (which we heard earlier) meshes the "Bo Diddley beat" with a steady rhythm in the maracas. By contrast, the beat in "Not Fade Away" is hard to

find. The first sounds we hear are the off-beat rhythms of the guitar and the bass, soon reinforced by the backup vocals. Even as the song gets under way, with guitar, bass, drums, and Holly's vocals all present, there is no instrument that marks the beat—rock or otherwise. Instead, we have Holly's take on the Bo Diddley beat and the drum style associated with it. The end of the song offers an ironic touch, fading away slowly even as Holly proclaims that his love will never fade away.

As in several of Holly's songs, the lyrics are similarly innovative. The words speak to a lukewarm partner. The "I" in the song is not the big man on campus but the gawky guy who loses his girl, or who never had her in the first place. Holly wrote and sang for the rest of us; in his music and his appearance, he was rock and roll's first everyman.

We can understand why "Not Fade Away" was not as popular as some of Holly's other songs; most teens still wanted to dance to rock and roll. But we can also understand why songs like this one so profoundly influenced the Beatles and other 1960s rock groups. "Not

CD 3:7

"Not Fade Away," Buddy Holly and Norman Petty (1957). Buddy Holly and the Crickets.

LISTENING GUIDE
CD 3:7 "Not Fade Away"

STYLE	Latin-tinged rock 'n' roll	
FORM	Strophic: same melody sets multiple verses.	
0:00	Introduction	
	Oo-bop-wop, bop-bop …	The five nonsense syllables are the (non)verbal sounds for the Bo Diddley beat-inspired riff that runs through the song.
0:10	First verse: vocal	
	I'm a gonna tell ya how it's gonna be …	Just two chords (IV and I): one more than Bo Diddley uses in "Bo Diddley"
0:42	Second verse (incomplete): vocal	
	My love is bigger than a Cadillac …	More of the story to the same music
1:16	Instrumental interlude	
	The guitar part elaborates the basic harmony of the verse.	
1:42	Third verse: vocal	
	I'm a gonna tell ya how it's gonna be …	Identical to first statement

5 to Listen For
"Not Fade Away"

INSTRUMENTATION
Lead and backup vocals, lead guitar, acoustic bass, and percussive sounds.

PERFORMANCE STYLE
Holly's hiccuppy vocal style is a rock-and-roll trademark; Jerry Allison played on a cardboard box instead of a drum set.

RHYTHM
The dominant rhythm—heard at first just by itself—sounds like a second-generation take on the clave rhythm of Afro-Cuban music, that is, a slightly altered version of the Bo Diddley beat.

RHYTHM
Fast tempo, but no steady timekeeping; only Bo Diddley beat measures time.

TEXTURE
Rich texture: voice/lead instrument plus secondary horn parts (riffs, sustained chords) and rhythm section

3 to Remember
"Not Fade Away"

TEEN LYRICS WITH FEELING
Lyrics like these project a more vulnerable image than the "mighty, mighty man" lyrics heard in so many rhythm-and-blues songs.

BEYOND DANCE MUSIC
In a single stroke, Holly opens the door to a new world of musical possibilities—he elevates rock 'n' roll from the dance floor to music just for listening.

THE RAPID EVOLUTION OF ROCK AND ROLL
Holly's apparent adaptation of the Bo Diddley beat suggests that recordings sped up the evolutionary pace: musicians would listen to a song, then use it as a point of departure for a new direction. "Bo Diddley" was a hit two years previously; Holly's songs would in turn strongly influence the Beatles.

his career. In 1959 Chuck Berry was arrested on a Mann Act violation and eventually sentenced to a two-year jail term.

The **payola scandal** of 1959 also contributed to the apparent decline of rock and roll. Because they controlled airplay of records, disc jockeys wielded enormous power. Some, like Alan Freed, used it to promote the music they liked. But many, including Freed, accepted some form of bribery in return for guaranteed airplay. The practice became so pervasive that it provoked a government investigation. Also at issue was the question of licensing rights. ASCAP, the stronger licensing organization, reportedly urged the investigation to undermine its major competitor, BMI, which was licensing the music of so many black and country performers. Establishment figures viewed the investigation results as proof of the inherent corruption of rock and roll.

By the early 1960s, it seemed as if rock and roll were just a fad that had run its course. In retrospect, it was just getting its second wind.

Fade Away" is a great example of how creative minds like Holly's recycled the sounds of first-generation rock and roll and sent a message that it could be more than dance music.

The Day the Music Died

On February 3rd, 1959, Buddy Holly died in a plane crash while en route from Iowa to North Dakota. As Don McLean noted in "American Pie," it was "the day the music died." The crash that killed Holly, Ritchie Valens, and J. P. "the Big Bopper" Richardson was one in a series of calamities that seemed to end rock and roll as suddenly as it had begun. The previous year, Elvis was drafted into the army. When he resumed his career two years later, he had lost the cutting edge that had defined his earlier work. Little Richard gave up his career to become a preacher. Jerry Lee Lewis married his thirteen-year-old cousin without divorcing his previous wife, and the ensuing scandal seriously damaged

By the early 1960s, it seemed as if rock and roll were just a fad that had run its course. In retrospect, it was just getting its second wind.

Rhythm and Blues, 1955–1960

Muddy Waters once remarked that "the blues had a baby and they called it rock and roll." We might add that if rock and roll was the baby of the blues, 1950s rhythm and blues was its older brother. Although it had been around longer, it came of age as a commercial music at about the same time rock and roll caught fire—the latter part of the fifties. It acquired a more distinct musical identity, one that often had greater crossover appeal. Several of its stars—Fats Domino, Sam Cooke, the Coasters, the Platters—appeared consistently on the pop charts, and R&B acts in general had a stronger market presence in the latter part of the decade.

Much commercially successful rhythm and blues

moved toward the pop charts by moving away from music that was rhythmic and/or bluesy, in favor of pop and gospel. **Gospel** had influenced doo-wop since the late forties; what changed was the range and the extent of its influence. Now gospel had also become a training ground for solo singing stars like Sam Cooke and Ray Charles. With the focus on individual voices, differences from artist to artist were more apparent. Vocal groups, most notably the Coasters and the Platters, also developed a recognizable sound. In general, production was more elaborate: recordings often featured richer instrumental accompaniment, more-complex arrangements, and trademark sounds. Even one- or two-hit wonders like the Marcels created recordings with a distinct personality.

> *Gospel had also become a training ground for solo singing stars like Sam Cooke and Ray Charles.*

"Am I Blue?" or Crosby's "I've Got the World on a String" as reference points, we can hear how thoroughly the Flamingos' version departs from traditional pop. Two obvious differences stand out: the singers and the tempo. The sound of lead singer Sollie McElroy and the close harmony of the Flamingos as a group are different from other pop singers we've heard. The tempo of the performance is much slower, less than half the speed of "Am I Blue." Indeed, the tempo is so slow that the recording, which lasts more than three minutes, includes only one statement of the chorus rather than two or three. To energize this slow tempo, the pianist plays repeated chords in a triplet rhythm.

Other notable differences are the "doo-wop-sh-bop" riffs of the backup vocalists during the verse and the long stretches over a single harmony. The vocal riff is the kind that earned doo-wop its name. The riff stands out in two ways: it is the main source of rhythmic energy in the song, and it replaces even the title phrase ("I only have eyes for you") as the song's melodic signature. In this respect it anticipates an important rock-era development: the distribution of melodic interest among several parts rather than concentrating it in the lead vocal line.

The harmony in this performance is bipolar. For long stretches, such as the opening verse and the first part of the chorus, there is no harmonic change. Upon arriving at the title phrase, the harmony suddenly becomes lush, with new chords on almost every syllable of the lyric. This kind of harmonic practice is unique to doo-wop.

All four style features—the timbre of the singers, the slow tempo, the signature vocal riffs, and the static harmony—give the recording a distinctive identity; it's not just another version of the song. In this respect it's in step with the move toward the recorded performance's being the primary document of a song, even though its starting point in this case is a pre-rock popular song.

Songs like "I Only Have Eyes for You" were the most typical doo-wop sound: pop standards or pop-like songs sung in close harmony at a slow tempo. There were hundreds of doo-wop groups singing in much the same style. During its peak period, from the late 1940s to around 1960, it offered a new kind of black pop and served as a bridge between pre–rock pop and the new black pop of the rock era.

Slow Doo-Wop

Among the most commercially successful trends in rhythm and blues styles in the latter part of the 1950s was slow doo-wop. The gospel influence is evident in the vocal sound, the interplay between lead and backup singers, and the slow tempo; black singers typically perform conventional hymns like "Amazing Grace" at a markedly slower tempo than white singers. The pop influence is in the choice of repertoire. Like doo-wop groups from earlier in the decade, groups like the Platters, the Drifters, the Flamingos—and the white groups that imitated them—recycled pop standards or sang new songs clearly rooted in conventional pop. The infusion of gospel style helped transform these songs into a distinctly different sound. We hear this in the Flamingos' 1959 recording of the 1934 hit "I Only Have Eyes for You."

CD 3:8

"I Only Have Eyes for You," Harry Warren and Al Dubin (1959). The Flamingos.

The Flamingos were a Chicago-based vocal quintet: two pairs of cousins and a lead singer. They were among the more successful doo-wop groups in the late 1950s, charting steadily on the R&B charts and occasionally crossing over to the pop charts, as they did with "I Only Have Eyes for You," their biggest hit.

As originally conceived, "I Only Have Eyes for You" is a beautiful foxtrot ballad. If we use songs like Waters's

LISTENING GUIDE
CD 3:8 "I Only Have Eyes for You"

| STYLE | Pop ballad sung doo-wop style |
| FORM | Pop song form (AA¹BA²), with verse and long tag |

0:00 Verse

My love must be a kind of blind love…. | The entire verse takes place over a single chord and the recurrent riff in the guitar and bass voice.

0:36 Chorus 1

A: Are the stars out tonight? … | The static harmony continues until the title phrase, which features the lush harmony of pre-rock pop.

A¹: (1:10) The moon may be high … | The "doo-wop-sh-bop" functions like a rhythmic pinprick.
B (bridge): (1:42) I don't know if we're | A rich texture: melody, backup vocals, piano triplets up high, and
in a garden, | other instruments.
A²: (2:14) You are here,
So am I,
Maybe millions …

2:57 Fadeout ending

A surprise at the end: instead of ending the song convincingly in the home key, the Flamingos return to the introduction, which leaves the ending open-ended. (Compare this with the definite ending in "Sh Boom"). The static harmony anticipates the approach used in soul and beyond since the mid-1960s.

4 to Remember
"I Only Have Eyes for You"

DOO-WOP VOCAL TIMBRE
The pleasant blend of a doo-wop singing group replaces the smooth crooning of a pop singer in the performance of pop standards.

HALF-SPEED TEMPO
The song moves at about half the typical speed of a fox trot: we hear the chorus of the song only once, rather than two or three times.

BIPOLAR HARMONY
Long stretches of a single chord contrast with lush harmonies, most notably on the title phrase.

INSISTENT TRIPLET RHYTHM
Triplets inject rhythmic energy into the song, helping to balance out the slow tempo.

5 to Listen For
"I Only Have Eyes for You"

INSTRUMENTATION
Lead/backup vocals, plus full rhythm, with electric guitar prominent at beginning and drummer using brushes

RHYTHM
Extremely slow tempo, with piano triplets providing momentum

HARMONY
Static in verse; rich in chorus

MELODY
Pop song: melody built from opening riff

TEXTURE
Rich sound: low guitar, high piano, close harmony or lead and doo-wop in middle

Solo Singers

Solo singers also fueled the growth of rhythm and blues in the late 1950s. Many, like Clyde McPhatter and Jackie Wilson, launched solo careers after starting as lead singers in doo-wop and R&B singing groups. (Both McPhatter and Wilson sang with Billy Ward's Dominos.) Sam Cooke bypassed doo-wop, going directly from gospel to a solo career. Ray Charles, the most important R&B singer of the late 1950s, followed the most roundabout route.

Ray Charles. Born at the beginning of the Great Depression, Ray Charles (1930–2004) faced a host of personal difficulties (he was blind since the age of six and kicked a serious drug habit) to endure as an icon of popular music—the most important and influential of the gospel-inspired solo performers of the 1950s. More than any other artist, he was responsible for the synthesis of blues and gospel. His music merged the emotional intensity of both styles. His singing came not out of the relatively smooth delivery of male quartets, as

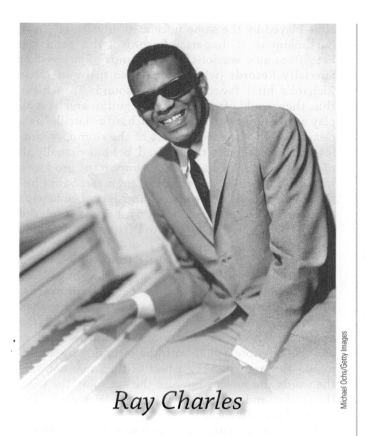

Ray Charles

Michael Ochs/Getty Images

Sam Cooke's had, but from the ecstatic, uninhibited shouting of holiness churches. Several of his songs, like "I Got a Woman," were thinly disguised adaptations of gospel songs fitted with new, secular lyrics.

Charles was a musician of eclectic tastes and a strong enough musical personality to put his own stamp on everything he tried. He broke through as a rhythm-and-blues artist in 1955. During this time he also gave expression to his interest in jazz, performing at jazz festivals as well as R&B events and recording with major jazz artists like vibraphonist Milt Jackson. In this respect he was the main rhythm-and-blues link to jazz's "return to roots" movement.

Like many R&B artists of the period, Charles included a few Latin numbers in his act and helped bring Latin music into rhythm and blues.

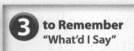

"What'd I Say," Ray Charles (1959).

The Latin numbers had an obvious effect on songs like "What'd I Say," his biggest hit of the 1950s. For rhythm-and-blues musicians like Charles, Americanized

Latin rhythms represented a more complex alternative to the relatively straightforward rhythms of rock and roll.

"What'd I Say" is not one song, but three: an instrumental, a solo vocal, and a rapid-fire call and response dialogue between Charles and The Raelettes. The instrumental section features Charles's take on Latin rhythm. The opening piano line sounds like an American cousin of the piano montunos of Afro-Cuban music, and the drum part is much closer to Americanized Latin drumming than it is to standard rock drumming, ca. 1959. In most other respects, the song is straight rhythm and blues.

The solo vocal section alternates between stop time and the instrumental riffs, which are now part of the background. Although the solo vocal section uses the by-now venerable verse/chorus blues form, it does not tell a story. Instead, it offers a series of images, mostly of dancing women. The sequence of the images in the live recording differs from the studio version, further suggesting that the real message is in the feeling behind the words, not the words themselves. The final section, whose moans often transcend verbal communication, confirms this impression.

"What'd I Say" defined a crucial juncture in the relationship between gospel and blues. The song revisits a blues tradition—in subject matter (the joy of sex), narrative style (pictures, not a story), upbeat mood, and form (verse/chorus blues)—that began with

5 to Listen For
"What'd I Say"

INSTRUMENTATION
Solo singer, backup vocals (at end), electric piano, bass, drums, horn section (trumpets, saxophones)

PERFORMANCE STYLE
Charles's vocal style fuses blues and impassioned gospel.

RHYTHM
Americanized Latin rhythm (no clave pattern)

HARMONY
Blues progression used throughout

TEXTURE
Frequent call and response at end: first horns, then backup vocalists

3 to Remember
"What'd I Say"

FROM INSTRUMENTAL TO VOCAL
Full version of "What'd I Say" begins as instrumental featuring Charles; middle section = solo vocal; end features full band, backup vocalists.

AMERICANIZED LATIN RHYTHM
Drumming, Charles's montuno-like opening riff show adaptation of Latin rhythm to R&B. Rhythms less insistent, more complex alternative to rock rhythm.

BLUES + GOSPEL + JAZZ
Charles brings together several streams in black music: jazz-like improvisation in opening, blues theme, style, and blues harmony, gospel-like call and response and screams, moans, etc., in Charles's singing

songs like Thomas A. Dorsey's "It's Tight Like That" (see Chapter 6). Soon after Dorsey recorded "It's Tight Like That," he brought the blues into African-American sacred music. Charles closes that particular circle by bringing gospel music into a "It's Tight Like That"–type blues song.

After establishing himself as the most important, innovative, and influential rhythm-and-blues artist of the 1950s, Charles reached out to two more styles: country and pop. While growing up he had listened to country music along with various forms of pop. After occasionally including country songs on earlier albums, he recorded two albums of country songs in 1962. Both were best-selling albums; the first topped all three charts (pop, R&B, and country) simultaneously. Charles's albums brought country songs to a wider audience and influenced a number of important country musicians, including Merle Haggard and Willie Nelson.

Charles's recordings of pop standards, like Hoagy Carmichael's "Georgia on My Mind," were similarly well received and influential. He was the first major rock-era performer to record an album of standards, a practice that a subsequent generation of singers—most notably Linda Ronstadt, Willie Nelson, and Rod Stewart—has followed.

For most of his career, Charles was in control of his own music. He charted his own direction—through jazz, R&B, country, and pop. For other R&B groups, the end result was often a partnership between performers, songwriters, and producers. Two such acts were the Coasters and the Shirelles.

Leiber and Stoller: The Rise of the Producers

"We don't write songs, we write records," said Jerry Leiber (b. 1933) and Mike Stoller (b. 1933). Leiber and Stoller's remark sums up the new reality of music making in the rock era. Increasingly, a song was not just a melody which singers could perform "their way," but the entire sound world captured on disc.

The Producer in the Early Rock Era. With this shift, the producer assumed an increasingly important role. The first producers wore several hats—artist and repertoire (A&R) man, songwriter, arranger, contractor—as well as recording engineer, in several cases. Because producers controlled so many elements, they often put their own stamp on the sound of a recording. For example, the New Orleans sound was the product of a distinctive arranging style played by the same nucleus of musicians. Dave Bartholomew at Imperial Records (who produced Fats Domino's sessions) and "Bumps" Blackwell at Specialty Records (who produced so many of Little Richard's hits) favored a heavy sound. To achieve this, they would often have saxes, guitar, and bass all play a low-register riff: Little Richard's "Lucille" is a clear example. It could be part of the sound, regardless of the featured artist. Indeed, behind virtually all of the major fifties stars was an important producer, who often doubled as recording engineer. Sam Phillips oversaw Elvis's early career and Jerry Lee Lewis's rock-and-roll records, while Leonard Chess produced Chuck Berry's hits, and Norman Petty, most of Buddy Holly's.

Leiber and Stoller stand apart from the others, if only because they wrote so many of the songs their acts recorded. Knowing that they operated within strict time constraints—by their measure, no more than 3 minutes 40 seconds (3:40) and no less than 2:20 (the upper and lower time limits of a 45 single)—Lieber and Stoller wrote a song with the recording session in mind. They crafted every aspect of the song: not only the words and melody but also the sax solos, the beat, the tempo, and just about every other element of the recorded performance.

They began as songwriters in love with the sound of the new black music. Among their first hits was "Hound Dog," originally written for Big Mama Thornton and covered a few years later by Elvis Presley. For Presley they wrote and produced such hits as "Jailhouse Rock." They left their imprint most strongly on the recordings of the Coasters and the Drifters.

Leiber and Stoller were among the first to elevate record production to an art. They were meticulous in both planning and production, often recording up to sixty takes to obtain the result they sought. Their most distinctive early songs were what Leiber called "playlets"—songs that told a funny story with serious overtones; Stoller called them "cartoons." As with print cartoons, the primary audience was young people—of all races—who identified with the main characters in the story. These were humorous stories, but with an edge.

The Coasters. The Coasters—so named because they came from the West Coast, unlike most of the other doo-wop groups—were really doo-wop in name only, because their music was so different from that of almost all the other groups of the time. They had formed as the Four Bluebirds in 1947 and became the Robins in 1950, singing backup behind Little Esther. They

|||||||||||||||||||||||||||||||||||||||||
"We don't write songs, we write records."
—Leiber and Stoller

reformed in late 1955, renaming themselves the Coasters.

The group's fortunes changed when they began working with Leiber and Stoller in 1954. The following year, Atlantic signed Leiber and Stoller as independent songwriters and producers. Together, they and the Robins/Coasters ran off a string of hits: "Smokey Joe's Cafe," "Charlie Brown," "Yakety Yak," and "Young Blood," which topped the R&B charts and reached the Top 10 in the pop charts in 1957.

CD 3:9

"Young Blood," Jerry Leiber and Mike Stoller (1957). The Coasters.7

The story told in "Young Blood" deals with youthful infatuation, but it is a far cry from the starry-eyed romance found in songs like "Sh Boom." As "Young Blood" shows, the Coasters' songs were the opposite of most doo-wop: steely-eyed, not sentimental, and darkly humorous. The Coasters' singing sounds slick, but not sweet. Although the Coasters have a black sound, the theme of the song is universal. Teens of all races could relate to it, and did.

The musical setting is a distinctive take on fifties rhythm and blues. The core instrumentation is typical: full rhythm section plus saxophone behind the vocal group. However, there are other instruments in the background. A shuffle rhythm with a heavy backbeat provides the underlying rhythmic framework. But the most prominent rhythm is the repeated guitar riff, which has a distinct rhythmic profile, and there are numerous shifts in the rhythmic flow—breaks that showcase the Coasters' trademark humorous asides that drop down the vocal ladder, with bass singer Bobby Nunn getting in the last word, and sections where the rhythm players sustain long chords instead of marking the beat. These and other features separate "Young Blood" musically from more straightforward R&B songs (like "Shake, Rattle and Roll"), just as the lyrics separate the song from both blues-oriented lyrics and romantic doo-wop.

Leiber and Stoller laid the groundwork for subsequent generations of producers. Such major figures as Phil Spector, Berry Gordy, George Martin, and Quincy Jones trace their roles back to Leiber and Stoller and the other producers of the 1950s who helped transform the making of popular music.

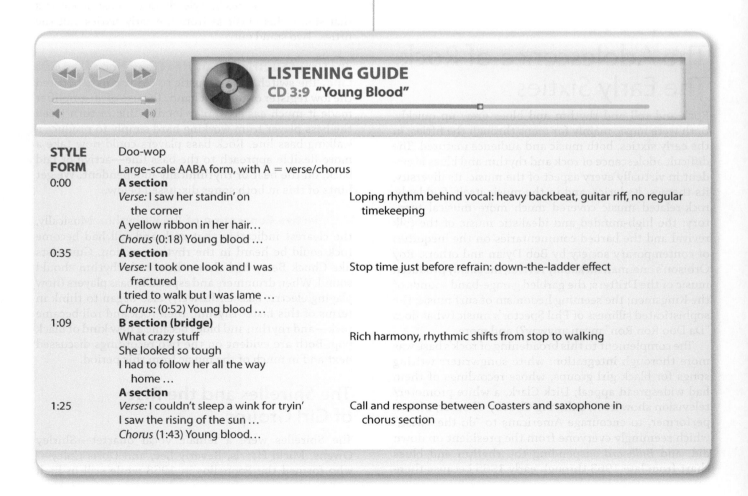

LISTENING GUIDE
CD 3:9 "Young Blood"

STYLE	Doo-wop
FORM	Large-scale AABA form, with A = verse/chorus

0:00	**A section**	
	Verse: I saw her standin' on the corner	Loping rhythm behind vocal: heavy backbeat, guitar riff, no regular timekeeping
	A yellow ribbon in her hair…	
	Chorus (0:18) Young blood …	
0:35	**A section**	
	Verse: I took one look and I was fractured	Stop time just before refrain: down-the-ladder effect
	I tried to walk but I was lame …	
	Chorus: (0:52) Young blood …	
1:09	**B section (bridge)**	
	What crazy stuff	Rich harmony, rhythmic shifts from stop to walking
	She looked so tough	
	I had to follow her all the way home …	
	A section	
1:25	*Verse:* I couldn't sleep a wink for tryin'	Call and response between Coasters and saxophone in chorus section
	I saw the rising of the sun …	
	Chorus (1:43) Young blood…	

5 to Listen For
"Young Blood"

INSTRUMENTATION
Vocal group (solo and together), plus electric guitar, bass, saxophone

PERFORMANCE STYLE
Contrast in vocal timbres an effective device, especially when voices heard in sequence

RHYTHM
Swing/shuffle rhythm at moderate tempo with strong backbeat

RHYTHM
Riffs and stop time in lieu of steady timekeeping

MELODY
Both verse and chorus-like sections built from short, slightly varied riffs

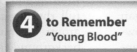

4 to Remember
"Young Blood"

WRY TONE OF LYRICS
A story of youthful infatuation that leads nowhere but trouble

DISTINCTIVE SHUFFLE RHYTHM
The loping guitar/bass riff and heavy backbeat give this shuffle-based rhythm a more open sound. There is no instrument consistently marking the shuffle rhythm.

SOUND OF THE COASTERS
The Coasters use the "down-the-ladder" breaks to showcase all of the voices, not just the lead singer and the bass.

PRODUCERS' IMPACT
Leiber/Stoller input is evident not only in song, but in setting: varied supporting rhythms and textures, including stop-time effects and strong contrasts.

● ● ● ● ● ● ● ●

The Adolescence of Rock: The Early Sixties

Rock and roll and rhythm and blues grew up quickly. Both were music mainly for teens through the fifties; in the early sixties, both music and audience matured. The difficult adolescence of rock and rhythm and blues is evident in virtually every aspect of the music: its diversity, its themes, its lyrics, and in the music itself. Suddenly, rock-related music covered much more musical territory: the high-minded and idealistic music of the folk revival and the barbed commentaries on the inequities of contemporary society by Bob Dylan and others; Roy Orbison's one-man rockabilly revival; the slickly produced music of the Drifters; the garbled garage-band sounds of the Kingsmen; the seeming hedonism of surf music; the sophisticated silliness of Phil Spector's music (what does "Da Doo Ron Ron" mean anyway?) and more.

The complement to this broadening of rock's base was more thorough integration: white songwriters writing songs for black girl groups, whose recordings of them had widespread appeal; Dick Clark, a white promoter/television show host, enlisting Chubby Checker, a black performer, to encourage Americans to "do the Twist," which seemingly everyone from the president on down did; and *Billboard* suspending the rhythm and blues chart from late 1963 through early 1965 because there

had been so little difference between the R&B and pop charts.

Rock's musical adolescence typically features an often appealing mix of innocence and immaturity with innovation and sophistication. The two songs presented next evidence this: the emotional fragility of Carole King's song "Will You Love Me Tomorrow" echoed in the voices of the Shirelles, but supported with a sophisticated accompaniment; Brian Wilson's complex and imaginative setting of "I Get Around," a song with an almost mindless lyric.

Common Musical Features of Early Sixties Music

Still, there is, overall, a sense of growth: of coming together into a new kind of music. Despite the significant differences in style, there are musical features that stamp this music as from the early sixties, not the fifties. Two stand out.

The Use of Electric Bass and the Liberation of the Bass Line. The switch from acoustic to electric bass boosted the low register of the rock band. The use of an amplifier made it much easier to play loudly. This in turn freed the bass player from working hard simply to produce a walking bass line. Rock bass players could now take a more flexible approach to the bass line—active or laid back, on the beat or rhythmically independent. We get hints of this in both songs discussed below.

A Collective Conception of Rock Rhythm. Musically, the clearest indication that rock and roll had become rock could be heard in the rhythm section. Guitarists like Chuck Berry had shown how rock rhythm should sound. When drummers and especially bass players (now playing electric bass exclusively) also began to think in terms of this faster rhythm, then rock and roll became rock—and rhythm and blues became a new kind of black pop. Both are evident on the two recordings discussed next and in much of the music from this period.

The Shirelles and the Rise of Girl Groups

The Shirelles were a female vocal quartet—Shirley Owens, Micki Harris, Beverly Lee, and Doris Coley—who formed the Poquellos in 1958 while still in high school. Their rise to the top of the charts is another of the happy accidents of the rock era. The group had won over the crowd at a high school talent show with a song they wrote themselves, "I Met Him on a Sunday." A classmate, Mary Jane Greenberg, introduced them to her mother, Florence, who, after some haggling, signed them to record the song for her fledgling label, Tiara Records. It was a local hit—big enough to be picked up by Decca. When released by Decca, the song charted nationally; it was the Shirelles' first hit.

CD 3:10

"Will You Love Me Tomorrow," Carole King and Gerry Goffin (1960). The Shirelles.

After a few more Decca-released recordings that went nowhere, Greenberg re-formed Tiara as Scepter Records and brought in Luther Dixon to produce the group. From 1960 to 1963, the Shirelles were almost always on the charts. Their biggest hit came in 1960 with a song written by Carole King and Gerry Goffin, her husband at the time: "Will You Love Me Tomorrow."

The song and its creation give us a wonderful preview of the tumultuous changes to come in the 1960s. It was written and performed by women, and the lyric gives us a woman's perspective on the fragility of new love.

> ❝ *In songs like "Will You Love Me Tomorrow," the Shirelles sang peer to peer about a meaningful issue.* ❞

And she had a Prince Charming find her out, eventually. But not me . . .

HOW CAN I EVER GET A DECENT BOY TO WALK ME HOME? THE FEW THAT HAVE I NEVER SEE AGAIN . . .

SHAME! DUNNO WHAT BOYS ARE COMING TO . . .

Image courtesy of The Advertising Archives

Before rock there had been few women songwriters (Kay Swift, who wrote the 1930 hit "Fine and Dandy" stands out). Moreover, the songs that they wrote were gender-neutral; there is no obvious clue in words or music that a song is written by a woman for women.

Before rock we get the woman's perspective on relationships mainly from female blues singers like Bessie Smith and country singers like Kitty Wells. Carole King's song gives us the other side of boastful, male R&B songs ("Good Rockin' Tonight"). The man thinks only of tonight; the woman worries about tomorrow. There is no mistaking the message of the song—the lyrics are simple and clear. This kind of frankness became possible in mainstream popular music only when society, or at least the audience for popular song, could accept this kind of straight talk. That change in attitude was under way by 1960. We hear this song as a transitional step between the Donna Reed façade of 1950s pop and the confessional songs of Carole King, Joni Mitchell, and other female singer-songwriters of the 1970s.

The music reinforces the message of the lyrics, not because it presents a coherent setting but because its main components send such different messages. There are three groups of sounds: the rhythm section, the string section, and the Shirelles. The rhythm section lays down a rather mundane rock beat, one that was fashionable during these years in rock-influenced pop. It remains constant throughout the song; there is almost no variation. But the string writing is bold and demanding—the most sophisticated part of the sound. The intricate string lines stand in stark contrast to the Shirelles' vocals, especially Shirley Owens's straightforward lead.

And therein lies the charm. The instrumental backup, and especially the skillful string parts, contrasts with the naïve schoolgirl sound of the Shirelles (none of whom was yet twenty years old when the song was released). All of this meshes perfectly with King's lyrics, the song's simple melody, and the group's look. Shirley sounds courageous enough to ask the question and vulnerable enough to be deeply hurt by the wrong answer. She, like the lyric, sounds neither worldly nor cynical.

The song and the singers reflect the changing attitudes of the early 1960s. It was written by a white woman, produced by a black man, supported with white-sounding string writing, and sung by young black women. The message of the song is colorblind: teens of all races could relate to it. The Shirelles crossed over consistently partly because of the changing racial climate (the civil rights movement was gathering steam) and partly because they were teens like their audience. In songs like "Will You Love Me Tomorrow," the Shirelles sang peer to peer about a meaningful issue.

LISTENING GUIDE

CD 3:10 "Will You Love Me Tomorrow"

STYLE	Early 1960s girl group
FORM	Considerably expanded AABA form
0:00	Introduction: instrumental
	Rhythm section lays down a straightforward, simple rock rhythm.
0:07	*First chorus*

A: Tonight you're mine, completely … A complete statement of the form takes almost two minutes. Each A
A: (0:35) Is this a lasting treasure … section unfolds slowly as it builds to the title phrase.
B: (1:03) Tonight with words
unspoken …
A: (1:31) I'd like to know that your
love …

1:30 *Second chorus (incomplete)*
A: Violins play a varied version of the The A section, shared by violins and voices. The Shirelles enter with the
melody. third line of the stanza, then repeat the title phrase.
A: So tell me now and I won't ask
again …

5 to Listen For
"Will You Love Me Tomorrow"

INSTRUMENTATION
Lead and backup vocals, full rhythm
(piano, bass, electric guitar, and drums),
and full strings (violins and cellos).

PERFORMANCE STYLE
The Shirelles' singing has a girl-next-door
quality: their voices are not classically
trained or modeled after mature pop,
blues, or jazz singing.

RHYTHM
Moderate tempo; straightforward rock
rhythm, with rebound backbeat (two taps
on the snare drum rather than just one)

MELODY
A section grows out of the opening
riff-like phrase, forming an arch, with the
peak on "so sweetly"; strong push toward
the title phrase.

TEXTURE
Distinct layers: lead vocal, backup vocal,
violins playing an obbligato, and low
strings and rhythm instruments laying
down steady patterns

4 to Remember
"Will You Love Me Tomorrow"

**VULNERABLE LYRICS, VULNERABLE
GIRLS**
Innocent-sounding girls' number 1
question; the Shirelles' vocal style and
look enhance the question in the lyric.

DRESSING UP
String writing adds a layer of
sophistication to simple vocal sounds and
rhythm-section accompaniment.

SIMPLE ROCK RHYTHM
The state of rock rhythm ca. 1960:
straightforward rock beat in drums,
slightly liberated bass line

BETWEEN ROCK, R&B, AND POP
Teen-themed song, black pop vocal
style, simple rock rhythm, pop-like string
writing

Regional Rock and Multitrack Recording: The Beach Boys and Surf Music

When I arrived at a Massachusetts college from California in the fall of 1963, one of the first questions my East Coast dorm mates asked me was "Do you surf?"

Regional Rock. For teens who had grown up with snowy winters and dreary, late-arriving springs, the beaches of southern California seemed like a hedonist's dream: sun, surf, cars, babes—the endless summer. Although *Beach Party*, the first in a series of films celebrating the surfing lifestyle, had been released just a month earlier, most teens, including my dorm mates, learned about the southern California lifestyle from the lyrics of songs by the Surfaris, the Ventures, Jan and Dean, and—above all—the Beach Boys.

Surf music was responsible for two important firsts in rock history. It was the first post-1959 rock style to add significantly to rock's sound world. Perhaps the most distinctive new sound was the high-register close harmony vocals of the Beach Boys and, to a lesser extent, Jan and Dean. More influential, however, were the array of new guitar sounds—intense reverb, single line solos in a low register (most famously in the Ventures' "Walk, Don't Run"), and down-the-escalator tremolos and other virtuosic effects popularized by Dick Dale, the "king of the surf guitarists" and one of rock's first cult figures, and those who imitated him. Indeed, Dale is arguably rock's first virtuoso guitarist—Hendrix, who like Dale was left-handed, copied Dale's guitar setup.

In large part because of these distinctive sounds, surf music acquired an indelible regional identity. A single vocal harmony or descending tremolo was all that was needed to put a listener on a Malibu beach watching the waves or cruising along the strip in a little deuce coupe or a station wagon with real wood paneling.

This was the first time in the short history of rock where the music evoked a strong sense of place. Rock and roll developed first in the center of the country, from Chicago through Memphis to New Orleans. There was a New Orleans sound, but the songs of Little Richard don't call to mind gumbo or wrought-iron railings the way jazz does. The music coming from Sam Phillips's studio had a distinct sound identity, but our images are of the performers, not the place; the same is true with Chuck Berry. By contrast, the name says it all: surf music is a sound about a place and a lifestyle. It would not be the last. A few years later, a street corner in San Francisco would become the geographic center of another rock-driven lifestyle; others would follow.

More generally, the new sounds coming out of California were the first clear signal of the

geographic diffusion of rock. The British invasion would be a far more potent sign, because it made an American music international. It is in this early sixties development that we see the first stages in what would become the global reach of contemporary rock-era music.

Multitrack Recording. From the start, Brian Wilson, the mastermind of the Beach Boys' sound, used a newly developed technology to craft the distinctive sound of the Beach Boys. According to his website, *www.brianwilson. com,* he worked it out before their first recording:

> It was a unique fusion that Wilson had been tinkering with in the family garage where, inspired by The Four Freshman and their complex vocal blends, and armed with a multitrack tape recorder, he'd spent hours exploring the intricacies of harmony and melody. By overlapping his own dynamic voice (which peaked in a soaring falsetto) and various instruments, he could create the effect of a full group.

Wilson's early exercises in multitrack recording show a new creative process at work. Before multitrack tape recorders, musicians had to imagine the sound that they wanted; perhaps try it out on an instrument, such as the piano; then write out what they heard and assemble a group of musicians to hear the actual sound of the musical mental image. If the final result were not to their liking, they rewrote the composition or arrangement and reassembled the musicians. In most stages of the process, the musicians had to convert sounds—real or imagined—into notation, which is necessarily an imperfect rendering of the musical sound. Then they had to rely on the musicians not only to play what was written but also to supply those elements of the performance that could not be notated. However, in multitrack recording, musicians like Wilson are working with actual sounds throughout the entire creative process. Further, they are able to experiment with their work at every stage of the process; they can add a part, and if it is not the desired result, they can remove it.

Today, creating music in a sound-only environment is commonplace. Buy an Apple computer, open up Garage Band (the audio workstation software that comes with the computer), drag and drop a few times, and you have an instant dance track. Wilson's work is among the most

> ❝
> ## Surf music is a sound about a place and a lifestyle.
> ❞

noteworthy early examples of this process; it would soon become the *modus operandi* in rock music, as we discover in the next chapter. It is a process that belongs to the rock era; it is the result of technology responding to musical needs, much as the technology of the 1920s responded to the musical needs of that time. It is a revolutionary change in the creative process, one that is as far reaching as the invention of musical notation and one whose possibilities are still being expanded. For those who have come of age in the twenty-first century, it may be hard to imagine a musical world without this technology. But fifty years ago, Wilson was on the cutting edge.

The Beach Boys. The most important and innovative of the surf music bands was the Beach Boys. Their band was a family affair. The original group consisted of three brothers, Carl (1946–1988), Dennis (1944–1983), and Brian Wilson (b. 1942); their cousin, Mike Love (b. 1941); and a friend, Al Jardine (b. 1942).

CD 3:11

"I Get Around," Brian Wilson (1964). The Beach Boys.

The Beach Boys' first recordings point out their debt to rock's first generation. They feature Chuck Berry riffs—even entire songs—borrowed almost note for note. (However, they combined Berry's riffs with a completely new vocal sound.) In their recordings released between 1963 and 1965, they glorified the surfer lifestyle in songs that subtly varied their innovative, immediately recognizable sound.

"I Get Around," a song that reached the top of the charts in June 1964, shows key elements of their style and the variety possible within it. The song begins with just voices, presenting the essence of the Beach Boys' vocal sound. In order, we hear unison singing, tight harmonies, and a soaring single line melody juxtaposed with harmonized riffs—all sung with no vibrato.

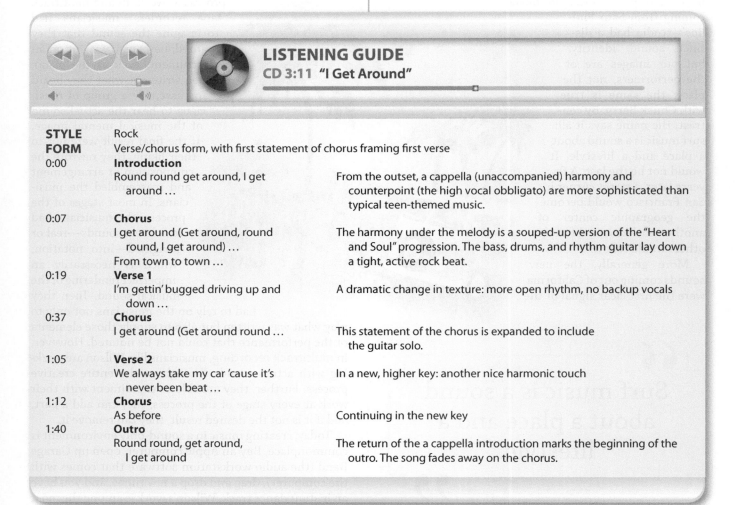

LISTENING GUIDE
CD 3:11 "I Get Around"

STYLE	Rock
FORM	Verse/chorus form, with first statement of chorus framing first verse

0:00 Introduction
Round round get around, I get around …

From the outset, a cappella (unaccompanied) harmony and counterpoint (the high vocal obbligato) are more sophisticated than typical teen-themed music.

0:07 Chorus
I get around (Get around, round round, I get around) …
From town to town …

The harmony under the melody is a souped-up version of the "Heart and Soul" progression. The bass, drums, and rhythm guitar lay down a tight, active rock beat.

0:19 Verse 1
I'm gettin' bugged driving up and down …

A dramatic change in texture: more open rhythm, no backup vocals

0:37 Chorus
I get around (Get around round …

This statement of the chorus is expanded to include the guitar solo.

1:05 Verse 2
We always take my car 'cause it's never been beat …

In a new, higher key: another nice harmonic touch

1:12 Chorus
As before

Continuing in the new key

1:40 Outro
Round round, get around, I get around

The return of the a cappella introduction marks the beginning of the outro. The song fades away on the chorus.

4 **to Remember**
"I Get Around"

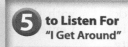

5 **to Listen For**
"I Get Around"

DISTINCTIVE VOCAL SOUND
The high lead singing with intricate, important backup vocal parts gave the Beach Boys' songs an unmistakable and virtually inimitable sound.

CLEAR ROCK RHYTHM WITH CONSIDERABLE VARIATION
Strong rock beat in chorus, with bass, drums, and rhythm guitar moving at rock beat speed. An open, loping long/short rhythm in verses provides contrast, as does the lack of an underlying rhythm during the a cappella introduction.

SOUND VARIETY IN INSTRUMENTATION AND TEXTURE
Overall low register of the instruments balancing high register vocals; innovative sound combinations, such as the organ doubling the guitar in the verse

STRONG BASS LINE THROUGHOUT THE SONG
The bass moves at rock-beat speed in the chorus and lopes along in the verses. This is the development that, more than any other, effects the musical transition from rock and roll to rock.

INSTRUMENTATION
Lead and backup vocals; electric guitar, electric bass, drums, organ

PERFORMANCE STYLE
High lead singing plus closely spaced vocal harmony

RHYTHM
Basic rock beat, reinforced by guitar, bass, and drums, predominates.

HARMONY
Rich harmony: well beyond I/IV/V

TEXTURE
Considerable variation in texture: a cappella vs. full band, steady timekeeping vs. loping rhythm or stop time, melodic interplay between lead and backup vocals

The refrain follows, its split melody supported by a driving rock rhythm played by the entire band. Unlike this rhythm, the distinctive vocal sound of the Beach Boys came from outside rock. Its source was the Four Freshmen, a slick, skilled, jazz-flavored vocal group who navigated complex harmonies as nimbly as Count Basie's saxophone section. Wilson, who admired the group and acknowledged them as a source of inspiration, used their sound as a point of departure. The song is harmonically richer than any other song that we have heard to this point; Wilson charts a distinctly new path in the fresh new chord progressions underneath the vocal.

The scene-painting verse sections are set off from the chorus by the substitution of an open-sounding, loping rhythm for the straightforward rock rhythm of the refrain. Even the instrumental solos have a characteristic, clearly defined sound. The short interlude in the verse combines a doubled organ and bass line with double-time drums, while the guitar solo is supported with sustained vocal harmonies.

The "fun in the sun" lyrics belie the considerable sophistication of the music: not only the harmonies and key changes that range well beyond the three-chord rock progressions of so many bands, but also the beautifully interwoven vocal parts, sharp contrasts in texture that outline the form of the song, varied timekeeping, and other subtle features. This sophistication was mainly the work of Brian Wilson; in their peak years, the sound of the Beach Boys was Brian Wilson's conception.

"Will You Love Me Tomorrow" and "I Get Around" show two aspects of the transition from the music of the 1950s to the music of the mid-1960s. The Shirelles' song bridges the gap between doo-wop and Motown and the other black pop of the 1960s. "I Get Around" evidences the assimilation of Chuck Berry's conception of rock rhythm. With them, rock and roll had become rock.

Looking Back, Looking Ahead

In 1954 rock and roll was on the verge of national recognition; in 1964 rock was on the verge of a revolution. During that same period, rhythm and blues crossed over to the pop charts so thoroughly that *Billboard* merged the pop and R&B charts for over a year.

Rock and roll and rhythm and blues energized young Americans. The active aggressive rhythms in so much of the music were matched by more assertive vocal styles and instrumental sounds, especially from electric guitars. The energy was in the look as well as the sound: Elvis's gyrations, Chuck Berry's duck walk, Little Richard's leg on the piano, Jerry Lee Lewis's manic piano pounding, the vigorously stylized choreography of the Coasters, even Ray Charles's pendulum-like rocking from side to side as he sang and played.

For their audience, the sounds and the looks promised freedom—freedom from the repressive mores of their parents, freedom from the restrained sound of their parents' pop, and freedom to assert their identity.

For blacks, the new music did not guarantee the freedoms that they had been denied for so long; that would not come until the mid-1960s. However, the rise of black and black-influenced music was one sign of the shift in consciousness that would ultimately lead to equality under the law, if not in practice.

In the decade that followed, rock would take over the music industry and become a truly international music. Rock, and what it represented, would undermine attitudes and values in North America and western Europe, and challenge centuries-old beliefs. We chart these momentous developments in the next chapter.

● ● ● ● ● ● ● ●
Terms to Know

Test your knowledge of this chapter's important terms by defining the following. If you can't recall the meaning of a certain term, refresh your memory by looking up the boldfaced term in the chapter, turning to the Glossary at the back of the book, or working with the flashcards on the Popular Music Resource Center.

doo-wop	obbligato
scat singing	payola scandal
bebop (bop)	gospel
rockabilly	surf music
overdubbing	multitrack recording

The Rock *Revolution*

Rock and Black Music in the 1960s

CHAPTER

10

© Peter Grosdek /Superstock

If it were possible to encapsulate the rock revolution in a single sound, it could easily be the opening chord of the Beatles' "A Hard Day's Night." In a single strum, George Harrison broadcast a new sound world, new freedoms, a new attitude, and a new way of creating music. The dissonant clangor was intentional: according to producer George Martin (the "fifth Beatle"), the group wanted a bold beginning because the song was the title track for the film of the same name.

The chord symbolized the search for new sounds and new ways of making them. Harrison played the chord on a Rickenbacker twelve-string guitar; underneath his sound is McCartney's bass note and Martin's supporting piano chord. The thoughtfully planned instrumental mix suggests that the quest for distinctive sounds was part of the new aesthetic of rock.

The chord symbolized harmonic freedom: it is more about sound than about structure. It relates tangentially to the key of the song but is not part of the standard progressions for that key. As a result, it previews the mix of conventional, blues, and modal harmonies that underpin the melody of the song—and in the rock of the 1960s and beyond.

The chord rings for an indeterminate time—about three seconds—before the band launches into the song proper, with Lennon's melody supported by a driving rock beat. As such, it implies that the more aggressive rhythms may be the heart of the new music, but that rock is not bound by its new rhythm.

The chord resonated not only at the beginning of the song (and the film) but also throughout the rapidly evolving world of rock. In effect, the Beatles threw down the gauntlet, even as they announced a new direction in their music that would ultimately lead to *Sgt. Pepper's Lonely Hearts Club Band*, their supreme accomplishment. In the process, they would spearhead the rock revolution.

● ● ● ● ● ● ● ●
The Rock Revolution: A Historical Perspective

To this day the rock revolution still seems like the most momentous change in the history of popular music. Nothing since has transformed popular music to such a degree, and only the modern-era revolution of the 1920s has had a comparable impact. There are several reasons for this perception:

- *It happened quickly.* The revolution was effectively over in just a few years.
- *Much of the music came from "outside."* In fact, the music that made the biggest splash came from abroad. The British invasion marked the first time

that music from beyond the United States became the commercially important music of a generation.

- *The memory of the music is still vivid.* The generation that grew up with it is still around, still working—still writing books about popular music. Oldies stations continue to feature this music, much of which now sounds comfortable rather than challenging. The music continues to sell well; several of the top acts of the era continue to tour; and the songs are used in films and commercials.
- *The music grew up very quickly, and we have it all down on record.* By 1965 a new Beatles album was an event; a year later, their album releases were an even bigger deal because the group had stopped touring. Their transformation over an eight-year period from the "Fab Four" to the creators of some of the most inspired and intriguing music of the century mirrored the maturation of rock from music for teenyboppers into a substantial musical language.
- *Seemingly everyone knew this new music.* In the sixties, a sizable majority of the audience knew—and liked—the top songs. This state of affairs contrasts strongly with the fragmented musical marketplace in the early twenty-first century.
- *The music was the soundtrack for a decade of extraordinary social change.* Civil rights, the Vietnam War, free love, the gradual empowerment of women, the environmental movement, a huge generation gap—all of this was a brutal challenge to the established social order. And it seemed even more revolutionary compared with the fifties, when the bland façade portrayed in the media promoted the American dream even as it covered up the abuses of McCarthyism, bigotry, big business, and the like.

A Revolutionary Music

Finally, though, it comes down to the music itself. Rock and roll and rhythm and blues promised a new musical direction; rock, Motown, and soul fulfilled that promise, and changed musical life in the process.

The rock revolution was comprehensive, not cosmetic. It affected every aspect of the music: its influences, creative process, authorship, sound, musical message, and end product. The music took advantage of brand new and still evolving technology in both performance and production. It reflected significant social shifts in both words and music. And despite the range of styles, it represented a coming together musically, the most important since the 1920s. Among the most significant new developments were these:

A Fully Integrated Music. Rock is an integrated music. It isn't just that the music of the sixties was more profoundly influenced by black music than any earlier mainstream style. It's also that the influence went both ways—we hear black influences in music by white bands and white influences in music by black performers. And, most important, these various influences are assimilated into a new sensibility and a new sound. Integration is about not only being together but also blending together.

Song Ownership and the Creative Process. From the outset rock changed the relationship between composer and performer. Most of the early rock stars, such as Chuck Berry, Buddy Holly, and Little Richard, performed original material—Elvis was an interesting exception to this trend. In their music the song existed as it was recorded and performed, not as it was written, if indeed it was written down at all. A song was no longer just the melody and the harmony but the total sound as presented on the record: not only the main vocal line but also guitar riffs, bass lines, drum rhythms, and backup vocals.

Increasingly, rock musicians took advantage of multitrack recording, an emerging new technology, to shape the final result even more precisely. Multitrack recording made it possible to record a project in stages instead of all at once. Strands of the musical fabric could be added one at a time and kept or discarded at the discretion of the artist or the producer.

This ability to assemble a recording project in layers fostered a fundamental change in the creative process. It was possible to experiment at every stage of a project, and it was normal for one person or group to stay in creative control of the project from beginning to end.

The Sounds of Rock. The sounds of rock were startlingly new. Rock and roll and rhythm and blues had laid the groundwork for these new sounds. Still, when they arrived—with Dylan and the folk rockers, the ascent of Motown, the British invasion, the "guitar gods," soul, Latin rock, proto-funk, and pop rock—the impact was stunning.

We think of the electric guitar as the signature instrument of rock, and so it is. But the instrument most responsible for the transition from rock and roll to rock was the electric bass. By the early sixties, it was standard equipment in a rock band. With good amplification the electric bass balanced the power of the electric guitar, giving rock bands the full bass sound they lacked in the fifties. James Jamerson, Motown's staff bassist, showed rock musicians what could be done with it.

Electric instruments benefited from a huge boost in amplification. Marshall stacks, the amps used by the Who, Cream, and so many other rock bands, weren't even available in 1960, but by the end of the decade their sound was filling arenas. Other companies kept pace, replacing tubes with transistors and boosting output many times over. A performance at Candlestick Park in San Francisco, at the time an outdoor baseball stadium with a capacity of almost 50,000, would have been a bad idea in 1960, the year it opened; in 1966, however, it was the venue for the Beatles' last public performance.

With increased amplification and a balance of power among the instruments, what had been the background component of a band became, in many cases, the whole band. In effect, this core nucleus—guitar(s), bass, drums, and keyboard—went from a supporting role to the center of the action. This shift flipped the balance between horns and rhythm instruments: horns, when used, were usually an extra layer; they were no longer in the limelight except for the occasional saxophone solo. And particularly in white rock, they were no longer an integral part of the band.

Rock Beat. This core nucleus laid down a new beat: a rock beat. Chuck Berry had laid the groundwork in the fifties with his boogie-woogie–inspired patterns that divided each beat into two equal parts. Played forcefully, this rock-defining rhythm is far more assertive than shuffle, swing, or 2-beat rhythms. However, Berry's recordings from the fifties lack the rhythmic impact of rock because no one else joins him in marking this more active rhythm. It wasn't until the whole band began playing with a rock conception that rock and roll became rock.

Moreover, in the rock of the sixties, producing a rock beat became a collective responsibility. With the liberation of the bass line to play a truly creative role, the instruments became both more independent and more interdependent. In other words, no instrument, not even the lead guitar, was absolutely locked into a specific pattern, like the bass player's walking pattern, the banjo player's "chunk" on the backbeat, or the drummer's ride pattern in prerock music. At the same time, the groove was the end product of the interaction of all the rhythm instruments. Take one away, and the groove was gone.

> *The instrument most responsible for the transition from rock and roll to rock was the electric bass.*

istockphoto.com

Sharing Melody. This sharing of responsibility also applied to melody. Up to this point, the main source of melodic interest in the songs we've heard was, appropriately enough, the melody—the vocal line when it was sung and the lead instrumental line when it was played. That changed with rock: melodic interest was spread out to the other instruments. In many of the songs we hear in this chapter, the song is immediately identifiable from an instrumental riff, generally the first of several melodic hooks. The hook identifies the song well before the singer enters. Typically, other instruments also had parts with some melodic interest. One result was a greater variety of texture, from delicate tapestries with a few parts to densely packed free-for-alls.

All of these changes—in instrumentation, rhythmic and melodic approach, and texture—applied to both white rock and the black music called "soul" through the mid-seventies. The difference from one style to the next was usually a matter of emphasis or interpretation; indeed, new ideas flowed freely in both directions.

Rock Attitudes and the Musical Message

These innovations give us a musical perspective on the wholesale shift in attitude that was at the core of the revolution. Three qualities of this new attitude stand out: sixties rock was egalitarian, it was eclectic, and it was real. Until 1960 most groups had a leader, who fronted the band, or a featured performer. In the thirties it was Benny Goodman with his orchestra. After the war it was Muddy Waters, or Louis Jordan and His Tympany Five. Even Buddy Holly fronted the Crickets. Vocal groups, from the Mills Brothers to the girl groups, were the almost singular exception.

By contrast, most sixties rock bands took group names: the Beatles, the Beach Boys, the Who, Jefferson Airplane. In so doing they projected a collective identity. There was nothing in their name that said one member was more important than the others. The interplay among voices and instruments was another key. In hooking the listener with a catchy riff or

in laying down the beat, no one person was consistently in the spotlight.

The sources of the new rock style, and the way in which they made their way into rock and soul, also evidenced this new attitude. Rock took a pragmatic approach to musical borrowing: musicians took what they needed, no matter what its source, and transformed it into something new.

Contrast that with music before 1960. Pop artists gave country songs a shower and a shave before putting them on record, as a pop cover of any Hank Williams song will attest. If the recordings are any indication, neither the singers nor the arrangers made much of an effort to understand either the sound or the sensibility of country music. Similarly, rhythm and blues usually got a bleach job: the Chords' cover of "Sh Boom" is one example among too many. Even many of the teen idols, from Pat Boone to Fabian to Frankie Avalon, dressed the part but neglected the sound and the style of rock and roll.

In the sixties, sounds came from everywhere: Delta blues, East Indian music, symphonic strings, jazz, music hall, folk, country—if it was out there, it was available for adoption. More important, rock musicians didn't necessarily privilege any particular style or family of styles. There is no sense of connection between the social standing of a style and its use in rock, unless it's an inverted one: the grittier the source, the more it was admired, as in the case of Delta blues. The Beatles' music epitomizes this egalitarian, eclectic approach: one track can be sublime, the next can sound like a children's song.

There was a hierarchy of importance within rock, especially in the wake of the Beach Boys' *Pet Sounds* and the Beatles' *Sgt. Pepper's Lonely Hearts Club Band*. The possibility of making an artistic statement in rock has been part of its collective understanding since the mid-sixties. But artistic statements were typically crafted out of seemingly ordinary materials. Even when rock emulated classical music and other established traditions, it did so on its own terms; the Who's *Tommy* was a rock opera but a far cry from conventional opera. For the best rock bands, the sound world of the sixties was like a well-stocked kitchen; bands simply took what they needed to create the feast.

> *Most sixties rock bands projected a collective identity. There was nothing in their name that said one member was more important than the others.*

istockphoto.com

> *The sound world of the sixties was like a well-stocked kitchen; bands simply took what they needed to create the feast.*

Finally, rock was *real* in a way that earlier generations of pop had not been. Rock formed a bond with its audience that was different from the connection between Tin Pan Alley popular song and its audience. Tin Pan Alley songs offered listeners an escape from reality, whereas rock songs often intensified the reality of life in the present. Moreover, the message of the song reached its audience directly because rock-era songwriters usually performed their own songs. Songs were not written so much *for* something—such as a musical or a film—as *to say* something.

Rock's concern with the present, combined with its direct and often personal communication between song, singer, and audience, elevated the role of the music for many members of that audience from simple entertainment to, in the words of noted rock critic Geoffrey Stokes, "a way of life."

Sixties rock and soul was a revolutionary music; the rock revolution is, in fact, the only widely acknowledged revolution in the history of popular music.

● ● ● ● ● ● ● ●

Bob Dylan and the Beatles: Making Rock Matter

On August 28, 1964, Bob Dylan and the Beatles met face to face for the first time. The Beatles were on tour in the United States and staying at the Delmonico Hotel in New York. They had acquired *The Freewheelin' Bob Dylan* album while in Paris in January 1964; according to George Harrison, they wore the record out, listening to it over and over. John Lennon in particular seemed drawn to Dylan's gritty sound and rebellious attitude. Somewhat later that same year, Dylan was driving through Colorado when he heard the Beatles for the first time on the radio. Later he would say, "I knew they were pointing the direction where music had to go." Each had something that the other wanted, and perhaps found intimidating: the Beatles, especially Lennon, wanted Dylan's forthrightness; Dylan responded to the power of their music and envied their commercial success.

Whatever initial uneasiness Dylan and the Beatles may have felt with each other went up in smoke. Upon learning that none of the Beatles had tried marijuana, Dylan promptly rolled a couple of joints and passed them around. As Paul McCartney later recalled, "Till then, we'd been hard Scotch and Coke men. It sort of changed that evening."

The Beatles' encounter with cannabis is credited with helping to change the course of their music. Ian McDonald, author of *Revolution in the Head*, a track-by-track account of the Beatles' recordings, observed, "From now on, the superficial states of mind induced by drink and 'speed' gave way to the introspective and sensual moods associated with cannabis and later LSD."

Still, there was more to this meeting than turning the Beatles on. It seemed to further motivate both parties to learn from the other. For the Beatles, Dylan raised the bar—the standard to which the Beatles would hold their music. More specifically, his music occasionally served as a model for their songs, especially those in which Lennon provided the more significant creative input. Later, in explaining their musical breakthrough in the mid-sixties, McCartney said, "We were only trying to please Dylan." Without question, the music they created after the meeting, especially from *Rubber Soul* on, represents a far more substantial legacy than their earlier work.

istockphoto.com

Pictorial Press Ltd/Alamy Limited

> "I knew they were pointing the direction where music had to go."
> —Bob Dylan, on the Beatles

As for Dylan, the experience gave him additional motivation to go electric. His next album, *Bringing It All Back Home,* which he recorded in January 1965, featured acoustic tracks on one side and electric tracks on the other. After that, he never looked back. In retrospect, his years as a folksinger, as important as they were to his career and to rock, were simply a prelude to his more substantial career as a rock musician.

There are obvious differences between Dylan and the Beatles: solo performer versus group; private versus public persona; seat-of-the-pants versus state-of-the art record production; talking, barely melodic songs versus tuneful melodies.

However, they were alike in at least two crucial ways: they came to rock from the outside, and they stretched rock to its outer limits. "Outside" for Dylan meant starting his professional career as a folksinger. "Outside" for the Beatles meant, more than anything else, Liverpool, England. The idea of foreigners' redefining American popular music—and thereby internationalizing it—was without significant precedent.

We focus on the most significant period in the careers of both acts—from the date of the meeting through the release of *Sgt. Pepper's Lonely Hearts Club Band.* We begin with Dylan.

From Folk to Rock

The folk revival that began in the late fifties had a short lifespan, even by pop standards. As a movement with mass appeal, it began in 1958, when the Kingston Trio's recording of "Tom Dooley" topped the pop charts. It ended seven years later, when Dylan went electric at the Newport Folk Festival, and folkies like Alan Lomax and Pete Seeger went ballistic.

In its revived form, folk music was an urban music. Recall that the earlier folk revival of the forties and early fifties, sparked by the work of the Lomaxes, Woody Guthrie, and—most popularly—the Weavers, had brought folk music into the city. The second revival, which began in the late fifties, made the separation between country roots and contemporary urban performance even wider. By 1960, this old/new folk music was flourishing in coffeehouses, often located in the more bohemian parts of major cities (Greenwich Village in New York, North Beach in San Francisco) or near college campuses.

The folk revival was apolitical at first. Its audience liked folk's tuneful melodies, pleasantly sung. That soon changed, as this new folk revival quickly rediscovered its activist past.

Bob Dylan and the Folk Revival. Dylan's music from the early sixties recaptures the substance and spirit of the songs of Woody Guthrie. The repertoire on his first few recordings includes mostly original material, which ranged from songs like "Talkin' John Birch Paranoid Blues," which he delivered in a "talking blues" style, often used by Woody Guthrie—resonant speaking over a strummed guitar accompaniment, with an occasional harmonica interlude—to anthem-like songs like "Blowin' in the Wind." In either case, the words were preeminent; the guitar accompaniment typically consisted of simple strumming of the I, IV, and V chords. The main musical variable was the melody—including whether there was one.

However, by the time he met with the Beatles, Dylan's lyrics were becoming more surreal and stream of consciousness. He had written "Mr. Tambourine Man" in February 1964 and performed it at the Newport Folk Festival that summer. Perhaps to counterbalance the more abstruse lyrics, Dylan began to add rock-oriented instrumental accompaniment to his music, to help communicate the general mood of the song.

Unlike CDs, vinyl albums contain content on both sides of the disc. So it was convenient, and perhaps expedient, for Dylan to dedicate one side of an LP to where he was coming from and the other side to where he was going: one side of *Bringing It All Back Home* is acoustic, the other side is electric. Dylan moved forward by returning to his roots; his first musical experiences were with a rock-and-roll band. To Alan Lomax, Pete Seeger, and other folkies who thought he'd committed musical blasphemy by going electric, this was the beginning of the end. But viewed in relation to the rest of his career, it was the end of the beginning. From that point on, Dylan was a rock musician, not a folksinger.

 "Subterranean Homesick Blues," Bob Dylan (1965).

Among the most provocative tracks on the album was "Subterranean Homesick Blues." The lyric is that of a proto-rap song: a stream of obscure references, inside jokes, stinging social commentary, and cinéma vérité–type images—all delivered much too fast to understand in a single hearing.

The density of the lyric and the speed of Dylan's delivery challenged listeners to become engaged; one could not listen to him casually and expect to get much out of the experience. For this song Dylan added a full rhythm section behind his acoustic guitar and harmonica. The band sets up a honky-tonk feel with a clear 2-beat rhythm. At the same time, it's a free-for-all for the guitarists; their interaction evokes electric blues. The ornery mood it sets up right at the start is an ideal backdrop for Dylan's words and voice.

What's so remarkable and significant about this song and others like it is that it simultaneously elevates popular music to a higher level of seriousness and brings

5 to Listen For
"Subterranean Homesick Blues"

INSTRUMENTATION
Voice, harmonica, acoustic and electric guitar, electric bass, piano, drums

PERFORMANCE STYLE
Dylan's raspy voice was a drastic departure from almost any other kind of popular singing—pop, R&B, folk, country, or blues.

RHYTHM
Strong two-beat rhythm with emphatic backbeat; fast delivery of words

MELODY
Not a conventional melody: rather, streams of words on a single note, occasionally interrupted by a riff-like idea ("Look out, kid")

HARMONY
Stretched-out blues progression

4 to Remember
"Subterranean Homesick Blues"

CONFRONTATIONAL TONE
Provocative lyrics, delivered very quickly

RAISING THE BAR
Street poetry with a bluesy, hard-country accompaniment = serious musical statement without classical sounds

BLUES/COUNTRY/ROCK FUSION
Honky-tonk beat, blues sounds and form, contemporary folk lyric, blended together

ROCK: ATTITUDE VS. STYLE
Rock in attitude but not in style features (no rock beat or rock band instrumentation)

popular music was, Dylan raised the bar, for rock and for popular music. Overnight the music grew up. It was no longer possible to mock rock—or at least Dylan's music—as mindless music for teens. Indeed, songs like "Subterranean Homesick Blues" would have left most adults in a state of incomprehension.

One of the acoustic tracks on *Bringing It All Back Home* was "Mr. Tambourine Man." A version by the Byrds was released within a month of Dylan's album; it topped the charts in June 1965.

The Byrds. The Byrds came together in the summer of 1964 to form what would become the first folk-rock band. The original lineup included guitarists Jim (later Roger) McGuinn, Gene Clark, and David Crosby; bassist Chris Hillman; and drummer Mike Clarke. McGuinn, Clark, and Crosby had formed a folk trio in Los Angeles in late 1963, which went nowhere. Adding Hillman and Clarke changed their sound and put them on the cutting edge of the mix between folk and rock. "Mr. Tambourine Man" was their first big hit, one of two No. 1 singles for the group.

A comparison of the two versions of "Mr. Tambourine Man" is instructive. Dylan's version is acoustic. The Byrds' cover uses a full band, including McGuinn's electric twelve-string guitar. Dylan's version lasts 5 minutes 30 seconds; the Byrds' version lasts only 2 minutes 29 seconds. And even that difference is deceptive, because the Byrds' recording has a slower tempo and includes McGuinn's introductory riff, which also serves as an extended tag.

The Byrds' version is also much more like a rock song in form. Two statements of the chorus frame just one of the four verses. This truncated version cut out over half of the lyrics—precisely the element that had made the song so special for Dylan fans. But the expanded instrumentation, simpler form, and slower tempo gave the song much wider appeal. McGuinn's famous opening riff, played on a twelve-string guitar, seemed to evoke the "jingle-jangle" of the chorus.

By using rock-derived points of entry—the distinctive sound of Roger McGuinn's twelve-string guitar, the guitar hook to start a song, and a comfortable rock beat—the Byrds converted Dylan's elusive and elliptical ramble into a tight pop song. Their folk-rock synthesis was both novel and appealing.

Dylan was not indifferent to the Byrds' success with his song; it would influence his next few albums,

it down to earth by wiping away traditional forms of pretentiousness. Dylan's lyric is far more complex than anything that had been done before. We've admired clever pop lyrics, deep blues lyrics, and meaningful country lyrics. But we haven't heard anything like this. Similarly, his singing is not pretty by any conventional standard—it was ordinary enough to convince Jimi Hendrix that he could start singing—but it's certainly appropriate for the song. And Dylan embeds words and voice in a down-home setting.

The combination of words and music reverses the traditional pop approach to artistry. Before, those who wanted to create artistic popular music emulated classical models: George Gershwin's *Rhapsody in Blue* or musical theater productions like *West Side Story*. Dylan's music sends a quite different message: one can be sophisticated without being "sophisticated"; that is,

CD 3:12

"Mr. Tambourine Man," Bob Dylan (1965). The Byrds.

without taking on the conventional trappings of sophistication, such as symphonic strings.

In essence, this kind of work formed a new definition of what artistry in rock—and by extension popular music—could be. By not only giving rock credibility but also redefining what credibility in

LISTENING GUIDE

CD 3:12 "Mr. Tambourine Man"

STYLE	Folk rock
FORM	Verse/chorus, with two statements of chorus framing verse
0:00	**Introduction**
	Roger McGuinn's famous riff, played on 12-string guitar, gets the song under way.
0:09	**Chorus**
	Hey! Mr. Tambourine Man, play a song for me … Much richer texture than in the original, with vocal harmony behind melody, plus consistently active guitar line, strong bass, drums, and tambourine
0:43	**Verse**
	Take me on a trip upon your magic swirlin' ship … McGuinn's vocal lacks the edge in Dylan's delivery of the lyrics. This is the second verse in Dylan's version.
0:32	**Chorus**
	Hey! Mr. Tambourine Man, play a song for me … As before
2:04	**Outro**
	The opening guitar riff leads to a long fadeout ending.

although he never truly compromised his vision in pursuit of commercial success. He wanted to be popular, but he also wanted to establish the terms of his popularity.

His next album, *Highway 61 Revisited*, recorded in the summer of 1965, brought into full flower the power latent in the electric side of *Bringing It All Back Home*. Following that album, Dylan gravitated toward country music. His next three studio albums—*Blonde on Blonde* (1966), *John Wesley Harding* (1967), and *Nashville Skyline* (1969)—used Nashville session musicians. His country excursion strengthened the connection between rock and country, just as his earlier work helped link folk and rock. This was another of Dylan's major contributions to rock in the sixties: he played the key role in bringing both folk and country into rock.

Dylan's work from the sixties remains a standard by which those who followed him have been measured. He inspired others not so much by providing a model that others would copy as by showing through example what could be said in rock. In this way, his influence was profound and pervasive.

5 to Listen For
"Mr. Tambourine Man"

INSTRUMENTATION
Lead, backup singers, 12-string electric guitar, electric guitar, electric bass, drums, tambourine

PERFORMANCE STYLE
12-string guitar sound: distinctive new timbre

RHYTHM
Straightforward rock rhythm

MELODY
Chorus melody consists of two long descending phrases: shows folk influence

TEXTURE
Rich texture, especially in chorus: vocal harmony, plus full rhythm and active guitar lines

3 to Remember
"Mr. Tambourine Man"

FROM FOLK TO ROCK
The famous opening guitar riff, rock beat, and full rock rhythm section, including prominent electric bass, connect the song stylistically to the new sounds of the 1960s.

NOT MUCH OF THE STORY
We only hear one verse of the song, so we know less of the story than we do in Dylan's original.

FROM WORDS TO MUSIC
In Dylan's version of the song, melody and accompaniment are in service of the words, which is where the real interest is. By contrast, the Byrds' version, with its richer accompaniment, distinctive guitar sound and riff, and emphasis on the refrain, shifts attention to the music. As presented in their version, Dylan's catchy melody and its setting seem more important than the lyrics.

The Beatles

By the time the Beatles got together with Dylan, they were riding the crest of Beatlemania. The band had scored their first U.S. No. 1 hit, "I Want to Hold Your Hand," in January 1964 and appeared on *The Ed Sullivan Show* for the first time in February. In little more than a month, the band developed a passionate following, one that would surpass Elvis's; the media dubbed it "Beatlemania." *A Hard Day's Night,* which opened in American theaters in early August, was filmed to capitalize on their runaway success before they faded away just as quickly. That didn't happen. Other British bands soon followed the Beatles to the United States, and within a year the British invasion was under way.

The British Invasion. The roster of British bands that made an impact in the sixties is substantial. The first wave, in 1964, included not only the Beatles but also the Rolling Stones, the Kinks, the Animals, the Dave Clark Five, and several others. By the end of the sixties, many more had joined them; the Who, Cream, and Led Zeppelin stand out.

The sudden popularity of British bands in America abruptly reversed the flow of popular music between the United States and the rest of the world. Up until the early sixties, popular music had been largely an American export. Before the sixties, few European musicians performing popular music enjoyed much of a following in the United States. All that changed with the British invasion.

Of course, the music that they played had deep American roots. Many of the bands began their careers by covering songs by Chuck Berry, Buddy Holly, and other rock-and-roll acts. The Rolling Stones' name underscores the musical impact of bluesmen like Muddy Waters and Robert Johnson. But what they brought back to the United States was an altogether new music. What's more, it was never exotic, and it soon became mainstream. Indeed, the British invasion, more than any other event, fueled the ascendancy of rock in the United States during the sixties.

What is surprising is the ease with which rock—and by extension popular music—became an international music. Up to this point, popular music *in* America and popular music *from* America were pretty much the same thing. After the Beatles that was no longer true. While Americans acknowledged, even celebrated, the Britishness of the Beatles and the other invading bands, there was no sense that their music was foreign. Perhaps it was because the sounds were at once familiar (because they were so deeply rooted in American culture) yet fresh (because they represented a new way of interpreting American music). Perhaps it was the open-minded spirit that seemed to pervade the sixties. Whatever the reason, their nationality was a nonissue.

The Musical Evolution of the Beatles. The Beatles are rock's classic act, in the fullest sense of the term. Their music has spoken not only to its own time but also to every generation since. Their songs are still in the air; they remain more widely known than any other music of the rock era. Beatles music is a cultural artifact of surpassing importance. No single source—of any kind—tells us more about the rock revolution of the 1960s than the music of the Beatles.

We can trace the beginning of the Beatles back to the summer of 1957, when John Lennon (1940–1980) met Paul McCartney (b. 1942) and soon asked him to join his band, the Quarrymen. George Harrison (1943–2001) joined them at the end of year; the group was then known as Johnny and the Moondogs. They went through one more name change, the Silver Beetles, and one more drummer, Pete Best, before settling on the Beatles and Ringo Starr (b. Richard Starkey, 1940), who joined the group after they had signed a recording contract.

The major phase of the Beatles' career lasted just under eight years. For all intents and purposes, it began on June 6, 1962, when they auditioned for George Martin, the man who would produce most of their records. It ended on April 10, 1970, when Paul McCartney announced that the Beatles had disbanded. After their breakup, all continued their careers as solo performers. But we remember the Beatles mainly through their recordings, made between 1962 and 1970.

The Beatles at the height of Beatlemania

LIFE

THE BEATLES
They're here again and what a ruckus!

AUGUST 28 · 1964 · 25¢

Time & Life Pictures/Getty Images

The Beatles' musical growth was unparalleled in popular music; the suddenness with which their music matured remains an astounding development. Like Dylan, the Beatles were expanding their sound world, but in a more adventurous and more encompassing way. Dylan drew mainly on existing popular styles and used them evocatively. By contrast, the Beatles reached farther afield, into musical traditions far removed from rock and its roots, such as classical Indian music (for instance, the sitar and finger cymbals heard in "Norwegian Wood") and string playing reminiscent of classical music. Moreover, they synthesized these extraneous sounds seamlessly into their music; they became part of the fabric of sound behind the vocals.

Among the most important reasons for the exceptional quality and appeal of their music are these three:

Knowledge of styles. They had firsthand familiarity with a broad range of styles. In their dues-paying years, the band performed not only rock-and-roll covers and original songs but also pop hits of all kinds. From their years of apprenticeship, they had a thorough knowledge of pop before rock, and they absorbed styles along with songs.

Melodic skill. Along with the Motown songwriting teams, the Beatles were the first important rock-era musicians to write melody-oriented songs that were in step with the changes in rhythm, form, and other elements that took place during this time. No one since has written so many memorable melodies.

Sound imagination. Aided by the development of multitrack recording and the consummate craftsmanship of their producer, George Martin, the Beatles enriched their songs with startling, often unprecedented, combinations of instruments and—occasionally—extraneous elements, such as the crowd noises and trumpet flourishes of "Sgt. Pepper."

As their music matured, it became bolder and more individual. The songs are more clearly the work of the Beatles—no one else could have made them—and less like each other. The contrast from song to song had clearly deepened. One can almost reach into a bag filled with song titles, pull out any five, and marvel at the distinctive identity in meaning and sound of each song and the pronounced differences from song to song.

For Beatles' historian Ian McDonald, the opening chord of "A Hard Day's Night" and the final chord of "A Day in the Life" frame the group's "middle period

… the sitar and finger cymbals heard in "Norwegian Wood"

of peak creativity." Certainly Harrison's chord immediately suggests that the group isn't just another rock band, and the seemingly endless chord at the end of "A Day in the Life" has a sense of finality, not just for the song, or even the album, but also a phase in the Beatles' musical evolution. A side-by-side comparison outlines their growth from a rock band with a difference into one of the creative forces of the twentieth century.

"A Hard Day's Night." "A Hard Day's Night" was a feature film shot in March 1964 and released that summer, first in England, then in the United States. It is about Beatlemania fans' hysterial response in both countries to the Beatles' live performances, and an attempt to capitalize on it—the more cynical parties in the production process expected the Beatles' star to fall as quickly as it had risen. The film came early in their career; the soundtrack was their third American album. Despite that, the Beatles enjoyed significant input into the film, choosing both the screenwriter and the director, Richard Lester. They also chose the title, which came from an offhand remark by Ringo that caught their fancy.

As they did in so many other areas, the Beatles confounded the experts with a film that broke new ground in almost every important respect. The

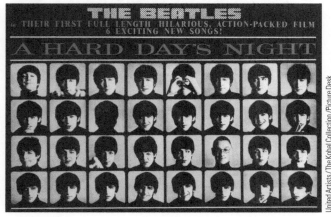

film was quasi-autobiographical: shot documentary-style in black and white, it purports to present a "day in the (incredibly hectic) life" of the band. It captured their cheeky good humor—Paul's cinematic grandfather was a running gag—even as it dramatized the relentless pressures of stardom, which would compel them to retire from public performance less than three years later. The group's naturalness in front of the camera, coupled with *cinéma-vérité*, resulted in a film far different from standard commercial fare and the rock and roll films of the 1950s.

"A Hard Day's Night," John Lennon and Paul McCartney (1964). The Beatles.

The title track from the album reveals the qualities that made their music stand out right from the start and anticipates the directions that it would soon take. In its sound and rhythmic approach, the band is leading the way in the transformation of rock and roll into rock. The band is locked into a rock beat (which Ringo enhances with double-time rhythms on bongos); the interplay among the rhythm instruments goes well beyond basic rock timekeeping. The sound of the band has an edge—the ring of the opening chord, the vocals, the strident guitar sound, and the relentless drumming. Compared to 1950s bands, and even the Beach Boys' sound, it is aggressive. At the same time, it is friendly: Lennon's song recalls pre-rock pop; so does the vocal harmony. The lyric is innocent enough, at least on the surface; in tone, it is more like "Sh Boom"—or even "Sunday" (also a song about getting together after long hours on the job) than the Rolling Stones' "Satisfaction," which would appear within a year. There are numerous innovations: the search for new sounds, the extensive use of multitrack recording, the opening and closing sounds, and use of modal harmony. (**Modal harmony** consists of chords built from modal scales, rather than the major and minor scales used in nineteenth- and early twentieth-century pop. Like major and minor scales, modal scales also have seven notes per octave, but in a different arrangement. Modal scales are common in British folk music; "Greensleeves" is a familiar example.) The mix of conventional, modal, and blues chords brought a fresh sound to rock harmony.

Like the film itself, the mix of old and new shows the Beatles beginning their move away from convention. Teen-themed songs would soon disappear, as both the band and their audience quickly grew up.

3 to Listen For
"A Hard Day's Night"

INSTRUMENTATION
Lead, backup singers, 12-string electric guitar, electric guitar, electric bass, drums, and bongos

PERFORMANCE STYLE
Both vocal sounds and instrumental support have an edge

RHYTHM
Straightforward rock rhythm, but with double time (twice as fast as rock rhythm) rhythm on bongos; syncopations in the melody

MELODY
Pop-style AABA song in which A section grows out of a riff

HARMONY
Basic harmony with occasional modal chords mixed in

5 to Remember
"A Hard Day's Night"

FROM ROCK AND ROLL TO ROCK: RHYTHM
Aggressive rock rhythm in guitars, drums, and free-moving bass line confirm collective conception of rock rhythm.

FROM ROCK AND ROLL TO ROCK: SOUND
Aggressive vocal sound, innovative opening chord, dense texture presage new sonic directions in 1960s.

MODAL AND TONAL
Beatles interpolate modal harmonies into standard pop harmony: e.g., under "working like a dog." Mix of tonal pop and modal chords expands rock harmonic vocabulary.

POP MELODY
Although a rock song, melody and form are more typical of pre-rock pop: AABA form, plus phrases developing from title-phrase riff.

DISTINCTIVE FEATURES
Opening chord/outro, vocal harmony, double-time bongos, shift in texture at bridge all show Beatles' keen ear for distinctive elements.

The Sound World of the Beatles: "A Day in the Life." The Beatles' "style" was not so much a particular set of musical choices, as was the case with Motown recordings heard next, but an approach to musical choices: write tuneful melodies and embed them in evocative sound worlds. Settings—instruments, textures, rhythms, even form—were purposeful; their function was to amplify and elucidate the message of the lyrics. There were strong contrasts from song to song, and occasionally within a song, as in "Lucy in the Sky with Diamonds" and the even more remarkable "A Day in the Life," both from *Sgt. Pepper's Lonely Hearts Club Band*.

"A Day in the Life," John Lennon and Paul McCartney (1967). The Beatles.

In "A Day In The Life," the Beatles create sound worlds that highlight the contrast between the mundane, everyday world and the elevated consciousness of an acid trip. It is projected by the most fundamental opposition in music itself, other than sound and silence: music with words versus music without words. The texted parts of the song are everyday life, while the strictly instrumental sections reflect the influence of tripping—they follow "I'd love to turn you on" or a reference to a dream.

This contrast is made even more striking by the nature of the words and music. The text of the song and the music that supports it paint four scenes. The first scene is the singer's response to a newspaper account of a man who dies in a horrible automobile accident while, one suspects, he was tripping. The second portrays Lennon attending a film—perhaps an allusion to the film *How I Won The War*, in which he had acted a few months prior to recording the song. The third depicts the singer in the workaday-world rat race. The last one is a commentary on another even more mundane news article. It is news reporting—and, by extension, daily life—at its most trivial: who would bother counting potholes? The music that underscores this text is, in its most obvious features, as everyday as the text. It begins with just a man and his guitar. The other instruments layer in, but none of them makes a spectacular contribution. This everyday background is opposed to the massive orchestral blob of sound that depicts, in its gradual ascent, the elevation of consciousness. The dense sound, masterfully scored by George Martin, belongs to the world of avant-garde classical music—it recalls Penderecki's *Threnody for the Victims of Hiroshima* (1960) and other works of that type.

The apparent simplicity of the vocal sections obscures numerous subtle touches. Starr's tasteful drumming and McCartney's inventive bass lines are noteworthy. So is the doubling of the tempo in the "Woke up ... " section. What had previously been the rock beat layer is now the beat. This expresses in music the narrator's frantic preparation for work without disturbing the underlying rhythmic fabric of the song. Perhaps the nicest touches, however, are found in the vocal line: the trill heard first on "laugh" and "photograph," then expanded on "nobody was really sure ... " before floating up to its peak on "Lords." It is precisely this melodic gesture—the trill, now set to "turn you on"—that presages the move from the vocal section to the orchestral section, and by extension the beginning of an acid trip. When the trill/leap material returns in the film-viewing vignette, this connection becomes explicit; the melodic leap is followed by the trill, which blends seamlessly into the orchestral texture. As a melodic gesture, the trill/leap sequence is also a beautiful surprise, strictly on its own terms.

5 to Listen For
"A Day in the Life"

INSTRUMENTATION
Simple rock band instrumentation: acoustic guitar, electric bass, drums, maracas, alternating with orchestral strings performing slow glissandos (gradual changes in pitch); orchestral winds and brass in "dream section"

RHYTHM
Strong contrasts in tempo: slow rock tempo; double time; pulse gradually disappears in instrumental sections.

MELODY
Tuneful melody with short phrases in narrative sections, which expand, then dissolve into trill, which dissolves into indeterminate pitch.

HARMONY
Simple harmony with occasional modal chords in vocal sections; dissonant blob of sound in instrumental section; simple tonic chord at the end

TEXTURE
Open texture in vocal sections: voice, light guitar, and maracas in midrange; bass and drums in a lower range; thick texture in instrumental sections

3 to Remember
"A Day in the Life"

CONTRASTING LEVELS OF CONSCIOUSNESS
Underlying message of song is contrast between everyday "reality" and altered consciousness. Expressed most fundamentally by opposition of words/ no words. Shift from pop to orchestral instruments and tuneful to avant-garde music underscores shift in consciousness.

NOVEL FEATURES
Song begins simply: strummed chords. It ends on an "OM" chord that lasts for over 30 seconds. In between are slowly elevating globs of string sounds, shifts in tempo, trills that dissolve into completely new music, and more. All are novel effects for rock (and the pop that preceded it) ca. 1967.

STYLISTIC DIVERSITY
Stylistic diversity of the song, so essential to its meaning, stretches boundaries of rock. The "altered consciousness" music has virtually no connection to rock, and even the ordinary music is some distance from conventional rock.

The final chord is an instrumental suggestion of the clarity of enlightenment after the transition, via the orchestral section, from mundane life in the "normal" world. It is a striking ending to a beautifully conceived and exquisitely crafted song, a song that is one of the most powerful metaphors for an acid trip ever created.

"A Day in the Life" encapsulates the art and achievement of the Beatles as well as any single track can. It highlights key features of their music: the sound imagination, the persistence of tuneful melody, and the close coordination between words and music. It represents a new category of song—more sophisticated than pop, more accessible and down to earth than pop, and uniquely innovative. There literally had never before been a song—classical or vernacular—that had blended so many disparate elements so imaginatively. Critics searched for a way to describe the song and the album. They labeled it a "concept album" and declared it the rock-era counterpart to the song cycles of nineteenth- and twentieth-century art music.

The Beatles had begun their career by affirming what rock was, in comparison to rock and roll and pop. As they reached the zenith of their career, they showed what it could become. Their contributions played a decisive role in reshaping rock, the music industry, and Western culture.

• • • • • • • •
Motown

When Berry Gordy Jr. (b. 1929) got out of the army in 1953, he returned to his hometown of Detroit and opened a record store. He stocked it with jazz, a music he loved, but he refused to carry rhythm-and-blues records in spite of a steady stream of customers asking for them. Two years later he was out of business. He would learn from the experience.

After a couple of years working on an assembly line at the Ford plant, Gordy returned to the music business, first as a songwriter, then as the founder of yet another independent record company. This time around, his goal was to create the first black pop style to cross over completely—to find a large audience among blacks, whites, and everyone else. He would succeed.

Gordy's Motown empire blended careful planning and tight control over every aspect of the operation with inspiration and spur-of-the-moment decisions. As it developed during the early sixties, Motown's organizational structure was a pyramid. At the top of the pyramid was Gordy. Underneath him were songwriters/producers like Smokey Robinson and the Holland/Dozier/Holland team. Underneath them were the house musicians. Berry recruited his core players from Detroit's jazz clubs. He relied on the skill and inventiveness of musicians such as bassist James Jamerson (the man most responsible for liberating the bass from its pedestrian 4-to-the-bar role), keyboardist Earl Van Dyke, and guitarist Joe Messina to bring to life the songs brought by the arrangers to the garage–turned–recording studio christened Hitsville U.S.A. The fourth level were the acts themselves: Stevie Wonder, Mary Wells, the Supremes, the Temptations, the Four Tops, Martha (Reeves) and the Vandellas, (Smokey Robinson and) the Miracles, and Marvin Gaye.

The Motown sound grew out of this pyramid structure. At its core was Gordy's guiding principle: to create music with the widest possible appeal. To that end he focused on the most universal of all subjects—love won and lost—and told the tales in everyday language. Smokey Robinson recalls Gordy's telling him early in their association that a song should tell a story; Robinson (and the other Motown songwriters) followed that advice.

Gordy's songwriters followed his plan, not only in words but also in music. Motown songs set the story to a melody with memorable hooks. The songs unfold according to a proven strategy: part of the story building to the chorus containing the hook; more of the story, followed by the repetition of the chorus; still more story—if there's time—followed again by the chorus. This template was easy for listeners to follow.

The house band created the beats, the grooves, the memorable riffs—within seconds we know both of the songs discussed next, before the vocalists begin singing—and the colors. These musicians, so essential to Motown's sound and success, were virtually anonymous. Often they would go to bars after a recording session and hear on the jukebox songs that they'd helped create; few if any of the patrons would know how much they had contributed.

It was the singers who moved into the spotlight. Not surprisingly, they received the lion's share of Gordy's attention. He determined what songs they recorded, what clothes they wore, their stage routines, and almost everything else related to their professional lives. Many artists came from disadvantaged circumstances, and Motown ran what amounted to a charm school to polish the public personas of its stars. Gordy did everything he could to have them project a smooth, cultivated image, both on stage and off.

The Motown Sound

The product of this multidimensional interaction among Gordy, the songwriters and arrangers, the house musicians, and the acts was the Motown sound. Among its most consistent and outstanding features were these four:

- *Melodic saturation.* Songs are full of melodic fragments. The lead vocal line is the most prominent, but there are many others: backup vocals, guitar and keyboard riffs, horn fills, string lines. The presence of so much melody, all of it easily grasped, helped ensure easy entry into the song; it also was a good reason to listen over and over again.
- *A good, but unobtrusive beat.* Motown songs typically feature a strong backbeat and an understatement of everything else. In particular, timekeeping in the

midrange register is subdued to give greater prominence to the voices.

- *A broad sound spectrum.* Motown recordings gave listeners a lot to listen for. The instrumental and vocal sounds cut across all social, racial, and economic lines. In the forefront are the relatively untutored singing styles of the vocalists, both lead singers and backup vocalists. There are sounds as simple as a tambourine and as sophisticated as French horn swoops and orchestral string sounds. The rhythm section typically included more than the minimum number of players; usually there were at least two guitars, several percussionists, and keyboards. With all of this richness, there were sounds for everyone, regardless of background.

- *A predictable form.* From the two songs, one could construct a pretty reliable template for a Motown song: layered instrumental introduction, solo two-phrase verse, bridge, title phrase, and commentary. There is enough variation in the form and in the other features of the song to keep it fresh, but we can certainly anticipate the events in the story.

These features were designed to provide easy entry into a song—and to keep us there. All four offer basic points of entry: melodic hooks, a clear backbeat, interesting and varied instrumental sounds, and an easy-to-follow form. The combination of easy entry and rich texture was a key element in Motown's success. We hear the Motown sound realized in two No. 1 Motown hits, the Supremes' "Come See About Me" and Marvin Gaye's memorable version of "I Heard It Through the Grapevine."

The Supremes

The Supremes—Florence Ballard (1943–1976), Diana Ross (b. 1944), and Mary Wilson (b. 1944)—went from a Detroit housing project to international celebrity in the space of a few years. The group was originally a quartet, the Primettes, the female counterpart to the Primes, who would soon become the Temptations. As the three-singer Supremes, they signed with Motown in 1961, started charting in 1964, and soon had five consecutive No. 1 singles. They became the most popular female vocal group of the 1960s and the main reason that Motown kept challenging the Beatles for chart supremacy.

The Supremes embodied the whole Motown package. In the television performances from their peak years, they appear in performance dressed in matching dresses or gowns, and with matching wigs. They move gently to the beat or step lightly; the athletic movements of today's divas are still well in the future. It's all slick and wide-eyed at the same time: the look, the gestures, the moves that match the vocal exchanges. The impression is of a more sophisticated version of the Shirelles, yet

The Supremes: (left to right) Mary Wilson, Florence Ballard, and Diana Ross

Pictorial Press Ltd/Alamy Limited

> " The Supremes embodied the whole Motown package. "

they still project the innocence of youth and inexperience. The visual impression of the group was one key to their success. It is also evidence of Gordy's overriding control in all aspects of performance.

The sounds of their voices match the look. Ross is clearly the most skilled of the three, but her vocal quality has a naturalness and naiveté that rigorous training would have disguised. The other two Supremes were less distinctive; by 1967, the group was called Diana Ross and the Supremes. (The name change may have had as much to do with Ross's favored status as Gordy's mistress as with her singing ability.)

The third hit in the string of five No. 1 singles was "Come See About Me," which topped the charts at the end of 1964 and the beginning of 1965. The song mines a familiar vein in Motown: the jilted lover.

CD 3:13

"Come See About Me," Holland-Dozier-Holland (1964). The Supremes.

LISTENING GUIDE

CD 3:13 "Come See About Me"

STYLE	Motown	
FORM	Verse/chorus, with bridge split between verse (new lyrics) and chorus (repeat lyrics)	
0:00	**Instrumental introduction**	
	Drums, then catchy harmonized riff (anticipates vocal)	
0:10	**Verse 1**	
	I've been crying / 'cause I'm lonely	Call and response between Ross and other Supremes, all over one chord
	(Bridge, Pt.1 [0:26]) That you're never ever gonna return	More agitated: longer vocal lines, with backup responses, more active harmony
0:33	**Chorus**	
	(Bridge, Pt.2) Keeps me cryin', baby, for you	Bridge extends and peaks here; this part repeats lyrics and melody.
	(Hook [0:46]) Come on boy, see about me	Again, rapid dialogue between lead and backup singers
0:52	**Verse 2**	
	I've given up my friends	Motown-style background: strong bass, hand claps, chord
	No matter what you do or say	instruments in background; light rock rhythm
1:16	**Chorus**	
	Keep on cryin', baby, for you	As before
	(Hook [1:27]) (come see about me) See about you, baby	
1:35	**Instrumental interlude**	
	Horn section briefly in the spotlight	
1:44	**Verse 3**	
	Sometimes up, sometimes down	Ross's line in a higher register = more impassioned
2:06	**Chorus + Outro**	
	Keeps me cryin', baby, for you	Gradual fadeout, with Ross comment over title-phrase riff

The lyrics present Ross's plea in everyday, if somewhat melodramatic, language. The song and the Supremes' singing of it suggest that the Ross's imaginary partner is a passing fancy; the song is relentlessly upbeat, as are the exchanges between the singers.

The musical setting follows the Motown template: instrumental introduction with catchy sound (the drums) and catchy riff; verse over static harmony; bridge to the hook; melodic hook repeated several times; repetition of the form two more times with an instrumental interlude. All of this takes place over an unobtrusive, bass-heavy accompaniment that lets the spotlight shine on the Supremes. And, as with so many Motown hits, there are features that deviate enough from the template to give the song a distinctive stamp: the handclaps on the beat, the extra phrase in the bridge, the other Supremes completing Ross's phrases.

By the time "Come See About Me" topped the charts, the Motown hit factory was a well-oiled machine. Songs from Motown acts such as the Supremes, the Temptations, and the Miracles poured out of car radios, jukeboxes, and fraternity houses. By 1966 three of every four Motown releases hit the charts, an astonishing percentage. Two years later, Motown released one of the great songs of the rock era, Marvin Gaye's version of "I Heard It Through the Grapevine."

Marvin Gaye

Of all the Motown artists, none sang with more emotional intensity than Marvin Gaye (1939–1984). His turbulent life—stormy relationships with his wife and other women, drug and alcohol abuse, and his death at his father's hand—seemed to find expression in

5 to Listen For
"Come See About Me"

INSTRUMENTATION
Lead and backup vocals; full rhythm, with electric bass, electric guitar, piano, drums, vibraphone, hand claps; horn section (trumpets, saxes) briefly between choruses

PERFORMANCE STYLE
Ross's wispy-voiced singing; untutored sound of other Supremes

RHYTHM
Light rock rhythm: beat keeping in handclaps, backbeat on guitar, rock layer in background, more varied rhythm in bass

MELODY
Vocal melody consists of short phrases—exchanged between Ross and Supremes.

TEXTURE
Vocals in the forefront, strong bass, open sound in midrange behind vocals

3 to Remember
"Come See About Me"

MOTOWN SOUND
Typical Motown sound: open midrange and light marking of rock rhythm to highlight voices; strong, free-moving bass line anchors sound.

MOTOWN TEMPLATE
Individual realization of Motown formal template: verse/bridge/chorus; chorus includes second part of bridge and title-phrase melodic hook.

SOUND OF THE SUPREMES
The Supremes offer a more refined and mature version of the girl-group sound. Ross's wispy-voiced singing mixes innocence and worldliness.

each statement. A Greek chorus–like commentary by the backup singers ends each section.

It's worth noting how well the musical setting of "Grapevine" helps project the lyric. From the first keyboard notes, the instrumental backing matches Gaye's despair. (Another version by Gladys Knight and the Pips, which charted the previous year, projects a quite different mood.) Some have accused Motown of being formulaic—pop music's answer to the Detroit auto assembly lines; but emotional, as well as musical, variety was possible within a consistent overall plan.

Motown: Updating Black Pop

Motown updated black pop. From Louis Armstrong and Ethel Waters, through Nat "King" Cole and the Mills Brothers, into doo-wop and the girl groups—one direction in black music had been a distinctly African American take on popular song. Motown offered not just a new take on pop but a new, black popular style—and a new kind of romantic music.

In this sense Motown was heading in the opposite direction from rock. Rock tended to look at love cynically (the Beatles' "Norwegian Wood" comes to mind), lustfully (the Rolling Stones' "Satisfaction"), or not at all. Motown songs preserve the romance in the popular songs of the thirties and forties even as they bring both lyrics and music into the present. Romance is evident not only in the sound—the rich string writing, the understated playing of the rhythm section—but also in the look. The groups wore tuxedos and gowns, like Las Vegas acts, not tie-dyed T-shirts and jeans, like the Woodstock crowd.

Motown was one of the remarkable success stories of the sixties. For the first time in history, a black style was on equal footing with white music. Motown would lose its toehold at the top in the seventies. The Jackson 5 was Motown's last big act. Stevie Wonder gained artistic freedom as a condition of his new contract, and he used it. Marvin Gaye also sought and got independence, eventually leaving Motown altogether. The company has remained an important player in pop music, and though it is no longer the dominant and innovative force that it was in the sixties, its legacy is still very much with us.

CD 3:14

"I Heard It Through the Grapevine," Barrett Strong and Norman Whitfield (1968). Marvin Gaye, vocal.

his music. Whether singing about love, as in "Grapevine," or contemporary life, as in several songs from his groundbreaking 1971 album *What's Going On*, he communicated an extraordinary range of feeling: pain, hope, joy, and frustration.

"I Heard It Through the Grapevine" is a drama in miniature. It is beautifully integrated: every element blends seamlessly to convey the sense of the text, in which story of love gone wrong gradually unfolds. The opening keyboard riff, harmonized with open intervals, immediately establishes a dark mood. Other instruments enter in stages, leading to the entrance of the voice. Each statement of the melody of the song contains four sections. The first two are blues-like in that they generally stay within a narrow range and go down more than up. The third builds to the final section for the hook of the song, "I heard it through the grapevine." It is the emotional center of

LISTENING GUIDE

CD 3:14 "I Heard It Through the Grapevine"

STYLE	Motown
FORM	Verse/chorus

0:00	**Instrumental introduction**	
	Ominous introduction—electric piano in the foreground playing famous riff; other instruments layer in, most notably the French horn swoop up, just before the verse.	
0:21	**Verse 1**	
	Ooh, I bet you're wondering how I knew ...	Phrases start high and end low, as in the blues.
	(Bridge [0:38]) It took me by surprise I must say ...	Surprising chord and sudden leap up underscores "surprise" in the lyric.
0:45	**Chorus**	
	(Hook) I heard it through the grapevine ...	Backup vocals, keyboard riff, and strings help bring back mood of opening.
1:09	**Verse 2**	
	I know that a man ain't supposed to cry ...	String response figures in low register behind voice + backup vocal harmony + Gaye and rhythm = rich texture
1:35	**Chorus**	
	I heard it through the grapevine ...	And for the restatement of the refrain
2:01	**Instrumental interlude**	
	Adapted from the introduction	
1:50	**Verse 3**	
	People say, believe half of what you see ...	Strings begin to soar on the bridge.
2:32	**Chorus**	
	I heard it through the grapevine ...	As before, followed by long fadeout ending
2:49	**Outro**	
	Gradual fading away, "muttering" of backup vocals help project the despondent mood of the song.	

Rock

In 1969 the Rolling Stones began to be billed as the "world's greatest rock and roll band." Whether the label came from the band itself or—as Jagger claimed—from an enthusiastic master of ceremonies is open to debate. Regardless of who used it first, the label has stuck; it has become as much as a part of their image as Jagger's tongue. One can attribute some of its staying power to the Stones' longevity—who would have predicted in 1969 that they would be the hottest ticket in 2005—and to media hype.

What's remarkable about their self-promotional assertion is that they chose to assert it—or at least assent to it. Because implicit in the billing is the assumption that in the space of five years, rock had evolved from a brand new sound to a timeless style. In 1964 the rules were just being written; by 1969 the essence of rock style had been worked out. From this point on,

rock becomes, in effect, a timeless style. For the Stones and others, "rock 'n' roll" is not a revival of Chuck Berry, but the purest form of rock.

When we think of timeless rock, we expect to hear bands with a core of electric guitar, electric bass, and drums playing songs with heavy riffs over a rock beat at a loud volume. Within these general parameters, there is considerable room for variation: solo-oriented versus group-oriented music; rhythmic play versus straightforward rock rhythm; different ways of assimilating the blues, the most profound outside influence on this music; differing textural densities, and instrumental effects. But in all cases, the essence remains present.

In this section, we observe rock's progress toward its timeless form through songs by the Rolling Stones and Cream. One is a group-oriented track; the other focuses on solo playing. Both reveal stages in the transition from rock ca. 1964 to rock ca. 1970. We begin with the Stones.

5 to Listen For
"I Heard It Through the Grapevine"

INSTRUMENTATION
Lead and backup vocals. Rhythm section with extra percussion (electric piano, electric guitar, electric bass, drums, tambourine, and conga), and orchestral instruments (violins and the French horn just before the voice enters)

RHYTHM
Moderate tempo; rock rhythm with strong backbeat but subdued marking of the rock rhythmic layer—mainly drums and conga on deep-sounding drums

MELODY
Vocal melody consists of short phrases—longer than the opening riff. Bluesy quality because of downward direction.

HARMONY
Minor key version of I-IV-V with a few additional chords (minor keys have often been associated with sad moods).

TEXTURE
Layered texture, distributed over wide range: bass and percussion are low, voices and keyboard in the middle, strings usually in a high register. Considerable variation from the empty sound of the opening to the full ensemble in the chorus.

3 to Remember
"I Heard It Through the Grapevine"

DEPICTING MOOD MUSICALLY
The dark mood of the song is established at the outset by such features as the ominous opening riff, the choice of an electric keyboard to play it, the open harmony, and the subtle, open-sounding rhythm. The melody of the song, which moves mainly from high to low, reinforces the mood.

FLEXIBLE TEMPLATE
The Motown template is predictable in its general features but accommodates considerable variation in detail and mood, as a comparison of "Come See About Me" and "Grapevine" reveals.

GAYE'S SINGING
The strained sound of Gaye's high-register singing also helps communicate the despair described in the lyrics

The Rolling Stones

"(I Can't Get No) Satisfaction," the Rolling Stones' first major hit, acknowledges the enormous influence of the blues, and Muddy Waters in particular, on the group. Both the band's name and the song title trace back to two of Waters's early recordings: a 1950 recording entitled "Rolling Stone" and a 1948 recording entitled "I Can't Be Satisfied."

The Rolling Stones grew out of a chance encounter in 1960, when Mick Jagger (b. 1943) saw Keith Richards (b. 1943) standing in a train station with an armful of blues records. It was not their first meeting; both had grown up in Dartford, England, and had attended the same school for a year, when they were six. Their meeting eleven years later would be the beginning of their band.

Both spent a lot of time at the London Blues and Barrelhouse Club, where they met Brian Jones (1942–1969) and Charlie Watts (b. 1941). At the time, Watts was the drummer for Alexis Korner's Blues Incorporated, which would also include Jagger after 1961. The band came together in 1962 when they added bassist Bill Wyman (born William Perks, 1936) after an audition. Keyboardist Ian Stewart (1938–1985) was also a member of the band at the time. He stopped performing with the group soon after their career took off, but retained a close connection with the Stones and performed on many of their recordings.

Like other British bands, the Rolling Stones began by covering blues and rock-and-roll songs. Within a year, Jagger and Richards, inspired by the success of Lennon and McCartney, started writing original songs for the band. They broke through in 1965: "(I Can't Get No) Satisfaction" and *Out of Our Heads,* the album from which it came, topped the charts that summer. By the time they recorded the song, they had pretty well defined their sound, style, and image.

Their conception of rock began with an attitude: sexually charged, down and dirty, swaggering, real. All of this was an extension of the bluesman's persona, and it is embodied most powerfully in Mick Jagger. Although he came from a comfortable middle-class family and was attending the London School of Economics in the early sixties, Jagger didn't simply imitate the bluesmen he admired—he forged his own identity, one that reverberated with their influence but was also different and credible. The rest of the band also assumed this attitude; Keith Richards's sneer is the visual counterpart to the nasty riffs for which he is so well known. Andrew Loog Oldham, who became their manager in 1964, actively promoted this image. By his own admission, he wanted them—or at least their public image—to be the opposite of the Beatles.

"(I Can't Get No) Satisfaction," Mick Jagger and Keith Richards (1965). The Rolling Stones.

Their music matched their image. They built a new sound from rock and roll, blues, and their own inspiration. From Jagger's sound to Wyman's bass lines, it was all of a piece. We highlight two of its qualities, the rhythmic groove and the dark, nasty sound.

- *The groove.* Like many other Rolling Stones songs, "(I Can't Get No) Satisfaction" starts with a syncopated riff; Watts enters only after the song is pretty well under way. The groove grows out of the interplay between the basic rock rhythm, the backbeat, and the layers of syncopated riffs and lines, much as the swing in swing is the product of riffs over a 4-beat rhythm.

- *A dark, nasty sound.* Jagger's singing—rough, highly inflected, almost drawled, and more speech-like than sung—is the most obvious expression of the nasty Stones sound. Complementing it is the thick, dark texture produced by Richards's fondness for the lower register of the guitar, Wyman's bass, and Watts's use of the bass drum. Typically, the highest sound in a Stones song is Jagger's voice, which stays in a midrange. The dark sound results from a lot of activity in the lower registers. Both Jagger's singing and the thick texture come directly from the blues; in the work of the Stones, blues become part of the sound of rock.

The compelling rhythms and the dense, riff-laden texture set the tone for the stories told in the songs. "(I Can't Get No) Satisfaction" is a study in sexual frustration: the music says what the words do not. As Jagger vents his sexual frustration with

5 **to Listen For**
"(I Can't Get No) Satisfaction"

INSTRUMENTATION
Lead vocal, electric guitar, acoustic guitar, electric bass, drums, tambourine

PERFORMANCE STYLE
Fuzztone guitar sound, Jagger's vocal sounds, from title-phrase whisper to verse-like rant: aggressive, edgy sound

RHYTHM
Rock rhythm, with strong beat keeping and even stronger syncopations

MELODY
Vocal melody constructed from simple riffs; verse-like section on one note; guitar riff most memorable melodic idea

TEXTURE
Thick texture: low-register electric guitar, low-tuned drums, electric bass, all under Jagger's vocal most of the time

5 **to Remember**
"(I Can't Get No) Satisfaction"

MEMORABLE GUITAR RIFF
Richards's fuzztone guitar riff sets mood for song and returns periodically throughout the song—one of several signature guitar riffs appearing ca. 1965.

BEAT-ORIENTED ROCK RHYTHM
Watts plays rock rhythm with heavy emphasis on the beat. The other rhythms—guitar riff, bass line, and Mick's tambourine and vocal line—weave around the strong beat.

DARK TEXTURE
Most of the sounds, including Richards's guitar riff, are in a low register; Jagger's singing is the highest sound = a dark-sounding texture, which helps convey mood of the song.

INVENTIVE FORM
The inversion of verse and chorus is an innovative twist on conventional verse/chorus form; it seems to help project the message of the song: Jagger's inability to get satisfaction.

BLUES INFLUENCE
The impact of blues style evident in dense, heavy texture, with interplay among the instruments, reliance on repeated riffs, Jagger's vocal style, aggressive sound, and subject of song.

In the work of the Stones, blues become part of the sound of rock.

Pictorial Press Ltd/Alamy Limited

The "world's greatest rock and roll band" in 1964: (left to right) Mick Jagger, Bill Wyman, Brian Jones, Charlie Watts, and Keith Richards

harangues about petty matters, the opening guitar riff never changes. It embodies Jagger's frustration because it tries (and tries) to go somewhere but never does. The form of the song also reinforces Jagger's frustration, because the sequence of verse and chorus are switched. What is usually the verse is the part that returns again and again. It builds to a peak, at which point Jagger begins to rant. There is no release, and the section ends futilely in a drum break.

To an audience raised on pop, all of this had the taste of forbidden fruit—it was a far cry from the teen-themed songs of the fifties or the early Beatles, or the surf music of the Beach Boys. The Stones' lives mirrored their public personas: Brian Jones's death "by misadventure," the Altamont riot, the occasional brushes with the law—all were real-life counterparts to the world depicted in their songs. In effect, the Rolling Stones brought a blues sensibility into the mainstream. Both words and music thrilled a new generation and repulsed an older one.

The group followed *Out of Our Heads* with *Aftermath*, released the following year. It was their first album to feature only original songs by Jagger and Richards. The group briefly fell under the spell of the Beatles; their *Their Satanic Majesties Request* was an ill-advised answer to *Sgt. Pepper*. They soon returned to rock and roll, recording such rock-defining hits as "Jumping Jack Flash" (1968) and "Honky Tonk Women" (1969). With songs like these, the group had refined its groove and defined its place in the history of popular music.

Guitar Gods

Among the most compelling new sounds of the late sixties were power trios such as Cream and the Jimi Hendrix Experience. These were bare-bones bands—just guitar, bass, and drums—set up to showcase the skills of their exceptionally able guitarists: Eric Clapton and Jimi Hendrix. These and other like-minded guitarists, such as Jeff Beck and Jimmy Page, took one additional element from blues—the guitar as the bluesman's "second voice." With the aid of the solid-body guitar, they used it as a point of departure as they introduced a new element into rock: virtuosic soloing.

The Solid-Body Electric Guitar. The idea of a solid-body electric guitar dates back to the 1930s, as guitar manufacturers worked to apply electric steel guitar technology to a standard guitar. Les Paul, a fine jazz guitarist and technical whiz, experimented with solid-body instruments as a means of reducing feedback (when part of a system's output signal is returned into its own input, causing a loud howl or squeal, which was considered undesirable at the time).

Leo Fender, a radio repairman turned instrument maker, began building solid-body electric guitar prototypes in 1944; he introduced his Broadcaster four years later, in 1948. Fender's Broadcaster, which became the Telecaster, and his Stratocaster, introduced in 1954, became standards by which other solid-body guitars were measured.

The sudden increase in amplification in the sixties made the instrument far more powerful. An array of sound modifiers, such as the wah-wah pedal, made the instrument more versatile.

Blues Guitar and Rock. Throughout the recorded history of deep blues, the guitar had been a melody instrument as well as a harmony and rhythm instrument in support of the voice. From Blind Lemon Jefferson on, bluesmen would answer sung phrases with vocal-like guitar lines, double the vocal line, or showcase the guitar's melodic capabilities in an instrumental solo. While Berry and others were creating rock guitar styles, electric bluesmen such as Guitar Slim, Buddy Guy, and Freddie King (one of Clapton's idols) were playing the guitar in a style that paralleled their raw, earthy singing, exploiting such novel effects as severe distortion. Their style served as a direct inspiration for a new generation of rock guitarists, most notably Eric Clapton and Jimi Hendrix.

Because they were the dominant soloists of their day, Clapton and Hendrix are inextricably linked. However, despite their strong connection in time, place, and purpose, they were two quite distinct musical personalities. Some of the differences between Hendrix and Clapton may have grown out of their early exposure to the blues. Hendrix grew up with the blues, hearing it as part of a broad spectrum of black music that also included jazz and rhythm and blues. Clapton approached the blues with the fervor of a convert, especially after his encounters with American bluesmen.

Although they used the blues as a point of departure, Hendrix and Clapton took these newfound capabilities several steps further. In so doing, they helped transform the electric guitar into the transcendental solo instrument of rock.

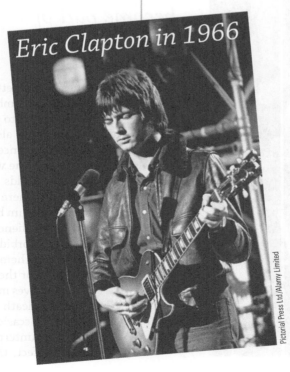
Eric Clapton in 1966

Pictorial Press Ltd/Alamy Limited

Eric Clapton and Cream. During the sixties, Eric Clapton (b. 1945) refined and purified his blues conception, especially during his short stint with John Mayall's Bluesbreakers in 1965 and 1966. The purity of this conception was important to him. He had left the Yardbirds just prior to joining Mayall when the band moved away from blues toward psychedelic rock.

By the time he formed Cream in 1966, with bassist Jack Bruce (b. 1943) and drummer Ginger Baker (born Peter Baker, 1939), Clapton had developed into rock's premier guitar virtuoso, although Hendrix would soon eclipse him. He was the

> *"With his impressive command of the instrument, Clapton makes all of this sound easy; his guitar becomes a miraculous prosthetic device."*

first major rock performer to play extended, improvised solos, especially in live performances. To accommodate his solo excursions, Cream dispensed with the rhythm guitar in live performance, although a second guitar was often added on recordings.

Cream was the first of the power trios: lead guitar, bass, and drums but no chord instrument. In live performance, the spotlight was on Clapton, although Bruce and Baker played active roles in support of his solos. They became a different band in the studio. The demands of AM radio airplay, with its 3-minute target, constrained Clapton's solo excursions. Their material gravitated toward the then fashionable psychedelic rock, although it still retained a strong blues connection. And, through the miracle of overdubbing, the band acquired additional instrumental voices without additional personnel—most notably, Clapton on rhythm guitar.

"Strange Brew," Eric Clapton, Felix Pappalardi, and Gail Collins (1967). Cream.

"Strange Brew" was not a singles hit but remains one of their best-remembered studio recordings. The lyric has psychedelic overtones—what *is* the "strange brew"?—but the real story is in the music. Here the blues influence runs deep, yet it's transformed into one of the most influential rock sounds of all time.

Blues influences begin with the form. The underlying harmony is a basic twelve-bar blues; the lyric and melodic form use the verse/chorus blues form first heard in "It's Tight Like That." However, the deeper blues influence is in Clapton's guitar playing. Clapton fills three distinct roles in this song. One is the sharp chords that come on alternate backbeats. A second is the rapidly rising riff that runs throughout the song. Third are the solo episodes: during the introduction, answering the vocal, and the brief solo in the middle of the song. The

deep blues influence is most evident in the solos, where Clapton adapts many trademark features of electric blues style: the fast vibrato, bent notes, free rhythms, extensive use of the pentatonic scale, and heavy inflection of individual notes. With his impressive command of the instrument, Clapton makes all of this sound easy; his guitar becomes a miraculous prosthetic device that creates vocally inspired musical gestures far surpassing what he could do with his voice.

Clapton's solo playing put him in the vanguard among the rock guitar soloists. Also innovative, however, are Clapton's riff-derived accompaniment, Bruce's syncopated bass lines, and the loose-jointed rhythm that they create. Clapton's repeated riff is a textural breakthrough for rock: it breaks away from the rhythmic and melodic regularity that are customary in rhythm guitar parts. In this respect, it is more like a repeated riff in an electric blues than anything commonly found in rock and roll.

Similarly, the texture created by the riff, Clapton's lead guitar line, and Bruce's bass line resemble the intertwined melodic strands of electric blues. (The connection shouldn't be surprising because Clapton claimed Waters to be a major influence.) At the same time, the concept is considerably updated, not only by the shift to rock rhythm, but also the emancipation of the bass line.

Cream helped loosen up rock rhythm. The basic beat is the 8-beat rhythm of rock, but all three instruments occasionally include patterns that move twice as fast as

---

⑤ to Listen For
"Strange Brew"

INSTRUMENTATION
Vocals, electric guitar(s) (overdubbed), electric bass, drums

RHYTHM
Rock rhythm with strong backbeat, double-time riff, fatback drums, syncopated bass lines, lead guitar riffs

MELODY
Riff-based vocal line

HARMONY
Basic blues progression

TEXTURE
Widely spaced sound: low bass, mid-range repeated riff, high vocal or lead guitar; drums in background

---

③ to Remember
"Strange Brew"

POWER TRIO PLUS
Power trio instrumentation (guitar, bass, drums) augmented with a second, active guitar line

BLUES INFLUENCE
Evident in form (refrain blues in the lyrics), texture, and especially Clapton's adaptation of blues guitar style; e.g., quick vibrato

LOOSER ROCK RHYTHM
Strong backbeat and steady tapping of the rock rhythm layer, but no marking of beat. Baker's drumming plays off this steady timekeeping, as do Bruce's free bass lines. Clapton's double-time riff (moving twice rock-beat speed) and lead guitar lines also play off the rock rhythm.

the basic rock beat. The most persistent and obvious is Clapton's riff, but there are also occasional double-time patterns in the drum part (a variant of the "fatback" beat so popular in soul music) and the double-time break toward the end. The double-time rhythms (that is, twice as fast as the rock beat layer) open up new paths toward greater rhythmic complexity.

Jimi Hendrix. Clapton's solo work demonstrates how he brought the essence of blues guitar style into rock. Hendrix went beyond that. He used electric blues as a point of departure, but he greatly increased the range, volume, and variety of sounds, even as he helped morph blues guitar styles into the dominant rock solo style. Hendrix was the trailblazer in both his expanded vocabulary of riffs, scales, and bent notes and his use of electronics. His was a virtuoso not only in speed—his ability to move around the instrument—but also in sound—opening up a world of new sound possibilities. As described by the *Rolling Stone Encyclopedia of Rock & Roll*, "Hendrix pioneered the use of the instrument as an electronic sound source. Rockers before him had experimented with feedback and distortion, but he turned those effects and others into a controlled, fluid vocabulary every bit as personal as the blues he began with."

Like too many of his musical contemporaries, Hendrix was a drug casualty. He died after a drug-alcohol interaction in September 1970 in the midst of plans for new projects that reportedly would have taken his music in quite different directions. While we regret his premature death, we remain grateful for his substantial legacy, made all the more impressive because it took only three years to compile.

Hendrix, like Eric Clapton with Cream, set up a powerful dialectic within hard rock: how to balance individual brilliance with group impact. The tradeoff is between the groove produced by the interplay of several lines (as we heard in the music of the Rolling Stones) versus the expressive power of a soloist's inspiration and virtuosity. In addition, these artists not only defined rock-based improvisation more than any others, but also helped redefine the possibilities of improvisation within popular music. Their influence, and particularly the influence of Hendrix, echoes through much of the music of the seventies and eighties, especially heavy metal and hard rock.

· · · · · · · · ·

Soul

For much of the 1960s, "soul" was the umbrella term for black popular music. Indeed in 1969, almost after the fact, *Billboard* changed the name of its rhythm-and-blues chart to "Soul." And much of it was popular, by any measure. The Motown success story was the most spectacular evidence of the ascendancy of black music, but Motown artists were not alone: twelve of the top twenty-five singles acts during the decade were black. It was a diverse group that included James Brown, Aretha Franklin, Ray Charles, Dionne Warwick, and the Supremes; they represented not one style but several.

Soul and Black Consciousness

Soul was more than a musical term. It came into use as an expression of the positive sense of racial identity that emerged during the decade. "Black is beautiful" was the slogan of many politically active members of the African American community. This shift in attitude, among blacks and some whites, was the social dimension of the relentless pursuit of racial equality. It went hand in hand with the enfranchisement of so many African Americans through the Civil Rights Act of 1964 and the Voting Rights Act of 1965.

As the drive for racial equality peaked, then deflated in the wake of the assassination of Martin Luther King Jr., black music occasionally became a vehicle for social commentary. James Brown released a series of exhortations, beginning with the 1968 song "Say It Loud—I'm Black and I'm Proud." Marvin Gaye's landmark album *What's Going On* appeared in 1971. But most of the music did not contain overt references to social conditions or racial issues. More often it dealt with the subjects that so frequently transcended race: love won and lost, and the good and bad times that resulted.

Soul Music

Black music charted a musical path different from white rock. Although much black music crossed over to the pop charts, black performers did not share much common ground musically with their white counterparts. There are three main reasons for this. The first and most significant is the strong gospel tradition. Most of the major African American performers of the sixties had grown up singing in church. There is no better example than Aretha Franklin, the "queen of soul": Aretha's father was pastor of one of the largest churches in Detroit, and she sang at his services from early childhood.

Another was the growing division between rock and roll and rhythm and blues. As we heard in Chapter 9, the differences between the two styles increased toward the end of the decade, not only because of the gospel influence in the singing but also because of differences in rhythm, instrumentation (horn sections were the rule in R&B but not in rock and roll), and texture (the bass was in the foreground, the guitar typically more in the background). Those black artists who began their careers in the sixties had also been listening to the major rhythm-and-blues artists of the fifties.

Their work continued the blues/gospel/pop syntheses of these artists.

A third reason for the array of distinctly black styles in the sixties was the artistic control of a few key producers. Berry Gordy was one. Another was Jerry Wexler, who had helped build Atlantic Records into a major pop label. Memphis-based Stax Records relied more on the musical intuition of its house musicians, who included Booker T. and the MGs and the Memphis Horns, to create a "house" sound.

Although, in the 1960s, virtually all new black music was called "soul," soul really refers to the emotionally charged black music of the sixties that draws deeply on gospel and the blues. It is best exemplified by the music that came from two southern cities—Memphis, Tennessee, and Muscle Shoals, Alabama—and two performers—Aretha Franklin and James Brown. This was music of real commitment: Percy Sledge bares his soul when he sings "When a Man Loves a Woman," and James Brown was, among other things, the "hardest working man in show business." The music expressed deep feelings, with little or no pop sugarcoating; when Aretha asks for respect, she spells it out.

The soul music of the mid- and late sixties came in two speeds: fast and slow. In either case, the music was raw. There was nothing particularly pretty about the voices of Otis Redding, Sam and Dave (Sam Moore and Dave Prater), Percy Sledge, or James Brown, but there was no mistaking the energy or the emotion. The instrumental sounds were painted in primary colors: strong bass at all times, powerful horns, vibrant sax solos, drums, guitar, and keyboard. Power won out over finesse.

The soul band of the sixties was an updated version of the jump bands of the late forties and the early fifties and Ray Charles's bands of the late fifties. Fast songs, propelled by agile bass lines, had a relentless rhythmic drive, the product of rhythmic play: a decisive backbeat, steady timekeeping, and lots of syncopated riffs. The balance within the band is different from rock: most of the syncopation comes in the bass line and the horn parts; compared with rock, the guitar part (usually there's only one guitarist) is typically less prominent. By contrast, slow songs provided a more subdued accompaniment; they surrounded the singer with a rich halo of sound.

Vocalists like Redding rose to the challenge of singing over this powerful and relentless backing. They sang, shouted, growled, moaned, and groaned. Their singing—laced with explosive consonants and short vowels—is almost percussive.

The songs continue to mine a familiar vein in rhythm and blues: in his sexual potency and his willingness to brag about it, Sam and Dave's "Soul Man" is a direct descendant of Roy Brown's "mighty, mighty, man" and so many other rhythm-and-blues heroes.

James Brown

CD 3:15

"Papa's Got a Brand New Bag," James Brown (1965). Brown, vocal.

James Brown (1933–2006) at once epitomized the "soul man" and stood apart from the other male soul singers. Not shy about positioning himself in the popular-music pantheon, Brown billed himself as "soul brother number 1" and the "godfather of soul." As with the Rolling Stones' claim to be the world's greatest rock and roll band, Brown's claim was based on fact: he *was* the most important male soul artist of the sixties.

The innovations that transformed Brown's music (and catapulted him to stardom) happened almost overnight. He had been working actively since the mid-fifties—his first R&B hit came in 1956—but he did little to set himself apart from other R&B artists until his breakthrough 1965 hit, "Papa's Got a Brand New Bag." (In sixties slang a *bag* is an area of expertise.) Brown's new bag was a breakthrough in rhythm.

We've detailed how the groove—the interplay that makes a rock beat a good beat—depends on the mix of regular timekeeping, syncopations, and other patterns that create conflict with the underlying rhythms. Brown created his unique rhythmic approach by addition and subtraction. He had a good-sized band—drums, bass, guitar, and keyboards (when Brown chose to play on recordings)—plus a full horn section: trumpets, saxophones (including a baritone sax), and trombone. This is the addition: his backup band is larger than most rock bands. Except for the bass, however, all the instruments have a reduced role. Guitar and drums are in the background, and often only the drummer supplies any kind of steady rhythm. The bass line is typically the most active and varied. The horns play riffs; the baritone

Julian Wasser/Getty Images

Brown's voice becomes a percussion instrument.

LISTENING GUIDE

CD 3:15 "Papa's Got A Brand New Bag"

STYLE	Soul	
FORM	Verse/chorus blues form, with one-chord interludes	
0:00	**Chorus 1**	
	Come here sister … Papa's in the swing.	Short riffs in vocal line and horns; single note on baritone sax
0:26	**Chorus 2**	
	Come here mama … and dig this crazy scene.	Rhythm section helps create open sound: strong bass, guitar on backbeat, rock beat tapped out on hi-hat.
0:48	**Interlude**	
	He's doing the Jerk … He's doing the Fly.	A preview of the future: grooving on a single chord
1:04	**Chorus 3**	
	Come here sister … Papa's in the swing.	Slight variation on refrain
1:26	**Blues**	
	Oh papa! He's doing the Jerk.	In performance, Brown would be demonstrating the steps.
1:48	**Outro**	
	Come on … Hey! Hey	A return to one-chord groove of interlude

sax part is usually just a note or two every eight beats. Brown sings only now and then; we imagine his footwork in the silences. This is the subtraction: less vocal and less involvement from most of the instruments.

All of this—more instruments doing less—creates an irresistible rhythm and an airy, open texture. There is no melody to speak of; Brown's voice becomes a percussion instrument—especially in the nonverbal sounds. (Try to emulate his voice and you'll find that your voice will explode and die away quickly, like many percussion sounds do.)

The interest comes in the interaction among the instruments. The beat and the rock rhythm are felt more than heard; everything else is over or against the time. It is a complex, if repetitive, rhythmic texture. And it is very close in principle to the rhythms and textures of West African music.

Brown's subsequent music brought popular music closer to its African roots than it had ever been before. Indeed, John Chernoff reported in his 1971 book, *African Rhythm and African Sensibility*, that African musicians felt more at home with James Brown's music than with that of any other popular musician of the time.

Brown's music has been profoundly influential. With its emphasis on intricate rhythms and de-emphasis of melody and harmony, it would create the blueprint for funk and rap. With deep roots in gospel, blues, rhythm and blues, and jazz, and its blending and modernizing of these styles, it represents a unique soul synthesis. In its originality and individuality, it stands apart from all the other music of the sixties. It remains one of the most influential styles from that decade.

Aretha Franklin

If James Brown was the godfather of soul, Aretha Franklin (b. 1942) became its reigning queen and one of the singular talents of popular music. Aretha grew up in a privileged yet painful environment. Her father was C. L. Franklin, pastor of one of the largest churches in Detroit and one of the most admired preachers in the African American community. Through him she came in contact with some of the great names in music: for example, gospel great Mahalia Jackson was a family friend. Aretha grew up in a hurry: singing in her father's church and then on the road as a child; a mother at sixteen; a pop/jazz singer on Columbia Records at nineteen (which turned out to be a dead end); and a series of abusive relationships.

Jerry Wexler jumpstarted her career in 1967 when he signed her to Atlantic Records and took her to Fame Studios in Muscle Shoals, Alabama, where Rick Hall had previously recorded such soul hits as Percy Sledge's "When a Man Loves a Woman." From the first note, Wexler knew he had something special. When the recording session ended disastrously (because of an alcohol-fueled fight between one of the session musicians and Ted White, Aretha's husband and manager at the time) and Aretha went into hiding, he tracked her down, brought her musicians to New York, and finished

5 to Listen For
"Papa's Got A Brand New Bag"

INSTRUMENTATION
Lead vocal, electric guitar, electric bass, drums. mixed horn section (trumpets, trombone, saxophones)

PERFORMANCE STYLE
Brown's singing is percussive.

RHYTHM
Light rock-beat timekeeping in drums only regular rhythm; strong backbeat, other parts (bass, vocal, horn riffs) mainly syncopated

HARMONY
Either blues progression or static harmony (in verse sections)

TEXTURE
Open

4 to Remember
"Papa's Got A Brand New Bag"

EMPHASIS ON RHYTHM
Song is about rhythm. No continuous melody, just fragments tossed back and forth between Brown and the horns. Harmony is basic blues progression or one chord. Absence of melodic and harmonic interest directs our attention to groove.

PERCUSSIVE SOUNDS
All of the instruments and Brown's singing are percussive: emphatic consonants (papa, bag), explosive single note on baritone saxophone, guitar chord, fingered electric bass sound, in addition to drums.

TEAMWORK
None of the parts is interesting enough to stand alone. Brown's voice stands out mainly because of the words and distinctiveness of sound, but it is not dominant. Collectively, the parts—vocal and instrumental—interlock to create a seamless flow.

OPEN SOUND
Because there is just enough activity to maintain groove, the musical flow is buoyant—no thick guitar chords or heavy bass lines to weigh it down. Brown's trademark groove was one of most distinctive and influential sounds of the 1960s.

the album. It was a huge success; it established her reputation as one of the supreme talents in popular music.

Many of Aretha's first hits explored the heartbreak of love, like most soul ballads of the time. However, her first up-tempo hits, most notably her cover of Otis Redding's "Respect" and her own "Think," emotionally redefined "fast soul." What had frequently been a forum for men to boast about their sexual prowess became the backdrop to a demand for dignity in "Respect" and a tongue-lashing in "Think." In both songs, the groove is as good as it gets, but it supports a call to arms rather than an invitation to sensual pleasure. "Respect," in fact, took on a meaning beyond the intent of its lyric: it became an anthem for the women's movement, which was just gathering momentum.

The musical formula for "Respect" is typical for 1960s soul: interlocked rhythm section, with horns playing riffs or sustained chords. The two major differences are Aretha's singing and the backup vocals, which give the song a churchier sound. The most memorable and individual section of the song is the stop-time

CD 3:16

"Respect," Otis Redding (1967). Aretha Franklin, vocal.

passage when Aretha spells out what she wants—"R-E-S-P-E-C-T"—so that there's absolutely no misunderstanding. What had been a straightforward verse/chorus song suddenly shifts up a gear. The remainder of the song features the dense texture previously heard in the chorus: a series of riffs from the backup vocalists—"sock it to me," "just a little bit," and finally the repeated "Re-re-re-re" (not only the first syllable of "respect" but also Aretha's nickname)—piled on top of the beat and horn riffs, with Aretha commenting on it all from above.

Having quickly established her credentials as the queen of soul, Aretha began to explore other musical territory. She has been one of the very few artists of the rock era who can cover songs convincingly. Her versions of Burt Bacharach's "I Say a Little Prayer," Sam Cooke's "You Send Me," Nina Simone's "Young, Gifted, and Black," and Paul Simon's gospel-influenced "Bridge over Troubled Water" are all standouts. Several of her own songs give further evidence of her expressive range: in "Rock Steady," she tips her hat to James Brown, while "Daydreaming" is as tender and romantic a song as any released in the early seventies.

Aretha's music is deeply personal and, at the same time, universal. The responsive listener feels her communicate one-on-one, yet her message transcends such a relationship. The best of Aretha's music seems to demand both empathy and ecstasy. We can give ourselves up to the groove even as we listen to her tough-time tales. No one in the rock era has fused both qualities more powerfully and seamlessly than she.

The Decline and Legacy of Soul

The soul movement went into a slow decline with the assassination of Martin Luther King Jr. in 1968. King's death touched off a series of inner-city race riots, which put a damper on the drive toward integration. James Brown and Aretha Franklin continued to perform and record successfully, but racial tension seemed to affect the chemistry within the interracial house bands at Stax in Memphis and Fame in Muscle Shoals, and between the bands and the performers they backed. There were still successes: Isaac Hayes produced "hot buttered

LISTENING GUIDE
CD 3:16 "Respect"

STYLE	Soul
FORM	Verse/chorus, with interlude and stop-time section at end

0:00 **Instrumental introduction**
Classic southern soul introduction: strong bass, locked horns, and guitar riff, all over a strong rock beat

0:09 **Verse/chorus 1**

What you want, Baby, I got	Aretha shouts out lyrics over simple two-chord oscillation, set to a strong groove
(Chorus [0:21]) Is for a little respect when you come home . . .	This part of the song remains fairly consistent in each verse

0:29 **Verse/chorus 2**

I ain't gonna do you wrong . . .	Backup vocalists play prominent role throughout song, sometimes taking lead role.

0:50 **Verse/chorus 3**

I'm about to give you all of my money . . .	Slight variation on refrain

1:11 **Sax solo**
The saxophonist is King Curtis, one of top R&B saxophonists of 1950s and 1960s.

1:28 **Verse/chorus 4**

Ooo, your kisses … Sweeter than honey . . .	Maintaining the same groove

1:48 **Stop time**

R - E - S - P - E - C - T	Stop time as she spells it out, then a gradual fadeout over chords of refrain

⑤ to Listen For
"Respect"

INSTRUMENTATION
Lead and backup vocals, electric guitar, electric bass, drums, tambourine, mixed horn section (trumpets, saxophones)

PERFORMANCE STYLE
Aretha's edgy gospel/blues mix; aggressive guitar sound; loud horns

RHYTHM
Rock rhythm with strong backbeat at moderate tempo; syncopation prominent in vocal, bass line, sax solo

MELODY
Melody = series of short riffs

TEXTURE
Thick texture = Aretha high, horn, guitar, piano, bass, drum parts fill in middle/lower range

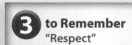

③ to Remember
"Respect"

CHANGE GENDER, CHANGE MEANING
Aretha's presence brings woman's point of view to fore.

ARETHA'S SINGING
Unmatched in expressive range, power, sensitivity, and emotional impact

SOUTHERN SOUL PLUS
Song adds backup vocal group to typical soul instrumentation of vocalist plus rhythm section and horns. They are integral to the impact of the song, especially in call-and-response sections.

soul" in Memphis, and Al Green, another exceptional voice, enjoyed considerable success in the early seventies. Green, who had grown up singing gospel, became an ordained minister shortly after a friend flung hot grits on his back, then killed herself. He finally left the pop world behind altogether in 1979, after injuring himself during a performance. His defection effectively brought the era of soul music to a close.

Soul music lasted less than a decade on the charts. The first soul hits appeared in 1965; by 1975 only James Brown was still carrying the soul banner. Its influence, however, has been evident ever since. Soul brought a more contemporary version of the deep feeling of the blues into black music. In this respect it is the insider's counterpart to the British blues bands: a new view of blues sensibility by those who grew up with it.

San Francisco and the Diversity of Rock

From the start, rock has been not a single style but a heterogeneous mix of styles linked by common musical features and shared attitudes. This became even more apparent during the latter part of the sixties, when rock became the dominant popular music and simultaneously went in several different directions, musically and geographically.

We may perceive the diversity of rock through geography in two ways. One is to note the numerous regional dialects of rock that surfaced in the sixties. In the United States, there was surf music from southern California, soul music from Memphis, Motown from Detroit. More significantly, rock became the first truly international popular music with the rise of the British bands. Their music added several dialects to the musical language that was rock. The other way is to observe the activity within a geographical region. During the latter part of the sixties, one good place to do this was the San Francisco Bay Area, the spiritual home of the counterculture.

The Counterculture

Those who came of age during the latter half of the sixties grew up in a world far different from the world of their parents. A decided majority experienced neither the hardships of the Great Depression nor the traumas of World War II and the Korean War. They were in elementary school during the McCarthy witch hunt; in most cases, it had far less impact on them than it did on their parents. A good number came from families that were comfortable financially, so that as teens they had money to spend and time to spend it.

A sizeable and vocal segment of these young people rejected the values of the group they pejoratively called the "establishment." They saw the establishment as excessively conservative, bigoted, materialistic, resistant to social change, obsessed with communism and locked into a potentially deadly arms race, and clueless about sexuality. Fueled by new technologies and drugs—both old and new—they incited the most far-reaching social revolution since the twenties.

For college-age youth of the mid-sixties, there were four dominant issues: minority rights, sexual freedom, drug use, and war. A generation that had grown up listening to rock and roll, rhythm and blues, and jazz found it difficult to comprehend the widespread discrimination against blacks that they saw as legitimized in too many segments of American society. They joined the drive for civil rights—through demonstrations,

sit-ins, marches, and, for some, more direct and potentially violent activities, such as voter registration in the South. The successes of the civil rights movement created momentum for other minority rights movements: women, Chicanos, gays, Native Americans.

Commercial production of an effective oral contraceptive—the Pill—began in the early sixties. For some women, this was the key to sexual freedom; it enabled them to be as sexually active as males with virtually no risk of pregnancy. It precipitated the most far-reaching revolution in sexual practice in the history of western culture. Moreover, it extended the drive for equal rights from the voting booth—in the United States, women were granted the right to vote only in 1920—into the bedroom and sparked a revival of feminism, which sought, among other things, to extend these rights into the workplace.

During this same period, the recreational use of mind-altering drugs spread to large segments of the middle class. Previously, drug use had been confined to small subcultures: for example, many jazz musicians in the post–World War II era were heroin addicts. Marijuana, always a popular drug among musicians and minorities, became the most popular drug of the sixties among young people, and especially the counterculture. However, the signature drug of the sixties was D-lysergic acid diethylamide, a semi-synthetic drug more commonly identified as LSD or acid. The drug was developed in 1938 by Albert Hoffman, a Swiss chemist; Hoffman discovered its psychedelic properties by accident about five years later. Originally, psychiatrists used it therapeutically, and during the Cold War, intelligence agencies in the United States and Great Britain apparently ran tests to determine whether the drug was useful for mind control. The key figures in moving LSD from the lab to the street were two Harvard psychology professors: Timothy Leary and Richard Alpert. They felt that the mind-expanding capabilities of the drug should be open to anyone. In reaction, Sandoz, Dr. Hoffmann's chemical firm, stopped freely supplying scientists with the drug, and the U.S. government banned its use in 1967. Underground use of the drug has continued despite this ban.

In the latter part of the sixties, the Vietnam War replaced civil rights as the hot-button issue for young people. In 1954, Vietnam, formerly French Indo-China, was divided—like Korea—into two regions: the north received support from the USSR and communist China, while the southern region received the support of western nations, especially the United States. A succession of presidents saw a military presence in South Vietnam as a necessary buffer against communist aggression.

As a result, U.S. military involvement gradually escalated over the next decade. Finally, in 1965 the government began sending regular troops to Vietnam to augment the special forces already there. This provoked a hostile reaction, especially from those eligible to be drafted. Many recoiled at the prospect of fighting in a war that seemed pointless; a few fled to Canada or elsewhere to avoid the draft. Massive antiwar demonstrations became as much a part of the news during the late sixties as the civil rights demonstrations were in the first part of the decade. The lies and deceptions of the government and military, which among other things reassured the American people that the war was winnable and that the U.S. forces were winning, coupled with news reports of horrific events such as the My Lai massacre, in which U.S. soldiers killed close to 500 unarmed civilians in a small village, further eroded support for the war.

The gulf between the older establishment positions and attitudes of young Americans on civil rights, sex, drugs, and war widened as the decade wore on. Still, there was a major shift in values: civil rights legislation passed, the role of women in society underwent a liberating transformation, recreational drug use became more common and socially acceptable in certain circles (although it was still illegal), and the war eventually ended in failure. As a result of this revolution, ideas and practices that seemed radical at mid-century—such as multiculturalism and equal opportunity in the workplace—are accepted norms in contemporary society, in theory if not always in practice.

Hippies

A small but prominent minority of young people chose to reject mainstream society completely. They abandoned the conventional lifestyles of their parents and peers; some chose to live in communes. They followed Timothy Leary's advice to "turn on, tune in, drop out." They dressed differently, thought differently, and lived differently. They were the ideological heirs of the Bohemians of nineteenth-century Europe and the Beats of the late 1940s and 1950s. Members of the group were known as hippies; collectively they formed the heart of the counterculture.

Throughout the sixties, the San Francisco Bay Area was a center for radical thought and action. The free speech movement led by Mario Savio got started at the Berkeley campus of the University of California in 1964; it led to confrontations between student protesters and university administrators over student rights and academic freedom. In 1966, in Oakland—next to Berkeley and across the bay from San Francisco—Huey Newton, Bobby Seale, and Richard Aoki formed the Black Panthers, a radical black organization dedicated to revolutionary social reform by any

istockphoto.com

means necessary, including violence. Hippies generally followed a less confrontational path.

For hippies, Mecca was San Francisco; their counterpart to the Sacred Mosque was Haight and Ashbury, an intersection in a heretofore ordinary neighborhood in San Francisco, near Golden Gate Park, the largest public park in the city. The area became a destination for those who wanted to "make love, not war" and travel the fast route to higher consciousness by tripping on psychedelic drugs. Migration to San Francisco peaked during the 1967 "summer of love," when an estimated 75,000 young people flocked to the city.

Rock music was the soundtrack for the counterculture. Music was everywhere—inside and outside—and especially at the Fillmore. Promoter Bill Graham turned the Fillmore Ballroom, a musty building in a rather seedy part of town, into the main venue for rock bands and their fans. Audiences flocked there for endless concerts; "live at the Fillmore" albums appeared regularly in record stores. The venue was so successful that Graham named its New York counterpart "Fillmore East." Because of Haight-Ashbury, "flower power," LSD, and the other trappings of the hippie scene, the music most associated with the Bay Area during the late sixties was acid rock (or psychedelic rock)—a rock substyle defined not by a musical feature but simply by the music's ability to evoke or enhance the drug experience.

Acid Rock: Jefferson Airplane

As tripping on acid became more widespread, words, images, and music were used to capture the psychedelic experience. Psychedelic art—rich in color, dense and distorted, and often suffused with religious and mystical images—became an important new direction in the visual arts. The images were not confined to canvas, or even

ABN Stock Images/Alamy Limited

album covers and posters. Perhaps the most famous and memorable visual image of the psychedelic sixties was a 1939 International Harvester school bus painted in a rainbow of colors; it was the vehicle for the cross-country tours of Ken Kesey, the patron saint of the psychedelic world, and his Merry Pranksters.

Music was even more integral to the psychedelic experience because it was used not only to evoke but also to enhance tripping on acid. Music could contribute to the experience (as we discover in "White Rabbit"), depict the experience (as we heard in the Beatles' "A Day in the Life"), and be a product of it (as was the case of much of the music from the mid- and late sixties). Indeed, the common bond that linked the widely varied music identified as acid or psychedelic rock was the connection to LSD. There was no specific musical feature, or set of features, that identified acid rock. (By contrast, consider the role of distortion in defining the sound of heavy metal, or the combination of horns and heavy bass in defining the sound of soul music.) Examples of acid rock ranged from the sprawling, blues-based improvisations of Jerry Garcia and the Grateful Dead to Jefferson Airplane's tight, flamenco-tinged "White Rabbit." The musical products were seemingly as varied as the acid trips themselves. The connection could be in the music, in the words, or both.

The band that first directed the spotlight to San Francisco and to acid rock was Jefferson Airplane. Vocalist Marty Balin (b. 1942) and guitarist Paul Kantner (b. 1941) formed Jefferson Airplane in 1965; the next year, Grace Slick (born Grace Wing, 1939) replaced Signe Anderson as the female vocalist with the group and soon became the face as well as the dominant voice of the group. Her good looks and extroverted and uninhibited stage personality were key elements in the success of the group. The rest of the group during the late sixties included lead guitarist Jorma Kaukonen (b. 1940), bassist Jack Casady (b. 1944), and drummer Spencer Dryden (1938–2005).

CD 3:17

"White Rabbit," Grace Slick (1967). Grace Slick, vocal, with Jefferson Airplane.

Slick brought two songs with her from the Great Society, the band she had formed with Jerry Slick, her husband at the time. As reworked by Jefferson Airplane, they became the group's two Top 10 singles: "Somebody to Love" and "White Rabbit." Both songs appeared on *Surrealistic Pillow* (1967), the first album the group recorded with Slick.

Of the two, "White Rabbit" connects more directly to the drug experience. The title of the song refers to the white rabbit in Lewis Carroll's *Alice in Wonderland*. In Carroll's tale, the rabbit, dressed in a waistcoat, leads Alice into a hole and into a fantasy world where she has all manner of strange experiences. The lyric comments on a scene in the story where she meets a caterpillar that seems to be smoking opium. Slick would later remark that the song was an indictment of parents who read stories like *Alice in Wonderland* to their children and then wonder why the children do drugs. However, the connection with LSD was oblique enough that the song made it past the censors, although the drug references (such as "feed your head") seem quite clear in retrospect.

In "White Rabbit," the lyrics (and Slick's singing) are primary; the music plays a supporting role. Among the defining features of the song are the flamenco-inspired instrumental accompaniment (adapted for a rock band) and the sustained crescendo to the final "Feed your head." Slick remarked that the inspiration for the accompaniment came from her repeated listening to *Sketches of Spain* while tripping on LSD. *Sketches of Spain* was an adventurous album by the jazz trumpeter Miles Davis; the most extended track was a drastic reworking of a guitar concerto by the Spanish composer Joaquin Rodrigo.

Another remarkable feature of the song is its slow, steady crescendo (a gradual increase in volume). The song begins quietly with an extended instrumental introduction in which the instruments enter one by one—bass, drums, then lead and rhythm guitars. Both the rhythm and the chord progression evoke Spanish music. Slick also enters quietly. The music gets louder as the song proceeds, reaching a climax on the line "Feed your head." As Slick belts out the lyric, the band shifts from the Spanish-flavored rhythm with which the song began to a straightforward rock rhythm; it is as if music, like the mind and Slick's voice, has been set free from the restrictive Spanish rhythm.

Jefferson Airplane remained one of the leading psychedelic rock bands into the early seventies, when the group reconstituted itself with Slick and Kantner as Jefferson Starship. Although their new name implied that they had become even more adventurous—starships fly higher than airplanes—the band actually became more mainstream and enjoyed even more commercial success during the seventies and eighties.

Both the psychedelic scene and psychedelic rock lost their potency around 1970. The 1967 "summer of love" devolved into a bad trip as the decade drew to a close. Haight-Ashbury went into decline; it would become gentrified a decade later. For many, LSD lost its status as the mind-expanding drug of choice.

The absence of a distinct musical identity made it difficult to sustain acid rock as a vital rock substyle; the style neither evolved (like heavy metal or country rock) nor achieved a more or less permanent stasis (like hard rock). It was—and remains—very much a period piece, a sound of a particular time and place.

LISTENING GUIDE

CD 3:17 "White Rabbit"

STYLE	Acid rock
FORM	Modified AABA form

0:00	**Introduction**	
	Flamenco-like introduction: bass, drums, then guitar	
0:28	**A**	
	One pill makes you larger …	Voice is dominant; band supplies exotic (for rock) background.
0:54	**A**	
	And if you go chasing rabbits …	As before
1:23	**B**	
	When men on the chessboard …	Shift to new melodic idea in higher key
1:51	**A'**	
	When logic and proportion …	Melody recalls the opening A, but it is more assertive, rising inexorably to title phrase, which Slick belts out.
	Feed your head!	Shift to rock rhythm just before key phrase of lyric

3 to Remember
"White Rabbit"

IMPORTANCE OF WORDS
Message of the song is mainly in the words; the melody is not a standalone melody, like those found in Motown or Beatles songs, nor is the accompaniment interesting enough to stand alone.

SPANISH FLAVOR
Like string sounds in "Eleanor Rigby," Spanish rhythms and harmonies connect to rock mainly by association; they are certainly not typical in rock music. In this case, it was Slick's obsession with Miles Davis's *Sketches of Spain* that provided the connection; in other respects, there seems to be little connection between words and music.

BIG CRESCENDO
Gradual crescendo makes final line of song sound like a call to action—an emphatic exhortation to take an acid trip.

5 to Listen For
"White Rabbit"

INSTRUMENTATION
Vocal, electric guitar, electric bass, drum

RHYTHM
Shifts between Spanish-flavored march rhythm and rock rhythm; little syncopation

MELODY
Slowly rising melody, built around long notes

HARMONY
Spanish modal harmony at start; rock modal harmony at ends of phrases

TEXTURE
Muted sound: vocal highest and strongest, guitar, bass in low register

One important reason that acid rock lacked a distinct musical identity was the fact that the drug experience was an overlay; it was not an integral element of the style. Indeed, most of the major acid-rock acts rooted their style in folk and blues. The Grateful Dead began as a jug band; the members of Jefferson Airplane had prior experience in folk, blues, and R&B; and both Jimi Hendrix and Eric Clapton, who were also associated with acid rock, had deep blues roots. For many of the top San Francisco–based acts, this connection with American roots music was a stronger musical bond than the drugs. Perhaps the clearest example of this came in the music of Janis Joplin.

Down to Earth: Janis Joplin and the Blues

The only female performer in the San Francisco rock scene with a more commanding presence than Grace Slick was Janis Joplin (1943–1970). Like Slick, Joplin fronted a band, had a let-it-all-hang-out stage personality, and wrestled with a severe substance abuse problem. Both looked the part of the counterculture diva—both dressed and undressed. But there

Grace Slick (left) and Janis Joplin (right)

album that was widely praised for the quality of Joplin's vocals, while the band was criticized for its ragged playing. Joplin soon separated from the band and became an important solo act for the rest of her brief life.

Joplin was rock's original blues diva. Before Joplin, few women sang with anything approaching the supercharged passion and freedom inherent in her singing; all of them were black—from Bessie Smith to Aretha Franklin. Indeed, Joplin's singing seems to owe more to Otis Redding and other male southern soul singers than to any woman, because what distinguishes Joplin's singing from that of other female singers is the rawness of her sound and the sheer exuberance of her performing style. She had a voice that often sounded like she had gargled with broken glass, although she could also sing as tenderly as any crooner. She combined that with a unique kind of vocal virtuosity. With its stutters, reiterations, rapid-fire streams of words, melismas, interpolations, and the like, her singing style is almost operatic in its exhibitionism.

Although Joplin thought of herself as a blues singer, most of the songs that she recorded were not blues, at least in the formal sense. Unlike the classic female blues singers of the twenties, who recorded mainly conventional blues songs, Joplin recorded a wide range of material. However, she brought blues feeling and style into everything she recorded, blues or not.

CD 3:18

"Piece of My Heart," Jerry Ragovoy and Bert Russell (1968). Janis Joplin, vocal, with Big Brother and the Holding Company.

> **"While Slick took her listeners into a fantasy world in songs like "White Rabbit," Joplin got real by drenching herself in blues and soul."**

were differences. Slick was beautiful and had come from a high-class background. Before joining Jefferson Airplane she had modeled for three years at a high-end San Francisco department store and had begun her undergraduate education at Finch College, a finishing school for young ladies. Joplin had grown up a social outcast in a Texas oil town; music was her escape. Joplin sipped while Slick tripped; Janis's taste for Southern Comfort was legendary. (Ironically, it was Slick who later developed an alcohol abuse problem, while Joplin died of a heroin overdose.) And while Slick took her listeners into a fantasy world in songs like "White Rabbit," Joplin got real by drenching herself in blues and soul.

Like many other young musicians of the time, Joplin migrated to San Francisco during the mid-sixties. Born in Port Arthur, Texas, Joplin began performing in coffeehouses in her native state before traveling to California in 1965. There, she began performing with a local blues band: Big Brother and the Holding Company. The group made an enormous impact at the 1967 Monterey Pop Festival, thanks mainly to Joplin's dynamic stage performance. Signed to Columbia Records, they cut one

"Piece of My Heart," which she recorded while singing with Big Brother and the Holding Company, was the only song of hers to reach the singles charts during her lifetime. It was a track on *Cheap Thrills*, the band's first album for Columbia and by far their biggest success; the album topped the charts for eight weeks in 1968.

"Piece of My Heart" remains the song most closely associated with her; two biographies include it in the title. "Piece of My Heart" had been a modest R&B hit the previous year for Erma Franklin, Aretha Franklin's younger sister. Her original version was a solid and straightforward slow soul song. Characteristically, the lyric tells the story of a troubled relationship, here from a woman's point of view: she is at once vulnerable and—as the lyric says—tough. Given Joplin's history and personality, it is easy to understand why she would be eager to cover it.

The thorough transformation of the song begins with the band; the instrumental accompaniment features

STYLE	Acid rock	
FORM	Verse/chorus form	
0:00	**Introduction**	
	Blues-influenced rock guitar solo gets the song underway; Janis enters with several statements of "come on," which also leads into chorus.	
0:28	**Verse**	
	Didn't I make you feel like you were the only man ...	Accompaniment suddenly quiets down to allow Joplin to begin softly.
	Bridge (0:42) And each time I tell myself that I ...	Sudden shift to more active double-time rhythms. The song builds to the hook as Joplin sings "come on" over and over. Backup vocals help.
0:59	**Chorus**	
	Take another little piece of my heart now, baby ...	Return to verse accompaniment, but stronger, and with backup vocals. The climax is mainly in Joplin's singing.
1:29	**Verse**	
	You're out on the streets looking good ...	As before in the accompaniment, but Joplin digs into her bag of vocal tricks to give the melody a more intense character.
2:05	**Chorus**	
	Take another little piece of my heart now, baby ...	As before
2:09	**Guitar solo**	
	An expanded version of the guitar solo during the introduction ... eventually it directs back to the chorus, as before.	
3:10	**Chorus**	
	Take another little piece of my heart now, baby ...	The refrain is sung twice (there is no third verse) before a brief return to the instrumental introduction, which ends with a chord that devolves into sci-fi-style electronic sounds.

the kind of blues-tinged rock that was characteristic of the San Francisco psychedelic scene, rather than a bass-heavy R&B sound. The instrumentation is standard: two guitars, with some distortion in the lead guitar, bass, and drums. The rhythms are more active and freer than in a straightforward rock song.

All of this is a foil for Joplin's soulful singing, which is considerably more passionate and virtuosic than Erma Franklin's. There is enormous contrast, in volume and vocal quality, from the almost screamed opening ("Come on") to the almost whispered verse ("Didn't I make you feel") to the half-spoken/half-sung ("Each time I tell myself") and the wailed chorus. As she delivers the song, she lays herself emotionally bare—as if she had stripped off all of her clothes. Few singers of any era were willing to throw themselves into a performance the way Joplin did, and fewer had the vocal agility and range to carry it off successfully.

Even more than Grace Slick, Janis Joplin redefined the role of women in rock. It was no longer simply being a pretty face in front of the band; Joplin matched men—black and white—in power and presence. In this respect, she paved the way for a larger role for women in rock: Patti Smith, Annie Lennox, Bonnie Raitt, Madonna, and many others benefited from her trailblazing efforts.

She paid a price for her passion. With her premature death, she joined the not-exclusive-enough club of rock icons who lived too hard and died too young. Ironically, she did not live long enough to enjoy her biggest hit; "Me and Bobby McGee," written for her by Kris Kristofferson, one of her ex-lovers, appeared on *Pearl*, an album released after her death. She left the album incomplete; she was to have added vocals to a track entitled "Buried Alive in the Blues" on the day she died.

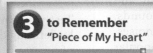
INSTRUMENTATION
Lead, backup vocal, electric guitars, electric bass, drums

PERFORMANCE STYLE
Joplin's raspy voice and vocal pyrotechnics—stutters, and so on; blues-influenced guitar style

RHYTHM
Rock rhythm in slow tempo, with frequent double-time rhythms; contrast between leisurely verse, busy verse, rock-rhythm chorus

MELODY
Active, almost instrumental melody because of Joplin's elaborations

TEXTURE
Strong contrasts: thin texture in verse, thick texture around Joplin's singing in bridge and chorus; all instruments active, mainly with riffs and busy lines, plus high backup vocals

BLUES-INFLUENCED ACID ROCK BAND
The standard instrumentation, blues-inspired riffs, and effects—such as the distortion and the spacey sounds and feedback at the end of the song—all connect the song to blues-oriented acid rock.

PASSIONATE SINGING
Joplin's singing is unique, not only for its basic quality, which recalls the voices of the great male soul singers, but also for its uninhibited use of an array of vocal devices and many shifts of mood.

ROCK THAT IS REAL
There were dozens of bands that dug into the blues in order to invest their music with the kind of emotional honesty heard in the music of the best blues artists. Few white singers, male or female, could match Joplin's intensity or emotional commitment.

The Bay Area music clearly evidences the stylistic explosion of the late sixties. As late as 1964, even an astute observer of rock music would have needed superior foresight to predict the many directions that rock-era music took in the latter part of the decade. The differences among songs and styles touch every aspect of the music—what songs are trying to communicate and how they communicate their message in words and music. No region more clearly exemplified this trend.

● ● ● ● ● ● ● ●
Looking Back, Looking Ahead

The sixties saw the wholesale transformation of popular music. It wasn't just that rock was a radically different kind of music. It was that everything about the music—how it was conceived and created, the tools with which it was made, the content of both words and music, the dynamics within musical groups and between musicians and their audience, and even what the music was—underwent significant change.

By 1970 rock music had become the new mainstream, a new family of styles. Virtually every other kind of music that was not rock or rock-influenced was out of fashion, a point we explore in the next chapter. In this respect it paralleled the coming together of popular music in the late twenties: the blend of fox trot song, jazz, and blues. But the range of styles within this new mainstream was much broader than in that earlier time. This is a reflection of the openness of rock musicians toward music of all kinds—and the openness of the rock audience toward musicians and music of many different kinds.

The Beatles were the poster boys of the rock revolution. Their invasion of America sparked it: their commercial and musical impact was crucial to rock's ascendancy. By the time they disbanded, the revolution was complete; the new music that they had helped usher in now ruled the popular music business. More important, the Beatles played a key role in reshaping the music and the industry that supported it. Among the most significant developments to which they contributed were establishing rock as the new popular music, making rock an international musical language, creating a new

Joplin and her music embody the tensions of the new womanhood that emerged in the sixties. On stage and in the studio, she is the equal of men, yet vulnerable in a specifically feminine way; she is modern in her sensibility, yet deals with timeless issues in her songs. For a new generation of women, she showed both what they might aspire to and the dangers of getting it.

The dramatic differences between "White Rabbit" and "Piece of My Heart" hint at the diversity of the music scene in the San Francisco Bay Area. Because of Haight-Ashbury, "flower power," LSD, and the other trappings of the hippie scene, the music most associated with the Bay Area during the late sixties was acid rock. The notoriety of the counterculture masked the diversity in the Bay Area music scene. Many of the important acts active during that time and place went beyond acid rock or had no connection with it. They included the Grateful Dead, whose music embraced much more than the drug culture; Creedence Clearwater Revival, one of the great singles bands of the era, playing down- to-earth rock and roll; Santana, Carlos Santana's one-band foray into Latin rock; and Sly and the Family Stone, whose music provided the crucial link between soul and funk.

kind of popular song, proposing rock as art, confirming the recording as the primary musical document, and expanding the range of musical influences and sounds, from sitars and calliopes to tape loops and crowd noises. These and other changes radically transformed popular music in the sixties.

The death of the Beatles as a group and the deaths of so many important rock stars—Jimi Hendrix, Janis Joplin, Brian Jones, Jim Morrison—might superficially seem to have echoed the troubles that plagued rock and roll at the end of the fifties. Although the losses were significant and tragic, rock didn't miss a beat. The revolution that had toppled pop was over. Rock was now big business and would grow even bigger in the coming decade.

Terms to Know

Test your knowledge of this chapter's important terms by defining the following. If you can't recall the meaning of a certain term, refresh your memory by looking up the boldfaced term in the chapter, turning to the Glossary at the back of the book, or working with the flashcards at the Popular Music Resource Center.

rock beat
modal harmony
Motown sound

soul
acid rock

Reactions to Rock
Established Styles in the Early Rock Era

CHAPTER

11

Superstock

8 TRACK STEREO TAPE PLAYER

For Frank Sinatra, the 1960s were like the month of March; he came in like a lion and went out like a lamb. After describing rock and roll as "the most brutal, ugly, desperate, vicious form of expression it has been my misfortune to hear," Sinatra swung into the 1960s as pop's biggest star. *Nice 'n' Easy*, his first album of the decade, topped the album charts. A year later, he formed his own record company and charted seven albums. However, with the rise of rock, his record sales declined. Hits and hit albums came less frequently, and several of his hit songs from the latter half of the decade ("Strangers in the Night," "Something Stupid," and "My Way") traded the trademark swing of the 1950s and early 1960s for a subdued rock rhythm. Later, he would cover George Harrison's "Something," calling it "the greatest love song ever written." It wasn't capitulation to rock, but it *was* accommodation. In 1971 he would briefly retire from show business. He returned about two years later (*Ol' Blue Eyes Is Back*) and redefined his place in the musical world once again, as an admired and appreciated elder statesman. In the 1990s he recorded two commercially successful duet albums with collaborators as diverse as Bono, Aretha Franklin, Julio Iglesias, and Chrissy Hynde.

Frank Sinatra on the eve of the rock revolution

Rocking the Establishment

The ups and downs of Sinatra's post-1960 career reflected on an individual level the same interplay that took place between established styles and rock during the rock era. We might describe the general pattern in this way: rejection, finding relevance through an accommodation with rock, then gradual rapprochement.

Rejection went both ways. As the 1960s began, it seemed that the place of pop, Broadway, jazz, country, and Latin music was not threatened by rock and roll. Sinatra belonged to a group of pop singers that spanned three generations: that of his roots, dating back to the swing era; that of singers like Nat Cole and Tony Bennett, whose careers took off in the years after World War II; and that of an even younger generation led by Johnny Mathis. Broadway was still big: the film soundtrack of Leonard Bernstein's *West Side Story*, released in 1962, spent over a year at the top of the album charts; the film soundtrack of Rodgers and Hammerstein's *The Sound of Music*, released in 1960, spent over three years there. The musical *Fiddler on the Roof*, which opened in 1964, would run for over three thousand performances. For

|||||||||||||||||||||||||||||||||||||||||

"The most brutal, ugly, desperate, vicious form of expression it has been my misfortune to hear"
—Frank Sinatra's definition of rock and roll

the most part, the leading jazz musicians, in particular John Coltrane and his circle, were too busy stretching jazz's boundaries to be concerned with rock. However, Herbie Hancock, like Coltrane a musical associate of Miles Davis, was one of the first to explore jazz/rock fusions. Country music for the most part romanced pop, not rock; the Nashville Sound backed smooth-voiced country singers like Eddy Arnold and Jim Reeves with violins and choirs instead of fiddles and steel guitars. Bluegrass hit the charts in 1962 with the theme song from the television show *The Beverly Hillbillies*. Ray Charles's two albums of country and western songs, both released in 1962, brought a new sound to country music and found a new audience for it. The sudden success of the bossa nova mainstreamed Brazilian music, much as the rumba had mainstreamed Cuban music. Musicians working in all of these styles could effectively ignore rock—even reject it, as Sinatra did. Their place in the music industry seemed secure.

However, the rapid rise of rock turned the tables. Audiences gravitated toward the appealing new sounds coming from England, Detroit, Memphis, and elsewhere, and left established styles scrambling for their slice of the pop music pie. Broadway continued to mount successful productions but seemed increasingly out of date and out of touch. The careers of other pop singers paralleled Sinatra's. Jazz lost its status as the hip outsiders' music; the new counterculture of rock supplanted bop and cool. The situation was more complex with country, in part because of rock musicians' interest in country music. Cuban-based Latin music meshed easily with rock, as we've noted. Brazilian music had a more jazz and pop orientation; its influence would ultimately be more pronounced there.

For those working in established genres, the most vibrant and innovative possible response to the rock revolution was to incorporate elements of rock style into their music. Rock elements ranged from cosmetic overlays—like those in Sinatra's late 1960s hits—to true fusions, which effectively created a new form of an established genre or a hybrid style. In this chapter, we present five interactions between rock and an established style: the pop rock of the 1960s and early 1970s, the rock musical, rock-tinged country, Latin rock, and jazz/rock fusion. Collectively, they offer another perspective on the impact of rock on the music industry. We precede them all with a brief discussion of the Brazilian bossa nova, the first and most influential new Latin music of the rock era.

● ● ● ● ● ● ● ●

The Bossa Nova and Brazilian Music

In 1959 *Black Orpheus,* a film that retold the Orpheus legend in Rio de Janeiro during Carnaval (the Brazilian Mardi Gras), won first prize at the Cannes Film Festival. The soundtrack for the film introduced bossa nova, a new Brazilian style, to new audiences in both Europe and North America. In the wake of its success and the collaboration of Brazilian musicians and American jazzmen during the early 1960s, Brazilian music quickly became part of American musical life.

Music from Brazil

For American audiences, Brazilian music has meant almost exclusively music from just one part of Brazil: the southern part, especially Rio de Janeiro. Rio is home to the samba, the dominant music in southern Brazil for

> " Samba schools work almost the entire year preparing for the parade. "

decades. This is particularly evident at Carnaval, Rio's last big splurge before Lent—a huge street party that culminates in a massive parade. Samba schools, each featuring hundreds of musicians, many of them percussionists, work almost the entire year preparing for the parade.

Bossa Nova and Its Impact

Bossa nova is Brazilian slang for "something new and different." The music emerged in Rio de Janeiro during the late fifties as a sophisticated, more melodic, and rhythmically less complex kind of samba. A small nucleus of musicians, notably songwriters Antonio Carlos Jobim (1925–1994), Luis Bonfa (1922–2001), singer/guitarist João Gilberto (b. 1931), and songwriter/guitarist Baden Powell (1927–2000), fell in love with American jazz, especially jazz-influenced pop singing and West Coast–based cool jazz. They blended the harmonic sophistication and cool of West Coast jazz with the rhythms of Brazil to produce this new style. The bossa nova craze peaked in the mid-sixties with authentic music by Jobim and Gilberto, Sergio Mendes's Brazilian crossover music, and the inevitable travesties, such as "Blame It on the Bossa Nova."

CD 3:19

"The Girl from Ipanema," Antonio Carlos Jobim (1963). Astrud Gilberto, vocal; João Gilberto, vocal and guitar; and Stan Getz, saxophone.

The landmark bossa nova recording appeared in 1963; it was a collaboration between singer/guitarist João Gilberto and jazz saxophonist Stan Getz. The signature track was "The Girl from Ipanema," which charted as a single the following year. The recording featured not only Getz and João Gilberto, but also Astrud Gilberto, his wife at the time, singing an English translation of the lyric. The opening of the song contains two keys to the style and the sound of bossa nova: João Gilberto's cool, flat, low-pitched voice and the complex off-beat rhythms of the guitar chords. Bass and drums flesh out the rhythmic texture, with bass on every slow beat and drums marking a steady rhythm four times as fast as the bass. Jobim plays the occasional fill on piano and takes a brief solo toward the end.

Jobim's song has the AABA form heard in so many pop songs of the twenties, thirties, and forties. The first phrase of the melody is deceptively simple—a simple riff that gently slides down over smoothly shifting chords. The bridge is more complex: bold harmonies support a sinuous melody. Jobim's songs favored both subtly shifting melodies and exotic, jazz-derived harmonies that were an ideal complement to the subtle rhythm of the guitar and Gilberto's low-key, almost monotonic

Ipanema is a famous beach in Rio de Janeiro.

LISTENING GUIDE

CD 3:19 "The Girl from Ipanema"

STYLE	Bossa nova	
FORM	Four choruses of an AABA-form song	
0:00	**Introduction**	
	Vocal introduction. Notice the almost total syncopation of the guitar chords.	
0:07	**First chorus**	
	A	Just voice and guitar. João Gilberto sings the lyric in Portuguese.
	A (0:22)	Rhythm section enters. Note rhythmic relationship between drums and bass: drums keep steady rhythm four times as fast as bass.
	B (0:37)	Bridge. Notice shift to longer phrases, which shift surprisingly. Bridge is twice the length of A section.
	A (1:06)	As before
1:21	**Second chorus**	
	A	Tall and tan …
	A	When she walks …
	B	Oh, but I watch her …
	A	Tall and tan …
2:34	**Third chorus**	
	Saxophone solo by Stan Getz; complete statement of melody (AABA)	
3:47	**Fourth chorus**	
	Piano solo by Jobim, the first two A sections. Note rich harmonies under melody.	
	(4:17) Astrud Gilberto sings bridge and last A section, with obbligato line from Getz.	
	(4:59) Gradual fade-out.	

In the Second chorus, "Vocalist is Astrud Gilberto, wife of João Gilberto at the time" appears beside the A sections.

5 to Listen For
"The Girl from Ipanema"

INSTRUMENTATION
Voices, acoustic guitar, saxophone, piano, bass, and drums

PERFORMANCE STYLE
Both Gilbertos, but especially João, sing with flat, uninflected voices

RHYTHM
Bass and drums establish a 16-beat rhythm at moderately slow tempo. Highly syncopated guitar chords conflict with this rhythm.

MELODY
A section spins out from three notes repeated several times. B section repeats a long, winding phrase three times before closing with new idea.

HARMONY
Rich chords shift underneath repetitive melody; far removed from I-IV-V in bridge.

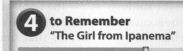

4 to Remember
"The Girl from Ipanema"

BOSSA NOVA AND JAZZ
Jazz, especially jazz harmonies, influenced Jobim and Gilberto.

COOL LATIN MUSIC
Hot Latin music is loud, fast, dense, and busy; bossa nova is slower, softer, and leaner.

SAMBA, BOSSA NOVA, AND AMERICAN ACCEPTANCE
Carmen Miranda was an exotic; bossa nova fit better with rock-era music.

BRAZILIAN MUSIC AND 16-BEAT RHYTHMS
The first 16-beat rhythms popular in the United States; "lite" alternative to rock rhythm

status quo, as evidenced by its role in the payola investigations that brought down Alan Freed. Pop and musical theater also had the most to lose: money (it was expensive to mount a Broadway production or film a musical), status, control—and face. Those who had belittled rock and roll had to eat crow when the music matured commercially and musically. So for many in the industry, acknowledging and accepting rock was a sign of capitulation. It did not go down easily.

In the end, though, everything happened—there was a full spectrum of reactions to rock by pop musicians. Some created pop rock by integrating rock elements—typically, rock rhythms and forms—into songs with a pop sensibility. Others continued to stay the course and remain completely outside of rock. Still others moved back and forth between old and new. We sample one of the most innovative of these possibilities in the music of Burt Bacharach.

Burt Bacharach and a New Kind of Pop

By 1960 Tin Pan Alley, originally a section of West 28th Street in New York, seemed to have shrunk to a single address: 1619 Broadway, otherwise known as the Brill Building. The building was home to several music publishers, most notably AlDon Music (named for partners Al Nevins and Don Kirshner), a company that set out to bridge the gap between rock and roll and traditional popular song. Staff songwriters included future star singer-songwriters Carole King, Neil Sedaka, and Neil Diamond.

The most inventive of the Brill Building–style songwriters was the team of lyricist Hal David (b. 1921) and songwriter Burt Bacharach (b. 1928). Bacharach came to popular song with a rich background in jazz, classical music (he studied composition with esteemed French composer Darius Milhaud), and traditional pop (he was serving as Marlene Dietrich's musical director even as he was turning out hits like the Shirelles' "Baby It's You"). He teamed up with lyricist Hal David in 1957; they recruited Dionne Warwick to sing their songs in 1963, and she was their voice for the rest of the sixties.

Warwick sang most of the Bacharach/David hits. Their association represented a kind of middle option between the singer-songwriters (like several of Bacharach's Brill Building partners) and the songwriter/singer separation

singing. This song offers an especially accessible example. Getz's playing is straightforward and lyrical; his sound has the restrained quality and smooth edge that the Brazilians admired so much. His contribution underscores the affinity between jazz and bossa nova.

The bossa nova fad lasted only a few years, but its impact touched American music in several important ways. Bossa nova rhythms became a pop alternative to rock rhythm; Dusty Springfield's version of Bacharach's "The Look of Love," heard below, is one example. Brazilian rhythms, from both bossa nova and samba, helped shape the rhythms of several new jazz styles that emerged after 1970. More generally, bossa nova reintroduced American listeners to the 16-beat rhythms of the samba, active patterns that move four times as fast as the beat. This time they took. Though there is no clear causal relationship between the rhythms of the samba and the active rhythms heard in the black music and jazz/rock fusions of the late 1960s and early 1970s, there is a decided similarity. Because of the bossa nova, the sounds had been in the air since the early 1960s.

● ● ● ● ● ● ● ● ●

Pop Rock

In 1960 the term *pop rock* might have been considered a contradiction in terms. A decade later it was reality. The pop establishment had fought hard to preserve the

CD 3:20

"The Look of Love," Burt Bacharach and Hal David (1967). Dusty Springfield, vocal.

of traditional pop. Hal David said that he and Bacharach had the sound of her voice in their ears when they wrote. By using Warwick consistently, in songs like "Alfie" and "Do You Know the Way to San José," and with their arrangements, Bacharach and David were able to gain a considerable degree of control over the final result, close to what the Beatles and Motown enjoyed.

Among Bacharach's most enduring hits has been "The Look of Love," a song written not for Warwick, but for *Casino Royale*, a 1967 spoof of the immensely popular James Bond films. For the soundtrack Bacharach used British pop singer Dusty Springfield, whose breathy voice seems ideally suited to the song and the steamy atmosphere that the words and music evoke.

David's lyric is understated; that gives it its power. What he says is mild enough, at least on the surface: "The look of love is in your eyes" or "Take a lover's vow and seal it with a kiss." Because of what he doesn't say and because of Bacharach's setting, we can imagine that love goes beyond a look and a kiss—especially in the late sixties and in a James Bond film, even a spoof.

"The Look of Love" reveals many of the qualities that set Bacharach's music apart from everyone else writing during that time. Among them:

- *A carefully constructed arrangement,* with little sound hooks embedded in the texture.
- *Unusual harmonies.* A Bacharach song typically contains harmonic surprises, and its harmonic language is far removed from more formulaic patterns, yet different from the new harmonic approaches of 1960s rock.
- *Rhythmic surprises.* Bacharach changes the length or the number of beats whenever he deems it musically necessary.
- *Innovative forms.* The form of the song, with phrases of varying length, does not conform to either the traditional pre-rock pop forms or rock-era verse/chorus forms.

Bacharach's song, like so much of the other music we've heard, is a real period piece, as much a part the sixties as Sean Connery's portrayals of James Bond. And, like Connery as Bond, the song does what it sets out to do very well indeed. That's why both have endured.

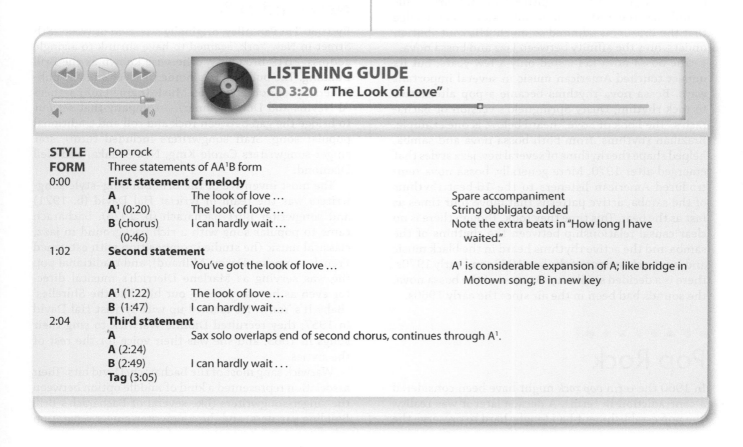

LISTENING GUIDE
CD 3:20 "The Look of Love"

STYLE	Pop rock		
FORM	Three statements of AA¹B form		
0:00	**First statement of melody**		
	A	The look of love …	Spare accompaniment
	A¹ (0:20)	The look of love …	String obbligato added
	B (chorus)	I can hardly wait …	Note the extra beats in "How long I have
	(0:46)		waited."
1:02	**Second statement**		
	A	You've got the look of love …	A¹ is considerable expansion of A; like bridge in
			Motown song; B in new key
	A¹ (1:22)	The look of love …	
	B (1:47)	I can hardly wait …	
2:04	**Third statement**		
	A	Sax solo overlaps end of second chorus, continues through A¹.	
	A (2:24)		
	B (2:49)	I can hardly wait …	
	Tag (3:05)		

5 **to Listen For**
"The Look of Love"

INSTRUMENTATION
Vocal, plus rhythm instruments (piano, electric bass, drum, and guiro), strings, and solo saxophone

PERFORMANCE STYLE
Wispy singing style; wispy sax sound

RHYTHM
Moderately slow tempo. Light, Latin-tinged rock beat. Break in meter at "How long I have waited" (six beats instead of four).

MELODY
Melody spins out from two-note riff. Second A section ranges more widely and becomes more active. B section is the most active.

TEXTURE
Transparent layered texture: voice in middle, bass on bottom, strings usually in high range, and piano fills behind voice; percussion constant and discreet

4 **to Remember**
"The Look of Love"

NEW KIND OF POP
Pop song for and by adults: contemporary lyric, new pop sounds

MODERNIZING POPULAR SONG: RHYTHM
Understated, Brazilian-tinged rock beat

MODERNIZING POPULAR SONG: MELODY AND HARMONY
Innovative development of melody from a short riff; surprising harmonies replace pop conventions

MODERNIZING POPULAR SONG: FORM
A well-connected verse/chorus form in which each section links to the next

Bacharach's Significance

Burt Bacharach and Hal David were among a new generation of songwriters who thoroughly transformed popular song into something quite different from the songs that Frank Sinatra, Johnny Mathis, and Tony Bennett were singing at the beginning of the decade. Although Bacharach's imagination and craft certainly played a big part in the transformation, there's no question that rock-era music, and especially Motown, played a crucial role in shaping Bacharach's new sound. It's particularly evident in the rhythm, the texture, the use of instrumental hooks, and the end-weighted form.

Although miles away from Dylan or the Rolling Stones in attitude and style, and directed to a different, more mature audience, "The Look of Love" demonstrates the trickle-down effect of the rock revolution: the way in which rock elements blended into other styles, reshaping and revitalizing them in the process. It reminds us that the impact of the rock revolution was felt not only in depth but also in breadth—we can gauge the extent of its influence not only by how dramatically this new music differed from the music that it replaced but also by how widespread its influence was.

The Bacharach/David style would profoundly influence the next generation of pop-rock songwriters, among them Barry Manilow, Paul Williams, and Marvin Hamlisch. One product of their efforts was soft rock, which blended the emphasis on melody and the clear forms of Tin Pan Alley song with an understated rock rhythm. This style flourished throughout much of the seventies, most notably in the recordings of the Carpenters, one of the top singles acts of the decade, and in the music of Barbra Streisand. It also found a home on Broadway.

Image courtesy of The Advertising Archives

> **"** *Bacharach's song is a real period piece, as much a part of the sixties as Sean Connery's portrayals of James Bond.* **"**

The Rock Musical

Musical theater entered the rock era on April 29, 1968. That evening, the first rock musical, *Hair*, opened on Broadway. Despite its drastic departure from typical Broadway fare, *Hair* received largely positive reviews. Critics lauded its "zestfulness" and "high spirits." *Hair* was as if someone had opened all the windows in a house that had been closed up for years.

The impact of *Hair* was sudden and invigorating, because of the musical itself and because of the Broadway tradition against which it was reacting. Through much of the 1960s, musical theater remained the most conservative segment of the popular music industry. Broadway producers continued to offer traditional fare, largely ignoring the rock revolution that was going on all around them. The Tony award winners for best musical the four previous years (*Hello, Dolly!* [1964], *Fiddler on the Roof* [1965], *Man of La Mancha* [1966], and *Cabaret* [1967]) varied little from the formula that had been so successful in the 1950s. They were typical Broadway. As a result, the contrast between these musicals and *Hair* was even more striking.

UNITED ARTISTS/THE KOBAL COLLECTION/Picture Desk

Hair *was as if someone had opened all the windows in a house that had been closed up for years.*

Hair

Hair was the brainchild of the actors James Rado and Gerome Ragni. The two had met in Los Angeles in 1964 and began putting the idea together the following year. They wrote the book and the lyrics to the songs, then performed in the production. Galt MacDermot (b. 1928), a jazz-oriented Canadian pianist and composer who had spent time in South Africa studying Bantu music, composed the music. The musical opened off Broadway in 1967, then moved to Broadway, where it ran for 1,750 performances.

Billed as "An American Tribal Love-Rock Musical," *Hair* rejected virtually every attitude and convention of traditional Broadway fare. Instead of building the music around a story about another time or place, *Hair* simply took a slice of counterculture life. The main issues for the counterculture—race, sex, war, and drugs—are the main themes of the musical. The plot, such as it is, is ambiguous and relatively insignificant. The racially integrated cast has no real stars, although Rado played Claude, the leader of the tribe, and Ragni played Berger. The songs focus on the various messages the musical intends to convey, instead of supporting the plot. There were sensational scenes—a burning of the American flag, a famous nude scene, with the actors' backs to the audience; provocative lyrics, with one song listing a series of sexual practices scorned by mainstream society; and novel features, such as actors going out into the audience.

To project this counterculture spirit, MacDermot drew on current and recent rock styles for the songs. The rhythm section, especially the electric bass, is prominent. Many of the songs are short—less than a minute—and longer songs typically use rock-era song forms. The singers range from amateurish to soulful; none sings in the light-classical style commonly heard in 1950s musicals. All of this purges the music of any association with conventional Broadway production. We hear all of these qualities in "Aquarius," the song that opens the musical.

Hair was one of a kind. The way it captured the spirit and substance of the counterculture was all but impossible to emulate. There were no significant sequels, either by Rado, Ragni, and McDermot or by others following their lead. Still, it opened the door for a number of important musicals that showed the influence of rock sensibility and style.

CD 3:21

"Aquarius," James Rado, Jerome Ragni, and Galt MacDermot (1967). *Hair* cast ensemble.

Rock's Influence on Broadway

First was Bacharach and David's *Promises, Promises*, which opened late in 1968. The musical, adapted by Neil Simon from Billy Wilder's 1960 film *The Apartment*, told

LISTENING GUIDE
CD 3:21 "Aquarius"

STYLE	Rock musical	
FORM	ABA, with title-phrase hook	
0:00	**Introduction**	
	"Found" sounds: tinkling, and so forth	
	(0:23) Instruments enter, setting up groove	
0:43	**A section**	
	Verse	When the moon is in the Seventh House …	Solo singer
	Chorus (1:02)	This is the dawning of the age …	Chorus = entire company singing
	Hook (1:13)	Aquarius!	Common element in A and B
1:25	**B section**	
	Verse	Harmony and understanding, Sympathy and trust abounding …	Contrast in melody, activity: functions like a verse
	Hook (1:41)	Aquarius!	Sung at a lower pitch
1:50	**A section**	
	Verse	When the moon is in the Seventh House …	Style aligned with Motown: strong bass, lighter timekeeping; richer harmony
	Chorus (1:02)	This is the dawning of the age …	
	Hook (1:13)	Aquarius	Extended in final statement

5 to Listen For "Aquarius"

INSTRUMENTATION
Solo voice, choir, electric guitar, electric bass, piano, drums voice, brass, assorted "found" sounds

RHYTHM
Motown-like understated rock rhythm at bright tempo; contrast in activity between A and B sections

MELODY
A section unfolds from a slow three-note idea; grows more active toward push to "Aquarius"; B section = short, fast phrases to continuous flow

HARMONY
Rich harmony that avoids conventional progressions and shifts through several keys

TEXTURE
Voice(s) dominant, bass next strongest voice, middle lighter; variation from solo voice (thinner) to chorus (thicker)

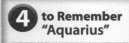

4 to Remember "Aquarius"

NO STARS
Solo voice not dominant; company sings most of song: expression of "we" attitude of 1960s

BEYOND RODGERS AND HAMMERSTEIN
Comprehensive departure from traditional musical: in plot, attitude, musical style

BLACK MUSIC INFLUENCE
Bass-heavy accompaniment, rich harmony, timekeeping in background, horn section suggest influence of Motown and soul

NEW AGE ANTHEM
Direct expression of new age values: 1960s peace, love, mind-expanding drugs, spirituality

the story of a young businessman who let his bosses use his apartment for extramarital affairs in return for job advancement. Bacharach's clever music complements the modern theme of the plot with up-to-date but adult-sounding music.

Stephen Sondheim's *Company* (1970) deals with a bachelor in his mid-thirties who is unable or unwilling to commit to a relationship and the efforts of five couples to find him a mate. There is no real plot, just a series of short scenes that reveal the flaws and foibles of the characters, and no real stars—the title refers both to the star-less cast and Bobby the bachelor's problem. Critics billed it as the first modern musical; certainly it adapts the "realness" of rock to the "over-30" generation (Sondheim was 40 when he composed it), and he typically conveys it musically through the pop rock style that emerged during the latter part of the 1960s.

Tim Rice and Andrew Lloyd Webber's *Jesus Christ, Superstar* (recorded 1970, staged 1971) retold the passion of Christ in contemporary terms. It portrayed the characters from a current psychological perspective and used rock-influenced music and everyday speech to make the story more up to date. Here, the relevance and immediacy associated with rock were evident not in the story, which is ageless, but in the way it was presented, in words and music. Some found the boldness of Lloyd Webber's setting of the passion shocking, even sacrilegious; others found it refreshing and inspiring.

Musical Theater After 1970

After a flurry of rock musicals in the late 1960s and early 1970s, including *Grease* (1972), the influence of rock became more indirect but still evident. Most obviously, rock became one of the styles on which theater composers could draw. Its more wide-ranging impact was less direct, but deeper. It took two forms. One was the use of musical style to evoke a sense of time and place. Sondheim's *Follies*, a musical about a theater scheduled for demolition that once presented *Ziegfeld Follies*–type revues, evokes the music popular between the two world wars; *Grease* samples a host of late 1950s rock 'n' roll styles; Lloyd Webber's *Evita* (1976), a musical about Eva Peron, the second wife of Argentine politician Juan Peron, is laced with tango rhythms. For Sondheim and Lloyd Webber, who would become the dominant figures in musical theater after 1970, this would become the norm. This practice has much more in common with the music of the Beatles, who shaped the sound world of a song to its lyric, than it does with the musicals of Rodgers and Hammerstein, which employed much the same musical language regardless of the plot.

The other was a more clear-eyed view of reality, a trademark of Sondheim's musicals. Beyond Sondheim, two exceedingly popular productions directed by Michael Bennett stand out in this regard. *A Chorus Line* (1975) gave its audience an unsentimental glimpse into Broadway's life behind the curtain. *Dreamgirls* (1981) did the same for Motown black pop groups of the sixties. Both offered a comparatively frank, unglamorous dramatization of the seemingly glamorous showbiz lifestyle.

The exchange between rock and Broadway went almost exclusively in one direction; theatrical music in rock assumed a radically different form. The Who's "rock opera" *Tommy* involved only the band members; so did the touring version of David Bowie's *Ziggy Stardust and the Spidermen from Mars*. Both began as recordings; live performances came later.

• • • • • • • •
Country Music

In the first decade of the rock era, country music was a part of rock yet apart from it. From the start, country music fed into rock, from Chuck Berry's "Maybellene" and the first rockabillies, through the folk revival and Ray Charles's country and western recordings. With

Roy Orbison, the last of the rockabillies and arguably the first country rocker, the boundary between country and rock became more blurred. An Orbison single released in 1963 that paired "Blue Bayou" with a remake of "Mean Woman Blues" brings the two together.

However, the dominant players in country music during the 1950s and early 1960s all but ignored rock and roll. During this time, Nashville reinforced its position as the spiritual and commercial center of country music. The Country Music Association, formed there in 1957, served as the primary trade organization for the industry, and Nashville served as its publishing and recording center. Already the publishing center of country music, Nashville also became its recording center. Most of the major record companies rented, then built, studios there. The "Nashville sound" was a marriage of country and pop. Inspired by the successful recordings of country songs by pop artists, some Nashville A&R (artists and repertoire) men, most notably guitarist Chet Atkins, sought to create a place in the mainstream market for country music. The result was a sound that supported smooth country vocalists like Jim Reeves with lush arrangements worthy of a Sinatra. A small number of musicians, including Atkins, pianist Floyd Cramer, and vocalist/choral director Anita Kerr, played or sang on many of these Nashville recording dates. Their continuing presence also contributed to the development of a consistent style, which remained largely independent of rock. That would change after 1965.

In the late 1960s and early 1970s, the country influence on rock was evident not only in Dylan's Nashville sessions, but also in projects involving Gram Parsons, first with the Byrds, then with the Flying Burrito Brothers; the southern rock of the Allman Brothers, Lynyrd Skynyrd, and others; the "American" sound of the Grateful Dead and Creedence Clearwater Revival; and the country rock of the early Eagles.

During that same period, rock influences also filtered into the hits coming from Nashville, as well as renegade outposts like Bakersfield, California, home to Buck Owens and Merle Haggard, and Austin, Texas, Willie Nelson's home base. Nelson and Waylon Jennings would defy the conventional Nashville wisdom and succeed; their 1976 *Wanted! The Outlaws* was the first album recorded in Nashville to be certified platinum. As it had done in the past, country simply absorbed and adapted the prevailing styles after they had taken root in the popular mainstream. Just as honky-tonk had borrowed the rhythm section and two-beat rhythm from mainstream pop, and western swing and rockabilly had adapted the swing and shuffle rhythms and horns of swing and R&B, so did 1960s country gently ease in rock rhythm—and other features of rock style. It also updated its most enduring theme.

Country's New Take on Reality

From Jimmie Rodgers's blue yodels to the latest hits on Country Music Television (CMT) or Great American Country (GAC), country music has chronicled the good times and the bad times of men and women, together and apart. Songs have expressed almost every conceivable point of view: the faithful wife, the wandering wife, the faithful husband, the philandering husband. Often songs seemed to be airing dirty linen in public, as we heard in Kitty Wells's answer song "It Wasn't God Who Made Honky Tonk Angels." By the late 1960s, the stories had acquired a more modern cast, as we hear in Tammy Wynette's "D-I-V-O-R-C-E."

Tammy Wynette (1942–1998) lived the stories she told in song so fully that it was difficult to discern where life ended and art began. She grew up without a father, married for the first time at seventeen, and divorced before the birth of her third child. While working as a beautician to pay the bills, she pursued a singing career. Within a year she was on her way, and by 1968 she had three No. 1 country hits, including "Stand By Your Man" and "D-I-V-O-R-C-E." The following year she married George Jones (they claimed to have married the year before), one of country music's great singers. It didn't work, except on recordings. Jones was an alcoholic by this time, and his drinking and its effects on his personal and professional lives ruined their marriage and nearly destroyed his career. Musically, however, they were a perfect match; both sang with real feeling and empathy, as documented by their duet recordings such as "Take Me" and "Let's Build a World Together."

Wynette excelled at expressing in song the pain of love gone wrong. She had experienced this pain firsthand and was able to translate it into music that touched listeners deeply. In "D-I-V-O-R-C-E," she presents the heartbreak of the end of a relationship. "D-I-V-O-R-C-E" tells the story in the present tense; we learn about the breakup of the marriage as it's happening.

The emotional impact of the song comes almost exclusively from the lyrics and her singing. The story unfolds gradually. It describes a painful situation in plain language, but with a gimmick: the spelling out of words in "D-I-V-O-R-C-E." The music is essentially neutral; there is nothing in the melody of the song that tells us about the pain—except when she reshapes it. The accompaniments are tasteful and very much in the background. We hear steel guitar, an electric guitar with reverb that recalls the surf music of the early 1960s, and a discreet rhythm section playing a discreet rock rhythm at a slow tempo. "D-I-V-O-R-C-E" also has a choir very much in the background, which surfaces only during the chorus.

"D-I-V-O-R-C-E" exemplifies Nashville at its most efficient: simple songs that are good vehicles for good singers, and professional musical settings appropriate to the mood of the song. Here they stay out of the way, letting Wynette and the lyric take center stage. In songs like this, the story and Wynette's telling of it are the expressive focus. Everything else should be in the background, and it is.

In this song, the musical influence of rock is slight—mainly the discreet rock rhythm—but it is present. As with pop and the rock musical, it evidences the trickling down of rock style into music far removed culturally and expressively from rock music.

Country Music in the 1970s

Country music continued to expand its audience in the 1970s, for several reasons. Among the most important were the greater openness of rock-era listeners to a range of musical styles and the continuing interchange between rock, country, and pop. This took place despite the conservative backlash and the rise of the "silent majority" during Richard Nixon's tenure in the White House. With the election of Jimmy Carter, the first president from the Deep South since Andrew Johnson, the White House became a major venue for country performers during his presidency. Pop-oriented country gathered the largest market share. Dolly Parton became the poster girl for country in the late 1970s and a mainstream star—and tabloid victim—in the 1980s after the release of the film *9 to 5*, for which she wrote and recorded the title track.

The essence of country music is embodied in its themes, its plainspoken way of presenting them, its distinctive vocal styles, and its characteristic instruments, especially fiddle, steel guitar, and dobro. These qualities would help the market for country music explode in the 1990s.

Tammy Wynette and George Jones in happier times

Wynette alluded to their disastrous personal life in songs that barely disguised their real-life troubles.

CD 3:22

"D-I-V-O-R-C-E," Tammy Wynette, Bobby Braddock, and Claude Putman (1968). Wynette, vocal.

STYLE	Rock-tinged country		
FORM	Verse/chorus: verse and chorus almost identical melodically		
0:00	**Introduction**		
	Guitar with reverb; steel guitar highlighted in intro		
0:14	**First statement**		
	Verse	Our little boy is four years old and quite a little man …	Simple setting spotlights Wynette's vocal.
	Chorus (0:52)	Our D-I-V-O-R-C-E becomes final today …	Country rock beat throughout
1:33	**Second statement**		
	Verse	Watch him smile, he thinks it's Christmas …	Shift to a higher key = more intensity
	Chorus (2:12)	Our D-I-V-O-R-C-E becomes final today …	Melody almost the same as verse; thicker texture (vocal harmony, high steel guitar) main difference

⑤ to Listen For
"D-I-V-O-R-C-E"

INSTRUMENTATION
Voice, choir, electric guitar, steel guitar, acoustic guitar, electric bass, drums

PERFORMANCE STYLE
Wynette's heartfelt singing a classic country vocal sound

RHYTHM
Gentle rock rhythm at moderate tempo

MELODY
Four long phrases in verse and chorus (almost identical)

TEXTURE
Voice(s) dominant, bass next strongest voice, middle lighter; variation from solo voice (thinner) to chorus (thicker)

④ to Remember
"D-I-V-O-R-C-E"

MODERN COUNTRY THEME
"D-I-V-O-R-C-E" updates personal themes of country music.

WYNETTE'S IMPASSIONED SINGING
Wynette's style—subtle timing, change in quality from strong to whispered—gives emotional credibility to lyric.

DOMINANT COUNTRY SOUNDS
In addition to Wynette's singing, steel guitar main obbligato instrument, guitar with reverb (borrowed from early 1960s rock)

COUNTRY ROCK BEAT
Rock rhythm on top of honky-tonk style two beat: bass alternating with crisp backbeat

Latin Rock: Carlos Santana

During the 1950s and 1960s, Latin music was only an occasional and subtle strand in the fabric of rock and rhythm and blues: the clave/hambone pattern in "Not Fade Away," bongo drums in "A Hard Day's Night," conga drums in "I Heard It Through the Grapevine," bossa nova rhythms in Bacharach songs. Around 1970, it became an equal partner, through the Latin rock of Santana.

CD 3:23
"Oye Como Va,"
Tito Puente (1971).
Santana.

Carlos Santana (b. 1947) was born and raised in Mexico. He moved to San Francisco in 1962. Santana first gained attention as a blues-inspired rock guitarist; his first commercial recording came from a live 1969 performance with blues guitarist Mike Bloomfield. That same year, he acknowledged his Hispanic heritage by forming Santana. Latin music has its roots in Cuba, as we've noted. Most Latin musicians at the time came from Spanish-speaking Caribbean countries or had roots there; New York was the American home of this music at the time. The music of Mexico (and Santana's father, a mariachi musician) is quite different. Nevertheless, Santana connected with Afro-Cuban music and merged it with rock into a one-band rock substyle.

A prime example of his synthesis of the two styles is his 1971 version of Tito Puente's "Oye Como Va." Here, Santana blends the sounds and rhythmic feel of Latin music into a rock song driven by Santana's guitar and Gregg Rolie's organ. The song begins with an irregular rhythmic pattern, played on the organ (and supported in the bass). It is not the clave rhythm of Afro-Cuban music, but it is similar in that it creates an asymmetrical rhythm over eight beats and serves as the main rhythmic reference. The performance consists mainly of several statements of Puente's simple melodic riffs, wrapped around strong organ and guitar solos.

As we listen to the guitar and organ solos in this song, we can hear how seamlessly Latin and rock rhythms merge. Both are built on the division of the beat into two equal parts, so the rhythms align when played together. One could easily imagine the solos of Carlos Santana or organist Gregg Rolie (b. 1947) taking place over a groove laid down by a rock bassist and drummer. They would not have to adjust the rhythmic feel of their playing to play the same music with a rock band.

Despite this comfortable correspondence between Latin and rock rhythms, those who wish to combine them must reconcile the two, because the beat and the clave pattern are

> # Santana connected with Afro-Cuban music and merged it with rock into a one-band rock substyle.

Sony Music Archive/Getty Images/Terry Lott/Getty Images

mutually exclusive ways of organizing a steady rhythmic stream. Marking the beat grounds the rhythm, because beat marking divides time into regular intervals. By contrast, organizing the rhythm mainly around the asymmetrical clave pattern helps the rhythm float, because it doesn't come to rest on the beat. Santana's effective compromise is to keep Puente's clave-like rhythm in the forefront throughout most of the song.

LISTENING GUIDE
CD 3:23 "Oye Como Va"

STYLE	Latin rock
FORM	Several short melodic fragments, all supported by two-chord pattern. Only one is sung. No consistent order to the fragments.
0:00	**Introduction**
	Three melodic ideas: the clave-like rhythm on a single note; a short phrase, played on guitar, which is repeated four times; and a stop-time pattern played by the entire band prepares the vocal. The stop-time phrase returns periodically to mark major sections in the form.
0:30	**Vocal**
	Oye como va . . . A rough translation: "Listen to how it goes, my rhythm; it's good for celebrating." A "mulata" is a cognate of "mulatto," referring to a woman of mixed race.
0:46	**Instrumental**
	Several new melodic ideas; the second (1:01) is expanded into a short guitar solo. A change in timbre accompanies the third. The fourth is the clave-like rhythm of the opening, and the fifth is yet another new idea with still another change in timbre. This sets up the organ solo.
1:55	**Organ solo**
	Rolie's flamboyant organ solo over two-chord pattern; Latin rhythms continue underneath. The clave-like rhythm and stop-time pattern announce return of vocal.
2:41	**Vocal**
	Oye como va . . . As before
3:03	**Guitar solo**
	Santana begins with earlier idea (1:01), then proceeds to develop it into a blues/rock-oriented solo over the relentless Latin rhythm, with clave-like pattern played on organ. Song ends with stop-time pattern.

5 to Listen For
"Oye Como Va"

INSTRUMENTATION
Vocals, electric guitar, organ, electric bass, drums, Latin percussion of timbales, congas, etc.

RHYTHM
Merger of rock and Latin rhythms at moderate tempo: rock beat plus clave-like rhythm

MELODY
Vocal melody formed from repeated riff; other melodies also riff based

HARMONY
Simple oscillation between two chords = no harmonic goal, helping produce open form

TEXTURE
Dense, percussion-rich texture, even during solos

3 to Remember
"Oye Como Va"

MULTINATIONAL INSTRUMENTATION
Santana's band includes his rock-style electric guitar, electric bass, and electric organ, plus an arsenal of instruments associated with Afro-Cuban music, including congas, timbales, and guiro (which produces the scraping sound).

CLAVE-LIKE RHYTHM
The foreground rhythm of Puente's song is asymmetrical and syncopated, like the clave rhythm, but the pattern contains six notes, not five, and does not line up with the clave rhythm. The result is a Latin feel, but not authentic Afro-Cuban rhythm.

ROCK-BASED GUITAR AND ORGAN SOLOS
The extended guitar and organ solos in "Oye Como Va" betray no Latin influence; they would sound just as effective in a rock song. The stylistic synthesis occurs because the Latin rhythms and percussion sounds continue underneath the solo.

What distinguishes **Latin rock** from Latin-influenced rock or rhythm and blues? In "Oye Como Va" it is, more than anything else, the sheer quantity of percussion instruments and the persistence of Puente's clave-like rhythm that place the Latin elements in the forefront. In this song, Afro-Cuban music and rock are more or less equal partners.

Santana was Latin rock's lone star. New York–based Latin musicians also attempted rock/Latin fusions: *bugalú*, a blend of Latin music and rhythm and blues, was a minor sensation in the Latin community during the sixties and early seventies. But none of this music had the crossover appeal of Santana's early music. In the mid-seventies, Santana gravitated toward jazz fusion; Latin rock faded away. However, the influence of Latin music—especially via Cuba and Brazil—would be even more pronounced, and more seamlessly integrated, in the seventies and eighties.

● ● ● ● ● ● ● ●

Jazz and Rock

In 1968, Miles Davis (1926–1991) went electric. For almost two decades, he had played a leading role in the jazz vanguard. A series of recordings in the late 1940s gave birth to cool jazz; his collaborations with Gil

Evans raised jazz to art and stretched its boundaries—recall that Davis's *Sketches of Spain* was the inspiration for Grace Slick's "White Rabbit"; he pioneered the use of modal scales and harmonies in jazz; and his early 1960s recordings continued to offer innovative approaches to swing, improvisation, and formal organization.

Through the early 1960s, he was on top of the jazz world. Miles was arguably the most admired jazz musician of his generation—by the top musicians who played in his groups, by critics who thoughtfully appraised his work, by fans who came to hear him despite his surly demeanor onstage, and by Columbia records, who continued to release his albums.

But Miles was restless. He recognized that jazz was at a crossroads. As much as any active jazz musician, he was aware that the evolutionary momentum of jazz had brought the music to a stylistic reckoning point. He had close contract with jazz musicians working to integrate rock into jazz. Herbie Hancock, the pianist in his quintet, was one of the first and most prominent jazzmen to explore this new territory.

So in 1968, he augmented his quintet with musicians playing electric guitar and keyboards to create what he claimed would be the "best damn rock band in the world." His new path was controversial—almost

Michael Ochs Archives/Getty Images

Miles was arguably the most admired jazz musician of his generation—by the top musicians who played in his groups, by critics who thoughtfully appraised his work, by fans who came to hear him despite his surly demeanor onstage.

as controversial as Dylan's electric conversion, as traditionalists accused him of selling out. But Miles had heard the future and was prepared to realize it. In two albums made in 1969, *In a Silent Way* and *Bitches Brew*, he created the most innovative and challenging synthesis of jazz and rock to that point.

CD 3:24

"Ssh," Miles Davis (1969). Davis, trumpet; John McLaughlin, guitar; Chick Corea and Joe Zawinul, keyboards; Wayne Shorter, saxophone; Herbie Hancock, piano; Dave Holland, bass; and Tony Williams, drums.

For the recording session of *In a Silent Way*, Davis added guitarist John McLaughlin and keyboardists Chick Corea and Joe Zawinul to his working quintet of saxophonist Wayne Shorter, pianist Herbie Hancock, bassist Dave Holland, and drummer Tony Williams. In a typical jazz environment, this would be extreme chord-instrument overkill. However, Davis relied on the good judgment and imagination of his musicians.

In a Silent Way consists of two long tracks: one is 18 minutes, the other is 20. Both are composite tracks created by engineer Teo Macero. Each long track is assembled from two shorter segments in an ABA pattern. The track from which our example is drawn is listed as "Ssh/Peaceful/Ssh"; we hear the concluding version of "Ssh."

On this album, Davis and his fellow musicians create a radically new sound world, typically via a three-layered approach. The foundational layer is an ostinato or riff that is repeated through a long stretch of time, accompanied by a relentless rhythm on the drums. In the background are the multiple keyboard instruments playing wisps of music in different registers and with different timbres. In the foreground is a solo instrument, the most prominent strand in this rich texture. "Ssh" begins with a sustained organ chord, which quickly gives way to a new texture with the bassist playing a two-note ostinato every four beats, the drummer playing a 16-beat rhythm, and the guitarist dreamily noodling over this base. The bass and drum parts run through the entire track, with intermittent elaboration of the ostinato. After about a minute, McLaughlin gives way to Miles; his eloquent trumpet playing is the outstanding element in the texture. The three keyboardists create a cloud of sound over the bass ostinato and around Miles. The improvisations by Miles and the keyboards use a modal scale (the scale that fits with the first chord in a blues); there is no harmonic change. Fragments of keyboard riffs, exotic harmonies, and complex figures color the texture.

The result is music without any obvious precedent. It is not rock—Miles's boast to the contrary—but it translates the dense, interactive textures, static harmonies, open forms, and active rhythms of rock and soul into a freer musical environment. Nor is it bop or post-bop jazz: rhythm, harmony, and form are radically different. Still, it retains the spontaneous feeling of great jazz.

Miles's music continued to evolve throughout his career. However, his more substantial influence was evident in the music of numerous alumni from his late-sixties bands, who took Davis's jazz rock, now called fusion, in several different directions: the Latin-tinged work of earlier editions of Chick Corea's Return to Forever; the electrically charged blasts of John McLaughlin

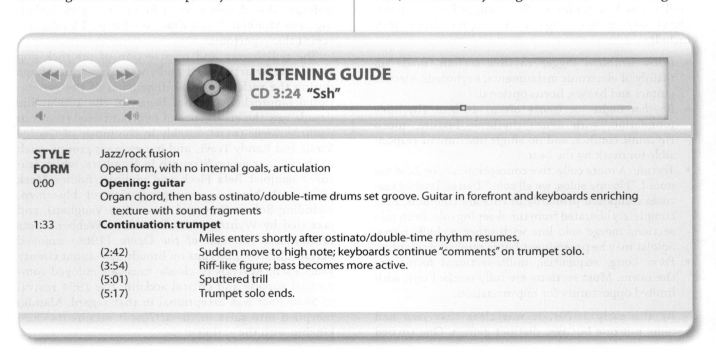

	LISTENING GUIDE CD 3:24 "Ssh"	
STYLE	Jazz/rock fusion	
FORM	Open form, with no internal goals, articulation	
0:00	**Opening: guitar**	
	Organ chord, then bass ostinato/double-time drums set groove. Guitar in forefront and keyboards enriching texture with sound fragments	
1:33	**Continuation: trumpet**	
	Miles enters shortly after ostinato/double-time rhythm resumes.	
(2:42)	Sudden move to high note; keyboards continue "comments" on trumpet solo.	
(3:54)	Riff-like figure; bass becomes more active.	
(5:01)	Sputtered trill	
(5:17)	Trumpet solo ends.	

5 to Listen For
"Ssh"

INSTRUMENTATION
Trumpet, electric guitar, organ, two electric pianos, string bass, drums

RHYTHM
16-beat rhythm at moderate tempo; kept in drums, highlighted in keyboard patterns, sometimes in trumpet

MELODY
No preexisting melody; strictly inspiration of moment; melody-rich with keyboard fragments behind guitar and trumpet

HARMONY
Foundation= no harmony, just bass ostinato and modal scale; rich harmonies circle around bass keynote and scale.

TEXTURE
Dense texture, with keyboard sound cloud around guitar and trumpet, plus bass pattern and busy drums

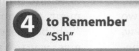

4 to Remember
"Ssh"

FUSION: FROM ROCK
Mainly via James Brown: collective conception, 16-beat rhythm, static harmony

FUSION: FROM JAZZ
Improvisation by lead and keyboard instruments, instrumentation

OPEN FORM
No harmonic structure or melody as basis for improvisation: limited only by imagination of soloists elaborating a single scale

BOLD DEPARTURE
Music goes beyond conventions of jazz (chord changes, soloist dominant) and rock (recurrent riffs, easy-to-follow form): radically new conception

and the mid-seventies Return to Forever that rivaled any rock band; the art funk of Herbie Hancock; and the soundscapes of Weather Report.

The music of these and other groups effectively created a new jazz tradition. The changes from straight-ahead jazz of the 1950s were comprehensive. They also include:

- *Instrumentation* Bigger rhythm section, made up mainly of electronic instruments: keyboards, electric guitars and basses; horns optional.
- *Rhythm* Eight- or (most often) 16-beat rhythmic foundation, with dense rhythmic texture, much rhythmic conflict, and no single instrument responsible for marking the beat.
- *Texture* A more collective conception: as Joe Zawinul noted, "No one solos, we all solo." Dense, layered textures composed primarily of riffs are common. Bass completely liberated from timekeeping role. Even solo sections merge solo line with other melodic parts. Soloist may be preeminent but is rarely dominant.
- *Form* Long, sequential, multi-sectional forms are the norm. Most sections are fully worked out, with limited opportunity for improvisation.

By the early 1970s, it was clear that jazz had become not one but two distinct genres. One turned

back on itself, preserving the swing-based jazz style of the past several decades in a precarious but often creative equilibrium. The other led to the formation of a new array of jazz/rock fusions, collectively so different that it marked the beginning of a new jazz tradition. The distinction between the two remains in place through our own time.

● ● ● ● ● ● ● ●

Looking Back, Looking Ahead

In 1978 Willie Nelson released *Stardust*, an album of pop standards. The track list included classics like "All of Me," "Georgia on My Mind," and the title track. It looked back to Ray Charles's *Genius Hits the Road*, his 1960 travelogue LP that also included "Georgia on My Mind" and anticipated the "Great American Songbook" CDs released by rock-era singers such as Linda Ronstadt, Rod Stewart, and Carly Simon. These recordings helped spark renewed interest in pre-rock pop—not only the songs but also the singers. Sinatra and Bennett were among the older stars to record duet albums with rock-era singers; Natalie Cole's extraordinary duet with her father on "Unforgettable" (1991), made possible by modern technology, remains unforgettable. A new wave of fine pop singers, including Jane Monheit, Diana Krall, and Michael Bublé, also revisit this repertoire.

The rediscovery and resurrection of pre-rock pop standards by artists and audiences who came of age during the rock era is one dimension of the generational rapprochement that began in the 1980s. The decade saw the emergence of neotraditional trends in country music (most notably in the music of George Strait and Randy Travis and in newgrass groups, such as the all-star group Strength in Numbers, which featured banjoist Bela Fleck and violinist/fiddler Mark O'Connor), blues (a new generation of bluesmen, including Robert Cray and Stevie Ray Vaughan), and jazz (led by Wynton Marsalis). Lloyd Webber's *Cats* (1982) and *Phantom of the Opera* (1986) enjoyed extraordinarily long runs on Broadway—about twenty years each. Revivals of classic musicals enjoyed commercial success and critical acclaim: the 1994 revival of *Show Boat* was exceptional in that regard. Mambo morphed into salsa in the 1970s; it retains its close kinship with the earlier style.

It's clear that the confrontational relationship between rock-era music and established styles that characterized the 1960s is well in the past. Similarly, the need to hop on the rock bandwagon is as dated as a leisure suit. The contemporary attitude is openness and easy coexistence. There was no more convincing demonstration of this than Tony Bennett's appearance on *MTV Unplugged* in 1994, which included duets with k. d. lang and Elvis Costello. The album from the show became the top-selling album of his career and won the Grammy award for Album of the Year in 1995.

What has come out of the interaction between rock-era music and established styles is a large and occasionally important body of music—from new kinds of musicals and new approaches to melodic song to jazz fusion and country rock—and a deeper appreciation of the past. This too is part of rock's legacy.

Terms to Know

Test your knowledge of this chapter's important terms by defining the following. If you can't recall the meaning of a certain term, refresh your memory by looking up the boldfaced term in the chapter, turning to the Glossary at the back of the book, or working with the flashcards at the Popular Music Resource Center.

samba	soft rock
bossa nova	rock musical
pop rock	Latin rock

Rock and R&B *in the* Early 1970s

istockphoto.com

CHAPTER

12

On May 13, 1971, Stevie Wonder (born Steveland Morris in 1950) turned twenty-one. On that day his contract with Motown Records expired. Up to that point, the arrangement had been good for both parties: Wonder was a child star, and both he and Motown reaped the rewards. However, when he came of age, Wonder took the $1 million in royalties that Motown had been holding in trust for him, formed his own record and publishing companies (Taurus and Black Bull, respectively), and negotiated a new record deal with Motown. For Wonder the crucial clause in the contract was complete artistic control. In effect, he made his records and Motown sold them.

Wonder assumed artistic control in an unprecedented way. He immersed himself in electronics, learning how to use synthesizers and electronic keyboards, a new and rapidly evolving technology at the time. With these newly developed skills, he played most—and sometimes all—of the parts on many of his recordings. On Wonder's recordings, a single artist with a lot of equipment replaced the multilevel Motown production pyramid (discussed in Chapter 10). The string of albums that he produced in the early seventies did well enough that he was able to renegotiate his contract with Motown in 1975. The new deal gave him a $13 million advance and a 20 percent royalty rate.

Wonder's emancipation from Motown and his subsequent contractual arrangements illustrate three key features of rock and R&B after 1970. First, this new music had become a big business. Second, important artists were determined to go their own way, no matter where it took them. Third, technology would play an increasingly important role in shaping the sound of popular music.

● ● ● ● ● ● ● ●
The Popular-Music Industry in the 1970s: Commerce and Technology

In the seventies, rock traded tie-dyed T-shirts for three-piece suits. In so doing, it turned its core values upside down. From the beginning, rock had portrayed itself as a music of rebellion, taking over popular music with a revolution. But as the market share of rock and R&B grew, so did the financial stake. It cost more to create and promote a record, to put on a concert, and to operate a venue. There was more money to be made but also more to be lost.

The Business of Rock

Not surprisingly, a corporate mentality took over the business side of rock. It was evident to some extent in the music itself, in that some artists seemed to make commercial success their highest priority and let that shape their music. Elton John, the bestselling rock star of the seventies, was the poster boy for this path. His early albums showed him to be a singer-songwriter of considerable gifts. As his star rose, he immersed himself in the Top 40 while adopting a Liberace-like stage persona, eventually donning elevator shoes, flamboyant costumes, and outlandish eyewear. His songs found the middle of the road, and he found megastardom. Somewhere along the line, he lost some of his musical individuality, trading it for familiarity and accessibility, and his visual identity at times deflected attention away from his real talent. John was not alone in this regard; others went down his yellow brick road to superstardom.

The impact of profit-oriented thinking was far more telling behind the scenes. It determined to a great extent which music would get promoted and how. Its impact was most evident in the media and in the use of new market strategies designed to maximize sales.

Media and Money. No medium showed the impact of the big-business mind-set more than radio. In the early years of rock, radio had been an important part of the music's outsider image—witness Alan Freed and other like-minded disc jockeys in the fifties and "underground" FM stations in the sixties. In the seventies, however, the most significant new trend was AOR (album-oriented radio). In this format, disc jockeys could no longer choose the songs they played. Instead, program directors selected a limited number of songs designed to attract a broad audience while offending as few as possible. Often stations bought syndicated packages, further homogenizing radio content. Free-form radio all but disappeared, and so did the adventurous spirit that it symbolized. As a result, distortion was out; tunefulness was in. Acts like Barry Manilow, the Carpenters, Stevie Wonder, Chicago, the Eagles, Fleetwood Mac, Paul McCartney and Wings, and, of course, Elton John got a lot of airplay and topped the charts.

Cross-Marketing. A major business innovation of the seventies was **cross-marketing**. In pursuit of greater financial rewards, record companies used tours to help promote record sales. With improved amplification, the stadium or large-arena concert became commonplace. More ritual than musical event, these concerts usually confirmed what the audience already knew about the music of a particular band. As a rule there was little, if any, spontaneity in performance, as bands drew their set list from current or recent albums.

istockphoto.com

" *By the early seventies, spectacle had become part of the business.* "

Often the performances were more about show than sound, although there were plenty of both. Flamboyance had been part of rock from the start, and by the early seventies, spectacle had become part of the business. Lights, fog, costumes, makeup, pyrotechnics, and the like were now commonplace at rock concerts. Such productions were almost a necessity because performers had to seem larger than life in such huge venues. At its most extreme, outrageous dress, makeup, and stage deportment replaced musical substance as the primary source of interest. Acts like Kiss epitomized this theatrical aspect of seventies rock.

Rock as Big Business. The seventies proved that there was money to be made in rock and R&B on a scale that was hard to imagine even a decade before. Record sales had increased enough that the Recording Industry Association of America (RIAA) created a new category in 1976, the platinum record, which signified the sale of 1 million units. (The gold record represented sales of 500,000 units.) Moreover, the album had replaced the single as the primary unit, so revenues were even higher.

The increased sales, which occurred during a long economic recession, certainly reflect the deeper bond between music and listener, the "rock as a way of life" state of mind. But there were other causes. The ever-growing diversity of the musical landscape meant that there was music for almost everyone's taste. Technology also played a role: the development of new playback formats made the music more accessible.

Technology and Music

One of the fruits of the Allied victory in World War II was the acquisition of a magnetic tape recorder that German scientists had developed. When brought to the United States after the war, it served as the prototype for the reel-to-reel tape recorders developed by Ampex and others. These reel-to-reel tape recorders belonged to the production side of the music business. They were expensive, difficult to use, and hard to tote around—factors that outweighed their superior fidelity for all but the most dedicated and well-heeled audiophiles. In an effort to make tape playback devices more accessible to consumers, RCA developed the first tape cartridge in 1958.

Tape Players. In the sixties two important tape-based consumer formats emerged. One was the four- or eight-track tape. These tape players began to appear in cars (and Lear jets—Bill Lear had the technology developed for his line of corporate jets) in 1965 and remained popular through the seventies. The other, more enduring playback device was the audiocassette. A number of manufacturers, most notably Philips, Sony, and Grundig, worked to develop cassettes and cassette players and to come up with an industry standard. By the seventies, this new technology had caught on: cassette sales grew much faster than LPs (vinyl) and by 1982 exceeded them.

This new format had many advantages. The units were smaller, and so were the playback devices. Some were portable; others went into car consoles. By the mid-seventies, boom boxes had appeared, offering a portable and low-priced alternative to the home stereo. The first Walkman came from the Sony factory in 1979; other companies quickly followed suit. All of these devices made listeners' personal recordings as accessible as the radio.

Cassette players also made it possible for consumers to assemble their own playlists, using blank tapes. With improvements in recording quality, most notably Dolby noise reduction technology, there was less loss in fidelity during copying. People could now take their music with them wherever they went.

Synthesizers. Most of the new sounds of the seventies came from synthesizers. A synthesizer is a device that creates sounds electronically. In early synthesizers, a tone generator would generate a sound wave, which other devices would modify. A piano-like keyboard was the most popular way to input the information necessary to generate a particular sound, but other devices, such as finger-activated metal bands, were also used.

Synthesizers are the ultimate musical application of technology. With synthesizers every aspect of the sound, from generation to final result, can be controlled electronically. Because of this, synthesizers opened up a new

Robert Moog with his pioneering (and massive) invention

Jack Robinson/Hulton Archive/Getty Images

sound world to musicians. Some of the sounds replicated the timbres of existing instruments, such as the violin. (That's why early synthesizers were called **analog synthesizers**: they created an analog, or likeness, of a conventional instrument.) Other sounds were simply not possible on acoustic instruments. They could be abrasive or soothing, simple or complex. The options were—and are—limitless.

The first synthesizers were cumbersome. The Moog synthesizer, as used by Wendy Carlos in her landmark 1968 recording *Switched-On Bach,* looked like an old-fashioned telephone switchboard, with plugs connecting the various oscillators. Carlos's recording, more than any other of that time, opened up the previously arcane world of electronic synthesis to the general public.

The synthesizer became a practical instrument for studio and performance with the application of transistor technology. Early synthesizers used vacuum tubes, but by the early seventies transistors were making them faster, smaller, and more flexible. These more streamlined synthesizers could now operate in real time, a crucial breakthrough for using them easily in live performance.

The first portable synthesizers were capable of performing only a single line, like a voice or saxophone does. But as transistors became smaller and more powerful, improved models capable of simultaneously playing several sounds began to appear. Another improvement was the ability to change sounds on the fly, rather than

If one had to reduce the relationship between sixties and early seventies music to a single word, that word might well be more.

having to stop and reset the parameters. These two changes made the instrument even more useful in both studio and concert.

The New Mainstream

By the early 1970s, the rock revolution was over. It was evident on the charts and in corporate offices. It was evident in the flurry of hastily arranged musical marriages between rock and pre-rock styles: pop rock, rock musicals, and jazz fusion. Most fundamentally, however, it was evident in the music itself.

If one had to reduce the relationship between sixties and early-seventies music to a single word, that word might well be *more.* Whatever happened in the sixties happened more in the seventies. Rock became diverse in the sixties; it became more diverse in the seventies as styles and substyles proliferated. Sixties musicians found the new grooves of rock and soul. Seventies musicians found them more easily; rhythms were freer and more daring, or more powerful. The sounds of bands got even bigger in the seventies through more powerful amplification and additional instruments. Contrasts between styles and the attitudes that they conveyed also became more pronounced: the seventies both heard the intimate confessions of the singer-songwriters and witnessed the bombast of David Bowie's grand spectacles. Sometimes these contrasts even appeared in the same song; Led Zeppelin's "Stairway to Heaven" is a memorable example. Some artists, such as Joni Mitchell, created highly personal music. Other acts hid behind a mask: David Bowie is an extreme example.

The eight examples discussed in this chapter reflect all of these trends, often in strikingly varied ways. The examples are paired to highlight themes; the contrasts in style simply underscore the ways in which diverse substyles manifested the dominant trends of the first part of the 1970s.

• • • • • • • •

The Liberation of Rock and Roll: Hard Rock and Heavy Metal

It took rock musicians about fifteen years to really get it—that is, to completely assimilate the numerous musical influences that fed into rock, transform them into the dominant style, and become comfortable with its conventions. Most fundamentally, this is evident in the top bands' approach to rhythm and sound. As the 1970s began, musicians approached rock rhythm with unprecedented freedom because they had reached a comfort zone with its essential elements. It is apparent in a wide range of music: the "American" rock of Creedence Clearwater Revival and the Grateful Dead, the southern rock of the Allman Brothers and Lynyrd Skynyrd, the art rock of Yes and Deep Purple, and the jazz/rock fusion of Miles Davis alumni John McLaughlin (Mahavishnu Orchestra) and Chick Corea (Return to Forever). However, it is most evident in the "dictionary definition" rock of bands like the Rolling Stones—their 1972 album *Exile on Main Street* is generally regarded as their finest work and one of the finest albums of the rock era—and in heavy metal, most notably in the music of Black Sabbath, Deep Purple (a band that straddled the boundary between heavy metal and art rock), and Led Zeppelin.

Two landmark recordings from the early 1970s, The Who's "Won't Get Fooled Again" and Led Zeppelin's "Black Dog," show in quite different ways the rhythmic independence achieved by elite rock musicians when they felt comfortable with the rhythmic foundation of rock. The Who use a novel instrument as a substitute for a rhythm guitar, whereas Led Zeppelin dispenses with persistent timekeeping altogether. That they can use this minimal timekeeping as a springboard for great rock is a testament not only to the excellence of both groups but also to the rapid and dramatic evolution of rock rhythm from the mid-1960s through the early 1970s.

The Who

In 1969 Alan R. Pearlman founded ARP Instruments in order to produce synthesizers capable of creating a variety of electronic sounds. His first synthesizer, released in 1970, was a fairly large machine. His second model, the ARP 2600, which was released in 1971, was portable and flexible enough to be used in live performance, although it was *monophonic*—that is, capable of playing only one sound at a time.

To promote his new instruments, Pearlman gave units to some of the top rock and R&B musicians of the era, in return for permission to use their names in promoting his product. Among his first clients was The Who's Pete Townshend. Judging by the almost immediate results, Townshend was fascinated by the synthesizer and the cutting-edge technology it represented. He featured it on several tracks of their 1971 album *Who's Next*, where it served as the best possible advertising for ARP and its instruments.

The Who had come together as a group in 1964. Vocalist Roger Daltrey (b. 1944), guitarist Pete Townshend (b. 1945), and bassist John Entwistle (1944–2002) had been part of a group called the High Numbers; they

became The Who when drummer Keith Moon (1947–1978) joined them. A year later, their music began to appear on the British charts. Their early hits, most notably "My Generation" and "Substitute" (both 1966), speak in an ironic tone. Indeed, "My Generation" became the anthem for the "live hard, die young, and don't trust anyone over 30" crowd. Musically, they were a powerhouse band with a heavy bass sound that displayed the strong influence of 1960s rhythm and blues. Townshend's power chords, Entwistle's talented bass playing, and Moon's flamboyant drumming gave Daltrey's searing voice a rock-solid foundation. Still, it seemed that they were no more than a singles band, incapable of anything more than a series of good 3-minute songs. That perception began to change with the release of the album *Happy Jack* (1967), which included an extended piece, "A Quick One While He's Away," and it was dramatically altered with the release of the rock opera *Tommy* in 1969.

"Won't Get Fooled Again," Peter Townshend (1971). The Who.

1970 Townshend conceived of a sequel to *Tommy*, called *Lifehouse*, which was to be even grander. He eventually put the project aside but incorporated some of the material into an album of singles, entitled *Who's Next*. Unlike *Tommy* and several subsequent efforts (such as *Quadrophenia*), *Who's Next* is not thematic. It's simply a collection of good songs, among them "Won't Get Fooled Again."

> ❝ The Who never forgot how to rock and roll. ❞

David Redfern/Redferns Music Library

3 to Remember
"Won't Get Fooled Again"

SYNTHESIZERS IN ROCK
Innovative use of ARP synthesizer as rhythm instrument: in its steady rock-beat speed timekeeping, synth effectively assumes role (if not the sound and register) of rhythm guitar.

EXPANSIVE FORM
Extended form, with strong contrasts among synthesizer alone, vocal sections, and instrumental sections. More than half the song comes from long instrumental sections.

RHYTHMIC LIBERATION
Steady timekeeping in synthesizer part liberates band rhythmically. All three instrumentalists are free to keep time, or play against the time. The result is an extraordinarily varied rhythmic texture, from heavy timekeeping by everyone, to the open sound of the synthesizer alone or the band playing riffs, lines, and rhythms that conflict with beat.

5 to Listen For
"Won't Get Fooled Again"

INSTRUMENTATION
Vocal, ARP synthesizer, electric guitar, electric bass, drums

RHYTHM
Complex, highly syncopated rock beat at moderately fast tempo, with synthesizer marking rock rhythm, and Moon's manic drumming playing against the beat

MELODY
Vocal line assembled mainly from short riffs

HARMONY
Harmony built around I-IV-V, but colored with modal chords and complex, shifting harmonies on synthesizer-only sections

TEXTURE
Dramatic shifts in density, with long synthesizer-only stretches contrasting with thicker sections featuring full band

The more compelling innovation is his integration of the synthesizer into the heart of the band—a real novelty at the time.

The synthesizer seems to expand not only the sound world created in "Won't Get Fooled Again" but also the size of the song. It is a sprawling song—over $8\frac{1}{2}$ minutes of music. The long synthesizer introduction and even longer interlude toward the end provide a dramatic contrast to the vocal sections, and its steady rhythm underpins the electrifying group jams in the extended instrumental passages.

In "Won't Get Fooled Again," innovative technology enhances the basic sound and rhythm of a rock band. In both its featured role (where it contrasts with the heart of the song) and in its supporting role, the synthesizer part adds a significant dimension to both sound and rhythm. The groove is so compelling that the lyrics almost seem incidental; we lose ourselves in the sounds and rhythms of the song. It makes clear that The Who never forgot how to rock and roll.

Led Zeppelin

A majority of the most important contributions to the development of rock-era music have come from two kinds of artists: those who help define or affirm its core values by doing one thing supremely well (for example, Chuck Berry, the Rolling Stones, James Brown) and those whose curiosity compels them to explore a wide range of influences and bring them into their music, thereby expanding the boundaries of rock (for example, Buddy Holly, Frank Zappa, Stevie Wonder). Few rock-era acts have been capable of contributing in both areas. One that did achieve this was The Who; another was Led Zeppelin.

Although often cited as a seminal heavy metal band, Led Zeppelin ultimately defies categorization. From *Led Zeppelin* (1969), the group's first album, it was clear that heavy metal was just one aspect of their musical personality. Their center is clearly the blues; their version of heavy metal evolved from it. At the same time, there seems to be nothing in their musical world that is not fair game for appropriation. What's particularly interesting in their music is the way in which influences bleed into one another. Their music may cover a lot of stylistic territory, but it is not compartmentalized.

In "Won't Get Fooled Again," Townshend spotlights the synthesizer right from the start. A steady stream of kaleidoscopically changing chords marking the eight-beat rhythm emerges from the opening chord. The band returns about 30 seconds later, at first intermittently, then settling into a groove. As the song proper gets under way, it's clear that the synthesizer chords serve a particular purpose. They are, in effect, a futuristic rhythm guitar, pitched in a high register instead of the more characteristic mid-range, but providing steady reinforcement of the rock rhythmic layer throughout the song. Musically, there is a direct line between Chuck Berry's transformation of boogie-woogie patterns and the synthesizer chords; both serve the same purpose.

In this song, the insistent rhythm of the synthesizer chords seems to liberate the rest of the band. Townshend's power chords and riffs, Entwhistle's active and free bass lines, and Moon's explosive drumming all play off this steady rhythm. It is this interplay between the steady rhythm of the synthesizer and the rest of the group that gives the song its extraordinary rhythmic energy.

Townshend's use of the synthesizer is innovative on two levels. One is simply the use of it—the ARP was a brand-new machine, and the Minimoog with which it competed had only been available for about two years.

The range of their music came mainly from guitarist Jimmy Page (b. 1944), whose curiosity led him not only to immerse himself in the blues, but also to seek out exotic musical styles (for example, flamenco and East Indian music). Led Zeppelin's front man was vocalist Robert Plant (b. 1948), who was Page's second choice as lead singer but turned out to be an ideal voice for the group. Bassist John Paul Jones (b. 1946) had been, with Page, part of the British music scene in the late 1960s; drummer John Bonham (1948–1980) was a friend of Plant's from their Birmingham days. Page also produced their albums. His production skills were as important a component of their success as his guitar playing; he brought a wonderful ear for sonority and texture to their music.

Page and Plant shared a deep interest in the mystic, the mythical, and the occult. This interest would increasingly inform their work, from untitled albums to cryptic covers, sparse liner notes, nonreferential lyrics, and numerous archaic musical influences.

Another quality that sets their music apart from every other group of the era is their ability to establish, then reconcile, extremes. The extremes are evident in virtually every aspect of their music making. Plant sang higher than most other male vocalists (and many females too). Their ensemble playing was more daring, their riffs more elaborate and beat defying, the contrasts

> # Heavy metal evoked supernatural, or at least paranormal, power.

within and between songs deeper and more striking. In some of their most memorable music—such as "Dazed and Confused" and "Stairway to Heaven"—they reconcile many of the extremes that characterize their music *within a single song*. These songs cover an enormous emotional and musical range: they can be tender one moment and overpowering the next.

The music of Led Zeppelin evolved considerably from their first album to *Physical Graffiti* (1975). That, coupled with the wide range of their music, makes it difficult to represent their achievement adequately with a discussion of a single album, much less a single song. However, the album that best captures the salient qualities of their music is the untitled fourth album, known variously as *Led Zeppelin IV*, *Zoso*, and the Runes LP. The music on the tracks ranges from the unbridled power of "Rock and Roll" to the delicacy of the acoustic "The Battle of Evermore," which provides clear evidence of the group's mystical/mythical bent. "Stairway to Heaven," perhaps the best-known song on the album, merges both.

"Black Dog," John Paul Jones, Jimmy Page, and Robert Plant (1971). Led Zeppelin.

"Black Dog," another track from the album, demonstrates Led Zeppelin's connection with heavy metal and their role in the continuing evolution of rock rhythm. From the very beginning of the song, it's clear that they've internalized the feel of rock rhythm. Consider how it begins.

- A noodle on the guitar
- Plant singing without accompaniment
- The band playing an extended, blues-based melodic line, without a vocal

This is a major step forward in rhythmic freedom from typical 1960s hard rock songs. Typically, these songs start with a guitar riff that sets the tempo. Other instruments layer in, setting up the groove. That doesn't happen here. Early on, we feel the beat strictly from Plant's vocal line. The silence that follows and the strung-out instrumental line make it difficult to group the beats into measures.

As they demonstrate in "Black Dog," Led Zeppelin became so comfortable with the rock groove that they could play with it—boldly. Even the chorus-like riff under Plant's "Oh, yeah" is completely syncopated. Throughout, the song has a great beat, but the timekeeping that does take place happens very much in the background. Indeed, in much

Led Zeppelin in concert: Robert Plant and Jimmy Page

Laurance Ratner/WireImageGetty Images

3 to Remember
"Black Dog"

RHYTHMIC PLAY
From very beginning to final fadeout, rock rhythm is implied but never clearly marked. Instead, Plant hints at it in his unaccompanied singing, and instrumental responses soar over it with long lines or bounce off it with syncopated riffs. Only Bonham marks the beat and rock rhythm consistently.

COMPLICATED LINES
Long instrumental responses in verse sections suggest solo-like lines worked out by entire group. Considerable expansion of typical answering riff in more conventional rock song.

VOCAL/INSTRUMENTAL BALANCE
Musical interest divided between Plant's abnormally high singing and more complex and melodically interesting instrumental parts. There is also more strictly instrumental music than vocal or vocal/instrumental music, both within verses and overall, because of Page's extended solo.

5 to Listen For
"Black Dog"

INSTRUMENTATION
Vocal, electric guitar, electric bass, drums (guitar overdubbed during solo)

PERFORMANCE STYLE
Plant's singing in extreme high range; moderate distortion in guitar and bass parts

RHYTHM
Highly syncopated rock rhythm at moderate tempo with long sections without steady timekeeping

MELODY
Contrast between opening, with long vocal and instrumental exchanges, and other sections, with rapid exchange of short riffs

TEXTURE
Contrast between open, voice-alone sound and dark, dense instrumental response; thick sound, with low-register guitar + voice in chorus

States far more than most of their peers. Their tours sold out and broke attendance records, and all of their recordings went platinum. They're still popular, almost three decades after they disbanded. There is no ambiguity about why: their music is a rare combination of almost unrestrained power and subtle artistry, of raw emotion and superbly calculated craft. For some, the mix was too heady; the band never attracted the broad-based audience of the Beatles or Elton John. But for a large core, it was just the right strength. Millions of loyal fans remain unsatiated.

Heavy Metal and Early 1970s Rock

Joe Elliot, lead vocalist for Def Leppard, was quoted as saying, "In 1971 there were only three bands that mattered. Led Zeppelin, Black Sabbath, and Deep Purple." Of the three, Black Sabbath stayed the closest to the musical features that defined early metal. By contrast, Deep Purple strayed far enough from metal basics that some critics considered them an art rock band, and Led Zeppelin was always much more than "just" a heavy metal band. The differences among the three bands make clear that heavy metal was anything but a monolithic style. Their similarities highlight the qualities that set heavy metal apart from other hard rock styles.

Two things stand out about heavy metal: power and craft. Most of the conventions of heavy metal—distortion; massive amplification; use of modes, pentatonic scales, and power chords; basic rhythms; power trio instrumental nucleus—were also part of the vocabulary of all hard rock music in the early 1970s. What metal bands did was to take these features and streamline or amplify them to give them more impact. Metal bands used *more* distortion and played *more* loudly. They took rock's shift away from traditional harmony several steps further by using conventional chords sparingly or, in some cases, abandoning harmony altogether. There is little harmony in "Black Dog" and it is based on modes instead of conventional harmony. Its guitarists played power chords with *more* "power"—that is, greater resonance—and used them almost exclusively, and they developed more flamboyantly virtuosic styles. Metal's riffs and rhythms were stronger and more pervasive: at times, vocal lines seemed to ride on the riffs like a whitewater raft.

of the song, we do not sense the beat at all, or sense it only from the rhythm of the main melody; what timekeeping there is in this song is purposeful and specific, rather than routine. In terms of freeing rhythm while still retaining the groove, "Black Dog" goes about as far as possible.

The extended instrumental lines in "Black Dog" also point out another feature of Led Zeppelin's approach to rock—one that would profoundly influence heavy metal bands. In effect, they harness solo-like lines within a tight group conception. In rock, guitar solos can be spectacular displays, but they can also undermine the collective conception that is at the heart of a rock groove. Page's solution was to work out these lines and integrate them into a group conception. For future heavy metal bands, this aspect of the recording was key: one of the marvels of good heavy metal performances is the tight ensemble of a band as they negotiate challenging and intricate passages. We can hear its roots in recordings like this.

Led Zeppelin gained a large, loyal audience. They were also one of the first British bands to concentrate on the United States as a fan base because of its huge population compared to Britain's; they toured the United

All of this supported nonmusical manifestations of power. Heavy metal evoked supernatural, or at least paranormal, power, especially in the group personas of Black Sabbath and Led Zeppelin. At a time when the women's rights movement was in the ascendancy—bras being burned, NOW being formed—metal bands projected masculine power, to the point where performers could sport skillfully styled long hair, wear makeup, and sing higher than many women without fear of abandoning their sexual identity.

The other was the mastery of craft. Like the alchemists of old, heavy metal performers diligently studied ancient formulas, from the modes of medieval music to the musical patterns of Bach and Vivaldi. These they adapted to rock, then juxtaposed them with elemental musical material. The best metal musicians, like Page and Ritchie Blackmore of Deep Purple, spent countless hours mastering their instruments. As a result, heavy metal has been, almost from the start, rock's most virtuosic substyle. It is evident not only in the individual brilliance of the many technically fluent performers, but also in the complex and intricate ensemble playing, often at breakneck speeds. Both individual and group virtuosity are evident in "Black Dog."

Power and craft put the focus on the music. The music is *there* more; one of the qualities that distinguishes heavy metal from most other styles is the sheer amount of nonvocal music. Even more important, music is the primary source of heavy metal's overwhelming impact and expressive power. Words serve a largely explanatory role. Most of the audience at a metal concert will know the lyrics to songs, but not from the vocal, which is often unintelligible.

In its emphasis on instrumental virtuosity and power, its distance from more mainstream practice (including intelligible, conventional lyrics), and its cult-like environment, heavy metal represents a more extreme point along the continuum of hard rock styles. This is evidenced in its reception during the 1970s: the relatively small but fervent audience, hand in hand with limited airplay on mainstream radio and negative press from rock critics. Still, it was one of the most influential and distinctive hard rock styles of the era.

A Timeless Music

"Won't Get Fooled Again" and "Black Dog" exemplify a key moment in the history of rock. It is around this time that rock emerged as a fully developed style; what makes rock rhythm rock becomes common currency. Up to this point, we hear rock musicians restlessly seeking to discover the optimal approach to rock rhythm; they find it around 1970. From this point on, rock becomes a timeless music, in the sense that its conventions are clear and widely understood, and that musicians feel comfortable

enough with them to play rock with great freedom. The rhythms and sounds of rock-era music would continue to develop beyond this point, as we will discover. But the rock that emerged around 1970 defines the core values of rock in a way that neither the rock that preceded it nor the rock that evolved beyond it does.

● ● ● ● ● ● ● ●

The Middle Ground in the Early 1970s: Rock and R&B

The breakup of the Beatles symbolized the fragmentation of the new mainstream of the rock era. After they dissolved in 1970, each of the band members went his own way. Paul McCartney was the most active and the most commercially successful; Wings, the group that he formed in 1971, was one of five 1970s acts to reach the Top 20 in both singles and album sales. Another was Elton John, the top pop artist of the decade.

A third was Stevie Wonder, whose declaration of musical independence upon turning twenty-one helped undermine Berry Gordy's overriding control of the Motown operation. Gordy faced pressures from within and without. The Jackson 5, their top act in the 1970s, left Motown for Epic in 1975. Like Wonder, Marvin Gaye also pushed for, and received, musical independence, which was good for both Gaye (his *What's Going On* remains one of the most important albums of the decade) and Motown. He would leave Motown in 1982. More pressing was competition from outside. The most formidable came from a group of Philadelphia-based producers, who expanded the Motown formula to churn out a string of hits. The Philadelphia acts were the most consistently successful segment of a wave of black pop in the early 1970 that also included more mature singers such as Roberta Flack and Bill Withers, as well as Barry White.

Much of this music evidenced the internal expansion of popular song: songs are longer and make use of larger ensembles. We sample the mainstream pop of the 1970s in songs by Elton John and the O'Jays.

Elton John and the Expansion of Mainstream Rock

The career of Elton John (born Reginald Dwight, 1947; his stage name came from the first names of fellow band members in his first band, Bluesology) is a testimony to the power of personality. Off stage, he is an unlikely looking rock star: short, chunky, balding, and bespectacled. On stage, his costumes and extroverted style made him larger than life; it rendered his natural appearance irrelevant. He was one of the top live acts of the seventies and the best-selling recording artist of the decade.

On stage, Elton John's costumes and extroverted style made him larger than life.

John's first hits were melodic, relatively low-key songs like "Your Song," but his albums also contained harder-rocking songs like "Take Me to the Pilot." As he repositioned himself in the mainstream, he retained his ability to tell a story in song, largely due to his partnership with lyricist Bernie Taupin, while infusing his music with pop elements; they helped expand the range of his music. He followed "Crocodile Rock," a fun take on fifties rock and roll and his first No. 1 hit, with "Daniel," a sensitive ballad. For the remainder of the decade, he veered from style to style.

"Tiny Dancer," Bernie Taupin and Elton John (1971). Elton John, vocal and keyboard.

At the center of his music was his husky voice, which changed character from the soul-tinged sound in songs like "The Bitch Is Back" to a much more mellow sound in songs like "Little Jeannie." Moreover, because of his considerable skill as a songwriter, he was able to fold external elements into his own conception, rather than simply mimic an existing sound.

In "Tiny Dancer," a track from his 1971 album *Madman Across the Water*, demonstrates both the craft and the range of his music at the start of his career. The lyric, written by his longtime collaborator Bernie Taupin, begins as if it is going to tell a story. However, as it develops, it resolves into a collage of vivid images. It is as if we see short video clips, which quickly cut away to another scene. There are oblique first-person references; some of the scenes seem to describe a relationship between John and the tiny dancer ("Piano man, he makes his stand"). But it is not a direct narrative.

John's setting of the lyric begins simply with John playing nicely syncopated piano chords, first to get the song underway, then to accompany his singing of the melody. Through most of the opening statement of the verse, it is as if the song will be set simply and intimately. However, other instruments enter in stages: steel guitar at the end of the first large section, other rhythm instruments upon the repetition of the opening section, then a choir at the end of the repeated section. At that point, John shifts gears, using the piano to give a stronger, more marked rhythm and shifting the harmony into uncharted waters. This builds toward the chorus, which adds a string countermelody to the many instruments and voices already sounding.

As recorded, "Tiny Dancer" takes over 6 minutes to perform: even at this length, there are less than two complete statements of the song. (In "Tiny Dancer," a complete statement consists of two verse-like sections that are melodically identical, a transition and a chorus.) This expands the verse/chorus template used, for example, in so many Motown songs. We can gauge the degree of expansion by noting that one verse-like *section* is equivalent to a complete chorus of a "Heart and Soul"–type *song*. To realize this larger form, John uses a huge ensemble: his voice and piano, plus bass, drums, guitar, steel

4 to Remember
"Tiny Dancer"

ARTY LYRIC
Taupin's arty, cinematic lyric shifts from image to image: there is no central narrative holding the lyric together. Even the chorus is deliberately obscure.

EXPANSIVE FORM
Form of "Tiny Dancer" follows a predictable verse/chorus pattern but unfolds on a much grander scale than a typical sixties rock or Motown song.

LAVISH INSTRUMENTATION
Piano, rhythm-section instruments, steel guitar, strings, and voices added layer by layer for maximum impact

RHYTHMIC CONTRAST
Rhythmic shifts, from active 16-beat rhythm of verse, through clearly marked rock rhythm in bridge, back to 16-beat rhythm; help outline form

5 to Listen For
"Tiny Dancer"

INSTRUMENTATION
Vocal, piano, steel guitar, electric guitar, electric bass, drums, strings, choir

RHYTHM
Slow 16-beat rhythm in verse; shift to rock beat in bridge; back to 16-beat rhythm in chorus; syncopation, especially in piano part

MELODY
Verse melody grows from short riff; title-phrase hook in chorus is longer

HARMONY
Dramatic shifts in harmony: verse = I-IV-V; bridge = new key; chorus = looping chord progression with delayed return to home key

TEXTURE
Texture "crescendos" through layering in of instruments, from just voice and piano to orchestral richness

Michael Ochs Archives/Getty Images

guitar, backup vocals, rich strings, and choir. The result is, when desired, a denser and fuller-sounding texture. Moreover, John adds and subtracts instruments to outline the form and accumulate musical momentum through the verse sections to the climax of the song in the chorus.

In the four albums following *Madman Across the Water*, John often integrated catchier riffs and rhythms into his songs. All four were number 1 albums; so was a subsequent "greatest hits" compilation. John remained active through the eighties and nineties, despite his short and difficult marriage to recording engineer Renate Blauel, acknowledgement of his sexual preferences, and numerous substance abuse issues. In the early nineties, he cleaned up his life and directed his energy to film and stage. He won his first Grammy in 1994 for one of the songs from the Disney animated film *The Lion King*, written in collaboration with lyricist Tim Rice. Another of their successful projects was what one reviewer called a "camp" remake of Giuseppe Verdi's famous opera *Aida*.

Two of the most impressive and fascinating aspects of John's career are its longevity—he is still an active performer—and the range of his collaborations. John Lennon's last public appearance came at an Elton John concert in 1974; about three decades later, John performed with Eminem at the Grammy awards ceremony. The list of those whom Elton John has performed with and befriended reads like a rock-era *Who's Who*. This speaks to not only his musical flexibility but also his generous nature.

The Sound of Philadelphia

In the early seventies, it seemed as if Motown had opened a branch office in Philadelphia. The most Motown-like records of the period appeared on Gamble and Huff's Philadelphia International label, not Gordy's. The basic formula was the same: lush orchestrations, solid rhythms coming from a rhythm section that had played together for years, jazz-tinged instrumental lines—all supporting vocal groups singing about the ups and downs of love. Only the details were different.

Three men engineered the **Philadelphia sound:** Kenny Gamble (b. 1943), Leon Huff (b. 1942), and Thom Bell (b. 1941). All were veterans of the Philadelphia music scene; they had worked together

off and on during the early sixties in a group called Kenny Gamble and the Romeos. By mid-decade, Gamble and Huff had begun producing records together. They enjoyed their first extended success with Jerry Butler, who revived his career under their guidance. Their big break came in 1971, when Clive Davis, the head of Columbia Records, helped them form Philadelphia International Records. The connection with Columbia assured them of widespread distribution, especially in white markets.

The artist roster at Philadelphia International included the O'Jays, Harold Melvin and the Blue Notes, Teddy Pendergrass (who left the group to go solo), Billy Paul, and MFSB, which was the house band. Their competition came mainly from Thom Bell, who produced the Stylistics and the Spinners, a Detroit group who went nowhere at Motown but took off when paired with Bell in 1972.

The O'Jays. Among the most successful of the Philadelphia groups were the O'Jays, whose members in the early 1970s included Eddie Levert (b. 1942), William Powell (1942–1977), and Walter Williams (1942). Formed as a quintet in 1958, the group languished on the fringes of the R&B scene throughout the 1960s, with only a few hits. The turning point in their career came in 1968, when they met Gamble and Huff. Chart success came in 1972, shortly after Columbia Records created the Philadelphia International subsidiary for Gamble and Huff. Their first hit, "Back Stabbers," began a run of 40 hit singles over the next fifteen years; nine of them topped the R&B charts and five reached the pop Top Ten.

"Back Stabbers," Leon Huff, Gene McFadden, and John Whitehead (1972). The O'Jays.

The O'Jays' "Back Stabbers" shows how Gamble, Huff, and Bell extended and updated the black pop style developed at Motown. The instrumental introduction of "Back Stabbers" runs for 40 seconds—far longer than any of the Motown intros. It begins with a quasi-classical piano tremolo, an ominous rumble that helps establish the dark mood of the song. The unaccompanied piano riff that follows simply hangs in sonic space; there is still no regular beat keeping. Finally, the rest of the rhythm section enters, with the guitarist playing a jazz-style riff.

The rhythm sound is fuller than late sixties Motown records, not just because of the addition of Latin percussion instruments (Motown

istockphoto.com

INSTRUMENTATION
Lead and backup vocals, plus large rhythm section (piano, electric guitar, electric bass, drums, extra percussion), vibraphone, strings, horns

RHYTHM
Brisk rock rhythm clearly marked by percussion instruments, with double-time riffs in vocal line, free rhythms in bass, syncopated riffs in melodic instruments

MELODY
Chorus = chain of riffs; verse and bridge have longer phrases; melodic material

HARMONY
Minor key supports dark theme of song: like Marvin Gaye's "I Heard It Through the Grapevine"

TEXTURE
Rich texture, with strong bass, active mid-range percussion, low/mid-range horns, high strings behind vocals, often in harmony

RHYTHMIC EFFECTS
Syncopated orchestral riffs and stop time dominant when they occur, overpowering steady rock rhythm in percussion

MULTIPLE MELODIC HOOKS
Motown influence evident in multiple melodic hooks, heard in vocal line, strings, and rhythm instruments

RICH ORCHESTRATION
Large, percussion-enhanced rhythm section, plus full string section and horns, support vocals

SPRAWLING FORM
Expansion of Motown-type form: big multistage, jazz-influenced instrumental introduction; chorus framing verse, extended bridge

only in the opening but also in the syncopated riffs that are the instrumental hooks of the songs. The formula behind the Philadelphia sound worked well for the better part of the decade. By the late seventies, however, it would be largely superseded by a more musically obvious version of itself: disco.

In distinctly different ways, "Tiny Dancer" and "Back Stabber" exemplify two dominant trends in the early 1970s: expansion and consolidation. Both of the songs are long by 1960s standards. In fact, John's hit songs in the 1970s average over 4 minutes in length. "Back Stabbers" is not a long song, but it is conceived on a grand scale, with a long instrumental introduction and rich orchestration. Both songs build on the music of the sixties; the freshness of the style comes from new ways of treating the conventions of 1960s music.

had been using them for years) but because there are more of them, and the reinforcement of the beat and the eight-beat layer is more prominent. After the conclusion of the opening phrase, the strings and, later, brass enter; all combine to create a lush backdrop for the O'Jays.

The song, co-written by Huff, advises a hypothetical person to guard against "friends" who are out to steal his woman. Like so much black pop, the song is about love, or at least a relationship. What's different about the lyric is that the narrator is an outside observer, rather than the person in the relationship. In effect, it's "I Heard It Through the Grapevine" told from the other side of the grapevine, but up-close and personal. It was the first of a series of such songs by the O'Jays.

As typified in this song, the Philadelphia sound is the Motown formula revised, expanded, and modernized. The instrumental introductions are more elaborate; the texture is richer; the songs themselves are more complicated; the spotlighted instruments are more contemporary sounding (in the case of the guitar); and there is greater rhythmic freedom, not

The Impact of Technology

Among the people of the African diaspora, the impulse to play with sound seems almost as strong as the impulse to play with rhythm. Two aspects of this impulse that seem especially persistent are the discovery of found sounds and the quest to make multiple sounds at the same time. Found sounds have taken many forms: making instruments out of everyday materials, like the cowbell in Cuban music, the steel drums of calypso, or the turntables of rap DJs; using everyday objects—a toilet plunger, the neck of a wine bottle—to modify the sound of a conventional instrument; or simply inventing new ways of making sound from an instrument, like "patting juba" by tapping out rhythms on various parts of one's body or slapping an electric bass.

The most familiar instance of the impulse to play multiple instruments simultaneously is the drum kit. More complex expressions of this practice range from jazz multi-instrumentalist Rahsaan Roland Kirk's ability to play the saxophone and two other instruments simultaneously to one-man bands like the obscure Abner Jay, the self-styled "last great southern black minstrel show," who accompanied himself with an electric guitar, bass drum, and hi-hat while he sang or played harmonica.

With his emancipation from Gordy's tight control, Stevie Wonder was able to combine both of these practices and take them high-tech. Both the electronic instruments—especially keyboards—that Wonder used on recordings like "Superstition" and the 24-track mixing boards that made the recording possible were new, rapidly developing technologies. Wonder was the first major artist, black or white, to take them to their logical extreme: make a complete recording by not only assembling it track by track but also recording each track himself.

Wonder's music represents a breakthrough in the "input" stage of the recording process; the music of Steely Dan evidences the refinement of the art of record production, the "output" stage in the process. We consider both.

Beyond Motown: The Music of Stevie Wonder

There's a certain irony that Motown's most powerful and original talent, and its longest running success story, is in many ways the antithesis of the Motown image and sound. Stevie Wonder is a solo act; most Motown acts were groups. The visual element was crucial to Motown's success: its groups, dressed in gowns or tuxedos, moved through stylized, carefully choreographed routines as they sang their songs. Our enduring image of Stevie Wonder: a blind man with sunglasses and long braided and beaded hair, sitting behind a keyboard and rocking from side to side in a random rhythm. Motown recordings were collective enterprises; behind the groups were largely anonymous songwriters and studio musicians. Wonder created his own recordings from soup to nuts: not only singing and playing all the instruments at times, but also performing the technical tasks—recording, mixing, mastering, and so on.

There are also differences in subject and attitude. In the mid-sixties,

Motown song lyrics talked mainly about young love, usually in racially neutral, often idealized language. Only reluctantly did they begin to address "real life" in songs like the Supremes' "Love Child." By contrast, Stevie Wonder took on social issues from his self-produced first album; the vignette of an innocent man's arrest in "Living for the City" is chilling. Stevie Wonder has advocated a long list of causes, from his firm push for a national holiday for Martin Luther King Jr. to rights for the blind and disabled.

Stevie Wonder was born Steveland Morris (some accounts say Steveland Judkins) in 1950. A hospital error at birth left him blind. By ten, he was a professional performer, singing and playing the harmonica (he also played piano and drums). Within two years, he had signed a Motown contract and was being billed as "Little Stevie Wonder, the 12-Year-Old Genius." (The "little" disappeared two years later, but the "Wonder" stuck.) He had a number of hits in the sixties, including "Uptight" (1966) and the beautiful love song, "My Cherie Amour" (1969), but emerged as a major force in popular music only when his contract with Motown guaranteed him complete control over his work.

Wonder was the most popular black artist of the seventies. A series of albums, beginning with *Music of My Mind* (1972), established his unique sound and cemented his reputation as a major player in popular music. Each album release was a major event within the black community, and his recordings also enjoyed enormous crossover success.

The widespread popularity of Wonder's music grows out of a style that is broad in its range, highly personal in its sound, and universal in its appeal. His music is a compendium of current black musical styles: in his songs are the tuneful melodies and rich harmonies of black romantic music, the dense textures and highly syncopated riffs of funk, the improvisatory flights of jazz, and the subtle rhythms of reggae and Latin music. Yet, even though he absorbs influences from all quarters, his style is unique.

"Superstition," a No. 1 single from the 1972 album *Talking Book*, is a funky up-tempo song with a finger-wagging lyric; in it he chastises those who would let their lives be ruled by superstitious beliefs. The melody that carries the lyric grows slowly out of a simple riff. Like so many Motown (and rock-era) songs, it builds inexorably to the title phrase.

Charlyn Zlotnik/Michael Ochs Archives/Getty Images

"Superstition," Stevie Wonder (1972). Wonder, vocal and keyboard.

> **❝Our enduring image of Stevie Wonder: a blind man with sunglasses and long braided and beaded hair, sitting behind a keyboard and rocking from side to side in a random rhythm.❞**

to Listen For
"Superstition"

INSTRUMENTATION
Vocals, drums, percussion, electric
keyboards and synthesizers, trumpet/sax
horn section, electric bass

RHYTHM
Rock beat at moderate tempo with
multiple syncopated double-time riffs

MELODY
Both vocal line and instrument figures
based on repeated riffs

HARMONY
Oscillation between static harmony on
pentatonic scale (verse) and rich harmony
leading up to hook

TEXTURE
Thick texture, with several keyboard
patterns and horn riffs weaving around
timekeeping and vocal

to Remember
"Superstition"

DARK LYRICS; UPBEAT GROOVE
Lyrics sermonize on real-life concern,
but Wonder's singing and song's rhythm
project optimism.

DENSE, RIFF-RICH TEXTURE
Dense texture woven together by
multiple repeated riff figures in low and
mid range

NOVEL ELECTRONIC SOUNDS
Numerous synthesizer sounds replace
conventional instruments.

FUNKY RHYTHMS
Layers of active, syncopated rhythms
at 16-beat speed over rock beat create
funky groove.

Steely Dan: The Pursuit of Studio Perfection

In 1959 the National Academy of Recording Arts and Sciences began presenting a Grammy Award for the "Best Engineered Album, Non-Classical." The award is given to one or more engineers for their work on a particular record date. The first winner of the award was Ted Keep, for his work on the novelty hit "The Chipmunk Song." Subsequent winners include the engineers responsible for *Sgt. Pepper* and *Abbey Road*. The only act whose recordings have won four awards is Steely Dan: their engineers won the award in 1978, 1979, 1982, and 2001.

The pursuit of studio perfection is just one of the qualities that distinguishes Steely Dan. Although it began as a band, Steely Dan became a popular and critically acclaimed act only after its two creative minds, keyboardist Donald Fagen (b. 1948) and bassist Walter Becker (b. 1950), dissolved the group and retained the name to label their studio-driven brainchild.

Becker and Fagen met at Bard College, where they played together regularly in a number of bands, including the Leather Canary. After Fagen graduated, they moved to New York, where they joined the backup band for Jay and the Americans. While in New York, they met producer Gary Katz, who would eventually invite them to Los Angeles to sign them up with ABC Records—first as songwriters, then as a working band. At ABC, they met recording engineer Roger Nichols; Nichols

The harmony shows the two main sources of his style: the verse sits on a bed of riffs, all built from the African American pentatonic scale; there is no harmonic change. By contrast, the transition to the hook is supported by rich, jazz-like harmonies.

Most distinctive element of Stevie Wonder's sound, however, is the rich texture that flows underneath the vocal line. The song begins simply enough, with a rhythmically secure drum part. Onto this, Wonder layers multiple lines: the signature riff, a repeated-note bass line, plus several more riffs in the background, all highly syncopated. Stevie played all the lines on synthesizers, overdubbing until he produced the dense, funky texture that became one of his trademarks. (Wonder was one of the first musicians to develop a sound based almost completely on synthesizers.)

"Superstition" shows us the rhythmic side of Wonder's musical personality; there is also a romantic side, as evidenced in songs like "You Are the Sunshine of My Life." In either mode, Stevie Wonder is an optimist, a "glass is half full" person. Even in his darkest songs, hope is implicit, if not in the lyric, then in the bounce of the beat: How can you be down if your hips are shaking and your foot is tapping? Wonder's optimism is remarkable in light of numerous personal problems. Not only has he been blind from birth, but he also suffered a devastating automobile accident in 1973 that left him in a coma for several days. He followed this adversity with some of his best music. He remains one of the icons of rock-era music.

Michael Ochs Archives/Getty Images

Steely Dan: (left to right) Jim Hodder, Walter Becker, Denny Dias, Jeff "Skunk" Baxter, and Donald Fagen

INSTRUMENTATION
Trumpet, electric guitar, organ, two electric pianos, string bass, drums

RHYTHM
16-beat rhythm at moderate tempo; kept in drums, highlighted in keyboard patterns, sometimes in trumpet

MELODY
No preexisting melody; strictly inspiration of moment; melody-rich with keyboard fragments behind guitar and trumpet

HARMONY
Foundation = no harmony, just bass ostinato and modal scale; rich harmonies circling around bass keynote and scale

TEXTURE
Dense texture, with keyboard sound cloud around guitar and trumpet, plus bass pattern and busy drums

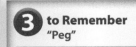

3 **to Remember**
"Peg"

WORDS VS. MUSIC
Clever, ironic lyrics with virtually no apparent connection to the music

FORMAL IMAGINATION
Conventional verse/chorus form: but verse is hip 12-bar blues form and chorus has rich harmony, in instruments and backup vocals.

INFUSION OF JAZZ VALUES
Evident in rich, varied harmony; rhythmic play; angular instrumental lines; virtuosic playing

Although many of their fans have spent long hours trying to decode the lyrics to Steely Dan songs, the exercise seems ultimately beside the point, because the songs are mainly about the music. More than anything else, the lyrics serve as window dressing, to entice those listeners who find lyrics important, or at least a necessary point of entry into the song. The lyrics are hip and provocative—Fagen was an English major, and he and Becker shared a strong interest in Beat literature. They often offer ironic commentary on life in Los Angeles—"Peg" is typical in that regard. But there is not the sense of connection between words and music that has informed so much of the music that we have heard.

The reason may well be Becker and Fagen's abiding interest in jazz, a largely instrumental music. Jazz values, such as melodic and harmonic complexity, rhythmic play, virtuosity, imagination, permeate their music, independently of the lyrics. In "Peg," the instrumental introduction evokes the angular lines and rich harmonies of bebop, while the harmony under the verse of the song is a clever reworking of a 12-bar blues progression. Throughout the song, there is extensive rhythmic play among the rhythm instruments, especially the bass. At the same time, in its overall design, the song follows the familiar rock-era verse/chorus pattern, and the chorus has a hook carved from a single, richly harmonized melody note: "Peg."

With their particular mix of rocklike accessibility, provocative lyrics, jazz influence, and perfectionist approach to recording, Steely Dan was one of a kind. In their music and their attitude toward music making, they were without any real precedent, and no band has really followed their lead. Becker and Fagen parted ways in 1981. Twelve years later, they came together, resurrected the Steely Dan name, and began recording and touring again. They remain active and productive through the early years of the twenty-first century: *Two Against Nature* won four Grammy Awards in 2001, including top album.

would record all of their music. On recordings, Becker and Fagen began using the cream of Los Angeles studio musicians, most of whom had extensive jazz experience. After 1974, Steely Dan became a studio band, in order to better realize Becker and Fagen's distinctive musical vision.

It's difficult to describe their "style," because each of their songs seems so different from the next: among their hits is an electronically enhanced "cover" of Duke Ellington's 1927 recording of "East St. Louis Toodle-oo." The three constants in their music seem to be impeccable production, stream-of-consciousness lyrics that offer slices of life in LA, and sophisticated, distinctive musical settings. There is often a jarring incongruity between the lyrics and the often complex music to which they are set. It is apparent in songs like their 1977 hit "Peg," one of the tracks from *Aja*, their sixth album and one of the first recordings to be certified platinum; *Aja* would win a Grammy for best engineered nonclassical recording.

The lyric of "Peg" offers a fragmentary account of a film star on the rise, told by someone who knew her when, but who is probably on the outside looking in now. It conveys a bittersweet mood: whatever connection he had with Peg has dissolved now that her career is on the way up.

"Peg," Walter Becker and Donald Fagen (1977). Steely Dan.

Gender, Art, and the Boundaries of Rock

The world of rock is a man's world. Or at least that's how the public at large has understood it. The stereotypical impression of rock features four or five aggressively heterosexual males singing and playing electronically amplified instruments loudly and rhythmically.

This is the core of rock. It's the "rock and roll" of the Stones and other like-minded bands: rock that is real and timeless. However, by the time it took shape in the years around 1970, it was an increasingly limited representation of the world of rock. The playlist for this chapter hints at this. We began with The Who and Led Zeppelin, two acts representative of this stereotype. The next pair of acts features rock's answer to Liberace and a post-Motown vocal group; both are backed by large ensembles with strings. The recordings of Stevie Wonder and Steely Dan effectively remove the visual component entirely: Wonder cannot sing and play all of the instruments simultaneously in performance; Steely Dan was a studio-only act.

Joni Mitchell and David Bowie, the final two artists discussed in this chapter, contradict this stereotype altogether, in radically different ways. In her early work, Mitchell is "real" but decidedly feminine. She paints intimate self-portraits that project a woman's perspective. Bowie made his first big splash as Ziggy Stardust, an androgynous alien who comes to save the world through rock and roll but is consumed by his own excesses. Ziggy masks Bowie so completely that even the character's gender is in doubt.

Mitchell and Bowie also approach rock as art from quite different directions. They were part of a larger movement to elevate rock musically and culturally.

Rock as Art

In its broadest meaning, *art* is the product of any human activity done skillfully and creatively. One can artfully manufacture an automobile, bake a soufflé, sew a quilt, or dunk a basketball. However, the artistic aspect of all of these activities is secondary to their function. A Ferrari may be beautiful to look at, but if it won't start, it's only an oversized ornament; a between-the-legs 360-degree dunk may garner style points, but in a game it's as unproductive as an air ball if it clanks off the rim.

We also use *art* more restrictively to refer to a product of a skilled and creative activity whose main purpose is to stimulate the mind, touch the heart, and delight the senses. This more specific connotation of art is most familiar in the visual arts, for example, the paintings of Rembrandt and the sculptures of Rodin. However, this meaning of *art* has also been used to describe music such as the symphonies of Beethoven and Brahms. In the early years of the rock era, this understanding of art was thought to apply mainly to classical music.

In the late sixties and early seventies, rock both co-opted and challenged the prevailing view of musical art, often at the same time. This is evident in a diverse body of music that includes the Beach Boys' *Pet Sounds* and the Beatles' *Sgt. Pepper*; Frank Zappa's *Freak Out*, which contains a long noncategorical list of Zappa's influences, from classical avant-garde composers to obscure folk musicians; The Who's rock opera *Tommy*; Pink Floyd's technologically enhanced concept album *Dark Side of the Moon*; and Miles Davis's jazz/rock fusion.

The most self-consciously arty branch of rock was the style known alternatively as **art rock** and **progressive rock**. Progressive rock musicians sought to elevate the status of rock by embracing a classical music aesthetic and adapting it to rock. Most often, this meant applying concepts and features associated with classical music, especially classical instrumental music, into their work. Occasionally, and more specifically, it could involve wholesale borrowing of classical compositions: Procul Harum's "A Whiter Shade of Pale" mixed rock and Bach; Keith Emerson of Emerson, Lake, and Palmer remade the Russian composer Modest Mussorgsky's *Pictures at an Exhibition*. Art rock/progressive rock became the mainly instrumental analog to concept albums and rock operas, which were typically more vocally oriented.

One quality that distinguished this activity from previous efforts to merge classical and vernacular was its range. It wasn't the work of a single person, such as Joplin or Gershwin, or even a single style, such as modern jazz. Rather, it encompassed music in which words were primary as well as strictly instrumental music; music that adapted the classics to music with no overt connection to the classics; music that reveled in virtuosity as well as simpler music that conveyed profound ideas and vivid images. What all of this music had in common was the desire to make a statement, to go beyond the conventional level of discourse in popular music.

The two examples considered here represent opposite ends of the rock spectrum: the singer-songwriters offered intimate and personal music; glam rock offered gaudy theater. Together, they hint at the range of artistic efforts in rock.

The Singer-Songwriters

The term **singer-songwriter** came into use during the early seventies to identify a group of performers who made personal statements in song, usually by themselves. Their songs were typically supported by a subdued, often acoustic accompaniment that put the vocal line in the forefront.

Within these general parameters, there has been astonishing variety: autobiographical confessions; *cinéma vérité* portraits or acerbic social commentary; cryptic accounts that leave the identity of the narrator in question. Most are songs in a restricted sense of the term, in that they have coherent melodies that help tell the story and make musical sense through an inner logic. They are seldom formulaic; formal and melodic imagination finds its greatest outlet in these songs.

Among the first wave of singer-songwriters were established acts who went solo: Neil Young left Crosby, Stills, Nash, and Young, and Paul Simon dissolved his long-time partnership with Art Garfunkel. They were joined by a new generation of folk-inspired performers, most notably Joni Mitchell and James Taylor. Randy Newman, by contrast, came from a family heavily involved in traditional pop and film music; Carole King had been writing hit songs for over a decade.

The music of the singer-songwriters of the late sixties and early seventies represents the continuing evolution of the folk/country/pop fusions of the mid-sixties. Bob Dylan was the dominant influence on its development, through inspiration and example. In his acoustic phase, he demonstrated better than any of his contemporaries the power of words set to music. In his electric phase, he showed how the impact of words and music could be amplified with the addition of other instruments. His songs set the tone. In them, he showed a new generation what they could say and how they could say it.

However, there were others within the rock tradition who helped shape its sound and sensibility. Buddy Holly, the Everly Brothers, Roy Orbison, and the Brill Building songwriters were important early sources. The Beatles and the Byrds were the most influential of Dylan's contemporaries. Other influences came from everywhere—folk and country especially, but also jazz, blues, pop, gospel, and Latin music.

Elevating the Feminine. The folk revival provided women with the most accessible point of entry into rock. With its intimate environment, emphasis on words and melody over rhythm, and understated acoustic accompaniment, the urban folk music of the postwar era was far less macho than rock and roll, jazz, or blues. Indeed, young women folksingers were fixtures in coffeehouses throughout the sixties; Joan Baez was the most notable.

Women performers who came out of the folk revival typically performed alone, accompanying themselves on the guitar. By contrast, girl groups and Motown acts depended on an extensive support system: songwriters, producers, musicians. Even strong solo acts like Janis Joplin and Aretha Franklin required accompaniment and seldom performed their own material.

During the sixties, the repertoire of many female folksingers

Michael Ochs Archives/Getty Images

mutated from reworked folksongs to contemporary songs in a similar style. Judy Collins's work in the sixties embodies this transition; Janis Ian's "Society's Child" (1965–1967), her first hit, helped mark this new direction.

Among the new voices of the early 1970s were Carole King and Joni Mitchell. Both enjoyed success as songwriters before breaking through as performers. After a decade of working behind the scenes writing songs for others, Carole King began a solo career after her divorce from Gerry Goffin in 1968. She broke through in 1971 with *Tapestry*, which remained on the charts for almost six years and eventually sold over 22 million units. Similarly, Mitchell's first foray onto the charts came as a songwriter: Judy Collins's version of "Both Sides Now" reached No. 8 in 1968.

Joni Mitchell. Joni Mitchell (b. 1943) was born Roberta Anderson in Fort Macleod, Alberta, Canada, and grew up in Saskatchewan, the neighboring province. As a young girl, she had equally strong interests in art and music. After high school, she enrolled in the Alberta College of Art and Design and played folk music in the local coffeehouse. Like many Canadians in search of a career, she gravitated to Toronto, where she met and married Chuck Mitchell, also a folksinger, in 1966. The couple moved to Detroit. After her divorce a year later, she moved to New York, where she connected into the folk scene, mainly as a songwriter, and then to southern California a year later.

Mitchell began recording under her own name in 1968. She found her musical voice, and her audience, in a series of albums released between 1969 and 1974. In them, Mitchell uses the folk style of the early sixties as a point of departure,

"All I Want," Joni Mitchell (1971). Mitchell, vocal and dulcimer; James Taylor, guitar.

It's as if we're inside Mitchell's head, with thoughts and images tumbling over each other in a stream of consciousness.

but she transforms every aspect of it—lyrics, melody, and accompaniment—into a highly personal idiom. We hear this in "All I Want," a track from her milestone 1971 album *Blue*.

Like so many of her early songs, "All I Want" has a romantic thread (or at least a relationship thread) woven through it. In this respect, she is right in step with so many other singer-songwriters, and—more generally—popular music, especially black pop. But there the similarity ends. Most love-related songs present their situation in a coherent narrative. Typically, both words and music follow a predictable path toward a goal that serves as the expressive high point of the song.

By contrast, Mitchell's lyrics to "All I Want" open the door to her subconscious. There are mercurial shifts in mood: one moment she's high on love ("Alive, alive, I want to get up and jive/I want to wreck my stockings in some juke box dive"), the next, she's licking her emotional wounds ("Do you see—do you see—do you see how you hurt me baby/So I hurt you too/Then we both get so blue"). The only consistent feature of the lyric is the emotional inconsistency of her relationship ("Oh I hate you some, I hate you some/I love you some"). It's as if we're inside Mitchell's head, with thoughts and images tumbling over each other in a stream of consciousness. There is no story; indeed, there is no sense even of time passing.

The music amplifies the temporal and emotional ambiguity of the lyric. The accompaniment begins with Mitchell playing an ostinato—a note repeated over and over—on an Appalachian dulcimer and James Taylor playing guitar. They deliberately avoid establishing a key or even marking the beat clearly. The song itself is strophic: the same melody serves three stanzas of poetry. It begins tentatively, echoing the indecision of the lyric. The most intense point comes in the middle. Shorter phrases and a more active, wide-ranging melodic contour echo the more active and frequent images in the text. They in turn lead to the heart of the song: "do you want." Like smoke rising from one of Mitchell's ever-present cigarettes, the melody gradually drifts up, reaching its peak on the words "sweet romance," the real issue of the song. It drops down quickly, but not to rest; the final sustained note is not the keynote. The instrumental introduction returns as the outro; it ends limply, as if it is a musical question mark. All of this underscores the message of the lyrics. Mitchell describes a complex, difficult

relationship and the emotional rollercoaster that it puts her through; there is no change in it during the course of the song, no resolution at the end.

As "All I Want" reveals, Mitchell's songs disdain the conventions of rock and pop. In her songs, ideas shape the forms, not vice versa. Melodies respond to the words, yet follow their own internal logic. Other aspects of the setting—most notably harmony, instrumentation, and rhythm—are individual to a particular song. They remain in a supporting role; the focus is squarely on the words and melody.

One measure of Mitchell's genius is that words and melody are separable yet indivisible. Her lyrics are studied as poetic texts; her songs are performed as instrumentals. Yet the sum is greater than the parts. Those searching for rock's counterpart to the art songs of classical music need look no further than the music of Joni Mitchell.

At the same time, they provide a postmodern perspective on love. In "All I Want," Mitchell opens herself up, so that we can experience the turmoil in her troubled relationship. It is an emotional breakthrough—for her, for rock, and for popular music.

After 1974 Mitchell turned in other directions. Through the rest of the seventies, she connected with jazz and the avant-garde. This culminated in the collaboration with jazz great Charles Mingus, which was cut short by Mingus's death in 1979. Her seventies experiments anticipated the world music movement of the

4 to Remember
"All I Want"

CONFESSIONAL LYRICS
Words reflect the turbulent state of mind of narrator by jumping from image to image.

OUTPOURING OF MELODY
Melody spins out from the opening phrase, finally peaking toward the end.

INDECISIVE HARMONY
Instrumental intro and outro that frame melody are harmonic question marks; harmony that supports melody is also unpredictable and unstable at times.

OPEN-ENDED FORM
Form of "All I Want" consists of three distinct sections; there is no sense of resolution at the end.

5 to Listen For
"All I Want"

INSTRUMENTATION
Voice, acoustic guitar, Appalachian dulcimer

RHYTHM
Subtle eight-beat pulse supports syncopated guitar chords, melody with varied rhythm

MELODY
Melody spins out from long idea; forms a long curve peaking toward end.

HARMONY
Ambiguous harmony frames song; accompaniment outlines key with rich harmony.

TEXTURE
Subdued but rich, rhythmically active accompaniment under melody

eighties. In the eighties, she continued to explore what some called "jazz/folk" fusion, as well as to develop her career in the visual arts as a photographer and painter.

Glam Rock: Rock as Spectacle

Rock has had a strong visual element ever since Elvis first combed his hair into a pompadour and curled his lips into a sneer. By the late sixties, the visual dimension of rock had become, in its most extreme manifestations, far more flamboyant and outrageous: flaming or smashed guitars, provocative gestures and body movements. This outrageousness was in part a consequence of larger venues. With arena concerts now increasingly common, performers had to appear larger than life to have visual impact.

In the first part of the rock era, the most spectacular form of theatrical rock was glam (or glitter) rock. It emerged in the early seventies, mainly in the work of David Bowie and T Rex, a group fronted by Marc Bolan.

Art as Artifice. As it took shape in the mid-sixties, rock prided itself on being real. It confronted difficult issues, dealt with real feelings, looked life squarely in the eye. The music of Dylan, the Doors, and the Velvet Underground are vivid examples of this attitude. This realism provoked a reaction. The Beatles followed *A Hard Day's Night,* a documentary-style film of their life on the run from fans, with *Help!* a psychedelic fantasy, in which they assumed personas, visually and musically.

Rock as artifice—rock behind the mask—found its fullest expression in glam rock, most spectacularly in David Bowie's first public persona, Ziggy Stardust. In portraying Ziggy Stardust, Bowie stripped identity down to the most basic question of all: gender. Was Ziggy

In Bowie's first tour of the United States, an interview tour in 1968, he insisted on wearing a long dress.

With his lithe build, flamboyant costumes, and heavy makeup, Bowie as Ziggy was a mystery.

male or female, or something in between? With his lithe build, flamboyant costumes, and heavy makeup, Bowie as Ziggy was a mystery. Particularly because he was not well known prior to Ziggy—unlike Roger Daltrey before *Tommy*—there was no "real" Bowie to compare with his Ziggy persona. As Bowie pranced around onstage, he rendered his gender—or at least his sexual preference—ambiguous. Add to that a fantastical story, and—when performed live—a spectacular production: glam rock, as exemplified by Bowie, was the opposite of real.

David Bowie as Ziggy Stardust. Bowie (born David Jones, 1947) began his career in the sixties as a British folksinger. Influenced by Iggy Pop, Marc Bolan, and the Velvet Underground, he began to reinvent his public persona. In 1972 he announced that he was gay. (However, he commented in an interview over a decade later that he "was always a closet heterosexual.") Later that year, he put together an album and a stage show, *The Rise and Fall of Ziggy Stardust and the Spiders from Mars*. It featured Bowie, complete with orange hair, makeup, and futuristic costumes, as Ziggy, a rock star trying to save the world but doomed to fail.

"Hang On to Yourself," David Bowie (1972). David Bowie, vocal.

The songs from *Ziggy Stardust* provide the musical dimension of Bowie's role playing. Their effect is not as obvious as his appearance, but without them, his persona would be incomplete. The three components of the songs—the words, Bowie's singing, and the musical backdrop—all assume multiple roles, as we hear in "Hang On to Yourself," one of the tracks from the album.

The lyric is laced with vivid images: "funky-thigh collector," "tigers on Vaseline," "bitter comes out better on a stolen guitar." These arrest our ear, without question. But Bowie continually shifts from person to person as he delivers them. He "reports" in the verse—"She's a tongue-twisting storm"—and entreats in the chorus—"Come on, come on, we've really got a good thing going." His voice changes dramatically from section to section. It's relatively impersonal in the verse and warm, almost whispered, in the chorus.

The music is both obvious and subtle in its role playing. Bowie embeds instrumental and vocal hooks into the song: the guitar riff and the whispered chorus, a shock after

Debi Doss/Hulton Archive/Getty Images

PROTO-PUNK
Loud, repeated power chords played on guitar with some distortion, in a basic rock rhythm and at a fast tempo: these are salient features of punk style. They inform basic feel of song throughout, although Bowie adds a number of sophisticated touches.

HOOKS
Loaded with instrumental (e.g., whiney guitar riff) and vocal hooks, which serve narrative of album/stage show (making the band appealing).

SOPHISTICATED FEATURES
Several sophisticated features not customarily found in straightforward rock (frequent shifts in mood, occasional addition of extra beats, sporadically active bass lines, and Bowie's ever-shifting vocal timbres) = song about a rock band rocking out, rather than simply a good rock song

INSTRUMENTATION
Lead and backup vocals, lead and rhythm guitar, electric bass, drums, handclaps, synthesizer

PERFORMANCE STYLE
Bowie's varied vocal timbres; heavy distortion on rhythm guitar, whiney lead guitar sound on riff

RHYTHM
Fast, insistent rock beat periodically reinforced by guitar and drums; rhythmic play = syncopated guitar chords, active irregular bass line, occasional "extra" beats

MELODY
Abundance of riffs in verse and chorus

TEXTURE
Sharp contrasts in texture between verse and chorus, mainly because of shift in dynamics, timekeeping, contrasting riffs, different timbres, and busy bass line in chorus

On to Yourself" was a model for punk and new wave musicians; indeed, Glen Matlock of the Sex Pistols remarked that "Hang On to Yourself" influenced "God Save the Queen."

Ziggy was Bowie's first and most outrageous persona. For the rest of his career, he has continually reinvented himself in a variety of guises, all markedly different from the others, including "plastic soul" man and techno-pop avant-gardist. Bowie has been rock's ultimate poseur. And that has been his art: assuming so many different personas—not only in appearance and manner, but also in music—that he has made a mystery of his real self. Given Bowie's constantly changing roles during the course of his career, it is small wonder that he has been the most successful film actor among post-Elvis rock stars.

Stretching the Boundaries of Musical Art

Mitchell and Bowie approach art from two different directions. In Mitchell's case, it is her craft as a lyricist and songwriter: the imagination and individuality of both and their synergistic integration. Her work ranks with the best popular songs of the century and they invite comparison with the art songs of classical music. Although Bowie's music also displays craft and imagination, what stands out with *Ziggy Stardust* is the boldness of the premise and the theatricality of the result. Interestingly, there is a precedent in classical music for Bowie's show. Operas in the late seventeenth and early eighteenth centuries were also spectacular events, with equally improbable characters and plots, as well as singers who communicated gender confusion: extraterrestrial beings—gods and demigods, rather than aliens—typically played significant roles, and the main male singers were *castrati*, men who had been castrated to preserve their voice in a higher range.

In the wake of the Beatles, *Tommy*, jazz/rock fusion, and the art-related rock of the early 1970s, the notion of relative musical value reached a tipping point. The sheer quantity and variety of expression opened the question of whether European classical music should be used as the benchmark for artistic worth. For those not constrained by traditional mindsets, complexity, virtuosity, imagination, innovation, and coherence were values independent of any particular tradition.

Rock's deepest immersion in art lasted about a decade, from 1966 (the year in which the Beach Boys'

the pile-driving verse. Both make the song immediately accessible and memorable.

But there are also subtle clues woven into the song that seem to tell us that, for Bowie, the hooks are the dumbed-down parts of the music. With such features as the extra beats after the first line of the verse ". . . light machine" and elsewhere, Bowie seems to be hinting that he's capable of a lot more sophistication than he's showing on the surface. Indeed, the spare style of the song was one of the freshest and most influential sounds of the seventies. Like Ziggy, he is descending down to the level of mass taste (even as he's reshaping it) because he wants the effect it creates, not because that's all he can do.

In Ziggy Stardust, Bowie creates a persona that demands attention but is shrouded in mystery. What makes his persona so compelling, both in person and on record, is not only its boldness but also its comprehensiveness. Precisely because accessibility and ambiguity are present in every aspect of the production—the subject of the show, Bowie's appearance, the lyrics, his singing, the music—Bowie raises role playing from simple novelty to art. This quality made him one of the unique talents of the rock era.

Bowie was also one of the most influential musicians of the decade. The "lean, clean" sound of "Hang

Pet Sounds and Frank Zappa's *Freak Out* were released) to the mid-seventies, when enthusiasm for the various art rock explorations seemed to wane. It was as if once rock had established its cultural credibility, it was time to move in other directions.

Looking Back, Looking Ahead

The music presented in this chapter has at least two things in common: it was created in the early and mid-1970s, and it charted. Only *Ziggy Stardust* and Joni Mitchell's *Blue* failed to reach the top ten. *Blue* reached No. 15 and eventually went platinum. *Ziggy Stardust* reached No. 5 in the United Kingdom, although it barely made the charts in the states; it too would go platinum.

From this short list, we can infer some of the major changes in rock and the industry that supported it. First, and in many ways most important, rock had become a bigger business. Listeners bought more albums (on vinyl, cassette, or eight-track) than singles, which meant that the potential profits were greater, but so were the potential risks. Recording became an art, a craft, and an expensive process: higher quality, higher risk, and higher reward. The platinum record (1,000,000 units sold) became an industry yardstick in 1976. Similarly, concerts were often spectacular events; stadiums and arenas were common venues.

Those making money in the music business worked to reduce risk. Album-oriented radio was an attempt to homogenize musical taste in an increasingly diverse environment. Cross-promotion between touring and recording packaged the artist and his product. Safety (performing the songs on the current recording) replaced spontaneity, except in the case of the Grateful Dead and a few others.

The commercially dominant music lost its cutting edge. Evolution—the continuing development of the breakthrough advances of the 1960s—replaced revolution; craft replaced discovery. The results were in some ways more satisfying. Typically, the songs and their settings are more polished; the performances are more skilled. But the excitement of encountering something startlingly new occurred far less frequently in the early 1970s than it did just a half-decade earlier.

No acts of the 1970s would match the popularity or familiarity of the music of the Beatles and the Motown acts. The- audience for rock and rhythm and blues became as diverse as the music: the songs presented in this chapter spoke to different constituencies.

The edge in the music of the seventies came from outside. Funk followed the lead of James Brown toward a more African music. Reggae, imported from Jamaica by way of the United Kingdom, recaptured the sense of social purpose that had informed so much music of the sixties. Disco, the most commercially successful outsider music, began by attracting an alternative audience: black, Hispanic, and gay. Punk revived the garage-band spirit of the sixties, incubated in small clubs, and promoted passion over perfection. We encounter these styles in the next chapter.

Terms to Know

Test your knowledge of this chapter's important terms by defining the following. If you can't recall the meaning of a certain term, refresh your memory by looking up the boldfaced term in the chapter, turning to the Glossary at the back of the book, or working with the flashcards at the Popular Music Resource Center.

album-oriented radio	Philadelphia sound
cross-marketing	art rock
synthesizer	progressive rock
analog synthesizer	singer-songwriter
heavy metal	glam (glitter) rock

Funk, Reggae, Disco, Punk
New Trends of the Late 1970s

istockphoto.com

CHAPTER

13

CBGB is a small club located in the Bowery section of New York City. Originally, it was the bar in the Palace Hotel. By 1973, the year that CBGB opened, the hotel had gone from palatial to poverty stricken: it had become a cheap rooming house for the alcoholics and druggies who inhabited the neighborhood.

The full and creative name of the club is CBGB & OMFUG—Country, Blue Grass, and Blues, and Other Music for Uplifting Gormandizers. Owner Hilly Kristal's original plan was to book those kinds of acts into his new club. However, one day Patti Smith, who had heard about the club from some of her biker friends, went over to ask Hilly to book her boyfriend Tom Verlaine's band. Kristal hired the band—Richard Hell, Richard Lloyd, and Tom Verlaine of Television—for a gig, followed by another with another newly formed band, the Ramones. Neither date attracted much of a crowd.

Nevertheless, Kristal persevered and promoted. After some success with Patti Smith early in 1975, he decided to present "A Festival of the Top 40 New York Rock Bands." He spent a lot of money on advertising and scheduled it in the summer to coincide with the Newport Jazz Festival, a big-time event. It was a gamble that paid off. Critics came to hear the bands, and the audience for punk exploded overnight.

Venues like CBGB recalled the early years of rock and roll, when crowds typically numbered in the hundreds, rather than the thousands drawn by the top rock and rhythm and blues acts of the seventies. The punk and new wave music that came from such clubs represented a grassroots movement that hearkened back to rock's early years. It was also one of the most influential new directions in rock.

The music of the seventies that was most responsible for shaping the sounds of the 1980s and beyond included not only punk, but also funk, reggae, and disco. Like the music that had shaped previous generations of popular music, all began as styles outside the mainstream. However, unlike earlier generations, they were all part of rock. Punk was in many ways a retro rock style; funk was one continuation of James Brown's distinctive approach to rhythm and sound; reggae evolved from the mixing of Jamaican music with rhythm and blues; and disco drew on black pop and the new electronic sound world.

The images we have of these various styles—the Ramones, with T-shirts and sunglasses, making a big noise in a small club; Rastafarian dreadlocks; the glitter of the disco ball and the platform shoes of disco dancers; the outrageous outfits worn by George Clinton and the members of his bands, Parliament and Funkadelic; the complete absence of a performance-related image for early techno—highlight the considerable differences from style to style.

However, they share common ground. None of these styles carved out and kept a significant share of the popular music market. Disco was the most commercially successful style, but among disco acts, only the Bee Gees and Donna Summer sustained any kind of chart presence. For the most part, all of these styles were outside the commercial loop.

The most common musical bond was rhythmic. All of these styles have more active rhythms than rock. Reggae has a strikingly new, multilayered beat. In the case of punk, the heightened activity is tempo driven; punk tempos are brisk. Funk and disco use a new, busier beat. This would be a primary source of their influence.

The discussion that follows presents a brief survey of each style, then considers the collective impact of the styles on rock-era music of the eighties.

● ● ● ● ● ● ● ●

Funk

Like *blues*, *jazz*, *rock*, *soul*, and *rap*, *funk* is a one-syllable word from African American culture that began as nonmusical slang, then found its way into music, and eventually became a style label.

"Funk" originally targeted not the ears but the nose. As far back as the late eighteenth century, *funky* meant foul or unpleasant; a person who neglected to bathe for several days usually gave off a funky odor. Over time it acquired another meaning: hip. Stylish clothes were "funky threads." When James Brown sings "Ain't It Funky Now," he is referring to the ambience, not the smell.

Funk and *funky* came into popular music through jazz. Beginning in the mid-fifties, *funk* referred to a simpler, more blues-oriented style—a "return to roots" and a departure from the complexities of hard bop. By the sixties it had also come to mean soulful. (It also retained the other meanings; context and delivery determined which meaning was appropriate.) By the early seventies, funk had come to identify a particularly rhythmic strain of black music.

> *James Brown was the "father of funk" as well as the "godfather of soul"—and the "grandfather of rap."*

From Soul to Funk: Sly and the Family Stone

James Brown was the "father of funk" as well as the "godfather of soul"—and the "grandfather of rap." Funk musicians built their music on both the basic concept of Brown's music and many of its key features. Whether he was talking about feeling good or exhorting his listeners to get up and get involved, Brown embedded his message in a powerful groove. However, it was Sly and the Family Stone who played the key role in the transition from soul to funk.

The band was the brainchild of Sly Stone (born Sylvester Stewart, 1944), a disc jockey turned producer and bandleader. More than any other band of the era, Sly and the Family Stone preached integration. The lineup included two of Stone's siblings (his brother Freddie and sister Rosie), Cynthia Robinson on trumpet, and several others, including trend-setting bassist Larry Graham: there were blacks and whites, and women as well as men.

In a series of hits spanning a five-year period (1968–1972), Sly and the Family Stone created an exuberant new sound. We hear it in "Thank You (Falettinme Be Mice Elf Agin)," which reached the top of the charts in January 1970. The music of James Brown is the direct antecedent of this song and this style: like Brown's music, there is a groove built up from multiple layers of riffs, played by rhythm and horns; there is no harmonic movement—everything happens over one chord; and the vocal part is intermittent, with long pauses between phrases.

"Thank You (Falettinme Be Mice Elf Agin)," Sylvester Stewart (1970). Sly and the Family Stone.

However, the sound is much denser and more active than that heard in "Papa's Got a Brand New Bag." Although the drummer marks off a rock beat along with

It was Sly and the Family Stone who played the key role in the transition from soul to funk.

Michael Ochs/Getty Images

4 to Remember
"Thank You (Falettinme Be Mice Elf Agin)"

DARK LYRICS, UPBEAT MUSIC
Words and music = conflicting messages? Party-time groove versus sobering portraits of ghetto life

EMPHASIS ON THE GROOVE
Focus on rhythm and texture; harmony = one chord; melody = repeated riffs

NEW BASS SOUNDS
New, more percussive style: string plucked, slapped, or thumped

BRIDGE FROM JAMES BROWN TO FUNK
Common threads include the great groove, static harmony, and percussive sounds.

5 to Listen For
"Thank You (Falettinme Be Mice Elf Agin)"

INSTRUMENTATION
Vocals (group singing most of the time), electric bass, electric guitar, drums, keyboards, and horns (trumpet and saxophone)

RHYTHM
Moderate tempo; rock rhythm with sharp backbeat; many layers of rhythmic activity, including several double-time (based on rhythm twice as fast as rock beat) rhythmic figures. Almost everything is syncopated.

MELODY
Repetitive melodies made up of short riffs in both the verse and the chorus

HARMONY
One chord throughout the entire song

TEXTURE
Dense, layered texture, made up of riffs in rhythm instruments and horns underneath the vocal. Texture remains much the same throughout the song.

the backbeat, the basic rhythmic feel of the song is twice as fast. It is what is now called a **16-beat rhythm**—analogous to two-beat (foxtrot), four-beat (swing), and eight-beat (rock) rhythms. We sense this faster-moving layer in virtually all the other parts: the opening bass riff, the guitar and horn riffs, and—most explicitly—in the "CHUCK-a-puck-a" vocalization. The more active texture opens up many more rhythmic patterns that can conflict with the beat; Sly's band exploits several of them.

And instead of Brown's spare, open texture, there are plenty of riffs: bass, several guitars, voice, and horns. Moreover, there is a spontaneous aspect to the sound, as if it grows out of a jam over the basic groove. It is this quality that gives the song (and Stone's music) its distinctive looseness—looseness that implores listeners to "dance to the music."

Social Commentary and Seductive Grooves

If we just listen to Sly's music, it can hypnotize us with its contagious rhythm. However, when we consider the words—the opening lines of "Thank You" are "Lookin' at the devil, grinnin' at his gun/Fingers start shakin',

reggae, seventies funk, calypso from Trinidad, and, from the late seventies on, rap.

The music provided one way to escape the pain of prejudice. Drugs were another. Sly Stone used them to excess and torpedoed his career in the process. He became increasingly unreliable, often not showing up for engagements; promoters stopped booking his band. Once again, drugs had silenced a truly innovative voice.

The influence of Stone's innovations is evident in a wide range of music from the seventies and beyond—directly in styles like the art/funk jazz fusion of Herbie Hancock and the film music of Curtis Mayfield, and indirectly in styles like disco. However, it led most directly to funk, especially the music of George Clinton.

George Clinton and Funk

George Clinton (b. 1940) was the mastermind behind two important funk bands, Parliament and Funkadelic. While still a teen, he formed the Parliaments, but as a doo-wop group. They signed with Motown in 1964 but did not break through. When Clinton left Motown, he had to relinquish the Parliaments name, so he formed Funkadelic while battling Motown to regain ownership of his group's name. Funkadelic represented a major change of direction. As the group's name implies, it brought together funk and psychedelic rock: James Brown and Sly Stone meet Jimi Hendrix. When Clinton regained control of the Parliament name in 1974, he used two names for the same band.

I begin to run"—we sense that the band is laughing to keep from crying, or burning down the house. As with many other Sly and the Family Stone songs, there is a strong political and social message. We sense that the music is the buffer between the band and society, a restraint against violent activism.

Lose yourself in the music, to avoid simply losing it.

This is our first example of what would become a growing trend in Afrocentric music, from the United States and abroad: powerful lyrics over a powerful beat. There is an apparent contradiction between the sharp social commentary in the lyrics and the seduction of the beat. They seem to be operating at cross-purposes: full attention and response versus surrender to the groove. Perhaps that's so, but it's also possible to interpret this apparent conflict in other ways. One is to view the music as a tool to draw in listeners, to expose them to the message of the words. Another is to understand the music as a means of removing the sting of the conditions described in the lyrics: lose yourself in the music, to avoid simply losing it.

||||||||||||||||||||||||||||||||||||||

Funk can not only move, it can re-move."
—George Clinton

Sly and the Family Stone became popular after the assassination of Martin Luther King and after the backlash from the civil rights movement had built up steam. Civil rights legislation removed much of the governmental support for the racial inequities in American life. It did not eliminate prejudice or racial hatred, as many had hoped it would. The lyrics of this and other songs by Sly and the Family Stone speak to that. We find this same combination of strong rhythm and sharp words in Jamaican

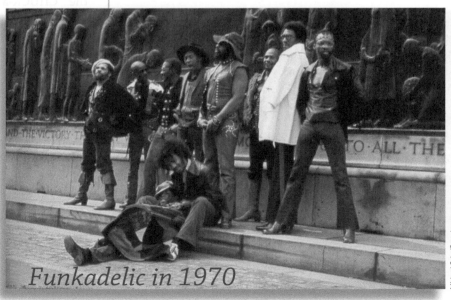

Funkadelic in 1970

INSTRUMENTATION
Voices, electric bass, drums, conga drum,
electric guitars, synthesizers, and horns

RHYTHM
Moderate tempo; basic beat is a rock
rhythm, but many parts move twice
as fast as rock (the opening "rap," the
bass patterns, and the conga part).
Lots of syncopation in the instrumental
background.

MELODY
Melody derived from blues-inflected
modal scale. First melody: long, unbroken
descending line. Second melody: short
riffs. Third melody: long sustained phrase.
All three melodies are simply repeated
several times; there is no development.

HARMONY
No harmonic change: decorative
harmonies (in voices and synthesizer)
derived from modal scale

TEXTURE
Dense texture, with voices, percussion,
bass, sustained chords on horns and
synthesizers, and high synthesizer
lines and chords. Strong contrast from
section to section ("Give up the funk" =
voices, bass doubling the melody, and
percussion)

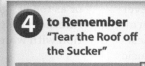

RHYTHM OVER MELODY
The rhythm, which features complex
interactions among the various
instruments, is more interesting than the
melody, which doesn't develop at all.

THE BASS AND BLACK MUSIC
Completely liberated bass: little
timekeeping; instead, intricate patterns
and riffs, occasional doubling of melody

IN THE GROOVE/IN THE MOMENT
The only focus is to give up the funk. No
story, no musical journey toward a goal.

ROAD TO RAP
The emphasis on rhythm and the chant-
like melodies are a prelude to rap and
techno

Without question there's an escap-
ist aspect to his work: his many aliases,
the flamboyant costumes he and his
bands wore in performance, and the
sci-fi world he created (the "Mother-
ship Connection") evidence that. Clinton seems to invite listeners to become
"one nation under a groove"; Surren-
dering to the rhythm offers momen-
tary relief from the pain of daily life
as a black person in the United States.
Whatever the motivation, there's no
question that Clinton's groups could
create a powerful groove. We experience
this in his 1976 hit, "Tear the Roof Off
the Sucker (Give Up the Funk)," which
his band recorded as Parliament.

The song shows Clinton's debt to
James Brown and Sly and the Family
Stone, and the ways in which his music
went beyond theirs. The instrumentation is similar—vocal, horns, and
rhythm—but the sound is fuller than
either James Brown's or Sly Stone's
because there are more instruments
and all of them are busy.

Clinton's debt to Brown goes beyond these general
features. After 1975 his roster included three significant
James Brown alumni: bassist Bootsy Collins, saxophonist Maceo Parker, and trombonist Fred Wesley. They
were key members of his large band, which included as
many as twelve musicians at a time.

Like Brown and Stone, Clinton creates the groove over
static harmony: this is a one-chord song. The texture is
dense: there are riffs and sustained chords from both
horns and keyboards, high obbligato lines from a synthesizer, an active but open bass line, lots of percussion, and
voices—both the choral effect of the backup singers and
Clinton's proto-rap. Clinton gives Bootsy Collins a chance
to stretch out. Collins's lines are active, syncopated, and
melodic, calling attention to the increasingly prominent
role of the bass in this branch of black music.

The rhythm has a 16-beat feel over the eight-beat
rhythm laid down in the drum part. Clinton's rap-like
introduction moves at this faster rhythm, and so do
the horn riffs, the bass line, and the guitar parts. This is
the same approach heard in the music of Brown and
Stone, but it is a thicker sound because there's so much
more going on. It is a darker sound as well, mainly because
of Clinton's voice and the prominence of the bass.

Clinton's various bands ran into trouble in the late
seventies, mainly because of bad money management,
sloppy business practices, and drug abuse. By 1981
Clinton had consolidated the two versions of the band
under one name, the P-Funk All Stars.

He recorded guitar-based material under the Funkadelic
name and more polished horn-section material with
vocal harmonies under Parliament's. This enabled the
two "bands" to perform on one stage at one time.

The formation of Funkadelic signaled Clinton's
transformation into Dr. Funkenstein (he also referred
to himself as Maggot Overlord); the title of his 1970

**"Tear the
Roof Off the
Sucker (Give
Up the Funk),"
George Clinton,
Bootsy Collins,
and Jerome
Brailey (1976).
Parliament.**

album *Free Your Ass and Your Mind Will
Follow* shows another side of his funky
sense of humor. Although Clinton certainly enjoyed being provocative and
playing with words, there is in many of
his songs a sense that he too is laughing to keep from crying. He tucks his
darker messages inside humorous packages set to a good-time groove. When
he tells listeners to "Tear the roof off
the sucker," he could be urging them to
party hard—or to riot.

Funk, by Clinton's band and other groups, never crossed over to the pop mainstream in its pure form. "Tear the Roof Off the Sucker" was Parliament's highest-charting song, and it made it only to No. 15. The music would prove to be enormously influential, however. It helped shape disco and other black styles, and with the advent of digital technology, rappers sampled Clinton's music mercilessly.

● ● ● ● ● ● ● ● ●

Reggae

Reggae is Jamaica's best-known music. It took shape in Jamaica around 1970 and found a second home in the United Kingdom by mid-decade. By the end of the seventies, it was known throughout the world, and its distinctive rhythms and sounds were seeping into other styles.

Reggae has spoken to and for Jamaicans of African descent. Its most powerful messages reverberated with the legacy of colonialism following political independence. Its distinctive sound is due in large part to Rastafarianism and rhythm and blues. We survey their impact on Jamaican music and encounter the style through the music of Jimmy Cliff and Bob Marley.

Jamaican Independence and Social Unrest

Most Jamaicans are of African descent—about 90 percent at the turn of the twenty-first century. Most trace their roots back to slavery; like the United States, Cuba, and Brazil, Jamaica was a destination for the slave traders. More than 600,000 slaves arrived in Jamaica between 1665 and 1838, the year in which the slave trade ended. British colonial rule continued for more than a century. Great Britain gradually transferred authority to Jamaicans, with the final step—independence—taken in 1962. Redress of the economic and social inequities of colonialism, however, did not keep pace with the political changes.

One result was a great deal of social unrest in the sixties. "Rude boys," disenfranchised young black Jamaicans who grew up in the most disadvantaged sections of Kingston, personified the violent dimension of this unrest. They were sharp dressers and often carried sharp knives and guns. For many Jamaicans, including the police, they were outlaws. Others, however, saw them as heroes, much as the James Brothers and Billy the Kid were heroes to earlier generations of Americans

or as today's gangsta rappers are to some young people. Another group with a much longer history of confrontation with white authorities were Rastafarians.

Rastafarianism

Rastafarianism was an important consequence of Marcus Garvey's crusade to elevate the status of people of African descent. Garvey, born in Jamaica, agitated for black power in the United States during the 1920s in response to the dire poverty and discrimination that the vast majority of blacks living in the New World faced. His efforts blended church and state; even as he pressed for an African homeland to which former slaves could return (it never materialized), he prophesied that Christ would come again as a black man. After serving half of a five-year sentence in an Atlanta prison, he was exiled from the United States and returned to Jamaica.

Rastafarians took Garvey's ideas several steps further. They claimed that Jesus had indeed come again, in the person of Haile Selassie (Prince Ras Tafari), the emperor of Ethiopia. Selassie claimed lineage back to King Solomon, which Rastafarians have taken as further proof of Selassie's divine status. In line with Selassie's personal genealogy, Rastafarians also claim to be descendants of the twelve tribes of Israel.

These beliefs, which have never come together as "official" doctrine—as has happened in organized religions—are the religious dimension of Rastafarians' efforts to promote a more positive image of Africa and Africans. This has largely come from within the movement. For those on the outside, the most vivid impressions of Rastafarianism are images, smells, and sounds: dreadlocks, ganja (marijuana, which they ingest as part of their religious practice), and music. To Jamaican music they gave a sound—Rastafarian drums—and reggae superstar Bob Marley. Another important musical influence was American rhythm and blues.

Rhythm and Blues and Jamaican Popular Music

The influence of rhythm and blues on Jamaican music is in part a matter of geography. Kingston, the capital city, is just over 500 miles from Miami as the crow flies and about 1,000 miles from New Orleans. Stations from all over the southern United States were within reach, at least after dark. So it should not surprise us that Jamaicans tuned in their radios to American stations in the years after World War II. For many young Jamaicans,

Dreamstime LLC

> *"Operators would drive around, pick a place to set up, and begin to play the R&B hits that the enterprising DJs had gone to the United States to fetch."*

Janine Wiedel/Digital Railroad

rhythm and blues replaced mento, the Jamaican popular music of the early fifties.

Sound systems, the mobile discos so much a part of daily life in Jamaica, offered another way to hear new music from America. Sound systems were trucks outfitted with the musical necessities for a street party: records, turntables, speakers, and a microphone for the DJ. Operators would drive around, pick a place to set up, and begin to play the R&B hits that the enterprising DJs had gone to the United States to fetch.

Ska: A New Jamaican Music. By the end of the 1950s, Jamaican musicians had begun to absorb rhythm and blues and transform it into new kinds of music. Ska, the first new style, emerged around 1960; it would remain the dominant Jamaican sound through the first part of the decade. Ska's most distinctive feature is a strong afterbeat: a strong, crisp *chunk* on the latter part of each beat. This was a Jamaican take on the shuffle rhythm heard in so much fifties R&B. It kept the long/short rhythm of the shuffle but reversed the pattern of emphasis within each beat. In the shuffle rhythm, the note that falls on the beat gets the weight; the afterbeat is lighter. In ska it is just the opposite, at times to the extent that the note on the beat is absent—there is just the afterbeat. It remains the aural trademark of ska.

From Ska to Reggae. As ska evolved into rock steady in the latter half of the sixties, musicians added a backbeat layer over the afterbeats. This created a core rhythm of afterbeats at two speeds, slow and fast: the characteristic offbeat *ka-CHUN-ka* rhythm of reggae. Because the bass had no role in establishing and maintaining this rhythm, bass players were free to create their own lines, and the best ones did. As rock steady evolved further into reggae, other rhythmic layers were added. The absence of beat marking, the mid-range reggae rhythm, the free-roaming bass, and the complex interplay among the many instruments produced a buoyant rhythm, as we'll hear in Jimmy Cliff's "The Harder They Come."

Jimmy Cliff and the Sound of Reggae

Jimmy Cliff (born James Chambers in 1948) was one of reggae's first stars. By the time he landed the lead role in the 1972 film *The Harder They Come,* he had gained an international reputation as a singer-songwriter. His appearance in the film, and the songs that he recorded for the soundtrack, cemented his place in popular music history. In *The Harder They Come,* Cliff plays Ivan O. Martin, a musician who becomes a gangster. Although his character is loosely based on a real person from the 1940s, Cliff 's title song brings the story into the present. The lyric resonates with overtones of social injustice and police oppression and brutality even as it outlines how the character will respond: "I'm gonna get my share now of what's mine."

The music sends a different message. Behind Cliff's vocal is a large rhythm section, with organ playing on the backbeat, another keyboard playing afterbeat chords, guitar and drums marking the rock rhythmic layer, and the bassist playing an active, bouncy, line. Their interaction produces the rich, complex, buoyant reggae rhythm, its most distinctive feature.

Reggae as Topical Music

In "The Harder They Come," we are faced with the seeming contradiction between words and music. The lyrics are dark, even menacing, but the music nevertheless brings a smile to one's face and a body movement somewhere. This is happy music, in its rhythm, in the lilt in Cliff's voice, in the form (a carbon copy of Motown's verse/bridge/chorus formula), and in the gently undulating melody. We are left to ponder: Is the music the candy that entices us to listen to the message of the lyrics, or a way to forget for the moment the situation that the lyrics depict? What we do know is that many of the songs that put reggae on the international

"The Harder They Come," Jimmy Cliff (1972). Cliff, vocal.

5 **to Listen For**
"The Harder They Come"

INSTRUMENTATION
Lead vocal, two keyboards (with organ sounds), piano, electric bass, drums, electric guitar

PERFORMANCE STYLE
Cliff's vocal style, with its use of falsetto and melisma, seems inspired by sixties American music. Choked guitar sound.

RHYTHM
Moderate tempo; rock-based rhythm with distinctive reggae feel; considerable syncopation and lots of activity, some of it double-time (moving twice as fast as the rock rhythm)

MELODY
Long phrases, which are repeated, in the verse and the first part of the chorus (bridge); the title phrase is a short riff.

TEXTURE
Densely layered, with several chord instruments, plus busy bass and drums behind the vocal

3 **to Remember**
"The Harder They Come"

REGGAE AS PROTEST MUSIC
Jamaican people's music: it came from them, and it spoke to them and for them, in direct, uncompromising language.

REGGAE RHYTHM
The interaction of the two organs produces the distinctive ka-CHUN-ka rhythm of reggae heard mainly in two organ parts.

WORDS AND MUSIC; WORDS VS. MUSIC
Combines lyrics that describe the harsh conditions in which the black underclass lives with irresistible, joyous music.

Is the music the candy that entices us to listen to the message of the lyrics, or a way to forget for the moment the situation that the lyrics depict?

"Is This Love," Bob Marley (1978), Bob Marley, vocal and guitar.

musical map, like this one and Bob Marley's "I Shot the Sheriff" and "Get Up, Stand Up," embedded hard messages within the music's infectious rhythms and sounds.

Like the music of Sly and the Family Stone and George Clinton, reggae contrasted hard lyrics and happy music. However, reggae was different in that it first became known outside of Jamaica as a music with a message. The music of Bob Marley, Jimmy Cliff, Peter Tosh, and other early reggae stars called attention to the social inequities in Jamaica. Moreover, it came at a time when rock had largely forsaken its role as a vehicle for social commentary. Marley would help fill that void, becoming a powerful voice on social issues.

Bob Marley and 1970s Reggae

Bob Marley (1945–1981) began his recording career in the early 1960s; it took off in 1964, after he formed the first edition of his backup group, the Wailers.

By the early 1970s, he was extremely popular in Jamaica. A recording contract with Island records propelled him to global stardom.

His success on record and in concert gave him and his country's music unprecedented exposure. For many people, Bob Marley *was* reggae. Worldwide, he was its most popular artist. His popularity gave him the leverage to work for meaningful change in Jamaican society. He became the decade's most visible spokesperson for peace and brotherhood, carrying the torch of sixties social activism and idealism into the seventies. Much of Marley's music was political: songs like "I Shot the Sheriff" and "Get Up, Stand Up" are familiar examples. However, he periodically displayed a more intimate side. In "Is This Love," Marley is speaking one-on-one with a special woman. In keeping with the content and tone of the lyric, the form of this song sprawls lazily through time.

Bob Dylan called Jimmy Cliff's "Vietnam" the best protest song ever written.

Hulton Archive/Getty Images

INSTRUMENTATION
Lead, backup vocals, several percussion instruments, including Rastafarian drums, bass, guitars, and keyboards

RHYTHM
Shuffle-based reggae rhythm at moderately slow tempo: light beatkeeping; ka-*chun*-ka pattern formed by offbeat/backbeat keyboard chords

RHYTHM
Slow-moving vocal line, free bass line over characteristic reggae rhythm

MELODY
Memorable extended instrumental riffs recur throughout; vocal line has widely spaced repeated riff in verse; flowing

TEXTURE
Rich texture, concentrated in mid-range (bass moves freely)

LOVE SONG
Song about love, not politics, sung at a leisurely tempo

REGGAE RHYTHM
Rich rhythmic texture with light percussive beat keeping, flowing melody, distinctive backbeat/afterbeat "ka-*chun*-ka rhythm in keyboards, free bass line

BUOYANT SOUND
Activity concentrated in mid-range, with keyboard and percussion providing steady but not beat-heavy rhythm, serves as musical cushion for vocal line.

The slower layer (marked by a sharp guitar "chunk") is the reference tempo, as it is in most rock steady and reggae songs. The vocal line implies the primacy of slower tempo, especially when Marley sings the title phrase over and over: "Is this love, is this love, is this love, is this love that I'm feelin'?"

The gentle pulsations of the drum and tambourine, prompted by the fast shuffle afterbeat rhythm in the organ (rather than the even, rock-like afterbeats in "The Harder They Come"), keep the rhythm afloat, while the vocal parts—Marley's slow-moving melody and the sustained harmonies of the "I-Threes"—and in-and-out bass slow the beat down to a speed below typical body rhythms—even the heartbeat at rest or the pace of a relaxed stroll. As a result, the rhythm of the song is buoyant and lazy at the same time. All of this evokes a feeling of languid lovemaking in the tropics, a perfect musical counterpoint to the lyric of the song.

Reggae as an International Music

Reggae's popularity outside of Jamaica owed much to the heavy concentrations of Jamaicans in England. As part of the transition from colonialism, Great Britain opened its doors—or at least its ports—to people from its colonies. More arrived from the Caribbean than from any other former colony—around 250,000 in the late fifties and early sixties. By the end of the sixties, the British government had put into effect legislation that severely restricted immigration. By that time, however, those Jamaicans already in England re-created much of their culture. All the Jamaican music of the sixties and the seventies found a supportive audience in England, among Jamaicans eager for this link to their homeland and among British whites intrigued by this quite different music.

For a new generation of British musicians in search of "real" music, reggae (and ska) provided an at-home alternative to the blues. Eric Clapton, who had immersed himself so deeply in the blues during the sixties, led the way with his cover of Marley's "I Shot the Sheriff"; the recording topped the charts in 1974. A wave of new British acts, among them the Clash, Elvis Costello, UB40, and the Police, wove the fresh sounds of reggae into their music.

Reggae's path to America seems unnecessarily roundabout. The music didn't find an audience in the United States until after it had become popular in England. Once known, however, its influence was even more diverse—and more divorced from the music's social context. For example, we hear echoes of the distinctive reggae rhythm in the Eagles' huge 1977 hit "Hotel California."

Jamaican music influenced African American music in two markedly different ways. Black pop musicians used the rhythmic texture of reggae to further liberate the bass from a timekeeping role, beyond advances of Motown and the Philadelphia sound. Because reggae embedded the pulse of a song in its distinctive mid-range rhythms, bass players were free to roam at will, largely independent of a specific rhythmic or harmonic role. Its influence was evident in such songs as "Sexual Healing," Marvin Gaye's 1982 ode to carnal love, and "What's Love Got to Do With It," Tina Turner's 1984 cynical rejection of it.

The other source of influence was not reggae, per se, but a characteristic element of the sound system–based Jamaican street parties. Between songs, DJs delivered a steady stream of patter. Much of it was topical, even personal: they would pick out, and sometimes pick on, people in the crowd that had gathered around. This practice was called **toasting**. It became so popular that Jamaican record producers like Lee "Scratch" Perry began releasing discs in which the B side was simply the A side without the vocal track. The instrumental track would then serve as the musical backdrop for the DJ's toasting—and save the producers some money.

Toasting is a direct forerunner of rap. Kool Herc, a Jamaican who moved to the Bronx as a young teen, brought toasting from Kingston to the streets of New York, where it quickly evolved into hip-hop. Grandmaster Flash, one of the seminal figures in early rap, described Kool Herc as his hero. Rap's first hit, the SugarHill Gang's 1979 "Rapper's Delight," is a classic example of the practice: extended raps over a loop of Chic's "Good Times."

• • • • • • • •

Disco

Disco is short for *discothèque*. *Discothèque* is a French word meaning "record library" (by analogy with *bibliothèque*, meaning "book library"). It came into use during World War II, first as the name of a nightclub—Le Discothèque—then as a code word for underground nightclubs where jazz records were played. Because of the German occupation, these clubs were run like American speakeasies during the Prohibition era.

The Roots of the Club Scene

Discothèques survived the war, becoming increasingly popular in France. The first of the famous discos was the *Whisky à Gogo* in Paris, which featured American liquors and American dance music, both live and on record. Others sprung up in the postwar years, eventually becoming a favored destination of jet-setters. Discothèques began to open in the United States around 1960. The first was Whisky a Go Go in Chicago, in 1958. The Peppermint Lounge, which Joey Dee and the Starlighters called home and where the rich and famous did the Twist, opened in 1961 in New York City.

This rags-to-riches-and-back-to-new-rags story would become the recurrent theme of dance music in the latter part of the century. As dance fads like the Twist moved out of the clubs and into mainstream society, the original audience sought out new dance music in different, less exclusive, and less pricey venues.

By the end of the sixties, a new club culture was thriving. It was an egalitarian, nonrestrictive environment. The new, danceable black music of the late sixties and early seventies provided the soundtrack: Sly and the Family Stone, Funkadelic, Stevie Wonder, Marvin Gaye, Curtis Mayfield, Barry White, and above all the Philadelphia acts, such as the Spinners, the Stylistics, the O'Jays, and Harold Melvin and the Blue Notes. Clubbers included not only blacks but also Latinos, working-class women, and gays, for whom clubbing had become a welcome chance to come out of the closet and express themselves. Despite the gains of the various "rights" movements in the sixties and seventies, these were still marginalized constituencies.

The Mainstreaming of Disco. By mid-decade, however, disco had begun to cross over. Integrated groups like KC and the Sunshine Band, which exploded onto the singles charts in 1975, began making music expressly for discos. *Saturday Night Fever* was the commercial breakthrough for the music. Almost overnight what had been a largely underground scene briefly became the thing to do.

In New York the favored venue was Studio 54, a converted theater on 54th Street in Manhattan. It became so popular that crowds clamoring to get in stretched around the corner. It was the place to see and be seen. Writing about Studio 54 at the end of the seventies, Truman Capote noted, "Disco is the best floor show in town. It's very democratic, boys with boys, girls with girls, girls with boys, blacks and whites, capitalists and Marxists, Chinese and everything else, all in one big mix."

||||||||||||||||||||||||||||||||||||||||||

"Disco is the best floor show in town."
—Truman Capote

Disco and Electronics. Meanwhile, the discothèque scene continued to flourish in Europe. The new element in the music there was the innovative use of synthesizers to create dance tracks. Among the most important musicians in this new domain were Kraftwerk, a two-person German group, and

Tom Gates/Hulton Archive/Getty Images

Giorgio Moroder, an Italian-born, Germany-based producer and electronics wizard who provided the musical setting for many of Donna Summer's disco-era hits.

Kraftwerk and Moroder exemplified the increasingly central role of the producer and of technology. Disco became a producers' music, even more than the girl groups of the sixties. Just as Phil Spector's "wall of sound" was more famous than the singers in front of it, so did the sound of disco belong more to the men creating and mixing the instrumental tracks than the vocalists in the studio. Here, the wall of sound was laced with electronic as well as acoustic instruments. Singers were relatively unimportant and interchangeable; there were numerous one-hit wonders.

Donna Summer: The Queen of Disco

"I Feel Love," Donna Summer, Giorgio Moroder, and Peter Bellotte (1977). Donna Summer, vocal.

If there's one performer whose career embodies disco—its brief history, its geography, and its message—it is Donna Summer (b. Donna Adrian Gaines, 1948). Summer grew up in the Boston area and moved to Europe while in her teens to pursue a career in musical theater and light opera. While working as a backup vocalist, she met Giorgio Moroder (b. 1940), who would collaborate with her on her major seventies hits. Her first international hit, "Love to Love You Baby," was released in 1975; it was a hit in both the United States and Europe. The most striking feature of the song was Summer's erotic moans. In its graphic evocation of the bedroom experience, it is in spirit an answer to Barry White's seductive songs.

As the song title suggests, "I Feel Love," her next big American hit, explores the erotic dimension of love, although not as blatantly as the earlier song. Here Summer's deliberately wispy voice floats above Moroder's sea of synthesized sound. Summer's vocal may be the most prominent element of the music, but the background is certainly the more innovative. The innovation begins with Moroder's use of electronic counterparts to a traditional drum set; there isn't one conventional instrument on the track. Even more noteworthy is the idiomatic writing for synthesizers. Moroder creates a

rich tapestry of sound by layering in a large quantity of repetitive patterns, some constantly in the foreground, others in the background and often intermittent. None of them really corresponds to traditional rock guitar or bass lines: it is not only the sounds that are novel, but also the lines that create the dense texture behind Summer's vocal.

Rhythmically, the song converts the 16-beat rhythms of funk and black pop into an accessible dance music by making the beat and the 16-beat layer more explicit. From the start we hear the steady thud of a bass drum–like sound on every beat and an equally steady synthesized percussion sound moving four times the speed of the beat in a mid-range register. Other parts, most obviously the synthesized ascending pattern that runs through the song, also confirm regular rhythms. Compared to previous examples that used this more active rhythm, "I Feel Love" is far less syncopated and much more obvious in its timekeeping. This is certainly due in large part to its use as dance music.

The busy rhythms of the accompaniment contrast sharply with Summer's leisurely unfolding vocal line and the slow rate

Donna Summer, queen of disco

Fotos International/Hulton Archive/Getty Images

3 to Remember
"I Feel Love"

ELECTRONIC SOUND WORLD
No conventional instruments; electronic substitutes for percussion, bass, and chord instruments

OBVIOUS RHYTHM
Beat marking in electronic bass drum, low synthesizer riff produces relentless timekeeping at three levels.

WOMAN VS. MACHINE
Contrast between Summer's gradually unfolding vocal line and slow harmonic change and active rhythms in many parts

5 to Listen For
"I Feel Love"

INSTRUMENTATION
Voice and array of synthesized sounds: bass, percussion, chords, and so on

PERFORMANCE STYLE
Summer's wispy voice vs. bright electronic sounds

RHYTHM
Regular timekeeping at three speeds: beat, 2x beat, and 4x beat; other rhythms unfold slowly

MELODY
Repeated riff in accompaniment; slow, narrow-ranged vocal line

TEXTURE
Rich texture made up of electronic sounds envelops Summer's vocal

of harmonic change. These two seemingly conflicting messages about time in fact invoke two aspects of the disco scene: the activity of the dancers to the throbbing beat and the endlessness of the experience, as one song mixes into the next. (The abrupt ending of the song suggests its use in a disco: the DJ would fade it away before the end as he brought up the next song.)

Summer's career started before disco went mainstream, then crested during the late seventies. Perhaps anticipating the imminent commercial decline of disco, she took her music in new directions in songs like "Bad Girls." This helped sustain her popularity through the end of the seventies; her last three albums of the decade went No. 1.

Among the most loyal members of Summer's fan base were gays. Their connection to disco took on a public face in the music of the Village People.

The Village People: Disco out of the Closet

The Village People was the brainchild of Jacques Morali, a French producer living in New York. Morali's various accounts of the formation of the Village People are conflicting, but what is certain is that he recruited the men who fronted his act literally off the street and in gay clubs.

> " The whole Village People act was an inside joke. "

The public image of the Village People was six guys dressed up as macho stereotypes among gays: the Indian (in full costume, including headdress), the leather man (missing only the Harley), the construction worker, the policeman, the cowboy, and the soldier. These expressions of hyper-maleness were, in effect, gay pinups. Their look was more important than their sound, although after a disastrous appearance on the television program *Soul Train*, Morali fired five of the six men and replaced them with new recruits.

The whole Village People act was an inside joke. Morali and gay audiences laughed behind their hands while straight America bought their records by the millions and copied the

"Y.M.C.A.," Jacques Morali, Henrio Belolo, and Victor Willis (1978). The Village People.

look—mustaches, leather jackets, and the like. Many listeners were not aware of the gay undertone to the lyrics—or if they were, they didn't care.

The group's song "Y.M.C.A.," their biggest hit on the singles charts (No. 2 in 1978), shows the macho men at work. In most cities and towns around the United States, a YMCA (established by the Young Men's Christian Association) is a place for families to participate in an array of activities. Some are athletic—basketball, swimming, and gymnastics—others are social and humanitarian, such as meals for senior citizens. In larger cities YMCAs can also accommodate residents. In cities like New York, these became meeting places for gays.

The lyrics of the song have fun with this situation. Seemingly innocuous lines like

They have everything for men to enjoy
You can hang out with all the boys

take on a quite different meaning when understood in the context of the Y as a gay gathering place.

The music is quintessential disco. It's apparent in the march-speed tempo, with the beat marked by the bass drum; active rhythms, especially the bass in the chorus and the string figuration; rich orchestration, with strings, oversize rhythm section, and electronic instruments; catchy chorus melody; and repetitive harmony.

Disco: Culture, Reception, and Influence

Although most disco artists came and went—Donna Summer was the biggest star, Chic the most successful band—disco was widely popular during the latter part of the seventies. During that three-year window, it spread from urban dance clubs to the suburbs, and its audience grew considerably. Disco had clear and strong gay associations, as "Y.M.C.A." makes clear, but it was more than music for gays and blacks. In this respect *Saturday Night Fever* was a slice of life: there were many working-class urban youth who used disco dancing as an outlet.

Disco was more than the music or even the culture that had produced it. For many it became a lifestyle. It was

CBS Photo Archive/Getty Images

5 to Listen For
"Y. M. C. A."

INSTRUMENTATION
Voices (a lead vocal, plus others occasionally reinforcing the lead line), drums, tambourine, handclaps, electric bass, keyboard, violins, and brass (especially trumpets)

RHYTHM
Disco tempo (about 120 beats per minute). Bass drum thuds out the beat; backbeat is also strong.

RHYTHM
Melody moves at a moderate pace with some syncopation. String and brass figurations often move four times as fast as the beat (16-beat speed)

HARMONY
Updated versions of the "Heart and Soul" progression (verse and chorus are slightly different). The progression cycles through the entire song; it never resolves

TEXTURE
Rich, layered texture: low = bass and bass drum; mid-range = voices, sustained strings, some brass riffs, and percussion sounds; high = brass riffs and string figuration. Always a thick sound.

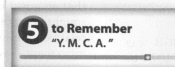

5 to Remember
"Y. M. C. A."

CODED LYRIC
NYC YMCA = gay meeting place. Lyric full of inside jokes

DISCO, A MULTIPLE-MINORITY MUSIC
Disco's original audience included gays, blacks, and Latinos; provoked homophobic and racially prejudiced reactions.

SLICK DANCE MUSIC
Amateurish singing, relentless dance beat, and fancy strings

FUNK, DISCO AND THE BEAT
Funk and disco are close musical relatives, but the more obvious beat in disco made it more popular.

CONTROL OF THE PRODUCER
With disco the producer assumed the main creative responsibility. Singer(s) were primarily for image.

hedonistic: dancing was simply a prelude to more intimate forms of contact. It was exhibitionistic: fake Afro wigs; skin-tight, revealing clothes; flamboyant accessories; platform shoes; everything glittering. And it was drug-ridden: with disco, cocaine and Quaaludes became mainstream drugs; the logo for Studio 54 showed the man in the moon ingesting cocaine from a silver spoon.

Reactions Against Disco. All this, plus the inevitable stream of mindless disco songs (the ratio of chaff to wheat in any genre is high; disco was no exception), gave disco's detractors plenty of ammunition. They trashed the music and the culture. Ostensibly, it was simply a reaction against disco's many excesses, but there was also a strong homophobic undercurrent. Perhaps the most notorious disco-bashing incident occurred in Chicago during the summer of 1979.

Steve Dahl, a disc jockey at a local rock station, organized Disco Demolition Night. Fans who brought a disco record to a Chicago White Sox doubleheader got into the park for 98¢. They spent the first game chanting "Disco sucks"; after the first game, they made a pile of records in centerfield. An attempted explosion turned into chaos.

Disco and Dance Fads. When disco disappeared from the charts and the radio, there was an "I told you so" response from those who hated it. But in retrospect it would have been surprising if it had lasted much longer. All the major dance fads in the twentieth century have had short life spans: the Charleston and the Black Bottom in the early 1920s, jitterbugging and Lindy hopping around 1940; the Twist and other rock-and-roll dances around 1960. The Charleston and the Twist were dance fads that caught on somewhat after the introduction of new rhythms: the two-beat foxtrot in the teens and early twenties and the eight-beat rhythm of rock and roll in the fifties. Disco, like the jitterbug, was a dance fad that emerged with the division of popular music into two related rhythmic streams. In the thirties it was sweet (two-beat) and swing (four-beat). In the seventies it was rock (eight-beat) and disco (16-beat).

The swing and disco eras were brief periods when the more active rhythms of black and black-inspired music became truly popular. In both cases much of the music was rhythmically more obvious than the music that had spawned it. Many of the hits of the swing era, especially by the white bands, laid down a strong beat but lacked the rhythmic play of music by Count Basie, Duke Ellington, or Benny Goodman. Similarly, disco was more rhythmically straightforward than funk or black pop. This made it accessible to a greater number of dancers but sacrificed musical interest in the process.

The Influence of Disco. It shouldn't be surprising that disco faded away so quickly. It was following much the same path as the other dance fads that signaled the arrival of a new beat. And it should not be surprising that a new beat took root in the music of the 1980s following disco's demise. In this way disco was influential, far more so than its brief life span would suggest.

Disco has also had a more underground influence—on two levels. It was, more than any other popular style, the gateway for the wholesale infusion of electronica. And it created a new kind of underground dance-club culture, which would continue through the eighties and flower in the nineties.

Punk

Among Hilly Kristal's first customers at CBGB was Malcolm McLaren, who came to New York in 1974 to attend a boutique fair. Three years earlier, McLaren had opened a clothing boutique in London called Let It Rock with Vivienne Westwood; it featured vintage and retro styles, as well as custom-made theater costumes. However, McLaren saw himself as a political provocateur. He wanted to be able to thumb his nose at the establishment and make money on it at the same time. McLaren viewed rock music as a vehicle for his politics; bands would make a statement with images as well as sound.

While in New York, McLaren persuaded the New York Dolls, who had just been dropped by Mercury Records, to let him manage them and design their outfits. He costumed them in red leather and had them perform in front of a hammer and sickle. For the Dolls, the shock strategy backfired: the blatant nod to the Soviet Union apparently turned off other labels, and the band broke up the following year. For McLaren, it was simply the prelude to an even bolder statement. After hearing early punk bands like the Ramones and the Neon Boys (who would become Television) and after seeing Richard Hell's torn clothing and studded collars, McLaren returned to England, changed the name of his boutique to SEX, and started carrying fetish clothing and original punk-inspired items. This in turn attracted a clientele from which McLaren would eventually assemble the Sex Pistols.

That a boutique storeowner and fashion designer would form and manage the U.K.'s seminal punk band says a lot about the movement. At least in McLaren's realization of it with the Sex Pistols, punk was part of a larger package. It was only one component of a presence designed to stand out, outrage, and affront those on the outside. Hand in hand with the noise of punk went the hostile attitude and—even more obvious from a distance—the look: spiked hair in a rainbow of colors, tattoos and body piercings, torn clothes ornamented or even held together with safety pins.

Punk was an extreme form of a wave of new music that emerged in the mid-seventies. In the sense that it sought to recapture the revolutionary fervor and the relative simplicity of early rock, it was a reactionary movement—a counterrevolution against what its adherents saw as the growing commercialism of mainstream rock. However, in its reconception of these values, it established an important and influential new direction in rock, which continues to the present.

The Punk Movement

The most powerful and enduring image in rock has been the rebellious outsider as hero. From Elvis, Little Richard, and Jerry Lee Lewis to the latest flavor of indie band, rock has glorified those who outraged a complacent, corporate-minded establishment while delivering their message loudly, if not always clearly. In rock's early years, it was rock on the outside versus the pop establishment. However, when rock became the dominant commercial music, the rebellion happened on the inside. As before, it was David and Goliath; with punk, however, Goliath was the rock establishment.

The power of this image can be gauged by the ratio of commercial success to critical attention. Few punk or new wave bands enjoyed much commercial success; nevertheless, far more has been written about the early years of punk than about more mainstream rock in the seventies.

The Roots of Punk. Punk took shape in New York. Much like the folksingers of the sixties, bands performed in small clubs located in Greenwich Village and Soho. CBGB, the most famous of these clubs, launched the careers of a host of punk and new wave bands. Among the CBGB graduates were Patti Smith, Richard Hell (in the Neon Boys, then Television, and finally as Richard Hell and the Voldoids), the Ramones, and the Talking

> ❝ *That a boutique storeowner and fashion designer would form and manage the U.K.'s seminal punk band says a lot about the movement.* ❞

Valentin Casarsa/istockphoto.com

Heads. Ohio was another spawning ground: Pere Ubu, from Cleveland, and Devo, from Akron, both had careers under way by 1975.

Among the major influences on punk in New York were the Velvet Underground and the New York Dolls. The Velvet Underground embraced the New York City subculture sensibility and nurtured it in their music. Their songs (for example, "Heroin") were dark, which foreshadowed punk's "no future" mentality, and the sound of their music was often abrasive and minimalist. They presented an anti-artistic approach to art, a rejection of the artistic aspirations of the Beatles and other like-minded bands. Moreover, their impresario was an artist, Andy Warhol, who packaged them as part of a multimedia experience (the famous Exploding Plastic Inevitable); this presaged McLaren's vision of punk as a fusion of image and sound in the service of outrage.

The New York Dolls, led by David Johansen, were America's answer to David Bowie, Marc Bolan, and the rest of the British glam bands. They lacked Bowie's musical craft and vision; their musical heroes were not only the Velvet Underground but also the MC5 and Iggy Pop and the Stooges. In effect, they dressed up the latter groups' proto-punk and made it even more outrageous, wearing makeup and cross-dressing outlandishly—they out-Bowied Bowie in this respect—and taking bold risks in performance. Brinksmanship came easily to them, as they were, in the words of one critic, "semi-professional" at best.

Patti Smith, a rock critic turned poet-performer, was the first major figure in the punk movement to emerge from the New York club subculture. Smith was its poet laureate, a performer for whom words were primary. There is nothing groundbreaking in the sound of her music. Indeed, she wanted to recapture rock's brief glory period in the mid-sixties, to have her music make a statement, not a spectacle. Her work had much of the purity and power of punk: purity in the sense that it returned rock to its garage-band spirit, and power in the outrage. But it was not outrageous, at least not by the Sex Pistols' standards. Smith was also important because she was a woman in charge; she played a seminal role in the creation of this new/old style. Partly because of her presence, punk and new wave music were much more receptive to strong women than conventional rock.

In the United Kingdom, punk was a music waiting to happen. All the components were in place, except for the sound. Disaffected working-class youth wanted an outlet for their frustration: pierced body parts, technicolor hair, and torn clothes made a statement, but they weren't loud enough, and they didn't articulate the message. Following McLaren's return to London and the Ramones' 1976 tour, punk took off in England as well as in the United States, most notably in the music of the Sex Pistols. Elvis Costello quickly became the bard of the new wave. The Clash, the Pretenders (fronted by Akron, Ohio, native Chrissie Hynde), and the Buzzcocks were among other leading U.K. bands in the late seventies.

The attitudes expressed in the punk movement reflected deeply rooted contradictions in everyday life during the seventies. The "we" mind-set of the sixties—the sense of collective energy directed toward a common goal—gave way to a "me" mindset, where people looked out for themselves. The various rights movements and the move toward a more democratic society eroded class distinctions at a rapid rate. Still, there was a strong conservative backlash in both Britain and the United States. At the same time, a prolonged recession, fueled in part by the absence of fuel due to the Arab oil embargo, gave working- and middle-class people little opportunity to take advantage of their new social mobility. And sky-high interest rates and inflation created the fear that today's savings would be worth far less in the future. "No Future," the nihilistic battle cry of the Sex Pistols, was in part a product of this bleak economic outlook.

The Power of Punk. Although the look screams outrage and the words scream rebellion, the power of punk is in the music; it is the sounds and rhythms of punk that most strongly convey its energy and attitude. Especially when experienced in its native environment—a small club overflowing with people—the music overwhelms, injecting the crowd with massive shots of energy.

Punk is to rock and roll what heroin is to opium: it gains its potency by distilling its most potent elements and presenting them in concentrated form. "Pure" punk songs are short; they say what they have to say quickly and move on. In their mid-seventies heyday, the Ramones would play 30-minute sets, in which all of the songs lasted about 2 minutes. Within such brief time spans, punk offers songs that intensify the dangerous aspects of rock and roll: the volume, the sounds, the rhythms.

Punk is loud. Subtlety is not part of the equation; typically, it's full-bore from beginning to end. Punk is noise: guitarists and bassists routinely use heavy distortion. Punk singing is the triumph of chutzpah over expertise. Indeed, the lack of vocal skill or sophistication was a virtual requirement; one couldn't credibly croon a punk song. Part of the message was that anyone could front a band if he or she had the nerve. Punk is fast: tempos typically exceed the pace of normally energetic movement—walking, marching, disco dancing. However, the most compelling feature of punk is its approach to rock rhythm.

Saturated Rock Rhythm. A brief recap of twenty years of rock rhythm: Recall that what distinguished rock and roll from rhythm and blues was the eight-beat rhythm. We heard it in the guitar lines of Chuck Berry and the piano playing of Little Richard and gradually in other rhythm instruments, as musicians caught on to this new rhythmic conception. Move ahead to the late sixties and early seventies: as rock musicians became comfortable with rock rhythm, the basic rock beat became a springboard for rhythmic play, as we heard in the music of The Who, Led Zeppelin, and others.

Punk restored the essence and power of rock rhythm by isolating it, saturating the rhythmic texture with it, and speeding it up. In punk, the "default" way of playing the rock rhythmic layer was simply to repeat a note, a chord, or a drum stroke over and over at rock-beat speed. Musicians could graft riffs onto this rhythm to create variety and interest, but this was an overlay; typically, the eight-beat rhythm continues through the notes of the riffs. By contrast, Chuck Berry's rhythm guitar patterns typically oscillate every beat between two chords. This oscillation creates slower rhythms that attenuate the impact of the faster rhythm. Punk strips away these slower rhythms, presenting rock rhythm in a purer form.

Punk made this "purer" form of rock rhythm stand out through a two-part strategy. First, the entire rhythm section typically reinforced it: guitar(s), bass, and drums all hammer it out. Indeed, depending on the speed of the song and the skill of the drummer, the reinforcement could be heard on the bass drum as well as the drums or cymbals. Second, it favored explicit timekeeping over syncopation and other forms of rhythmic play. This reverses the prevailing direction of the evolution of rock rhythm, which was toward greater rhythmic complexity—more syncopation, more activity, more implicit timekeeping—as we heard in Chapter 12. We sample the power of punk in a song by the Sex Pistols.

The Sex Pistols

We think of rebels as independent figures standing apart from the crowd. So there is an uncomfortable irony to the fact that the most rebellious act in the history of rock music was part of an extraordinarily complex and manipulative artist/manager relationship. Malcolm McLaren made the Sex Pistols: vocalist Johnny Rotten (John Lydon, b. 1956), guitarist Steve Jones (b. 1955), bassists Glen Matlock (b. 1956) and Sid Vicious (John Ritchie, 1957–1979), and drummer Paul Cook (b. 1956); he also made them an instrument that enabled him to realize his own provocative ends.

McLaren found the Sex Pistols in his shop. Matlock, the original bassist with the group, worked for McLaren. When he let McLaren know that he and two of his friends, guitarist Steve Jones and drummer Paul Cook, were putting together a band, McLaren found

them rehearsal space, took over their management, and recruited a lead singer for them. John Lydon, who became Johnny Rotten (allegedly because of his less than meticulous personal hygiene), had been hanging around SEX for a while. McLaren had gotten to know him and felt that he had the capacity for outrage that he'd been looking for. (Another SEX shop hanger-on, Sid Vicious [John Ritchie], would eventually replace Matlock.)

In fact, none of the four had much musical skill at the time they formed the band. Jones was more adept at thievery than guitar playing: he stole the group's first sound system. McLaren booked the group into small clubs, where they acquired more of a reputation for outrageous conduct than for musicianship. Word spread about the group through word of mouth, newspaper reviews, and subculture fanzines. The term *punk* itself was originated by Billy Altman, a *Creem* magazine contributor, in 1972, and popularized by *Creem* writer-editor Lester Bangs throughout the seventies.

> The Sex Pistols acquired more of a reputation for outrageous conduct than for musicianship.

The Sex Pistols. Left to right: drummer Paul Cook, bass player Sid Vicious, singer Johnny Rotten, and guitar player Steve Jones

AFP/Getty Images

The Sex Pistols found their musical direction after hearing the Ramones and learning the basics of their instruments. What they had from the beginning, however, was the ability to shock, provoke, confront, and incite to riot. When they added the musical energy of the Ramones to this stew, they were ready to overthrow the ruling class, a stance that is evident in two of their best-known songs, "Anarchy in the UK" and "God Save the Queen." Johnny Rotten opens "Anarchy in the UK" with "I am an Anti-Christ; I am an anarchist" and ends with a drawn out "Destroy." The opening line lances both church and state; the final word makes clear their agenda. Rotten, a skinny kid who knew no bounds, sings/screams/snarls the lyrics. In "God Save the Queen," we can imagine the sneer on Rotten's face as he delivers the opening line, "God Save the Queen, the fascist regime."

All of this was music to McLaren's ears. He hated the liberal attitudes of the sixties and was canny enough to exploit their openness, so that he could take aim at both the ruling class and the "peace and love" generation. In his mind, punk was nihilistic: "no future" was the motto. For McLaren, the Sex Pistols were another expression of his business philosophy. The bondage gear sold in McLaren's boutique promoted sex as pain, not pleasure. Although Rotten railed against the "fascist regime," punk's use of the swastika image evoked the ultimate fascist regime. And the Sex Pistols' sets often ended in some kind of fracas; their attitude was more than words and symbols.

The music behind the words was, if anything, even more provocative. It wasn't just that it was loud—

"God Save the Queen," Cook, Jones, Matlock, and Rotten (1977). The Sex Pistols.

particularly when heard in the small venues where the punk bands played. Or simple—power chords up and down the fretboard. It was the beat. Punk fulfilled the confrontational promise of the very first rock-and-roll records. It was the subversive element that got the revolutionary message across loud and clear, even when the lyrics didn't.

In "God Save the Queen," guitar and bass move in tandem to hammer out a relentless rock rhythm almost all the way through; only the periodic guitar riffs that answer Rotten's vocals give it a distinctive shape. The drummer reinforces this rock rhythm by pounding it out on the bass drum and either a tom-tom or hi-hat. Like the Ramones, the band distilled and intensified rock and roll's revolutionary rhythmic essence. There

③ to Remember
"God Save the Queen"

INCENDIARY LYRICS
Song lyrics slam British royalty, establishment; "no future" = hard times for underclass

SOUND WITH AN EDGE
Abrasive vocal, distilled, aggressive, saturated rock rhythm, distorted power chords produce classic punk rock sound

POWER OF PUNK
Inflammatory message in lyrics reinforced by aggressive musical setting

⑤ to Listen For
"God Save the Queen"

INSTRUMENTATION
Vocal, guitar, bass, drums

PERFORMING STYLE
Abrasive vocal style: loud speech; less than singing; heavy distortion in guitar and bass

RHYTHM
Distilled, intensified rock rhythm at moderately fast tempo

MELODY
Most distinctive melodic material = guitar riffs; vocal not distinct melodically, even in chorus

TEXTURE
Thick, heavy sound: low-range power chords stand out.

is no way that a rock beat could be more pervasive or powerful.

The power of the song comes from its stylistic coherence. Every aspect of the song—the lyrics, Rotten's vocal style, the absence of melody, simple power chords, the heavily distorted sounds, and the relentless, fast-paced beat—conveys the same basic message: they are mutually reinforcing.

The message of the Sex Pistols resonated throughout the United Kingdom. Many working- and middle-class youths were tired of the rigid class system that they inherited and foresaw a bleak future. The Sex Pistols' songs encapsulated the frustration and rage they felt.

Despite their meteoric rise and fall (Lydon announced the breakup of the group in January 1978), the Sex Pistols were enormously influential. No group in the history of rock had more impact with such a brief career. They embodied the essence of punk in every respect. No one projected its sense of outrage and its outrageousness more baldly.

New Wave and the Talking Heads

New wave was the umbrella term used to identify the music that emerged in small clubs, mainly in New York and London, during the mid-seventies. It embraced not only punk acts but also other bands seeking a similar audience. Among the more important were the Talking

Heads and Devo in the United States and Elvis Costello and the Attractions in England.

These diverse acts shared considerable common ground. Both bands and audience assumed an anti-mainstream position. With few exceptions, their music, whatever form it took, was a reaction against prevailing tastes. The reaction could be rage, weirdness, cleverness, humor, and more; but it was typically a reaction.

As this new music emerged, it was labeled "punk" or "new wave" more or less interchangeably. In retrospect, one of the significant distinctions between punk, or at least the "pure" punk of the Ramones and Sex Pistols, and the new wave styles that emerged at the same time is the aim of the music. Punk aims for the gut; new wave aims for the brain, or perhaps the funny bone. Perhaps more precisely, punk was the new rock, and new wave the new pop. All-guitar was usually punk; the presence of a keyboard indicated new wave. The songs of new wave acts such as the Talking Heads and Elvis Costello demand attention to the words, and the musical setting puts the lyrics in the forefront.

To support clear delivery of the lyrics, new wave bands favored a stripped-down, streamlined sound: guitar(s), bass, and drums, with the occasional keyboard. (Elvis Costello seemed fond of cheesy-sounding synthesizers.) The rhythmic texture was relatively clean, with little syncopation or rhythmic interplay. This energized the songs without overpowering or deflecting attention from the vocals. Instrumental solos were at a minimum; the primary role of the music was to enhance the words.

Like so many British rock musicians, the Talking Heads started out in art school. Lead singer David Byrne (b. 1952) and drummer Chris Frantz (b. 1951) attended the Rhode Island School of Design together before moving to New York. They formed the group in 1975, with Tina Weymouth (b. 1950), Frantz's then-girlfriend (and later wife), playing bass, and added guitarist/keyboardist Jerry Harrison (b. 1949) two years later.

Although they operated in the same CBGB milieu as the Ramones and other similar punk bands, the Talking Heads came from an opposite place conceptually. Where the Ramones' sound

"Psycho Killer," David Byrne, Chris Frantz, and Tina Weymouth (1977). The Talking Heads.

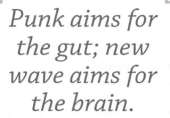

Punk aims for the gut; new wave aims for the brain.

remained remarkably consistent from song to song, the Talking Heads' music, beginning with their debut album *Talking Heads '77* and continuing throughout their sixteen-year career together, offers considerable variety. In their earlier albums, this is especially remarkable, given their limited instrumental resources and Byrne's vocal limitations.

Their music reflects both their seemingly insatiable curiosity regarding the world of music and their art-school training. Byrne would become one of the leaders of the world music movement in the eighties; *Naked*, their last studio album, released in 1988, featured African musicians. Many of their early songs draw on the rock and rhythm and blues with which they were surrounded in their formative years. However, they process it in their songs much as cubist painters like Picasso and Braque processed the scenes and objects that they portrayed in their paintings. These once familiar sounds often occur as distorted or fragmented in the Talking Heads' music, to the extent that the connection with an earlier style is all but broken. This manipulation of familiar sounds provided an instrumental setting that enhanced the impact of Byrne's quirky lyrics and quavery voice, which was ideally suited to convey a person who has drunk way too much coffee or is simply over the edge.

"Psycho Killer," a surprise hit from their first album, evidences salient features of their sound: lyrics and Byrne's singing in the forefront, varied accompaniment, with several subtle features in support. Rhythm and texture are simple and clean; the bass line marks the beat with a repeated note, while guitar and keyboard move at rock-beat speed. The jangly guitar—first in the arpeggiated accompaniment of the verse, then in the chords under the chorus—echoes Byrne's words and sound. This spare backdrop—perhaps a musical counterpart to the white cell of the psycho ward—is an ideal foil for Byrne's vocal. The lyric is inflammatory. Byrne announces quite clearly that he's crazy ("a real live wire"), and his neutral delivery makes his portrayal especially

David Byrne of the Talking Heads

Michael Ochs/Getty Images

5 to Listen For
"Psycho Killer"

INSTRUMENTATION
Vocal, guitar, bass, drums, keyboard

PERFORMANCE STYLE
Byrne's quavery vocal sound, which gets more intense as song progresses

RHYTHM
Understated rock beat: more emphasis on beat than rock rhythm; little syncopation

MELODY
Mainly repeated phrases in narrow range in verse and chorus; wider ranging as song unfolds

TEXTURE
Widely spaced, open sound, with variety from section to section

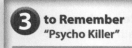

3 to Remember
"Psycho Killer"

PROMINENT LYRICS
Byrne's lyrics describe a person in the process of losing it; his depiction of a serial killer. Switch to French in chorus a distinctive touch.

PORTRAYING A DEMENTED PERSON
Byrne's untutored and uninhibited singing and melody grow more unrestrained from verse to chorus; dynamic depiction of madness

INSTRUMENTS IN BACKGROUND
Modest instrumentation, understated rhythm, spare texture provide neutral background, like sterile room in psycho ward, for Byrne's vocal

of *Rolling Stone*'s list of the 500 greatest albums of all time. Its critical acclaim, at the time and subsequently, attests to the rapid evolution of punk beyond the raw, manic energy of the Ramones and the Sex Pistols and the Clash's role in that evolutionary process.

Like the Rolling Stones, the Clash grew out of a chance encounter. However, the meeting between guitarists Mick Jones and Joe Strummer took place not in a train station over an armful of blues records, but while waiting in line for an unemployment check. As in the United States, rampant inflation in the United Kingdom had had a devastating effect on the economy. An influx of people from the former British colonies (Jamaicans, East Indians, Nigerians, and others) strained social services and heightened racial tension. At the same time, the class distinctions that had been part of British life for centuries were under assault—as was made manifest in "God Save the Queen."

The Clash came together in 1976 when Strummer (1952–2002) and Jones (b. 1955) teamed up with bassist Paul Simonon (b. 1955) and drummer Terry Chimes (b. 1955). Topper Headon (b. 1955) soon replaced Chimes. Simonon gave the group its name, which suited the confrontational personality of the group and their on-stage persona. In the summer of 1976, Strummer and Simonon found themselves in the middle of a riot between Jamaican immigrants and police. "White Riot," the song that they wrote in response to the incident, was the group's first major hit. It not only got the group noticed but also set the tone for their career: many of their songs railed against political and social injustices.

"White Riot" and many other early songs follow the lead of the Ramones: they are fast, loud, and crude. However, the group quickly evolved into a much more skilled and versatile band. By 1979, the year when they released *London Calling*, the Clash were at home in a variety of styles. However, they never lost the passion that informed their first work. It is evident in virtually all of their music, regardless of subject.

"Death or Glory," a track from the album, comments on a central issue for the group: whether money will motivate a group to sell out. The lyric oozes attitude. The cast of characters includes a "cheap hood" and a "gimmick hungry yob" ("yob" is British slang for a young working-class thug). The images are brutal: the hood beats his kids; bands

effective—as if he's a time bomb waiting to explode. In contrast to "God Save the Queen," which goes full bore from beginning to end, there are numerous changes in accompaniment, from the edgy beginning to the brutal beat-by-beat chords in the interlude where Byrne shifts to French.

As "Psycho Killer" demonstrates, the sound of the Talking Heads was fueled more by imagination than by craft. There's nothing particularly challenging in any of the instrumental parts, nor is Byrne a vocalist with a wide expressive range. There is no obvious virtuosity or lavish instrumentation. Yet the Talking Heads created one of the most innovative sound worlds of the seventies.

In "Psycho Killer," the Talking Heads explored a dark and difficult theme, via a song that put the words in the forefront and that backed them up with musical settings that helped evoke the ominous lyrics, despite relatively modest instrumental resources. The song illustrates how new wave often projected rage or frustration, but with more finesse: a sharp stick instead of a bludgeon.

The Clash and the Evolution of Punk

The Clash released the double album *London Calling* in the United Kingdom in December 1979. It is the only album by a band formed after 1970 to make the Top 10

"Death or Glory," Mick Jones and John Mellor (1979). The Clash.

5 to Listen For
"Death or Glory"

INSTRUMENTATION
Lead and backup vocals, lead and rhythm guitar, electric bass, drums, keyboard

RHYTHM
Clean, active rock rhythm at moderately fast tempo, with most parts moving at eight-beat speed except during interlude, when activity doubles

RHYTHM
Distinctive, often syncopated rhythm in guitar accompaniment

MELODY
Contrast between rapid rhythm, flat contour in verse, hooks in chorus, musing instrumental riffs in intro/interludes

TEXTURE
Thick texture, with much melodic interest in guitar parts underneath plain vocal line and in instrumental sections

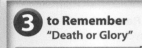

3 to Remember
"Death or Glory"

LYRICS IN FOREFRONT
Both verse and chorus put words in forefront; lyrics laced with brutal images of wannabes who fail as musicians and people.

ROCK SONG CONVENTIONS
Verse/chorus form and melodic hooks make the song easy to follow and appealing.

STRONG SECTIONAL CONTRASTS
Musing introduction, straight-ahead verse, chorus with can't-miss hook, instrumental interludes shift to more or less relaxed rhythms.

More than any other group of the late seventies, the Clash demonstrated by example how to revitalize rock with words and music that mattered, because, unlike the "gimmick hungry yob," they refused to compromise. (Interestingly, their record company undermined their integrity by marketing them as the "The Only Band That Matters," a phrase created by their fans.)

The Reverberations of Punk

Punk and new wave restored the soul of rock and roll. The important bands resurrected rock's sense of daring and amped it up well beyond what had gone before. As with Dylan's pre-electric and early electric work, the anthemic sixties songs of The Who and the Rolling Stones, and reggae, there is a powerful message: political, social, and personal. However, in punk, the rock can be as brutally blunt in its musical message as in the lyrics. There is a synergy among attitude, words, and music that gives both punk and new wave unprecedented impact. Once again, this is rock music that sought to change the world, or at least shake it out of its complacency.

In punk, the message is primary, whether it is expressed directly or obliquely. This helps account for the relative simplicity of the musical materials—whether presented as a sound blitz (as in the Sex Pistols' music) or with imagination (as in the music of the Clash and the Talking Heads). If the musical setting were too elaborate, it would deflect attention away from the underlying intent of the song.

As with any significant new music, punk and new wave would reverberate through the music of the next generation. Punk, and especially the music of the Clash, served as a bridge between the significant rock of the sixties and the significant rock of the eighties, most notably the work of U2. It introduced a new conception of rock rhythm that would filter into numerous mainstream and alternative styles. This was one reason why much of the rock from the eighties sounds as though it is from that decade and not from an earlier time. It sharpened the edge of much rock-era music, even the pop of Michael Jackson and Madonna. It opened the door for those outside corporate rock; the alternative movement that began in the early eighties continues the independent spirit that typified the punk and new wave music of the late seventies. That spirit lives on most fully in the post-punk bands that have emerged since 1980.

that haven't got it should give it up. The chorus sums up the disillusionment that pervades the song.

The music that supports it is simply good rock, rather than high-energy pure punk. The song uses the conventional verse/chorus form; the chorus features catchy melodic hooks that embed themselves in listeners' ears. Once under way, the song maintains a driving beat enriched with rhythmic interplay among the rhythm section players, except for an adventurous interlude that spotlights Headon. The texture is dense in a way that is typical of rock, with melodic lines in both guitars and bass, and there is an array of timbres, from the distorted chords that announce the chorus to the more mellow bass and guitar sounds in the introduction.

"Death or Glory" is not representative of *London Calling*, a double album with nineteen tracks. Neither is any other track on the album; each song has a distinct character and musical setting; they range from swing-evoking "Jimmy Jazz" and reggae-inspired "Revolution Rock" to the clever punk-style "Koka Kola." However, throughout the album, the Clash infuse their music with the power and passion of punk. Regardless of the style or influences of the music, the songs matter—because of the lyrics and because the music backs up the lyrics.

Looking Back, Looking Ahead

Funk, reggae, disco, and punk were extraordinarily influential and would resonate through the music of the eighties and beyond. The new music from the early eighties to the present sounds like it comes from this time, not from the sixties or seventies, for a number of reasons: new electronic sounds and effects, new voices, outside influences, and the like. Most fundamentally, however, there is a new approach to rhythm. Rock rhythm got a makeover from punk; 16-beat rhythms became the dominant style beat; and even more active rhythms surfaced in rap, techno, and related styles. These rhythmic innovations help place the music chronologically after 1980.

By the eighties, rock-era music had evolved well past the rock-defining music of the late sixties and early seventies. Rap and techno, punk/funk/disco fusions, the new pop of Michael Jackson and Madonna, and the significant rock of U2 and Springsteen—all evidenced the new attitudes, sounds, and rhythms. Indeed, the rock styles that remained truest to the spirit and sound of the 1960s were mainly "alternatives." We sample this music in the next several chapters.

Terms to Know

Test your knowledge of this chapter's important terms by defining the ones listed here. If you can't recall the meaning of a certain term, refresh your memory by looking up the boldfaced term in the chapter, turning to the Glossary at the back of the book, or working with the flashcards at the Popular Music Resource Center.

funk	reggae
16-beat rhythm	toasting
mento	disco
ska	punk
rock steady	new wave

Electronica and Rap

istockphoto.com

CHAPTER 14

The welcome page of Joseph Saddler's website (www.grandmasterflash.com) features a video in which Saddler, better known as Grandmaster Flash, explains how DJs from the seventies never put their hands on the grooves of the vinyl discs they played. He goes on to say that he was the first to put his hands on the grooves, which enabled him to develop an array of innovative techniques, including cutting, scratching, back spinning, and flaring. Soon, he would mark particular spots on a disc with tape or crayon so that he could access a particular spot on the fly. Armed with two turntables, a mixer, and a stack of discs, including doubles of the tracks he planned to use, Flash could transform the playback of a song—to this point as predictable an event as the sun rising in the east—into a unique, spontaneously crafted experience.

In the sense that it became a device in which one could shape musical sound in the moment, Flash turned the turntable into a musical instrument. But because the musical sounds involved an extra layer of creativity—the sounds had already been recorded—the turntable was different in kind from more conventional instruments, such as those used in a rock band. Although the use of prerecorded sounds in live performance was not new, Flash's techniques brought a new, richer, and more improvisatory dimension to the experience. They were one sign of a movement that would radically transform cutting-edge rock-era music in the eighties and beyond.

It should be noted that there was a good reason that other DJs handled recordings by the edge: bringing the grooves into contact with anything—fingers, crayons, errant tone-arm needles—would damage the disc and eventually render it unplayable. While Grandmaster Flash was perfecting his novel techniques, another revolution was under way that would render them all but obsolete. In this chapter, we discuss the digital revolution and consider its impact on electronica and rap, the two styles that would benefit most directly from it.

●●●●●●●●

The Digital Revolution

What made electronic technology—the microphone, the radio, and improved recording quality—possible was the ability to convert sound waves into electrical signals and electrical signals back into sound. What made digital audio possible was the ability to encode the waveform generated by the electrical signal into a binary format, then reverse the process for output. This was accomplished by **sampling** the wave at regular intervals, with several possible gradations. On a standard CD, the wave is sampled 44,100 times a second; there are 65,536 (16 × 16 × 16 × 16) possible gradations of the wave. What happens is that this high sampling rate, coupled with the thousands of gradations, makes it possible to simulate the shape of the wave so closely that the original waveform and the digital sampling of it are virtually identical.

Digital audio fools our ears in much the same way that digital images fool our eyes. Open a visual image on your computer and magnify it. You'll notice that it is a grid of squares, each a single color or shade of gray. However, the size of each square is so small that our eyes are fooled into seeing color blends, curves, and other continuous images.

This ability to encode waveform data digitally has had several benefits. First, it eliminates signal degradation. In analog tape recording, there were inevitably some unwelcome sounds: one can hear tape hiss on predigital recordings that have not been remastered or on cassette copies of recordings. The more a tape is copied, the more pronounced the extraneous sounds become. By contrast, digital information can be copied an infinite number of times with no loss of audio quality, as anyone who has burned a CD or used a file-sharing service knows.

Second, it became possible to maintain quality despite unlimited use. Because of the physical contact of a stylus with a record groove, or tape with the tape head, the quality of sound degraded over time. A recording played for the one-hundredth time on a turntable or cassette player will sound worse than the first time, no matter how much care is taken. This problem disappeared with digital audio.

> "Digital information can be copied an infinite number of times with no loss of audio quality."

Dan Wilton/istockphoto.com

Third, the high sampling rate has enabled those working with computer audio to isolate musical events with a precision that earlier generations could only dream about. Instead of shuttling a tape head back and forth to find the right starting point, those working in the digital domain can quickly identify and mark the beginning and end of a musical event. Once isolated, they can manipulate it at will—compressing or expanding it, changing its pitch higher or lower, changing its timbre, enhancing it with special effects.

The New Digital Technologies

It was one thing to have the capability of using digital technology; it was quite another to actually have the hardware that made it possible. After years of research and development, two crucial technologies emerged in the early eighties: audio CD and MIDI.

Audio CD. The **audio CD** (compact disc) required more than the ability to convert sound into digital data; it was also necessary to apply laser technology to encode and decode the data from the storage medium (hence "burn" a CD). Research on the laser dates back to a 1958 paper by a physicist at Bell Labs. By the early seventies, lasers were being used to read digital data stored on discs. By 1980 Philips and Sony, two of the leaders in audio research, had agreed on a standard for CD audio: 16-bit sampling and a 44.1K sampling rate. Other sampling precisions and sampling rates have also come into use; streaming audio generally uses less precise sampling (8-bit sampling produces 1/16 the data of 16-bit sampling) and slower sampling rates.

Perry Kroll/istockphoto.com

In 1984 the first CD pressing plant in the United States—in Terre Haute, Indiana—started producing CDs. The first CDs were expensive because the production process was seriously flawed; only a relatively small percentage of the CDs produced were good enough for release. As a result, the cost of a CD was high—higher than cassette or vinyl. Not surprisingly, given the nature of the music business, the cost of a CD remained higher than that of a cassette, even though production costs were soon much lower.

MIDI. **M**usical **I**nstrument **D**igital **I**nterface, or simply MIDI, is an industry standard that allows electronic instruments to communicate with one another and with a computer. In theory, this seems like a natural and modest step. In practice, it was a tremendous breakthrough for two main reasons. First, it enabled a single person to simulate an orchestra, a rock band, or a swing band, using just one instrument. Using a MIDI-enabled electronic keyboard or other similarly configured device, musicians could choose from an array of MIDI-out sounds—usually no less than 128. They could play the passage as if playing a piano or organ, but the sound coming out would be like a trumpet, or bells, or violins, or a host of others.

Second, MIDI devices could interact with sequencers. A **sequencer** is a device that enables a person to assemble a sound file, track by track. Using a sequencer that can store eight tracks, a person can re-create the sound of a band: one track for the bass, another for the rhythm guitar, and so on.

Sequencers can also be used to create loops. A **loop** is a short sound file—such as a drum pattern or a bass line—that can be repeated and combined with other loops or freely created material to create a background for a song, whether it's rap, pop, techno, house, or something else. To make this process easier, loops are usually a standard length: eight beats (two measures), sixteen beats (four measures), and so on. With these kinds of resources, assembling the rhythm track to a song can be like building with LEGO®: users simply snap them into a track in their digital audio software.

Sampling. A **sample** is a small sound file. (Please note that this meaning of *sample* is different from the sample of a waveform; the two meanings are related but different, much like the multiple meanings of *beat*.) There are two basic kinds of samples in common use. One is the recorded sound of a voice or group of voices, an instrument (for example, a grand piano) or group of instruments (such as a violin section), or some other sound. This sound can then be activated through some other device. For instance, one can buy a disc with the sampled sound of several cellos playing every note on the usable range of the instrument, recorded in many different ways. Then the buyer can install it on a computer, activate it inside the appropriate software, and produce a passage that sounds like a recording of the cello section of a first-rate symphony orchestra.

This kind of sampling has been available since the sixties. The first commercial "sampler" to achieve any kind of currency was the Mellotron®. It was a keyboard instrument in which depressing a key would activate a looped tape of a string sound. It was not very flexible, but it was a cost-efficient alternative to hiring violinists. However, sampling didn't really become practical until digital technology.

Now, sampling has reached such a level of sophistication that it is often impossible to determine whether a passage was recorded live or created using samples. In effect, this kind of sampling is a more advanced version of MIDI playback because the sounds are rendered more accurately.

The other primary kind of sampling involves lifting short excerpts from existing recordings to use in a new recording, much like a visual artist will use found objects to create a collage or assemblage. It has been a staple of rap background tracks since the technology became available in the mid-eighties.

Computer Audio. In 1965 Gordon Moore, one of the founders of Intel, predicted that the number of transistors on a computer chip would double every couple of years. Moore's law, as it has been called, has largely held true. What this has meant is that the amount of computing power one can buy for $1,000 has doubled every eighteen months or so.

Because CD-quality digital audio requires over 1 million samples per second, the first personal computers could not handle audio processing in real time. Fast-forward to the turn of the century, though, and it's a different story. One can burn CDs at … I hesitate to write a number here, because by the time this book gets into print it will be out of date. Digital audio workstations, sequencers, special effects plug-ins, notation software—there is nothing in the process of creating and producing a recording that cannot be done on a computer supported with the right software and peripherals except the invention of original material.

Those who have come of age with this technology in place may not find it to be unusual. However, for those of

> *For just a few thousand dollars, anyone can create a home studio that can do just about anything that could have been done only in a million-dollar studio less than a generation ago.*

Chris Schmidt/iStockphoto.com

us who have seen it emerge, it is awe inspiring. For just a few thousand dollars, anyone can create a home studio that can do just about anything that could have been done only in a million-dollar studio less than a generation ago. One of the images of this time that is sure to endure is the creative person sitting not at an instrument or a desk, but at a workstation, surrounded by displays, keyboards, CPUs, and other computer audio equipment.

The advances in computer-based digital audio have put high-end music production within almost everyone's budget. For the aspiring creative artist, the financial investment is a fraction of what it once was. The larger investment is time—not only to develop the necessary musical skills but also to master the applications necessary to create the desired result. And there are plenty of role models, from Stevie Wonder, Brian Eno, and Grandmaster Flash, to Trent Reznor, Moby, Juan Atkins, Richard James, and hundreds more. And it will only get better.

Digital technology has made it easier to make well-crafted music, both for those with well-developed musical skills and those with little or no skill. But it has also allowed for a less immediate kind of music making. In performance or recording, there can be a world of difference between having a drummer playing and having a drum loop playing, simply because the drummer can respond in the moment. For those who want to keep their music real, the challenge is to use the technology in ways that enhance the personal dimension of their music rather than undermine it. Another option is to create a radically new esthetic, one that builds naturally on the innovations of digital technology. We explore this new esthetic in a discussion of electronica.

● ● ● ● ● ● ● ●

Electronica

Among the most enduring images in twentieth-century music is the singer with guitar. The image transcends style, race, gender, locale, theme: Blind Lemon Jefferson,

Jimmie Rodgers, Gene Autry, Maybelle Carter, Robert Johnson, Woody Guthrie, Bob Dylan, Joan Baez, Joni Mitchell, and countless others—country and city, traditional and topical.

Now imagine a sound that is this image's complete opposite. There's little or no singing—and what vocals there are have been filtered through an electronic device. There's no melody with accompanying chords; instead there might be wisps of riffs or some sustained notes. Instead of the simple rhythm of the accompaniment, there is the thump of a low percussion sound marking the beat, several fast-moving patterns, plus other electronically generated loops. Instead of the strumming of an acoustic guitar, there's an array of electronic sounds, complete with special effects (fx). Instead of a story with a beginning and an end, there's total immersion in a sound world with no apparent time boundaries. Instead of a single performer singing and playing while a few others listen, there's a DJ in a booth, surveying a dance floor filled with bodies moving as he mixes the music.

You'll find examples of this totally opposite sound in the dance/electronica section of your favorite music store—on the street, in the mall, or online. Electronica has become the umbrella term for a large and varied family of styles: house, techno, trance, ambient, jungle, drum 'n' bass, industrial dance, and many more.

The almost total contrast between electronica and the folk/blues/country singer underscores how radically different the electronic-based music of the eighties, nineties, and the twenty-first century is from so much earlier music, including much of the music of the early rock era. The differences begin with its origins and continue with its venues, its performance, and ultimately its intent.

The Antecedents of Electronica

Most popular music genres have evolved through the influence of music from "below"—that is, music from "plain folk" who live outside and beneath the realm of high culture. We often use the word *roots* to convey this. Electronica is different. Its origins are in the most cerebral and esoteric music of the mid-twentieth century, the classical music avant-garde.

During the middle of the twentieth century, composers in Europe and the United States, using equipment as sophisticated as the first tape recorders and synthesizers and as everyday as nuts and bolts, explored virgin musical territory. Shortly after World War II, French composer Pierre Schaeffer began creating music using recorded sounds, rather than musical ideas inside his head, as raw material. The recordings could be of any sounds at all, and they could be modified or transformed before being assembled into a music event. Schaeffer called this process *musique concrète* ("concrete music").

Others—among them German composer Karlheinz Stockhausen, French American composer Edgard Varèse, and American composer John Cage—assembled compositions completely from synthesized sounds, recorded, then spliced together to form a complete composition. In 1958 Lejaren Hiller set up the first computer music studio at the University of Illinois. Among these new electronic works were the first examples of the recording as the creative document—with no performer involved in the creative process.

Much of this music was conceptual: it grew out of a particular idea that the composer wanted to explore. The results explored every possible extreme. American composer Milton Babbitt created works in which every musical parameter was regulated by a predetermined mathematical series: total serialism. In effect, his compositions using this procedure were precomposed. At the other end of the spectrum were works by John Cage. One famous work required the performer to sit perfectly still for the entire performance, 4 minutes, 33 seconds in length; the composition was the ambient sounds in the performing space. Stockhausen composed a work for piano in which fragments of music were printed on an oversized score; the performer determined the sequence of the fragments during the performance. Cage created works in which events were determined by chance. Varèse created *Poème électronique*, an electronic piece that mixes synthesized and *concrète* sounds, for the 1958 World's Fair in Brussels, where it played over 425 loudspeakers.

All of these concepts have found their way into the various electronica styles. For example, the loudspeaker setup for *Poème électronique* anticipates the "total immersion" sound systems of dance clubs. Stockhausen's piano piece, where the performer switches arbitrarily from fragment to fragment, anticipates the DJ mixing on the fly. *Musique concrète* anticipates the found sounds that appear in so much electronica and related styles like rap. And totally electronic pieces anticipate the millions of synthesizer-generated dance tracks.

This isn't to say that there's a straightforward causal connection between mid-century avant-garde music and the electronica of the last twenty-five years. Rather, it should suggest three things. First, even the most esoteric ideas and concepts have a way of filtering down; in this case, they made it all the way to the underground—the club scene that has nurtured this music. Second, electronica could blossom only when the necessary equipment became accessible and affordable. Third, electronica involves more than simply making dance music on computers. Its most imaginative creators have radically altered or over-turned conventional assumptions about music making.

Music for Dancing, Places to Dance

The dance club is the home of electronica. The dance scene that has nurtured the music since the early eighties has been an underground continuation of disco: the music of Donna Summer and Giorgio Moroder were among the best and most successful examples of early electronica. In essence, there were people who still wanted to dance after disco declined in popularity; the club scene, and the music created for it, gave them the outlet.

During the eighties, two major club scenes emerged in the Midwest: **house music** in Chicago and **techno** in Detroit. Both would have a profound influence on dance music throughout the world. House music was a low-budget continuation of disco; DJs like Frankie Knuckles would use bare-bones rhythm tracks as part of mixes that included disco hits and current disco-inspired songs. The Detroit scene was almost exclusively the work of three friends and colleagues—Juan Atkins, Derrick May, and Kevin Saunderson—who had known one another since junior high. Despite their Detroit base, they were more interested in techno pioneers like Kraftwerk than in Motown. As Atkins said in an interview, "I'm probably more interested in Ford's robots than in Berry Gordy's music." As DJs and producers, they delivered a stark, dark kind of dance music under numerous guises, including Atkins's Model 500 and May's Rhythim Is Rhythim.

By the mid-eighties, the music had migrated to Great Britain. The event that brought the music, the culture, and the drugs up from the underground and into the public eye was the 1988 "Summer of Love," a rave that went on for weeks. A **rave** is a huge dance party conducted in a large space: outdoors, an abandoned warehouse, or even a large club. Ecstasy and other designer drugs were very much part of the scene; they suppressed the need to eat or sleep. (Never mind that the drugs are dangerous—even deadly—especially when consumed with alcohol.)

Ambient music, a quite different branch of electronica, dates back to the seventies. Its early history

A rave is a huge dance party conducted in a large space: outdoors, an abandoned warehouse, or even a large club.

istockphoto.com

||||||||||||||||||||||||||||||||

"I'm probably more interested in Ford's robots than in Berry Gordy's music."
—Juan Atkins

includes Pink Floyd, Kraftwerk, and Tangerine Dream. The father of ambient music, though, is Brian Eno; his recording *Ambient I: Music for Airports* (1979) is seminal.

As its name suggests, ambient music is more atmospheric and less dance driven, with more attention to texture and less emphasis on rhythm. As a genre within electronica, it hasn't had a home, but it has merged with both house and techno, introducing a more varied sound world into both. In these hybrid genres, it began to catch on in the late eighties and early nineties.

Fueled in part by the growth of the club scene, a host of other styles have emerged in the nineties and the first years of the twenty-first century. The proliferation of styles came about not only through the combination and recombination of existing styles (such as "ambient house") but also through the absorption of outside influences, which led to an array of hardcore techno substyles. Electronica has begun to appear on the pop charts, in the music of acts such as Bjork, Chemical Brothers, and Moby.

Hearing Electronica

Dance music has defined a new performance paradigm for popular music. The nature of the venue—the dance club, rather than the arena, auditorium, night club, or coffeehouse—has fundamentally altered what is performed, how it's performed, how it's created, and how it's experienced.

The obvious difference, of course, is the use of recordings, rather than live musicians, to create the music being heard. That doesn't mean that there isn't the spontaneity and performer–crowd interaction that can be part of a live performance; it's just that it comes from a different source: the DJ.

The idea of stringing together a series of songs has a long history in popular music. From the thirties on, dance orchestras and small dance combos would occasionally play a **medley**, a group of songs connected by musical interludes. Often medleys were slow dance numbers; bands would play one chorus of each song rather than several choruses of one song. But they could be any tempo.

Medleys were harder to create in the moment during the early years of the rock era, because the identity of a song was more comprehensive. It was more than just the melody and harmony; it included every aspect of the song as preserved on the recording. It was more difficult to alter songs so that one would flow easily into the next. Still, the idea of connecting songs did not disappear, as landmark albums such as *Sgt. Pepper* and *The Dark Side of the Moon* evidence.

However, it wasn't until disco that the idea of creating medleys resurfaced, in a much updated form. It was the DJ who transformed the practice of connecting songs into an art. A DJ with a two-turntable setup was able to **mix** a series of songs into a **set**, an unbroken string of songs that could last longer than even the most extended Grateful Dead jam.

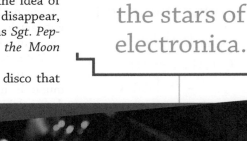

The art of the DJ begins with music that he or she selects. For this reason, many DJs create their own music; it helps them develop a signature style. In performance—in the dance club—skilled DJs string together a series of dance tracks with seamless transitions. It is not just that they blend one record into the next without dropping a beat—unless they plan to. They orchestrate the sequence of songs, how much they'll use of each song, and the kind of transition they'll use to give a sense of architecture to the set. It is in this context that they can respond to the dancers' energy, building to a climactic moment or moments as the set unfolds.

In the discussion of rock and rhythm and blues in the sixties, we noted that the record had become the document, the fullest and most direct expression of the musicians' creative intent. This changes in dance music. The musical unit is no longer the *recording*—which is seldom if ever played in its entirety—but the *set*. The recording is the raw material for the set; recordings are the building blocks—much as riffs are the building blocks of so many songs.

This in turn changes the nature of a dance track. It isn't just that it's music for dancing. Instead, the dance track is often created with the idea that it is a component of a larger structure—the set—rather than an entity complete unto itself—the song. This is a radical departure from mainstream rock; rock gave the song an integrity that it could not have had in earlier generations.

Moreover, music for club use employs a different sonic spectrum. Since the early sixties, popular music designed for airplay concentrates on mid-range frequencies because these come across better on radio than high or low frequencies do. By contrast, dance clubs typically have good sound systems, so producers can take advantage of the entire range of audible frequencies. Electronica styles typically make full use of this, especially low-end frequencies.

This combination of a full sonic spectrum and relentless dance beat, all in an enclosed space, produces a kind of sensory inundation. It is virtually the opposite extreme of sensory deprivation, and it seems to have many of the same mind-altering consequences.

Jovana Cetkovic/istockphoto.com

Electronica and Dance Music

We hear an influential example of electronica: "Nude Photo" by Rhythim Is Rhythim (Derrick May, b. 1963), is a good early sample of Detroit techno. "Nude Photo" establishes a characteristic techno groove almost immediately. The heart of it is the beat: a bass drum–like sound on every beat, a strong backbeat, and a fast-moving percussion part. Layered over that is some more melodic material: complicated, syncopated synthesizer figures, one in mid-range and two in a lower register.

> DJs are
> the stars of
> electronica.

After the track gets underway, a slow-moving melodic fragment comes in and out. There is some variety: a short rap-like vocal, some other vocal sounds, addition and subtraction of the various layers, some new versions of the melodic figures toward the end. These are the musical counterparts to the disco ball—rotating, and slightly different because of that, but essentially the same throughout. The track begins and ends abruptly; one can imagine it as part of a mix where we would never hear beginning or end.

"Nude Photo,"
Derrick May
(1987). Rhythim
Is Rhythim.

This example can only hint at the range of sounds, rhythms, and textures possible within the world of electronica. Still, it highlights key features of the genre: a steadily marked beat at about 120 beats per minute; rich, complex textures featuring electronically generated percussive and pitched sounds; very little singing; subtle changes within a generally repetitive, modularly constructed form; and little sense of beginning or end.

These tracks are not telling a story; rather, they're sustaining a mood.

Electronica has been the most faceless music of the last twenty-five years. Its creators work anonymously in studios—often alone—and assume aliases: Aphex Twin is Richard James; Rhythim Is Rhythim is Derrick May. The music they produce—largely instrumental and without the melodic points of entry common to other kinds of popular music—does little to encourage the listener to identify with them in the same way that they would identify with the lead singer or lead guitarist of a rock band. In many ways, this recalls the structure of the music business at the turn of the previous century, when largely anonymous songwriters turned out reams of songs for Tin Pan Alley publishers. For the most part, DJs are the stars of electronica, but it is a very localized form of stardom. However, there are signs that the music, as a genre, is beginning to develop a larger audience and a more mainstream presence.

Rap

Several years ago, students at the university where I was teaching asked me to participate in a discussion titled "Is rap music?" To get the discussion started, one of the students read a definition of music. As it turned out, rap wouldn't have been music according to the dictionary definition. However, at no time in the discussion did anyone challenge the question itself. For me, the correct answer to the question "Is rap music?" is simply "It doesn't matter." Rap is rap.

Rap is a form of creative expression that uses musical sounds to help get its message across. (Indeed, one could argue convincingly that the rap video is the first total-arts genre, because it combines poetry, drama, visual arts, dancing, and music.) Whether it is music should be a nonissue, as it is to the millions who enjoy it.

Forerunners of Rap

The practice of talking over a musical accompaniment has a long history in popular music. Al Jolson used to talk over instrumental statements of the melody in the twenties; bluesmen and contemporary folk artists like Woody Guthrie would routinely strum and

5 to Listen For
"Nude Photo"

INSTRUMENTATION
All sounds except for vocal fragments are generated electronically: drum machines and synthesizers use a variety of timbres.

RHYTHM
Moderately fast beat (about 120 beats per minute); 16-beat rhythm with a strong beat (bass drum–like sound) and a stronger backbeat

RHYTHM
Most other rhythms (pitched and percussive synthesized sounds) move at 16-beat speed; riffs and patterns map onto a rhythm moving four times the beat speed. Lots of syncopation; variation in beat keeping.

MELODY
Pitched lines are melodic in the sense that they have a contour and do not outline chords. They are not tuneful: low and midrange patterns are too jagged and syncopated to sing; the high synthesizer line is singable but repetitive.

TEXTURE
Dense, layered texture is made up of percussive and pitched patterns. Variation in texture as parts leave and return is a main source of interest.

5 to Remember
"Nude Photo"

WHERE'S THE BAND?
Except for voice clips, all sounds are electronically generated; no one "plays" an instrument.

MIXING
In a dance club "Nude Photo" would be part of a seamless mix; neither beginning nor end would be heard.

NEW WAY OF MAKING MUSIC
No one has to perform in real time at any stage in the creation of the music.

RHYTHIM'S RHYTHM
"Nude Photo" mixes obvious beat keeping and the backbeat with several layers of active, often complex rhythms.

MANIC MINIMALISM
"Nude Photo" is high-energy music with little variation or change.

talk. Within the popular tradition, the practice of reciting poetry over a musical accompaniment goes back to the fifties, when Beat poets like Kenneth Rexroth presented their work backed by a jazz combo. Somewhat later, black poets like Amiri Bakara (LeRoi Jones) often delivered their work with jazz in the background. In the sixties, acts as different as Bob Dylan and James Brown delivered words that were both rhymed and rhythmic, using a vocal style that fell somewhere between everyday speech and singing. However, the most direct antecedent of rap was the toasting of the Jamaican DJs who ran mobile sound systems and kept up a steady stream of patter as they changed discs. Another source of rap, this one closer to home, was George Clinton's funk; we heard a proto-rap at the beginning of "Tear the Roof Off the Sucker (Give Up the Funk)."

Rap and African American Culture. There are numerous parallels between the Mississippi Delta in the first half of the twentieth century and the South Bronx in the latter half. Both regions are heavily black. Both are heartbreakingly poor; there is either no work or work at such low pay that one cannot make ends meet. They are violent, even lawless places. Health and living conditions are closer to life in a Third World country than the suburbs of New York or Memphis: out-of-wedlock children born to young teens; rats and roaches everywhere; segregated, underfunded schools, where the playground may become a battleground.

There are differences, of course. The Delta was—and is—rural. Geography, prejudice, and poverty kept the people who lived there thoroughly isolated from mainstream culture. The South Bronx is urban. Fifth Avenue in Manhattan is a short subway ride away. But it might as well have been another world for those who lived in the ghetto. In effect, there has been, in both cases, an invisible barrier that has prohibited meaningful contact between blacks and whites. However, television brought the rich and famous into the living rooms of South Bronx residents; they had a much sharper sense of what they didn't have than their Delta counterparts.

Both are depressing, demoralizing environments, environments that can suck hope out of one's mind, body, and spirit. So it is a testament to the resiliency of African Americans and the vitality of their culture that the Delta and the South Bronx have been home to two of the most vital, important, and influential forms of artistic expression to emerge in the twentieth century. Just as the Delta is the spiritual home of the blues, the South Bronx is home to rap.

Ask those who listen to rap what draws them to it. Chances are they'll say, "It's real." Like the blues, the realness of rap is not just in what it says, but in how it says it. Rap gives us a window into life in the ghetto: the good, the bad, the ugly ... and the beautiful. There is humor; bleak visions of the past, present, and future; posturing; misogyny and responses to it; slices of gang life and pleas to bring an end to it; brutal depictions of current conditions and forceful demands for action. Like other roots music—blues, folk, country—this is music by and for its constituency. That rap has found a much wider audience is incidental to its original mission. The power comes from its emotional urgency: as with the blues, we can feel it's real. It has an edge, in words and sound.

> **"Just as the Delta is the spiritual home of the blues, the South Bronx is home to rap."**

Doug Schneider/istockphoto.com

Rap is a contemporary instance of a popular style's speaking to and for its audience. In a 1992 *Newsweek* article, Public Enemy's Chuck D called rap "Black America's CNN." In his view, it provides information and opinions for the inner city, viewpoints not available through conventional media. Chuck D feels that rap and rap videos give whites exposure to a side of black life that they could not get short of living in a ghetto.

Rap and Hip-Hop. Rap emerged as one artistic dimension of **hip-hop** culture, along with break dancing and graffiti. All three were unconventional forms of expression that required considerable skill and preparation. **Break dancing** is extremely athletic; its vigorous moves parallel the energy of the music to which it's performed. Graffiti artists prepared their work much like a military campaign. They would plan the graffito through a series of sketches, scout out the train yards, sneak in and paint the cars, then sneak out. Their use of trains and buses as "canvases" suggests that graffiti was another way to get their message out of the ghetto.

Rap emerged as one artistic dimension of hip-hop culture, along with break dancing and graffiti.

There is a kind of defiance built into all three: rap, graffiti art, and break dancing. The implicit message is "You can put us down, but you can't keep us down." You—the man, the establishment—can subject us to subhuman living conditions. You can ignore us. But you can't break our spirit. We can create something that comes from us, not you, and you can't do what we do, even though you want to. (Keep in mind that before Eminem there was Vanilla Ice.)

Grandmaster Flash: Messages and Techniques

Among the pioneers was Grandmaster Flash. Flash (born Joseph Saddler, 1958) was born in Barbados but moved with his family to the Bronx at a young age. He grew up with passionate interests in his father's jazz records and electronics, which he merged as a budding DJ at block parties and in public parks.

> In the twentieth century, there have been three groups of musicians who have routinely assumed performing aliases: rappers, rural bluesmen, and calypsonians. For every Grandmaster Flash, Ice-T, or Notorious B.I.G., there were bluesmen like Lead Belly, Lightnin' Hopkins, and Howlin' Wolf, and calypsonians such as Attila the Hun, Lord Kitchener, and Mighty Sparrow.

Inspired by Kool Herc, the first great hip-hop DJ, Flash developed the array of turntable techniques that would revolutionize rap. Even more significantly, he translated these techniques into a radically new musical conception: the **sound collage**. In the visual arts, an artist creating a collage assembles found materials (artifacts such as print materials, photographs, or machine parts) or natural objects (such as seashells, flowers, or leaves) into a work of art. The collage can consist exclusively of the preexisting materials, or it can be integrated into the work of the artist. What the visual artist does with found materials, Flash did with sound. In effect, he cut and pasted sound clips from recordings into his music. The clips could range in length from a fraction of a second to several seconds; in either case, Flash completely recontextualized them.

The first song in which he showcased these skills was "The Adventures of Grandmaster Flash and the Wheels of Steel," which he recorded with the Furious Five, featuring Melle Mel (Melvin Glover) and ex–Sugarhill Gang percussionist Duke Bootee (Ed Fletcher). The song, a minor R&B hit in 1981, included excerpts from Chic's "Good Times," Blondie's "Rapture," and Queen's "Another One Bites the Dust," as well as samples from other songs and sources; it would become a textbook for the creative possibilities of sampling. This was a radical transformation of the age-old practice of musical quotation. Instead of inserting snippets of melody, Flash mixed in the entire musical event as preserved on record.

"The Message," Grandmaster Flash (1982).

Flash's other major contributions came with "The Message," which reached No. 4 on the R&B charts in 1982 and also crossed over to the pop charts. It was innovative in both subject and setting. "The Message" presents a brutal picture of life in the ghetto. Its impact begins with the rap itself, which describes the oppressive and parlous circumstances of everyday life for those who live there. Another noteworthy feature was the "arrest" at the end of the track, a "slice of life" interpolation that interrupts the musical accompaniment for several seconds. When the accompaniment resumes, it is as if the arrest were barely a blip on the radar screen—a virtual nonevent in the ongoing misery of life in the ghetto. Such real-life nonmusical sounds were not an innovation with rap; in rock-era music they date back at least to the Beatles. However, rap captured more powerful clips and used them more extensively. Both the rap and the arrest scene convey a much more serious message. With "The Message,"

5 to Listen For
"The Message"

INSTRUMENTATION
Rapping (no singing) plus electronically generated pitched and percussive sounds

RHYTHM
16-beat rhythms kept mainly in the rap; no consistent time keeping in the instrumental setting except for strong backbeat

RHYTHM
Clave-like syncopation in rap "chorus"

MELODY
Melodic material: repeated synthesizer riffs

TEXTURE
Open texture with wide registral gaps between bass and high synthesizer riff

3 to Remember
"The Message"

DEPRESSING ACCOUNT
Lyrics paint a dismal picture of ghetto life.

EMPHASIS ON RHYTHM
Rap plus repetitive riffs and percussion sounds; no melodic development but rhythmic interest

BLEAK MUSICAL SETTING
Open texture—high synth riff, low bass, other percussion/riffs/rap in mid-range; repeated riffs (they go nowhere musically) reinforce bleak message of rap.

rap graduated from party music to serious social commentary.

The other major innovation in "The Message" is the coordination of the musical setting with the message of the rap. There are many layers of activity, most of it generated on synthesizers and drum machines. The most prominent are the strong backbeat and the high synthesizer riff, the closest thing to melodic material on the entire track. However, none of the many layers establishes a consistent, active rhythm: the bass part, percussive guitar-like mid-range part, and the multiple percussion parts dart in and out of the texture; the overall effect evokes James Brown's music, but it is much emptier sounding than the textures typically heard in his music. The 16-beat rhythm that is implicit in the instrumental sections becomes explicit only when the rap begins. An abrupt change in the rhythm of the rap, from the 16-beat stream to a variant of the clave pattern, signals the arrival at the "chorus": "Don't push me cuz I'm close to the edge."

The spare, widely spaced sounds, and the way the synthesizer riff trails off seem to communicate the desolation of the ghetto environment; the lack of change in the setting seems to imply

the difficulties faced in ameliorating this depressing environment.

Rap crossed over to the mainstream with Run-D.M.C.'s version of "Walk This Way." As with earlier rap songs, "Walk This Way" built the rap on a preexisting musical foundation, in this case, Aerosmith's 1976 hit "Walk This Way." The new twist was that Aerosmith members Steven Tyler and Joe Perry participated in the recording session. This new version made the charts exactly a decade after the original, in 1986. A year later, LL Cool J and the Beastie Boys (who were signed to Def Jam Records, the most prominent rap label) found the charts; with their emergence, rap burst out of the ghetto and into the 'burbs.

Public Enemy: Rap as a Political Music

Among the major rap acts of the late eighties and nineties was Public Enemy. The group's key figures were Chuck D (born Carlton Ridenhour, 1960), Flavor Flav (born William Drayton, 1959), and DJ Terminator X (born Norman Rogers, 1966). They surrounded themselves with a substantial posse, some of whom contributed to their work.

"1 Million Bottlebags," Ridenhour/ Robertz/ Rinaldo/ Depper (1991). Public Enemy.

Public Enemy was the most political of the rap acts to emerge during the late eighties. Their look rekindled memories of the black radicals from the sixties: paramilitary uniforms, Black Panther evocations, fake Uzis carried by their entourage as they appeared on stage. The look was the smaller part of the equation. Far more telling were the raps themselves.

Public Enemy circa 1990

Public Enemy's Chuck D called rap "Black America's CNN."

5 to Listen For
"1 Million Bottlebags"

INSTRUMENTATION
Rap, electronic percussion, synthesizer, "found" sounds

RHYTHM
Aggressive 16-beat rhythm, reinforced by rap and percussion

RHYTHM
Syncopated synthesizer chords and riffs, mainly in chorus.

MELODY
Melodic fragments highlight chorus-like sections

TEXTURE
Main focus rap and percussive sounds; other sounds, low and high, are intermittent

3 to Remember
"1 Million Bottlebags"

EQUAL-OPPORTUNITY DENUNCIATION
Rap indicts both the abusers and the producers of alcohol: the former for their unwillingness to clean up, the latter for targeting the black community in their advertising.

RICH SOUND WORLD
Five different sound sources: rap, spoken elements, real-world sounds, percussion sounds, and pitched sounds—the siren-like sounds and the synthesizer chords

RAP, RHYTHM, AND MESSAGE
Rap delivery and rhythm create a 16-beat rhythm at a fast tempo, which conveys the anger and frustration of the rap; so do aggressive sounds (percussion sounds, siren).

In "1 Million Bottlebags," a track from their 1991 album *Apocalypse 91 … The Enemy Strikes Black*, Public Enemy takes on everyone. The rap is an indictment of alcohol abuse. It takes on all of those responsible for the problem—not only those who consume it and can't stop, but also the companies that prey on blacks by advertising their liquor products heavily in the ghetto. The language is powerful and direct; it is from the street. The frustration and anger behind it are palpable.

The rap begins with a collage of sounds: a bottle breaking, a "news bulletin" about target advertising by liquor companies in the black communities, the rhythm track, the sound of beer (or malt liquor) being poured, a beer belch, then horn-like synthesizer chords. The rap begins. Sirens and more prominent rhythm sounds signal the arrival of a chorus-like section. The end of the track simulates changing stations on a radio. Juxtaposed are a long statement about the immorality of making money off the impoverished and a scathing critique of the way in which racist corporate types dismiss the problem.

There are five kinds of sounds here: the rap, the spoken elements, the real-world sounds (for example, the bottle breaking), the rhythm tracks, and the pitched sounds, such as the siren screeches that mark the chorus. Collectively, they amplify the message of the rap through the sharp juxtaposition of sounds and images. The siren screeches are at once a musical sound—a two-note riff—and an evocation of a too-familiar real-life sound. There is complexity in the density of information, which matches the multiple levels of commentary.

The rhythm track, which combines a strong backbeat with interlocked patterns that collectively mark the 16-beat rhythm, serves several purposes. It is the glue that holds the track together, through the changes of voice, the spoken clips, and other sounds. It reinforces the delivery of the rap. Because both move at 16-beat speed, the percussion sounds give the rap support and strength. And it creates a groove: even more than in funk, you can move to the groove even as you take in the message.

"1 Million Bottlebags" is even less melodic than "The Message." The only easily identifiable melodic elements are the siren-like sound and the repeated chord; in both cases, the same pitch is repeated again and again. The absence of melody is a strength, not a shortcoming. Its presence would dilute the impact of the rap. It would soften the edge that is present everywhere else: in the delivery of the rap, in the rhythm track and other musical sounds, and in the sound clips.

The moral high ground staked out by Public Enemy in tracks like "1 Million Bottlebags" was undermined by incidents such as the 1989 *Washington Post* interview with Professor Griff (born Richard Griffin, 1960), Public Enemy's "minister of information," in which he made numerous provocatively anti-Semitic remarks, including claiming that Jews were responsible for the majority of wickedness that goes on throughout the world. It was the most flagrant of several anti-Semitic public incidents in Public Enemy's career; others included an endorsement of Nation of Islam leader Louis Farrakhan. The controversy surrounding such incidents created dissension within the group and a sudden decline in their fortunes. By 1993 Chuck D put the group's career on hold; he would revive Public Enemy later in the decade, where they recaptured some of the success that they had previously enjoyed. Still, their most substantial contribution came in the late eighties and early nineties; more than any other group of the era, they made rap relevant—the black CNN—to both blacks and nonblacks and created sound worlds that amplified the impact of the lyrics.

Mainstreaming Rap: The Case of Gangsta Rap

In rap the boundary between life and art is all but invisible. The work of rappers often comes directly from their life experiences; the raps may simply document them.

Nowhere has this been more evident than in gangsta rap. **Gangsta rap**, which emerged in the latter part of the eighties, brought the violence of inner-city life into the music and out into the world. A visual image of this life was the 1988 film *Colors,* starring Robert Duvall and Sean Penn as police officers trying to control violence between the Bloods and the Crips, two rival Los Angeles gangs. Ice-T, among the first of the gangsta rappers, recorded the title track of the film.

Tupac Shakur, M. C. Hammer, and Snoop Doggy Dogg

Although Schoolly D, a Philadelphia-based rapper, is credited with the rap that sparked the genre (the 1986 single "P.S.K."), gangsta rap has been perceived as a West Coast phenomenon because of the success of rap artists and groups such as N.W.A. and Ice-T, then Dr. Dre (a former N.W.A. member), Snoop Doggy Dogg, M. C. Hammer, and 2Pac (Tupac Shakur). The success of these groups escalated the territorial animosity from rival gangs within a community to the communities themselves. Bad blood developed between West Coast gangsta rappers and New York hip-hop artists; both groups used lyrics to dis the opposing camp. The violence portrayed in the lyrics often spilled over into real life. Snoop Doggy Dog and Tupac Shakur were among the notable gangsta rap artists who served jail time ("California Love" was Shakur's first recording after his release from jail); the shooting deaths of Shakur and Notorious B.I.G. are commonly regarded as gang retribution for earlier offenses.

The violence was not the only controversial aspect of the music. Raps were often pornographic and misogynistic, and richly scatological. Most recordings routinely earned the "parental advisory" label from the RIAA (Recording Industry Association of America). For suburban whites, gangsta rap must have seemed like forbidden fruit; the genre would enjoy a large following among whites, most of whom experienced the rappers' world only vicariously.

Although its audience had grown steadily throughout the late eighties and early nineties, gangsta rap crossed over to the mainstream in large part because of a musical decision: to work pop elements into hardcore rap in an effort to give the music more widespread appeal. It first appeared in the music of New York hip-hop artists such as Notorious B.I.G. and Nas and quickly spread to the west coast: Tupac Shakur's "California Love," which topped the pop, R&B, and rap charts in 1996, epitomizes this new approach.

Tupac Shakur. If ever an artist seemed destined to live and die by the sword, it would be Tupac Shakur

"California Love," Tupac Shakur (1996). Tupac Shakur and Dr. Dre.

(1971–1996). His parents were active in the Black Panthers; his mother was acquitted on a conspiracy charge only a month before Shakur's birth; his father is currently incarcerated in Florida; and others close to his mother during his childhood were either in and out of prison or fugitives.

What made his too-short life doubly tragic was the terrible conflict between the sensitive and violent sides of his personality. He was intelligent and curious—reading Machiavelli during his prison term—and creative and multitalented, with obvious gifts as an actor, poet, dancer, and musician. Yet in his personal and professional lives, he gave vent to the violent side: run-ins with the law, a sexual abuse lawsuit, and scandal. "Hit 'Em Up" was a personal attack on Notorious B.I.G.; in it, he claimed to have slept with B.I.G.'s wife. That his life would end prematurely as a result of the ultimate violent act seems in retrospect almost a foregone conclusion.

Shortly before his death, Shakur recorded "California Love" with Dr. Dre for Death Row Records, the label headed by Suge Knight, who was also repeatedly in trouble with the law. The opening scene and the action during the song itself seem inspired by the Mad Max films: they purport to present a desolate, lawless world a hundred years in the future. Although it is skillfully produced, the video has no obvious thematic connection with the song, which is very much in the present—the "'95" that Dr. Dre mentions is clearly 1995, and Tupac's first words are "out on bail/ fresh outta jail." Both the video and the song evidence the mutation of rap from an outsiders' music flourishing in inner-city parks to a big business.

The song shows how rap found a mainstream audience by bringing in non-rap elements. It begins with a striking processed vocal riff; the instrumental introduction that follows spotlights the bass. The next section features a tuneful melody with a rich accompaniment; this becomes the main chorus of the song. The chorus returns after Dr. Dre's rap. It is followed by another sung section, "Shake it," which gives way to Tupac's rap.

The rap lyrics offer a sizeable dose of gangsta rap posturing. There are references to violence, gangs, prostitution, money, clothes, and jewelry. But the prevailing mood, in both words and music, is party hard, because "we keep it rockin'!" Especially in the chorus, it sounds more like a promo for the chamber of commerce than an incitement to riot.

Jim Smeal/Getty Images

5 to Listen For
"California Love"

INSTRUMENTATION
Vocals, raps, synthesized percussion, bass, and chord-instrument sounds, "natural" percussion sounds (cowbell, whistle)

PERFORMANCE STYLE
Electronic modification of sung vocal parts

RHYTHM
16-beat rhythm kept in percussion and rap; other rhythms moving more slowly.

MELODY
Sung chorus built from repetitive riff frames raps

TEXTURE
Rhythmically dense, melody-rich texture with heavy bass, high mid-range percussion and synth chords, vocal in between, plus active high-range synthesizer riffs

3 to Remember
"California Love"

RAP + MELODY = CROSSOVER SUCCESS
Sung chorus plus instrumental melodic fragments underneath sung vocals and raps

SLICE OF CALIFORNIA LIFE
Raps mix a salute to California with personal remarks: jail, jewelry, clothes, and the obligatory commentary on street life.

RICH SOUND WORLD
Imaginative instrumental and vocal sounds, collage-like melodic fragments, and dense, active rhythms create rich, constantly varying sound world, far richer and more interesting musically than previous two raps.

instrument. In rap, it has become the dominant instrument, period. This sound—strong, freely moving bass and active percussion—distills the most characteristic elements of black music to their essence and pushes them into the forefront, much as the saturated rock rhythm played by a punk rock band reduces, intensifies, and projects the most basic elements of rock rhythm and sound.

In particular, the bass sound, made dark and fat by stripping away the overtones so that only low-frequency sounds remain, is a logical extension of the dark sound of electric blues. Electric blues made rural blues darker by adding a bass instrument and guitar riffs in a low register; the characteristic bass-driven sound of rap simply continues this progression.

In "California Love" we hear this essential sound by itself for about seven seconds. During the course of the song, the other elements of the song—vocal choruses, raps, and other instrumental sound—cover over this foundation, which continues through the song. Especially in light of the fact that the more tuneful elements were added as a conscious effort to enhance the appeal of the style, the effect of this short interlude is striking; it is as if we get a glimpse of a public figure in an unguarded moment and see him as he really is, not as he portrays himself.

The rich texture created by the numerous melodic fragments and sustained chords are an important source of the enormous crossover appeal of the song. It makes the song more accessible and more familiar, and there is more to connect to—not only the two raps and the beat, but also the melodies and the sound variety. The strategy to mainstream rap through melody succeeded on both coasts, and it has remained a common practice up until the present.

Fortunately for Death Row Records, Shakur had recorded a substantial amount of unreleased material. Six albums were released posthumously, the last in 2004. All went platinum. His legacy extends beyond his recordings. Following his death, his mother, Afeni Shakur, established the Tupac Amaru Shakur Foundation to "provide training and support for students who aspire to enhance their creative talents."

The Messages of Rap. Gangsta rap has been the most visible rap style since the late eighties, because of its appeal and because of its notoriety, but it is only one of many rap styles to emerge during this period. Because it

Its most surprising feature, and undoubtedly one of its most appealing features, is its melodic and textural richness. The vocal melodies are the most apparent evidence of this, but woven into the texture behind both the sung sections and the raps are lush synthesizer harmonies and multiple fragments of melody. The return of the chorus features even more supplementary melodic activity, both vocal and instrumental. Almost all of this activity, and especially the synthesizer chords and lines, occurs in middle and high register, above the vocal range of the rap. This counterbalances the characteristic dark bass sound that runs throughout the song.

Additionally, several layers of percussion sounds mark the backbeat and 16-beat rhythms or play against these regular rhythms; the whistle stands out as a source of rhythmic play. The rhythmic texture of the song is even denser than that heard on "1 Million Bottlebags," although the tempo is considerably slower.

The sound world of the song, and the genre, is defined most fundamentally in the brief instrumental interlude just after the title-phrase riff. For a brief moment, there is only the active bass line and several percussion sounds, most prominently the high-pitched percussion sound marking the 16-beat rhythm. It is a sound that we associate with rap; we hear it above everything else emanating from car stereos. In Motown, soul, seventies black pop, and funk, the bass is the dominant rhythm is so integral to hip-hop culture, it may be hard to divorce rap from its trappings and particularly the baggage that it carries: the controversial pronouncements, the violent world it portrays and realizes, and the hedonistic lifestyle it often projects. So it is not surprising that rap, like so many other genres with aggressive postures and outsider status (heavy metal, punk, techno), has gotten its share of bad press. Its critics focus on the language, the lifestyle, the lyrics, and the emergence of substyles like gangsta rap to condemn the entire genre. There is no denying rap's edge; the speed and tone of the rap and the busy rhythms underneath virtually guarantee it.

However, the act of rapping is inherently value neutral. It can be, and has been, used to deliver a variety of messages—not only dark gray portraits of life in the 'hood and expletive-filled rants but also humor and hope. Whether the message is negative or positive depends on the content, not the genre. A case in point: Christian rap (or, more alliteratively, holy hip-hop) also emerged in the nineties. The music of groups such as the Gospel Gangstaz sends a message far different from that heard in "California Love," "Hit 'Em Up," and other gangsta rap tracks.

At the beginning of the twenty-first century, rap—in all of its manifestations—is an enduring and significant part of the rock-era musical world. The numerous rap/rock syntheses—such as rapcore, rap rock, and rap metal—offer one more indication of its strong presence in popular music. At the same time, some have looked back almost nostalgically to "old school," the rap from the late seventies and eighties, when the message, whether it talked about good times or bad, seemed purer.

● ● ● ● ● ● ● ●

Looking Back, Looking Ahead

The common features of the music considered in this chapter offer compelling evidence of the way electronica and rap, arguably the two most progressive musical styles since 1980, have moved beyond rock. Here are key differences:

- 16-beat rhythms, instead of a rock beat
- A good beat of far greater complexity because of the more active rhythms and a richer texture
- Electronic instruments and samples instead of a core rhythm section of guitar, bass, and drums
- Few if any sung riffs and no melody to speak of; no hooks in a sung chorus or in a lead guitar part

And while there is a sense of verse/chorus form in the three rap songs and recurring musical ideas in the techno track, there is little sense of arriving at the chorus and highlighting it with a memorable melodic hook.

Moreover, the very *idea* of a song as a fixed, discrete document contained on a recording comes under attack in both styles. Tracks like "Nude Photo" are just a single element in a DJ's mix. And in both techno and rap, remixing songs into new or alternate versions is standard practice. Electronic sounds, percussive effects, and more active rhythms would infiltrate pop, rock, and rhythm and blues in the 1980s, as we hear in the musical examples in Chapter 15.

● ● ● ● ● ● ● ●

Terms to Know

Test your knowledge of this chapter's important terms by defining the ones listed here. If you can't recall the meaning of a certain term, refresh your memory by looking up the boldfaced term in the chapter, turning to the Glossary at the back of the book, or working with the flashcards at the Popular Music Resource Center.

audio CD	rave
MIDI (Musical Instrument Digital Interface)	ambient music
	medley
sequencer	mix
loop	set
sample	rap
electronica	hip-hop
musique concrète	break dancing
house music	sound collage
techno	gangsta rap

Beyond Rock

The 1980s

CHAPTER

15

istockphoto.com

Joel Whitburn is the guru of the *Billboard* charts. He heads Record Research, a company he founded to collect and publish chart information, and has published about 100 reference books. Whitburn developed a complex rating system to evaluate commercial success of rock-era acts based on chart performance. By his measure, the top ten acts on the album charts of the seventies and eighties were:

	1970s	1980s
1	Elton John	Prince
2	Chicago	Michael Jackson
3	Paul McCartney and Wings	Bruce Springsteen
4	The Bee Gees	Whitney Houston
5	The Rolling Stones	Madonna
6	Eagles	The Rolling Stones
7	Fleetwood Mac	Billy Joel
8	Led Zeppelin	The Police
9	Carole King	U2
10	Bob Dylan	John Mellencamp

Whitburn's system is only one way to measure popularity. Still, his data prompt us to ask: Where's the rock?

● ● ● ● ● ● ● ● ●

Beyond Rock

The seventies list is dominated by white male acts. The only exception is Carole King, and there are no minorities. By contrast, only one of the top five acts of the eighties is a white male. The Rolling Stones are the only act to appear on the list for both decades—improbably, not because of the music but because of their lifestyle. The music of Billy Joel ranges far beyond conventional rock. U2 and the Police created new sounds based on the sounds and rhythms of late 1970s music. The new act closest to the core rock sounds of the late sixties and early seventies was John Mellencamp; even Springsteen consistently incorporated the new sounds of the eighties into his music.

Rock-era music entered a new phase in the eighties. Unlike the music of the early seventies, which seems in many respects a continuation of the music of the late 1960s, much of the music of the eighties sounds as if it could not have been created before 1980. Two reasons for this development stand out. One was the use of sounds and rhythms that were not common currency, or even available, in the early seventies. The other was the integration of style elements from "outsider" styles into pop, rock, and rhythm and blues.

Advances in electronic synthesis opened up a broad new palette of sounds to the musicians of the 1980s. Digital sound generation made both the replication of existing timbres and the creation of new timbres easier; it also streamlined the enhancement of conventional sounds through various effects. As a result, music that did not incorporate synthesized sounds became the exception rather than the rule. These sounds are integral to the distinctive styles of acts as diverse as U2 and Madonna.

The music of the eighties also stands out because of new rhythms. Three were widely used: the energized rock beat derived from punk; adaptations of the afterbeat rhythms of reggae; and, most commonly, the 16-beat rhythms first heard in funk, black pop, and disco. These took various forms, often in combination, as in the relentlessly pulsing rhythms in the music of U2 and the syncopated, dance-oriented rhythms in Madonna's music. As a result, the timeless rock groove of the Stones and others was less common in the middle-ground music of the eighties than these new, more active rhythms.

Fusions

Punk and disco seem about as easy to blend as oil and water. As they emerged in the late seventies, they seemed to demarcate contrasting ideologies and musical approaches. Punk was real, whereas disco, as experienced in a club, was an escape into a timeless world. Punk was about grit; disco was about glitter. Punk was performed by live bands on conventional rock instruments, hammering out a concentrated rock rhythm; disco was performed by DJs mixing a string of recordings, most of which combined a strong beat with active 16-beat rhythms. The lyrics of punk songs usually said something; disco lyrics often descended into banality.

> " Punk and disco seem about as easy to blend as oil and water. "

However, in *Christgau's Record Guide*, a 1990 survey of 3,000 recordings from the eighties, Robert Christgau, the "dean of American rock critics," cited "post-punk/post-disco fusion" as a key development of the decade. He described a synthesis of the two in **DOR**, or **dance-oriented rock**, an umbrella term used by DJs in 1980s disco pools to identify an array of eighties styles. Because pools helped spur the sale of nonradio records, some acts made sure there were dance-oriented tracks on their albums.

The fusion of disparate inside/outside styles was nothing new in rock; it had been common practice from the start. However, the innovations resulting from the fusions of the eighties were different from those of the previous generation, for at least three reasons. First, the eighties was the first generation of rock music (and, for that matter, twentieth-century popular music) that was not nurtured by the blues; the final infusion of blues into popular music came in the late sixties. Second, the fusions did not involve blending rock or rhythm and blues with an established outside style, such as folk, blues, or jazz. Instead, the outside styles came from *within* rock-era music. Third, because of the blending of rock styles, the boundaries between rock, rhythm and blues, and pop became more fluid and transparent; the list of the top artists of the eighties hints at that.

Finally, another fusion profoundly affected the dissemination of music: the music video brought together sound, image, and movement into a newly emergent genre—the music video—that became a staple on a new network—MTV—in a new medium, cable television.

• • • • • • • •

MTV and Music Videos

Those who have grown up with hundreds of networks may find it difficult to imagine a time when television viewing options consisted almost exclusively of three networks: NBC, CBS, and ABC. Larger metropolitan areas had public television and a few independent stations, but until the early seventies most viewers had only the three major networks from which to choose.

Cable TV is almost as old as commercial broadcasting. The first cable TV services were launched in 1948; a well-situated antenna brought television signals to homes in remote rural regions. There was some growth during the fifties and sixties, but cable TV as we currently know it didn't get off the ground until the latter part of the seventies. Two key developments—the launching of communications satellites and significant deregulation of the broadcast industry—made cable television economically viable.

Cable changed the economics of the television industry and transformed it in the process. Networks relied exclusively on advertising for their revenue; the signal was free. Cable TV services charged subscribers a fee and passed on a percentage of that fee to the channels that they offered their subscribers. This new source of revenue made possible the fragmentation of the television market. A network that could command only 1 or 2 percent of the market would have no chance for success against the major networks; but that same 1 or 2 percent of the cable market could provide enough income to make the network viable.

MTV. Among the first of these new cable networks was **MTV**. The network began broadcasting in 1981. Symbolically, the first music video that MTV broadcast was "Video Killed the Radio Star." The original format of the network was analogous to Top 40–style radio stations: videos replaced songs, and VJs (video jockeys) assumed a role similar to radio disc jockeys.

Perhaps because cable originally serviced mainly rural parts of the country, MTV took an AOR-type approach to programming. For the first couple of years, programming targeted a young, white audience. Bands were almost exclusively white—Duran Duran, a British pop group with a keen visual sense, was one of the early MTV bands. Black acts cried "racism" with some justification.

It was Michael Jackson who broke MTV's color barrier. The demand for his spectacular music videos—made in conjunction with his 1982 album *Thriller*—was so overwhelming that the network changed its policy.

The Cable Act of 1984 effectively deregulated the television industry. In its wake the cable industry wired the nation. With new revenues came new and improved programming. MTV started VH1 in 1985 and diversified its programming in several ways, adding documentaries, cartoons, and talk shows. In particular, its segments on rap helped bring it out of the inner city.

MTV has affected both consumers and creators. The network has become a key tastemaker for young people around the world. It has influenced not only what they

Symbolically, the first music video that MTV broadcast was "Video Killed the Radio Star."

istockphoto.com

listen to but also many other aspects of youth culture: dress, looks, body language, vocabulary, and attitudes. The fact of MTV has also reshaped the sound of pop, as we consider below.

Music Videos. Rock had been a look as well as a sound from the start. Elvis was a sensation on television, then in films. Other rock-and-roll stars made their way into films as well, although not as stars. The 1956 film *The Girl Can't Help It,* which starred Jayne Mansfield, featured Little Richard, Gene Vincent, and Fats Domino. The Beatles' breakthrough film feature, *A Hard Day's Night* (1964), showed the power of film to enhance music, especially when the visual element was so well in tune with the music and the spirit of the band.

In the late sixties, the idea of using videos as a promotional tool took hold. At the same time, live performances were captured on video or film. Documentaries of the 1967 Monterey Pop Festival and Woodstock in 1969 remain treasures. Further experiments, especially by new wave acts like Devo, moved closer to the integration of sound and image that characterizes contemporary music video. With the arrival of MTV, the music video became a key component of the music industry.

The music video inverted the conventional relationship among story, image, and sound. In musical theater and film musicals, songs were written for the story, ideally enhancing those moments when what the character felt was too much for mere words. In earlier music videos, the relationship was the opposite: the visual element was designed to enhance the song. Now the music video is such an essential component of pop success that acts create song and video as an integrated whole. In either form it is a relatively new expressive medium.

The most obvious, and most widely discussed, consequence of music videos was the suddenly increased emphasis on the look of an act, and the look of the video, as a determinant of success. The two artists who leveraged this new, integrated medium to gain overwhelming commercial success were Michael Jackson and Madonna.

● ● ● ● ● ● ● ●

Pop in the Eighties

The early eighties ushered in a new generation of pop stars. In many respects, their music was dramatically different from the music of the previous decade. Six qualities distinguish it:

- *It made gender, race, and sexual preference nonissues.* The eighties' leading acts were Michael Jackson, Prince, and Madonna. None of them are heterosexual, white

males. Other successful pop performers during that decade included Boy George, Cyndi Lauper, and Tina Turner.

- *It exploited new media resources.* Michael Jackson wasn't the first to make music videos, but he raised the music video to an art form. Video and film were essential in boosting both Prince and Madonna to superstardom; the three set the tone for the pop music videos of the next decades.

- *It brought back the multifaceted entertainer.* It was no longer enough to be just a good singer or musician; one had to be able to move well, although no one topped Michael Jackson in skill or imagination. Conversely, those who could present themselves well, dance expressively, and use the music video as a new meaningful medium could achieve stardom with more limited vocal ability.

- *It was a musical melting pot.* Although the new pop of the eighties and beyond connects most directly to the black pop tradition of the sixties and seventies, the music was certainly open to other influences: disco, punk, reggae, funk, Latin music, dance music, and rap.

- *Synthesizers played an increasingly important role in the sound of the music.* Some replaced guitars, basses, and conventional keyboards as the main sources of harmony; synthesized percussion sounds enriched, or even replaced, drum kits and other acoustic instruments; and sustained synth sounds put a lot of string players out of work.

- *It has been extraordinarily popular.* Michael Jackson's *Thriller* album easily surpassed the sales of the previous best-selling album. Prince and Madonna also had impressive sales figures. As rock critic Robert Christgau pointed out, the sheer sales volume of *Thriller* was part of its significance.

Precisely because its artists drew from so many sources, there has been no single "middle-ground" style. It has not been defined by a distinctive kind of beat keeping, like punk; or a rhythmic feel, like funk; or a special sound quality, like the distortion of heavy metal. Indeed, all three are used in middle-ground music. The opening of Prince's "When Doves Cry" or Eddie Van Halen's solo in Michael Jackson's "Beat It" are familiar examples of metal-style guitar playing.

Instead, it was a set of principles that defined the music that topped the charts during the eighties. The songs typically have intelligible lyrics that tell a story— usually about love or its absence or about a slice of life. They are set to a singable melody. The melody in turn is embedded in a rich, riff-laden texture; most layers—if not all—are played on synthesizers. The songs typically have a good beat—easy to find and danceable, neither too monotonous nor too ambiguous.

The Legacy of Motown: Michael Jackson

This set of principles is, more than anything else, an updated version of the Motown sound. The lyrics are more worldly, the rhythms are more complex, and synthesizers replace many of the conventional instruments. Novel elements, most notably rap, can give this more recent music a different sound. Still, the basic approach is clearly the same.

The Motown middle-ground connection extends beyond the music. The elaborate movement and dance captured on music videos upgrade the choreography of the Motown acts, and Motown's pyramid-like creative structure evolved into the elaborate production of post-eighties pop.

Berry Gordy's vision was a black pop style whose appeal transcended the black community. One branch of its legacy was the post-eighties pop middle ground marked out by Michael Jackson, which continues to flourish in the music of women and men of many races and ethnic heritages. Motown was not a force for social change during the sixties drive for civil rights. The very fact of Motown—the enduring appeal and popularity of the music—has helped bring us to a musical world where the boundaries between black and white—and Hispanic—are all but invisible and inaudible. This is in turn both cause and consequence of more open attitudes with regard to race and gender, not only in music but in society.

Michael Jackson is the direct link between the two traditions: as a member of The Jackson 5, he was part of the last great act in Motown's heyday. As a solo performer in the late seventies and early eighties, he helped define the new pop middle ground musically, revive the all-around performer, and establish the music video as a new, integrated mode of expression. Moreover, his dancing raised the bar to a virtually unattainable height. His growth as an artist parallels the evolution and transformation of the Motown paradigm into the new pop of the eighties.

Although only twenty-four when *Thriller* (1982) was released, Michael Jackson had been a professional entertainer for three-fourths of his life and a star for half of it. He had released solo singles in the early seventies, but Jackson's solo career didn't take off until 1978, when he starred in the film *The Wiz*. During the filming, he met composer/arranger/producer Quincy Jones, who collaborated with him on *Off the Wall* (1979), his first major album, and *Thriller*. Jones's skill and creativity proved to be the ideal complement to Jackson's abilities.

There are precedents for Michael Jackson's exuberant dancing in rock-era music: for example, Elvis's stage and film performances; the stylized choreography of the

"Thriller," Rod Temperton (1982). Michael Jackson, vocal.

Motown groups, including The Jackson 5; James Brown's stage shows, which featured "the hardest working man in show business" moving and grooving all over the stage; and the dance scenes in films like *Saturday Night Fever*. However, it was the musical that offered a more direct precedent for the integration of song, dance, and story. This connection is evident in the video of "Thriller": the group dance scene recalls the marvelous dance scenes in the film version of Leonard Bernstein's landmark musical *West Side Story*.

Michael Jackson was fortunate to be in the right place at the right time. MTV had gone on the air in 1981; *Thriller* was released a year later. Jackson helped transform the music video from a song-with-video into a mini-film that used a song as the focal point; for example, the video of "Thriller" is over twice the length of the track on the album. Jackson made it work through his dancing: no earlier rock-era performer had danced with his virtuosity and expressiveness.

The title track to *Thriller* shows the musical side of these changes. It is a long song by pop standards, in part because of the long buildup at the beginning and the voiceover at the end by Vincent Price, one of Hollywood's masters of the macabre. But the heart of the song is a Disneyesque version of scary. Michael's voice, the skillful orchestration, the security of the four-on-the-floor bass drum and heavy backbeat, and the busy rhythms all ensure a cartoonish kind of spooky music more reminiscent of *Scooby Doo* than of *Friday the 13th*. The video reinforces this as each of the nightmarish scenes dissolves into fiction. This isn't to say that it wasn't well done or that it didn't deserve its enormous popularity. But compared to the Black Sabbath version of a scary night, this one is safe—at least until the music drops out and Price has his last laugh—or Jackson's cat's eyes return.

"Thriller" also reveals several distinctive characteristics of post-1980 pop. One is the extensive use of electronic instruments in combination with conventional instruments. Among the most prominent electronic sounds are the repeated bass riff, the sustained harmonies behind Michael's vocals, and the brash chords of the opening, all played on synthesizers. The basic rhythm grows out of disco: we hear a strong backbeat, a relentless bass-drum thump on each beat, and several layers of percussion marking off a 16-beat rhythm. However, the other instrumental parts, especially those played on rhythm section instruments or their electronic counterparts, create a texture that is denser and more complex than that heard in a conventional disco song. (This is certainly appropriate, because the dancing of Jackson and his cohorts is more expressive and complex than social dancing to disco.) Jackson's vocal line is simply one strand in the texture; in the verse, it is in the forefront, but in the chorus sections the backup vocals and instruments playing the title-phrase riff all but drown him out. It floats on the busy rhythms and riffs that provide much of the song's momentum—indeed, in the video, the basic rhythm track sustains the flow through the graveyard scene, and, after a short break, through the first part of the extended dance number that is the heart of the video.

Although only three of the tracks were shot as music videos, all of the songs on *Thriller* have a distinct identity. There is considerable contrast from song to song, as the musical settings capture the tone and content of the lyric. For example, the hard-edged riffs that open "Wanna Be Startin' Somethin'" anticipate the lyric's schoolyard-style provocation. The punk-inspired beat and Eddie Van Halen's guitar underscore the message of "Beat It." The loping rhythm (a shuffle beat on top of a rock beat), the use of pre-rock pop harmony, and the soft synth sounds reinforce the friendly rivalry between Michael and Paul McCartney in "The Girl Is Mine." And a setting that mixes an open middle range—just a simple synthesizer riff—with the irritation of a persistent bass riff and percussion sound characterizes the emptiness of the groupie-style relationship in "Billie Jean." Both the songs and Quincy Jones's masterful settings give the album an expressive range that compensates for the one-dimensional quality of Jackson's singing.

There is no doubt that *Thriller* would have been a successful album without the videos. But it also seems certain that the videos, and the fact that the songs were so "video-ready," played a crucial role in its overwhelming success. *Thriller* has been the crowning achievement of Jackson's career; nothing before or since matched its success.

to Listen For
"Thriller"

INSTRUMENTATION
Lead and backup vocals, electronic analogues to conventional instruments (bass, horns, percussion, chord instruments) percussion, guitar; non-musical sounds, spoken commentary

PERFORMANCE STYLE
Jackson's light, not-scary voice balanced by Price's macabre "rap"

RHYTHM
Active rhythms at march/disco tempo: bass riff at rock-beat speed; busy 16-beat percussion parts, fast horn riffs; many riffs syncopated

MELODY
Short title-phrase riff at chorus; verse = longer phrase

TEXTURE
Dense texture formed mainly from layers of riffs: bass, mid-range, vocal, higher range horn-like riffs; sustained sounds behind riffs

to Remember
"Thriller"

EXTENSIVE ELECTRONICS
Electronic versions of conventional instruments: bass riff throughout, plus horn-like riffs, sustained chords

EXPANSIVE FORM
In both audio track and video, instrumental interlude; in video, allows the action/dance scene to unfold

MOTOWN INFLUENCE
Bright rhythms, bass-heavy texture, melodic saturation, and verse/chorus form build on Motown formula

Madonna

In Renaissance-era Italian, *madonna* was originally a variant of *mia donna*, or "my lady." The term eventually came to refer more specifically to Mary, the mother of Jesus. For example, the phrase "madonna and child" identifies those works of art that depict Mary with the infant Jesus. In the eighties, "Madonna" acquired an even more concrete image: the pop star whose given name soon was enough to identify her to the world at large.

Madonna (born Madonna Ciccone, 1958) was born the same year as Michael Jackson. In 1978, while Jackson was starring in *The Wiz*, Madonna moved to New York to further her career as a dancer. She soon became active in the club scene, while she struggled to pay the rent. Her star rose quickly. Her first records, released in the early eighties, gained her a following, mainly among clubbers. Although these songs didn't cross over, they created enough of a buzz that she received a contract to record her first album, *Madonna*, which was released in 1983.

In 1984, she took one of the many bold steps that have characterized her career, releasing the video of "Like a Virgin." Shot in Venice, Italy, the video rapidly juxtaposes images of Madonna in a white wedding dress with her in street

Madonna in 1984, combining provocative, shocking, and controversial themes and images with bright, accessible music.

Michael Ochs Archives/Getty Images

"Like a Prayer," Madonna Leonard (1989). Madonna, vocal.

clothes and a provocative evening dress—attire that suggests she is anything but a virgin. The video established a formula that would set the tone for her subsequent work: combine provocative, shocking, and controversial themes and images with bright, accessible music.

Among her most controversial projects of the eighties was the video "Like a Prayer." The song was the title track from her 1989 album of the same name. The video conflates religious images (for example, a scene in which she grasps a knife, and it cuts her in a way that evokes the stigmata of the crucified Christ); symbols of racism (burning crosses); numerous incongruities and impossibilities (a black gospel choir in a Catholic chapel; the statue of a black saint who comes to life, then doubles as the black man wrongly accused of murdering a woman); and the one constant—Madonna in a revealing dress. All of this outraged numerous religious groups, who threatened to boycott Pepsi, which had recruited Madonna as a spokesperson. The controversy served as free publicity: the album topped the charts.

The video of "Like a Prayer" dramatically evidences the emergence of the music video as an entity distinct from the song that spawned it, and from other expressive forms that merge song, image, and movement. The messages of the song—among them, racism is wrong, we are all brothers and sisters in Christ, and Madonna is sexy—come through mainly in the rapid-fire series of images/scenes/song fragments. There is little sense of continuity in the narrative, visually or in the lyric, and there are long stretches where Madonna makes no attempt to sing in the video, even as we hear her voice in the song. This shows the rapid evolution of the music video, not only in Madonna's own work but also in the medium overall. It has moved well beyond simply capturing a live performance, as was the case in "Everybody," her first video; at this point in her career and in the brief history of the medium, such videos seem a distant memory.

Musically, Madonna's winning formula has been to combine a simple, catchy melody with trendy sounds and rhythms and skillful production. The melody of "Like a Prayer" flows in gently undulating phrases, with little or no syncopation. When isolated from its setting, the melody bears a closer resemblance to a children's song or a folk melody than to a dance-inspired song from the eighties. And like a folk melody, it is easily absorbed and remembered. The support for this melody oscillates

between sustained chords sung by a choir and played on an organ and a Caribbean-flavored background that bears a striking resemblance to Steve Winwood's 1986 No. 1 hit "Higher Love." As with much post-1980 pop, the active accompaniment is dense, rhythmically active, and rich in both electronic and conventional instrumental sounds. The steady flow of Madonna's melody allows her to alternate between the dance-like sections and those sections with only sustained harmonies and extremely light percussion sounds.

"Like A Prayer" breaks no new ground musically, but it does merge disparate and seemingly contradictory musical features into an effective song, just as the video does.

The most ground-breaking aspect of Madonna's career has been her ascension to a position of complete control of her career: writing her songs, producing her recordings, choreographing her performances, and making the key decisions about every aspect of production and promotion. This owes more to her ambition, business acumen, and chutzpah than it does to her talent. In achieving elite celebrity status (single-name recognition, constant tabloid fodder) as she directed her career, she has become a role model for a new generation of women performers.

Many have found her public persona liberating. Without question, her success added a new dimension to sexual equality within the pop music business: women, or at least women like her, no longer had to be front persons for men. Cynical observers have dismissed the provocative images that she presents, such as those encountered in the "Like a Prayer" video, as attention-getting stunts whose shock value obscures a lack of talent and imagination. It is true that Madonna is not spectacularly creative

⑤ to Listen For
"Like a Prayer"

INSTRUMENTATION
Vocal, choir, organ, guitar, multiple percussion instruments, bass, keyboards

PERFORMANCE STYLE
Madonna's straightforward, plain singing; guitar distortion

RHYTHM
Busy 16-beat rhythms at dance tempo

MELODY
Abundance of riffs in verse and chorus

TEXTURE
Contrast between sustained harmonies under vocal and active, dense, percussion-rich texture

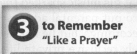

③ to Remember
"Like a Prayer"

SIMPLE SONG/POP HOOK
Simple melody offers easy point of entry.

CONTRASTS
Striking contrasts in sound, rhythm, and texture: melody plus sustained chords from dense texture with Madonna, choir, and lots of rhythm, including distorted guitar

FROM PRAYER TO POP
Melody, choir, organ connect to religious service; pop sections have no religious overtones musically

in any artistic dimension of the music business: she is not Michael Jackson's equal as a dancer, Prince's equal as a songwriter or an instrumentalist, or Tina Turner's equal as a vocalist. However, to dismiss her talents out of hand would be to ignore the sense of conviction with which Madonna presents these controversial juxtapositions and to dismiss their role in challenging value systems that have grown rigid over time.

Post-Punk/Post-Disco Fusions: The Music of Prince

It would be difficult to find any rock artist who embodies more confluences and contradictions than Prince (born Prince Rogers Nelson, 1958). His music is a rock and rhythm-and-blues melting pot: one hears elements of funk, punk, hard rock, disco, black and white pop, and more, in varying proportions. His touring bands have included blacks and whites, women and men. His particular syntheses came to be known as "the Minneapolis sound," after the city where he was born and where he has continued to make his home base (he opened Paisley Park Studios there in 1987). The confluences extend to his personal life; the unpronounceable symbol that he used in lieu of his name from 1993 to 2000 (when he became "the artist formerly known as Prince") reputedly represents a merging of the symbols for male and female.

The contradictions are present in his life and his music. He created a public persona so blatantly erotic at times that his music sparked the campaign to put parental advisory labels on recordings, but he has led an extremely reclusive private life, which has a strong spiritual dimension. (He claimed that God directed him to change his name to a symbol.) He has been an artist sufficiently drawn to the spotlight that he co-authored and starred in a quasi-autobiographical film (*Purple Rain*) and a musician who willingly and anonymously writes for, produces, and accompanies other artists. (Prince often uses aliases when he appears on others' recordings.) His music has been deeply rooted in the valued music of earlier generations: in a 1985 *Rolling Stone*

interview he acknowledged artists as diverse as Stevie Wonder, Joni Mitchell, Miles Davis, Santana, and George Clinton. Yet his music has grown by absorbing numerous contemporary influences some distance from his musical roots—such as new wave—and by blending sounds produced by cutting-edge technology—for example, drum machines in the early eighties—with more conventional instruments, all of which he plays masterfully.

One measure of Prince's greatness as an artist has been his ability to reconcile the contrasting, even contradictory, elements of his musical life into a personal style that retains its identity despite its great stylistic and emotional range. Listening to a Prince album can be like taking a course in rock history. Prince has mastered virtually all rock-era styles. For Prince, style mastery isn't simply the ability to cover a style; he seldom does just that. Instead, he draws on disparate style elements and mixes them together to evoke a particular mood. For him, beat patterns, sounds, and rhythmic textures are like ingredients in a gourmet dish; they are used to flavor the song. More important, he also adds original ideas to create the nouvelle cuisine of eighties pop.

> " Even by rock standards, Prince is an eccentric. "

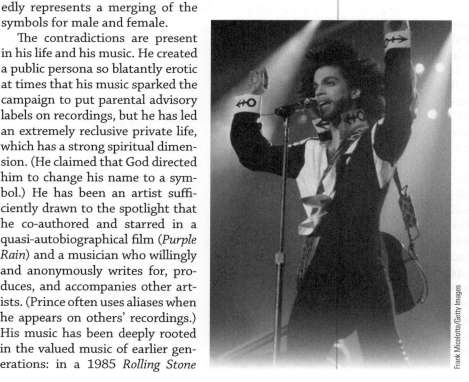

Frank Micelotta/Getty Images

Prince is the son of musicians: jazz pianist John Nelson and singer Mattie Shaw. To escape his parents' troubled relationship (they divorced when he was ten), Prince sought refuge in music. By his teens, he had not only mastered the full array of rhythm instruments but also begun writing his own material and learning production skills. Although not a child star, he was more precocious in some respects than Michael Jackson as both musician and producer. He played all the instruments on his first five albums and produced the albums as well. Stevie Wonder had pioneered this electronic version of the one-man band in the early seventies; Prince grew up with it.

He secured his first recording contract, which gave him total freedom in the studio, in 1977. The hits began coming two years later, beginning with "I Wanna Be Your Lover." The success of *Purple Rain* (1984) brought him commercial success (sales of 13 million units; three hit singles) and critical recognition (the soundtrack won three Grammy awards). In its wake, he became one of the few super-stars of the eighties. His subsequent work continued to explore new territory. As he remarked in the *Rolling Stone* interview, "I always try to do something different and conquer new ground." He reached what many commentators feel was an artistic high point in 1987 with the release of the double album *Sign 'O' the Times*.

"Sign 'O' the Times," Prince (1987). Prince, vocal.

"Sign 'O' the Times," one of three singles from the album to chart, presents a bleak vision of contemporary life: gangs, AIDS, drugs, and natural disasters, interlaced with anecdotal accounts of the fallout from drug use. The music is correspondingly bleak. The track begins with an intricate rhythm formed from a syncopated synthesizer riff and two electronically generated percussion sounds. This texture continues throughout the song. In the larger context of Prince's music, the repetition seems purposeful. It seems to suggest a despair that knows no end. In effect, it serves as a substitute for a standard rhythm section, and it is the accompaniment for Prince's vocal in the verse section. Other consistent elements include a strong backbeat and a synthesized bass riff, which often provides a response to the vocal line. Funky, jazz-influenced guitar figures, then sustained synthesizer chords, which provide the first harmonic change, high-light the buildup to the crux of the song: one finds hap-piness only in death. To underscore this difficult idea, the music returns to the empty sound of the opening—an abrupt and disconcerting return to reality. Only a blues-tinged guitar solo, again over the relentless synthesizer riffs and intricate percussion rhythms, provide relief from the misery portrayed in the lyric; this is interrupted by percussion sounds that evoke the fire of a machine gun.

"Sign 'O' the Times" gains its impact as much from what's missing as from what's present. There is no rhythm guitar, no bass line, and no routine timekeeping on a drum set. There is no hook at the highpoint of the chorus to latch onto. There are no familiar chord progressions and few other clues that help us navigate through the song. The rhythms are com-plex, as in funk, but disciplined; the tex-ture is spare, not dense. These features help create a sound world that is as vivid and powerful as a black and white photo-graph of a gray day in the ghetto.

"Sign 'O' the Times" shows how Prince mixes dispa-rate elements into a coherent and effective whole. From punk, via rap, he took realness—there is no fantasy, or escape, in this song. From funk, he took complex lay-ered rhythms, which he pared down to convey the mood of the song. He adapts blues-influenced rock guitar to the context, supporting it unconventionally with the minimalist synthesizer riffs and rhythms.

Almost any other Prince song will sound quite differ-ent in many respects; that is one reason for his commer-cial and critical success. The most consistent elements are likely to be the mix of synthesized and conventional instruments; an open-sounding, intricately worked-out texture that puts a different spin on the conventional interplay between regular timekeeping and syncopated patterns; and a few distinctive features that help set the song apart from the sources that inspired it. In this song, it is the absence of bass and drum set and the rich sus-tained harmonies in the first part of the chorus. But the distinctive element can be anything: "U Got the Look," another top hit from *Sign 'O' the Times*, offers a radically transformed version of the 12-bar blues progression.

Even by rock standards, Prince is an eccentric. Still, the odd, often contradictory aspects of his personal life cannot obscure or diminish Prince's remarkable musical achievement. He remains one of the most multitalented, multidimensional musicians in the history of rock.

5 **to Listen For**
"Sign 'O' the Times"

INSTRUMENTATION
Vocal, electric guitar, synthesizers (riffs, percussion, sustained chords)

RHYTHM
16-beat rhythm at moderate tempo implied throughout by interaction of layers, percussion parts

MELODY
Mainly long phrases in verse and bridge; no hook at chorus

HARMONY
No harmony in verse; sustained, slowly changing chords in bridge

TEXTURE
Spare texture: no bass, chord instrument much of the time; mainly repeated riffs

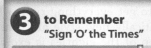

3 **to Remember**
"Sign 'O' the Times"

DARK SONG
Loud, repeated power chords played on guitar with some distortion, in a basic rock rhythm and at a fast tempo: these are salient features of punk style. They inform basic feel of song throughout, although Bowie adds a number of sophisticated touches.

UNDERMINING POP FORM
Verse/chorus form that subverts the arrival at the chorus by subtracting instruments and returning to bleak opening texture

DARK SETTING
Music reinforces mood of lyrics through empty-sounding texture, form without conventional hook, absence of conventional rock band sounds (no bass, rhythm guitar, steady timekeeping in drums)

The Maturation of Black Pop

The more traditional black pop, the one that charted the ups and downs of romantic love, got a makeover in the eighties. A new generation of singers—among them Lionel Richie, Natalie Cole (daughter of the great Nat Cole), Whitney Houston, and Luther Vandross—were some of the brightest stars of the eighties and nineties. Top acts from the past continued to make great music: Tina Turner, Marvin Gaye (until his untimely death in 1984), Aretha Franklin, Stevie Wonder, and Diana Ross stand out.

Tina Turner scored her first No. 1 hit as a solo act in 1984 with "What's Love Got to Do with It." At forty-four, she was the most senior of the prominent black pop singers, but most of the others weren't far behind. Not surprisingly, these artists sang about love in a more mature and real way than the black pop artists from the sixties usually did. They and their audience had grown up in the intervening years. In most cases, the tone of the lyrics connected more directly to the mature black romantic music of the early seventies, most notably the music of Roberta Flack and Bill Withers, than it did to the bright-eyed, more innocent lyrics of sixties black pop.

The music is comparably more mature. In the songs of the early sixties girl groups and early Motown recordings, there is a sense of discovery; the occasional rough edges in conception and production evidence that it is hard to get everything right when you're inventing a dramatically new style and sound. By contrast, the black pop of the eighties is exquisitely produced. The maturity is also evident in the words. These are songs about love—or more accurately, about the problems of relationships—and the singers deliver them in a manner that makes the lyrics credible.

Musical Features of the New Black Pop

The sound of the eighties black pop resulted mainly from two significant changes: the use of synthesized sounds to replace most, if not all, of the traditional instruments, and more adventurous rhythms. The sumptuous backgrounds that were so much a part of the sound of later doo-wop, Motown, Philadelphia, and Barry White are part of this updated black pop sound. The difference is that producers use electronic analogues to the strings, horns, and even rhythm instruments. Their function is much the same, but the sounds are new. This fresh sound palette gives the music a more contemporary flavor.

The other major change had to do with rhythm. By the beginning of the eighties, 16-beat rhythms were the norm throughout much rock-era music, and especially black music. We hear these more active rhythms in most of the songs discussed in this and the previous chapter and in much of the music in the subsequent chapters. At comparable tempos, 16-beat rhythms offer many more opportunities for rhythmic play than rock rhythm, simply because there are so many more combinations of sound and silence. When applied to a Motown-style conception of rhythmic texture, the results are liberating.

Recall that one of the distinctive features of Motown songs was subtle timekeeping, except for a strong back-beat. Generally, only the drummer (and conga player, if present) kept the rock rhythm; no instrument marked the beat. In the black pop of the eighties, timekeeping became not only more active but also often more implicit. Any regular timekeeping was generally in the background, and at times it was dispensed with altogether. The dominant rhythms moved either much more slowly (for instance, sustained chords) or faster than the beat; the faster rhythms typically played against the beat, with irregular patterns or syncopations.

In this connection, it is worth noting the impact of reggae on this new kind of rhythmic freedom. Recall that the black pop and R&B of the late fifties and early sixties was a major influence on Jamaican music in the sixties, which developed into reggae by the end of the decade. The characteristic sound of reggae comes largely from the offbeat rhythms in the middle of the texture and the free bass line underneath. In the late seventies and eighties, both black and white acts wove reggae rhythms into other styles. Its impact on black music can be heard in such songs as Marvin Gaye's "Sexual Healing" (1982) and Tina Turner's "What's Love Got to Do with It" (1984). With this development, the exchange between black pop and Jamaican music has come full circle. We hear the influence of reggae in "What's Love Got to Do with It."

Tina Turner

If anyone were entitled to be cynical about love, it would be Tina Turner (born Annie Mae Bullock, 1939). In 1956, as a young woman still in her teens, she connected with Ike Turner, eight years her senior and already a music business veteran. The connection soon became personal as well as professional. They married in 1962, and for more than a decade, they prospered professionally as the Ike and Tina Turner Revue; they had a huge hit in 1971 with a cover of Creedence Clearwater Revival's "Proud Mary."

However, for much of their relationship, Ike abused Tina emotionally and physically. The abuse grew worse as their career declined; Ike's alleged drug use and almost paranoid distrust of outside management was a main factor. Their professional relationship complicated any personal breakup. When she finally broke free of

> If anyone were entitled to be cynical about love, it would be Tina Turner.

black artists.) The next year saw the release of *Private Dancer*, an album that included "What's Love Got to Do with It" among its three charting singles. The song would win three Grammys the following year.

Turner's song and her singing project an embittered view of love; any excitement found in the physical aspects of a relationship is tempered by the foreknowledge that the relationship will never mature into love. She sings from the heart; close to two decades of pain spill out in her soulful singing.

The song uses the verse/chorus template as a point of departure. The verse builds inexorably to a magnetic hook, which Turner's gritty voice invests with deep feeling. By contrast, the musical setting is muted—almost arid. Synthesizer sounds are prominent: sustained synthesizer chords and obbligatos. The rhythm shows the influence of reggae in the persistent rebound pattern on the offbeat, the open texture, and a free-roaming bass in the chorus. The accompaniment never matches the intensity of Turner's singing; it is almost as if the accompaniment is indifferent to her despair. This has the effect of casting Turner's pain into relief; in the song, she grieves alone.

Race and Romance

The rebirth of Turner's career was not only a personal triumph but also a symbolic milestone for mature women, black and white. Ever since Bing Crosby began to croon into a microphone, audiences, or at least those of the opposite sex, personified their relationship with the singer. They could imagine Crosby and other crooners singing to them alone, and meaning it. Frank Sinatra would soon become the first pop-singing heartthrob; thousands of adoring fans swooned during his performances, much as they would for Elvis fifteen years later. Sinatra, Crosby, and several other singers parlayed their pop success into film careers; even Fred Astaire, in appearance an extremely unlikely leading man, succeeded in winning the affection of Ginger Rogers, at least on the screen.

By contrast, Ethel Waters, the top black pop singer, could sing "my man and I ain't together" (from Harold Arlen's bluesy standard "Stormy

Hulton Archive/Getty Images.

"What's Love Got to Do with It," Terry Britten and Graham Lyle (1984). Tina Turner, vocal.

Turner—in the middle of a tour—she also broke contractual obligations. Because of this, the divorce settlement devastated her financially; she retained only her name.

It took Tina the better part of a decade to get her solo career on track. Her break came in 1983, when she covered Al Green's "Let's Stay Together" for B.E.F. (British Electric Foundation), the production side of a synth-pop group doing some serious soul searching. (B.E.F. would eventually record not only with Turner but also Chaka Khan, Mavis Staples, and other major

---

5 to Listen For
"What's Love Got to Do with It"

INSTRUMENTATION
Vocal, bass, drums, percussion, synthesizers (sustained chords, riffs)

PERFORMANCE STYLE
Turner's soulful, passionate singing

RHYTHM
Slow rock beat, more active rhythms in background, including reggae-like rebound backbeat

MELODY
Long phrases in verse; repeated title-phrase riff highlights chorus

TEXTURE
Several layers, but open sound (sustained chords, subtle riffs) encases Turner's rich voice

---

3 to Remember
"What's Love Got to Do with It"

ANTI–LOVE SONG
Lyric speaks directly and honestly about the hurt of a broken heart.

TURNER'S PASSIONATE SINGING
Turner's singing is comparably direct; it makes the lyric emotionally credible.

80S POP SOUND
Instrumental accompaniment dominated by synthesized sounds; rhythm features open texture with light rock-rhythm timekeeping, more active rhythms darting in and out

Weather") to Cotton Club audiences and on disc, but her most significant film role before 1950 came as Petunia in the 1943 all-black film *Cabin in the Sky*. In it, she sings another great pop standard, "Taking a Chance on Love," to Eddie Anderson, who would later become famous as Jack Benny's servant Rochester. She is dressed dowdily and simply rolls her eyes back and forth as she sings. The song and the singing are great, the message is romantic, but their interaction is anything but romantic. Indeed, the scene reminds contemporary viewers that minstrelsy was not ancient history in 1943; Hollywood refused to portray blacks in a romantic relationship. In the late forties and fifties, Nat Cole thrilled black and white audiences with beautiful love songs like "Unforgettable," but his appeal was limited to his voice, at least among white audiences.

The personification of romantic song in popular music began to transcend race in the sixties, with the popularity of the girl groups and Motown acts. By the time Turner recorded "What's Love Got to Do with It," Turner's sex appeal was certainly not delimited by her ethnicity in North America, and even more in Europe, where she has had an ardent fan base (and where she currently resides). By the end of the century, race and ethnic heritage were nonissues in romantic music, as a parade of contemporary pop divas evidences.

The Go-Go's circa 1980

GAB Archives/Redferns Music Library

> *Lead singer Belinda Carlisle had been a cheerleader in high school; it was as if someone put a yellow smiley face on Johnny Rotten.*

Punk-Inspired Pop

Rock got a "beat lift" around 1980. The new sound was lean, clean, vibrant, and colored with an array of synthesizer timbres and effects. It harnessed the energy of punk, but its most direct antecedent was the music of David Bowie, himself one of punk's seminal influences. From these sources, it distilled a purer form of rock rhythm, typically spread throughout the texture, from bass and kick drum to high-pitched percussion and synth parts. Its leanness and cleanness came in large part from an open-sounding mid-range: crisp single-note lines and sustained chords replaced thick guitar chords and riffs.

Bowie himself was a major contributor to this new sound. So were new wave artists such as Elvis Costello, Blondie, the Pretenders, the Talking Heads, Devo, and the B-52s. However, there were also groups that had neither punk's rage nor new wave's weirdness.

The Go-Go's' "We Got the Beat" (1981) could easily be the signature song of this new rock sound. Like a typical Ramones' song, it has a simple lyric, mostly the repeated title phrase. And it has punk's saturated rock rhythm—not only in the drum part but also in repeated notes and chords from top (high piano chords) to bottom (bass and low guitar). But the spirit of the song is completely different. It is almost mindlessly happy—much closer to fifties rock and roll than it is to punk or new wave. However, the rhythmic approach clearly places it in the eighties. So does the makeup of the band. The Go-Go's were among the first of the all-girl rock groups.

"We Got the Beat" also shows how the point of punk's rhythmic innovation had been turned completely on its head within five years. In the Sex Pistols' music, the rhythm was aggressive and confrontational. Here it's simply bouncy. Lead singer Belinda Carlisle (b. 1958) had been a cheerleader in high school; it was as if someone put a yellow smiley face on Johnny Rotten.

Van Halen

Among the bands to utilize this new approach was Van Halen, an excellent second-generation heavy metal band. Two brothers, drummer Alex (b. 1953) and guitarist

Eddie (b. 1955) formed the band with bassist Michael Anthony (b. 1954) and lead vocalist David Lee Roth (b. 1954). Their 1978 debut album, simply titled *Van Halen*, showcased Eddie Van Halen's breathtaking virtuosity. The appropriately titled "Eruption," a freeform solo by Van Halen, immediately raised the bar for guitarists. The album was an immediate success and one of the most spectacular debut albums in rock history. It would be the first of an almost unbroken string of platinum albums by the band.

David Lee Roth and Eddie Van Halen

Michael Ochs Archives/Getty Images

Although associated with heavy metal because of the guitar-centric songs and Eddie Van Halen's playing, Van Halen was, from the start, more than a heavy metal band. During the early eighties, in the latter part of Roth's tenure with the band, Eddie Van Halen sought to move more toward the mainstream, in part by incorporating synthesizers into their sound—he is also a skilled keyboardist. Among the fruits of this particular direction was "Jump," from their sixth album, *1984*; it was the band's first No. 1 single.

"Jump," Alex Van Halen, Eddie Van Halen, and David Lee Roth (1983). Van Halen.

"Jump" exemplifies the new sound of punk-inspired and pop-oriented rock that emerged in the early eighties. The features that most clearly identify this sound are prominent synthesizer parts, open texture, and the contemporary approach to rock rhythm. For most of the song, including the opening signature riff, synths rule. In addition to replacing the lead guitar as the source of the opening instrumental hook, they provide most of the accompaniment for Roth's vocal. Van Halen plays guitar only in the contrasting section and in a brief tantalizing solo, which only hints at his technical mastery and sonic imagination. This soon gives way to a synthesizer solo that is more extended but less virtuosic. The synth riff lies mainly in a medium-high register; it is in a higher range than Roth's vocal line much of the time. By contrast, the bass line, played by Anthony (on bass) and Van Halen, is in a low register. What's missing—or very much in the background—most of the time are chords played by a rhythm guitarist. By omitting this typically prominent part of the texture, Van Halen gives the song a more spacious sound.

Underpinning Roth's vocal and the synthesizer and guitar parts is a bass line that is mostly a single note repeated at rock-beat speed. It changes infrequently in the heart of the song—mainly at the end of phrases, in the contrasting section, and during Van Halen's guitar solo. By presenting the rock-rhythm layer most prominently in a repeated-note bass line, Van Halen (and the other eighties bands that also used this strategy) further concentrates this already distilled form of rock rhythm. Here, the bass part turns rock rhythm into a musical trampoline on which the rest of the texture bounces. In this form, the rhythm is vibrant, not aggressive. Indeed, "Jump" is a good-humored song; we can almost see Roth smirking as he sings the song.

Shortly after recording *1984*, Roth left the band. Sammy Hagar (b. 1947) replaced him for the better part of a decade. He too left, in 1996. Gary Cherone (b. 1961) then began his brief tenure as lead vocalist. The band, inactive since 2004, undertook a reunion tour with Roth in 2007.

5 to Listen For
"Jump"

INSTRUMENTATION
Vocal, synths, electric guitar, drums

RHYTHM
Basic rhythm: bouncy rock beat at moderate tempo; time kept in bass; signature riff syncopated

MELODY
Instrumental riffs most prominent melodic strand; different versions of same rhythm

HARMONY
Fresh approach to I/IV/V throughout most of song; bridge uses more wide-ranging harmony

TEXTURE
Open sound: strong bass, high synth riff, vocal, drums in middle; bridge = sudden shift in texture—more fluid rhythm, thicker texture in midrange

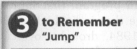

3 to Remember
"Jump"

HAPPY SONG
Good mood in lyrics echoed by syncopated riff, guitar and synth solos, and clearly outlined rhythm at a moderate tempo

FROM PUNK TO POP
"Saturated" rock rhythm (bass repeated note/drums) recontextualize more aggressive punk approach to rock rhythm.

80S POP ROCK SOUND
Prominent synths: main solo voice, as well as bass line support, dominant riff, and background color augment traditional rock instrumentation.

The sounds and rhythms popularized in songs like "Jump" were one of the freshest trends in rock during the eighties. Other acts—including the Eurythmics, Cyndi Lauper, and the Smiths—also featured it in their music. The livelier, cleaner rhythmic textures and the expanded sound palette created by the new synth timbres make the music sound distinctly different from almost all of the music of the seventies and before. A similar approach underpins some of the most significant rock of the decade.

- - - - - - - -

Significant Rock

Music, like the musicians who produce it, can mature; and maturation, in music as in life, is ideally a never-ending process. The earlier discussion of the maturation of rock rhythm described an early stage in the musical development of rock, comparable to changes from adolescence to young adulthood. The music that we explore next is a markedly later stage in this process. We might think of it as a successful response to a mid-life crisis, as if a man asked himself where the idealism of his youth had gone and resolved not only to recapture it but also to convert those ideals into positive actions. Altruism returned to rock in the mid-1980s, mainly through a series of spectacular -Aid events.

Making Rock Relevant

In Ethiopia, a country in northeast Africa, the vast majority of people depend on farming for their livelihood. In the seventies, the Soviet-backed government instituted a land-reform program that limited the acreage that individuals could farm. In 1984, drought, overcultivation, and the government's poorly conceived and ineptly executed marketing program created a famine that devastated the country.

British journalist Michael Buerk, aided by Kenyan cameraman and journalist Mohammed Amin, traveled to Ethiopia in the fall of 1984. On October 24th, the BBC broadcast a 7-minute film that showed thousands of people dying from starvation. The other major news agencies quickly picked up the film. Over a billion people around the world soon saw Buerk and Amin's account of the Ethiopian famine.

Among those who saw Buerk's broadcast was Bob Geldof (b. 1954), the lead singer with the Irish new wave band the Boomtown Rats. Geldof was so moved that he resolved to organize a musical event to raise money for famine relief and to raise people's awareness of the crisis; he would call his project Band Aid. He enlisted the help of Midge Ure (born James Ure, 1953), a member of Ultravox, another U.K. new wave band. Together they wrote the song "Do They Know It's Christmas?" then recruited an all-star cast to perform it, and obtained 24 hours of free studio time to record it. Among the guest performers on the recording were Paul McCartney, Bono, Sting, Boy George, and Phil Collins. The recording was released on December 15, less than two months after Geldof viewed Buerk's broadcast. It quickly topped the charts in the United Kingdom. Geldof donated all the revenues from its sale to assist the Ethiopian people through the Band Aid Trust, which he formed for that purpose.

Around the time "Do They Know It's Christmas?" was released in Great Britain, another equally bleak news report of the famine aired in the United States. After viewing the broadcast, Harry Belafonte (b. 1927), a singer and actor who had parlayed his spectacular success as a calypso singer in the fifties into a long and distinguished career in entertainment, called his manager Ken Kragen, who also managed several other top entertainment stars, about organizing a project for famine relief. Within short order, Lionel Richie, Stevie Wonder, and Michael Jackson were on board; Jackson and Richie wrote the song "We Are the World." The principals scheduled a recording session right after the American Music Awards ceremony. An all-star cast—including Paul Simon, Tina Turner, Diana Ross, Willie Nelson, Bruce Springsteen, Bob Dylan, and Ray Charles—recorded the song on January 28, 1985; Quincy Jones, who included Jackson's *Thriller* album among his numerous significant credits, produced the session. The single came out in March. On Good Friday (April 5 that year), 5,000 radio stations played the song simultaneously. The single and an album spun off from the single both went multiplatinum. The project, called USA (United Support of Artists) for Africa, raised over $50 million for famine relief.

Capitalizing on the goodwill generated by the Band Aid project, Geldof organized Live Aid, the most massive fund-raising event in the history of the music business. His idea was to create a "global jukebox" with broadcasts of concerts from stadiums in London and Philadelphia. The concerts—over 22 hours between the two venues—and live performances from other venues throughout the world—for example, Moscow, Sydney, the Hague—would be broadcast throughout the world via satellite. The roster of acts performing at the multiple venues reads like a Who's Who of rock. Live Aid, performed July 13, 1985, drew a worldwide audience estimated at over 1 billion viewers. At one point during the broadcast, Billy Connolly, a Scottish comedian and actor who was opening for Elton John, announced that he had been informed that 95 percent of the world's television sets were watching the event. Live Aid eventually raised over $260 million for famine relief in Africa. Even more important, the events and the recordings called attention to the plight in Africa. Shipments of grain surpluses from the United States and elsewhere soon alleviated the suffering in Ethiopia.

These events and others like them (such as Farm Aid) put the "we" back in rock. In the sixties, rock had defined itself as a "we" music: first in the bands themselves (names like the Beatles, the Beach Boys, the Who, the Rolling Stones gave bands a collective identity), then in the bond between music and audience. The "we" in rock was a generation that didn't trust anyone over thirty. The seventies, by contrast, have been dubbed as the "me" decade; in music, self-involvement (what about me?) and the pursuit of success seemed to negate the sense of community created in the sixties.

The massive fund-raising events of the eighties signaled the return of rock's conscience, but with a huge difference. In the sixties, rock gave voice to a generational revolution. It provided the soundtrack for an

Putting the "we" back in rock. George Michael, Bono, David Bowie, Paul McCartney, and Freddie Mercury onstage at the Live Aid concert at Wembley Stadium in London

Dave Hogan/Getty Images

assault on the establishment and, by overthrowing the pop music establishment, it led by example. In the eighties, rock *was* the establishment, the dominant segment of the music industry. As a result, it could leverage the celebrity of its artists in projects that served a greater good. In the eighties, "we" in rock not only included the musicians, the music industry, and the audience, but also those whom they sought to help.

The sense of purpose that these events symbolized was one sign of a renewal in rock. Leading this renewal were Bruce Springsteen and U2.

Bruce Springsteen

Asbury Park is a New Jersey beach town about an hour's drive from New York City. Bruce Springsteen (b. 1949) grew up in and around the town. Early on, he forged the musical split personality that has been his trademark: he worked with bar bands close to home and also played solo gigs in Greenwich Village clubs, where he mingled with Patti Smith and other early punk rockers. This helps account for the huge swings in his music, from the all-acoustic *Nebraska* album to the hard-rocking *Born in the U.S.A.*

His enormous success comes in part from his ability to integrate seemingly contradictory aspects of his life and work. He is a superstar and a man of the people, a musician who plays to sold-out arenas and shows up unannounced to sit in with local bands. Throughout his career, he has stayed close to his working-class roots and has written songs that reflect their concerns. At the same time, he is larger than life—the "Boss" to his fiercely loyal fans.

In 1974 rock critic Jon Landau went to a Springsteen concert at the Harvard Square Theatre. In a long, rambling review, he wrote, "I saw rock and roll's future and his name is Bruce Springsteen." Landau turned his words into action, becoming Springsteen's manager.

Landau's evaluation was right on the mark in the sense that Springsteen became the biggest star of the next two decades to consciously continue the core tradition of rock. While others branched off in new directions, Springsteen stayed close to his rock-and-roll roots, even as he updated and expanded the sound. For example, his first big hit, the 1975 song "Born to Run," features an oversized band (several guitars, saxophone, keyboards, bass, and drums), an extended guitar hook, a sprawling form, and a powerful, obvious beat.

After "Born to Run," Springsteen's career was primed for takeoff. However, a drawn-out legal battle involving Landau and Springsteen's first producer, Mike Appel, kept Springsteen out of the studios for about three years. He returned with a string of critically acclaimed and mildly (for 1980) popular albums: *Darkness on the Edge of Town* (1978), *The River* (1980), and the acoustic *Nebraska* (1982). He finally broke through to a

> "I saw rock and roll's future and his name is Bruce Springsteen."
> —Jon Landau

mass audience in 1984 with *Born in the U.S.A.* It was in this album that Springsteen fully realized the big conception first expressed in songs like "Born to Run."

In the title track, Springsteen mixes a strong story line, simple riffs and rhythms, and subtle details. The lyric paints a brutal portrait of a Vietnam War veteran through powerful,

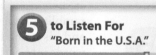

"Born in the U.S.A.," Bruce Springsteen (1984). Bruce Springsteen, vocal, with the E Street Band.

almost posterized images: "sent me off to a foreign land/to go and kill the yellow man." The verses telegraph defining moments in the protagonist's life, from early childhood to his inability to get a job and the insensitivity of the government in supporting veterans. Springsteen's words put an ironic spin on the title phrase. In this context, what could be a prideful affirmation of patriotism becomes a jingoistic mantra—a badge of shame for a country that sends its less fortunate off to fight in a senseless war, then does little to help those who return.

Springsteen sets his trenchant lyric in an almost minimalist musical environment. The song begins with only a single octave on the piano, a heavy backbeat, and a synthesizer riff. The spacing of these three elements—low, middle, high—and a judicious amount of reverb (which makes the backbeat sound uncomfortably close to a rifle shot) give the introduction a big sound by defining a wide open space waiting to be filled in. As the song unfolds, Springsteen fills in the middle; the most prominent of the additional parts either strengthen the bass or fill in the upper range—most notably, the piano part presents a more active version of the synthesizer riff. These and

David Mcgough/DMI/Time Life Pictures/Getty Images

other instruments weave in and out of the texture, but the riff and backbeat are constants—even through Max Weinberg's "war zone" drum solo.

Springsteen is at once simple and subtle. The prominent elements in "Born in the U.S.A." stand out vibrantly, whereas the spacing of the texture and the balance between the prominent features and background support is more sophisticated. Springsteen has maintained this strategy in his subsequent music, most notably in *The Rising*, his response to 9/11. He remains one of the few artists in rock music with a truly powerful presence.

Springsteen's "significant" sound, as evidenced in "Born in the U.S.A.," was one of several musical options that he would employ in his music from the early eighties on. Other tracks on the album range from the punk-drenched "No Surrender" and the country-flavored "Darlington County" to the synth rock of "Dancing in the Dark" and the moody ballad "My Hometown." Another significant band of the eighties would define themselves musically by developing and refining one of the truly distinctive styles of the decade.

5 to Listen For
"Born in the U.S.A."

INSTRUMENTATION
Vocals, synthesizers, drums, keyboard, bass,

PERFORMANCE STYLE
Springsteen's strained vocal sound = intense conviction

RHYTHM
Rock rhythm at moderate tempo with overpowering back beat; rock timekeeping off and on

MELODY
Main melodic feature: title-phrase riff, played, then sung, dominates song.

TEXTURE
Open sound dominated by high riff, strong backbeat, low sustained bass notes

3 to Remember
"Born in the U.S.A."

ANTIWAR SONG
Lyric a scathing indictment of war and its costs

SIGNIFICANT ROCK
Open texture with Springsteen's raspy voice in the middle conveys a sense of importance

SPRINGSTEEN STRATEGY
Combine easily grasped features (riff, backbeat) with subtle touches (piano doubling synth riff)

SYNTHS AND 80S ROCK
Dominant presence of synthesizer sounds = fresh sound in 1980s rock

U2

From the start, U2—lead vocalist Bono (born Paul Hewson, 1960), guitarist-keyboardist The Edge (born David Evans, 1961), bassist Adam Clayton (b. 1960), and drummer Larry Mullen (b. 1961)—have had a sense of their destiny. In 1981, three years after the group came together, Bono told *Rolling Stone*, "Even at this stage, I do feel we are meant to be one of the great bands. There's a certain spark, a certain chemistry, that was special about the Stones, The Who, and the Beatles, and I think it's also special about U2." They have fulfilled their destiny because they have stayed together and because they have never lost their passion for rock and what it can be. As recently as 2000, after more than two decades of touring, recording, and sending their message out into the world, Bono told *USA Today* that "There is a transcendence that I want from rock. . . . I'm still drunk on the idea that rock and roll can be a force for change. We haven't lost that idea."

U2 soon made Bono a prophet. In their first two albums, *Boy* (1980) and *October* (1981), the group addressed personal issues, among them relationships and their faith. By 1983, the year that they released *War,* their third album, the band had defined its purpose, found its audience, and begun to define its sound. With this album, their music took on the politically and socially aware edge that would characterize it through the rest of the eighties. "Sunday Bloody Sunday," a track from the album and their first No. 1 hit in the United Kingdom, for example, recounts an especially bloody incident in the ongoing strife between Catholics and Protestants in Northern Ireland, and the musical setting reinforces the message of the lyrics: the five-note bursts played by the entire band underneath Bono's vocal line evokes the sound of gunfire.

The following year, U2 began their long and fruitful collaboration with Brian Eno (b. 1948)—a founding member of Roxy Music, an electronica pioneer, the father of ambient music, and by 1984, a much-in-demand producer. (More recently, Eno has identified himself as a "sonic landscaper," a label that also applies readily to his work with U2.) Eno brought a polish to U2's music while preserving the distinctive sound world that they had begun to create. Their first album together was the 1984 release *The Unforgettable Fire*; he would collaborate on four of their albums. By 1985 *Rolling Stone* had dubbed them the band of the eighties, but it wasn't until *Joshua Tree* (1987) that they achieved the overwhelming commercial success to match their critical acclaim.

Virtually from the start of their career, U2 cultivated a sound world that made their music sound significant. They put the essential components in place in their first albums, enhanced them with the help of Brian Eno, and maintained them through the eighties. The sound grows out of punk but already has a distinct identity in songs like "Gloria" (1981) from their second album. Surrounding Bono's vocals is a four-strand texture, separated into low, middle, and high:

- Two low-range sounds: repeated notes at rock-beat speed in the bass and beat keeping on the bass drum
- A mid-range percussion sound: a rock-rhythm layer on the sock cymbal
- A medium-high-range sound: the angular guitar line, also moving at rock-beat speed

The insistent rock rhythmic layer, played by the entire band, derives from punk, but U2 has already put their personal stamp on it in the spacing of the instruments and in The Edge's asymmetrically patterned single-line guitar figures. Because of the registral openness and the angular guitar lines, the effect is quite different from punk. Whereas the sound of Ramones-style punk rams the listener head on, the sound of U2, even at this early stage, envelops the listener.

This distinctive sound world is built on contrast: between high and low and between slow and fast. As the band's music evolved during the eighties, the contrast deepened. One significant change came from within the band. The active rhythms doubled in speed, from rock rhythm to a 16-beat rhythm, while such features as chord rhythm often moved at even slower speeds. In his work with U2, Eno enriched the "sonic landscape" by deepening the contrast between slow and fast with sustained synthesizer sounds and introducing stronger textural contrasts. These changes

George Rose/Getty Images

||||||||||||||||||||||||||||||||

"I'm still drunk on the idea that rock and roll can be a force for change."
—Bono

"Where the Streets Have No Name" Adam Clayton, Dave Evans, Paul Hewson, and Larry Mullen Jr. (1987). U2.

gave U2's music an even more sharply defined profile, as we hear in "Where the Streets Have No Name," a hit track from their 1987 album *Joshua Tree*.

"Where the Streets Have No Name" continues U2's predilection for meaningful words encased in meaningful-sounding music. The lyrics describe a universal longing for the harmony that can be created when divisions by class, race, and wealth disappear. They are general enough to have spawned multiple interpretations. Some connect the song's message to Ethiopia, where Bono and his wife had done relief work. Others link it to Los Angeles, where the video of the song was filmed. Still others associate it with Dublin, where the street one lives on could identify one's social and economic status. And most connect it to the world beyond.

Bono presents the lyric through a melody whose simplicity is obscured by the rich instrumental backdrop. If we tune out the instruments and simply listen to Bono's voice, we hear a folksong-like melody: short phrases that gently rise and fall within a narrow range. Like "Barbara Allen," the Scottish folksong heard in Chapter 2, this melody is coherent even without accompaniment, and it would work with a simple folk guitar accompaniment.

It is U2 and Eno's grand setting that relocates this simple melody from the front porch to the stage. The extended instrumental introduction—almost 2 minutes in length—begins with sustained organ and synthesizer sounds. The Edge's busy guitar pattern slowly emerges out of this sound cushion. At first it is in a rhythm that oscillates once for every six notes, like a jig in slow motion. Imperceptibly, he converts the pattern to the 16-beat rhythm that is sustained through the rest of the song. The rhythmic patterns range from the sustained synthesizer chords, which may last four measures before changing, through the beat-speed thump of Mullen's bass drum, Clayton's rock-beat-speed repeated note, and the 16-beat rhythms of the guitar(s)—there are two guitar sounds much of the time—and drums. All of this encases Bono's singing in a musical halo.

The sound world that U2 created in "Where the Streets Have No Name" was the band's musical signature during the eighties. It is heard in many of their hits during that decade, and it becomes progressively more sophisticated from album to album. It has the effect of elevating the simple melody that lies at its

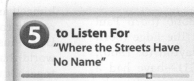

5 to Listen For
"Where the Streets Have No Name"

INSTRUMENTATION
Vocal, synths, guitar, bass, drums

RHYTHM
Steady timekeeping at moderate tempo in bass (8-beat) and drums (16-beat); steady rhythm in guitar but irregular patterns; contrast with slow-moving vocal line, sustained chords

MELODY
Tuneful, simple melody

HARMONY
Slow-moving melody

TEXTURE
Open sound: low bass, bass drum, midrange timekeeping on cymbal, guitar upper midrange, vocal in center

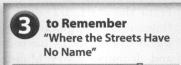

3 to Remember
"Where the Streets Have No Name"

POSITIVE MESSAGE
Lyrics that send a message of hope: for a world that is not divided by class, wealth, race, or any other arbitrary criterion

IRISH BARD
Simple, folk-like melody; Bono's singing: Irish tenor with blues-like grittiness

U2 SOUND
Characteristic 1980s U2 sound: slow-moving, tuneful vocal melody, steady rock-speed bass line; 16-beat rhythm on drums; complex patterns at 16-beat speed in guitar; sustained synth harmonies in background

SIGNIFICANCE ≠ SYNCOPATION
Persistent rhythms at several speeds, with very little syncopation (except in melodic pattern of guitar part) plus spacious texture send message that this is important music

center, investing it with a power and impact that it could not have had in a simpler setting. In this sense, the music of U2 is the ultimate folk rock, one in which the power of the words is matched by the power of the music.

Significant-Sounding Rock

For many, Bruce Springsteen and U2 were the only two truly important acts of the eighties. Both confronted difficult problems in which they had a deep personal involvement: the Vietnam War, the conflict in Northern Ireland, and the suffering in Africa. And both wore their hearts on their sleeves: they would rather be too passionate than too reserved.

The power of their music comes from applying two principles: simplifying and highlighting basic rhythms and creating a full, yet open sound. By emphasizing regular timekeeping over syncopation, and maintaining the same basic texture with only subtle variation through long stretches of time, the instrumental settings convey both simplicity and seriousness. Their function is to enhance the power and presence of the lyric.

The rhythmic approach used by both Springsteen and U2, while realized in strikingly different ways, has the same effect: it cuts the cord with good-time rock. As we have noted in earlier chapters, the rock groove that makes people want to get up and dance grows out of the interplay between regular rhythms and rhythms that conflict with it or transcend it. Both of the songs discussed in this section minimize or all but eliminate this interplay. In "Born in the U.S.A." it is confined almost exclusively to the dominant riff and the backbeat; in "Where the Streets Have No Name" it occurs only in the irregular *patterns* of The Edge's active accompaniment, not in the rhythm itself, which is regular. It is as if both Springsteen and U2 are saying that they want listeners to hear the message in the lyrics. Listeners can draw power from the music, but they should not be distracted by rhythms that are too playful for the lyric. In post-punk rock, a serious message virtually demands music with minimal syncopation.

⬤ ⬤ ⬤ ⬤ ⬤ ⬤ ⬤ ⬤

Renewing Rock and Roll

Among the most important debuts of 1988 was a group known as the Traveling Wilburys. They presented themselves as half-brothers of the late Charles T. Wilbury Sr.: Lucky, Otis, Charles T. Jr., Nelson, and Lefty. In fact, the Traveling Wilburys were one of the great super-groups of any era. On their first album, released in the fall of that year, the Wilburys included Bob Dylan, Jeff Lynne, Tom Petty, George Harrison, and Roy Orbison. This recording was the only one to include all of the original members; Orbison passed away later that year.

Lynne (b. 1947) was the catalyst for the formation of the group. After leading the Electric Light Orchestra through-out the seventies and into the eighties, Lynne dissolved the band in 1986 to move into solo work and production. While at lunch, Harrison and Lynne called Bob Dylan to ask whether they could use his home studio to record a song. Orbison was in town and agreed to sing on the track. Petty (b. 1950) and Dylan joined in. The good times led to an album assembled over a ten-day period.

The Traveling Wilburys. Clockwise from top left: Jeff Lynne, Bob Dylan, Tom Petty, George Harrison, and Roy Orbison.

There is symbolic significance to the coming together of Dylan, Orbison, and Harrison just before Orbison's death. The road from Anglo-American folk music to rock divided with the birth of country music in the twenties and the reclamation of the folk heritage in the thirties. Until the sixties, they evolved along largely separate paths. Rock-and-roll acts found little common ground with folk counterparts other than their shared heritage and a mostly young audience; Buddy Holly and The Kingston Trio were in different worlds musically. Their intersection with—and through—rock began in the early sixties, in large part because of the work of Orbison and Dylan. By the late eighties, the schism was ancient history; the formation of the Wilburys celebrated that fact.

Neo-Traditional Trends of the Eighties

The Wilburys' collaboration was one branch of a **neo-traditional movement** within rock during the eighties and nineties. The Rolling Stones breathed life into their career in the early eighties, while boogie bands such as ZZ Top kept trucking along. Also, many newer rock acts—such as John Mellencamp, Tom Petty and the Heartbreakers, and Dire Straits—carved out a niche in the rock marketplace.

Flashing back to an even more distant past was a jump-band revival led by the Stray Cats; it would gain momentum in the nineties in the music of groups such as the Brian Setzer Orchestra. Fresh voices breathed new life into two of rock's most influential antecedents: the blues and the socially conscious song. The blues revival that began in the mid-eighties gave a boost to the careers of established bluesmen and introduced new stars, such as Stevie Ray Vaughan and Robert Cray. Later in the decade, a new generation of socially aware female singer-songwriters, among them Tracy Chapman and Suzanne Vega, would evoke the spirit of early Bob Dylan.

John Mellencamp

Perhaps the most down-to-earth of the newer rock acts was John Mellencamp—literally. "Rain On The Scarecrow" (1986), one of his most powerful songs, tells the plight of the small-time farmer through a tale about a family that's losing their farm. So it's not surprising that Mellencamp was one of the main forces behind the Farm Aid benefits.

Mellencamp, known as John Cougar at the beginning of his career ("Cougar" was his first manager's invention; Mellencamp learned about it only after seeing the name on the cover of his debut album), began his career in the mid-seventies, but it didn't take off until the early '80s. His breakthrough album was *American Fool* (1982), which included the No. 1 single "Jack And Diane." It was the first of five Mellencamp albums released in the 1980s to reach the Top Ten on the album charts and go platinum.

"Paper In Fire," John Mellencamp (1987). Mellencamp, vocal.

Mellencamp's "Paper In Fire," a hit single from the 1987 album *The Lonesome Jubilee*, shows his connection with, and expansion of, the American rock and roll tradition exemplified by Creedence Clearwater Revival, the Dead, and the Band. Mellencamp encases an excellent story, which unfolds slowly and suspensefully, in a well-grooved rock and roll setting. The lyric tells a cautionary tale about the fate of those who get but don't give. Mellencamp sets up the chorus beautifully by presenting the verse with a subdued, static accompaniment, then exploding with siren-like syncopated chords at the chorus.

Through the instrumentation of the song, Mellencamp deepens the country/blues fusion that typified the "American" sound, ca. 1970. Among the backup instruments are a banjo (bluegrass), slide guitar (deep blues), fiddle (country), and accordion (zydeco); the tambourine shaking out a double-time rhythm throughout the song was a staple in the minstrel show and in numerous rock bands of the 1960s.

"Paper In Fire" is an especially successful continuation of the storytelling tradition within rock that dates back to Bob Dylan. Like Dylan, Mellencamp uses the musical setting to amplify the sense of the text; the music behind the words and melody are integral to the impact of the song. It demonstrates that fresh approaches to the by-now-timeless rock style produce memorable music.

Looking Back, Looking Ahead

In the eighties, pop, rhythm and blues, and rock reinvented themselves. Of the eight tracks presented in this chapter, only one—Mellencamp's "Paper in Fire"—could reasonably have been created before 1980. The others belong to the 1980s, mainly because of the increased prominence of synthesized sounds and new punk/funk/disco/reggae-influenced rhythms. Also evident in several of these tracks is a return to relevance; the songs by Madonna, Prince, Turner, U2, Springsteen, and Mellencamp have meaningful messages, although they convey them in markedly different ways.

Among the most outstanding developments of the decade was the modernizing of pop and its emergence as a new middle ground in popular music. Pop stars, and particularly Michael Jackson and Madonna, led the way in reconceptualizing the music video as an integrated expressive form rather than a visual accompaniment to the song.

With the introduction of the CD, music-related cable TV channels, and the overwhelming popularity of music videos, the music industry continued to expand during the 1980s. The top pop, rock, and rhythm and blues acts achieved unprecedented commercial success. However, even as more middle-ground acts co-opted

5 to Listen For
"Paper in Fire"

INSTRUMENTATION
Lead and backup vocal, lead guitar, slide guitar, violin, harmonica, accordion, electric bass, banjo, drums, tambourine

PERFORMANCE STYLE
Mellencamp's husky voice ideal for storytelling

RHYTHM
Rock rhythm at fast tempo, with double-time rhythm in tambourine and abundant syncopation, especially "fire siren" riff

MELODY
Abundance of riffs in verse and chorus

TEXTURE
Sharp contrast between verse and chorus, mainly because of subtraction/addition of instruments

3 to Remember
"Paper in Fire"

COMPELLING STORY
Three vignettes relate in different ways how those who take without giving get burned.

SOUND PAINTING
Musical setting amplifies impact of lyric: verse = suppressed energy; chorus explodes, with siren-like sounds.

AMERICAN SOUND
Mellencamp's down-home vocal style, solid rock rhythm, bluegrass and blues instruments (banjo, slide guitar, fiddle, etc.) all project "American" rock sound, ca. mid-1980s.

the cutting-edge music of the 1970s, alternative sounds emerged in towns and cities like Athens, Georgia, and Aberdeen, Washington.

● ● ● ● ● ● ● ●
Terms to Know

Test your knowledge of this chapter's important terms by defining the ones listed here. If you can't recall the meaning of a certain term, refresh your memory by looking up the boldfaced term in the chapter, turning to the Glossary at the back of the book, or working with the flashcards at the Popular Music Resource Center.

dance-oriented rock (DOR)
MTV
neo-traditional movement

Alternative, Heavy Metal, and Grunge After 1980

istockphoto.com

CHAPTER

16

Aberdeen, Washington, is a town of about 16,000 people. It is situated at the eastern end of Grays Harbor, an inlet along the Pacific Coast in the west-central part of the state. The town bills itself as the gateway to the Olympic Peninsula, a beautiful temperate rainforest. However, timber, not tourism, is the main industry. It is not a wealthy town. Unemployment runs high, especially among younger residents.

The dominant colors in Aberdeen are green and gray. As in other towns along the coast in northern California and the Pacific Northwest, the climate is relatively mild: not too cold in the winter and not too warm in the summer. Trees and other plants thrive there. However, it rains frequently—about 85 inches a year—and fog and overcast skies are far more common than sunshine, especially in winter.

Though it's hard to establish a causal connection between artists and the environment in which they were raised, one can't help wondering whether Kurt Cobain's music would have taken a radically different form had he been born in Miami, Florida, which is about as far southeast as Aberdeen is northwest. As it happened, grunge, the alternative music that Cobain and Nirvana helped bring to a mass audience, seems to reflect the depressed circumstances and depressing weather that one encounters in Aberdeen.

Grunge brought alternative music into the mainstream and made Seattle a rock hotspot during the nineties. However, by the time Nirvana crossed over in 1992, the alternative movement was a decade old and rapidly diversifying from its punk base.

● ● ● ● ● ● ● ● ●

The Alternative Movement

Alternative is an umbrella term for a large family of rock-related, punk-inspired styles that began to develop in the early eighties and continues to flourish in the early twenty-first century. "Alternative" has lost its original connotation as the music it identifies has become more familiar. However, the alternative movement began as a musical alternative not only to the pop of Michael Jackson and others but also to the more commercial, MTV-oriented rock of the eighties.

istockphoto.com

Alternative bands sought the artistic freedom to make the music they wanted to make, uncorrupted by a corporate mindset

"Our band could be your life."
—The Minutemen, pioneer alternative band

The Alternative Ecosystem

The elevator-trip version of alternative rock: in the sixties, rock mattered; in the seventies, it sold out—except for punk; in the eighties, alternative bands mattered; in the nineties, they sold out.

Such a simple paradigm cannot help but distort the reality of the situation. Integrity is not incompatible with popular success, as the Beatles and many other acts have demonstrated. Nor is all pop necessarily bad. But there's no question that the bottom-line mentality of the major players in the music business has made mainstream pop more calculating and less daring. In this respect, the paradigm rings true.

What the paradigm does describe, with greater accuracy, is the us-versus-them attitude of those who inhabited the world of alternative rock. As the movement took shape, musicians and audiences believed passionately that their music mattered. For them, rock was a way of life, as it had been in the sixties. Like the punk and new wave music from which it developed, early alternative flourished in a largely closed ecosystem. Control was the key. Alternative bands sought the artistic freedom to make the music they wanted to make, uncorrupted by a corporate mindset.

Alternative was a grassroots movement to restore integrity and importance to rock. Bands toured relentlessly, going from one small club to the next. (The Bird, Seattle's first punk rock club, had an official capacity of ninety-nine people, although twice that many routinely crowded into the club.) They recorded low-budget albums on their own or on independent labels and sold many of them at performances. Some got airplay on college radio stations; during the eighties, commercial stations seldom programmed songs by alternative bands. Many developed loyal, even fanatic, followings; some fans published or wrote for fanzines. Occasionally, bands attracted attention from outside critics and fans: *Rolling Stone* selected *Murmur*, R.E.M.'s first album, as the best album of 1983.

Because it started out on such a small scale, the world of alternative music was far more personal. Fans, writers, and others who supported the music felt a sense of ownership. Usually, they had gone the extra mile or two to seek out bands to follow. They bought their recordings. Perhaps they had gotten to know members of the band, done some of the grunt work, or written for a fanzine. The sense of connection went beyond the music; as the Minutemen, one of the pioneer alternative bands, sang, "Our band could be your life." So when a band caught on—signed with a major label; played on big, well-organized tours; made videos; appeared on MTV—fans felt betrayed, or at least marginalized.

Success was also a concern for the musicians. The experience of becoming a rock star helped drive Kurt Cobain to suicide. His suicide note alludes to this.

> "I feel guilty beyond words about these things, for example when we're backstage and the lights go out and the manic roar of the crowd begins. It doesn't affect me in the way which it did for Freddie Mercury, who seemed to love and relish the love and admiration from the crowd, which is something I totally admire and envy. The fact is, I can't fool you, any of you. It simply isn't fair to you, or to me. The worst crime I can think of would be to pull people off by faking it, pretending as if I'm having one hundred percent fun. Sometimes I feel as though I should have a punch-in time clock before I walk out on-stage. I've tried everything within my power to appreciate it, and I do, God believe me, I do, but it's not enough."—Kurt Cobain

It is painful to read how fame caused Cobain to lose the thing that he valued the most. In 1994 he cancelled Nirvana's appearance at Lollapalooza, the Woodstock-like touring festival that helped catapult alternative into the mainstream, then took his life.

It's ironic that "rock that mattered" became an alternative to mainstream music, rather than the heart of it, in less than two decades. Even though many of the sixties artists whose music mattered the most—such as Bob Dylan, Frank Zappa, the Velvet Underground—were never mainstays on the singles charts, there was a sense of common purpose between them and acts, such as the Beatles and the Rolling Stones, that did have a real pop presence. Moreover, they had the support of those behind the scenes, from major labels eager to book the next important act to free-form radio and festivals like Woodstock.

That wasn't the case in the eighties. For the most part, the mainstream

had evolved away from this change-the-world attitude. Acts like Springsteen and U2—acts that said something important to a lot of people—were the exception, not the rule. Most of the other integrity-first bands were simply an alternative to the mainstream.

Alternative: A Neo-Traditional Trend

Alternative began as a neo-traditional movement: recapturing the sense of importance that characterized rock in the sixties and punk and new wave music in the seventies was its primary goal. However, the message was different. Alienation replaced the heady optimism of the sixties as the dominant theme. Musically, alternative derived most directly from punk and new wave. Tempos were fast, rhythms were busy, sound levels were generally loud—and sounded louder because of the small spaces in which they played. The point of departure was the garage band. The core instrumentation was typically vocals, a guitar or two, bass, and drums, although bands often went beyond this basic lineup.

As the movement gained momentum in the latter part of the eighties, it diversified by infusing elements of other rock-era substyles—such as funk,

Kurt Cobain

Terry McGinnis/WireImage/Getty Images

Sound levels were generally loud—and sounded louder because of the small spaces in which they played.

istockphoto.com

metal, and electronica—into its punk core or by imparting a more modern sensibility to genres that had come and gone, such as ska and the music of the early seventies singer-songwriters. Common ground became more a matter of attitude and commercial presence (or lack of it—bands flew under the radar of big music) than musical similarity. The first **Lollapalooza** tour (1991)—an important outlet for alternative music in the nineties—featured such diverse acts as Jane's Addiction (the festival was band member Perry Ferrell's idea), Nine Inch Nails, and Ice-T and Body Count. None of these is a "pure" post-punk band.

With the sudden and surprising success of grunge in the early nineties, alternative music wrestled with the tension between high-mindedness and commercial success. In the early twenty-first century, alternative is as much a music industry label as it is a statement of purpose.

The discussions that follow highlight the music of five acts: R.E.M., Metallica, Ani DeFranco, Nirvana, and Radiohead. All but Metallica have been labeled "alternative" acts; the considerable differences among them underscore the extent to which "alternative" is defined as much by what it isn't as by what it is. Heavy metal isn't strictly an alternative style, but the music of high-minded bands like Metallica has more in common with the music of alternative acts—in intent, result, and audience—than it does with the pop middle ground of the eighties and nineties.

• • • • • • • •

From Punk to Alternative

The boundary between punk and new wave on the one hand and alternative on the other seems more geographic than temporal or musical. The formation of the first alternative bands occurred around 1980, when the careers of bands like the Clash, Elvis Costello and the Attractions, and the Talking Heads were at a high point. Their music represents a stylistic continuation of punk and new wave; there is no radical difference between the two at the beginning, although alternative would soon diversify into a much more varied music.

However, alternative took root in college towns throughout the United States rather than in major

Eddie Vedder of Pearl Jam, showing off his grunge footwear at the second Lollapalooza concert in 1992

metropolitan areas. The size of the town wasn't as important as the size of the university; it was the student body that provided the most enthusiastic support for these bands. Active regional scenes, in the United States and ultimately throughout the world, would become a hallmark of alternative music.

Early Alternative

The two bands most responsible for starting the alternative music movement were Hüsker Dü, based in St. Paul, Minneapolis (home of the University of Minnesota), and R.E.M., formed in Athens, Georgia (home of the University of Georgia). Both locales were well outside the New York–London axis where punk and new wave flourished. Hüsker Dü (the group took their name from a Swedish board game whose name means "Do you remember?") began as a hardcore punk band trying to out-Ramone the Ramones. Their music occasionally ventured beyond this frenetically paced music toward a more moderate and melodic style. Although admired as an important influence on the new alternative movement, Hüsker Dü never crossed over to a more mainstream audience. That wasn't the case with R.E.M.

R.E.M. was formed in 1980 by guitarist Peter Buck (b. 1956) and vocalist Michael Stipe (b. 1960). Buck and Stipe recruited bassist Mike Mills (b. 1958) and drummer Bill Berry (b. 1958), agreed on a name (REM is the acronym for "rapid eye movement," a defining characteristic of the lightest stage of sleep), then performed relentlessly. They quickly became favorites of the local underground rock scene, playing college bars and parties while waiting for their big break, which came quickly.

"Radio Free Europe," Bill Berry, Peter Buck, Mike Mills, Michael Stipe (1981). R.E.M.

"Radio Free Europe," their first hit, helped put the band on the rock music map and establish the essentially retrospective orientation of alternative music. It has the bright tempo, clean rhythm, and lean sound associated with David Bowie and new wave bands. The texture is spare in the verse; by contrast, the chorus features a much richer texture because of the jangly, reverberant guitar figuration and the active bass line underneath Stipe's vocals.

Characteristically for R.E.M., the lyric is as elliptical as the music is clear. The words are intelligible, but what do they mean? By their own admission, the band

5 to Listen For
"Radio Free Europe"

INSTRUMENTATION
"Radio" noises: vocals, guitars, bass, drums

PERFORMANCE STYLE
Nice contrast between detached guitar sound in verse, more resonant and sustained sound in chorus

RHYTHM
Punk-influenced fast, basic rock beat, with strong backbeat, repeated notes in bass/guitar in verse; chorus adds sustained vocal sound.

MELODY
Verse = short, separated statement on repeated melodic phrase; chorus = string of long notes in different key

TEXTURE
Shift in texture underscores verse/chorus contrast: spare sound in verse; richer sound, with moving bass line, guitar figuration in chorus

3 to Remember
"Radio Free Europe"

WHAT IS THE SONG ABOUT?
Non-narrative lyrics whose meaning is at best abstruse

POST-PUNK ROCK
Clean, prominent rock rhythm in drums and bass at fast tempo, but active bass line, harmonies in different key departure from conventional punk approach: less aggressive, more subtle

SHARP CONTRASTS
Open sound of the verse and warmer, guitar-enriched texture of the chorus, with more melodic bass line

the tone for the alternative movement. And the simplicity of their sound—basic instrumentation, clear textures, little if any electronic wizardry—was a model for the alternative bands that followed.

• • • • • • • •

Extreme Virtuosity: Heavy Metal After 1980

Heavy metal, such a powerful force in rock during the early seventies, seemed a caricature of itself by mid-decade. The most visible metal band was Kiss, who gained their reputation more from their clownish makeup and over-the-top stage show than their music. However, metal didn't go away; it simply went on the road.

Although dismissed or ignored by rock critics—Lester Bangs pronounced it all but dead in the late seventies—heavy metal developed a loyal and steadily increasing fan base through the late seventies and eighties through frequent touring. Fans packed arenas to hear their favorite bands, bought their recordings, and kept up to date through fanzines. By contrast, mainstream exposure on radio and MTV was minimal, especially early in the 1980s.

The Revival of Heavy Metal

However, by the end of the 1980s, it was clear that heavy metal was the most popular genre in a heavily segmented rock marketplace. To cite just one piece of evidence, Guns N' Roses' debut album, *Appetite for Destruction* (1987), sold over 20 million units. Numerous other metal bands, among them Van Halen, Def Leppard, and Metallica, also racked up platinum/multiplatinum record sales.

Male teens and males slightly older made up most of the heavy metal fan base in the eighties. In the wake of the economic hard times in both Great Britain and the United States, many faced a bleak future. They felt out of the

has deliberately written nonspecific lyrics. As Michael Stipe said in a late-eighties interview, "I've always left myself pretty open to interpretation."

The sharp and sudden contrasts between verse and chorus provide a foretaste of what would become a defining feature of alternative music: dramatic, often jarring contrasts within songs. And Buck's flashback to a guitar sound directly descended from the Byrds' Roger McGuinn provides an early instance of the infusion of alternative's punk base with elements from other retro styles.

By the late eighties, R.E.M. had begun to bring alternative into the mainstream: "The One I Love" (1987) was their first Top 10 single. They would remain a popular band through the nineties, although Berry retired from performing in 1997.

In their determination to follow their own creative path, even if it circled back to the past instead of moving toward the future, the group set

||||||||||||||||||||||||||||||||||||||

"I've always left myself pretty open to interpretation."
—Michael Stipe of R.E.M.

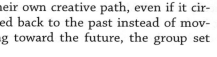

Tom Hill/WireImage/Getty Images

loop, especially during the eighties, when the gap between rich and poor widened so dramatically. They responded to the recurrent themes in heavy metal: the occult, sexual dominance (often to the point of misogyny), rage, frustration, protest, and—above all—power. Band names tell the story—Megadeth, AC/DC, Motörhead, Judas Priest, Slayer, Iron Maiden, Twisted Sister, Scorpions—all worthy sequels to the original: Black Sabbath.

And it was the music above all that conveyed the power. Most characteristically, heavy metal was loud to the point where a listener *felt* it as much as heard it. And the sound was heavily distorted, a sign both of power (distortion originally came from overdriving amplifiers) and defiance (distortion was originally an undesirable byproduct of amplification, to be avoided if possible).

Performances were a communion between musicians and their audience. Bands preached to the converted. Fans knew the words to songs (from liner notes), even though they were often unintelligible in performance. Stage shows were typically spectacles on a grand scale, comparable to an elaborate pagan ritual. In response, metalheads engaged in **headbanging**, heavy metal's version of dancing. In the familiarity of the audience/congregation with the songs, in their involvement in the performance, and in the sense of power that they experienced during the event, a heavy metal concert was more like a religious rite than anything else.

All of this occurred outside the purview of the mainstream media. Few "unconverted" listeners were willing to go past the distortion, the lyrics, and the visual images. The music, and what it stood for, was almost universally misunderstood and underappreciated. Those who attended the symphony would probably have been horrified to learn of the wholesale expropriation of classical music by metal guitarists like Eddie Van Halen, Randy Rhoads, Yngwie Malmsteen, James Hetfield, and Dave Mustaine. They might well be scandalized at the suggestion that Eddie Van Halen expanded the sound possibilities and raised the level of virtuosity on his

> *A heavy metal concert was more like a religious rite than anything else.*

istockphoto.com

instrument more than any performer in any genre—classical, jazz, rock, or country—since the diabolical nineteenth-century violinist Niccolo Paganini and his pianist counterpart, Franz Liszt. For the most part, heavy metal remained insulated in its own world: the bands and their fans. Indeed, Van Halen's 1978 self-titled debut album helped bridge the gap between the early seventies and the metal renaissance of the eighties.

Heavy metal was never a monolithic style, as we've seen, but in the eighties it became even more diverse. Substyles, often based on a single feature, proliferated. By the end of the decade there was speed metal, thrash metal, death metal, industrial metal, and more. Its diversity was also due to its blending with other styles; during the eighties, heavy metal came in several grades of purity. Distortion remained metal's sound signature, but "pure" heavy metal was far more than a rock song played with distortion.

As evidenced in the music of top eighties bands such as Metallica and Megadeth, a heavy metal song is a far cry from standard rock, rhythm and blues, or pop fare. Here are some of the most striking differences:

- *Distortion is typically more extreme.* Because it is the most easily borrowed feature of heavy metal style, serious metal bands compensated by increasing the distortion to the point that the notes being played may be almost impossible to discern because of the halo of white noise around them.
- *Instrumentation is basic.* It consists of one or two guitars, bass, and drums. Use of additional instruments—synths, saxes, extra percussion—is a stylistic impurity, as we noted in the earlier discussion of Van Halen's "Jump."
- *It is not tuneful music.* This is especially evident in the vocal line, which is typically more incantation than melody. The vocalists chant, wail, even spit out the words. They seldom sing a catchy melodic phrase.
- *The ratio of instrumental sections to vocal sections is much higher than in most other rock-based styles.* In

addition to extended solos, where lead guitarists show off their prowess, there are also long passages with no vocal lines. These typically consist of a series of intricate riffs.

- *It typically avoids conventional harmony.* Bands may play power chords, but complete harmonies and chord progressions are the exception rather than the rule. Instead, the music tends to be linear, with both solos and group riffs built on modes. Variety in pitch choice comes about through shifts from one mode to another or shifting the central tone of a mode. (It should be noted that the avoidance of conventional harmony in heavy metal is a choice, not a limitation. Numerous metal songs begin with delicate, slow introductions; these often contain sophisticated harmony. Apparently, eighties metal bands, like their predecessors from the early seventies, felt that the use of standard or even alternative chord progressions would undermine the power of their music.)
- *The best metal bands are virtuosic.* This applies not only to the guitarist(s) who solo, but also to the entire band, who create and perform intricate riffs, often at breathtakingly fast tempos, with a level of precision comparable to that of a fine string quartet or tight jazz combo.
- *Metal "songs" tend to be long, sprawling, multisectional works.* They avoid the standard verse/bridge/chorus formula of rock-era music. Instead, the work typically consists of blocks of sound, often in different tempos and with different key centers, all arranged in complex, unpredictable sequences.

These features occur in heavy metal tracks undiluted with other stylistic elements. What passed for heavy metal in the eighties ranged from mainstream rock covered with a metal sheen (for example, Def Leppard's "Photograph") to the music of such conscientious bands as Metallica. We consider "One," a track from their 1988 album *And Justice for All.* The song was released as a single during the following year; it was also the song used for the band's first music video.

Metallica

Metallica began the eighties, toiling in relative obscurity. The group, formed in 1981 by guitarist-vocalist James Hetfield (b. 1963) and drummer Lars Ulrich (b. 1963), built an ardent cult following during the first part of eighties even as it burned through a string of guitarists, including Dave Mustaine (b. 1961), who would later form Megadeth. In 1983 Hetfield and Ulrich recruited Kirk Hammett (b. 1962); Hammett remains the lead guitarist with the group. Cliff Burton (1962–1986), the bassist for Metallica's first three albums, died in a freak

James Hetfield of Metallica

accident during a 1986 Swedish tour. Jason Newsted (b. 1963) replaced him; he would remain with the group through 2001.

"One," James Hetfield and Lars Ulrich (1988). Metallica.

Like those of other top metal bands, Metallica's record sales were brisk, although the band got almost no exposure on radio or television. The group eventually broke through on radio in 1988 with "One," a single from their fourth album (and first with Newsted), *And Justice for All,* which peaked at No. 6 on the charts.

Even a cursory listening to "One" makes clear that the market came to Metallica, not the other way around. "One" is a grim antiwar statement that unfolds on a large scale: the work is well over 7 minutes long. It makes few concessions to mainstream rock—in lyrics, music, or length. The form of the song takes its shape from the images in the lyrics; it is an especially graphic depiction of the horrors of war, as experienced by one of its many casualties.

The song unfolds slowly and gently at first, after the faint chatter of machine guns and other war noises; the extended instrumental introduction features a guitar duet. The first flash of typical metal comes about 2 minutes later, in the chorus; the burst of distortion seems to depict a flashback by the protagonist. For the next 2 minutes, the track alternates between the gentler flamenco-tinged music and the more aggressive and distorted music of the chorus, as the protagonist moves back and forth from faint memories to the painful present. About halfway through, the music abandons the gentler sound of the opening section. With the entry of the "machine gun" rhythm—first on drums, then with the entire band—it is as if the scene shifts from the hospital ward to the battlefield. The action escalates, first in an ensemble section dominated by the "machine gun" rhythm, then in a guitar solo. The song ends abruptly.

In its sprawling form, relatively little emphasis on vocal lines, musical sophistication (for instance, there

INSTRUMENTATION
War sounds; vocal, guitars, bass, drums

PERFORMANCE STYLE
Growling vocal, extreme distortion in guitars, bass in latter part of track

RHYTHM
Frequent shifts between four-beat and three-beat measures; rock rhythm implied throughout

MELODY
Multiple melodies in vocal sections: verse deliberately flat—several repeated notes—chorus short, simple

TEXTURE
Numerous textures ranging from guitar solo/duet to full band in low register: massive dark sound

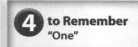

PROTEST SONG
Lyrics and music send grim, powerful antiwar message.

SPRAWLING FORM
"One" unfolds slowly with Spanish-flavored guitar intro, dramatic shifts in pacing, rhythm, texture, extended instrument sections: episodic form, with several "scenes."

UPDATED METAL SOUNDS
Intense distortion, tight ensemble (especially in the latter half of the song), fluent guitar solo

STRONG CONTRASTS
Shifts from section to section amplify "flashback" elements in lyrics

may have scorned it early on, musicians didn't. Not only did it develop into one of the important directions of the late eighties and nineties, it also bled into the exciting new fusions of the alternative bands that began to surface at the end of the decade. It remains a significant part of the rock music scene.

● ● ● ● ● ● ● ●

Women's Voices

Women quickly found a home in the alternative movement. Their growing presence can be understood as still another dimension of the more prominent place of women in popular music; the eighties were the decade not only of Madonna but also of Joan Jett, the Go-Go's, and the Bangles. What made the work of women in alternative music distinctive was that their voices were not constrained in any way by the expectations of more mainstream music. Alternative gave feminists a forum and enabled women of every persuasion to speak their mind.

The women's movement within alternative music took root in the latter part of the eighties and flourished in the nineties. Among the important trends was the **riot grrrl** movement, which supported a militant feminist agenda with post-punk music that favored confrontation over chops (that is, musical skill). The music was part of a self-contained subculture; Bands like Bratmobile and Bikini Kill played in clubs and at music festivals that promoted feminist solidarity. Feminist fanzines nurtured and promoted them and other acts, and independent labels released their recordings The **queercore** movement, which reacted against more mainstream gay and lesbian views, found a musical voice in the work of bands such as Sister George, Tribe 8, and Team Dresch, whose founder Donna Dresch also created the fanzine *Chainsaw*, which she spun off into a still active record label.

Alternative music also supported a revival of singer-songwriters, many of them women. Even as artists like Tracy Chapman, Suzanne Vega, k.d. lang, and Alanis Morrissette garnered major label contracts and the occasional Grammy award (Tracy Chapman's "Give Me One Reason" won a Grammy in 1996 for Best Rock Song), other singer-songwriters, such as Patty Larkin, Dar Williams, and Ani DiFranco, also toured and recorded extensively.

That the music of women within the alternative movement would take these two directions should not

are several shifts from four-beat to three-beat measures), and deep contrast from dark and moody beginning to powerful conclusion, "One" demands a lot from its listeners. The music is as uncompromising and grim as its message.

"One" has more in common with a film soundtrack than a conventional rock song. Indeed, after recording the song, Metallica discovered the similarities between their song and *Johnny Get Your Gun,* a 1939 antiwar novel that author Dalton Trumbo later turned into a film. The music video of "One" juxtaposes scenes from Trumbo's film with footage of the band and adds dialogue from the film to the music. Curiously, many of Metallica's fans objected to the video, the band's first. Perhaps it was the fact of the video that troubled them, because the video, with its skillful mixing of band scenes with film footage, makes the antiwar message of the track even more compelling.

Metallica's "One" is significant rock. With its long, narrative-based form, dramatic shifts in mood, masterful playing, and vivid sound images, "One" makes its statement through a style that is in many ways more complex than that heard in the songs of Springsteen or U2. It exemplifies Metallica's principled approach to music making; there is nothing in "One" that suggests any effort to accommodate more mainstream tastes. Despite this, the band has enjoyed commercial success as well as critical acclaim.

Despite its growing popularity, no rock music of the eighties was less understood or less appreciated than heavy metal. However, even though critics and audiences be surprising, because they have their roots in the two seventies styles most open to women. Patti Smith was a punk pioneer, and musicians like Talking Heads bassist Tina Weymouth made women instrumentalists less exceptional—Kim Gordon, the bassist with Sonic Youth, followed in her footsteps. Similarly, singer-songwriters like Joni Mitchell and Carly Simon brought a feminine perspective to the forefront of popular music; the music of contemporary artists such as Ani DiFranco continues that tradition.

Ani DiFranco

Although her music has evolved away from what she calls the "folk punk" of her early recordings, Ani Di Franco (b. 1970) embodies the entrepreneurial spirit of alternative music as fully as any artist. Rather than wait for a major label to offer her a contract, she started her own record company, Righteous Babe Records, in 1989 and put out her first album the following year. While in college at New York City's New School, she began touring actively, performing in small clubs and other venues where she built up a loyal following. As she and her label grew more successful (it now offers all of her recordings, plus recordings by twelve other acts), she established the Righteous Babe Foundation, to give support to causes in which she believes, including queer visibility, opposition to the death penalty, and historic preservation. (The new headquarters of Righteous Babe is a formerly abandoned church in Buffalo.)

Like Joni Mitchell, whose music has reflected a similarly wide-ranging curiosity and a from-the-heart perspective, DiFranco's music has ranged from contemporary takes on the urban folk style

"32 Flavors," Ani DiFranco (1995). DiFranco, vocal; Andy Stochansky, percussion.

to collaborations with major artists such as Prince, Janis Ian, Maceo Parker, and the Buffalo Philharmonic Orchestra. The three constants have been incisive lyrics, which usually speak either to social and political issues dear to her heart or the current take on her personal life; her affecting voice; and her fluent and imaginative acoustic guitar playing. We hear her mordant view on a failed relationship in "32 Flavors," a track from her 1995 album *Not a Pretty Girl*.

"32 Flavors" is the product of just two musicians: DiFranco and percussionist Andy Stochansky, a longtime collaborator. Together, they update the work of the great singer-songwriters of the early seventies. DiFranco's guitar accompaniment, which remains consistent throughout the song, is more elaborate and melodic than the accompaniments typically heard in the folk and folk-inspired music of the sixties and seventies. Guitar(s)—DiFranco added a discreet bass guitar part—and percussion provide a buoyant cushion for DiFranco's scathing indictment of a former partner. Lines like "cuz some day you are going to get hungry/ and eat most of the words you just said" cut like a scalpel because they are funny and true. DiFranco's warm, low-key vocal style in this song resonates with the gentle accompaniment; its understated quality gives the lyrics even more bite because of the contrast between the message and its delivery. The extended percussion outro is a nice bonus, although not connected thematically to the lyric.

The gently flowing music of Ani DiFranco heard here is some distance stylistically from the punk-inspired sounds that typify alternative music. However, her do-it-yourself approach to all aspects of her career—performing, recording, managing, promoting, and support for other grassroots efforts in causes that are important to her—embodies the spirit of alternative music. Her enterprise and determination in charting her own career path, unbeholden to authority figures

Interestingly, just as DiFranco's career began, alternative began its move into the mainstream, in the music of groups like Nirvana.

> "DiFranco's enterprise and determination in charting her own career path, unbeholden to authority figures in any branch of the music industry, has been an inspiration to numerous young musicians."

C. Flanigan/FilmMagic/Getty Images

Alienation

The final two tracks discussed in this chapter are Nirvana's "Smells Like Teen Spirit" and Radiohead's "Paranoid Android." One typically finds them identified

INSTRUMENTATION
Lead/backup vocal, guitar, bass, percussion, drums

PERFORMANCE STYLE
Understated vocal, instrumental styles put lyrics in forefront

RHYTHM
Gentle 16-beat rhythm with persistent syncopation in accompaniment pattern

MELODY
Two repeated melodic ideas: stream of descending notes for verse; shorter wordless chorus

HARMONY
Vocal sections: cycling progression avoids conventional sequence.

STORY OUT FRONT
Sharp-edged lyric that describes a relationship gone bad with vivid images and imaginative, occasionally humorous wordplay

BUOYANT UNOBTRUSIVE SETTING
Low-key vocal style, repetitious melody, and rhythmically active and melodically imaginative guitar/percussion accompaniment create a buoyant cushion: melody, vocal style, and accompaniment an ideal foil for lyrics

RHYTHMIC NON SEQUITUR
Extended percussion jam = last half of song = no apparent relation to vocal section

(another term coined by Coupland), felt completely estranged from their baby-boomer parents and the world portrayed in the media. They saw little hope for advancement in their work; many felt that their odds of enjoying the lifestyle of the rich, if not the famous, were about as good as winning the lottery. They were more in tune with the "no future" mindset broadcast by the disaffected youth in Great Britain and North America and the punk bands that set it to music. The "X" used to identify them underscored their lack of identity and power. As a result, they turned away from mainstream society and turned toward the music that expressed their anger, frustration, and alienation. Their anthem was Nirvana's 1991 hit "Smells Like Teen Spirit."

as representative examples of grunge and art rock or prog rock, respectively. The musical resources used on each of these recordings differs markedly. Still, there is an undercurrent that connects them despite their obvious musical differences.

Both project a sense of alienation. It pours out of the lyrics and the music. And it comes from and speaks to a group dubbed Generation X.

Generation X

Generation X was a term popularized by Canadian novelist Douglas Coupland: it identifies the children of the baby boomers—those born mainly in the latter part of the sixties and the seventies. Most were born during the hangover from the sixties, with race riots, the squalid end to the Vietnam War, the rise of the "silent majority," the impeachment of Nixon, and rampant inflation all but obliterating the optimism with which the decade began. The members of Generation X, some of whom came from counterculture families, came of age during the "greed is good" eighties. Many, especially those stuck in service-industry "McJobs"

Grunge

The pivotal song in the history of alternative rock as a commercial music was Nirvana's "Smells Like Teen Spirit," from their 1991 album, *Nevermind*. For this recording, Nirvana consisted of singer-guitarist Kurt Cobain (1967–1994), bassist Chris Novoselic (b. 1965), and drummer Dave Grohl (b. 1969). Grohl replaced the drummers on Nirvana's first album, *Bleach* (1989), which the group made for just over $600. In the wake of its surprising success, Nirvana signed with Geffen Records. As a result, *Nevermind* was a far more elaborately produced album.

The album soared to No. 1, dethroning Michael Jackson's *Dangerous* album, which had been on top of the charts. "Smells Like Teen Spirit" got incessant airplay from MTV. All of a sudden the nineties had an anthem: it is still among the best-known songs of the decade. Alternative had crossed over.

Nirvana's particular brand of alternative came to be called **grunge**, though those involved in the scene hated the term. Grunge fused punk disaffection with the power and distortion of heavy metal. Like so many other alternative styles, it started on the fringes—literally: Cobain and Novoselic formed Nirvana in

Nirvana's sudden success made Seattle the mecca for grunge

Aberdeen, Washington, which is on the fringe of North America. The group's first single appeared on one of the many indie labels: the appropriately named Sub Pop, which was based in Seattle. Nirvana's sudden success made Seattle the mecca for grunge, but the sound had already surfaced in several locations around the United States.

In retrospect, it is easy to understand the enormous appeal of "Smells Like Teen Spirit," especially to its target audience: angry young people who were not ready to buy into the system. The lyrics jerk from image to idea, like a trigger-happy video editor. Their power comes not from their coherence but from the jarring juxtapositions—mulatto, albino, mosquito, libido; hello, how low.

The music amplifies this sense of dislocation. The song begins with a distinctive four-chord pattern. It is barely amplified; it sounds almost as if Cobain is trying it out for a song he's writing. Suddenly, we hear the same riff, this time with the whole band in heavy metal mode. Just as suddenly, the middle falls out—we are left with just bass, simple drum timekeeping, and a haunting two-note riff, which serves as an introduction to the verse; it continues underneath Cobain's singing. The two-note riff speeds up under the "hello/how low." The two-note vocal riff that sets "hello" then becomes the raw melodic material for the climactic

"Smells Like Teen Spirit," Kurt Cobain (1991). Nirvana.

section of the refrain. Here Cobain sings as if his throat is being ripped out. A short instrumental interlude, which interrupts the four-chord progression, bridges the chorus and the verse that follows.

We hear this same sequence of events, then a loud instrumental version of the verse and "hello" section. Instead of the refrain, however, the song shifts to a third verse; we hear the entire verse/bridge/chorus sequence again, followed by primal screams on the word "denial."

"Smells Like Teen Spirit" is a dark song. Everything about it conveys that message; its enormous impact comes in part from the reinforcement of this mood on so many levels. The chord progression does not follow a well-established path; because of this we respond more to its rise and fall. It is like a hole that one cannot climb out of: every time the band arrives at the fourth and highest chord, they drop back down. Because the bass line/outline runs through almost all of the song, despite all of the contrasts, it seems to suggest a depressed state of mind that's impossible to shake. In this context, the instrumental break following the refrain sounds absolutely demonic; it is purposefully ugly, even mocking.

The big innovation—and perhaps the biggest stroke of genius—is the schizophrenic shift from section to section. Nirvana creates sharply defined sound worlds within each section of the song. They are haunting, mocking, and angry in turn. They create sharp contrasts from section to section: the kind one would more likely encounter between one song and the next, rather than within a song. When combined with the relentless chord progression and the repetition of the two two-note melodic fragments, they project a mood of utter despair: one can rage against the wind—or the machine—or fall into an almost apathetic state, but it is impossible to shake off the dark mood.

"Smells Like Teen Spirit" is a remarkable synthesis of several different, almost contradictory, elements. The melodic material—especially the several instrumental hooks, the "hello" section, and the vocal chorus—embed themselves in the listener's ear; they offer immediate points of entry. At the same time, they don't sound like music calculated to be appealing. Rather, they seem to be a direct expression of the mood of the song; that they are catchy at the same time is a bonus.

The sharp contrasts and abrupt shifts from section to section help "Smells Like Teen Spirit" portray the darkest depression: an oppressive weight that cannot be thrown off. It is easy to understand why "Smells Like Teen Spirit" was the song of the nineties.

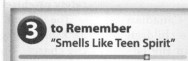

5 to Listen For
"Smells Like Teen Spirit"

INSTRUMENTATION
Vocal(s), guitar, bass, drums

PERFORMANCE STYLE
Screamed vocals, extreme distortion in loud section; modified vocal sound in "hello/how low"

RHYTHM
Active rock rhythm at moderate tempo

HARMONY
Distinctive progression cycles throughout song

TEXTURE
Dramatic contrasts between three sections: first section = empty sound, "hello" = reverberant guitar sound, third section = loud, with thick sound: vocal/distorted guitar/drums/bass

3 to Remember
"Smells Like Teen Spirit"

STRONG CONTRASTS
Three distinct sound worlds through most of song: empty verse, ringing bridge, screamed chorus

HARMONIC GLUE
Unresolved progression cycles throughout song, links contrasting sections.

SCHIZOPHRENIC SONG
Chord progression like depressed state impossible to shake; contrasting textures, sounds, dynamic levels suggest shift in mood.

And it makes Cobain's subsequent suicide even harder to take; it is as if he let us into his mind so that we can feel his despair.

"Smells Like Teen Spirit" is a punk song in spirit: it expresses rage, alienation, and frustration in both words and music. But the eclectic mix of styles—power trio intro, understated verse, metal breaks—serves an expressive purpose here. It extends the emotional range of punk, if only because the quiet of the verse makes the louder sections, especially the chorus with its short vocal riffs, more powerful by contrast. Classic punk drove in only one gear; here, Nirvana shifts back and forth among several.

Radiohead: The New Art Rock of the Nineties

The members of Radiohead all went to the same high school: Abingdon School, a private institution outside of Oxford. Drummer Phil Selway (b. 1967), guitarist Ed O'Brien (b. 1968), guitarist-vocalist Thom Yorke (b. 1968), bassist Colin Greenwood (b. 1969), and multi-instrumentalist Jonny Greenwood (b. 1971)—Colin's younger brother—formed the band On A Friday in 1986. They went to different universities but continued to practice together over vacations during their college years and came together again as Radiohead in 1992 (their name comes from a 1986 Talking Heads song, "Radio Head.").

Their first album made it quite clear that the group would find their own direction. The album name *Pablo Honey* came from a bit by the Jerky Boys, a comedy group whose CDs consist of irritatingly funny phone calls. "Creep," the single that got them noticed, is very much in the spirit of the times: it is Buddy Holly, deeply depressed. Musically, however, it does little to predict the group's future.

The alienation that marked Radiohead's early work becomes even more apparent in subsequent albums. This may be evident before the first sound: The booklet that comes with *OK Computer* (1997) contains the lyrics displayed almost randomly amid collage-like images. Both words and images are hard to decode. *Kid A* (2000) is even more frugal with content: there are simply fragments of images and no lyrics. It is as if the group is challenging its audience: we have something of value to say to you, but you have to work hard to discover what it is. This attitude extends to their songs, as we hear in "Paranoid Android," from *OK Computer*.

"Paranoid Android," Ed O'Brien, Jonny Greenwood, Colin Greenwood, Phil Selway, and Thom Yorke (1997). Radiohead.

"Paranoid Android" was a boundary-stretching single. This is apparent on even the first hearing, because the song is almost 6½ minutes long, more than double the length of a typical single. The lyrics are at once unremittingly depressing and incoherent. We have the impression of someone (human or android) holding his head and screaming, "I can't stand this any more!" as he goes mad.

The song is profoundly disturbing, not because the music is as dark as the lyrics, but because it is often so beautiful. It begins with a pan-Latin sound: intricate guitar figuration outlining exotic harmony, plus the shaker associated with Brazilian music and the claves of Cuban music, then a higher-pitched classical guitarlike line. There is no bass yet; the music floats. Yorke delivers the lyric slowly and in measured fashion, which directs our attention more to the haunting, plaintive quality of his voice. The refrain of this part has only two syllables: "what's then." Because these are only two words, our attention goes even more to the sound of his voice. A beautiful halo of sound surrounds it, as bass and a high synthesizer part enrich the texture. All this seems to resonate with the melancholy that is so much a part of Latin culture. Radiohead seems to have captured its essence in this part of the song, although they apply it to a quite different end.

A long transition to a new section begins with a guitar riff set against the Latin percussion. The riff appears on two levels and in two forms. The first statement lines up with four-beat measures. The higher-pitched restatement has a beat removed (four beats plus three). The sense of imbalance that the foreshortened riff creates helps set up the next vocal section, which has no apparent connection to the previous section. We get a spark of distortion, then another statement of the riff with full-bore distortion. It gains in power because of the contrast with the two previous sections. After a brief guitar solo, we hear a sustained chord, then a slower section with wordless vocal harmonies. Yorke sings over these simple but beautiful harmonies. Little by little, other layers are added; by the time the guitar riff interrupts again, the sonority is rich with vocal parts and sustained string-like synthesizer sounds. The reprise of the guitar riff is strictly instrumental; with its abrupt ending, it seems to signal a descent into madness.

The facts of the song—its sprawling length; the three distinct sections and the reprise of the second section; the strong contrast in character within and between sections; the deliberate delivery of the lyrics—are there. The reading of it is necessarily subjective.

The more significant point is that the conflicts and discontinuities within the words, within the music, and between the words and music demand that listeners engage with the song in more than a casual way. In particular, the music is complex and rich enough—even though it is also quite accessible—to admit multiple levels of meaning. Not since the Beatles' demise has a

INSTRUMENTATION
Vocal, Latin percussion, synthesizer, acoustic and electric guitars, bass, drums, keyboard

PERFORMANCE STYLE
Yorke's plaintive singing; sharp contrasts in instrumental timbre, from delicate acoustic guitar to heavily distorted

RHYTHM
Latin-like rhythm in first part/rock rhythm in second section; occasional three-beat measures create imbalance; slow rock rhythm with sustained harmonies in third section

MELODY
Tuneful fragments in opening section

TEXTURE
Jarring contrasts in texture, but all are rich, with several melodically interesting layers; extended sections without vocal

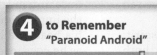

WORDS OF ALIENATION
Dark lyric, rich in obscure allusions, and as violently contrasting as the music

MUSIC OF ALIENATION
The contrast between sections shocks because the sections are so completely different in musical features such as instrumentation, rhythm and tempo, dynamics, and melodic style, and in the moods that they project. The opposition seems to be beauty vs. ugliness; the unifying element is the terrible sadness that runs through the entire track.

INTRASONG CONTRASTS: AN AESTHETIC FOR THE 1990S
In 1990s alternative music, jarring disjointedness often replaces internal coherence as an organizational principle.

ROCK AS ART REDUX
In their evocative use of rich, complex, contrasting sound worlds, Radiohead follows the lead of the Beatles.

sections create their own moods; we are violently whipped from one to the next. This kind of sonic fragmentation within a song is common in recent alternative music, in part because of the critical and commercial success of both bands.

Looking Back, Looking Ahead

There are numerous parallels between the alternative movement and early rock. Both grew out of the most rhythmically aggressive music of its time: the eight-beat rhythms of rock; the saturated eight-beat rhythms of punk. Both took shape on the fringes of the music industry, in out-of-the-way locales. Both were originally recorded on independent labels, then crossed over to the majors when the music gained commercial traction. Both developed passionate followings: rock as "a way of life" evolved into "our band could be your life." Both diversified stylistically over time by drawing in a wide range of influences. By the 1990s, "alternative" was an umbrella term for a disparate family of styles, much as "rock" was in the 1960s. And both saw their market share grow over time. This comparison also largely applies to second-generation heavy metal, although it is not identified as an "alternative" music because of its direct connection to the heavy metal of the early 1970s.

There are significant differences beyond the generation gap: 1950s–1960s; 1970s–1980s. Rock fomented a revolution. Punk, new wave, and alternative were, more than anything else, a counterrevolution, an attempt to reclaim the energy and attitude of early rock. To convey this musically, alternative bands often intensified those qualities that had distinguished rock from more established styles. They were often louder, more abrasive sonically, and aggressive rhythmically. Strong, almost schizophrenic, contrasts within songs, arguably the most widespread and significant musical innovation of alternative music, produced intensification by compression.

Unlike rock, alternative never became the dominant music of its time; it has remained a relatively small segment of the industry despite the unquestioned critical and commercial success of acts such as Radiohead. We

group blended accessibility, challenge, sound imagination, and sound variety so artfully. This is rock aspiring to significance.

Alienation and Fragmentation

Although "Smells Like Teen Spirit" and "Paranoid Android" create dramatically different sound worlds, they share two common elements that place them in the nineties. One is the sense of alienation that the lyrics project. In both there is palpable tension between the outside world and the world inside the protagonist's head. The other is sudden and jarring musical contrasts. In each song, the abrupt shifts from soft to loud seem to suggest a sudden loss of control: flying into a violent rage because one can't stand it anymore. These shifts magnify the message of the words; as used here, they provide the most consistent and powerful expression of the alienation depicted in the lyrics.

The strong sectional contrasts—sometimes to the point of discontinuity—describe a formal approach that is precisely the opposite of that used in more conventional rock songs. There, the chorus establishes the mood of the songs; the function of the verses is to amplify and explain that overall mood. Here, the various sample other significant trends in the early twenty-first century in the next chapter.

● ● ● ● ● ● ● ●

Terms to Know

Test your knowledge of this chapter's important terms by defining the terms listed here. If you can't recall the meaning of a certain term, refresh your memory by looking up the boldfaced term in the chapter, turning to the Glossary at the back of the book, or working with the flashcards at the Popular Music Resource Center.

alternative
Lollapalooza
headbanging

riot grrrl
queercore
grunge

A World
of Music
Popular Music at the
Turn of a New Century

istockphoto.com

CHAPTER

17

On April 3, 2008, Apple issued a press release announcing that "the iTunes Store surpassed Wal-Mart to become the number one music retailer in the United States, based on the latest data from the NPD Group. With over 50 million customers, iTunes has sold over four billion songs and features the world's largest music catalog of over six million songs." The date of the announcement was just shy of the fifth anniversary of Apple's online record store's opening for business on April 23, 2003.

• • • • • • • •

The Internet and the Music Industry in the Early Twenty-First Century

Apple's announcement underscored the suddenness with which the Internet has transformed the distribution of recorded music. The legal and illegal distribution of music over the Internet has helped democratize the music industry, returning much of the power to artists and audience. Those with access to what is now basic technology can make their own music and deliver it online to a global audience, bypassing the established industry channels. Listeners have much broader access to music and can choose exactly what music they would like to listen to—and pay for.

The Internet

The first attempts to create an Internet, or network of networks, date back to the seventies. By 1980 a protocol that enabled different networks to communicate with one another was in place. During its early years, the Internet was mainly under government supervision and control; the National Science Foundation managed it in the United States. However, in 1993 the Internet backbone was opened to the private sector in the United States, and Mosaic, the first browser, became available. (Mosaic became Netscape the following year.) Browsers simplified access to the Internet by providing a graphical user interface similar to those found on Windows and Mac operating systems. Rapid development in every aspect of the Internet experience, from increased bandwidth to faster computers and more capable browsers, has made downloading and—more recently—uploading audio and video routine. For listeners, the Internet has collapsed time and space; music from around the world and from every era of sound recording is increasingly available online.

The Internet offers consumers unprecedented choice. With the emergence of iTunes and other Internet-enabled delivery services, buyers can choose between buying an album or buying individual tracks, and buying the album digitally or physically. Similarly, subscription services such as Rhapsody are in effect an online jukebox—with millions of choices and a monthly fee instead of three plays for a quarter.

Consolidation of the Majors and Rise of Indies

These developments have provided a paradigm-shifting counterpoint to the continuing consolidation of the record industry. In 1980 there were six major record labels: Columbia, RCA, EMI, Polygram, MCA, and WCI. Collectively, they sold about four-fifths of the recordings released that year. By 2005 there were four majors, with the possibility of only three on the horizon. Seagram acquired MCA in 1995 and Polygram in 1998; they became the Universal Music Group. Columbia (bought by Sony) and RCA (bought by BMG) merged in 2003. An attempted merger between EMI and Warner in 2000 was called off; it may still happen. The four companies continue to control a decided majority of recorded music, although they market it under numerous labels. In 2005, about 82 percent of the recordings sold in the United States came from one of these majors.

The majors are as international as the music they sell. Currently, three of the four companies have headquarters outside the United States. Their operations have been similarly diverse. They have served, in effect, as large holding companies, providing administrative structure for numerous smaller labels targeted to specific markets. As a result, the recording industry has continued to diversify.

What the majors lack is the flexibility or the mindset to respond to variation and change. This has opened the door for independent labels, and even independent artists, to market quickly and specifically, using all available resources. Computers and the Internet enable them to do so at a fraction of conventional marketing costs. The use of a website for promotion, distribution, and online delivery eliminates upfront production expenses, such as pressing a large quantity of CDs, and the need for middlemen and conventional channels of distribution. At the same time, it makes music immediately available to a global audience. Because of these technological advances, artists and entrepreneurs have been able to create their own independent labels—including netlabels that deliver music only online, launch personal websites, start online artist cooperatives, and establish interest groups. All of this has enabled artists and labels to extend the sense of personal connection to a potentially much wider audience and return to the artists a much bigger chunk of a smaller pie.

To this point, the most spectacular instance of this new initiative was Radiohead's online pre-release of *In Rainbows* (2007), their first album in four years and the first created after their contract with EMI expired. The band initially offered it via direct download from their website, with consumers determining whether to pay for the album and, if so, how much. Although only 40 percent of downloaders paid something, the band still netted $3 million from online sales. All of this preceded the release of the physical CD in January 2008.

Such a step had been on the band's collective mind for years; earlier, singer Thom Yorke told *Time* magazine, "I like the people at our record company, but the time is at hand when you have to ask why anyone needs one. And, yes, it probably would give us some perverse pleasure to say 'F___ you' to this decaying business model." In an interview with David Byrne after the release of *In Rainbows*, Yorke acknowledged that Radiohead was in an almost unique position to take such a step, but pointed out that emerging artists have unprecedented leverage regarding the retention of digital rights to their material.

||||||||||||||||||||||||||||||||||||||||||

"It probably would give us some perverse pleasure to say 'F___ you' to this decaying business model."
—Thom Yorke of Radiohead

The Legacy of Rock: A World of Popular Music

Like the business that it supports, popular music has gotten both bigger and smaller. Rock is a truly global music: the U.S.–U.K. international style is accepted and understood as the dominant musical language around the world. At the same time, there is not a commercially dominant body of music, as there was in the sixties, with Motown and the British bands. Data on music consumption in the early twenty-first century details this audience fragmentation.

Each year, the RIAA—Record Industry Association of America—issues a survey of consumer taste in recorded music, broken down by genre, format, age, and distribution channel. A research firm gathers the information via a survey of more than a thousand past-month music buyers. Genre distribution is determined by asking buyers to identify the genre(s) of their purchases. It is at best an imperfect system. "Rock" is clearly a grab bag of many substyles, and the "other" category, which amounts to about 7 percent, is truly eclectic, including everything from big band and Broadway shows and electronic, emo, and ethnic, to Latin and love songs and Top 40 and trip hop. The chart below shows those genres that have averaged more than 10 percent market share between 2000 and 2007. These results generally corroborate the artist distribution on *Billboard's* comprehensive album chart.

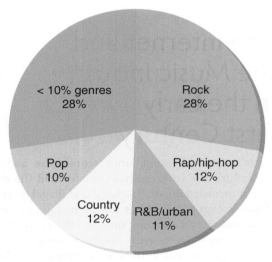

Source: Compiled from RIAA 2007 consumer profile.

Billboard's charts present a more detailed view of the current musical landscape. Currently, the journal lists forty-nine singles charts and forty-nine album charts; among the album charts are three rock charts, country and bluegrass charts, five Latin/Mexican charts, plus charts for Christian and gospel music, reggae and world music, and much more.

The RIAA data and *Billboard's* various charts highlight the extraordinarily fragmented musical landscape that we enjoy at the beginning of the twenty-first century; no one genre is dominant, as pop was in the decade after World War II. Cable television, satellite radio, and the Internet have made catering to niche markets economically viable.

Globalization and Multiculturalism

It has long been said that music is the universal language. There is some truth to that. The fact that audiences in Beijing can appreciate the music of Beethoven and audiences in London can enjoy the music of Ravi Shankar suggests that music has the power to transcend geographical and cultural boundaries.

This kind of universality, however, is akin to the study of Latin or classical Greek. Both classical music and classical

Indian music are long-established traditions. In Western culture, "classical" music is largely a fixed or, at best, a slowly evolving repertoire. Beethoven has been dead for almost 200 years. While performances bring his music to life, they do not change what he wrote (travesties like Walter Murphy's "A Fifth of Beethoven" notwithstanding) or add to his output. Beethoven's music may speak to non-Western listeners, but it is not changed in the process.

Rock-era music is different. Rock has grown from the first truly international popular music style in the sixties into the first truly global music. It goes well beyond the importation of an existing genre into another culture, as with jazz in Europe or classical music in Asia. Rather, the international family of rock/R&B styles coexists with rock/regional fusions emanating from almost every corner of the world. It is a musical language with numerous constantly evolving dialects. For instance, in the United States, one finds the "tribal rock" of Robert Mirabal, a Native American from the Taos Pueblo in New Mexico; the Cajun music of Michael Doucet and Beausoleil; and the contemporary Tejano music of Selena. All of these have attracted listeners beyond their core audience.

Their success not only underscores the inherent flexibility and openness of rock-era music, it also makes clear that race, ethnicity, and gender are, for the most part, nonissues in twenty-first century popular music. In a quite different way, so does the broad commercial appeal of the divas of contemporary pop.

• • • • • • • •

Pop: The Divas

Diva is the feminine form of the Latin word for god or godlike; it shares a common etymology with *divine*. *Diva* came into English through Italian, where it identifies a female opera singer performing a leading role. More recently, it has come to refer to female pop singing stars and, even more generally, to any woman with star quality.

The Emergence of the Divas

In 1998 VH1 sponsored its inaugural Divas concert, an all-star event presented to raise funds for the station's "Save the Music" foundation. The concert brought

> *Music has the power to transcend geographical and cultural boundaries.*

Superstock

together two rock-era queens—Aretha Franklin (the queen of soul) and Gloria Estefan (the queen of Latin pop)—and three rising stars: Mariah Carey, Céline Dion, and Shania Twain. The Divas concert series ran for six more years; the last concert took place in 2004. The format remained much the same: bring together established stars and new talent. Younger invitees included Mary J. Blige, Faith Hill, Jewel, Beyoncé, Brandy, Shakira, and Jessica Simpson.

These and other young female performers, such as Alicia Keys, Jennifer Lopez, Christina Aguilera, and Britney Spears, formed a new generation of pop singers. Their numbers show Madonna's enormous impact; it is clear that Madonna's unprecedented commercial success paved the way for their entry into the music business.

Frank Micelotta/Getty Images

> 66 *The diva label wasn't just show-business hype: for the most part, these women are skilled singers with pleasant, accessible voices and, in some cases, distinctive, even unique, vocal abilities.* 99

Not surprisingly, in light of this connection, image has been as important as sound. Most look as good as they sing, and all are portrayed as glamorous on album covers and in the media. A few—for example, Britney Spears, Jennifer Lopez—enjoy a tabloid-driven celebrity apart from their music.

The diva label wasn't just show-business hype: for the most part, these women are skilled singers with pleasant, accessible voices and, in some cases, distinctive, even unique, vocal abilities. For example, Mariah Carey's vocal range is more than twice that of a typical pop singer (her songs have often included extensive reminders of this fact), and the fluency of Christina Aguilera's melismatic singing deserves comparison not only to great black singers like Aretha but also to opera singers.

They are a diverse group: Shania Twain and Céline Dion are Canadian. Twain took the name Shania, an Ojibwa word, to affirm her connection with Native Americans; her stepfather is a full-blooded member of the nation. Dion is from French-speaking Canada. Shakira is Colombian. Jennifer Lopez is a child of Puerto Rican parents. Christina Aguilera's father is from Ecuador. Beyoncé, Mary J. Blige, and Brandy are black; Mariah Carey has white, black, and Latino blood. Several gravitated toward pop from their "home" styles. Twain and Hill began as country singers; Dion's first songs were in French; Alicia Keys, Beyoncé, and Mary J. Blige have strong R&B roots.

Their common ground extends beyond gender, appearance, success, and on-stage compatibility. They and their producers have incorporated the defining elements of eighties/nineties pop into their music. Their music may retain features of their home style— Jennifer Lopez singing in Spanish, rapper Jay-Z on a Beyoncé track, steel guitar in a Faith Hill song. Still, the use of rich textures with synthesized instruments and active rhythms in support of a tuneful melody that sets a lyric about love brings much of their music into the pop middle ground. Their chart success evidences that.

Aretha and Kid Rock at VH1 Divas Live in 2001

> They may have modeled their image and performance style after Madonna, but the divas' musical and vocal conception derives most directly from Aretha and her peers.

It is fitting that Aretha was one of the five artists invited to perform at the first Divas concert. Clearly, she was the dominant musical personality, although she only sang with others, and she has been the dominant influence on the vocal style of many of the younger divas— black, white, or Latina. Indeed, the prevailing vocal style of these performers might be described as "Aretha lite."

Her influence is evident in these singers' diction, which has something of the intonation and cadence of black speech; in the vocal quality, typically a more restrained echo of her soulful sound; and in the forms of expressive nuance, especially the use of melisma. Each of the divas has personalized her style to some degree, but most share a connection to the more soulful black vocal style of the sixties and beyond, which Aretha's singing epitomizes. They may have modeled their image and performance style after Madonna, but the divas' musical and vocal conception derives most directly from Aretha and her peers. We hear evidence of both influence and individuality in Christina Aguilera's hit, "What a Girl Wants."

Christina Aguilera: "What a Girl Wants"

If *American Bandstand* was required after-school viewing for teens in the late fifties, then the *Mickey Mouse Club* was the must-watch show for their younger siblings. Both shows aired on ABC every afternoon. The *Mickey Mouse Club* was one of Walt Disney Productions' first excursions into television programming. The show featured two older men guiding a group of perky kids through an hour of kids' news, singing, dancing, cartoons, and stories. All sported the mouse-eared beanies that were as required an accessory for pre-teens as coonskin caps had been a few years previously (the Davy Crockett fad) and as a single white sequined glove would be for Michael Jackson fans in the early eighties. The show ran from 1955 to 1959, when Disney elected to cancel it.

In 1989, thirty years after its initial cancellation, the Disney Corporation revived the show for a second time. (The first attempt, which went on the air in 1977, was a failure.) This time the show aired on the Disney Channel, a premium cable channel that began broadcasting in 1983. This would prove to be the longest-running version of the show; *MMC*, as it was called, would air for seven seasons. It would also help launch the careers of three top pop acts: the male vocal group 'N Sync and two pop divas, Britney Spears and Christina Aguilera.

By the time Christina Aguilera (b. 1980) joined the *Mickey Mouse Club* in 1992, she had been an active performer for half of her life. By the age of six, she was performing in talent shows around Pittsburgh, where she grew up; she competed on *Star Search*, an *American Idol* precursor, at nine. Aguilera's star rose quickly. In 1998 she was chosen to sing "Reflection" for the animated Disney feature *Mulan*. This led to the release of her self-titled first album, which quickly went to the top of the album charts in 1999. So did "Genie in a Bottle" and "What a Girl Wants"—the top two singles from the album; the latter track was the first new No. 1 single of the new millennium on *Billboard's* Hot 100 singles chart.

"What a Girl Wants," Guy Roche and Shelley Peiken (1999). Christina Aguilera, vocal.

"What a Girl Wants" puts a contemporary sheen on the well-established, rock-era, black pop style, even as it showcases Aguilera's considerable vocal ability. The lyrics impart a post-feminist flavor to a discussion of love. Aguilera asks her significant other to give her some space as she looks around (but never touches). That she asks for it and that he assents to her request show that, in song at least, relationships should offer equal opportunity to both parties.

The story unfolds in typical fashion: a series of verses build smoothly to a catchy chorus with a can't-miss hook. The melody unfolds in smooth undulations, and at a pace that allows the words to be easily understood; Aguilera saves most of her vocal acrobatics for interludes and obbligato flights during the chorus.

Although the song is based on the familiar verse/chorus model, "What a Girl Wants" is anything but formulaic. From the introduction that features just Aguilera and percussion sounds, through the pseudo-classical synthesizer interlude, through the chorus that never really ends (perhaps to suggest that Aguilera's looking-but-not-touching will not stop anytime soon), the song evidences the considerable skills of songwriter-producer

Christina Aguilera at ten, at the First Annual Teen Choice Awards.

Steve Granitz/WireImage/Getty Images

Guy Roche, who co-wrote the song with Shelley Peiken. Both have supplied numerous hits for Aguilera and other leading pop acts.

Roche created a rich setting for Aguilera's singing. It combines backup vocals plus synthesized percussive and pitched sounds, with subtle colors added via conventional instruments. The strummed acoustic guitar gives warmth to the largely synthesized accompaniment.

The rhythms of "What a Girl Wants" belong to the new century; they show the influence of post-Motown black pop and dance music. From the pop of the eighties, it takes the largely implicit beat keeping and highly syncopated patterns; its especially active rhythms show the influence of dance music. The basic tempo of the song, which we sense from the alternation of bass note and backbeat, is quite slow—about 75 beats per minute, or just over half the speed of a disco track or rock song. In the verse, both Aguilera's vocal and the strummed guitar move at 16-beat speed. The dance music influence becomes most evident in the rhythms that move twice this fast, that is, eight times as fast as the beat. These especially animated rhythms include synthesizer noodles, percussion bursts, and, most spectacularly, Aguilera's flawless melismas, which are the contemporary pop counterpart not only to the melismatic flourishes of Aretha Franklin, Patti LaBelle, and other top black singers but also to the florid embellishments heard in operatic arias for sopranos. Especially in these moments, Aguilera earns her diva status.

The stylized melismas are one dimension of Aguilera's black-influenced vocal style. Her delivery of the verse "sounds" black; it is quite different in inflection and intonation from her everyday speech—as heard in television interviews, for example. The basic quality is rich and resonant, although not as gritty as Aretha's or Tina Turner's. The inflection of the vocal line—for instance, the occasional bluesy bent note—also betrays black influence.

Especially when considered in the context of the pop music landscape at the turn of the century, Aguilera's vocal sound and style seem a case not so much of Aguilera's deliberately trying to sound black as of her singing in the prevailing popular style. Pop singing, like so many other aspects of the style, evidences the profound influence and the continuing evolution of the black pop tradition that took shape in the early sixties. By the end of the century, it was so thoroughly assimilated that the music of black, Latino, and white pop performers

5 **to Listen For**
"What a Girl Wants"

INSTRUMENTATION
Lead; backup vocals; numerous electronic counterparts to chord, bass, percussion, and melody instruments; guitar

PERFORMANCE STYLE
Aguilera's elaborate melismas evidence her vocal virtuosity.

RHYTHM
16-beat rhythm implied by interaction of several layers; no persistent beat keeping; occasional double-time melismas, figuration

MELODY
Chorus built from catchy hook

TEXTURE
Open texture, with dark bass, high synth

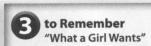

3 **to Remember**
"What a Girl Wants"

MODERN POP THEME
Lyric asks for freedom and understanding in a relationship from a feminine perspective.

BUSY RHYTHMS
Turn-of-the-century pop: complex, syncopated rhythmic texture, with a slow-moving beat overlaid with extremely active (eight times beat speed) rhythms

MODERNIZING BLACK POP
Busy, implied rhythm; Aguilera's black-influenced vocal style; bass-heavy, melody-rich texture all update and universalize black pop of '60s/'70s.

Garth Brooks has sold over 128 million units.

Frank Micelotta/Getty Images

represented a smooth stylistic continuum rather than several distinct styles.

Aguilera and the numerous other young divas have been a commanding presence in pop music at the turn of the new century. They join an earlier generation of stars that included Whitney Houston and Janet and La Toya Jackson. No group of pop performers was more frequently heard or was more in the public eye. They reaped the fruit of the efforts of Madonna and the many other women who worked to break down the gender barrier in popular music. Their success evidences the fact that the pop music world was a level playing field with respect to race and gender.

Country Music at the Turn of the Century

The Beatles remain the best-selling act of all time, having sold 170,000,000 units as of May 2008. A quick question: Who is second? The answer isn't Michael Jackson or Madonna, or Elvis or Elton John, or any pop, rock, or R&B act. It's Garth Brooks, who has sold over 128 million units since beginning his recording career in 1989.

A Not-So-Silent Plurality: The Popularity of Country Music Since 1990

For country music, Brooks's spectacular sales figures are neither an aberration nor an isolated instance. The RIAA publishes a list of acts whose albums have sold 10 million units. Of the 100 best-selling acts of all time, 24 began their recording careers in the 1990s or later. Of these 24, 8 are country acts: Brooks and Dunn, Kenny Chesney, Dixie Chicks, Faith Hill, Alan Jackson, Toby Keith, Tim McGraw (Faith's husband), and Shania Twain.

Joining them in the Top 100 were five country acts whose careers began in the 1980s: Brooks, Alabama, Vince Gill, Reba McIntire, and George Strait. All remained active through the 1990s, and all but Alabama are still active performers. Newer artists like Taylor Swift and Dierks Bentley, as well as *American Idol* winners Kelly Clarkson and Carrie Underwood, routinely join them on *Billboard's* comprehensive album charts. For country, the Top 100 is end-weighted: only two other country singers, Willie Nelson and Kenny Rogers, appear on the list.

One reason for country music's recent surge in popularity is the use of a more accurate and efficient method of calculating sales. Toward the end of 1991, *Billboard* began using Nielsen SoundScan, an information system that tracks sales through the use of barcodes scanned at registers in retail centers and record stores throughout the United States. Around the same time, the music industry started using computers to track radio airplay. In combination, the two information sources provided much more precise—and eventually more reliable—data about popularity.

Not coincidentally, the market share of country music just about doubled between 1990 and 1993, from 9.6 percent to 18.7 percent. This alerted industry executives on both coasts to something that country fans had known for decades: country music was much more popular than the music industry thought it was.

The dramatic jump in market share (which has since declined somewhat) was just one indication that country music had become a major player in the popular music industry. Country music television networks, country stars in advertisements, the emergence of Nashville as an important music center, crossover chart success—these also show the growing presence of country music.

However, the unprecedented popularity of country music at the turn of the twenty-first century would seem to be more than a matter of better accounting. More than any other kind of rock-era music, contemporary country music has retained familiar points of entry: a good story told in an easy-to-understand lyric; a singable melody, sung with feeling but without histrionics; a good beat; a predilection for conventional instruments, although electronic sounds occasionally appear on tracks; and forms that are easy to follow. Stylistically, there's a smooth continuum between middle-ground country and much of the AOR rock of the seventies; the slight twang of the singers is typically the most obvious—and sometimes the only—country element.

By contrast, many of the best-selling artists of the last two decades have abandoned this approach. Pop divas typically embellish melodies with elaborate melismas; they are surrounded by hyperactive electronic rhythm tracks. Rap is, by definition, not a melodic music, although rap fusions with rock and rhythm and blues include singable parts. Much of the rock of the 1990s and 2000s has explored extremes, in vocal style, volume, and contrast. So, some measure of the success of contemporary country music comes from its filling the "accessibility void" created by new directions in pop, rap, rock, and R&B.

As it has in the past, country music absorbs and adapts the music of earlier generations. In this case, it was the middle-ground rock of the 1970s and early 1980s. We hear this explicitly in the Dixie Chicks' 2002 cover of Fleetwood Mac's 1975 hit "Landslide."

The Dixie Chicks

While performing in London in April 2003, Natalie Maines, the lead singer of the Dixie Chicks, remarked, "Just so you know, we're ashamed the president of the United States is from Texas." She would later apologize for disrespecting the president but not for her antiwar position. It was not her first antiwar statement; previously, she had taken fellow country star Toby Keith to task for his ardent support of the war and the president. The remark provoked death threats and boycotts, and another thinly veiled barb at Keith continued to erode their support among country fans, to the point that Martie Maguire told a German reporter later that year, "We don't feel a part of the country scene any longer; it can't be our home any more." Despite a disappointing tour, the group refused to back down from their earlier position. In the lyrics to "Not Ready to Make Nice," a single from their acclaimed 2006 album *Taking The Long Way*, they recounted their ordeal—the death threats, a mother telling her child to hate a stranger—and made clear that they would continue to stand by their principles. Fortunately, what might have been professional suicide in an earlier time redefined their career and broadened their audience. The album entered the Top 200 album charts at No. 1 and won several Grammys.

The attention surrounding the Bush incident and their subsequent distancing of themselves from their core audience has deflected attention from the group's deep connection with traditional country music. The Dixie Chicks—currently Natalie Maines (b. 1974), Martie Maguire (b. Martha Erwin, 1969), and Emily Robison (b. Emily Erwin, 1972)—began as a four-person, all-girl bluegrass group busking on Dallas street corners. The sisters are excellent instrumentalists: Maguire on violin, mandolin, and other string instruments; Robison on banjo, dobro, and numerous other instruments. As their career took off, they moved away from bluegrass toward contemporary country. The pivotal point in their career came in 1995, when Maines, the daughter of top

> Some measure of the success of contemporary country music comes from its filling the "accessibility void" created by new directions in pop, rap, rock, and R&B.

The Dixie Chicks performing with Stevie Nicks, who originally recorded "Landslide." Left to right: Emily Robison, banjo; Natalie Maines, guitar; Stevie Nicks; and Martie Maguire, mandolin.

Frank Micelotta/ImageDirect/Getty Images

"Landslide," Stevie Nicks (2002). The Dixie Chicks.

session steel guitarist Lloyd Maines, joined the group, now down to just three, as lead vocalist. Maines's singing gave the group a more mainstream sound, which in turn made them a top country act, with multiple multiplatinum albums.

Home (2002), their third album with Maines, simultaneously looked back to the past and ahead to the future. Unlike the previous two albums, it was an all-acoustic recording. In addition to the traditional bluegrass instruments—fiddle, banjo, dobro, mandolin, bass—there were steel guitar and Celtic instruments on several tracks. Despite this traditional orientation, the group scored a huge crossover hit with their cover of Fleetwood Mac's "Landslide."

For the Dixie Chicks, adapting "Landslide" was a relatively straightforward affair. Maines's vocal style isn't that far removed from that of Fleetwood Mac lead singer Stevie Nicks, and the original version of the song features an intricate acoustic guitar accompaniment. The group simply adapted the guitar accompaniment to banjo and mandolin, added acoustic bass, guitar, and dobro, and sang the chorus in their trademark three-part close harmony.

Like the Carter Family's "Wildwood Flower" and Hank Williams's "Lovesick Blues," "Landslide" is a country cover of a popular song. Unlike the two earlier examples, the two versions of "Landslide" sound like not-too-distant points on a continuum, despite the Dixie Chicks' use of traditional instruments. It is a measure of the extent to which rock absorbed country influences.

Not "A Bunch of Hillbillies": Country Music in the Twenty-First Century

The music video of "Landslide" alternates between Maines standing in surreal settings; Robison, who is proudly pregnant, lying in a stylized grassy field with a house that grows roots; and Maguire walking through an urban neighborhood. All three women are dressed fashionably: Maines and Robison wear long gowns but are barefoot; Maguire is wearing a sexy pantsuit. They are clearly worldly women, and the backgrounds have more to do with the art of Salvador Dali than with actual farms and forests. At the same time, we hear and see Robison play the dobro and Maguire play mandolin—after she plucks it out of midair. In its mix of traditional and modern, rural and urban, and real and surreal, the video seems to encapsulate the creative balance between tradition and innovation, and between down-home and sophisticated, that characterizes much contemporary country music.

It was during the tour supporting *Home* that Maines made her controversial comment. Despite the fallout from

to Listen For
"Landslide"

INSTRUMENTATION
Lead and harmony vocals, banjo, mandolin, acoustic guitar, dobro, bass

PERFORMANCE STYLE
Country twang in lead and harmony vocals: no vibrato, pure sound

RHYTHM
Bluegrass-type activity over two-beat rhythm at a moderate tempo; not much syncopation

MELODY
Moderate-length phrases in narrow range unfold gently, peaking to the title word.

TEXTURE
Rich texture concentrated in mid-range, with several melodically interesting accompaniment figures; vocal, with and without harmony, in the forefront

to Remember
"Landslide"

TRADITIONAL SOUND; MODERN SONG
Remake of AOR rock hit given a fresh sound with bluegrass instrumentation

CLOSE HARMONY
Dixie Chicks' distinctive vocal sound comes from Maguire and Robison's harmonizing above and below the melody.

COUNTRY CROSSOVER
Huge success of song evidence of enduring appeal of tuneful melody presented directly, freshly, and skillfully

her remark, the Dixie Chicks continued to tour, but they did not record another studio album until 2006. In *Taking the Long Way* (2006), the group once again moved away from their traditional roots and away from their traditional audience. Super-producer Rick Rubin was called in to produce the album; Martie Maguire recalls him telling her, "I think this should sound like a great rock act making a country album, not a country act making a rock album." The Dixie Chicks' gravitation toward rock puts them at the cutting edge of country music, just as their political views separate them from the "my country right or wrong" mindset associated with country music's core audience.

The career of the Dixie Chicks encapsulates the evolution of country music and the expansion of its audience. They began as bluegrass-playing buskers earning spare change; country began as a folk tradition suddenly put on recordings and played over the air by amateur or semiprofessional performers. Today, they are a major act with broad commercial appeal, just as country is a major force in the music industry. They and country produce music with a distinct regional identity, but it is no longer a regional music. Their seamless transition from country traditionalists to a "great rock act making a country album" mirrors the open-ended two-way exchange between rock and country since the 1960s.

• • • • • • • •

Tropical Latin, ca. 2000

To celebrate its fortieth birthday, the National Academy of Recording Arts & Sciences went international. The organization was formed in 1957; a year later, it awarded the first Grammys. In 1997 the academy formed a separate branch for Latin music, the Latin Academy of Recording Arts & Sciences (LARAS), which the parent organization describes as "a unique, multinational membership-based association composed of music industry professionals, musicians, producers, engineers and other creative and technical recording professionals who are dedicated to improving the quality of life and the cultural condition for Latin music and its makers both inside and outside the United States."

Three years later, LARAS sponsored the first Latin Grammy Awards. The event took place at The Staples Center in Los Angeles and was broadcast over CBS. It was the first prime-time programming in which Spanish and Portuguese were used extensively. In keeping with its international orientation, awards are given for Latin recordings made both inside and outside the United States.

Between 2000 and 2007, Mexican and Brazilian artists dominated the awards, with seventy-nine and seventy-seven artists, respectively. Artists from Spain were third, with forty-two awards. Artists from the United States and the Dominican Republic tied for eighth, with fifteen. For American listeners the number of Brazilian winners might not be surprising, given the familiarity of Brazilian music since the 1960s. By contrast, Mexican music in the United States is a more regional phenomenon, although Mexican and Tejano music accounted for over half of Latin-music sales in 2007.

The winners of the first Latin Grammy for Best Short Form Music Video were Gloria Estéfan and her producer/husband Emilio Estéfan, Jr. for the song "No Me Dejes de Querer." The song topped three Latin music charts and was Estéfan's first Spanish-language song to reach the *Billboard* Hot 100 charts. The song and *Alma Caribeña*, the album on which it appeared, represented another return to the Spanish language; the majority of her recordings have been in English. "No Me Dejes de Querer" exemplifies what is now called "tropical Latin"; it moves back and forth between a more generic Latin style and salsa.

Salsa

Salsa (Spanish for "sauce") was an American-based Latin "return to roots" movement. It successfully reinvigorated the uptown mambo style that went out of favor during the ascendancy of rock. Salsa updated this 1950s sound mainly by assimilating elements of other styles, both Latin (Puerto Rican music, for example) and American (jazz, R&B). Nevertheless, according to accounts by both older and younger musicians, salsa retained its Cuban core, even though few of the first-generation salsa musicians were Cuban or of Cuban descent.

During the late 1960s and early 1970s, the purest form of salsa, that is, the sound and style closest to the music's Afro-Cuban roots, had a limited audience: mainly Latinos and a small minority of non-Latinos drawn to the music. However, with the emergence of disco in the latter part of the 1970s, salsa had also acquired a more generic connotation. It referred to music with a Latin flavor, but not Afro-Cuban in the most important respects. For example, "Salsation," one of the songs used in the *Saturday Night Fever* soundtrack, has a Latin sound because of the brass riffs, the Latin-like rhythm, and Latin percussion. But its rhythmic foundation owes more to disco than to Afro-Cuban music. This gave the song more crossover appeal but diluted its essence.

Like their country-music counterparts, salsa musicians have wrestled with the conflict between artistic freedom and commercial success. As in these other styles, there are artists in both camps. Musicians like vocalist Celia Cruz (the queen of salsa until her passing in 2003) and pianist/bandleader Eddie Palmieri have remained true to the Afro-Cuban roots of salsa even as they absorb other influences. Palmieri has been especially bold in his exploration of new possibilities and has enjoyed the acclaim of both critics and aficionados.

At the other extreme of the Latin/American musical spectrum were tropical Latin artists whose sound was weighted toward mainstream pop. Among the most prominent was Gloria Estéfan and Miami Sound Machine.

Gloria Estéfan

Both Gloria (Fajardo) Estéfan (b. 1957) and her husband Emilio Estéfan Jr. (b. 1953) fled with their families to Miami in the wake of the Cuban revolution. The couple met in 1975 when Emilio, who was moonlighting as a musician from his job as a sales manager, heard Gloria sing and asked her to join his band, which would quickly evolve into Miami Sound Machine. They married three years later.

Miami Sound Machine made seven studio albums between 1977 and 1983, playing what amounted to contemporary American music sung in Spanish and intended primarily for a Spanish-speaking audience: disco, pop, ballads, and the occasional Latin number. They became a mainstream pop act in 1984 with the release of *Eyes of Innocence*, their first English-language album. They would follow it with two others before Gloria started to receive top billing. In many of the group's early hits, like "Dr. Beat," their style was indistinguishable from American/international pop.

A broken vertebra suffered in an accident involving the band's bus during a 1990 tour kept Gloria at home for a

"No Me Dejes de Querer," Gloria Estefan, Emilio Estefan, Jr., and Robert Blades (2000). Gloria Estéfan, vocal.

year. Upon her return, she began recording in both Spanish and English; *Mi Tierra* (1993), her first Spanish-language album as a headline act, drew much more deeply on her Cuban heritage, in words and music. So did *Alma Caribeña*, which was released in 2000.

The set for the "No Me Dejes de Querer" music video is a posh Mediterranean-looking nightclub, with arched entries and palm trees. Estéfan begins the video leaning alluringly against a column; in the course of the video, she flits from table to table and takes a turn on the dance floor, leaving a string of men pining after her. Most of the men, including the musicians, are dressed in white suits and are wearing fedoras;

Frank Micelotta/Getty Images

Estéfan's rich, expressive voice is an ideal complement to the lyrics; the melody floats over the pulsating salsa rhythms.

most of the women wear clingy dresses. There is dancing throughout. The scene evokes prerevolutionary Havana, or Rio or Buenos Aires, as seen in numerous films, but the look is up to date, with black, brown, and white dancers moving sinuously over the dance floor.

The music is salsa. The verse is a Cubanized Caribbean sound—Latin rhythms and instruments, plus guitars strumming. During the chorus, the traditional salsa sounds and rhythms kick in: piano *montuno*, bass playing the offbeat *tumbao* pattern, vocal line in clave. There is a modern-sounding solo in the middle of the song by Puerto Rican pianist Papo Lucca, a contemporary of Palmieri. The blazing trumpet solo at the end underscores the affinity between salsa and jazz. In all of this the connection

5 to Listen For
"No Me Dejes de Querer"

INSTRUMENTATION
Lead/backup vocals; piano; guitars; electric bass; Afro-Cuban percussion; brass, with trumpet featured; saxophone

PERFORMANCE STYLE
Estefan's passionate singing, always with a slight edge

RHYTHM
Alternates between Latin rhythms not in clave and Afro-Cuban rhythms in clave at a moderate tempo

MELODY
Verse contains moderate-length phrases in narrow range; chorus exchanges short riffs sung by chorus with longer responses.

TEXTURE
Dense texture, especially thick in middle, with guitars, voices, and horns

3 to Remember
"No Me Dejes de Querer"

SALSA LOVE SONG
Flowing rhythms at moderate tempo ideal for salsa song about love

FROM "LATIN" TO SALSA
Song shifts back and forth between generic "Latin" rhythm and authentic salsa/mambo rhythms.

LA CANTANTE
Estefan's rich voice, which verges on cracking at passionate moments, clearly conveys the emotions in the lyric.

between contemporary salsa and the mambo of the 1940s and 1950s is apparent.

There is a striking difference in intent, however. Mambos like "Complicacion" were frenetic dance music. "No Me Dejes de Querer" is a love song: the title phrase is usually translated as "Don't Stop Loving Me." The lyrics are intensely romantic: the opening line, translated into English, reads "I don't ever want to imagine/That your eyes will not gaze upon me," and it goes on from there.

Estéfan's rich, expressive voice is an ideal complement to the lyrics; the melody, built from short phrases and featuring exchanges between a male chorus and Estéfan, floats over the pulsating salsa rhythms. It inverts the Latin lover stereotype: a sultry woman on a sultry evening promising unending love as she leaves one man for another.

"No Me Dejes de Querer" is salsa as song—danceable song, to be sure, but song in which the focus is on the words, the melody, and the singer. In this respect, it compares to mambo much as bossa nova compares to samba. In this way Estéfan expands the expressive range of this hybrid Cuban/American music.

World Music

They're found in museum stores, coffee shops, bookstores, and health-conscious groceries. They have bright, attractive covers that catch the eye. They offer sounds from around the world, from Asian Lounge music and African Grooves to zydeco. They are the CDs released by Putumayo World Music. Since its founding in 1993, Putumayo World Music has sold over 20,000,000 recordings, expanded its catalog (currently over 125 recordings), and given over $1,000,000 from their sales to nonprofit organizations.

The idea to found a world music label came to Dan Storper in 1991 when he heard the Afropop group Kotoja while strolling through San Francisco's Golden Gate Park. He would start the company two years later. For millions of listeners around the world, Putumayo World Music has been the point of entry into other musical cultures. Their success points up the still small but vibrant market for what is commonly called "world music."

The Roots of the World Music Movement

The global music of the past twenty years has grown out of a movement that, in the United States, dates back to the early fifties, in the music of the Weavers. Among their biggest hits were songs from Israel ("Tzena, Tzena, Tzena") and South Africa ("Wimoweh"). Later in the decade, Harry Belafonte would enjoy comparable success with his versions of calypso songs like "Banana Boat (Day-O)." Although the music of the Weavers and Belafonte doesn't sound very authentic, their advocacy of folk music from then exotic locales and their effort to capture something of its spirit planted the seed for the world music movement. Belafonte also played a key role in introducing South African singer Miriam Makeba to American audiences. She would enjoy a long run in the sixties, but her success did not lead to widespread interest in South African music.

Brazilian music and the Beatles played a big part in expanding the popular music worldview. Brazilian music was an early example of an international/regional fusion; jazz met samba and returned as bossa nova. The Beatles spearheaded a more inclusive musical attitude on several levels. One was the simple fact of their success. The British invasion of the mid-sixties made rock—and by extension popular music—an international music. It didn't matter that the Beatles were from Liverpool instead of Los Angeles; audiences went wild over them. The second level of influence was their musical daring. They weren't afraid to try anything or to use music from any source. By their example they nurtured the open-mindedness of rock and folk artists. More specifically, they helped bring East Indian music to a much wider western audience. George Harrison's flirtation with the sitar and his use of it in songs like "Norwegian Wood" helped open the door for Indian musicians like Ravi Shankar.

The Emergence of World Music

All of this laid the groundwork for the world music movement that began to take shape in the seventies and flowered during the eighties. Four key ingredients were in place: the development of regional popular styles, deep interest from a few mainstream popular musicians, the drive to reclaim folk heritages around the world, and audience interest.

Reggae was the first of the Afrocentric popular styles to gain notice. It had several advantages: strong musical connections to R&B yet its own distinctive sound; an audience base in England because of the Jamaicans who had moved there; a powerful message; and—perhaps most important—lyrics in English.

Other Afrocentric music followed reggae's path to international recognition. The eighties saw a renewed interest in calypso and soca (**soul ca**lypso, a regional/international hybrid that had emerged during the seventies) from Trinidad, zouk and cadence from the French Caribbean, samba from Brazil, Afropop styles like highlife from Ghana and juju from Nigeria (King Sunny Ade was the best-known Nigerian musician), mbalax from Senegal, plus a variety of music from South Africa.

None of these styles has succeeded on the same scale as reggae—many, especially the West African styles, must overcome the language barrier—but all have an international presence. Collectively, this music, by musicians from Africa and of the African diaspora, is often identified as worldbeat; the generic term for the fusions involving West African music is Afropop.

Many styles were already in existence well before the eighties (calypso, for example, dates back to the teens, highlife to the twenties). Their emergence in the eighties reflects both the changes in the music—a more updated sound through the addition of electronic instruments and the incorporation of elements from the international style—and the interest of musicians and audiences in new sounds.

The complement to regional musicians' blending elements of the international style with their local music was mainstream musicians' bringing these regional styles into their music. Three stand out: Paul Simon, David Byrne, and Peter Gabriel. All played an active role in promoting world music by using regional musicians on their recordings (Ladysmith Black Mambazo with Paul Simon; Youssou N'Dour with Peter Gabriel) and by seeking out and promoting regional music (David Byrne assembled several anthologies of Brazilian music; Gabriel co-founded WOMAD, the world festival of music, art, and dance).

The eighties also saw a revival of folk traditions around the world. Chief among them was Celtic music, but other regional folk and folk/international styles found enthusiastic international audiences, for example, music from Bulgaria (Le Mystère des Voix Bulgares, clarinetist Ivo Papasov), flamenco (the Gipsy Kings), and indigenous Australian music.

The Sound of Afropop

In 1991 Senegalese singer Youssou N'Dour (b. 1959) was appointed a Goodwill Ambassador for UNICEF. Eleven years later, Angélique Kidjo (b. 1960), a native of Benin, also became a UNICEF Goodwill Ambassador. Senegal and Benin are former French colonies in sub-Saharan Africa. Senegal is along the west coast: Dakar, the capital city and N'Dour's hometown, is the westernmost city on the African continent. Benin is a small country directly west of Nigeria and southeast of Senegal.

Kidjo and N'Dour are, respectively, the best-known African female and male singers. They have earned widespread critical acclaim: both have won Grammys, and the New York Times labeled N'Dour "one of the world's greatest singers." Both have been extraordinarily active on behalf of causes that they believe to be important: Kidjo for education and human rights—she founded the Batonga foundation to provide young African girls with upper-level education to prepare them for leadership

positions—and N'Dour for technology and health—N'Dour helped organize the 2006 Africa Live: The Roll Back Malaria Concert, which was given in Dakar.

Kidjo moved to Paris in 1983, where she obtained work as a backup vocalist. By 1989 she had a recording contract and a career in Europe. Within a few years, she had become the best-known African female vocalist since Miriam Makeba. N'Dour's international career also took off in the 1980s after Peter Gabriel recruited him for his first WOMAD concert.

Both won Grammys for Best Contemporary World Music Album: N'Dour in 2005 for *Egypt* and Kidjo in 2008 for *Djin Djin*. For Kidjo, *Djin Djin* was a conscious effort to return to her roots, to recapture and integrate into her music the rhythms and sounds of her home country. She had grown up listening to native musicians and rock, funk, and pop from abroad; the album is an expression of that rich heritage. The album features an impressive list of guest artists, including Peter Gabriel, Alicia Keys, saxophonist Branford Marsalis,

"Ae Ae," Angélique Kidjo (2008). Kidjo and N'Dour, vocals.

Josh Groban, and Carlos Santana. "Ae Ae," the opening track, appears only once on the American version of the physical CD; however, the iTunes version of the album includes a second version with N'Dour. The tracks are identical except for the vocals: Kijdo shares solo material with N'Dour and he improvises a vocal obbligato over an otherwise instrumental interlude.

"Ae Ae" features three of the most common features of African/international fusions: the extensive and prominent use of traditional African instruments; complete western rhythm sections, typically laying down a 16-beat rhythm; and melody and harmony that puts a distinctively African spin on the major scales and three basic chords of European tonal harmony. In addition to a large array of unpitched percussion instruments, "Ae Ae" uses a *balafon*, a xylophone-like instrument, and a *kora*, a harp-lute made from a calabash. Both play moving lines behind the vocal throughout the song.

The rhythm section on "Ae Ae" includes drum set, electric bass, guitars, and organ, in addition to the African percussion instruments. The musicians lay down a vibrant groove based on the by now ubiquitous 16-beat rhythm, with an active bass line and a dense, percussive texture. The sound of the guitar, typical of much west African music, and the African instruments, both pitched and unpitched, color the sound to give it a specifically African flavor. Still, it is a version of the international groove so popular around the turn of the century.

The approach to melody and harmony represent a common feature of pop styles throughout west Africa: an adaptation of European tonality in which melodies are constructed entirely from the seven notes of diatonic scales (rather than pentatonic scales) and harmony consists of progressions built from two or three chords that cycle with little or no change throughout the song. In "Ae Ae," there are three progressions, all built from I, IV, and V: one for the solo verse, the second for the bridge, and the third for the chorus.

> " *As Kidjo said in the video about* Djin Djin, *she wants to "entertain each other but learn at the same time."* "

The Afropop approach to melody and harmony has more in common with the hymns and other religious music brought to Africa by missionaries than with western popular music. The choral singing heard on this recording—a sound popularized in America most prominently by the South African a cappella choral group Ladysmith Black Mambazo—support this connection.

Weaving through the buoyant rhythms are the voices of Kidjo and N'Dour. Kidjo's lyric is part commentary on the plight of Africans who immigrate to Europe to escape the poverty, poor health, and political turmoil there and part exhortation to Africans to become self-sufficient. In this respect, the song continues the practice among members of the African diaspora (Kidjo now lives in New York) of sending a powerful message over a compelling groove. As Kidjo said in the video about *Djin Djin*, she wants to "entertain each other but learn at the same time."

In "Ae Ae," as in much of the music by African artists who have enjoyed international success, there is something of the atmosphere of a family reunion. It is not so much a coming together of people as of styles and cultures—music from the mother continent meeting up with its offspring in the Americas. What Africa had sent to the Americas via the slave trade came back to Africa transmuted but still compatible, so that they could be easily blended. A second wave of African music, mixed from traditional sounds and their evolutionary mutations among the diaspora, has found a welcome audience in America and around the world.

Youssou N'Dour and Angélique Kidjo

We end our survey of popular music where we began: in Africa. Looking back to the beginning, in Chapter 2, we can see a symmetry that invites comparisons highlighting dominant themes in our discussion: the blending of disparate musical traditions and the enormous impact of technology (compare "Woodman, Spare That Tree" with "What a Girl Wants"), the creative tension between old and new, and the spread of regional styles to larger, even global, audiences.

Looking Back, Looking Ahead

As this is written, the rock era is over half a century old. Yet, as the music industry data presented earlier suggest, rock no longer commands a majority of the market share, and the rock that is closest to the attitude of the 1960s is now an "alternative." It would seem that we remain in the rock era by default, mainly because no new style has supplanted it as the dominant music of a generation. Our survey suggests a reason for this.

The most surprising development at the turn of the twenty-first century was what *didn't* happen: there *was* no revolution. Recall that there were two revolutions in twentieth-century popular music. The first occurred in the teens and twenties, when a wholesale infusion of black music—ragtime, hot dance music, blues, and jazz—and new technology transformed the sound of popular music and changed American culture. The second was the more familiar rock revolution of the fifties and sixties, in which a further infusion of black music and new technology transformed popular music and changed the world.

A third revolution was "due" around the turn of the century, but it hasn't happened, although new technologies that affected both the creative process and music delivery were in place; another important new black music emerged; and lively underground scenes eventually crossed over to more mainstream audiences. One reason for the nonrevolution is rock's inherent openness to new styles; another is the diversity of contemporary music. In the two previous revolutions, there was a dominant popular music establishment supported by a

CRIS BOURONCLE/AFP/Getty Images

5 to Listen For
"Ae Ae"

INSTRUMENTATION
Lead and backup vocals, guitars, organ, bass, drums, extra percussion, African pitched instruments—balafon, kora

RHYTHM
Vibrant 16-beat rhythm at a bright tempo, with active timekeeping on several percussion instruments; persistent syncopations in chord instruments, bass

MELODY
Long phrases in verse, bridge; chorus (A-E, A-E) spun out from title-phrase riff

HARMONY
Song built mainly on I, IV, and V; shift to new key after false start in middle

TEXTURE
Rich texture, with multiple melodic strands in lead vocals, choir/backup vocals and African instruments; frequent call and response

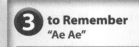

3 to Remember
"Ae Ae"

AFROPOP SOUNDS
The African instruments are one source; guitar and bass sonorities are another.

INTERNATIONAL/REGIONAL FUSION
A seamless blend of international elements—core rhythm section, active rhythms, layered textures, verse/chorus form—with regional elements (language, native instruments)

UPBEAT SONG
Active, vibrant rhythms; basic three-chord harmony; frequent call and response; and tuneful chorus all project an upbeat mood.

mainstream culture that viewed minorities, and especially blacks, as inferior. Rock changed the attitude toward minorities—of all kinds—and their culture: multiculturalism is a rock-influenced and rock-era phenomenon. Moreover, the diversity of the music and the numerous outlets for it have made it impossible for the dominant players in the industry to concentrate their efforts in support of one particular style. Still another reason is that, unlike the previous two revolutions, the future direction of the music is not at all clear.

Minstrelsy opened the door for blacks to enter mainstream culture. They walked through it—first as minstrels; then as ragtime pianists, dance musicians, jazzmen, blues and pop singers; then as major players in rock-era music. Their music set in motion two evolutionary trends that have now run their course. One was a shift in musical emphasis from melody to rhythm; the other was a regular—even predictable—progression of style beats.

At the turn of the twentieth century, the most popular songs were flowing melodies set to a piano accompaniment in a bright waltz rhythm: the evergreen "Take Me Out to the Ball Game" remains the most familiar example. The musical interest in these songs resided almost exclusively in the melody; accompaniments were typically generic. There was none of the rhythmic interest that we associate with popular music, certainly since the twenties. Ragtime, a rhythmically interesting music, was on the fringes of the music business; its notoriety far exceeded

its popularity. By the turn of the twenty-first century, the pendulum had swung to the other extreme: rhythm is the dominant element in contemporary music, often to the exclusion of melody. Rap and dance music are familiar styles, and active rhythms are a prominent feature in pop, rock, and R&B, as we have noted.

More specifically, ever since a black-based rhythmic conception became the rhythmic foundation for popular music, the speed of the defining rhythmic layer has doubled every twenty years or so: the two-beat rhythms of the fox-trot in the twenties and thirties; the four-beat rhythms of swing in the thirties, forties, and early fifties; the eight-beat rhythms of rock in the latter part of the fifties, sixties, and seventies; and the 16-beat rhythms in a variety of styles, mostly since the mid-seventies.

The logical next step in this progression, 32-beat rhythms, occurred right on schedule, in the dance music of the nineties; however, drum machines were required to produce them at all but the slowest tempos. They haven't caught on in other kinds of music, nor are they likely to, because of their speed. In the earlier style beats, melodies and other supporting parts moved at the same speed as, or faster than, the style-beat-defining layer. In rock-era music, Chuck Berry's vocal line moves in step with his rhythm guitar part; the cadence of a rapper lines up with the 16-beat rhythms supporting the rapper. By contrast, 32-beat rhythms are simply too fast to be usable at a dance tempo. A melody with lyrics that moved at 32-beat speed would be all but impossible to deliver, and even harder to understand. For this reason, 16-beat rhythms represent the last stage in this rhythmic progression.

So where does popular music go from here? We close with two reflections on the future of popular music and its place in the world.

• • • • • • • •

Terms to Know

Test your knowledge of this chapter's important terms by defining the terms listed here. If you can't recall the meaning of a certain term, refresh your memory by looking up the boldfaced term in the chapter, turning to the Glossary at the back of the book, or working with the flashcards at the Popular Music Resource Center.

majors   salsa
netlabels   worldbeat
tropical Latin   Afropop

Outro

Two Perspectives on the Future of Popular Music

It's clear that innovation within the music of a generation is still possible: Radiohead's "Paranoid Android" is hauntingly beautiful and without significant precedent, as we heard. However, innovation on a larger scale—creating a new musical vocabulary for a new generation—may prove to be more problematic. The current imbalance between rhythm and melody and the exhaustion of usable new style beats suggests that further innovation in popular music may well require a completely new paradigm. It would seem that the forces that impelled the evolution of popular music during the twentieth century have reached the evolutionary end of the line; they can no longer generate a revolutionary new music.

Twenty-first-century musicians may find the path to our musical future by reflecting on its past. If there has been an overriding theme in the history of popular music, it is that innovations in popular music have come from syntheses of dissimilar, even disparate, musical traditions. It goes back to the beginning: one such synthesis resulted in the music for the minstrel show, and it continued through the twentieth century in the ongoing interplay between mainstream and "outsider" styles.

Today, we have access to a world of music. Much of our recorded legacy is available to anyone with an Internet connection and a computing device. Moreover, creative minds of today are more likely to be open to musical traditions of all kinds than they would have been a half-century ago. Appreciation of the musical traditions of diverse cultures was an important consequence of the rock revolution, and knowledge of these traditions has grown dramatically. In this rich environment, it would seem that it is not a matter of whether, but rather when, new directions in popular music will emerge.

—Michael Campbell, author
Westerly, Rhode Island
USA

Although it's not a purely musical concern, the current crisis over how popular music is consumed will, I think, play a role in the actual content of the music, although I'm not sure how. With acts forced to make their living through touring and the potential lack of affordability of that mode, it would appear that another crisis is on the horizon.

Furthermore, the combination of low-price production, both of the music itself and of what the Germans call "tone carriers," or delivery media—free, if you count mp3s—has caused what I think is an unsustainable glut of mediocre music. The graph of bad-to-good is no longer a bell curve, but more like a mesa with a huge plateau on it. This could well result in frustration or a conservative sticking to a single micro-genre by the consumer.

I came back from Japan in 2001 telling people that the Next Big Thing might not be music at all, but rather cell phones. That was both a little off the mark and a little true, but I wonder if the future of popular culture will be shaped as much by music in the future as it was in the past. It could well be that it won't.

—Ed Ward, guest commentator
Berlin
BRD

12-bar blues form The most widely used form for one chorus of a blues song. It is defined principally by its chord progression, which features I, IV, and V in a consistent pattern over 12 bars: I(1), I(3) / IV(5), I (7) / V(9), I(11). The 12-bar blues form is used in both vocal and instrumental songs. In sung 12-bar blues songs, the typical lyric is a rhymed couplet, with the first line repeated:

> I write these words to try to explain the blues *1st line of couplet*
> Yeah, I write these words to try to explain the blues *1st line of couplet repeated*
> Hope these words are something you can use. *2nd line of couplet, the rhyme*

16-beat rhythm A style beat in which the fastest rhythmic layer moves four times the speed of the beat: 4 times per beat × 4 beats = 16-beat rhythm. First popularized in disco and funk, it has been the most widely used style beat since the early 1980s.

45 rpm single 7-inch vinyl discs, first brought out by RCA in 1949, that held about 3 minutes of music, or one song.

78 rpm recording First records, these shellac discs delivered about 3 minutes of popular music on 10-inch discs and about 4 minutes of classical music on 12-inch discs.

accent A musical event that stands out from its neighbors because of a change in one or more musical elements. The most common sources of accent are intensity (the event is louder), duration (longer), density (the event contains more parts), or pitch (higher or lower).

acid rock (psychedelic rock) The music most associated with the Bay Area during the late sixties; a rock substyle defined not by a musical feature but simply by the music's ability to evoke or enhance the drug experience.

acoustic recording An early recording process in which sound vibrations were transferred directly to the recording medium (cylinder or disc) by means of a large horn or cone. In 1925 it was replaced by electric recording.

Afropop A generic term for the fusions involving West African music.

album-oriented radio (AOR) A type of FM radio format that emphasized a restricted playlist.

alternative An umbrella term for the music and the culture that continued to reverberate from punk. Stylistically, alternative is defined by what it *isn't*—mainstream pop—more than by what it is.

amplifier A piece of equipment that can increase the strength of an electric signal.

analog synthesizer A synthesizer in which musical variables are controlled by adjusting voltages. In many cases the waveforms generated in this manner were similar (i.e., analogous) to the waveforms of acoustic instruments; hence the designation *analog* synthesizer. Analog synthesizers were used until the early 1980s, when they were gradually replaced.

animal dance A popular dance such as the grizzly bear, the chicken glide, the turkey trot, and the foxtrot, adapted or borrowed from black folk dances, that became popular around 1910.

ambient music A more atmospheric, less dance-driven branch of electronica, with more to texture and less emphasis on rhythm.

arpeggio A chord whose pitches are performed one after the other instead of simultaneously. Also called *broken chord*.

art rock A rock substyle that sought to elevate rock from teen entertainment to artistic statement, often by drawing on or reworking classical compositions (e.g., Emerson, Lake, and Palmer's version of Mussorgsky's *Pictures at an Exhibition*). Art rock was often distinguished by the use of electronic effects and mood music–like textures far removed from the propulsive rhythms of early rock.

audio CD A compact disc containing audio files.

backbeat A percussive accent occurring regularly on the second beat of beat pairs: 1 **2** 1 **2** or 1 **2** 3 **4**.

ballad (1) a folk or folk-like song that tells a story in several stanzas. (2) In twentieth-century popular music, a popular song performed at a slow tempo.

beat (1) The rhythmic quality of a piece of music that invites a physical response ("that song has a good beat"). (2) The (usually) regular marking of time at walking/ dancing/moving speed (usually between 72 and 144 beats per second). (3) The rhythmic foundation of a style or substyle, distinguished by the consistent use of regular rhythms and rhythmic patterns: a two-beat, a rock beat, a shuffle beat.

bebop See *bop*.

beguine   In American popular music, an Americanized form of the Cuban rumba. It has a similar rhythmic feel but lacks the clave rhythm heard in authentic Afro-Cuban music.

big-band swing   Swing-era or swing-style music performed by a big band.

bluegrass   An updated version of country's old-time string band music. Bluegrass developed in the late 1940s under the guidance of mandolinist Bill Monroe.

blue note   An African-inspired alteration of certain conventional scale tones.

boogie-woogie   A blues piano style characterized by repetitive bass figures, usually in a shuffle rhythm.

bop   A jazz style that developed in the 1940s, characterized by fast tempos, irregular streams of notes, and considerable rhythmic conflict.

bossa nova   A samba-based, jazz-influenced Brazilian popular-song style that became popular in the United States in the early 1960s.

break dancing   Along with rap and graffiti, an expression of hip-hop culture; this extremely athletic, vigorous dance parallels the energy of the music to which it's performed.

broadside   A topical text sung to a well-known tune.

burlesques   In a minstrel show, humorous parodies of cultivated material.

cakewalk   A dance fad of the 1890s; also the music to accompany the dance.

call and response   A rapid exchange, usually of riffs, between two different timbres: e.g., solo voice and guitar; solo voice and choir; or saxophones and trumpets.

cha-cha-cha   A Latin dance that became popular in the 1950s. Its name comes from the signature rhythm that ends each phrase.

Charleston   The most popular of the vigorous new dances of the early 1920s.

chord progression   A sequence of chords. Many of the chord progressions in popular music follow well-used patterns, such as the chord progressions for "Heart and Soul" and the 12-bar blues.

chorus   (1) A large singing group. (2) In verse/chorus and rock songs, that part of a song in which both melody and lyrics are repeated. (3) In blues and Tin Pan Alley songs, one statement of the melody. Also called *refrain*.

classic blues   The popular blues style of the 1920s, which typically featured a woman singing the blues (e.g., Bessie Smith) accompanied by one or more jazz musicians.

clave rhythm   The characteristic rhythm of Afro-Cuban music. It can be represented as:

$$//\mathbf{X} \text{ x x } \mathbf{X} \text{ x x } \mathbf{X} \text{ x } // \text{ x x } \mathbf{X} \text{ x } \mathbf{X} \text{ x x x } //$$

The x's indicate an eight-beat rhythm; **X**'s are accented-notes. In a *reverse* clave rhythm, the two measures are switched.

claves   Two cylindrical sticks, about 1 inch in diameter, used to tap out the clave rhythm.

collective improvisation   An improvisational context in which more than one performer is improvising a melody-like line. Collective improvisation is standard practice in New Orleans jazz, free jazz, and much rock-era jazz fusion.

commercial blues   An umbrella term for blues styles performed by professional entertainers during the first part of the twentieth century, as opposed to folk or country blues.

comping   In bop jazz style, chordal accompaniment played in rhythmically irregular or unpredictable patterns.

concert band   A band (woodwinds, brass, and percussion instruments) that performs in a concert-like setting (seated on-stage, in front of an audience) rather than while marching.

country blues   A family of African American folk blues styles that flourished in the rural South. Country blues differs from commercial blues mainly in its accompanying instrument—usually acoustic guitar—and its tendency toward less regular forms.

country music   A commercial form of the music of white southerners, which began with the advent of commercial radio in the early 1920s. The different styles of country music mix elements of the traditional folk music of the South with other popular styles, such as jazz, pop, and rock.

country rock beat   Most characteristically, a strong honky-tonk two-beat combined with a clear, simple rock rhythm.

cover version   A version of a song by someone other than the original artist.

crooner   A singer (usually male) who sings with a sweet sound in a conversational, low-key manner. Amplification made crooning possible. Bing Crosby was the most successful of the early crooners.

cross-marketing   The practice of using media in tandem so that each helps promote the other. The practice began in the early 1970s, when rock bands toured to promote a newly released recording. Robert Stigwood, producer of *Saturday Night Fever,* was the first to adapt this promotional strategy to film in a big way by using songs from the soundtrack to spark interest in the film.

cubop   A fusion of bop and Latin rhythms. It developed in the late 1940s, primarily under the guidance of trumpeter Dizzy Gillespie.

dance-oriented rock (DOR)   American versions of the post-punk/post-disco fusions of the early 1980s.

deep blues   A term coined by Robert Palmer to describe blues least influenced by other styles, e.g., pop, jazz, or gospel.

diatonic scale   Either of the two most common musical scales, the major scale and the minor scale, each containing seven pitches per octave, with intervals of five whole steps and two half steps.

disc jockey   A host of a radio show that features recordings, rather than live music.

disco   A dance music that rose to popularity in the mid-seventies. Disco songs typically had a relentless beat; a complex rhythmic texture, usually with a 16-beat rhythm; and rich orchestration, typically an augmented rhythm section with horns and strings.

doo-wop   A pop-oriented R&B genre that typically featured remakes of popular standards or pop-style originals sung by black vocal groups. Doo-wop died out in the early 1960s with the rise of the girl groups and Motown.

downtown Latin style   A watered-down version of Afro-Cuban music intended for the white American market.

duration   The length in time of a musical event.

dynamics   Levels or changes in intensity. The dynamic level of a Ramones song is very loud.

electric blues   A post–World War II blues style characterized by the use of a full rhythm section, including electric guitar. It is the most popular form of contemporary blues.

electric recording   A recording procedure developed in the 1920s that converts sound into an electric signal before recording and then converts the electric signal back into sound for playback. With its far superior sound quality, it immediately—made acoustic recording obsolete.

electric steel guitar   Invented in the early 1930s, it soon replaced the dobro as the instrument of choice for lap guitarists.

electronica   The umbrella term for a large and varied family of musical styles that rely mainly or exclusively on synthesized musical sounds: house, techno, trance, ambient, jungle, drum and bass, industrial dance, and many more.

elements of popular music   The elements of music—instrumentation, dynamics, harmony, melody, rhythm, texture, and form—as typically used in popular music.

endman   A comic in a minstrel troupe. Minstrel performers sat in a semicircle on-stage; an endman sat at one end or the other.

folk music   Music made by a group of people (e.g., Cajuns, Navahos, or whites from rural Appalachia), mostly without formal musical training, primarily for their own amusement or for the amusement of others in the group. Within the group, folk music is transmitted orally. Within the popular tradition, folk music has also referred to folksongs sung by commercial musicians (e.g., the Kingston Trio) or music with elements of folk style (e.g., the folk rock of the late 1960s).

form   The organization of a musical work in time.

four-beat rhythm   A rhythmic foundation in which each beat receives equal emphasis; the common rhythmic basis for jazz.

foxtrot   A popular dance created in the teens by Irene and Vernon Castle. Also, a song with a two-beat rhythmic foundation suitable for dancing the foxtrot.

front line   The horns (or other melody-line instruments, such as the vibraphone) in a jazz combo. The term comes from the position of the horn players on the bandstand: they stand in a line in front of the rhythm instruments.

funk   An R&B-derived style that developed in the 1970s, primarily under the guidance of George Clinton. It is characterized mainly by dense textures (bands may include eight or more musicians) and complex, often 16-beat rhythms.

gangsta rap   A rap style of the late eighties that depicted the violence of inner-city life.

genre   A body of music linked by such features as instrumentation and form. A genre, such as blues, can appear in several different styles.

glam (glitter) rock   A rock style of the early 1970s in which theatrical elements—makeup, outlandish dress—were prominent. David Bowie, in his various incarnations, is considered by many to be the major figure in glam rock.

gospel   A family of religious music styles: there is white and black gospel music. Black gospel music has had the more profound influence on popular music by far. Created around 1930 by Thomas Dorsey and others, gospel has influenced popular singing, especially rhythm and blues, since the early 1950s.

griot   In West African culture, the tribe's healer (witch doctor), historian (preserver of its history in his songs), and, along with the master drummer, most important musician.

grunge   A rock substyle that emerged around 1990 that fused punk disaffection with the power and distortion of heavy metal.

habanera   A dance created in Cuba during the early nineteenth century that became popular in both Europe and South America. Its characteristic rhythm resurfaced in the Argentine tango and the cakewalk.

half step   On a keyboard instrument, the interval between any pitch and the immediately adjacent pitch.

harmony   Chords and the study of chord progressions.

headbanging   Heavy metal's version of dancing.

heavy metal   A hard rock style that developed in the early 1970s. Its most distinctive feature is heavy distortion.

hip-hop   A term used to describe the African American culture from which rap emerged. Its artistic expressions include not only rap but also break dancing and graffiti.

hokum   An upbeat, good-humored, light-hearted blues novelty style popular between the two world wars.

honky-tonk   (1) A working-class bar. (2) Country music associated with honky-tonks. It developed around 1940 and was distinguished from other country music of the period in its use of drums, a heavy backbeat, and electric guitar.

house music   An early techno style based originally in Chicago; it was a low-budget continuation of disco.

improvisation   The act of creating music spontaneously rather than performing a previously learned song the same way every time. Improvisation is one of the key elements in jazz.

inflection   Moment-to-moment changes in dynamic level. Aretha Franklin sings in a highly inflected style.

instrumentation   Literally, the instruments chosen to perform a particular score; broadly, the instrumental and vocal accompaniment for a recording.

intensity   The degree of loudness of a musical sound.

interlocutor   The straight man in a minstrel show. The interlocutor would sit in the middle of the semicircle and ask questions of the endmen, who would give comic replies.

interval   The distance between two pitches.

interpolation   The insertion of a song into a musical comedy for which it was not written. Interpolation was common in the early years of musical comedy, when producers would insert a song into a show simply because it was a hit.

jazz   A group of popular related styles primarily for listening. Jazz is usually distinguished from the other popular music of an era by greater rhythmic freedom (more syncopation and/or less insistent beat keeping), extensive improvisation, and more-adventurous harmony. There are two families of jazz styles: those based on a four-beat rhythm and those based on a rock or 16-beat rhythm.

jump band   In the late 1940s, a small band—rhythm section plus a few horns—that played a rhythm-and-blues style influenced by big-band swing and blues. Saxophonist/vocalist Louis Jordan was a key performer in this style.

keynote   The focal pitch on which a scale begins.

Latin rock   A fusion of Afro-Cuban music and rock.

libretto   The text for a sung stage production, from opera to musical comedy.

Lollapalooza   Woodstock-like touring festival that was an important outlet for alternative music in the nineties.

long-playing (LP or 33 rpm) record   First issued by Columbia Records in 1948, these vinyl discs could hold over a half-hour of music and didn't break when dropped.

loop   A short sound file—say, a drum pattern or a bass line—that can be added to a track in a song to supply a rhythm, harmony, riff, or other similar element.

mainstream   A term commonly used to identify the most popular style(s) during a given time period.

major scale   A diatonic scale with a particular arrangement of whole and half steps. The sequence of whole and half steps can be heard (and seen) by playing the white keys on a keyboard from C to C. However, a major scale can use any of the 12 keys within an octave as a keynote. (*see also* minor scale)

majors   The "big four" recording companies—Sony BMG, EMI, Universal, and Warner—that control a decided majority of recorded music.

mambo   A Latin dance fad of the late 1940s and '50s that combined the rhythms of the Afro- Cuban *son* with the horn sounds of big-band jazz.

maracas A percussion instrument made by putting handles on dried, seed-filled gourds; the shaking of seeds against the interior walls makes the distinctive sound.

march Music composed in regularly accented, usually duple meter that is appropriate to accompany marching; a composition in the style of march music.

measure A consistent grouping of beats. A waltz has measures containing three beats; a march has measures with two beats. Also called *bar*.

medley A group of songs connected by musical interludes.

melisma Several pitches sung to a single syllable. In popular music melisma has been most widely used by African American singers, especially blues and gospel-influenced artists.

melody The most musically interesting part of a musical texture. The melody is typically distinguished from other parts by the interest and individuality of its contour and rhythm.

mento The Jamaican popular music of the early 1950s.

microphone A device that converts sound waves into an electric signal. The microphone has been in use in popular music since the 1920s.

MIDI Stands for *Musical Instrument Digital Interface*; a protocol that enables digital devices such as instruments and computers to communicate with each other.

minor scale A diatonic scale with an arrangement of whole and half steps different from both the major scale and modal scales. In many styles, it is used to help convey darker moods. (*see also* major scale)

minstrel show A form of stage entertainment distinguished by cruel parodies of African Americans. Minstrel shows were popular from the early 1840s to the end of the nineteenth century.

mix A series of songs or dance tracks seamlessly connected by a disc jockey.

modal harmony A term that identifies chords created from modal scales, which are different from the major and minor scales heard in nineteenth- and early-twentieth-century popular music.

modern era In popular music, the period from the early 1910s to the early 1960s.

montuno In Afro-Cuban music, a syncopated accompanying figure, usually played on the piano, that is repeated indefinitely.

Motown sound A consistent set of characteristic style features heard in sixties Motown recordings.

MTV A cable television network that began broadcasting music videos in 1981.

multitrack recording The process of recording each part of a performance separately, then mixing them into a complete performance. The Beatles, along with their producer George Martin, were among the first to take full advantage of multitrack recording techniques.

musique concrète A process of creating music, invented by French composer Pierre Schaeffer shortly after WWII, that uses recorded sounds as raw material.

neo-traditional movement A style that offers a new take on an established, or traditional, style.

netlabels Independent music labels that deliver music only online, launch personal websites, start online artist cooperatives, and establish interest groups.

New Orleans jazz Style of jazz performance based on the early bands that performed in and around New Orleans; revived in the late 1940s, it typically features collective improvisation and quick tempos. The front-line instruments usually include cornet or trumpet, clarinet, and trombone, with a rhythm section partial or complete. Also called *Dixieland jazz*.

new wave The "back to basics" movement within rock beginning in the late 1970s, featuring simplified instrumentation and basic chords and melodies. An early new wave band was the Talking Heads.

obbligato A second melody playing under the main melody.

octave The interval between two pitches that vibrate in a 2:1 ratio. Pitches that vibrate in such a simple ratio to each other share the same letter name.

olio The second section of a minstrel show—the variety portion that featured a wide range of unrelated acts, much like the later vaudeville shows.

operetta Originally a kind of European musical drama that was less serious than opera, with speech instead of singing between songs, but with more dramatic integrity than musical comedy. Generally, plots told a fairy tale–like story. European operettas were popular in the United States through World War II. *Show Boat* began an American operetta tradition.

overdubbing The process of recording an additional part onto an existing recording.

parlor song A song composed mainly for domestic use by amateur musicians; Stephen Foster's "Jeanie with the

Light Brown Hair" is a familiar example. The parlor song remained popular through most of the nineteenth century. Also called *household songs* or *piano bench music*.

patriotic song   A song with a patriotic theme.

patting juba   A practice among slaves (and their descendants) in which they tapped out tricky rhythms on their thighs, chests, and other body parts.

payola scandal   The late 1950s scandal that resulted from the investigation of the practice of record companies' bribing disc jockeys to secure airplay for their records.

pentatonic scale   A scale with five notes per octave. Two pentatonic scales are used widely in popular music: the Anglo-American pentatonic scale, heard in minstrel songs (Stephen Foster's "Camptown Ladies" begins with such a scale) and some country music; and the African American pentatonic scale, heard in blues and blues-influenced styles.

Philadelphia sound   A popular black pop style in the early and mid 1970s created by Philadelphia-based producers. It was a more elaborate and complex sequel to the Motown sound.

piano rag   A march-like, syncopated composition for the piano.

pitch   The relative highness or lowness of a musical sound, determined by the frequency with which it vibrates.

pop rock   A rock-era substyle that grafted elements of rock style onto prerock popular song.

popular-music   Music that appeals to a mass audience, is intended to have wide appeal, and has a sound and a style distinct from classical or folk.

progressive rock   A rock style that sought to elevate the status of rock by embracing a classical music aesthetic and adapting it to rock.

psychedelic rock   *See* acid rock.

punk   A rock style that emerged in the late 1970s, characterized musically by relatively simple instrumentation, fast, insistent rhythms, and extremely high volume. The Ramones and the Sex Pistols were among the best-known punk bands.

queercore   A music movement of the 1980s that reacted against more mainstream gay and lesbian views and found a musical voice in the work of bands such as Sister George, Tribe 8, and Team Dresch.

race record   A term that came into use in the early 1920s to describe recordings by African American artists intended for sale primarily in the African American community.

ragtime   A popular style at the turn of the twentieth century that mixed European forms, harmony, and textures with African-inspired syncopation. Ragtime began as a piano music, but soon the term was applied to any music—song and dance as well as piano music—that had some syncopation.

rap   A musical style of the 1980s and '90s characterized by a rhymed text spoken in a heightened voice over a repetitive, mostly rhythmic accompaniment.

rave   A huge dance party conducted in a large space: outdoors, an abandoned warehouse, or even a large club. Ecstasy and other "designer" drugs were very much part of the scene.

refrain   *See* chorus.

reggae   The most widely known Jamaican popular music, it has a distinctive, intoxicating rhythm. It emerged around 1970 in the music of Jimmy Cliff, Bob Marley, and others.

reverse clave rhythm   A version of the clave rhythm, in which the second half of the pattern comes first.

revue   A type of stage entertainment popular in the first third of the century. Revues were topical; they often lampooned prominent public figures. They had a flimsy plot, designed to link—however loosely—a series of songs, dance numbers, and comedy routines.

rhythm   The time dimension of music. The cumulative result of musical events as they happen over time.

rhythm and blues (R&B)   A term used since the mid-forties to describe African American popular styles, especially those influenced by blues and/or dance music.

rhythm section   The part of a musical group that supplies the rhythmic and harmonic foundation of a performance. Usually includes at least one chord instrument (guitar, piano, or keyboard), a bass instrument, and a percussion instrument (typically the drum set).

riff   A short (two to seven pitches), rhythmically interesting melodic idea.

riot grrrl   A music movement of the 1980s that supported a militant feminist agenda with post-punk music that favored confrontation over musical skill.

rock beat   Eight evenly spaced sounds per measure (or two per beat)—over a strong backbeat.

rock musical   A musical that uses rock rhythms and generally incorporates some of its ideas and attitudes. *Hair* was a prototypical rock musical.

rockabilly   According to Carl Perkins, a country take on rhythm and blues, performed mainly by white Southerners, that combined elements of country music with rock and roll. Rockabilly was most popular in the mid-fifties.

rumba An Afro-Cuban-inspired dance popularized in the United States during the early 1930s.

salsa A term that came into use in the 1960s and '70s to describe an updated form of the mambo. It is now the most popular traditional form of Afro-Cuban music in both the United States and Cuba.

samba The most popular Afro-Brazilian dance music of the twentieth century in Brazil and elsewhere. The samba has been popular in the United States since the early 1930s. The 16-beat rhythms of samba influenced the new jazz and African American popular styles of the 1970s and '80s.

sample A small sound file. There are two basic kinds of samples in common use. One is the recorded sound of a voice or group of voices, an instrument (such as a grand piano) or group of instruments (a violin section), or some other sound. This sound can then be activated through another device. The other main kind of sampling involves lifting short excerpts from existing recordings to use in a new recording, much like a visual artist will use found objects to create a collage or assemblage.

scale A conventional arrangement of pitches in a series separated by small intervals. The two most widely used families of scales in popular music are *diatonic scales,* with seven pitches per octave, and *pentatonic scales,* with five pitches per octave.

scat singing A type of wordless singing, usually at a fast tempo, in which the singer uses nonsense syllables in place of lyrics. Typically scat singers imitate instrumentalists.

sequencer A device that enables a person to assemble a sound file track by track. Using a sequencer that can store eight tracks, a person can re-create the sound of a band: one track for the bass, another for the rhythm guitar, and so on.

set A group of songs performed by a band or presented by a disc jockey. Popular and jazz musicians play a set of songs, then take an extended break. A DJ may mix songs into a set that provides continuous music for a half hour or more.

singer-songwriter A term that came into use around 1970 to describe songwriters who performed their own music. The music of singer-songwriters was generally characterized by an emphasis on melody, a folklike accompaniment, and a relatively low dynamic level.

ska The dominant Jamaican popular music through the first part of the 1960s. The most distinctive feature of ska is a strong afterbeat: a strong, crisp *chunk* on the latter part of each beat.

skip An interval larger than a whole step on a musical scale.

soft rock A family of rock styles characterized mainly by sweeter singing styles; more melodious, even Tin Pan Alley–esque vocal lines; richer instrumentation; and a gentle dynamic level. Soft rock blended the emphasis on melody and clear forms of Tin Pan Alley song with an understated rock rhythm.

son The most characteristic style of Afro-Cuban music, popular in Cuba during the early part of the twentieth century. Some of the Cuban musicians who migrated to New York in the 1930s and '40s blended *son* with big-band swing to produce the mambo.

song interpretation the practice of personalizing a song performance, often thoroughly altering the contour and the rhythm of the melody, begun in the 1930s by singers such as Armstrong, Waters, Holiday, and Crosby.

song plugger A publishing-house pianist who could play a new song for a professional singer or a prospective customer.

songster A book with just the lyrics to popular songs of the day, published in the mid-nineteenth century.

songster A black entertainer who sang and played many different kinds of music, including blues, ballads, work songs, children's songs, and familiar folk songs, both black and white.

soul A term used widely in the 1960s by both white and black Americans to describe popular music by African Americans, particularly music, like that of James Brown, marginally influenced by pop or white rock styles.

sound collage Music by cutting and pasting sound clips into music. The sound collages of Grandmaster Flash were seminal.

speakeasy A nightclub in which alcoholic beverages were illegally sold; despite their illegal status, they flourished during Prohibition.

standard A song that remains popular well after its initial appearance; songs that live on in recordings, films, and live performances.

step A small interval between pitches. There are two kinds of steps: half steps and whole steps. A half step is the interval between two adjacent pitches; a whole step is equivalent to two half steps. Most diatonic scales are comprised exclusively of whole and half steps.

stride piano An offshoot of ragtime that typically featured a more complex bass/chord accompaniment and elaborate figuration in the melody.

strophic A song form in which two or more verses of text are sung to the same melody. A hymn is strophic.

style The set of those common features found in the music of a time, place, culture, or individual.

style beat A term used to identify the rhythmic foundation of the music of an era. Since about 1920, four main style beats have emerged in popular music: the rhythm of the foxtrot (or two beat) in the 1920s and 1930s; swing (or four beat) rhythm in music popular from the late 1930s through the 1950s; rock (or eight beat) rhythm from the late 1950s through the 1970s; and the 16-beat rhythm popularized in disco during the 1970s and used extensively since that time in a variety of styles.

surf music A term that came into use to describe the late 1950s/early 1960s rock styles that glorified the Southern California lifestyle.

sweet As opposed to swing, so-called sweet bands played songs in a two-beat rhythm, with little syncopation, slow tempos, and flowing melodies.

swing (1) The sense of rhythmic play—the result of various kinds of rhythmic conflict—that characterizes good jazz performance. (2) Music, often jazz or jazz-influenced, based on a clearly marked four-beat rhythm. The Swing Era in popular music lasted about a decade, from 1935 to 1945.

syncopation Accents that come *between* the beats of a regular rhythm rather than *with* them.

synthesizer An instrument in which sounds are generated electronically. Synthesizers typically use a keyboard as the primary input device.

Tambo and Bones Nicknames for the endmen in a minstrel show, so called because one usually played a tambourine and the other a pair of bones.

techno Post-disco dance music in which most or all of the sounds are electronically generated.

tempo The speed of the beat.

texture The relationship of the parts in a musical performance.

third-stream music A concerted effort by the Modern Jazz Quartet, Gunther Schuller, and the Beaux Arts String Quartet to fuse jazz and classical music.

thumb-brush style An early country guitar style in which the performer plays the melody on the lower strings and, between melody notes, brushes the chords on the upper strings. It was first popularized by Maybelle Carter.

timbre The distinctive tone quality of a voice or an instrument.

Tin Pan Alley A nickname for a section of East 28th Street in New York City, where many music publishers had their offices. Also, the styles of the songs created in the first half of the century for these publishers: a *Tin Pan Alley song* refers to songs by Irving Berlin, George Gershwin, and their contemporaries.

toasting The practice developed by Jamaican disc jockeys of delivering a steady stream of patter. Much of it was topical, even personal: they would pick out, and sometimes pick on, people in the crowd that had gathered around. Toasting is a direct forerunner of rap: both initially featured topical, humorous commentary over preexisting music.

torch song A song about unrequited or lost love.

traditional country vocal sound The flat, nasal, relatively uninflected vocal sound associated with country music.

trio (1) A group of three musicians. (2) The second half of a march, rag, and other composition in multisectional form. In a march the melody of the trio is often lyrical.

triplet A division of the beat into three equal parts.

tropical Latin A generic term for music influenced in varying degrees by Afro-Cuban music.

tumbao A syncopated bass pattern characteristic of Afro-Cuban music.

two-beat rhythm The style beat characterized by the alternation of bass note and backbeat; the rhythmic basis of the foxtrot and other early syncopated instrumental styles.

unison Two performers playing the same pitch.

uptown Latin style The sound of authentic Afro-Cuban music in the 1940s and '50s.

vaudeville A form of stage entertainment popular from the 1880s to about 1930. It consisted of a series of acts: singers, dancers, novelty performers, and comics. It differed from the revue and musical comedy in that there was no attempt to link vaudeville acts into a dramatically coherent whole.

verse/chorus form The most popular song form of the late nineteenth century. The verse tells a story in several installments, with different text set to the same melody.

The chorus, which follows each verse, repeats both words and melody to reinforce the main message of the song. In early verse/chorus songs, the chorus was often sung by a small group, usually a quartet.

vibrato　A slight oscillation in the basic pitch of a musical sound. Vibrato is used by most popular singers and instrumentalists (except for pianists and percussionists).

walkaround　The conclusion of a minstrel show, featuring the entire troupe in a grand finale of song and dance.

waltz song　A type of song popular around 1900 in which a flowing melody is supported by a simple, waltz-time accompaniment.

western swing　A Texas country style popular in the 1930s and early 1940s. Western swing added drums, horns, piano, and steel guitar to the instrumentation of the standard country band.

whole step　An interval formed from two half steps.

worldbeat　A general term to describe the rhythms in music that fuse a prevailing international style with a regional music, such as rhythm and blues plus a regional African style.

Supplements

Dizzy Gillespie on the cover of "Ray's Idea,"
published in 1948 and billed as "Be-Bop
(The New Jazz)."

Copyright © 1948 Robbins Music. Used by permission of Warner Bros. Publications, Inc.

THE BEBOP ERA

WE THINK OF THE "MODERN JAZZ" ERA as beginning with bebop in the midforties, but what makes bebop "modern," distinguishing it from the preceding swing era? This chapter explores bebop's most significant characteristics:

- General aesthetics grounded in improvisation and solo playing—that is, in individual solos, not in melody, popular song, and arrangement
- The emergence of bebop melodies—"heads"—that stylistically complement the improvisations
- Smaller groups favored over big bands
- Musical performances in jazz clubs rather than large dance halls
- De-emphasis on commercial or popular success
- De-emphasis on dancing:
  - ▶ Tempos that are considerably faster or slower than in swing
  - ▶ Rhythmic pulse that is less obviously articulated than in swing
- Rise in black consciousness resulting from a new perception of African Americans' contributions to jazz

Many of these points provided the cultural context of jazz for the remainder of the twentieth century. Besides defining a more modern sensibility, these characteristics helped transform jazz from popular entertainment into an art form in many of its substyles. Before exploring the characteristics of bebop further, we look at the origins of bebop in the 1940s.

Revolution Versus Evolution

The emergence of *bebop* in the 1940s irrevocably altered the jazz landscape. In contrast to the well-polished big bands of the swing era—many of them incredibly successful—some jazz musicians began gravitating toward smaller groups. Initially, they developed their musical ideas in impromptu jam sessions, especially in such after-hours Harlem clubs as Monroe's Uptown House and Minton's Playhouse. By the end of World War II, these cutting-edge musicians had moved downtown to appear at the nightclubs on West Fifty-second Street. Dozens of clubs—such as the Three Deuces, the Onyx, the Downbeat, the Famous Door, the Spotlite, Kelly's Stables, and the Hickory House—opened their doors on what became known as "The Street." They called the new music *rebop* (eventually to fall into disuse), *bebop,* or just *bop.*

Many of the architects of bebop—such as Charlie "Yardbird" or "Bird" Parker, John Birks "Dizzy" Gillespie, and Kenny Clarke—began their careers playing in big bands, but bebop represented a radical rejection of the musical conventions of the swing era. Instead of elaborate dance halls, bebop players performed in bars and nightclubs, and many seemed indifferent to commercial success as entertainers—they played for listening rather than dancing. Rather than the slick show-business theatrics of the big bands, beboppers aimed to capture the informal spirit of the jam session. Its groups often comprised only five or six musicians—two or three horn players and a rhythm section of piano, bass, and drums. Whereas the big-band arrangers of the swing era carefully inserted improvised solos within longer written arrangements, the smaller bebop bands avoided elaborate charts and emphasized, above all, virtuosic improvisational skill.

Many older musicians were perplexed by these new sounds. Bandleader Cab Calloway is said to have derided trumpeter Dizzy Gillespie's playing as "Chinese music." In 1948 trumpeter Louis Armstrong dismissed bebop as an annoying novelty performed by overly competitive musicians. He said:

> All they want to do is show you up, and any old way will do as long as it's different from the way you played it before. So you get all them weird chords which don't mean nothing, and first people get curious about it just because it's new, but soon they get tired of it because it's really no good and you got no melody to remember and no beat to dance to.[1]

Drummer Dave Tough, a "Chicagoan" in the 1920s who later became an important drummer during the swing era, reacted with less hostility but was clearly confused by the music. After first hearing Dizzy Gillespie and Oscar Pettiford's band on Fifty-second Street, he noted:

> As we walked in, see, these cats snatched up their horns and blew crazy stuff. One would stop all of a sudden and another would start for no reason at all. We never could tell when a solo was supposed to begin or end. Then they all quit at once and walked off the stand. It scared us.[2]

Reactions such as these were not uncommon in the music world, but the fans of traditional jazz were the most disappointed: the music they loved was being called passé, old-fashioned, and—the worst insult of all—unhip. While bebop was taking root, many traditionalists bemoaned the demise of classic jazz and argued that bebop abandoned jazz music's most treasured principles. Modernists called these listeners *moldy figs.* Arguments between the two sides enlivened much jazz discourse in the late 1940s.

Bebop and *bop* are terms that came about in the 1940s to describe the nervous, energetic style of the younger jazz musicians. The terms probably developed from the nonsense syllables used by scat singers to re-create the characteristic melodic phrases of the new style.

Moldy figs was a term used by younger musicians and fans in the 1940s to describe older jazz fans who clung to the music of the 1920s and 1930s and derided the newer bebop style.

Bebop began in the early 1940s as "insider's" music—a music for musicians. Despite the efforts of the moldy figs, bebop would become the dominant jazz style by the end of the decade. Among other factors, a wartime tax on dance halls triggered the decline of the big bands. Small jazz clubs, such as the ones found on Fifty-second Street, boomed. Younger players, who had fewer outlets for musical employment than the stars of the big bands, joined small groups and experimented with the new musical language.

Bohemianism added an attractive element to the music. Performers and their *hipster* audiences often took on the affectations and inside slang of beboppers. Some of these affectations—such as Dizzy Gillespie's beret, goatee, and horn-rimmed glasses—were benign; others—such as Charlie Parker's heroin addiction—were not.

With bebop, jazz ceased to be a strongly commercial music. Some musicians, such as Dizzy Gillespie, felt that bebop should try to adapt to dancing. Many of its devotees, however, interpreted the music as a political statement, a rejection of all things conformist and mainstream. This view included a reaction against American racism and segregation. Many players felt that Louis Armstrong and other older musicians conformed to racial stereotypes of black entertainers. Bebop challenged and defied these stereotypes. Indeed, political activism among some black musicians can be traced to the nonconformity of the beboppers. As institutional segregation came under attack in the 1950s and 1960s, black musicians often used their music as a public statement of their political beliefs. Thus the conventions of bebop laid the foundation for modern jazz, both in musical style and in the convictions of its players.

The word **hipster** was used to describe a young follower of jazz who affected the dress, speech, and manner of jazz musicians working in the new jazz styles of the late 1940s and early 1950s.

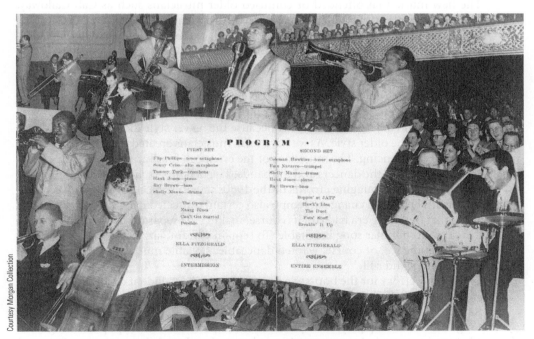

In 1943 the "zoot-suit riots"—named for the stylized clothing of young Chicanos—erupted in Los Angeles and continued for a week as whites, including soldiers and sailors on leave, attacked Hispanics. A future recording supervisor of jazz for Mercury Records, Norman Granz, organized a concert at the Philharmonic Auditorium in Los Angeles to benefit Mexican youths, and an enduring concert series began. Here is the 1949 program for Jazz at the Philharmonic, picturing, among others, Ron Brown on bass and Shelly Manne on drums. Notice the integrated seating, part of an anti-discrimination clause Granz wrote into all his contracts.

Courtesy Morgan Collection

Despite these dramatic, possibly revolutionary, developments, much of the musical style of bebop evolved naturally from swing style. Players carried over to bebop features of earlier jazz:

- Improvisation on the following:
  - ▶ Popular songs in 32-bar AABA or ABAC form
  - ▶ Rhythm changes (a 32-bar set of changes in AABA form)
  - ▶ The 12-bar blues chord progression
- Improvisation based mostly on eighth-note melodic lines
- Characteristic instrumentation of rhythm-section plus horns
- Overall performance formats of head-solos-head (although bebop emphasized this far more than earlier styles did)

Seen in this light, bebop was a natural next step in the musical development of jazz. This should not be surprising because the musicians who innovated bebop had trained extensively in swing bands. Although many of the revolutionary aspects of bop were more social than musical, jazz musicians and fans at the time were indeed caught up in what they perceived as the radical newness of its language. In the description of bebop style to follow, we emphasize these innovations rather than the older swing elements.

Characteristics of the Bebop Style

The new music that offended or confused older musicians such as Cab Calloway, Louis Armstrong, and Dave Tough differed from earlier jazz in improvisational style, melodic language, and harmonic language. Much of the repertory changed considerably. In typical bebop compositions, the horns played the melody, improvised solos followed, and a reprise of the melody formed the ending. The horns frequently stated the melody in unison or in octaves, creating a starker, leaner sound than the full-voiced chords played by big bands. Bebop groups played at faster tempos than those of swing bands but played their ballads much more slowly.

Bebop also departed from swing because the newer style did not support dancing as well as the older style. As we have seen, musicians created the jazz of the 1920s and 1930s for dancing. The musicians of the era speak fondly of the energizing give-and-take between the dancers and the bands. The beboppers, however, disassociated jazz from the jitterbugging crowds of the 1930s to win respect for their music as an art form. The radical change in tempo also certainly affected dancing. Further, some argue that the swing era had run its course, making the separation of the music from dancing and popular song inevitable. To remain vibrant, jazz needed to evolve. The popular audience, of course, wanted danceable, singable music—a void soon to be filled by rock and roll.

The repertory for the bop-style bands remained dependent on the 12-bar blues and compositions based on the chords of "I Got Rhythm"—both a legacy of the Kansas City style—as well as the 32-bar AABA or ABAC form in standard popular songs. But the bebop players emphasized recomposition of these popular songs into a bebop framework. In recomposition players abandoned the original melody and composed a new one, sometimes called a *contrafact*, over the harmonic structure of the original. Although this practice did occur in earlier jazz—"Tiger Rag," for example,

A ***contrafact*** is a new melody composed to fit the harmonic and formal structure of a previously composed popular song.

A Contrafact: Dizzy Gillespie's "Groovin' High"

Here is a contrafact of the original melody of "Whispering" with Gillespie's recomposition, "Groovin' High":

The "Whispering" melody, which is primarily diatonic, almost masks its harmonic progression. In "Groovin' High" Gillespie writes a new melody mostly in eighth notes and with more notes than in the original composition—typical of the bebop melodic language. Here are some features of Gillespie's recomposed melody:

▶ It is much more chromatic

▶ It is jagged and angular

▶ It outlines and highlights the harmonic progression through a repeated motive, marked as (b)

▶ It has accents that crop up in unexpected places

These are the features of bebop that swing fans sometimes found hard to understand. Gillespie's melody too has the typical double-eighth-note figure prevalent in bebop melodies and improvisations, marked as (a). This characteristic two-note figure may very well be the source of the word *bebop*.

provided the chords to some jazz tunes—the beboppers turned recomposition into a standard practice (See the box "A Contrafact: Dizzy Gillespie's 'Groovin' High.'") For the bebop player, such recompositions had two advantages:

▶ The new melody resembled the bebop improvisations that followed and kept the musical language unified.

▶ Performers and record companies did not have to pay song royalties to the original composers because they did not use the original melodies.

Many of the significant early works of the bebop era were contrafacts:

BEBOP-STYLE TUNE (COMPOSER)	ORIGINAL (COMPOSER)
"KoKo" (Charlie Parker)	"Cherokee" (Ray Noble)
"Hot House" (Tadd Dameron)	"What Is This Thing Called Love?" (Cole Porter)
"Crazeology" (Benny Harris)	"I Got Rhythm" (George Gershwin)
"Groovin' High" (Dizzy Gillespie)	"Whispering" (Vincent Rose–Richard Coburn–John Schonberger)

Dizzy Gillespie, one of the founders of the new style, acknowledged the obvious differences in bebop from earlier jazz but was keenly aware of how the music evolved logically from swing. When asked to contrast the newer bebop music with the older style, he cited several differences:

> Chords. . . . And we stressed different accents in the rhythms. But I'm reluctant to say that anything is the difference between our music of the early forties and the music before that, of the thirties. You can get records from the early days and hear guys doing the same things. It just kept changing a little bit more; one guy would play a phrase one way, and another guy would come along and do something else with it. . . . Charlie Parker was very, very melodic; guys could copy his things quite a bit. [Thelonious] Monk was one of the founders of the movement too, but his playing, my playing, and Charlie Parker's playing were altogether different.[3]

The one characteristic that players most frequently singled out as new was the harmony. As saxophonist Illinois Jacquet pointed out, "The major difference in the new music was the chord changes."[4] The harmonies used by the bebop players sometimes emphasized the upper parts of chords such as ninths, elevenths, and thirteenths. These additions to chords, called *extended chord tones*, or *tensions*, would be contributed not only by the accompanying pianist but also sometimes by the soloist. Hearing the emphasis on these extensions, early critics of the music thought the improvisers were playing "wrong notes."

Music Example 7-1a, the opening of Gillespie's "A Night in Tunisia," shows a prominent use of the seventh, ninth, and thirteenth as arpeggiated chordal extensions. Also prominent in bebop was the so-called flatted fifth, the use of a pitch a *tritone* away from the root of the chord. The melody of measures 7 and 8 of "A Night in Tunisia" illustrates the use of the flatted fifth: here E♭ is used in conjunction with the A7 chord:

Extended chord tones, sometimes called **tensions**, are notes added to seventh chords to make the harmony richer and more pungent. These tones are usually ninths, elevenths, and thirteenths. Extended chord tones usually resolve to more-stable pitches, such as roots, thirds, and fifths.

A **tritone** comprises a diminished fifth or an augmented fourth—a popular interval in bebop melodies. Sometimes called a *flat five* by jazz musicians.

Music Example 7-1
"A Night in Tunisia."

Reharmonization refers to the bop practice of inserting different chords into the fundamental chord structure of a well-known song to freshen the interpretation and expand harmonic options for the soloist.

Reharmonization was another important new aspect of bebop harmony. Bebop players often inserted new chords and chord progressions into a standard composition; this gave soloists more chords to improvise over and made the harmonies more chromatic, often aligning them with the tensions or extended chord tones. Reharmonization was popular at the jam sessions in Harlem in the early 1940s. "We'd do that kind of thing in 1942 around Minton's a lot," Dizzy Gillespie recalled. "We'd been doing that kind of thing, Monk and I, but it was never documented because no records were being made at the time."[5] Historians have frequently cited pianist Art Tatum's influence on bebop reharmonization because of his extensive harmonic reworkings of popular songs. (See Tatum's performance of "Tiger Rag" in Chapter 4.)

Running the changes refers to a kind of improvisation, particularly associated with bebop, where the player maintains mostly up-tempo eighth-note lines that articulate the chord changes.

Bebop players also became known for *running the changes*: improvising by maintaining mostly up-tempo eighth-note lines that articulate the chord changes in a virtuoso manner. Some swing improvisation can also be seen as running the changes, but the practice is particularly associated with bebop, where it became widespread.

The way rhythm players accompanied soloists also changed. In particular, because of the influence of Kenny Clarke, Max Roach, and others, bebop drummers kept time very differently. Many swing-era drummers marked all four beats of a 4/4 measure with the bass drum, but bebop drummers such as Clarke switched to the ride cymbal to maintain the pulse. They used the bass drum for *dropping bombs*—sharp, irregular accents that were far more disruptive than the accents of the swing drummers. Bebop drummers used the snare drum to punctuate the musical texture with accents, or "kicks," or to maintain a kind of irregular chattering as an aside to the principal beat on the ride cymbal. (Accents on the bass drum are also called kicks.)

The faster tempos of the bebop players lay behind some of these changes in drumming. Clarke admitted that he was unable to maintain the breakneck speeds and keep his foot playing the bass drum on all four beats, so he switched the time-keeping role to the ride cymbal. Clarke, nicknamed "Klook" or "Klook-mop" (those syllables mimicked the sound of his unpredictable accents), played a fundamental role in developing this new style of drumming.

The faster tempos also brought about changes in piano playing. Bebop pianists abandoned the left-hand striding style that kept steady time. Instead they broke up the texture with chords, often syncopated, leaving the timekeeping role to the bass and the drummer's ride cymbal. This type of accompanying came to be called *comping*. During their improvisations the bebop pianists also played with the right hand lines like those of horn players while the left hand accompanied with short, staccato chords.

With the pianist's left hand and drummer's bass drum no longer projecting the pulse, bands relied on their bassists to keep time, usually by walking the bass on each beat of the measure. Following the influence of Ellington's bassist Jimmy Blanton (see Chapter 6), bebop bassists played in a more linear fashion instead of merely playing the root notes of each chord. Blanton also influenced such bassists as Oscar Pettiford and Ray Brown, who became renowned for their ability to improvise solos as well as accompany and keep time.

The Historical Origins of Bebop

Many factors, both musical and social, contributed to the rise of bebop in the 1940s. In this section we look at the people, places, and political forces that helped create this musical phenomenon. Later we focus on the specific contributions of several key players in bebop's early development.

THE EARLY FORTIES: JAMMING AT MINTON'S AND MONROE'S

The earliest stirrings of bebop took place in the informal jam sessions in Harlem. In 1940 Minton's Playhouse on West 118th Street hired drummer Kenny Clarke as a bandleader. For the house band, Clarke hired trumpeter Joe Guy, bassist Nick Fenton, and an eccentric pianist named Thelonious Monk. Musicians would stop by Minton's and sit in after they had completed their gigs. The atmosphere was informal, so they could try out ideas, network, and engage in friendly (or not so friendly) competition with the other players. In other words the jam sessions helped the players make connections, develop new ideas, and establish a rough pecking order of talent. The club, as trumpeter Miles Davis pointed out, was "the music laboratory for bebop."[6]

Guitarist Charlie Christian (see Chapter 6), a member of the Benny Goodman band, was a regular participant at Minton's—he even kept a spare amplifier at the club. Thanks to a jazz fan named Jerry Newman, who had a portable recorder, some

Dropping bombs is a term describing how bebop drummers used the bass drum for sharp, irregular accents in the rhythmic accompaniment.

Comping refers to the chordal accompaniment provided by pianists or guitarists in jazz bands. This accompaniment is often syncopated. The term *comp* is probably derived from a contraction of the word *accompany* or *complement*. Listen to Al Haig's syncopated comping behind Charlie Parker and Dizzy Gillespie on "Salt Peanuts" (CD 1, Track 24). For an early example of piano comping, listen to Count Basie's accompaniment to Carl Smith's trumpet solo on "Shoe Shine Boy" (CD 1, Track 18).

of these sessions were captured and eventually released. The recordings reveal a music in transition. The rhythm section plays with a lighter, more buoyant sound than the steady chugging of swing-era rhythm: Kenny Clarke accents off-beats on the bass and snare drums, and Christian supplies supple guitar lines in which the eighth notes are more evenly spaced than the swing eighths of earlier players.

Pianist Thelonious Monk composed regularly for the band at Minton's. While a member of the house band there, he wrote some of his most enduring compositions, including two haunting ballads, "'Round Midnight" and "Ruby My Dear," which showed the unique harmonic sense that characterized Monk's style. Other musicians adopted the Monk tunes heard at Minton's. Trumpeter Cootie Williams used "Epistrophy," which Monk wrote with Kenny Clarke, as his radio theme song in 1942, although he changed the title to "Fly Right." Williams was also the first to record Monk's "'Round Midnight," in 1944. Even when playing standard tunes, Monk often made unusual reharmonizations, especially in introductions. One musician in the audience remembered that Monk "generally started playing strange introductions going off, I thought to outer space, hell knows to where."[7]

Monroe's Uptown House on West 134th Street was another site for jam sessions. Run by pianist Allen Tinney, they normally began at 3 a.m. and lasted until daylight. The house band included Max Roach, a brilliant drummer who eventually recorded with Charlie Parker. Many new musical ideas came out of these competitive jam sessions. As one participant at Monroe's remembered, "The musicians used to go there and battle like dogs, every night, you know, and just playing for nothing and having a good time."[8] Charlie Parker, in town with the Jay McShann band, was so stunned by the level of musical activity at Monroe's that he left the McShann band and remained in New York:

> At Monroe's I heard sessions with a pianist named Allen Tinney; I'd listen to trumpet men like Lips Page, Roy [Eldridge], Dizzy, and Charlie Shavers outblowing each other all night long. And Don Byas was there, playing everything there was to be played. I heard a trumpet man named Vic Coulson playing things I'd never heard. Vic had the regular band at Monroe's, with George Treadwell also on trumpet, and a tenor man named Pritchett. That was the kind of music that caused me to quit McShann and stay in New York.[9]

BIG BANDS IN THE EARLY 1940S

If the uptown Harlem clubs like Minton's and Monroe's functioned as the "laboratories" for bebop, the more commercial format of the big band also provided opportunities for many of the newer players to develop and test their ideas. Particularly significant in the early part of the 1940s were the big bands of Earl Hines and, shortly thereafter, Billy Eckstine. These bands included both Charlie Parker and Dizzy Gillespie, so they were especially notable. Because of the record ban, however, most of their music went unrecorded. (See the box "The American Federation of Musicians Strike in 1942.")

In 1942 Hines recruited Gillespie on trumpet and Parker on tenor saxophone (there was no opening for an alto saxophone player). Outside of Harlem jam sessions, this was the first time Parker and Gillespie had worked together on the bandstand. Also playing trumpet with the Hines band was another player in step with the latest musical developments: "Little" Benny Harris. Harris's composition "Ornithology," a contrafact of the swing standard "How High the Moon," became a bebop classic.

The American Federation of Musicians Strike in 1942

Unfortunately, much of the music that marked the transition from swing to bebop in the early 1940s was never documented on studio recordings because the American Federation of Musicians (AFM) called a strike in August 1942. Protesting the lack of payment to musicians for records played on the radio, the union insisted on a recording ban—with the exception of V-discs (Victory discs) produced specifically for the armed forces overseas. Decca settled in September 1943, Columbia and Victor held out another year, and eventually the strike ended. These three record companies held the lion's share of the market before the ban, but several smaller labels sprang up shortly afterward and focused their attention on recording the younger players.

The band also featured two outstanding singers who would develop major careers: Sarah Vaughan and Billy Eckstine.

Sarah Vaughan (1924–1990) became a preeminent jazz singer, possibly the greatest to develop in the bebop era. Her leap to the limelight came during the heyday of bop, when she sang with both the Earl Hines and Billy Eckstine big bands in the early 1940s. There her associations with Parker and Gillespie established her reputation and refined her ability to sing with the looseness and unexpected vocal twists and turns of the newer style. (We return to Sarah Vaughan in our discussion of jazz singers in Chapter 8.)

Billy Eckstine (1914–1993) was a suave baritone vocalist who also played trumpet and valve trombone. In the early 1940s, he had a hit with the Hines band in the slightly bawdy blues song "Jelly, Jelly." Persuaded to form his own band, Eckstine left Hines and hired Gillespie as musical director. Gillespie convinced many of the most forward-looking of Hines's musicians to join Eckstine's band, including Parker, pianist John Malachi, and eventually drummer Art Blakey.

The Eckstine band of 1944 has frequently been called the "first bebop big band," but the group did not achieve significant commercial success. Although they played at dance halls in the South, the band's bop-oriented compositions—many written and arranged by Gillespie—kept most people off the dance floor. Parker soon left the band, never having recorded with Eckstine, and Gillespie remained a short time afterward. In April 1944 Gillespie recorded some blues-oriented compositions with Eckstine, including "I Stay in the Mood for You" and "Good Jelly Blues," both cut in the mold of Eckstine's "Jelly, Jelly" hit. At the end of the year, Gillespie played on "Blowing the Blues Away," a tenor saxophone "battle" between Gene Ammons and Dexter Gordon. Eckstine, long one of the principal singers in jazz, would continue with a distinguished career as a jazz vocalist.

BEBOP MOVES TO FIFTY-SECOND STREET

Around the middle of the 1940s, the clubs of West Fifty-second Street became the primary venue for bebop bands. "The Street" comprised two blocks between Fifth Avenue and Broadway. The jazz clubs were tiny, crowded, and often poorly lit—far removed from the elaborate dance halls played by the big bands. In fact, most had no dance floors, merely tables for listening and an area where listeners were not required to buy drinks. During the war an immense concentration of jazz players developed in the city. For the cost of the cover charges, a listener could stroll down The Street and stop in to hear Sidney Bechet, Art Tatum, Coleman Hawkins, or Fats Waller anytime between 9 p.m. and 3 a.m. Gradually, the newer bebop bands worked their way into Fifty-second Street.

As Dizzy Gillespie remembered it, the birth of the bebop era came after he left the Eckstine band in 1944. With bassist Oscar Pettiford, Gillespie formed a band to play at the Onyx Club, one of several acts on the bill. Gillespie and Pettiford hired Max Roach on drums and George Wallington on piano; both had been in the house band at Monroe's Uptown House. Gillespie tried to contact Charlie Parker, who had returned to Kansas City after leaving Eckstine, but Parker never received the telegram. When tenor saxophonist Don Byas, an accomplished player with a big sound reminiscent of Coleman Hawkins, began sitting in, they eventually invited him to join the band. With the horns playing in unison, the group's repertory was new and startling:

> In the Onyx Club, we played a lot of original tunes that didn't have titles. We just wrote an introduction and a first chorus. I'd say, "Dee-da-pa-da-n-de-bop . . ." and we'd go on into it. People, when they'd wanna ask for one of those numbers and didn't know the name, would ask for bebop. And the press picked it up and started calling it bebop. The first time the term *bebop* appeared in print was while we played at the Onyx Club.[10]

The group itself did not record, but much of the band—Gillespie, Pettiford, Roach, and Byas—assembled in the studio in early 1944 under the auspices of Coleman Hawkins for a series of historic recordings. Hawkins, some twenty years into his career, placed himself into the musical vanguard by hiring the more talented young players on the scene. According to many this attempt resulted in the first bebop recordings. Although half of the six tunes were ballads for Hawkins, the rest were in the newer style: Gillespie's "Woody n' You," Budd Johnson's "Bu-Dee-Daht," and a blues piece called "Disorder at the Border." In these recordings bebop had an embryonic sound: the ponderous big band, the rhythm section, and many of the solos still seemed weighted down by the conventions of swing. Only Gillespie's energetic start-and-stop solos hinted at the music to come—the music fundamentally indebted to the innovations of Gillespie and Parker.

The Architects of Bebop

Numerous musicians contributed to the formation of bebop, but none were more significant than Charlie Parker and Dizzy Gillespie. Kenny Clarke, whose role in modifying drum styles also greatly affected bebop, was discussed earlier. Among pianists, the preeminent contributors included Thelonious Monk and Bud Powell.

CHARLIE PARKER

Charlie Parker was probably the greatest, most brilliant jazz saxophonist of all time. His influence on jazz history rivals that of Louis Armstrong: both generated a major jazz style while radically increasing the level of technical proficiency on their instruments. Parker's improvisations left a mark on almost every subsequent jazz musician.

Born in Kansas City, Kansas, on August 29, 1920, Parker and his family moved across the river to Kansas City, Missouri, seven years later. At first he played baritone and alto horns in his school bands, but in 1933 he turned to the alto saxophone. Within two years he left school to play full-time with a local bandleader known as Lawrence "88" Keyes.

Parker's talent was not immediately apparent. Bassist Gene Ramey described Parker as the "saddest thing in the Keyes band."[11] In the cutthroat world of the Kansas City jam session, Parker learned about competition the hard way. In a radio interview, Parker recalled his first jam session:

> I'd learned how to play the first eight bars of "[Up a] Lazy River," and I knew the complete tune to "Honeysuckle Rose." I didn't never stop to think about there was other keys or nothin' like that. [Laughter] So I took my horn out to this joint where the guys—a bunch of guys I had seen around were—and the first thing they started playing was "Body and Soul," long beat [implied double time] you know, like this. [*Demonstrates.*] . . . So I go to playin' my "Honeysuckle Rose" and [unintelligible], I mean, ain't no form of conglomeration [unintelligible]. They laughed me right off the bandstand.[12]

But Parker was diligent. Known for carrying his horn in a paper bag, the teenager learned a few Lester Young solos note-for-note while studying basic harmony with some of the local guitarists. He joined the band of Buster Smith, a saxophonist who was an early influence on Parker. Then in 1938 he joined the band of Jay McShann, a pianist based in Kansas City but originally from Oklahoma.

Charlie Parker pictured on the cover of a Gil Fuller transcription of bebop themes, including "Oop Bop Sh-Bam" and "Ray's Idea."

Copyright © 1949 Robbins Music. Used by permission of Warner Bros. Publications, Inc.

In early 1939 Parker moved to New York for the first time, playing sessions at Monroe's Uptown House and washing dishes at Jimmy's Chicken Shack so that he could hear pianist Art Tatum, who often performed there. Undoubtedly, Tatum's sophisticated harmonic sense influenced Parker, and his effortless virtuosity and streams of high-speed runs quite likely helped determine the mature Parker style. In a famous anecdote, Parker credited a guitarist named Biddy Fleet with teaching him more-advanced harmonies: playing "Cherokee," which would become one of his signature tunes, Parker realized that he could emphasize the higher chordal extensions—ninths, elevenths, or thirteenths. These, too, became a feature of his mature style.

In 1940 Parker returned to Kansas City and the McShann band to become one of its musical directors. An amateur recording, probably from 1940, is the first we have of Parker. This recording preserved a solo practice session on "Honeysuckle Rose" followed by "Body and Soul"—significant choices given the story of Parker's first jam session.

Parker cut his first professional recordings informally at a radio station in Wichita, Kansas, on November 30, 1940, with the McShann band. These tunes, known as the Wichita transcriptions, revealed the group's Kansas City origins: "Moten Swing," "Honeysuckle Rose," and "Oh, Lady Be Good." In 1941 and 1942, still with the McShann band, Parker made his first studio recordings, including "Swingmatism," "Hootie Blues," "Sepian Bounce," and "The Jumpin' Blues." "Hootie Blues" featured Parker's first important solo—one that dramatically announced the arrival of a new saxophone stylist.

Parker and the McShann band returned to New York in late 1941 or early 1942 to play at the Savoy Ballroom. At that time he immersed himself in the New York scene, frequently attending the after-hours sessions at Minton's and Monroe's. Parker shared the stand with trumpeters Roy Eldridge, Dizzy Gillespie, and Charlie Shavers, as well as saxophonist Don Byas. Drummer Kenny Clarke, who in 1941 considered himself among the newer innovators, was stunned by Parker's playing:

> Bird was playing stuff we'd never heard before. He was into figures I thought I'd invented for drums. He was twice as fast as Lester Young and into harmony Lester hadn't touched. Bird was running the same way we were, but he was way out ahead of us. I don't think he was aware of the changes he had created. It was his way of playing jazz, part of his own experience.[13]

Surrounded by this high level of musical activity, Parker decided to remain based in New York, playing in the big bands of Earl Hines and Billy Eckstine. Earning awestruck respect from his fellow musicians, he was rapidly becoming an underground hero. Increasingly during this time, he found himself jamming and sitting in with various groups in the heart of Fifty-second Street.

Parker's performances with the band of guitarist Tiny Grimes became especially significant. On September 15, 1944, Grimes invited Parker to cut four sides with the band, which included Clyde Hart on piano, Harold "Doc" West on drums, and Jimmy Butts on bass. Parker was featured in all four tunes, including his own composition "Red Cross." In the two takes of "Red Cross," we hear Parker's first recorded solos with *rhythm changes*. More generally, as Parker's first small-group records featuring him as soloist, we hear the early crystallization of Parker's bebop playing.

Rhythm changes are derived from the harmonies of the 1930 George and Ira Gershwin song "I Got Rhythm." The bridge in rhythm changes consists of two-bar harmonies following a circle-of-fifths pattern that returns to the tonic. For example, if rhythm changes are performed in B♭, the harmonies of the eight-bar bridge are D7 (2 bars), G7 (2 bars), C7 (2 bars), and F7 (2 bars). The F7, as the dominant of the tonic B♭, leads back to the A section. Extremely popular since the 1930s, rhythm changes are still commonly used by jazz musicians for improvisation and composition. (Listen to Track 10 of the 🅟 Audio Primer CD to hear an example of rhythm changes.)

Although the Grimes band was more of a swing than a bop group, Parker plays his solos superbly, presenting several of his trademarks:

▶ A lean, edgy tone

▶ Use of blues inflections

▶ Double-time sixteenth-note runs

▶ Bebop-style licks that were to become the mainstay of the new style

After the Grimes recordings of late 1944, Parker began working with small groups as his bebop style matured. His most significant partnership was with Dizzy Gillespie, and their musical relationship flourished. By May 1945 the two were fronting a band at the Three Deuces on Fifty-second Street, where they remained until July. The group recorded several tunes that became mainstays of the bebop era, including "Groovin' High," "Dizzy Atmosphere," "All the Things You Are," and "Salt Peanuts."

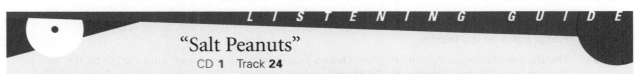

L I S T E N I N G   G U I D E

"Salt Peanuts"
CD **1** Track **24**

Dizzy Gillespie and His All Stars: "Salt Peanuts" (Gillespie). Guild 1003. New York, May 11, 1945. Gillespie, trumpet and vocal; Charlie Parker, alto saxophone; Al Haig, piano; Curley Russell, bass; Sidney Catlett, drums.

"Salt Peanuts" may be the best-known bebop tune, perhaps because its humorous motivic idea is unforgettable. The tune is a crowd pleaser, less often adopted for performance by Parker, who generally refused to play up to his listeners. Yet there are instances of Parker's performing—and singing—"Salt Peanuts" in live versions! This classic recording, an early instance of Parker and Gillespie together on record, has a remarkably complex layout for an early bebop tune. Compare it with the modern version by Steve Coleman (CD 2, Track 15).

Introduction—16 bars as 8 + 8

0:00   Introduction, part 1. A driving drum solo sets a very bright tempo—typical for a tune in bebop style. Catlett sets the tempo with the first four measures, then states the rhythm of the head (played by the horns at 0:12) for the next four measures.

0:06   The rest of the ensemble enters. The transcription below includes the beginning of the introduction played by the horns and the first four bars of the head. Notice the prevalence of tritones played by the horns—the first pitches heard are B♭ and E, followed by G♭ and C. The last two bars of the introduction (measures 7 and 8) feature a break for pianist Haig playing the "Salt Peanuts" (SP) octave motive.

1st chorus head—32-bar AABA

0:12 The head consists of two licks, the second of which is the SP motive. (The transcription on the previous page also contains the opening four bars of the head.) Parker and Gillespie divide the SP motive, with Parker on the lower note and Gillespie on the upper.

0:19 Repeat of the A section.

0:26 The bridge features Parker and Gillespie in octaves. There are alterations in the harmonies, which themselves are based on rhythm changes. Some of the melodic leaps include tritones.

0:32 The third A section completes the first chorus.

Interlude A—8 bars

0:39 A composed line for Parker and Gillespie on the A section changes.

2nd chorus head—32-bar AABA

0:45 Parker takes the first lick of the tune himself, while Gillespie sings the SP motive.

0:52 Repeat of the A section.

0:58 Parker solos on the bridge.

1:05 The third A section completes the two-chorus presentation of the head, with Parker on the tune's first lick and Gillespie singing the SP motive.

Interlude—16 bars as 8 + 8

1:11 The rhythm section plays alone for the first eight bars.

1:18 Parker and Gillespie rejoin the band for the second section of the interlude, which features prominent tritones. Haig takes the last two bars as a solo break.

3rd chorus—32-bar AABA piano solo

1:24 Haig solos on a full chorus. Haig's left hand is relatively inactive, while the right hand concentrates on "running the changes," as is typical in up-tempo bebop.

4th chorus—32-bar AABA alto saxophone solo

1:50 Parker's solo is virtuosic and features the edgy tone for which he was well known.

Interlude—8 bars

2:16 An interlude to set up Gillespie's entrance and solo break in the last two bars.

5th chorus—32-bar AABA trumpet solo

2:23 The first two bars of Gillespie's solo continue the break from the interlude. His use of extreme high notes is typical of his style as is the fleet dexterity of the entire improvisation.

Drum solo

2:50 Catlett's drum solo maintains the time, leading into the introduction.

Introduction—As coda

3:09 The second part of the introduction repeats, with the band singing the final SP motive.

From "Salt Peanuts" we can summarize these characteristic features of Parker's up-tempo style:

▶ Disjointed, irregularly accented melodic lines, mostly comprising eighth notes with occasional arpeggiations

▶ Little space between phrases

▶ Melodic connections based on extremely subtle motivic interrelations and voice leading

▶ A commanding, insistent tone quality

▶ Use of melodic chord extensions

▶ Intense, powerful expression

▶ Frequent blues inflections

▶ Concentration on middle and upper range of instrument

▶ Scale-chord relationships generated from the use of altered and extended chord harmonies

Gillespie's style echoes Parker's, and bop melodic playing in general, in its use of the following elements:

▶ Angular melodic lines made up largely of eighth notes

▶ Less rhythmic variety because of the eighth-note emphasis

▶ Phrases of irregular length

▶ Long phrases that may complete a section or more of a chorus

▶ Use of extended and chromatic extended chord tones

▶ A lack of vibrato in up-tempo playing

▶ Emotional though virtuosic playing

▶ Emphasis on the middle and upper range of the instrument

▶ Melodic continuity based on voice leading and large-scale phrasing

▶ De-emphasis of motive structure, at least in up-tempo playing

▶ Few blues inflections in up-tempo playing

▶ Adventurous chord-scale associations

On November 26, 1945, Parker supervised his first session as a leader. These recordings for Savoy Records included some of his most important performances as well as the original compositions "Billie's Bounce," "KoKo," "Now's the Time," and "Thriving on a Riff." "KoKo," a contrafact of "Cherokee," also featured Dizzy Gillespie on trumpet, but a nervous, nineteen-year-old trumpeter from St. Louis named Miles Davis played the other cuts. The title "Now's the Time" was later said to have prophesized two important trends: the acceptance of bebop and the growing importance of the civil rights movement. "Koko" became one of Parker's most famous solos—a classic statement of bebop virtuosity. Interestingly, earlier live recordings of Parker performing its source tune, "Cherokee," demonstrate that he was developing the principal ideas for the solo since at least 1942. (Parker was performing "Cherokee" since 1939.)

In December 1945 Parker traveled to the West Coast with a band led by Gillespie for an engagement in Hollywood. In one sense the trip was an experiment, an attempt to see if bebop, developed largely on the East Coast, would generate excitement elsewhere. The gig, at a club called Billy Berg's, was not successful. Gillespie and the band returned to New York within a few months, while Parker stayed on. Reputedly, he had pawned his plane ticket to support his heroin habit. His addiction, which had developed when he was a teenager, caused Parker increasingly intense physical and emotional problems.

While still in California, Parker continued to record, thanks to the interest of Ross Russell, founder of Dial Records and an ardent admirer. Some of the recordings from early 1946 were brilliant, particularly a session on March 28 that featured "Moose the Mooche" (named after Parker's drug supplier) and "A Night in Tunisia." The latter cut featured one of the most spectacular saxophone breaks ever recorded—Russell even issued it as "Famous Alto Break." But Parker's addiction was growing worse. The breakdown came during a recording session on July 29, in which Parker was virtually unable to play. Back at his hotel, Parker (it was claimed) set fire to his mattress and was seen walking around nude. Arrested by the police, he was eventually sentenced to a term in Camarillo State Hospital, where he remained for six months. Later, much to Parker's anger, Russell issued the recordings from Parker's July 29 session. Parker was ultimately released from Camarillo, and after several performances and recordings he returned to New York in April 1947.

The following four years proved to be the most intensely productive period of Parker's career, in part because he was temporarily free of his heroin dependency and because bebop had, while Parker was on the West Coast, become even more popular back East. Indeed, Parker returned to New York as one of the most famous musicians in jazz. He formed his most long-lived working quintet with trumpeter Miles Davis, pianist Duke Jordan, bassist Tommy Potter, and drummer Max Roach—a group that remained together for a year and a half. The band recorded many Parker compositions that became jazz standards. For example, "Scrapple from the Apple" was a kind of double recomposition: the A section used the harmonies from Fats Waller's "Honeysuckle Rose," and the B section took the chords from "I Got Rhythm."

"Confirmation" became one of Parker's best-known bebop heads. It was also one of his few tunes not based on recomposition over preexisting chord changes. The melody for "Confirmation" was itself tricky to negotiate, a repository of bebop melodic devices.

A 1947 recording of "Crazeology" presents Parker in his prime, working with innovative variants to rhythm changes. An unusual chord change to G♭ in the A section forces Parker to rethink how he plays rhythm changes in B♭ because he cannot rely on his established note patterns. As we discussed in Chapter 6, such established patterns are called *formulas* or, more popularly, *licks*. Parker excelled at developing formulas for use in up-tempo improvising.

A unique item among Parker's formal recordings is a session in which he played tenor saxophone. Recall that Parker played tenor in the Hines band but was never formally recorded at the time. This session, under the direction of Miles Davis on August 14, 1947, shows another side of Parker's artistry, with a tenor style that recalls Don Byas.

Charlie Parker's Use of Formulas

Part of the genius of Parker's improvisational skill lay in his ability to use and reuse formulas, or licks, in creative and ingenious ways. Parker had a vast repository of licks to call upon, and he played them in a variety of improvisational settings and tempos. Jazz players have adopted many of these licks, which have since become part of the general language of jazz. Thomas Owens catalogued some sixty-four formulas (and their variants) in Parker's recorded solos, based on their frequency of occurrence.* The transcription here shows two: the first lick Parker typically played over the chord progression Gm7–C7; the second lick was played over the progression Dm7–D♭m7–Cm7 (usually heard as iii7–♭iii7–ii7 in the key of B♭ major and often played by Parker in the measures 8 and 9 of a 12-bar blues).

* Thomas Owens, "Charlie Parker: Techniques of Improvisation." Ph.D. diss., University of California, Los Angeles, 1974.

As he gained wider public acceptance and acclaim, Parker undertook other new and interesting projects. In November 1948 he signed a contract with Norman Granz of Mercury Records; most of the Parker's recordings for the remainder of his life were under Granz's supervision. In addition, Granz organized several concerts and tours of top-flight jazz performers under the title Jazz at the Philharmonic, a venue that became extremely well known in the late 1940s and 1950s. Parker often participated in these concerts and tours under Granz's direction.

Parker made two European tours, playing Paris in 1949 and Sweden the following year. Thanks to Granz, Parker recorded in many different settings, including sessions with Machito's Afro-Cuban band, whom we discuss later in this chapter. Most significant was the unusual step of recording with string accompaniment, in which Parker fulfilled a long-held ambition. In *Charlie Parker with Strings,* Parker played standards in a subdued mood. His recording of "Just Friends," from the first strings session on November 30, 1949, became a classic; it was not only Parker's best-selling record but reputedly his favorite of his recorded solos. The strings recordings became so popular that Parker took a string quartet (along with an oboe player) on the road for several clubs dates in 1950 and 1951.

While Parker recordings, both studio and live, abound, it is disappointing to learn that he was filmed performing only once, on a television broadcast on February 24, 1952. There he appeared with Dizzy Gillespie for a performance of "Hot House." (Pianist Dick Hyman also appeared on the show.) Although the television program was the only instance of Parker performing live on film, he did *appear* in a Gjon Mili film of 1950 (with Coleman Hawkins) for Jazz at the Philharmonic publicity, but the sound was overdubbed afterward.

Copyright © Bettmann/Corbis

The original caption for this photo read: "The show at the new Birdland Restaurant, which opened on Broadway, December 15 [1949], offers music to suit just about every taste. Entertaining at their specialties are (left to right), trumpeter Max Kaminsky, Dixieland style; saxophonist Lester Young, swing; [Oran] "Hot Lips" Page, famed for sweet swing; Charlie Parker on the alto sax, representing bop; and pianist Lennie Tristano, exponent of a new style called 'music of the future.' It marked the first time that these noted musicians, representing completely different schools of modern music, were gathered on the same stage."

One of Parker's most significant devices, not new to jazz but one that he developed extensively, was his tendency to quote other music in his solos. The quotations ranged from classical themes to well-known pop tunes, jazz heads, and children's songs. For example, in a solo on "Salt Peanuts" performed in Paris in 1949, Parker quoted the beginning of Igor Stravinsky's *The Rite of Spring*, a famous classical work that had premiered in Paris in 1913. At the other extreme, in a solo on "Just Friends" recorded in 1950, Parker quoted "Pop Goes the Weasel." Both of these performances were live; Parker tended to quote more often in live settings than in studio recordings. Perhaps he chose the live venue because he realized that the humor implied in a quotation would quickly become stale on repeated listening. He also may have needed the informal atmosphere of a live audience to feel comfortable making a joke. Of note is the unequaled ingenuity with which Parker wove his quotations into the flow of his solos. Parker's freewheeling quotations greatly influenced later generations of players.[14]

Parker spent his final years in a downward slide both physically and mentally. He suffered from ulcers, became overweight, and drank heavily. When one of his daughters, Pree, died of pneumonia, Parker became severely depressed. In 1954 he twice attempted suicide and voluntarily committed himself to Bellevue Hospital in New York. Parker last performed at a club named for him, Birdland. The performance was disastrous, a visible airing of his feud with pianist Bud Powell. A week later, on March 12, 1955, he died at the apartment of the Baroness Pannonica de Koenigswarter, a jazz patron who had befriended him. His body was ravaged by years of substance abuse. Although the story is not authenticated, jazz legend has it that the examining doctor listed Parker's age as fifty-three. He was only thirty-four.

DIZZY GILLESPIE

Along with Charlie Parker, John Birks "Dizzy" Gillespie (1917–1993) played a crucial role in promoting the new bebop style in the 1940s. "Bird might have been the spirit of the bebop movement," said Miles Davis, "but Dizzy was its 'head and hands,' the one who kept it all together."[15] Despite Gillespie's reputation for clowning around—which earned him the nickname "Dizzy" early on—he was dedicated to his craft as a musician. He made a point of working out experimental harmonies and chord progressions at the piano, often enthusiastically teaching and coaching the other players. Gillespie clearly rejected the stereotype of the untutored, "natural" jazz musician. As he told *Time* magazine in 1949,

> Nowadays we try to work out different rhythms and things that they didn't think about when Louis Armstrong blew. In his day all he did was play strictly from the soul—just strictly from the heart. You got to go forward and progress. We study.[16]

Although his style had originally been influenced by trumpeter Roy Eldridge, Gillespie soon developed an improvisational technique that was much more distinct. With his impressive command of the upper register of the trumpet, he punctuated his solos with wild leaps into the "stratosphere." He could play much faster than previous trumpeters, with sinuous chromatic lines in dramatic contrast to the diatonically based solos of swing.

As a composer and an arranger, Gillespie was prolific. Many of his bebop heads became jazz standards in their own right, such as "Groovin' High," "Woody n' You," "Salt Peanuts," and "A Night in Tunisia" (see Music Example 7-1). Written while Gillespie was a member of the Hines band during the early 1940s and originally titled "Interlude," "A Night in Tunisia" was perhaps his most famous piece. Although unusual in its exoticism, it showed many of the hallmarks of the nascent bebop style. The use of the Latin-tinged rhythm in the opening section reflected Gillespie's interests in Afro-Cuban music.

Gillespie was born in Cheraw, South Carolina, on October 21, 1917. Years later, after receiving a scholarship to the Laurinburg Institute in North Carolina, he moved with his family to Philadelphia and there joined a band led by Frankie Fairfax. In 1937 he left Fairfax to move to New York, where he rapidly made his way into the better-known bands, working as the featured soloist with Teddy Hill and, in 1939, Cab Calloway. He was summarily dismissed from the band in 1941 after Calloway mistakenly accused Gillespie of hurling a spitball at him during a performance.

Like Parker, Gillespie frequently participated in the after-hours sessions at Minton's and had been a member of the big bands of Earl Hines and Billy Eckstine. Gillespie soon achieved success as a composer-arranger, contributing original numbers to the bands of Boyd Raeburn and Woody Herman. After winning the New Star Award in the *Esquire* magazine jazz poll in 1944, Gillespie formed the band with bassist Oscar Pettiford that performed at the Onyx Club on Fifty-second Street. It was the recordings and performances with Charlie Parker, however, that thrust Gillespie squarely into the front line of the bebop movement. The 1945 performances and recordings of the two principal talents of bebop culminated in the disastrous West Coast trip at the end of the year (discussed earlier).

After his split with Parker, Gillespie returned to the large-group format and led his own big band with increasing commercial success through 1950. On many of their recordings, we hear the successful translation of bebop from small group to big band,

Latin Jazz

Latin music has had a continuous influence on jazz throughout the twentieth century. For example, it is quite possible that Latin rhythms helped furnish the characteristic syncopation of New Orleans hot melody in the teens. Moreover, many of the important early New Orleans musicians had Latin roots from a variety of countries.

Latin rhythms also appear in ragtime. As early as 1902, it appears in the ragtime hit, "Under the Bamboo Tree" (Cole-Johnson); moreover, the habanera rhythm can be heard in Scott Joplin's "Solace—A Mexican Serenade" from 1909. The habanera rhythm was probably the most common Latin ingredient in jazz until the 1940s. In the habanera and other Latin rhythms, the beat is divided into two even halves, contrasting with the "swung" eighth notes more typical of swing.

The habanera beat appears in what is undoubtedly the most important blues tune of classic jazz: W. C. Handy's "Saint Louis Blues." Handy, in his autobiography *Father of the Blues,* recalls that around 1910 he saw the effect on the dancers of the Latin-tinged tune "Maori" by Will Tyer. At that moment he made the decision to try to incorporate the habanera rhythm into his works. That same beat crops up with one of the more famous techniques associated with Jelly Roll Morton: his so-called Spanish tinge is also based on the habanera beat. This rhythm can be heard on Morton's 1923 recordings of "Mamanita" and "New Orleans Joys"; it also appears in Morton's "The Jelly Roll Blues," which was published in 1915, although Morton claimed to have written it in 1905.

Meanwhile, Latin dances in the United States supplemented the exploding number of ballroom dance fads through the teens, twenties, and thirties. Well-known Latin bandleaders such as Desi Arnaz and Xavier Cugat promoted the tango, the rumba, and other Latin dances, many of which became highly popular with the public. Among the important percussion instruments that set the style and pace

Machito, an important innovator in blending Afro-Cuban music with bebop, plays the maracas; the young woman is playing the claves.

William P. Gottlieb/Ira and Leonore S. Gershwin Fund Collection, Music Division, Library of Congress.

for these dances was the *claves,* essentially two thick wooden sticks that, when struck together, produce the characteristic *click* of the Latin percussion sound. The impulse of the clave beat is syncopated over the duple meter of the underlying beat and is one of the characteristic sounds of much Latin rhythm.

Most of the Latin influence in early jazz can be traced to Mexico and South America, although there is a decisive Caribbean influence as well. In the late 1920s, there began a major immigration of Cubans to New York City. Their music, which was distinguished from earlier Latin music, was called *Afro-Cuban* and was often more aggressive in its rhythmic power, possibly because of its closer connection to African roots. As an addition to the claves among the Latin percussion, the *conga drum* was popularized by Afro-Cuban musicians. Their music grew in popularity through the 1940s. Among the influential promoters of the Afro-Cuban sound was Machito (born Frank Grillo), a Cuban vocalist who came to New York in 1937 and teamed up with trumpeter Mario Bauza, who had played with numerous jazz big bands. Machito called his group "the Afro-Cubans" and often worked with well-known jazz performers as soloists.

Since **cubop** of the 1940s, Latin music has sustained a major presence in jazz. For many decades the best-known Latin musician with jazz associations was percussionist and bandleader Tito Puente (1923–2000), a New York native raised in Spanish Harlem. Puente's first big break in the music business—when he was all of thirteen years of age—was becoming Machito's drummer.

Separate contributions came from Brazil, although we note that some commentators classify Brazilian music as distinct from Latin. (Latin music is typically more driving and rhythmically aggressive; moreover, it is normally associated with Spanish-speaking countries, whereas the primary language of Brazil is Portuguese.) The *samba,* a fast, syncopated dance, was introduced in the United States from Brazil in the 1930s and 1940s. During the 1960s a blend of jazz harmonies with softened, sultry melodies and textures, known as **bossa nova**, became extremely popular.

Many Brazilian musicians became well known in jazz circles through the bossa nova fad as it developed through the 1960s. Jazz musicians such as tenor saxophonist Stan Getz did much to popularize the samba and the bossa nova. The most important composer of bossa nova tunes was Antonio Carlos Jobim (1927–1994), who wrote "Desafinado," "The Girl from Ipanema," and many other hits. On CD 2, Track 14, we hear Brazilian pianist Eliane Elias playing one of his best-known songs, "One Note Samba."

including the exciting "Things to Come," a prophetically titled piece written and arranged by Gillespie and Gil Fuller. Gillespie, always attracted to Afro-Cuban elements in jazz, hired conga player Chano Pozo to perform with his band and featured him in a Carnegie Hall concert in 1947. This Afro-Cuban element, which Gillespie felt complemented and expanded the rhythmic resources of jazz, became an important facet of Gillespie's work. We hear it, for example, on the Gillespie-Pozo composition "Manteca" as well as on "Cubana Be/Cubana Bop," written by Gillespie, Pozo, and George Russell.

Compared with Charlie Parker, Gillespie presented a more commercial side to bebop. He insisted that the music be entertaining and lamented its separation from dancing. To the mainstream audience, his stage persona—which included hipster posturing with beret, goatee, and glasses—became at least as well known as his music. His many innovations and tireless championing of the music, however, made Gillespie a significant founder and a fundamental contributor to the development of bebop. He continued to perform bop-based jazz with groups both large and small for decades to come as one of the great personalities and elder statesmen of the jazz scene. He died on January 6, 1993.

LISTENING GUIDE

"Manteca"
CD 1 Track 25

Dizzy Gillespie and His Orchestra, with Chano Pozo: "Manteca" (Pozo-Gillespie-Fuller). Victor 20-3023-A.
New York, December 30, 1947. Gillespie, trumpet, leader; Dave Burns, Elmon Wright Jr., Benny Bailey,
trumpets; William Shepperd, Ted Kelly, trombones; John Brown, Howard Johnson, alto saxophones;
Joe Gayles, George "Bick Nick" Nicholas, tenor saxophones; Cecil Payne, baritone saxophone;
John Lewis, piano; Al McKibbon, bass; Kenny Clarke, drums; Pozo, conga.

Introduction

0:00   In much Afro-Cuban music, the groove, projected by the rhythm section, is an essential part of the composition. In the introduction to "Manteca," we hear a groove that builds through the addition of instruments and leads to a solo statement by Gillespie. The transcription below shows the opening bass riff that establishes the groove. Notice that its placement within the two-bar unit avoids downbeats or other means of regularly marking the 4/4 pulse. Such syncopation is often heard in Afro-Cuban bass lines. After the bass-and-conga beginning, we hear the baritone saxophone entering at 0:08, overlaying another vamp to add to the groove. The rest of the brass enter at 0:16, and finally Gillespie at 0:19. The accumulated forces culminate in chords for the full band at 0:31 with a "fall-off" on the last chord, leaving just the bass, drums, and conga.

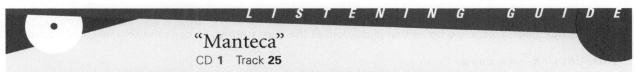

Head—40-bar AABA

0:38   The groove, continuing from the introduction, leads into the head. Here there is a pickup figure in the saxophones that is answered by the full brass in a call-and-response pattern. The eight-bar A section builds into its pattern, repeated intensely in measures 7 and 8 (0:46).

0:49   Repeat of the eight-bar A section.

1:00 The bridge is unusual in being 16 bars instead of the customary eight. For the first eight bars, we hear lush saxophone chords that provide a fine contrast to the A section. For the second eight bars (1:11), Gillespie solos over the chordal cushion provided by the saxophones.

1:22 Return of the eight-bar A section.

Interlude

1:34 The groove of the introduction returns and leads to entries of intense brass figures. These figures culminate in a restatement of the basic AABA form of the tune but with the AA as a tenor solo.

Tenor saxophone solo—16-bar AA

1:48 The groove changes to a swing beat as the band provides a background for the first eight bars of the tenor solo.

1:59 The second eight bars of the tenor solo use the rhythm section alone as accompaniment.

B section—Bridge, 16 bars

2:10 The bridge returns, scored for full band.

2:21 Gillespie returns to solo with the second half of the bridge. He is accompanied by chords in the saxophones in addition to the rhythm section.

A section—Head, 8 bars

2:33 The call-and-response figure that characterizes the head returns, as does the original Latin groove.

Introduction—As coda

2:44 The groove established in the introduction returns, but now grows quieter until a sudden surge in the drums ends the piece.

BUD POWELL

Earl "Bud" Powell (1924–1966), generally considered the finest of the bop pianists, transferred Parker's and Gillespie's bebop techniques to piano. He gained acclaim for playing up-tempo lines at blistering speed and exercised a profound influence on a generation of pianists. He best codified the right-hand bop piano style, in which sparse, sharply articulated chords in the left hand punctuated and rhythmically set off linear improvisations in the right. But he was also an immensely capable player in the more two-handed style derived from Art Tatum and the classic stride masters.

A New Yorker, Powell began gigging around town when he was a teenager. He soon joined the scene at Minton's, where house pianist Thelonious Monk took an early interest in his development. As the pianist with trumpeter Cootie Williams's band in 1944, Powell made his earliest recordings, which demonstrate his style in transition—equally at home in the swing of Earl Hines as well as in the nascent bebop style. He became a mainstay on Fifty-second Street, where he played with Gillespie, John Kirby, Don Byas, Dexter Gordon, and others.

Early on, Powell showed signs of mental instability. "Bud was always—ever since I've known him—he was a little on the border line," recalled tenor saxophonist Dexter Gordon. "Because he'd go off into things—expressions, telltale things that would let you know he was off."[17] During a racial incident with a policeman, Powell took a beating, especially to his head. Afterward his erratic behavior increased, and he was institutionalized five times between 1945 and 1955. Despite his often moody and withdrawn behavior, however, Powell's playing astounded his contemporaries.

Powell's performances are well documented by recordings. In January 1947 Powell made his first recording as a leader, with Curley Russell on bass and Max Roach on drums. Powell later recorded frequently with Roach. Although he did not often record with Charlie Parker (they supposedly never got along), Powell joined Parker's first studio session when Parker returned to New York from Los Angeles in May 1947. The group recorded "Donna Lee," "Chasin' the Bird," and "Cheryl."

Powell's trio recordings of 1949, with bassist Ray Brown, showed him to be not only a stunning pianist but also a gifted composer. One of Powell's tunes, "Tempus Fugit," showcased the pianist playing at breakneck speed. Another, a fine solo track called "I'll Keep Loving You," revealed a tender side of his playing and contains references to Art Tatum.

Several of Powell's compositions were elaborate. For example, "Un Poco Loco" was a complex Latin-oriented composition in which Powell soloed over a repeated single-chord vamp and made use of exotic pitches and scales. Another complex piece, "Glass Enclosure," written in four sections, was a disturbing evocation of his time spent in mental asylums. A third example, "Parisian Thoroughfare," was recorded twice in 1951, once with a trio and again as a solo piano feature.

Courtesy Morgan Collection

The influential pianist Bud Powell. His piano style combined up-tempo bebop lines in the right hand with sparse chordal punctuations in the left hand.

Powell displayed his fiery spirit in a famous concert recorded at Massey Hall, Toronto, on May 15, 1953, in which he performed with Charlie Parker, Dizzy Gillespie, Max Roach, and bassist Charles Mingus—a recording justly acclaimed as reuniting Parker and Gillespie in a "summit meeting" of the top talents in bebop. His work after 1953 was less even. He recorded for Blue Note, Verve, and Victor, but his mental problems, often made worse by drinking, interfered with his playing. Powell moved to Paris in 1959 and recorded with another American expatriate, tenor saxophonist Dexter Gordon. Unfortunately, Powell continued to suffer health problems and was diagnosed with tuberculosis in 1963. He died in 1966.

The quintessential bebop pianist, Powell had a direct impact on the piano styles of Barry Harris, Hank Jones, Tommy Flanagan, and Sonny Clark. Indeed, no pianist who followed Powell could escape his influence. His right-hand-dominated style became the prime technique for nearly all jazz pianists and made Powell the father of modern jazz piano.

THELONIOUS MONK

Thelonious Sphere Monk was an original. Avoiding the virtuosic flamboyance of Art Tatum and the up-tempo facility of Bud Powell, Monk instead created a piano style that struck many of his contemporaries as erratic, awkward, or just plain odd. But all of Monk's peers considered him one of the prime movers of bebop. "Monk's contribution to the new style of music was mostly harmonic," Dizzy Gillespie said, "but also spiritual."[18]

Photo by Frank Malcolm. Courtesy Frank Driggs Collection.

Thelonious Monk performing at the Beehive Club, Chicago in 1955.

Although Monk's technique was rooted in the Harlem stride tradition, his solos were devoid of the flashy virtuosity of the older school. His playing was lean and spare, making abundant use of silence around the notes. A noted characteristic of his playing used clusters and "crushed notes"—a dissonant group of pitches out of which Monk would release all but one or two notes.

Much of Monk's influence on bebop came from his practice of reharmonizing popular standards, a practice evident early in his career. In his introduction to "Sweet Lorraine," as recorded by Jerry Newman at Minton's in 1941, Monk played the melody of the song with an accompaniment that departs radically from the original. Even in this early recording, he displayed much of the wit and quirkiness that would come to be associated with his style. As Miles Davis put it, "Monk had a great sense of humor, musically speaking. He was a real innovative musician whose music was ahead of his time. . . . He showed me more about music composition than anyone else on 52nd Street."[19]

Born in 1917 in Rocky Mount, North Carolina, Monk came to New York with his family when he was four. Largely self-taught, he played piano and organ in church.

Monk and Metric Displacement

Some of Thelonious Monk's compositions and improvisations rely on the technique of *metric displacement*. The transcription below shows that in Monk's composition "Straight, No Chaser," the main idea of the melody (indicated as *X*) first begins with a pickup to the downbeat of the measure. Yet when it is restated, it appears one beat earlier in the measure,

> ***Metric displacement*** is a technique whereby the soloist implies or states a rhythm in the melody line that seems to go against the underlying basic rhythm of the piece. It also can be achieved by placing melodic phrases irregularly against the underlying rhythm.

anticipating the fourth beat. Because this second statement of *X* is now displaced in the measure relative to the first statement, it distorts the sense of the underlying 4/4 meter. This happens again in the third and fourth measures. The fifth statement of *X* appears in yet another metric position by anticipating the third beat of the measure.*

---

* For further discussion of these techniques of metric displacement in Monk's compositions and improvisations, see Cynthia Folio, "An Analysis of Polyrhythm in Selected Improvised Jazz Solos," an essay contained in *Concert Music, Rock, and Jazz: Essays and Analytical Studies*, ed. Betsy Marvin and Richard Hermann (Rochester: University of Rochester Press, 1995), 111–118.

He also acquired some European classical technique in his youth but abandoned it early in favor of his own idiosyncratic jazz style.

As house pianist at Minton's during the early 1940s, Monk was positioned to have his pieces performed frequently by the up-and-coming bebop players. Curiously, however, they rarely asked Monk to record with them. He made his first studio recording with Coleman Hawkins in 1944, but he did not record in earnest for Blue Note Records until 1947. Blue Note's producer, Alfred Lion, was intrigued by Monk's dramatically innovative style, but Lion cautiously insisted on recording fourteen selections before agreeing to release a single 78 rpm record.

Working with both trios and sextets, Monk continued to record for Blue Note for the next five years. These recordings highlight his strengths as a composer. His poignant ballads "'Round Midnight," "Ruby My Dear," and "Monk's Mood" featured a rich harmonic vocabulary. A medium-tempo number, "In Walked Bud," was a tribute to pianist Bud Powell that outlined both the melody and the harmony of Irving Berlin's "Blue Skies" in an effective recomposition. Some of his melodies, such as those in "Straight, No Chaser" and "Criss Cross," seemed to shift the beat around by using motives repeated in different parts of the measure. (See the box "Monk and Metric Displacement.")

Monk's distinctive approach to jazz dramatically foreshadowed the minimalism and abstract objectivity that were to become fashionable in the West from the 1950s on. Monk's performances draw us into a conscious awareness of each note and ask us to judge it, to place it in its context, and to enjoy its unique occurrence at that particular moment. In his decision to revamp traditional jazz piano values, Monk addressed the problem of how to imbue each pitch—out of the few pitches available—with special significance and still create good music. Hence, Monk did not rely on dazzling the listener with ornate, previously worked-out licks.

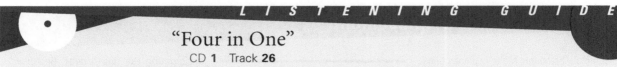

"Four in One"
CD **1** Track **26**

Thelonious Monk Quintet: "Four in One" (Monk). Blue Note 1589. New York, July 23, 1951. Monk, piano;
Sahib Shihab, alto saxophone; Milt Jackson, vibraphone; Al McKibbon, bass; Art Blakey, drums.

"Four in One" is a characteristic Monk composition. This piece also shows off to excellent advantage
Monk's idiosyncratic piano playing in a group setting.

Introduction—8 bars

0:00   Piano solo. Blakey taps the hi-hat lightly on the second and fourth beats of each bar. The third and
fourth bars contain the syncopated whole-tone runs from the tune's A section.

Head—AABA, first two A sections

0:12   The entire band first plays the melody in unison and then moves quickly to notes occasionally
harmonized in seconds and thirds. During the third and fourth bars, listen for syncopated and
repeated whole-tone runs in thirds.

0:20   The eight-bar A section ends humorously with a "bebop" figure. In a piano voicing below the alto
saxophone melody, Monk adds a lowered major ninth—a "wrong-note" D—a ninth below an E♭
melody note in an E♭ major chord.

0:24   The A section repeats.

Head—AABA, B section (bridge)

0:37   The eight-bar bridge begins with the vibraphone and the alto sax on the melody. The II–V
harmonic patterns are conventional for the first two bars, then move up a half step for the third
bar and back down for the fourth bar.

The second four-bar group begins as though it were a transposition of
the first group; but instead of following the pattern, it turns to Monk-
style humorous "wrong-note" chords for measures 6 and 7. The
downbeat chord of measure 6, shown at right, is especially sharp.

A dominant-seventh harmony at the end of the bridge sets up the return to the A section.

Head—AABA, final A section

0:49   Repeat of the A section.

Monk piano solo—1 chorus (AABA)

1:02   As the solo begins, Monk refers to the head's melodic motives.

1:34   At the downbeat of the sixth bar of the bridge, Monk repeats the sharply dissonant chord from
the B section of the head. He ends the bridge with a paraphrase of the head, which continues
during the first two bars of the last A section.

1:41   During the whole-tone sequence of measures 3 and 4 of the last A section, however, Monk develops an alternate higher-register whole-tone syncopation. The solo is remarkable in its imaginative
references to the head.

Shihab alto solo—First half of chorus (AA)

1:51   Shihab has a Parker-like quality to his tone, lines, and bebop phrasing.

2:04   At the start of the second A section, he refers directly to the melody.

Jackson vibraphone solo—Second half of chorus (BA)

2:15   Entering at the bridge, Jackson continues the pattern of clear melodic references. His final A
section is freer.

2:17–2:21	Monk's accompaniment in the B section ranges from single notes in octaves . . .
2:23–2:39	. . . to dense chords.
2:30–2:35	He then moves on to parallel tenths in the final A section.

Reprise of the head

2:39	The head repeats almost exactly. As a brief coda, Monk plays a witty "bebop" cutoff in measure 7 of the last A section.

Monk's compositional and pianistic trademarks, heard in such pieces as "Four in One," include the following:

▶ Unusual rhythmic irregularities in the melodic line

▶ Use of the *whole-tone scale*

▶ A conventional large-scale form (AABA with eight-bar sections) that, because of its predictability, sets off the more personal, stylistic elements

▶ From time to time, intriguing harmonies that break the conventional "rules" of jazz harmony

▶ A whimsical effect created by the contrast between Monk's personal idioms and bebop norms

A **whole-tone scale** has whole steps only and thus no dominant, making it impossible to form major or minor triads. There are only two whole-tone scales: C–D–E–F#–G#–B♭ and D♭–E♭–F–G–A–B. Notice that they share no notes. The scale is often associated with French twentieth-century composers such as Claude Debussy. (Listen to Track 1 of the ⏺ Audio Primer CD; the whole-tone scale is the fifth scale played.)

Although Monk would eventually leave a legacy of jazz standards, he was slow to achieve recognition as a performer. During the 1950s he recorded with such musicians as Sonny Rollins and Gigi Gryce, and he continued to innovate rhythmically. His solo from "Bags' Groove" with the Miles Davis All Stars in 1954 was a tour de force of the techniques of metric displacement—Monk deliberately repeats motives in different parts of the measure, in effect "turning the beat around."

In the later fifties, Monk gained visibility and praise from his masterly album *Brilliant Corners* (1956) and his celebrated 1957 engagement at the Five Spot in New York with saxophonist John Coltrane. In 1959 at New York's Town Hall, he appeared in a concert that featured his big-band compositions. By 1964 his visibility and reputation had increased so much that *Time* magazine pictured him on its cover. Interestingly, his solo piano recording from that same year, *Solo Monk*, revealed Monk's indebtedness to the Harlem stride school.

Although Monk continued to perform and record into the midseventies, he spent his last years living in seclusion at the home of his patron, Baroness Pannonica de Koenigswarter. He died in 1982.

Slightly outside the mainstream bop tradition, Monk's playing nevertheless enormously influenced several generations of pianists. For example, Herbie Nichols and Elmo Hope both owed a debt to Monk during the 1950s; and Andrew Hill, Randy Weston, and Chick Corea all took something from Monk's style. Some aspects of Monk's style prefigure the *free jazz* that burst on the scene in the late 1950s. Although Monk was relatively neglected during his lifetime, devoted players and groups have kept his music alive. For instance, the jazz group Sphere (taking Monk's middle name) formed in the early 1980s to perform Monk's compositions.

Free jazz refers to the 1960s jazz substyle that overturned many of the traditional elements of the music. It's also known as *avant-garde* and the *New Thing*.

Other Bebop Artists

Apart from Parker, Gillespie, Powell, and Monk, many other players contributed in various ways to bebop. Here we look at three artists who provided stylistic innovations on trombone, trumpet, and tenor saxophone, respectively: J. J. Johnson, Fats Navarro, and Dexter Gordon.

J. J. JOHNSON

Although common enough in all types of jazz ensembles, the trombone has never enjoyed the popularity of the other horns. The up-tempo single-note lines pervasive in jazz wind styles are difficult to execute on the trombone because of the slide mechanism. Because this is especially true for the low register, agile trombone playing usually occurs in the upper register.

J. J. Johnson (1924–2001) shook up jazz trombone playing in the late 1940s, although his technical developments followed logically from the work of the swing players. Johnson emphasized the high register and astonished everyone with boplike lines—at the time thought to be impossible on the trombone—that were reminiscent of Parker and Gillespie.

After working with big bands in the 1940s, Johnson made a series of significant records with smaller groups in the late 1940s and early 1950s. He eventually teamed up with fellow trombonist Kai Winding (1922–1983) to jointly lead a two-trombone quintet in 1954. With a distinguished career that continued into the 1990s, Johnson became well established as both a trombonist and a composer.

FATS NAVARRO

In addition to Dizzy Gillespie, a notable trumpeter of the bebop era was Theodore "Fats" Navarro (1923–1950), who in 1945 replaced Gillespie in Billy Eckstine's band. Over the next five years, he recorded frequently as a sideman, playing with Kenny Clarke, Coleman Hawkins, Illinois Jacquet, Dexter Gordon, and Bud Powell. He also performed with the band of composer-arranger Tadd Dameron, playing an impressive solo on Dameron's "Good Bait," based on rhythm changes. Navarro transferred Charlie Parker's bebop language to trumpet, playing chromatic melodic lines that were dexterous and cleanly executed. Navarro set the standard for a future generation of trumpeters that included Clifford Brown (see Chapter 8). Like many bebop players, Navarro succumbed to the ravages of heroin addiction, leading to ill health and death from tuberculosis in 1950 at the age of twenty-six.

DEXTER GORDON

Despite Charlie Parker's overwhelming influence on alto saxophone, significant bebop tenor players emerged during the 1940s. Chief among them was Dexter Gordon, whose career lasted into the 1980s. Gordon's bebop playing was confident and extroverted, offering a rich, muscular, and warm sound on the tenor. He also often played with humor, picking up Charlie Parker's habit of quoting melodies from other pieces within his improvisations. Initially influenced by such Basie regulars as Herschel Evans, Gordon's relaxed, behind-the-beat phrasing owed a special debt to Lester Young.

Gordon was born in Los Angeles in 1923. While still a teenager, he became a member of Lionel Hampton's group and shared the bandstand with saxophonist

Illinois Jacquet, an early role model for Gordon. In 1944 Gordon joined the Billy Eckstine band, which was staffed with many of the fiery young bebop players of the day. Shortly after, Gordon was featured in a saxophone "duel" with Gene Ammons on Eckstine's "Blowin' the Blues Away." This was the first of many saxophone "duels" for Gordon; his 1947 recording "The Chase" pitted him against another important bebop tenor player, Wardell Gray (1921–1955).

Like so many others of the bebop era, Gordon was plagued by heroin abuse; but despite incarceration and parole in the 1950s, he continued to evolve as a player. Gordon influenced two upcoming tenor players—John Coltrane and Sonny Rollins, but the impact was reciprocal: Coltrane's hard-edged sound attracted Gordon, and in the late 1970s he took up soprano saxophone, which was largely popularized by Coltrane. Gordon also displayed a talent for theater: he provided the music for, played for, and acted in the 1960 Jack Gelber play *The Connection*.

Prior to moving to Europe in 1962, Gordon recorded for Blue Note, issuing *Go, Doin' Alright*, and *A Swingin' Affair*. He lived in Copenhagen, played frequently at the Club Montmartre, and toured, recorded, and taught. When he returned to the United States in 1977, the *Down Beat* readers' poll pronounced him "Musician of the Year." He also received that title in 1980. Gordon starred in the 1986 movie *'Round Midnight*, in which he played an expatriate jazz musician living in Paris, and was nominated for an Academy Award. Gordon died in 1990.

Bop-style Big Bands of the Late 1940s

As we have seen, the bebop revolution emphasized the small ensemble. Further, the late 1940s witnessed the demise of many celebrated big bands. Despite all this, bebop proved attractive to some of the large bands. Dizzy Gillespie's big band was probably the first to commit completely to the new music. Other large ensembles soon followed and built much of their repertory along bebop lines. Some bands achieved even more popularity than Gillespie's band.

WOODY HERMAN

Woody Herman (1913–1987), a white clarinetist from Milwaukee, brought the bebop sounds to a wider audience and probably achieved the greatest commercial success in this style. Primetime radio shows, sponsored by Old Gold cigarettes and Wild Root hair tonic, broadcast Herman and his band. These broadcasts—largely unavailable to the black bands, whose mass media exposure was severely limited—made Herman's band the first bebop-oriented music that many people in the United States heard.

Herman started with a swing group in the midthirties, and in 1945 Herman's Herd earned a jukebox hit with "Caldonia." This novelty tune made deliberate and humorous use of the hip vernacular that was emerging from the clubs on Fifty-second Street. Largely a head arrangement, "Caldonia" featured a celebrated five-trumpet unison passage, written by trumpeter Neal Hefti, that had obviously originated in the solo lines of Gillespie. The band's rhythm section—Ralph Burns on piano, Greig "Chubby" Jackson on bass,

Bandleader and clarinetist Woody Herman on the cover of "Early Autumn." This number featured saxophonist Stan Getz.

Copyright © 1952 Cromwell Music. Used by permission.

Swing Bands in the Bebop Era

The big bands that made it through the end of the 1940s all seemed to jump on the bebop bandwagon. Swing drummer Gene Krupa and his band redid "Lemon Drop," written by bebop pianist George Wallington and popularized by Woody Herman in 1948. In Krupa's 1949 version, "Lemon Drop" trombonist Frank Rosolino supplied a bebop scat vocal in the style of Dizzy Gillespie. Krupa's staff arranger, Gerry Mulligan, created a hit for Krupa with his bop-oriented "Disc Jockey Jump." The more-commercial bebop recordings of Herman and Krupa did much to popularize the music among white audiences. As we saw in Chapter 5, even Benny Goodman briefly tried his hand at leading a bop-style group in the late 1940s.

Billy Bauer on guitar, and Dave Tough on drums—created a furious drive on the up-tempo arrangements of "Northwest Passage" and "Apple Honey."

Herman reformed his band in 1947 into a group known as the Second Herd. The band boasted several rising stars, including tenor saxophonists Stan Getz and Zoot Sims, both of whom based their distinctive sounds on that of Lester Young. In contrast to the normal saxophone section of two altos, two tenors, and one baritone, Herman's band featured the three tenors and one baritone. Known as the Four Brothers after a Jimmy Giuffre composition of the same name, the section was renowned for its clean, swinging ensemble sound. (See the box "Swing Bands in the Bebop Era.")

CLAUDE THORNHILL

Less successful commercially but largely committed to the new bebop music was the band of pianist Claude Thornhill (1909–1965). Like Woody Herman and Gene Krupa, Thornhill's career began during the swing era of the midthirties (he even recorded with Billie Holiday in 1938), but he devoted some recordings of 1947–1948 to big-band arrangements of bebop compositions by Charlie Parker and others. The arrangements were unusual and original. Thornhill's arranger, Canadian Gil Evans (1912–1988), was influenced by the French Impressionist composers as well as by jazz, and he experimented with coloristic sounds and instruments not often heard in a big band: French horn, tuba, and bass clarinet. The absence of vibrato in the horns gave the band a stark, moody sound. For Thornhill, Evans arranged Parker's compositions "Yardbird Suite," "Anthropology," and "Donna Lee." (The authorship of "Donna Lee" was credited to Charlie Parker, although it was probably composed by Miles Davis.)

Despite the use of bebop compositions, some listeners still found the spirit of Thornhill's band at odds with the small groups of Fifty-second Street. Miles Davis, who would collaborate with Gil Evans in the following years, noted, "I didn't really like what Thornhill did with Gil's arrangement of 'Donna Lee,' though. It was too slow and mannered for my taste. But I could hear the possibilities in Gil's arranging and writing on other things."[20]

Miles Davis and many of Thornhill's players—Gil Evans, baritone saxophonist and arranger Gerry Mulligan, and alto saxophonist Lee Konitz—eventually retreated from the prevailing bebop style. The result was known in the following decade as *cool jazz*, which we explore in Chapter 8.

See the following table for a summary of bebop characteristics.

Bebop-era Melodic Features

TIMBRE

▶ Tougher, edgier sound than swing; often raspy
▶ Little use of vibrato except on ballads
▶ Little use of instrumental effects
▶ Strong attacks combined with legato lines
▶ Little use of blue-note effects on up-tempo pieces
▶ Instrumental ranges extended upward, especially for brass

PHRASING

▶ Highly irregular, perhaps to offset symmetrical AABA forms
▶ Little space between phrases

RHYTHM

▶ Great reliance on eighth-note lines in up-tempo pieces
▶ Ballads featuring more rhythmic variety

THEMATIC CONTINUITY

▶ Voice leading almost exclusively in up-tempo pieces
▶ Motivic relationships less obvious, except on ballads

CHORD-SCALE RELATIONS

▶ Inside, but based on more-complex scales that include extended chord tones

LARGE-SCALE COHERENCE

▶ Voice leading
▶ Occasional reliance on use of climax followed by relaxation
▶ Balance of gesture

Questions and Topics for Discussion

1. What are some of the differences between swing and bebop? What are some of the similarities? In what ways are the differences revolutionary or evolutionary?

2. How was Charlie Parker the consummate bebop musician? Refer to aspects of his life and music.

3. How did the lives of Dizzy Gillespie and Thelonious Monk differ from that of Charlie Parker? Refer to big bands, compositions, attitudes toward music, and personal history.

4. How did the repertory of bebop change from that of swing? What aspects of the repertory stayed the same?

5. Is it appropriate to regard bebop as the beginning of "modern jazz"? Cite both musical and sociological factors in arguing your case.

Additional Listening Downloads

Search for these classic jazz performances at your favorite online music store.

- Dizzy Gillespie: *Dizzy Gillespie: Ken Burns's Jazz;* "Groovin' High" (1945)

- Thelonious Monk: "'Round About Midnight" (1947)

- Thelonious Monk: *Straight, No Chaser;* "Straight, No Chaser" (1966–67)

- Charlie Parker: *Charlie Parker with Strings: Complete Master Takes;* "Just Friends" (1949)

- Charlie Parker and His Orchestra (with Dizzy Gillespie): "Bloomdido" (1950)

- Bud Powell: *Ultimate Bud Powell;* "Tempus Fugit" (1949)

- Bud Powell (with Fats Navarro and Sonny Rollins): *Best of Bud Powell;* "52nd Street Theme" (1949)

What kind of computers will be needed tomorrow?

...owl-
...ome
...ing
...em.

...iters
...sec-
...the

The
...giv-
...very

day. They point to the eventual need
for faster speeds and greater capaci-
ties. After years of dealing in millionths
of a second, IBM scientists now talk of
billionths of a second.

How do they hope to achieve such
speeds? By tapping completely new
principles for the operation of computer
circuits. IBM scientists and engineers,
for example, are developing computer
circuits and high-speed memories of thin
magnetic films of metal. They also are

investigating the application to computers of tunnel diodes, and of cryo-
genic circuits which function at tem-
peratures approaching absolute zero.

From these research directions will
come new generations of computers.
IBM is exploring them all now, to as-
sure businessmen and scientists that
computer technology will be ready
for new generations
of information-
handling problems. **IBM**

Courtesy Morgan Collection

A It's the first thing you
should know about
is for personal
computers.

The era of the
personal com-
puter is here.
Apple will challenge
your imagination for years to
come. Thousands of uses,
from finances to fun and
games. For information,
call toll-free (800)
538-9696.* Or write:

Apple.

apple computer

*In California, call (408) 996-1010.   10260 Bandley Dr., Cupertino, California 95014.

The 1970s witnessed the entrance of the personal
computer into U.S. society. *Above right:* In a 1961
advertisement that shows the former size of
computers, IBM wonders what kind of computer
people will need in the future. Immediately above is
one of the answers—the Apple computer of 1978.

JAZZ-ROCK, JAZZ-FUNK FUSION

THE DEVELOPMENT of *jazz-rock* and *jazz-funk fusion* during the 1970s remains controversial. *Fusion* involved the incorporation of rock, soul, and funk elements into jazz, and it drastically altered the musical directions taken in the postbop era. The key elements of jazz-rock and jazz-funk include the following:

Jazz-rock, *jazz-funk*, or **fusion** is a form of jazz that combines elements of rock (or R&B funk) and jazz.

- Replacement of the 4/4 swing feel with rock or funk rhythms
- Harmonies and progressions that were usually simpler and often characterized by a slow harmonic change or use of long vamps
- Electric and electronic instruments as the norm; specifically:
    - ▶ Replacement of the acoustic bass with the electric bass
    - ▶ Replacement of the acoustic piano with electric piano and synthesizers (so pianists became "keyboardists")
    - ▶ Rise to prominence of the electric guitar as a characteristic instrument of the fusion ensemble
- Intense amplification and use of electronic effects

An important element in fusion was the addition of the *synthesizer* to the ensemble. As synthesizers underwent development in the seventies and became less expensive and more convenient to play (smaller and more portable), the typical fusion ensemble became more likely to adopt them. (See the box "Synthesizers" for more.)

Synthesizers

Synthesizers were originally developed for musical use in the early 1950s. Unlike acoustic instruments, the synthesizer produced sound electronically: in analog synthesizers an oscillator supplies a voltage to an amplifier, from which it is routed to a speaker. The earliest models pioneered by RCA, Bell Laboratories, and European companies were cumbersome: they did not have attached keyboards and were unsuitable for live performance.

In the sixties manufacturers produced the first synthesizers that allowed keyboardists to conveniently control and manipulate the sound during live performances. During the seventies synthesizers became cheaper and more compact, leading to the familiar sight of the rock band multikeyboardist surrounded by stacks of electric pianos, synthesizers, mixers, and other gear. The Minimoog was perhaps the first widely used synthesizer, a standard keyboard accessory in rock bands and fusion groups in the early seventies.

The midseventies witnessed the dual breakthroughs of polyphonic and digital synthesizers. *Polyphonic* models enabled

> **Sampling** is the practice of digitally recording sounds for musical use in playback. Any kind of sound can be sampled, from a note on an acoustic instrument, to natural sounds, to a passage of music already recorded. For playback the sound is usually activated by computer or by pressing a key on a keyboard. **Sound modules** play back recorded samples, which can be digitally stored on a computer for playback. **Samplers** are used to both sample and play back sounds.

the keyboardist to play chords. *Digital* synthesizers were even more flexible: their numerical translations of complex sound waves allowed for the creation of a greater number of timbres, or sound qualities, for each note.

In addition to synthesizers, *samplers* were gradually developed: when acoustic instrumental sounds (or in fact any kinds of sounds) are recorded and reproduced for musical use, the practice is known as *sampling*.

Curiously, even early jazz synthesizer solos reflected the instrument's potential. The synthesizer was then at the forefront of the developing jazz-rock and jazz-funk styles. Musicians were intrigued by the expressive qualities of the new instrument, and many imaginative solos were created.

Feedback is a distorted effect created when the sound coming from a speaker is picked up by the electronic sensing device of an instrument (or a microphone) and routed back to the speaker. As this process multiplies, harsh electronic wails are created. Feedback commonly (and annoyingly) occurs in PA (public address) systems when the microphones pick up the sound coming from the speakers.

In addition to adopting the new timbre of the synthesizer, jazz musicians began modifying the role of the electric guitar. The traditional mellow timbre of the hollow-body electric guitar had been defined by such players as Charlie Christian in the late 1930s and maintained in jazz through the 1960s. In fusion this sound was superseded by the steely, cutting timbre; the sustained notes; and often the distortion obtained from the solid-body electric guitar. (Listen to Tracks 39 and 40 of the 🅟 Audio Primer CD to compare these sounds.) A common form of distortion was created by intentional *feedback*. Musicians such as Jimi Hendrix in the rock world showed how feedback could be controlled and used as a musical quality.

The radical changes of instrumental timbre associated with fusion were accompanied by changes in the roles of the players themselves. In particular the concept of solo accompaniment was radically modified: instead of the improvised comping of the pianist or guitarist, the group often relied on repeated vamps or ostinato figures.

For the most part, seventies jazz fusion can be broken down into either *jazz-rock* or *jazz-funk*. The latter term, though less common, was often more accurate because the music incorporated elements of R&B and funk more often than rock.

In a very general sense, differences between rock and funk are perhaps best understood by their rhythmic underpinning. Music Example 11-1 compares a rock drum pattern with a funk drum pattern.

The funk drum pattern is more complex because it is based on a sixteenth-note subdivision and incorporates more syncopation; the rock rhythm is based on an eighth-note subdivision. Hence funk music is more likely to be syncopated and

Music Example 11-1
A rock drum pattern and a funk drum pattern.

rhythmically complex; rock music is generally less syncopated and often characterized by the use of "straight" or "even" eighth notes. Both drum patterns incorporate a heavy use of *backbeats,* almost always played on the snare drum.

The first experiments in fusion took place in the late sixties. Much of the impetus for and early development of the style came from Miles Davis and his sidemen. Davis's watershed albums *In a Silent Way* and *Bitches Brew,* both from 1969, helped introduce both electric keyboards and rock/R&B rhythms and harmonies to the jazz audience.

The first wave of popular jazz-rock groups in the early seventies—Mahavishnu Orchestra, Weather Report, Return to Forever, and Herbie Hancock's Headhunters—were formed by former Davis sidemen. These groups earned extensive critical and popular acclaim. Using electronic instruments and the rhythmic grooves of rock and funk, these new groups displayed first-rate improvisational skills and strongly defined compositional structures. Recordings by these groups sold well, too, surpassing many of the musicians' expectations for commercial success. For the first time since the swing era, a form of jazz had become popular again.

Despite the potential of these early fusion groups, two trends occurred that helped, as musician/critic Bill Laswell described, "assassinate the promise of fusion"[1] during the second half of the seventies. The first negative trend, according to some critics, was an overreliance on flashy but largely empty technique. Some of the fusion players relied on faster and faster playing in their improvisations. As guitarist Al Di Meola candidly admitted, "I really wanted to become the fastest guitarist in the world. Just like the track stars want to become the fastest runner in the world."[2]

The second negative trend in fusion's evolution was its commercialization. Whereas a typical jazz record might sell 10,000 to 20,000 copies, some of the most popular fusion records (such as Herbie Hancock's *Headhunters*), sold more than a million. To tap into this market, record companies put subtle—and sometimes not so subtle—pressure on musicians to simplify their music. The more commercially oriented fusion products gravitated toward slickly packaged, danceable, ingratiating music, with catchy melodic hooks replacing the substance of an improvisational or compositional core.

Because of these commercial trends, fusion musicians soon sustained withering critical scorn for "selling out." For example, in a telling interview with keyboardist George Duke in 1977, *Down Beat* interviewer Lee Underwood soundly reprimanded Duke for his commercial leanings: "There are some artists who shoot for immortality,"

Backbeats are heavy emphases on beats 2 and 4, as played by the drummer (usually) on the snare drum. (Other drums or the hi-hat can be used for quieter backbeats.) They can be added to a 4/4 swing rhythm as well. Backbeats increase danceability by clarifying the rhythm and adding to the excitement of the music.

Underwood pontificated, "not just for a heated swimming pool and a house in the Hollywood hills."[3]

Although some fusion artists continue to break new ground, one of the legacies of fusion—*smooth jazz*—is unabashedly oriented toward extensive radio airplay (see Chapter 12). Although one can argue that smooth jazz is simply satisfying popular demand—much like the cookie-cutter swing tunes of the late 1930s—one can also contend that latter-day fusion has not fulfilled its earlier artistic promise. Its detractors disdainfully refer to the music as "lite jazz," "hot-tub jazz," or "fuzak" (a combination of *fusion* and *Muzak*).

Smooth jazz is a popular form of fusion jazz that is common today. It combines rock or funk grooves with an electronic ambience to create an "easy listening" feel. Although improvisation may be present, the pleasant quality of the groove and the melody are its dominant features.

The Appeal of Rock and Funk

Many jazz musicians developed a fascination with rock and soul music as these styles developed during the 1960s. These types of music were popular with youth to an unprecedented degree and largely embodied the rebellion of the sixties against the mores and values of the previous generation. The new generation of jazz musicians—often naturally rebellious—grew up listening to rock and funk; it was natural for them to incorporate these elements into their experimentation with jazz.

Soul and, later, funk developed out of rhythm and blues, which itself was the offspring of the so-called race records of prewar African American music. The rhythm and blues of the 1940s embraced a danceable style with a heavy beat and often syncopated rhythms. As the sounds of the swing-era big bands faded away and bebop proved to be uncommercial, rhythm and blues filled the demand for popular music among black audiences.

The soul and funk groups of the sixties and the early seventies strongly influenced the development of fusion. The band of singer James Brown, the self-proclaimed "hardest working man in show business," featured horns, electric guitar, electric bass, and drums. Brown's hits such as "Papa's Got a Brand New Bag" and "I Feel Good" made prominent use of harmonies heard in jazz, such as ninth chords. Brown's music was also rhythmically complex, with strong backbeats and highly syncopated, rhythmically interlocking parts for the bass, guitar, and drums. The dense interplay of the rhythm-section instruments in funk suggested a way for upcoming jazz-fusion players to integrate their jazz-oriented harmonies with syncopated rhythms.

Herbie Hancock made explicit the connection between Brown's funk rhythms and the new jazz fusions:

> In the popular forms like funk, which I've been trying to get into, the attention is on the interplay of rhythm between the different instruments. The part the Clavinet plays has to fit with the part the drums play and the line that the bass plays and the line that the guitar plays. It's almost like African drummers where seven drummers play different parts. They all play together and it sounds like one part. To sustain that is really hard.[4]

Slap bass is a technique in which the bass player percussively hits the low strings of the instrument while picking melodies on the higher ones. This "slapping and popping" style was created by Larry Graham and subsequently imitated by jazz, funk, and pop bass players.

Another influential soul band, particularly admired by Miles Davis and Herbie Hancock, was Sly and the Family Stone, whose hits in the late sixties and the early seventies included "There's a Riot Going On," "I Want to Take You Higher," and "Everyday People." The group's electric bassist was Larry Graham, who developed a technique of thumping the low strings while plucking the higher strings, creating a percussive funky sound. This *slap bass* style was picked up by other funk players and by fusion electric bassists such as Stanley Clarke, Alphonso Johnson, Marcus Miller, and Jaco Pastorius, who made the "slapping and popping" sound an important component of their playing.

In addition to soul and funk, rock also made an impact on the development of fusion. Rock, which came of age in the 1950s, developed out of a complicated mix of 1940s R&B, country and folk music, and Delta and electric blues, among other elements. With the so-called *British invasion* of the midsixties, groups such as Cream and the Rolling Stones earned phenomenal popularity by covering compositions by African American blues and R&B artists such as Chuck Berry, Muddy Waters, and Robert Johnson.

After first performing in the United States in 1964, the Beatles became cultural icons impossible to ignore. In 1966 jazz drummer Art Taylor conducted a series of interviews for his book *Notes and Tones*, asking jazz musicians what they thought of the Beatles.[5] Intense opinions about them, pro and con, also arose in George Simon's interviews with big-band leaders Count Basie, Woody Herman, Stan Kenton, and Artie Shaw in Simon's book *The Big Bands*.[6] Eventually, many of the jazz stalwarts gave in to pressure from the record companies and other musicians to incorporate rock tunes into their recordings and performances. On the recording *Ellington '66*, Duke Ellington recorded versions of the Beatles' compositions "All My Loving" and "I Want to Hold Your Hand." Count Basie recorded *Basie's Beatle Bag*, consisting entirely of Beatles compositions. Jazz guitarist Wes Montgomery's albums *Michelle* and *A Day in the Life* were titled after the Beatles compositions included on each record. Woody Herman's late-sixties group played the Fillmore auditoriums and recorded rock songs such as the Doors' "Light My Fire."

Despite such experimentation, covering popular rock tunes in a jazz setting proved to be relatively infertile. As fusion developed, the music retained the rhythms, harmonic concepts, and electric ambience of rock music but used these elements to support improvisation and original composition. Covering hit tunes became far less common.

Early fusion artists expressed admiration for the solos of rock guitarist Jimi Hendrix. Hendrix (born Johnny Allen Hendrix) was a self-taught guitar virtuoso who used feedback, distortion, and electronic devices in his extended and flamboyant solos. His hit "Purple Haze" (the title based on a nickname for the hallucinogenic drug LSD) prominently featured a sharp ninth chord, a harmony frequently found in jazz settings. Hendrix took part in two of the most famous rock festivals of the late sixties: the Monterey Pop Festival and Woodstock. His psychedelic performance of "The Star-Spangled Banner" at Woodstock is one of the most compelling and famous moments in the film of the concert. He also had an interest in jazz. For example, he recorded with fusion guitarist John McLaughlin and organist Larry Young late in his career, and he had several discussions with Miles Davis about recording an album, which sadly never materialized. Hendrix died of a drug overdose in 1970 at the age of twenty-seven.

Other rock-oriented bands of the late sixties and the early seventies managed to fuse jazz with rock while appealing to a wider public. Blood, Sweat & Tears thrived on a formula of horns and jazz-based solos to augment their rock compositions, which featured the soul-based singing of David Clayton-Thomas. The group penned a string of Top 40 hits, as did the band Chicago, which used similar instrumentation. Some experimental rock groups, such as the British bands Soft Machine and King Crimson, featured even more extended improvisation. Jazz artists Chick Corea and Gary Burton both acknowledged the influence of King Crimson on their work.

The Fusion Music of Miles Davis

In a remarkable jazz life in which he was always at or near the center of the action, Davis managed to pioneer jazz development yet again with his groundbreaking work in fusion. Davis was increasingly drawn to the popular rock and soul music of James Brown, Jimi Hendrix, and Sly and the Family Stone, as well as Cannonball Adderley's soul-jazz hit, "Mercy, Mercy, Mercy." Davis began experimenting with rock rhythms and electric instruments (such as the Fender Rhodes electric piano) on *Miles in the Sky* and *Filles de Kilimanjaro* (see Chapter 10).

But Davis's *In a Silent Way* was even more radical, presenting music that was both harmonically and rhythmically far simpler than his previous work. The riff-oriented album featured three electric keyboardists—Herbie Hancock, Chick Corea, and Josef Zawinul—as well as British electric guitarist John McLaughlin. In place of the usual recorded performances of individual compositions, *In a Silent Way* was assembled by producer Teo Macero, who edited the studio sessions to create two compositions, each of which took up the entire side of an LP. "In a Silent Way/It's About That Time" was a medley, with the opening drumless section providing a four-minute introduction that was spliced in again at the end to provide a frame for the entire work.

L I S T E N I N G   G U I D E

"It's About That Time/In a Silent Way" (excerpt)

CD 2   Track 9

Miles Davis: "It's About That Time" (Davis)/"In a Silent Way" (Zawinul), from *In a Silent Way*. Sony C3K 65362. New York, February 1969. Davis, trumpet and leader; Wayne Shorter, soprano saxophone; Chick Corea, electric piano; Herbie Hancock, electric piano; Josef Zawinul, organ; John McLaughlin, electric guitar; Dave Holland, acoustic bass; Tony Williams, drums.

The original album side consisted of a medley, beginning with "In a Silent Way" (lasting about four minutes), followed by "It's About That Time" (eleven minutes), and concluding with the four-minute "In a Silent Way," spliced in again to create an overall ABA structure. The excerpt here, beginning about five minutes into "It's About That Time," consists of the soprano saxophone solo and the trumpet solo and concludes with the first statement of the melody to "In a Silent Way."

"It's About That Time" includes two repeated sections for the improvisations. The first (part I) is a repeated three-note bass riff around E♭; the second (part II) is a two-bar groove riff.

"It's About That Time"—Soprano saxophone solo

0:00   For part I the bass riff repeats every bar. Above it the electric piano repeats a six-chord pattern, setting up three-bar phrases. Drummer Williams plays in a subdued manner, keeping time by playing a rock beat that articulates all four beats of the measure. Although the use of rock rhythms in a jazz context was fairly new, a single repeated bass riff beneath shifting harmonies in the piano had already been used in modal jazz, and it is instructive to compare this excerpt with John Coltrane's "Acknowledgement" from *A Love Supreme* (CD 2, Track 6).

0:22   Shorter begins his solo with simple rifflike ideas that emphasize the pitches C and F. Notice that each of his melodic ideas seems to build on and develop the previous idea. Just before part II he begins to spin out longer melodic lines.

1:19 The band begins part II with the groove riff heard in the bass. The riff is shown in the transcription below. Playing over the riff, Shorter relies on fairly short, simple blues riffs. Around 2:02 he begins to play longer, more jazz-inflected lines. He winds up his solo after the band returns to part I by echoing the three-note bass riff.

"It's About That Time"—Trumpet solo

2:42 In part I Davis begins his solo by referring to the melody played by the keyboardists in their six-chord vamp. Note that this induces the keyboardists to move away from that original vamp and begin comping in a more rhythmic manner. Many of their comping figures now echo the three-note bass riff.

3:32 Over the groove riff of part II, Davis uses a generous amount of space between his phrases. Most of his phrases stay concentrated in the middle register, and they seem often to return to the pitch F, the underlying key center.

4:01 Still in part II, Williams begins playing in a high-energy rock style, drumming loudly and energetically. Despite the intensity, Davis still plays with characteristic restraint, although in his first phrase he briefly moves to the higher register.

4:40 The band returns to part I. Davis often uses short, clipped phrases. Although many of Davis's lines stay within the overall tonal center of F, he once responds to the keyboardists' comping when they move outside the tonal center: at 5:22 he plays and holds a G♭, a dissonant note a half step above the tonal center. Organist Zawinul's comping on organ frequently echoes the three-note bass motive.

5:31 While the band plays part II, Davis often plays longer and more-chromatic lines. His solo winds down, and he stops playing while the band continues the groove riff.

"In a Silent Way"—Melody played by guitar

6:29 Here the recording is spliced to merge with "In a Silent Way," a haunting, dreamy composition written by Zawinul. (Zawinul described the composition as a "tone poem" that recalled his boyhood in Austria.) Guitarist McLaughlin plays the melody, accompanied by bowed bass and keyboards. Although Zawinul's original version of the composition was faster and had far more harmonic changes, the musicians played this version out of tempo and adhered to a single harmonic center.

Davis's next studio recording, *Bitches Brew*, was pivotal. From here on his music centered on rock-based rhythms and completely abandoned the 4/4 swing feel that had defined it for twenty-five years. The compositions amalgamated rock and soul influences; a steady, insistent rock or funk beat underscored the freewheeling improvisations by Davis or bass clarinetist Bennie Maupin. Davis also augmented the group's personnel, often including three drummers and a percussionist to create a densely textured and layered rhythmic foundation. For many of the compositions, Davis provided only a general sketch consisting of melodic ideas and a tonal center. The recording sold well, although most of the tracks were long and uncompromising.

Davis's watershed albums *In a Silent Way* and *Bitches Brew* were notable for the following reasons:

▶ Adoption of electric keyboards

▶ Rock-based rhythms

▶ Simplified harmonic foundations often based on repeated ostinato figures

▶ Dense percussion textures and Davis's use of electric effects such as the *Echoplex* (on *Bitches Brew*)

▶ Use of sidemen who formed the first wave of the major fusion groups in the early seventies (Chick Corea, Herbie Hancock, John McLaughlin, Wayne Shorter, and Josef Zawinul)

The **Echoplex** is a commercial electronic device that adds echo to a sound. The rate of speed of the echo can be altered to make the delay effect slight or more pronounced. This device was popular in the late 1960s and the 1970s.

Davis never turned back. After his fusion experiments in the late sixties, he continued to explore creative, improvised music within rock, funk, and computer-controlled synthesizer frameworks. By doing this he gained an even higher degree of popularity and commercial success. After releasing *Bitches Brew,* Davis began playing at rock music venues, such as the Fillmore East in New York and the Fillmore West in San Francisco. In this astute professional move, Davis tapped into a wider audience by opening for rock acts such as the Grateful Dead, the Band, Santana, and Crosby, Stills, and Nash. (See the box "Miles Davis in the Early 1970s.")

Davis stopped performing between 1975 and 1981 because of declining health. He had developed problems from cocaine addiction and had an arthritic hip and stomach ulcers exacerbated by alcoholism. He returned from seclusion with the 1981 album *The Man with the Horn,* which included saxophonist (not pianist) Bill Evans,

Miles Davis in the Early 1970s

With his move to fusion and accompanying popularity, jazz traditionalists such as singer Betty Carter accused Davis of selling out by cashing in on a popular trend: "It's all about money. . . . They [Davis, Herbie Hancock, and Donald Byrd] have a 'reasonable' excuse for the why of what they're doing, but the only excuse is money."*

Nevertheless, a review of Davis's early 1970s recordings shows just how uncompromising and uncommercial much of his music actually was. In contrast to the well-rehearsed, high-octane precision of fusion groups like the Mahavishnu Orchestra and Return to Forever or to the dance-floor grooves of Herbie Hancock,

Davis's groups often performed dissonant, atmospheric, seemingly free-form medleys stitched together loosely by a rock or funk beat. With a band consisting of keyboardists Chick Corea and Keith Jarrett, drummer Jack DeJohnette, bassist Dave Holland, and saxophonist Steve Grossman, Davis gave his musicians plenty of improvising space. As a result, many of the pieces seemed to rewrite themselves each night: "Friday Miles" (named for the night the group performed), from his 1970 recording *At Fillmore,* combined versions of "Sanctuary," "Bitches Brew," "Miles Runs the Voodoo Down," "I Fall in Love Too Easily," and "The Theme." The recordside length of each composition on the double album was created by splicing together chosen segments of longer, live performances.

In the live performances themselves, Davis developed a musical system to signal the group to segue into another piece, as Enrico Merlin shows here:

I have discovered three types of what I call "coded phrases" corresponding to particular characteristics of the relative piece:
1. The first notes of the tune
2. The bass vamp
3. The voicings of the harmonic progressions

For example, in the case of "It's About That Time" the coded phrase is taken from the voicings of the descending chord progressions played by the electric piano.†

* Linda Prince, "Betty Carter: Bebopper Breathes Fire," *Down Beat,* May 3, 1979, p. 14.

† Enrico Merlin, "Code MD: Coded Phrases in the First 'Electric Period.'" Talk given at "Miles Davis and American Culture II," May 10–11, 1996, Washington University, St. Louis. Available at *www.plosin. com/milesAhead/codeMD.html.*

bassist Marcus Miller, drummer Al Foster, and guitarist Mike Stern, whose heavy-metal, Hendrix-like solos jazz critics loved to hate. Davis again showed his flair for hiring rising young stars of jazz by picking up guitarist John Scofield in 1982. Scofield inspired Davis to return to his blues roots: the trumpeter featured a 12-bar blues on "It Gets Better" from *Star People*.

As in the past, these newer sidemen continued with prominent careers after their association with Davis. Guitarists Stern and Scofield are among the outstanding guitarists of today; Miller flourished with an accomplished career as a bassist, synthesist, and producer. Saxophonist Bill Evans recorded a number of albums after leaving Davis.

Although Davis continued to tour and perform, he turned more often to the studio for his albums rather than recording live as he had in the early seventies. For example, Davis created a landmark album in 1985—*Tutu*—which was named after Archbishop Desmond Tutu, winner of the Nobel Peace Prize for his work in ending apartheid in South Africa. *Tutu* made extensive use of studio technology; the tracks were arranged and the synthesizers were programmed by Davis's former bass player, Marcus Miller, with the help of Jason Miles. The album was constructed by introducing layers of synthesized drum tracks, percussion, and keyboards. The funk grooves and the catchy melodic ideas provided a foundation over which Davis later added his trumpet solos. In some ways Miller was something of a fusion-era Gil Evans, providing lush dense backdrops for Davis. (See Chapter 8 for Gil Evans's collaborations with Davis.)

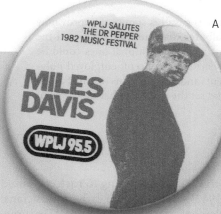

Courtesy Morgan Collection

A promotional button from WPLJ Radio advertises a Miles Davis 1982 concert in New York City.

Merlin's observations have been corroborated by musicians who played with Davis during this period. Interestingly, Merlin notes that Davis developed the medley concept before he turned to fusion. For example, with his acoustic bands of the midsixties Davis would often begin the next piece while the previous piece was ending.

Captivated by the guitar playing of Jimi Hendrix, in the seventies Davis

began incorporating guitar into his ensembles, at times recording with two and sometimes even three guitarists. He soon dispensed with acoustic bass by hiring Michael Henderson, an electric bassist who had played R&B and soul in the Motown studios with songwriter-vocalist Stevie Wonder. Henderson provided the anchor for Davis's group, establishing the tonal center and two- or four-bar ostinato riffs over which the soloists would improvise. Al Foster was often the drummer called on to set the groove with Henderson.

In contrast to the funk-based rhythm sections, Davis's horn lineup was more in keeping with his bands of the past. For his saxophonist Davis often used a player strongly influenced by John Coltrane, such as Dave Liebman, Gary Bartz, or Sonny Fortune. Usually, these players played soprano saxophone. Davis himself

played both trumpet and organ. Like the rock guitarists and keyboardists of the era, he often used a *wah-wah pedal* on trumpet. During live performances Davis would stalk the stage, often directing the musicians from the organ with cues that were sometimes overt and sometimes imperceptible to the audience.

A *wah-wah pedal* is a pitch-frequency filter, operated by the foot, that is usually used by guitarists or electric keyboardists. When the pedal is pressed, the note or chord being held makes a *wah* sound. (An acoustic *wah* sound can be achieved by brass players' using their left hands or mutes over the bells of their instruments.) The up-and-down movement of the pedal creates the repeated *wah-wah* effect. (Listen to Track 41 on the ⓟ Audio Primer CD to hear jazz-rock guitar with wah-wah pedal.)

A **harmon mute** is a hollow metal mute that, when placed in the bell of the trumpet, gives the sound a distant, brooding quality. Miles Davis's use of the harmon mute from 1954 onward helped popularize its use. (Listen to Track 14 of the Audio Primer CD to hear an example of a harmon mute.)

Despite the elaborate studio technology used on *Tutu,* Davis's playing was unmistakable. Over the funky vamp on "Splatch," for example, Davis displayed his trademark *harmon-muted* trumpet—the same subtlety of phrasing and the same start-and-stop ideas that had characterized his playing for four decades. Despite the sometimes radical change of musical circumstances, his style was remarkably consistent throughout his career. Trombonist and composer J. J. Johnson sums up this point neatly:

> Miles is doing his natural thing. He's just putting in today's setting, on his own terms. If you put Miles and his new group in the studio and record them on separate mikes and then you cut the band track and you just played the trumpet track, you know what you'd have? The same old Miles. What's new is the frame of reference.[7]

On his final albums, Davis continued to experiment with studio technology. His work from the late eighties featured sampled, electronically derived soundscapes—much like Miller's work on *Tutu*—over which Davis added trumpet improvisations. Davis died of a stroke on September 28, 1991, at the age of sixty-five. Shortly before his death, he returned once to playing in a more traditional format, performing at the Montreux Jazz Festival in a retrospective of his collaborations with Gil Evans. His last recording, *doo bop,* was released posthumously and incorporated hip-hop grooves and rap. Davis had been an integral part of the jazz scene for more than four decades, always moving and changing. Interestingly, nearly half of his career was dedicated to fusion music after he helped spark the trend in the late sixties.

Regarding Davis's role in incorporating aspects of R&B, rock, and funk music into the jazz idiom, pianist Ramsey Lewis noted:

> It was not until the late sixties when Miles Davis gave his stamp of approval by incorporating some of these ideas into his albums that musicians accepted the fact that rock rhythms and influences other than the traditional ones could be integrated with jazz. . . . Davis extended the harmonic concept, employed polyrhythmic patterns, added electronic instruments and devices to his trumpet along with his highly unique and creative ability, and set the pace for what has come to be known as fusion music.[8]

Other Fusion Pioneers

Miles Davis was not the only prominent jazz musician responding to rock and funk in the sixties. Jazz guitarist Larry Coryell (b. 1943) was one of the earliest musicians to incorporate rock, blues, and even country elements into his jazz playing. Like some of the other young players in the midsixties, Coryell took a wildly eclectic approach. He later remembered, "We were saying, We love Wes [Montgomery], but we also love Bob Dylan. We love Coltrane but we also love the Beatles. We love Miles but we also love the Rolling Stones."[9]

In 1966 Coryell was part of the Free Spirits, one of the very earliest jazz-rock groups; the following year he joined the Gary Burton Quartet, recording with Burton the albums *Duster* and *Lofty Fake Anagram.* Most of Coryell's solo from "Walter L." (from *Gary Burton in Concert*) could have come from a late-sixties rock band. Coryell used blues-based licks, playing with sustain and distortion that approached feedback in one spot. Coryell's performance with guitarist John McLaughlin on Coryell's 1970 recording *Spaces* provided one of the high points of early fusion guitar. In the seventies

Courtesy Morgan Collection

Guitarist Larry Coryell was one of the first guitarists to bring a rock-based approach into a jazz idiom.

Coryell formed the group Eleventh House, but his playing was eclipsed by emerging fusion guitarists such as McLaughlin.

Another early form of jazz-rock fusion was played by the Fourth Way, a San Francisco–based band led by New Zealand pianist Mike Nock (b. 1940). Nock was one of the first players to make extensive use of electric keyboards, playing synthesizers and a Fender Rhodes electric piano and using devices such as the wah-wah pedal on the three albums the group recorded between 1968 and 1971.

The late sixties also witnessed the formation of an influential band called Dreams. Among its players were many of the up-and-coming stars of the fusion movement,

CTI Records

Another notable development in the early seventies was the founding of CTI Records, named after record producer Creed Taylor. Many sixties-era jazz musicians who were on the verge of moving into fusion were still maintaining a postbop approach on their records for this label. These included drummer Billy Cobham, pianists Chick Corea and Herbie Hancock, guitarist George Benson, and saxophonist Joe Farrell. Despite its fine roster, however, CTI's critical reception was often mixed, largely because of Taylor's frequent practice of overdubbing string or orchestral accompaniments. Taylor also supposedly discouraged drummers from using brushes, so on many of the slower ballads the listener was treated to the unusual sound of the drummer keeping time with sticks. On the best of the CTI recordings, such as Milt Jackson's *Sunflower* and George Benson's *White Rabbit*, the quality of the improvisations made up for the string accompaniments.

including drummer Billy Cobham (b. 1944); tenor saxophonist Mike Brecker (b. 1949); Mike's brother, trumpeter Randy Brecker (b. 1945); and guitarist John Abercrombie (b. 1944). Abercrombie's use of feedback and distortion on "Try Me," from the 1970 recording *Dreams,* showed the attraction of high-energy rock guitar playing.

LIFETIME

One of the most important early fusion bands was Lifetime, a dynamic trio formed by Tony Williams, the drummer who had earned tremendous acclaim with Miles Davis in the sixties. Originally from Boston, Williams had been a drumming prodigy, playing regularly around the city by age fifteen. In 1963 at age seventeen, Williams recorded for Blue Note in New York with saxophonist Jackie McLean and was soon asked to join Miles Davis's quintet. Williams's style changed along with Davis's: for example, on Davis's 1969 album *In a Silent Way,* Williams kept up a steady, regular rhythm, abandoning the explosive, unpredictable playing that had previously been his trademark with the Davis quintet. (Listen to CD 2, Track 9.)

In a Silent Way included an astounding British guitarist who had arrived in the United States only two weeks before: John McLaughlin. Born in Yorkshire in 1942, McLaughlin had played in British rock and jazz groups during the fifties and sixties and had participated in studio sessions with pop singers Tom Jones, Petula Clark, and David Bowie. McLaughlin's 1969 album *Extrapolation,* recorded while he was still living in England, demonstrated his remarkably fast execution in an acoustic jazz format. Instead of the syncopated phrasing of traditional jazz guitarists, McLaughlin's playing was even, hard, and cutting. He occasionally used *bent pitches* in the manner of rock guitarists.

A ***bent pitch*** is a small glissando or slide from one frequency to (usually) a slightly higher one. On guitar it is achieved by pushing against the string on the fret board, thus "bending" it.

Invited by Williams, McLaughlin left Britain to come to the States and join Lifetime. The group began as a trio; along with Williams on drums and McLaughlin on guitar was organist Larry Young. Lifetime not only was indebted to the jazz tradition but also drew inspiration from jam-oriented rock bands such as Cream and the Jimi Hendrix Experience. On the title track from the Lifetime recording *Emergency!,* the group alternated a repeated four-bar figure with a half-tempo improvisation by McLaughlin. "Spectrum" probably best showcased the group's hybrid approach: it moved from a Hendrix-like rock vamp to improvisational sections with a 4/4 swing feel, with walking bass played by Young on the organ. The rapid unison line of "Spectrum," played by guitar and organ, foreshadowed McLaughlin's later work with the Mahavishnu Orchestra.

Blending jazz and rock rhythms and held together by Williams's high-energy style of drumming, Lifetime never achieved a wide popularity. The group's raucous energy, propelled by the distortion and the sheer volume of the guitar and the organ, was too extreme for mainstream jazz fans, and its often dissonant and extended improvisations proved too esoteric for mainstream rock fans. Lifetime's second album, *Turn It Over,* was even more explicitly rock-based: it included bassist Jack Bruce of Cream on three of the tracks.

Tony Williams's work with Miles Davis and Lifetime earned him almost legendary status among jazz drummers of the eighties and nineties. He continued with a variety of projects involving both jazz and rock, including reunions with the Miles Davis rhythm section of Herbie Hancock and Ron Carter in a group known as V.S.O.P. ("Very Special One-time Performance"). He also performed with some up-and-coming younger players such as Mulgrew Miller and Donald Harrison. The jazz world was greatly saddened in 1997 by Williams's early death from heart failure at age fifty-one.

His final albums, *Wilderness* and *Young at Heart,* are interestingly varied: the former includes experiments with merging the classical and jazz worlds, and the latter is a piano trio record featuring Mulgrew Miller and bassist Ira Coleman. In 1997 Williams was elected to the *Down Beat* Hall of Fame.

MAHAVISHNU ORCHESTRA

Lifetime was short-lived—the group broke up in 1971—but the hard-driving energy of the music was something fresh. John McLaughlin was emerging as one of the paramount guitarists on the jazz scene. McLaughlin and Larry Coryell were perhaps the two musicians most responsible for bringing the sound of rock guitar into the jazz idiom.

McLaughlin's concept of jazz-rock guitar included elements of non-Western musical traditions, especially classical Indian styles, along with the blues licks typical of fifties and sixties R&B guitar playing. During this time McLaughlin adopted as his guru Sri Chimnoy; accordingly, the titles of McLaughlin's solo albums *Devotion* and *My Goal's Beyond* reflected his newly formed spiritual interests. On *Devotion* McLaughlin hired two of Jimi Hendrix's sidemen, drummer Buddy Miles and bassist Billy Cox; *My Goal's Beyond* used two Indian musicians, Badal Roy and Mahalakshmi, along with such jazz players as saxophonist Dave Liebman, bassist Charlie Haden, and drummer-percussionist Airto Moreira. One side of *My Goal's Beyond* was merely solo acoustic guitar.

After Lifetime broke up, McLaughlin assembled one of the first—and most significant—fusion bands of the seventies. The Mahavishnu Orchestra was named by McLaughlin's guru. McLaughlin hired drummer Billy Cobham, who had played with Horace Silver and the band Dreams; Czech keyboardist Jan Hammer, who had been a member of Sarah Vaughan's trio; Irish bassist Rick Laird; and violinist Jerry Goodman, who had been a member of the rock group The Flock.

The success of the Mahavishnu Orchestra was phenomenal. Their 1971 recording *The Inner Mounting Flame* reached number 89 on the *Billboard* chart; the following year their second album, *Birds of Fire,* reached an astounding 15 on *Billboard.* (The *Billboard* chart records the Top 200–selling albums on a weekly basis; jazz albums have rarely shown up even at the bottom of the chart.) Like that of Miles Davis, the Mahavishnu Orchestra's popularity enabled them to play concerts and tour on the rock music circuit.

In contrast to the loose, often ethereal jazz-rock improvisations of Miles Davis, however, the Mahavishnu Orchestra was tightly rehearsed. The group played dazzling unison figures, complex meters (such as 7/8 or 5/16), ostinato figures—sometimes indebted to Indian music—and rock rhythms pounded out at a ferocious velocity by drummer Billy Cobham, who used a drum set with double bass drums, one played by each foot. On *double-necked guitar,* using a wah-wah pedal and other electronic devices, McLaughlin tore through rapid-fire sixteenth-note solo passages, bending notes and using distortion at deafening volume.

A ***double-necked guitar*** has two necks. Sometimes the second neck has twelve strings rather than the usual six.

The Mahavishnu Orchestra did not rely exclusively on high-octane, blisteringly fast playing. For example, "A Lotus on Irish Streams," from *The Inner Mounting Flame,* and "Open Country Joy," from *Birds of Fire,* are pastoral, acoustic reveries. Much of the band's impact derived from the dramatic juxtaposition of acoustic works such as these with high-energy electric compositions.

All in all, as one writer has observed, the Mahavishnu Orchestra's recordings "remain benchmarks for ensemble cohesion and inspired jazz-rock improvisation."[10]

The group seemed to awaken new possibilities at a time when many jazz musicians were excited by the potential of jazz-rock. Keyboardist George Duke recalled:

> When fusion was first happening, it was the most interesting music I had heard in my life. It reached its peak with the Mahavishnu Orchestra. . . . But it seemed like after that everybody was copying each other and getting too technically oriented, playing so many notes and scales that the feeling was going out of the music.[11]

The group disbanded in 1973. McLaughlin formed a second Mahavishnu Orchestra in 1974. The short-lived, eleven-piece group included Jean-Luc Ponty, a highly talented French violinist who went on to create his own fusion recordings during the seventies and eighties, including the albums *Imaginary Voyage* and *Enigmatic Ocean*. After the Mahavishnu Orchestra broke up, much of McLaughlin's work abandoned the fusion directions he had helped chart. He concentrated on acoustic guitar, playing with the Indian-based group Shakti and later in an acoustic guitar trio with Paco de Lucia and Al Di Meola.

HERBIE HANCOCK AND HEADHUNTERS

With his work as a member of the breakthrough Miles Davis Quintet between 1963 and 1968 and with his own Blue Note recordings, Herbie Hancock distinguished himself as one of the most outstanding jazz pianists and composers of the sixties. Hancock was Davis's first sideman to use the Fender Rhodes electric piano, on the album *Miles in the Sky*. After leaving Davis's band, Hancock continued to use electric piano on his recordings *Crossings, Mwandishi*, and *Sextant*. Hancock's group for these recordings—usually a sextet—was booked into rock music venues such as the Fillmore, but their spacey, open-ended improvisations proved unsuccessful, and Hancock was forced to disband the group in 1973.

Before abandoning the rock circuit, however, Hancock had the significant experience of opening for the R&B pop group the Pointer Sisters at the Troubadour club in Los Angeles. Hancock was impressed by the direct audience appeal of the Pointer Sisters. He started thinking about taking his music in a direction that had more popular appeal, one rooted in the funk and R&B styles of James Brown, Stevie Wonder, and especially Sly and the Family Stone. Introduced to Nichiren Shoshu Buddhism by his bassist, Buster Williams, Hancock experienced a revelation while chanting:

> My mind wandered to an old desire I had to be on one of Sly Stone's records. It was actually a secret desire of mine for years—I wanted to know how he got that funky sound. Then a completely new thought entered my mind: Why not Sly Stone on one of my records? My immediate response was: "Oh, no, I can't do that." So I asked myself why not. The answer came to me: pure jazz snobbism.[12]

Although Hancock never recorded with Stone, he did achieve a breakthrough into popular culture with his phenomenally successful album *Headhunters*. The album reached number 13 on the *Billboard* chart, then eventually went platinum (sold a million copies). With the exception of reed player Bennie Maupin, who was with his earlier group, all the members of Hancock's new quintet had been steeped in funk music. His intent, Hancock claimed, was to hire not jazz musicians who could play funk, but funk musicians who could play jazz. *Headhunters* made extensive use of overdubs and studio technology, including tape loops. In addition to playing the Fender Rhodes electric piano, Hancock also played *Arp synthesizers*, the *Mellotron*, and other electronic keyboards.

Arp synthesizers were among the first synthesizers made specifically for live performance.

The **Mellotron** is an electronic instrument that was used for string-ensemble effects in the 1970s. An early, analog sound module, the Mellotron produces notes by activating short tape recordings of a string ensemble playing each note of the scale. When a key is pressed, the tape recording of the chosen note plays.

Hancock's solo on "Chameleon" established him as one of the finest live per- formers on synthesizer. Much of the success of the *Headhunters* album was due in fact to "Chameleon," which became a hit largely because of its syncopated, danceable two-measure bass riff and catchy melody. (See the box "Herbie Hancock's Synthesizer Solo on 'Chameleon.'")

L I S T E N I N G   G U I D E

"Chameleon" (excerpt)
CD **2**   Track **10**

The Herbie Hancock Group: "Chameleon" (Hancock), from *Headhunters*. Columbia KC 32731. San Francisco, 1973. Hancock, keyboards; Bennie Maupin, soprano saxophone, tenor saxophone, saxello, bass clarinet, alto flute; Paul Jackson, electric bass and marimbula; Harvey Mason, drums; Bill Summers, percussion.

Because of its infectious funk groove, "Chameleon" was an enormously successful hit for Hancock, earn- ing him a huge crossover audience. Most of the composition is based on a simple riff in the bass texture, played by the synthesizer.

Opening riff

0:00	The piece begins with a repeated funk riff played on the synthesizer. This riff forms the backbone of the entire composition. The riff is played twice by itself.
0:11	The other instruments gradually add to the texture, one by one, beginning with the drums.
0:31	A guitarlike synthesizer sound plays a simple, rhythmic line.
0:51	Hancock plays a funky rhythmic accompaniment on the clavinet, a percussive keyboard instru- ment, adding to the texture.
1:11	(Fade out and back in.)

Synthesizer solo

1:53	The synthesizer solo begins. (See the box "Herbie Hancock's Synthesizer Solo on 'Chameleon.'")
3:44	Listen here for Hancock's repeated riff.
4:54	The tenor saxophone/synthesizer melody returns, now stated along with Hancock's synthesizer solo.

On *Headhunters* Hancock revived his earlier hit "Watermelon Man," a composi- tion recorded on his first album more than ten years earlier. On the updated version, percussionist Bill Summers plays an African-like rhythm by blowing on a beer bottle. Although Hancock was later criticized for "selling out," not all of the compositions on *Headhunters* were overtly commercial. "Sly," a homage to Sly Stone, included several drastic tempo changes and featured daring improvisations by both Hancock and saxophonist Bennie Maupin.

Compositional subtlety and extended improvisation gradually faded from Hancock's later recordings. The group's next project, *Thrust,* used repetitive funk and dance rhythms, although Hancock's composition "Butterfly" was haunting and evocative, reminiscent of some of his earlier impressionistic recordings for Blue Note in the sixties. Hancock's subsequent recordings were marketed squarely as commercial products, placing strong dance grooves in the forefront. Hancock's *Manchild* was aimed at the burgeoning seventies disco market; nevertheless he found space for an impressive acoustic piano solo on "Hang Up Your Hangups."

In response to the sometimes hostile comments from jazz critics, Hancock insisted that his dance music recorded in the seventies and eighties was not jazz:

> Jazz fusion is another idiom. It uses elements of jazz and elements of popular forms, but it established its own idiom. I'm not concerned with changing that idiom, or changing disco. I want to play the music I'm playing and still have it be dance music. Making some music that is fun to dance to and really nice to listen to, some music that has emotion in it. . . . It's funny because many of the elements are simpler than before. For example, a lot of the music happening today has simpler

Herbie Hancock's Synthesizer Solo on "Chameleon"

The synthesizer performs most advantageously when its unique timbral qualities are imaginatively exploited. Hancock's solo succeeds because it does what cannot be done on any other instrument, particularly the segments with the modulated sounds and the *portamenti*.

> A **portamento** is a smooth, uninterrupted slide from one tone to another, especially with the voice or a bowed stringed instrument.

Hancock's synthesizer solo is so effective partly because of the beautiful balance among three distinct elements: free blues lines, repeated funky riffs, and nonpitched sounds. Unlike the controlled voice leading and motivic structure that tend to unify bop and traditional jazz solos, the funky jazz-rock solo tends to be sectional, that is, to feature a single idea until it settles in.

The bass line establishes the harmonic orientation of the piece by alternating B♭7 and E♭7—the standard I and IV harmonies of the B♭ blues. Hancock's solo responds to these blues harmonies with an emphasis on the B♭ blues scale.

Hancock begins his solo with several very funky blues licks, generously separated by space. The repeating pattern of measures 38 through 43 is gradually transformed by the addition of modulated sound. As "noise" this passage cannot be transcribed exactly into notes on the staff, so only the rhythm is suggested

chord structures and simpler harmonies than in the past. The complexity is now in the textures and in keeping the groove going.[13]

Hancock's biggest success came with "Rockit," from the 1983 album *Future Shock*, which stayed on the pop-music charts for more than a year and became a classic MTV video. The album went platinum and won a Grammy for best R&B instrumental. Musically and commercially successful, Hancock's work within fusion and funk-based styles numbers among the most important of any jazz artist in the seventies and eighties.

for the most part. Noise or nonpitched sound of this sort is usually produced by frequency or amplitude *modulation* of the signal.

> ***Modulation*** of a sound wave occurs when the sound is modified by being fed through another wave. In ***amplitude modulation*** the amplitude (the range of loud and soft) of the wave is modified by another wave. In ***frequency modulation*** the frequency (the range of high and low) of the wave is modified by another wave. Both of these techniques produce sounds vastly different from the original.

This modulated section is the first of two such passages that are similarly syncopated. The continuous dotted quarter notes of this section effect a fascinating cross-rhythm with the underlying 4/4 meter.

The drummer moves to the bell of the ride cymbal to complement the funky patterns beginning in measure 102. The repetitions help drive the solo forward but not at the expense of its funky earthiness.

Hancock's pattern beginning in measure 116 shows a 3/4 rhythm superimposed on the basic underlying 4/4 of the bass line and the rhythm section. Such a polyrhythm begins to create a sense of *polymeter* because the rhythms are maintained for a considerable length of time and are clearly delineated.

> ***Polymeter*** is the juxtaposition of two or more musical lines in different meters at the same time.

(continued on the following page)

Despite success in the pop-funk market, Hancock frequently returned to an acoustic jazz format, playing in a hard bop idiom with the V.S.O.P. Quintet. The group reunited Hancock with his former band mates from the Miles Davis Quintet—bassist Ron Carter, drummer Tony Williams, and saxophonist Wayne Shorter—and included trumpeter Freddie Hubbard. The group performed a number of compositions recorded earlier with the 1963–68 Davis quintet. Hancock also returned to the hard bop and modal idiom in recordings with trumpeters Wynton Marsalis and Wallace Roney. On his 1996 album, *The New Standard,* Hancock performed jazz arrangements of pop hits by the Beatles and others, succeeding where many earlier attempts to cover such tunes failed.

On the 1998 album *Gershwin's World,* Hancock teamed up with an impressive array of players from the jazz, popular, and classical fields, such as jazz pianist Chick Corea, classical soprano Kathleen Battle, the Orpheus Chamber Ensemble, and pop musicians Stevie Wonder and Joni Mitchell. We return to Hancock and this album in Chapter 12 because it both embodies the eclecticism of the 1990s and hints at a possible direction for jazz in the twenty-first century.

Herbie Hancock's Synthesizer Solo on "Chameleon"

(continued from the previous page)

Beginning in measure 134, the rhythmic component of the modulated sound becomes very complex: the 4:5 notation signifies that four notes are played in the time of five beats. This rhythm interlocks with the 4/4 meter in such a way that the pattern begins first on the downbeat, then on the second beat, and so on. In addition to the overall 4:5 polyrhythm, each large pulse is subdivided into three or four smaller note values, thus generating a multilevel polyrhythmic texture.

When Hancock chooses to step out of the blues scale, he usually does so with a patterned riff. A strikingly effective deviation from the blues scale occurs toward the end of the solo (measures 156 through 162), where Hancock gradually bends the pitch of the synthesizer (probably using a left-hand control device such as a pitch-bend wheel) a half step higher, thus simulating the upward blue-note bend on a larger scale. The bounce back to the correct intonation comes across as the large-scale resolution of the inflected blue note.

More recently, Hancock's 2001 album *FUTURE2FUTURE* finds the keyboard-ist continuing to explore new fusions with performances that link jazz players with hip-hop, turntable, and techno artists.

CHICK COREA AND RETURN TO FOREVER

Herbie Hancock's replacement in the Miles Davis Quintet was Chick Corea, who joined Davis in the fall of 1968. In summer 1970 Corea gave notice to Davis to pursue his own projects and an interest in what he called musical "abstraction." His recordings *Song of Singing* and *Circle: The Paris Concert* made extensive use of free improvisation. The next year, however, Corea became interested in communicating with a wider audience, as Hancock had. His two solo piano albums, *Piano Improvisations,* volumes 1 and 2, showed Corea in a transitional stage: the first side of each contained songs marked by relatively simple forms, structures, and lyrical melodies; the second side of both albums were free atonal improvisations.

The solo reaches its climax with the return of the full band, in call-and-response exchanges with Hancock. Here, Hancock plays solo breaks that blend the ubiquitous blues licks into chromatic scale segments. This procedure winds up the solo in a logical and satisfying manner.

Courtesy Columbia Records and CBS Inc.

The members of Return to Forever were Chick Corea, Stanley Clarke, Lenny White, and Al Di Meola; here is an advertisement for their 1976 album *Romantic Warrior* for Columbia Records.

With his group Return to Forever, Corea abandoned free playing, moving decisively toward airy, Brazilian-influenced music. He hired bassist Stanley Clarke, saxophonist-flutist Joe Farrell, drummer Airto Moreira (who often went by his first name only), and Airto's wife, singer Flora Purim. The group made two recordings, *Return to Forever* and *Light as a Feather*, which highlighted Corea's sophisticated compositions. Some of these—such as "Spain" and "La Fiesta"—were playful references to Spanish music. "Spain," in fact, opened with a solo piano introduction that borrowed material from composer Joaquín Rodrigo's *Concierto de Aranjuez*—a melody that was used earlier on the Miles Davis/Gil Evans collaboration *Sketches of Spain*. Both Airto and Purim were Brazilian, and the group played Brazilian sambas and Latin-influenced rhythms with astonishing clarity and freedom. Corea's tunes caught on. "It seemed like after we made that record," said saxophonist Joe Farrell about *Light as a Feather*, "Everybody and their brother started playing sambas and songs with melodies. It became very popular."[14]

The title *Light as a Feather* characterizes the album as a whole. The lightness is achieved by the relative lack of bass drum in the rhythm section. Instead the bass—itself never too heavy—dominates the lower frequencies. The amplified acoustic bass here offers a delicate sound, more akin to an unamplified bass than the heavier electric bass usually heard in jazz-rock. The prominent Latin rhythms and the lively character of the performances imbue the work with a feeling of joy and exhilaration throughout.

Corea reorganized Return to Forever in 1973, converting the group into an electric quartet. Only Stanley Clarke remained from the earlier band, but he switched from amplified acoustic bass to electric bass. Lenny White, who had performed on Miles Davis's *Bitches Brew*, was the drummer. The electric guitarist on *Hymn of the Seventh Galaxy*, the first album of the revamped Return to Forever, was Bill Connors, but he was soon replaced by Al Di Meola. As for the repertory and the overall style of the group, Corea drew on his own experiences playing with Miles Davis, but he was equally inspired by John McLaughlin's Mahavishnu Orchestra. "John's band, more than my experience with Miles," Corea admitted, "led me to want to turn the volume up and write music that was more dramatic and made your hair move."[15]

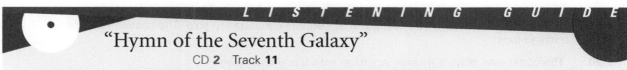

"Hymn of the Seventh Galaxy"
CD **2** Track **11**

Chick Corea and Return to Forever: "Hymn of the Seventh Galaxy" (Corea), from *Hymn of the Seventh Galaxy*.
Polydor 825 336-2. Hollywood, August 1973. Corea, electric piano and organ; Stanley Clarke, electric bass;
Bill Connors, electric guitar; Lenny White, drums and percussion.

Hymn of the Seventh Galaxy reflects the first wave of popular jazz-rock fusion of the early seventies. The first electric Return to Forever album features not only rock rhythms and high-energy improvising but also sophisticated writing and ensemble playing. In fact, much of "Hymn of the Seventh Galaxy" is given over to composition, with the guitar improvisation inserted between the composed passages. Although the composition loosely follows the format of head-solos-head, some of the returns to the head sections are rewritten dramatically. Moreover, rather than relying on a repeated chorus structure, the guitar solo consists of several different sections. Note that the final statement of the head overlaps the end of the guitar solo, and it is altered considerably from the statements of the head at the beginning of the composition. By moving away from the chorus structure of the jazz tradition, the work shows an attempt to develop more-elaborate and ambitious compositional structures in a small-group format.

1st section—Introduction and head

0:00   The composition begins with synthesized sound, which ushers in the introduction played by the organ and the guitar (at 0:08).

0:14   The first part of the head consists of short, rock-based melodic ideas played in unison by the organ, guitar, and bass. These melodic ideas are punctuated by White's energetic drum fills and Corea's electric piano chords.

The opening measures are shown in the transcription below and identify three basic melodic ideas (indicated as motives A, B, and C). Notice that A is a four-note motive; B is an eight-note motive (B is a type of elaboration of A); and C is an eight-note motive reconstructed similarly to B.

0:42   The second part of the head occupies nine bars and initiates a new idea, stated by the bass and the organ. This is punctuated by statements of motive C, before returning to a reprise of the first part of the head.

0:50   The first part of the head is restated.

1:18   The reprise of the second part of the head is elaborated. Unlike its initial statement at 0:42, this restatement is not punctuated by statements of motive C. Following the initial four bars, the section also makes use of mixed meter by including bars that are not in 4/4.

Guitar solo

1:43   Launched by repeated chords in the electric piano, the guitar solo begins. Connors relies on the sustained notes and the cutting texture of rock guitar. Rather than keep time, White fills by playing rolls on the cymbals and the drums.

2:07 White begins to keep time while guitarist Connors continues to solo. The section runs for sixteen bars.

2:20 The guitar now plays a melody in unison with the electric piano.

Guitar solo continues—Reprise of head

2:40 The head returns with motive B. Connors both states the motive and continues to solo between statements of the motive.

2:58 The group continues the head, now without the guitar soloing. They state motive C, but now it's heard in rhythmic augmentation (i.e., the motive consists primarily of quarter notes rather than eighth notes). This is followed by motive A, motive B (in augmentation), and motive C.

3:09 The coda, played in unison, is based on motive C and sets up a self-consciously dramatic ending.

3:17 The composition concludes with the synthesized sound heard at the beginning.

Like the Mahavishnu Orchestra, Return to Forever excelled in playing exciting, impressive unison lines at breathtaking speed. Corea performed not only on electric piano but also on Moog and Arp synthesizers, clavinet, and organ. As heard on "Vulcan Worlds" from the album *Where Have I Known You Before*, Clarke was one of the fastest and most facile electric bassists around. Adept at both improvising and accompanying, he made effective use of the slap-and-pop techniques of funk bass. *Where Have I Known You Before* also contained occasional solo interludes on acoustic piano, with the free-flowing harmonies of the title cut sounding like an homage to Bill Evans's "Peace Piece." At its best Return to Forever's music was compositionally sophisticated: the group effectively blended complex forms, meter and tempo changes, and well-written ensemble passages with dynamic and virtuosic improvisation.

The group's follow-up recordings, *No Mystery* and *Romantic Warrior*, pursued the path begun with the earlier albums, although some of the compositions were shorter and contained less improvisation. It is possible that the group and its record company were aiming for selections suitable for commercial radio airplay. On these recordings the group experimented with numerous subgenres of jazz-rock, rock, and funk; there were funk grooves ("Sophistifunk" and "Jungle Waterfall"), "art-rock" orchestral effects ("Romantic Warrior"), and even heavy metal ("Excerpt from the First Movement to Heavy Metal").

Corea broke up the electric group in 1975. Bassist Stanley Clarke (b. 1951) worked sporadically with Corea during the remainder of the decade but also issued a series of commercially oriented recordings under his own name. Among them "School Days" was a successful hit; even more popular was "Sweet Baby," a collaboration between Clarke and keyboardist George Duke that made the Top 20 in 1981.

Like Clarke, guitarist Al Di Meola (b. 1954) continued as one of the most successful names in fusion. He released a series of albums in the Return to Forever mold, most notably *Elegant Gypsy* and *Casino*. These emphasized Di Meola's brilliant though flashy technique and were testaments to his desire to become "the fastest guitarist in the world." Among later projects, Di Meola played in an acoustic guitar trio with John McLaughlin and Paco de Lucia and experimented with synthesizer textures as accompaniment to the acoustic guitar.

Courtesy Morgan Collection

Stanley Clarke in an early promotional photograph. Clarke made the switch to electric bass as a member of Return to Forever when Corea turned the group electric.

Corea went on to create a larger, more orchestral version of the Return to Forever concept by making use of strings and horns. A series of "thematic" albums followed in the second half of the seventies. *Mad Hatter,* with its Alice in Wonderland motif, included lesser efforts such as the "The Trial," distinguished by the repeated phrase "Who stole the tarts, was it the Queen of Hearts?" On one cut, however, Corea returned to a postbop, acoustic jazz format, playing in a straight-ahead swinging quartet context on "Humpty-Dumpty" with drummer Steve Gadd, saxophonist Joe Farrell, and bassist Eddie Gomez. Similarly, *MusicMagic* featured dazzling solos as well as stunning, complicated written ensemble passages for horns side-by-side with simpler pop-style tunes sung by Corea's wife, Gayle Moran, and bassist Stanley Clarke. One of Corea's most dramatic and sparkling improvisations was played over a Latin-based rhythm on "Armando's Rhumba" (from *My Spanish Heart*), played with Clarke and violinist Jean-Luc Ponty.

Like Hancock, Corea's subsequent career in the 1980s and 1990s included work in both electric and acoustic formats. His group, Chick Corea's Elektric Band, with bassist John Pattitucci and drummer Dave Weckl, was a significant fusion band of the eighties, playing dynamic and well-rehearsed music that recalled the electric Return to Forever group of the 1970s. Corea also returned to the acoustic trio format on two recordings: *Trio Music* (featuring the compositions of Thelonious Monk) and *Live in Europe.* The trio reunited Corea with bassist Miroslav Vitous and drummer Roy Haynes, who had performed on Corea's 1968 *Now He Sings, Now He Sobs.*

Corea's compositional inventiveness and brilliance have led him to undertake musical projects that combine extensive written composition with improvisation, such as *Three Quartets* and his *Sextet* recording. In the 1990s and early 2000s, Corea returned to his musical roots, recording a tribute to Bud Powell and performing with his group Origins.

WEATHER REPORT

One of the longest-lasting and best-known fusion groups, Weather Report first formed in 1970. They recorded fifteen albums in their fifteen-year history. The band underwent numerous personnel changes, with only founding members keyboardist Josef Zawinul and saxophonist Wayne Shorter—both of whom worked with Miles Davis in the sixties—remaining through the band's tenure. In addition to personnel turnover, Weather Report also undertook several changes in musical direction. They began as an acoustic group, using collective improvisation that was sometimes metrically free. By their third album, 1973's *Sweetnighter,* however, keyboardist and composer Zawinul was moving the group toward more strongly defined compositional

A 1979 publicity photo of Weather Report: Joe Zawinul, Wayne Shorter, Peter Erskine, and Jaco Pastorius.

Courtesy Morgan Collection

structures and more rock- and funk-based rhythms and grooves. They reached the apex of their popularity when electric bassist Jaco Pastorius joined the band and they recorded their hit composition "Birdland," from the album *Heavy Weather*.

Born in Austria in 1932, Zawinul was raised in Vienna and studied at the Vienna Conservatory. Arriving in the United States in 1959, he worked early on with bandleader Maynard Ferguson and singer Dinah Washington. But it was his ten-year stint, from 1961 to 1970, with alto saxophonist Cannonball Adderley that gave Zawinul national exposure. Foreshadowing his later interest in synthesizers and fusion, Zawinul played electric piano with Adderley during the late sixties. His use of the instrument helped bring its sound into the jazz idiom. (Zawinul was not first to promote the electric piano in jazz, however: Ray Charles and Sun Ra had performed on electric keyboards in the late fifties, and Earl Hines had both performed and recorded on a Storytone electric piano as early as 1940.)

Showing a natural talent for pop-jazz crossover, Zawinul wrote the Adderley band's prominent soul-jazz hit, "Mercy, Mercy, Mercy." On this cut Zawinul played the Wurlitzer electric piano; on the group's other big hit, "Country Preacher," he played a Fender Rhodes. In the latter performance, he altered the tone bars to give the instrument a more percussive sound. In 1969 Miles Davis paid the distinct compliment of recording Zawinul's composition "In a Silent Way" (CD 2, Track 9) while hiring him to play keyboards alongside Chick Corea and Herbie Hancock. Zawinul rerecorded the composition on his own album, *Concerto Retitled,* the following year.

In 1970 Zawinul and Wayne Shorter formed Weather Report with Czech bassist Miroslav Vitous. The quintet was initially filled out by drummer Alphonse Mouzon and percussionist Airto Moreira (who did not tour with the group but who overdubbed the percussion parts). With Zawinul on electric piano and Shorter primarily on soprano saxophone, Weather Report's first two albums, *Weather Report* and *I Sing the Body Electric,* emphasized mood, color, and collective improvisation.

By *Sweetnighter* the group had moved toward danceable grooves underlying the solos. In "Boogie Woogie Waltz," for example, the band maintained a consistent 3/4 rock beat beneath Shorter's oblique saxophone lines and Zawinul's Fender Rhodes parts, colored by the sound of the wah-wah pedal. The composition also showed new directions that the group would continue to explore: the use of electric bass (on the piece, both electric and acoustic bass are heard) and a short, catchy four-measure melody that is repeated. The latter highlighted Zawinul's ability to write brief melodic ideas as song hooks.

Sweetnighter was the first of Weather Report's recordings on which Zawinul also played synthesizer. He would soon become one of the premier synthesists in fusion, mining the vast compositional and coloristic possibilities of the instrument. By the group's next album, *Mysterious Traveller,* Zawinul was behind a stack of Moog and Arp synthesizers as well as electric piano augmented by wah-wah pedal, *phase shifter,* and Echoplex. With electric bassist Alphonso Johnson replacing Miroslav Vitous, the group also took a decisive turn toward funk rhythms and grooves. Johnson, who played fretless electric bass, laid down a syncopated, funky, repeated figure on "Cucumber Slumber"; as on Hancock's "Chameleon," the bass figure dominated the groove.

Beginning with the 1976 album *Black Market,* electric bassist Jaco Pastorius joined the band. Pastorius redefined electric bass playing with ripping, staccato funk

A *phase shifter* is an electronic device that alters the sound of an instrument by altering the sound wave's shape. The resulting sound has a bubbling or slightly hard-edged quality.

Vibrato is a method of varying the pitch frequency of a note, producing a wavering sound. A vibrato brings a note to life. Heard mostly on wind instruments, strings, and vocals.

accompaniments; fast, clean solos; interjections of surprising harmonics and entire chords; and a liquid sound that often incorporated *vibrato* at the ends of phrases. Born in Morristown, Pennsylvania, in 1951, Pastorius began his career playing in local soul and jazz bands. He made the trio recording *Bright Size Life* with guitarist Pat Metheny, but it was his own 1975 recording *Jaco Pastorius* that showcased his remarkable abilities. On "Donna Lee," accompanied only by percussion, Pastorius glided effortlessly through the melody of the bebop classic, then followed with an astounding solo; on "Come On, Come Over," with vocals by soul singers Sam [Moore] and Dave [Prater], Pastorius's percussive accompaniment revealed new and exciting approaches to funk bass playing.

With Weather Report, Pastorius's outgoing exuberance brought more and more fans to the band's live performances, which generally showcased the bassist in a solo feature that might combine Jimi Hendrix's "Purple Haze" and "Third Stone from the Sun" with "Donna Lee" and the Beatles tune "Blackbird." Pastorius was "an electrifying performer and a great musician," noted Zawinul. "Before Jaco came along we were perceived as a kind of esoteric jazz group . . . but after Jaco joined the band we started selling out concert halls everywhere."[16]

Pastorius was a talented composer too, writing "Teen Town" and "Havona" for Weather Report's best-selling album, *Heavy Weather*. Largely on the popularity of Zawinul's composition "Birdland," *Heavy Weather* reached 30 on the *Billboard* chart and became a gold record, selling more than 500,000 copies. The tune was later recorded by bandleader Maynard Ferguson and, with added vocals, by Manhattan Transfer. "A Remark You Made," also from *Heavy Weather,* was a hauntingly evocative ballad featuring Wayne Shorter on tenor saxophone.

On some subsequent Weather Report albums of the late seventies—as with other promising fusion bands, such as the Brecker Brothers—the group turned to formulaic disco rhythms. Their 1978 album *Mr. Gone,* with Peter Erskine on drums, received negative reviews. *Mr. Gone* earned only a one-star "poor" rating in *Down Beat;* according to the critic, Weather Report had abandoned its creative moorings:

> It seems that the general Weather Report idea is to fill each composition with a mechanical bass ostinato, dense synthesized chording, and funky, cluttered drumming. . . . Where earlier Weather Report albums possessed a sense of adventure, *Mr. Gone* is coated with the sterility of a too completely pre-conceived project.[17]

The review generated enormous controversy, and the group angrily responded to the criticisms in a *Down Beat* interview the following month.

Nevertheless, the group remained enormously popular. In 1980 Weather Report won the reader's poll category in *Down Beat* for the ninth year in a row. Pastorius left the group in 1982, forming his own group, Word of Mouth, which recorded two albums. Unfortunately, alcohol and cocaine addiction brought about severe personal problems for Pastorius, who died after a barroom fight in 1987.

After Pastorius left, Weather Report persisted, releasing several albums—*Procession* (1983), *Domino Theory* (1984), *Sportin' Life* (1985), and their final recording, *This Is This* (1986). After the group broke up in 1986, Zawinul formed Weather Update, a short-lived group that played Weather Report compositions; in 1988 he put together the Zawinul Syndicate with guitarist Scott Henderson.

The Zawinul Syndicate has continued to explore musical styles that blend different cultures. For example, Zawinul's album *Stories of the Danube* (1996) unites orchestral music and jazz in a tapestry linked thematically by the Danube and the cultures influenced by the river. In 1998 the band toured the world and released a two-CD set called *World Tour*. Zawinul has also been involved in staging multicultural festivals throughout the world.

As mentioned in Chapter 10, Wayne Shorter has also pursued a variety of projects. For example, he recorded an interesting duo album with Herbie Hancock in 1997, *1 + 1*. Other projects include large-scale orchestral works that sometimes feature Shorter on saxophone.

Weather Report remains Shorter and Zawinul's legacy from the seventies and eighties. During the fifteen years they kept the band together, Weather Report explored a remarkable abundance of compositional styles and approaches. As Stuart Nicholson summarizes:

> Despite being routinely described as a "jazz-rock" band, their stylistic outlook was extremely broad, perhaps the most inclusive in jazz. Their range extended from classical influences such as the French Impressionists to free jazz, from World music to bebop, from big-band music to chamber music, from collective improvisation to tightly written formal structures, from modal vamps to elaborately conceived harmonic forms, from structures with no apparent meter to straight-ahead swing. . . . Both Zawinul and Shorter created a large body of work that, outside of Duke Ellington, numbers among the most diverse and imaginative in jazz.[18]

PAT METHENY

Guitarist Pat Metheny was one of the most original and popular fusion artists to emerge in the midseventies. Much of his work avoided the cutting, hard-rock sound favored by other fusion guitarists such as John McLaughlin. Metheny preferred bright, lyrical, and often gentle timbres.

Pat Metheny in the 1970s.

Courtesy Morgan Collection

Chorus reverberation is an electronic effect that guitarists use to "fatten," or fill out, sounds. The sound signal is enriched through the addition of reverb (echo) and a chorus effect (that is, added frequencies complement the sound, giving the effect of several voices or tones sounding at once).

Digital delay is an electronic effect that creates an echo or secondary sound so that a guitarist can, in effect, play several parts at once.

Metheny's distinctive sound was created by his use of electronic devices, such as *chorus reverberation, digital delay,* and phase shifters. He used them not for distortion and power effects but rather to give his instrument a fatter, richer sound. In addition, Metheny shunned the pyrotechnics of other fusion guitarists, such as John McLaughlin and Al Di Meola. "I'm not," he made clear, "drawn to the athletic approach to the music." Rather, he saw his lyricism as part of the midwestern melodic tradition of Lester Young and Kansas City: "Even today I think of what I'm playing as sort of a Kansas City style, evolved or modernized. It's that melodic, lyrical thing."[19]

Metheny was born in Lee's Summit, Missouri, in 1954. A musical prodigy, he taught guitar at the University of Miami at age eighteen. Two years later he was invited by vibraphonist Gary Burton to join the faculty at the Berklee College of Music in Boston. Metheny continued his association with Burton by recording and performing in the vibraphonist's quartet.

Metheny's first album, *Bright Size Life,* was released in 1976. Created with bassist Jaco Pastorius and drummer Bob Moses, it showed Metheny's penchant for clear melodic lines with an occasional country twang. "Unity Village" was a quiet solo guitar piece on which Metheny overdubbed himself. Elsewhere he displayed his affinity for the music of Ornette Coleman—whom Metheny called "one of the most melodic musicians ever"[20]—by recording two of Coleman's compositions in a medley, "Round Trip/Broadway Blues."

After *Bright Size Life,* Metheny put together a quartet for touring, consisting of drummer Danny Gottlieb, electric bassist Mark Egan, and keyboardist Lyle Mays. The group built a national reputation by playing one-nighters throughout the country. *Watercolors,* his next album, was followed by the lyrical *The Pat Metheny Group* in 1978. The moody, gentle "Phase Dance" from the latter album featured simple, spacious, diatonic harmonies, with pianist Lyle Mays capturing the folksy quality sometimes heard in Keith Jarrett's playing.

Metheny's next several albums explored a variety of genres. For example, in contrast to his earlier work, *American Garage* was more rock-oriented and was dedicated to the garage bands across the country. "Heartland"—one of his many compositions recalling his midwestern roots—had a decidedly country flavor. Metheny brought Brazilian percussionist Nana Vasconcelos into his group for *As Falls Wichita, So Falls Wichita Falls,* but the dreamy ostinatos featured on many of that album's compositions caused some to dismiss the recording as musically thin—a cross between Muzak and New Age. For his album *Offramp,* Metheny made use of what was then the most sophisticated synthesizer, the Synclavier.

Metheny also performed superbly in acoustic jazz settings. His recording *80/81* included Ornette Coleman's former bassist Charlie Haden along with drummer Jack DeJohnette and saxophonists Michael Brecker and Dewey Redman. The group engaged in open-ended improvisation on Ornette Coleman's "Turnaround." On *Rejoicing*—recorded with bassist Charlie Haden and another Coleman alumnus, drummer Billy Higgins—Metheny featured three of Coleman's compositions. On *Song X* Metheny finally recorded with Ornette Coleman himself. The record was an uncompromising enterprise that both enhanced Metheny's status in the jazz world and brought Coleman to a larger listening public.

On subsequent recordings Metheny merged his neo-romantic streak with Brazilian elements, as on the 1987 *Still Life Talking,* which won a Grammy award, and on *Letter from Home* (1989), which brought to the fore another aspect of Metheny's music: the use of wordless vocals. Metheny's albums have enjoyed both popular and critical success. *Still Life Talking, Letter from Home,* and *Secret Story* all went on to become gold records.

More recently, Metheny—by now an eminent and respected elder statesman of fusion—was involved in several related projects that built on his previous work and reputation and that sometimes involved nonfusion concepts as well. In 1999, for example, he released albums with his longtime hero, guitarist Jim Hall, and saxophonist Dave Liebman. He has continued working in trio formats, most recently with bassist Christian McBride and drummer Antonio Sanchez.

The Pat Metheny Group, now recording for more than twenty-five years, owes some of its current commercial success to receiving airplay on smooth-jazz radio stations (see Chapter 12 for a discussion of smooth jazz); however, the group's recordings—such as "The Gathering Sky" on the 2002 CD *Speaking of Now*—continue

Other Fusion Bands: The Brecker Brothers and Steps

Following the first wave of popular fusion groups in the early 1970s (Mahavishnu Orchestra, Headhunters, Return to Forever, and Weather Report), other fusion bands were quick to emerge. The Brecker Brothers, named for trumpeter Randy Brecker and tenor saxophonist Michael Brecker, released their first album in 1975. *The Brecker Brothers* featured funky R&B grooves, energetic improvising, and exciting ensemble passages. "Some Skunk Funk" contained a rapid-fire melody that moved inside and outside the harmony, and it became something of a test case for aspiring fusion horn players. On later albums the group responded to pressure from record executives by channeling the formulaic disco rhythms that were becoming omnipresent in the late seventies. Still their 1981 recording *Straphangin'* showed Randy and Michael Brecker to be formidable improvisers and composers. Both were comfortable in a number

of settings, including mainstream jazz, fusion, and studio pop work.

Michael Brecker also played with the group Steps (later renamed Steps Ahead). Started in 1979 by vibraphonist Mike Mainieri, the group began with players known for their mainstream jazz work, such as bassist Eddie Gomez (an acoustic bassist who played with the Bill Evans Trio). The band changed personnel several times: their first American-released recording, *Steps Ahead,* featured Brazilian pianist Eliane Elias (CD 2, Track 14). Owing in part to the use of vibraphone, acoustic bass, and acoustic piano, the group successfully negotiated a détente between fusion and more-mainstream jazz.

By the mideighties the group changed personnel and moved more decisively toward electronic instruments and commercially oriented fusion. Mike Mainieri and Michael Brecker remained in the group, and several of the group's newer

players were known for their fusion work, especially guitarist Mike Stern, who had toured and recorded extensively with Miles Davis. With changing personnel Steps Ahead continued to record and perform through the 1990s.

Michael Brecker is now one of the most widely imitated and influential tenor saxophonists of the past several decades. His playing boasts a virtuoso technique that combines some of the improvisational approaches of John Coltrane with the earthiness of R&B saxophonists such as Junior Walker. In addition to tenor saxophone, he has been playing the EWI (Electronic Wind Instrument), which allows different timbres and looping effects. He has returned to more-acoustic jazz formats in recent years, as both a leader and a sideman, with such jazz stalwarts as Herbie Hancock, McCoy Tyner, and Pat Metheny.

to offer inspired lyrical improvisations and sophisticated compositional structures. In a recent article, Metheny summed up his beliefs:

> I made a commitment to focus on and bring into sound the ideas I heard in my head that might not have existed until my time, to try to represent in music the things that were particular to the spiritual, cultural and technological potentials that seemed to be actively available to me in the shaping of my own personal esthetic values.[21]

This statement may serve as a general credo for the ideals of jazz-rock fusion. At its best it is a happy marriage of rock, funk, technology, and jazz. Despite reactions against fusion on the part of some musicians (see Chapter 12), its basic philosophy has provided an important direction for jazz in the twenty-first century.

Jazz-Rock, Jazz-Funk Styles

TIMBRE

▸ Electronic; either
- Very hard-edged, raucous
- Smooth, vague
▸ Upper instrumental ranges emphasized
▸ Use of blue note effects, particularly in funky substyles
▸ Ambience of rock with many electric and electronic instruments in addition to more-traditional instruments
▸ High volume in many forms

PHRASING

▸ Highly irregular in improvisation, but thematic heads often composed in two- and four-bar units

RHYTHM

▸ Wide variety of rhythmic values, but eighth notes emphasized in up-tempo improvising
▸ Highly energetic
▸ Very relaxed; sometimes out of tempo

THEMATIC CONTINUITY

▸ Motivic

CHORD-SCALE RELATIONS

▸ Inside, although can become outside in high-energy modal rock performances
▸ Blues scale usages in funky styles

LARGE-SCALE COHERENCE

▸ Motivic

Questions and Topics for Discussion

1. What are the principal differences between rock and funk?

2. What changes in rhythm and instrumentation did fusion bring to jazz? Describe the new instrument that the fusion bands of the 1970s began to use.

3. How did the performance and sound of the electric guitar change in the fusion bands compared with electric guitar in earlier jazz groups?

4. How does the keyboardist's accompaniment in a fusion band generally differ from that of a pianist in an acoustic jazz group?

5. How can Miles Davis's career be seen as a virtual history of jazz from the late 1940s to the 1970s?

6. What were some of the most significant fusion bands? Who were their key musicians?

Additional Listening Downloads

Search for these classic jazz performances at your favorite online music store.

- Miles Davis: *Miles Davis at Fillmore: Live at the Fillmore East;* "It's About That Time" (1970)

- Miles Davis: *The Complete Jack Johnson Sessions;* "Right Off" (1970)

- Mahavishnu Orchestra: *The Inner Mounting Flame;* "The Dance of Maya" (1971)

- Chick Corea. *Light as a Feather;* "Spain" (1972)

- Herbie Hancock: *Headhunters;* "Sly" (1973)

- Weather Report: *Sweetnighter;* "Boogie Woogie Waltz" (1973)

I HAVE A DREAM

DR. MARTIN LUTHER KING
★ ★ ★ APPEARING AT THE ★ ★ ★
SOUTHERN BAPTIST CHURCH
APRIL 4th - 1968
MEMPHIS, TENNESSEE

Courtesy Morgan Collection

The fight for civil rights was the hallmark of the 1950s and 1960s. Dr. Martin Luther King Jr. (1929–1968) was at the forefront of nonviolent protest against segregation. This poster advertises his last speech, given at a rally in support of striking garbage collectors; later that evening James Earl Ray shot and killed King as he stood on his motel balcony.

THE 1960s AVANT-GARDE

THE STYLISTIC INNOVATIONS in jazz during the 1950s led directly to the formation of a controversial avant-garde in the 1960s. Heated debates arose, recalling the vitriolic exchanges between the beboppers and the moldy figs during the 1940s. The principal issue in the 1960s (as in the 1940s) was disagreement between innovators and populists: innovators felt that the music must progress, while populists thought that the music should attract and please a mass audience. Even today these controversies remain far from settled. In many respects they mirror the general tension in the West between popular and fine art. What ultimately validates an art form? Acceptance by a large audience (the popular) or the originality resulting from cutting-edge experimentation (the avant-garde)?

Given that this issue had been around a while, what made the 1960s *free jazz* or the *avant-garde* so controversial? The principal reason was that the avant-gardists radically rejected aspects of the jazz tradition that many players and listeners considered fundamental. Improvisation still remained, but other elements were drastically altered—changes that made the music seem incoherent to some. These changes included the following:

▶ *Absence of a steady pulse or meter.* The 4/4 swing feel, often considered essential to the jazz tradition, was frequently abandoned.

▶ *Absence of a predetermined harmonic structure.* For the avant-garde soloists, improvisations did not have to be bound by an underlying harmonic progression. Horn soloists sometimes resorted to a *nontempered intonation* that could

Free jazz, the ***avant-garde***, and the ***New Thing*** are terms used to describe the 1960s jazz substyle that overturned many of the traditional elements of jazz.

Nontempered intonation is the use of pitches unrestricted by the "equal-tempered," twelve-note chromatic scale. For example, a nontempered pitch might be a note between D and E♭. Pitches between the tempered notes of the chromatic scale are sometimes called ***microtones***.

conflict with a pianist or guitarist comping the changes. Many groups did away with the instruments that normally provided harmonic support, such as piano or guitar.

▶ *Altered role for rhythm-section instruments.* Avant-garde bassists and drummers often no longer performed their typical timekeeping roles but instead participated in collective improvisation.

▶ *Freer formal structures.* Before the 1960s, musical structures were based on smaller groupings of four, eight, and sixteen measures, helping listeners orient themselves within the form. Many avant-garde players eschewed this regularity in composing and improvising.

▶ *Use of extended or unusual instrumental sounds.* The avant-garde soloists cultivated new timbres and sounds. Percussion became more prominent; saxophonists and trumpeters explored the highest registers and incorporated shrieks and wailing, often imitating the human voice.

This chapter considers the key figures of the avant-garde of the 1960s along with some of the larger social and cultural upheavals taking place during the decade.

Ornette Coleman and Free Jazz

With the arrival of alto saxophonist Ornette Coleman on the New York scene in 1959, avant-garde jazz—also called *free jazz* or the *New Thing*—received its strongest initial boost. In fact, free jazz received its label from the 1960 Coleman album of the same name. A cover painting by abstract expressionist Jackson Pollock reinforced its avant-garde statement. Coleman, who initially played a plastic alto saxophone, polarized the jazz community in New York in the late 1950s: some hailed him as a genius, while others denounced him as a charlatan.

Coleman's music was controversial. His quartet—with trumpeter Don Cherry, bassist Charlie Haden, and drummer Billy Higgins (replaced by Ed Blackwell in 1960)—had no chordal instruments such as the piano. Some listeners dismissed his music as a radical rejection of the jazz tradition, but those who praised him considered his music an extension of historical practice. Among Coleman's earliest champions was pianist John Lewis of the Modern Jazz Quartet, who had heard Coleman's group in California:

> I've never heard anything like Ornette Coleman and Don Cherry before. Ornette is, in a sense, an extension of Charlie Parker—the first I've heard. This is the real need . . . to extend the basic ideas of Bird until they're not playing an imitation but actually something new.[1]

As his album titles *Change of the Century* and *The Shape of Jazz to Come* suggested, Coleman's music was new. The improvised solos were not necessarily tied to traditional harmonic progressions but instead were based on loose and shifting tonal centers. Without any harmonic accompaniment, the soloists could move freely to different harmonic areas, although Haden's bass lines sometimes retained the pieces' original forms.

Courtesy Morgan Collection

With his pianoless quartet in the late 1950s, Ornette Coleman was one of the key figures of early avant-garde jazz.

Coleman was an astonishingly prolific composer whose tuneful, sometimes cheerful compositions were written to be interpreted freely. Coleman noted:

> I don't tell the members of the group what to do. I want them to play what they hear in the piece themselves. I let everyone express himself just as he wants to. The musicians have complete freedom, and so, of course, our final results depend entirely on the musicianship, emotional make-up, and taste of the individual members.[2]

Unlike traditional jazz improvisation, in which the soloist and the accompaniment often follow a repeating 32-bar structure, Coleman's work sometimes abandoned this form. Most of his compositions, however, retained the large-scale organization of head-solos-head associated with more-conventional jazz.

Coleman was born in Fort Worth, Texas, in 1930. After beginning his career performing in rhythm-and-blues (R&B) bands in the midforties, he briefly moved to New Orleans in 1948, working mostly in nonmusical jobs, then returned to Fort Worth. Joining the R&B band of Pee Wee Crayton, Coleman traveled to Los Angeles, where he settled in 1954 after being fired by Crayton. He worked for a while as an elevator operator—a job that allowed him to read and study music theory while parked on the tenth floor. Participating in Los Angeles jam sessions, he occasionally encountered scorn from other musicians, but he also found like-minded players interested in his music and in his freer approach to improvisation.

In 1958 Coleman signed with Contemporary Records and recorded two albums for the label. His first, *Something Else!!!! The Music of Ornette Coleman,* was cut in 1958 and featured a conventional rhythm section with drummer Billy Higgins and pianist Walter Norris; the second, *Tomorrow Is the Question,* was recorded the following year and abandoned the use of piano.

The forms for Coleman's early compositions were frequently conventional, following the structure of the 12-bar blues and the 32-bar AABA song form. Of his irregular pieces, "Mind and Time" used a 10-bar form, and "Giggin'" was a 13-bar blues. Coleman's unique contribution, however, was his ability to veer into different tonal directions, dissociating himself from a fixed harmonic scheme in his solos. Although his albums for Contemporary were less radical than his work to come, they show how his music was evolving toward complete freedom from syntactic constraints.

After signing with Atlantic Records in 1959, Coleman recorded *The Shape of Jazz to Come* and *Change of the Century* with his own quartet, comprising Cherry, Haden, and Higgins. Coleman's approach to the alto saxophone was unique: he emulated the human voice, using bent pitches and unusual intonation. "There are some intervals," he stated, "that carry that human quality if you play them in the right pitch. You can reach into the human sound of a voice on your horn if you're actually hearing and trying to express the warmth of a human voice."[3] Coleman's unusual intonation and motivic playing was often embedded in a relatively simple rhythmic language, creating, as one writer put it, "a touch of folksong naiveté."[4]

These features summarize Coleman's style:

▶ Fragmented, angular melodies instead of the long, spun-out eighth-note phrases of bebop

▶ Melodic connections based on motivic structure and large-scale gestures and more-abstract relations among sets of pitches

▶ Little if any use of conventional harmony and voice leading, but solos often establish loose, shifting tonal centers

▶ Variety of melodic rhythm but avoidance of even-note phrases

▶ Nasal, insistent tone

▶ Rhythm at times loosely connected to background pulse

▶ Concentration on middle and upper range of instrument

▶ Passionate expression

▶ Deviations from standard intonation

As tightly controlled as Coleman's playing was, his pitch structure and his rhythmic fluidity created an impression of freewheeling spontaneity. He combined a sensuous, linear approach to the instrument with a strikingly original sound, created in part by his unique, well-controlled intonation. Although harmony in the conventional sense of chord changes did not often factor into Coleman's music, harmony in the larger sense of related intervals and control always appeared. Without conventional harmony Coleman shaped large-scale form by establishing loose, shifting tonal centers and through musical gestures such as dynamic climax, melodic contour, and sectionalization. All in all Coleman succeeded in allying passionate expression to rigorous linear structure; his playing was emotional, powerful, and thoroughly individual.

John Lewis arranged for Coleman and Don Cherry to attend the Lenox School of Jazz in Massachusetts in the summer of 1959. That November, Coleman and his group came to New York for their legendary gig at the Five Spot. Despite the acclaim of Lewis and other famous musical figures such as Gunther Schuller and Leonard Bernstein, the group experienced derision by some of the older established players. For example, trumpeter Roy Eldridge claimed, "He's putting everybody on. They start with a nice lead-off figure, but then they go off into outer space. They disregard the chords and they play odd numbers of bars. I can't follow them."[5]

In December 1960 Coleman took the unprecedented step of bringing together eight players (two quartets) in a composition titled *Free Jazz*. Coleman had expanded his quartet—Cherry, Haden, and Blackwell—with Higgins, bassist Scott LaFaro, and bass clarinetist Eric Dolphy. The group recorded two takes (one of them lasted thirty-six minutes): they combined solo improvisation, collective improvisation, and prearranged ensemble passages.

To many listeners *Free Jazz* was daunting: it seemed formless and chaotic, a radical rejection of all jazz conventions. Careful listeners, however, heard within its collective freedom a musical conversation in which motives and ideas were stated, then drawn out, reinterpreted, and developed by other players. The role of the rhythm-section players seemed predetermined as well: Haden and Blackwell maintained the fundamental rhythmic pulse, while LaFaro and Higgins played against the time.[6] Coleman's written ensemble passages were used as transitions between the improvised sections.

Free Jazz profoundly influenced the emerging jazz avant-garde. It suggested new sets of relationships among improvisers and allowed the rhythm section to jettison routine timekeeping. Both the use of collective improvisation based on freely improvised motives and the abandonment of cycling harmonic-metric forms redefined the possibilities of group interaction. Other players, such as pianist Cecil Taylor, may

Ornette Coleman's Chamber and Orchestral Compositions

Coleman revealed his interest in contemporary concert music and the third stream by his appearance on Gunther Schuller's 1960 album *Jazz Abstractions;* Coleman was the alto saxophone soloist on "Abstractions," a serial work by Schuller for alto, string quartet, two double basses, guitar, and percussion.

Continuing in a third-stream vein, Coleman premiered in England a chamber music work, *Sounds and Forms for Wind Quintet,* performing trumpet interludes between all ten movements. It showed his ability to create extended compositional structures. This work helped Coleman win the prestigious Guggenheim award for composition; he was the first jazz composer to be so honored.

Several years later, in 1971, Coleman completed a large-scale work for orchestra entitled *Skies of America,* with movements that included "Foreigner in a Free Land" and "The Men Who Live in the White House." The New York Philharmonic revived this work at Lincoln Center in 1997.

also have been experimenting with freely improvised music, but Coleman's greater visibility forced many players to reevaluate their own approaches to the inherited practices of the jazz tradition.

By 1962 Coleman had temporarily withdrawn from public performance; he returned in 1965, playing not only saxophone but also trumpet and violin in a trio with drummer Charles Moffett and bassist David Izenzon. An even more radical player than Haden, Izenzon contradicted the pulse at times, provided melodic commentary, and often used the bow. Coleman brought an intensely percussive, furious, driving approach to the violin, while he centered his trumpet playing in the instrument's higher register, alternating rapid runs with smeared notes and strong accents. Approaching new instruments in an unorthodox manner, Coleman continued to generate controversy among musicians and listeners, although his European tour in 1965 had a significant impact on the avant-garde overseas. On his recording from Stockholm, *Live at the Golden Circle,* Coleman's alto saxophone solos remained highly organized motivically, as can be heard in his compositions "Dee Dee" and "European Echoes."

In 1997 Lincoln Center presented an entire evening dedicated to Coleman—*Civilization: A Harmolodic Celebration*—that featured performances of his group, Prime Time, and reunited Coleman with Charlie Haden and Billy Higgins. Among the other guests were Lou Reed and Laurie Anderson. (See the box "Ornette Coleman's Chamber and Orchestral Compositions.")

Coleman's work in the 1970s and 1980s has been influenced by what he calls *harmolodic theory,* a term first discussed in the liner notes to *Skies of America.* Coleman noted that *harmolodics* presented "melody, harmony, and the instrumentation of the movement of forms." He later wrote that they "had to do with using the melody, the harmony, and the rhythm all equal."[7] Gunther Schuller suggested that harmolodics relates to the use of similar melodic material in different clefs and keys, producing a texture of predominantly parallel motion, although Schuller freely admitted that it was unclear how this idea related directly to Coleman's own compositional technique. The term is characteristic, Schuller noted, of Coleman's obscure and often contradictory yet often poetic pronouncements on music.[8] Despite Coleman's own writing on the subject, the theory remains vague.

During the early 1970s, Coleman worked sporadically, sometimes insisting on compensation for recordings and appearances that was too large for a jazz musician

Harmolodics is a theory of music devised by Ornette Coleman. Although its meaning is unclear, harmolodics has provided the theoretical motivation behind Coleman's work since the 1970s.

of his celebrity and audience appeal. He preferred to remain underemployed and underrecorded rather than sacrifice his artistic principles.

Coleman regained the jazz limelight during the midseventies, combining his free style with funk rhythms and re-emerging as a notable and innovative player. Coleman formed the group Prime Time to incorporate these changes in his style and in his interests. As with his earlier music, much of the improvisational material was not governed by conventional harmonic structure. This time, however, Coleman used electric instruments.

Prime Time began as a quintet, with two electric guitarists and an electric bassist; it was later expanded to a sextet, with the addition of a second drummer. The group featured an interesting amalgam of rhythm and blues, free jazz, and other influences, including Moroccan music. Against an unusual combination of rock and funk *backbeats* (heavy emphases on beats 2 and 4) alongside rhythm-and-blues vamps, Coleman improvised atonally, often using microtonal pitches. Clearly, he was attempting to broaden his status as an avant-garde figure and reconnect with his R&B origins.

Coleman achieved a wider degree of recognition after touring and recording with fusion guitarist Pat Metheny between 1985 and 1986. He recorded with Metheny on the 1985 album *Song X.* In 1987 Coleman recorded *In All Languages,* in which his original 1959 quartet including Don Cherry, Charlie Haden, and Billy Higgins was juxtaposed with his Prime Time electric ensemble. This album, now considered a Coleman classic, was reissued on CD by Verve/Harmolodic in 1997. It provides a remarkable summary of Coleman's distinguished career.

Backbeats are heavy emphases on beats 2 and 4, as played by the drummer (usually) on the snare drum. (Other drums or the hi-hat can be used for quieter backbeats.) They can be added to a 4/4 swing rhythm as well. Backbeats increase danceability by clarifying the rhythm and adding to the excitement of the music.

L I S T E N I N G   G U I D E

"Street Woman"
CD **2** Track **5**

Ornette Coleman: "Street Woman" (Coleman), from *Science Fiction.* Original issue Columbia KC31061.
Reissued on Sony SRCS 9372. New York, September 9–13, 1971. Don Cherry, pocket trumpet;
Coleman, alto saxophone; Charlie Haden, bass; Billy Higgins, drums.

"Street Woman" shows the joyful, up-tempo sound of Coleman's best-known quartet. Like so many of Coleman's pieces, "Street Woman" projects a basic tonal center (in this case, G), although it avoids standard chord progressions. The motivic tightness of the melody is remarkable: after the opening three figures present their abrupt flourishes, the remainder of the melody releases the built-up tension with descending three-note ideas. These three-note descents are either two steps or a step and a third.

Head—1st time through

0:00   The following transcription shows the melodic basis of "Street Woman" in nine numbered melodic figures:

Articulates G, the piece's tonal center, at the end of the sixteenth-note flourish.   Reinforces the same pitch.   Horns begin to slow their presentation.

In perfect fifths, the melody begins to move into a series of descending three-note ideas.

In minor thirds.

Perfect fifths (with one perfect fourth) return.

Horns return in unison to a culminating phrase of three descending three-note figures. The stretching of the melodic line F#–E–D, as heard in figure 4, reinforces the melody's conclusiveness.

▶ Note the pattern of intervals in the horns' presentation underlying the nine figures: unison, sixths, perfect fifths, minor thirds, perfect fifths, unison.

▶ An outline of the bass line is shown in the lower staff throughout the example. Haden's bass accompaniment consists largely of rapid alternations between single-pitch octaves. He follows the horns through the figures of the melody, while his bass line imparts a sense of harmonic movement to the head without detailing specific chords.

Head—2nd time through

0:15   The principal melody is repeated in virtually the same manner.

Coleman alto saxophone solo

0:31   This solo begins with a flourish up to high G that recalls melodic figure 2. He works largely with pitches from the G major scale, then deviates, then returns to the basic G pitch center, which he articulates in numerous ways.

1:28 and 1:56   Coleman returns to the high G in a passionate statement several times toward the end of his solo. The reiteration of the high G helps unite the work, giving it a focus on an emotional high point. At the same time, the G is the overall tonality of the composition and performance.

Haden gradually assumes a walking bass as accompaniment, although he will return to octaves from time to time.

Haden bass solo

2:07   Haden works with the idea of keeping one pitch constant and moving the other.

2:46   Later he moves into a freer statement that ushers in Cherry's pocket trumpet solo.

Cherry trumpet solo

3:11   Cherry presents ideas that recall strongly the figures of the head, particularly melodic figure 1. His solo begins energetically with a flurry of notes. Haden returns to the octave idea of the head.

3:35   Cherry's lines become more lyrical and tonal, emphasizing G minor.

4:02   Cherry ends his solo with an almost classical F#–G (leading tone–to–tonic) phrase.

Head—Reprise

4:07   The head is played twice, as it was heard at the beginning of the performance.

Coda

4:41   Melodic figure 1 is repeated three times with a follow-up high G. Haden closes the bass line on E♭, avoiding the traditional cadence to the tonic G.

The career of John Coltrane was marked by a restless search for musical growth and the transcendental.

By the 1990s Coleman was accepted as one of the elder representatives of the jazz avant-garde. He was inducted into the French Order of Arts and Letters in 1997 and was elected to the prestigious American Academy of Arts and Letters the same year.

John Coltrane

In the twelve years from 1955, when he joined Miles Davis's quintet, to his death in 1967, John Coltrane, initially an obscure and often criticized tenor player, became the leading saxophonist of his generation and one of the most important jazz artists of all time. His influence was profound. He was consistently devoted to his craft, to technical proficiency, to musical exploration, and to endless practicing and studying. His album titles, such as *A Love Supreme* and *Om*, revealed the connection of his music to his religious beliefs and spiritual quest. Fans and listeners heard his extended solos as reaching for the ineffable. Particularly with his quartet of 1960–1965, Coltrane became the symbol of the improvising musician as exploratory seeker. Even in his later, successful years, Coltrane remained uncompromising in his musical ideals and overall goals.

OVERVIEW OF COLTRANE'S CAREER

Although Coltrane underwent many changes and transformations in his sound and his style, his career encompasses three general periods:

▶ 1955–1960: Hard bop and "sheets of sound"

▶ 1960–1965: Classic quartet and modal compositions

▶ 1965–1967: Avant-garde

In the first period, Coltrane and Sonny Rollins competed to be the premier tenor saxophonist in jazz. At that time Coltrane was often described as a hard bop player with an edgy sound. Jazz critic Ira Gitler coined the phrase *sheets of sound* to describe Coltrane's rapid-fire execution, irregular groupings of notes, unusual phrasing, and technique of inserting several harmonies over a single chord. Coltrane's 1959 composition "Giant Steps" was a tour de force of improvisation over rapid and unusual harmonic shifts, which showed off his dazzling ability to execute eighth-note lines over a difficult sequence of chord changes.

Coltrane launched his second period by bringing together his well-known and long-lived quartet, which included McCoy Tyner on piano, Jimmy Garrison on bass, and Elvin Jones on drums. The repertory of the quartet emphasized modal composition, often with particular attention to minor modes such as the Dorian. (See the box "What Is Modal Jazz?" in Chapter 8.) The group's extended improvisations, such as in their performance of "My Favorite Things," featured fewer and slower-moving harmonies. The quartet's modal approach reached its zenith in the December 10, 1964, recording *A Love Supreme,* a four-movement suite. (Listen to CD 2, Track 6, to hear one of these movements.)

Coltrane's third and final period spanned the last two years of his life, when he became increasingly involved in the jazz avant-garde. His album *Ascension,* which used several young, radical musicians, provided a significant document of the free jazz movement.

Sheets of sound, an expression coined by jazz critic Ira Gitler, describes a method of playing that features extremely fast notes with irregular phrase groupings. Sometimes unusual harmonies are introduced over the given chord change. This method originated with John Coltrane.

EARLY YEARS

Born in Hamlet, North Carolina, on September 23, 1926, and raised in High Point, North Carolina, Coltrane played, at age thirteen, alto horn, clarinet, and then alto saxophone. Initially influenced by Johnny Hodges, who played in Ellington's group, he eventually came under the inescapable spell of Charlie Parker. After moving to Philadelphia in 1943, Coltrane studied at several local music schools; he then joined the U.S. Navy band and was stationed in Hawaii between 1945 and 1946. The following year while on tour in California with the King Kolax band, Coltrane met Parker, recently released from Camarillo State Hospital. Coltrane attended Parker's February 19 recording session for Dial—which included pianist Erroll Garner—and later took part in a jam session with the altoist.

In 1948 Coltrane joined the band of Eddie "Cleanhead" Vinson. It was at that time that Coltrane took up the tenor saxophone, which opened up a range of possibilities:

> When I bought a tenor to go with Eddie Vinson's band, a wider area of listening opened up for me. I found I was able to be more varied in my musical interests. On alto, Bird had been my whole influence, but on tenor I found there was no one man whose ideas were so dominant as Charlie's were on alto. Therefore, I drew from all the men I heard during this period, beginning with Lester [Young], and believe me, I've picked up something from them all, including several who have never recorded. The reason I like Lester so was that I could feel that line, that simplicity. . . . There were a lot of things that [Coleman] Hawkins was doing that I knew I'd have to learn somewhere along the line. I felt the same way about Ben Webster. . . . The first time I heard Hawk, I was fascinated by his arpeggios and the way he played. I got a copy of his "Body and Soul" and listened real hard to what he was doing.[9]

Dizzy Gillespie is shown here with Adam Clayton Powell. For many years Powell represented New York's Harlem in Congress, where he was especially effective in helping create the "Great Society" programs that attempted to generate economic and social opportunities for blacks and the poor.

Photograph copyright © 1955 by Lehman Hamilton. Courtesy Morgan Collection.

This quotation reveals Coltrane's ability to absorb a huge array of influences. Throughout his career he remained profoundly interested in the musical developments of his colleagues and was extremely supportive of many of the younger musicians. In addition to his appetite for music, however, Coltrane displayed an inclination toward substance abuse. He began using heroin in the late 1940s, and he frequently drank and ate obsessively. He remained addicted to heroin for nearly ten years.

In 1949 Coltrane joined Dizzy Gillespie's band, with which he made his first commercial recording. During this time Coltrane continued to study and absorb the styles of other tenor saxophonists, particularly bebop pioneers Dexter Gordon and Wardell Gray, as well as Sonny Stitt, a bop altoist who also doubled on tenor.

Taking on a staggering variety of gigs as a sideman, Coltrane appeared in the R&B bands of Earl Bostic, as well as Gay Crosse and His Good Humor Six. In 1954 he joined the band of one of his earliest idols, alto saxophonist Johnny Hodges. Coltrane appreciated Hodges's musical sincerity and confidence and noted that "I liked every tune in the book."[10] Unfortunately, Coltrane's problems with drugs and alcohol caused him to leave the band and return to Philadelphia to recuperate. Although he had already accumulated numerous professional experiences, his most significant ones were yet to come.

HARD BOP WITH MILES DAVIS

Flush with success from his 1955 appearance at the Newport Jazz Festival, Miles Davis formed a working quintet that year, hiring Coltrane on tenor. Although Davis had been using tenor saxophonist Sonny Rollins, Rollins had moved to Chicago, taking the first of his extended sabbaticals from performing. Davis's drummer, Philly Joe Jones, and pianist Red Garland—both Philadelphians—persuaded Davis to hire Coltrane, who was then working with organist Jimmy Smith. In September 1955, in the same week that he married his fiancée, Naima Grubbs, Coltrane played his first performance with Davis.

"When Coltrane joined Miles Davis's quintet in 1955," writes Thomas Owens, "he formed a musical alliance that would have a great impact on the evolution of jazz."[11] Coltrane's years with Davis were indeed formative. Although some critics were initially hostile to Coltrane's aggressive technique and steely tone, his virtuosity was dazzling. Phrases frequently began with an upward glissando, moving to a longer-held vibratoless pitch.

Despite his technical advances, Coltrane's drug habit, along with that of Philly Joe Jones, was causing problems on the bandstand. Miles Davis's biographer, Jack Chambers, recounts the story of Coltrane's falling asleep on-stage during an entire set. Present was a record executive intent on signing him to a major record label; after seeing his condition, he left without talking to Coltrane.[12]

The year 1957 was pivotal in Coltrane's career. Exasperated by his behavior, Davis fired him. Shaken, Coltrane managed to get off heroin and quit drinking alcohol. During the spring and summer, he worked with pianist Thelonious Monk; later that fall the two teamed up for a famous engagement at New York's Five Spot. Monk gave Coltrane further freedom to experiment, with extended solos often backed by only bass and drums. In Coltrane's words Monk was "a musical architect of the highest order. . . . I felt I learned from him in every way—through the senses, theoretically, technically."[13] Coltrane also claimed that Monk was the first to show him how to produce two or three notes simultaneously on the tenor saxophone.

Saxophonist Sonny Rollins was working and recording with the Miles Davis Quintet before Coltrane. Jazz writers and analysts singled out Rollins's musically inventive and thematically coherent solos.

Around this time Coltrane also recorded his first album as a leader. On the LP *Coltrane,* his version of "Violets for Your Furs"—a song earlier recorded by singer Frank Sinatra (and later by Billie Holiday)—showed the depth of tone and emotion that Coltrane could summon on ballads. For these slower, more sensitive solos, he frequently balanced melodic paraphrase with florid runs.

Other Coltrane improvisations showed a turn to the long, sixteenth-note phrases and patterns that were to become a distinctive part of his style. Some of Coltrane's hard bop compositions, such as "Moment's Notice" from his 1957 recording *Blue Train,* contained unusual and quick-moving harmonic twists.

As his technique and approach to the instrument continued to evolve, Coltrane rejoined Davis in 1958. Gitler's term *sheets of sound* was an apt description for Coltrane's torrid scalar passages. In addition, Coltrane made conscious use of unusual and irregular phrasing:

> I found there were a certain number of chord progressions to play in a given time, and sometimes what I played didn't work out in eighth notes, sixteenth notes, or triplets. I had to put the notes in uneven groups like fives and sevens in order to get them all in.[14]

Similarly, Coltrane was candid about harmonic experimentation, sometimes superimposing extra chords on the tunes' basic changes. His solo in "Straight, No Chaser" (from Miles Davis's *Milestones*) contained unusual harmonic substitutions. Referring to Davis's music, Coltrane said, "Due to the direct and free-flowing lines in his music, I found it easy to apply the harmonic ideas that I had. I could stack up chords—say, on a C7, I sometimes superimposed an E♭7, up to an F♯7, down to an F. That way I could play three chords on one."[15]

Davis's modal music supplied the ideal repertory for Coltrane's experiments in *harmonic superimposition*. On his solo on Davis's "So What," from *Kind of Blue* (CD 2, Track 4), Coltrane "stacked" harmonies over the given D Dorian and E♭ Dorian modalities. In the spring of 1959, the same time he recorded *Kind of Blue* with Davis, Coltrane took his own group into the studio and recorded one of his most famous works, "Giant Steps." This imaginative composition used the harmonic patterns of hard bop but reworked them into a large-scale format with fast key changes linked by major thirds. Its fast-moving harmonies differed drastically from the slow-moving harmonic progressions of *modal jazz*. In this tour de force, Coltrane showed his mastery of bebop harmonies and unusual progressions in a driving, up-tempo format.

COLTRANE'S CLASSIC QUARTET

In 1960 Coltrane took the decisive step of leaving the Davis sextet and forming his own quartet, which opened at the Jazz Gallery in May. At first the personnel was unstable. Coltrane initially tried pianist Steve Kuhn, bassist Steve Davis, and drummer Pete LaRoca, but he quickly replaced Kuhn with Philadelphian McCoy Tyner, a hard-driving, percussive pianist who had been a member of the Art Farmer–Benny Golson Jazztet.

In McCoy Tyner (b. 1938) Coltrane found a pianist in sympathy with his own modal interests. Tyner's harmonic sound was based on chords built in fourths. In backing up Coltrane, he frequently intoned a bass-register open fifth in his left hand, operating as a kind of drone that created a tonal center. This open-fifth drone focused the tonality, leaving Coltrane free to depart from and return to the tonal center within his improvisations. Tyner's own solos projected an extremely forceful and clipped staccato touch on improvised lines, which sometimes culminated in thunderous tremolos. On his earliest recordings—including his own *Inception* and *Reaching Fourths*—Tyner played his staccato and even eighth-note lines in a hard bop idiom, skillfully negotiating each harmony. During his five years with Coltrane, however, he interpreted the harmonies more freely, ranging both inside and outside the tonal centers, often through *pentatonic scales*.

Renowned for his powerful touch and almost demonic energy, Tyner has remained one of the most popular pianists in jazz. He continues to work with his own groups, including a big band, and has appeared as a special guest both live and on recordings with other major artists.

Like Tyner, Coltrane's drummer, Elvin Jones, was also a fiery, intense player. Born in Pontiac, Michigan, Jones (1927–2004) came from a musical family that included his equally renowned brothers, trumpeter Thad Jones (1923–1986) and pianist Hank Jones (b. 1918). Before joining Coltrane, Elvin Jones had recorded with Miles Davis, Art Farmer, J. J. Johnson, and Sonny Rollins. Jones's years with Coltrane brought him fame not only for his complex polyrhythms but also for sheer physical endurance. In the context of the band's extended improvisations, Jones generated unbelievable energy and drive as both a powerful timekeeper and a complementary voice to Coltrane's

---

Harmonic superimposition is the technique of adding chords on top of the harmonies already present in a song. It creates further harmonic complexity.

Modal jazz is a body of music that makes use of one or more of the following characteristics: modal scales for improvising, slow harmonic rhythm, pedal points, and the absence or suppression of functional harmonic relationships. Significant early examples of modal jazz come from Miles Davis's recording *Kind of Blue* (1959) and the recordings of John Coltrane's classic quartet (1960–1964).

A **pentatonic scale**, or pentatonic set, is a five-note set that avoids the interval of a tritone and can be arranged as a series of perfect fourths or perfect fifths. The black notes of the keyboard form one such scale.

Publicity photo by Phil Bray. Courtesy Morgan Collection.

Pianist McCoy Tyner's powerful playing is based on modal harmonies built in fourths.

own style. Their performances often included extended duets without piano or bass accompaniment. The level of energy generated by Jones's playing brought about an increased participation for the drummer relative to the bassist and the pianist. Jones was aware of this role. In discussing his playing with Coltrane, he said:

> I always realize I'm not the soloist, that John is, and I'm merely the support for him. It may sound like a duet or duel at times, but it's still a support I'm lending him, a complementary thing. . . . It's being done in the same context of the earlier style, only this is just another step forward in the relationship between the rhythm section and the soloist. It's much freer—John realizes he has this close support, and, therefore, he can move further ahead; he can venture out as far as he wants without worrying about getting away from everybody and having the feeling he's out in the middle of a lake by himself.[16]

Coltrane's classic quartet was rounded out by bassist Jimmy Garrison (1934–1976), who joined at the end of 1961. Like its other members, Garrison had played and recorded with numerous hard bop musicians in the late fifties. Garrison had even performed with Ornette Coleman on *Ornette on Tenor* and was a regular member of Coleman's band just before joining Coltrane. Less technically oriented than Tyner and Jones, Garrison was a thoroughly solid player who often relied on drones and fixed patterns in addition to the more customary walking lines when he was accompanying soloists. In his own solos, Garrison featured unusual bass techniques, sometimes strumming the bass with three-note chords in a quasi-flamenco style.

The quartet became one of the premier groups in jazz; at the same time, Coltrane continued to expand his musical interests and influences by studying the music and the scales of Africa and India. He also took up the soprano saxophone, which provided further inspiration and new paths to explore. Coltrane featured the soprano on some

Coltrane's Modal Compositions

The Coltrane quartet built much of its repertory on a modal foundation. Instead of negotiating a set of changes, modal jazz players often piled up chords, sometimes in fourths, freely chosen from the modal scale. The relationship of their melodies to the chords could also be quite free, often extending chromatically beyond that modal scale. In Coltrane's performance of "My Favorite Things," for example, the song's original harmonic progression was simplified to single modal areas during the solos, which the Coltrane quartet then stretched to the breaking point. The length of each modal area was not predetermined but emerged spontaneously during performance. (Miles Davis used a similar strategy in his recording of "Flamenco Sketches" from *Kind of Blue*.)

Another important tune in the quartet's repertory was Coltrane's "Impressions," which bore an interesting resemblance to Miles Davis's "So What." The pieces had identical 32-bar AABA forms and modal areas: D Dorian for the A sections and E♭ Dorian for the B section. The E♭ Dorian bridge was largely a transposition of the A section—again, resembling "So What."

As Coltrane continued to explore the outer limits of modality, he also incorporated a shift in his improvisational language. In place of the hard bop formulas carefully integrated into his earlier solos (such as "Giant Steps"), Coltrane more and more worked from short motivic ideas, which he would explore through repetition with extensive, sometimes obsessive variation. As Coltrane worked through the variants of these *motivic cells*, the effect

> *Motivic cells*, also called *thematic cells*, are short melodic ideas subject to variation and development.

on the listener was hypnotic, often recalling the incantational atmosphere created by some Eastern musical styles. In part this effect derived from Coltrane's deep interest in the music of Asia and the Near East.

of his best-known performances, including "My Favorite Things," recorded in 1960. (See the box "Coltrane's Modal Compositions.")

During 1961 and 1962, Coltrane's quartet was frequently expanded to a quintet, incorporating Eric Dolphy on flute and bass clarinet. (Dolphy also arranged and conducted the big band on Coltrane's 1961 *Africa/Brass*.) Dolphy's influence on Coltrane's group was liberating: his extended improvisations on such compositions as "India," based on the G Mixolydian mode, triggered hostility from music critics. Some of them attacked what they perceived as Coltrane's move toward free jazz, and they criticized Dolphy's use of speechlike cries in his playing. *Down Beat* editor John Tynan dismissed the music as "anti-jazz":

> At Hollywood's Renaissance club recently, I listened to a horrifying demonstration of what appears to be a growing anti-jazz trend exemplified by these foremost proponents [Coltrane and Dolphy] of what is termed avant-garde music. I heard a good rhythm section . . . go to waste behind the nihilistic exercises of the two horns. . . . Coltrane and Dolphy seem intent on deliberately destroying [swing]. . . . They seem bent on pursuing an anarchistic course in their music that can but be termed anti-jazz.[17]

Nevertheless, Coltrane's 1964 recording *A Love Supreme* was enormously successful and was hailed as a masterpiece. *A Love Supreme* represented the crystallization of the musical ideas Coltrane had developed since he had formed his quartet: modal improvisation, extended *pedal points*, and the motivic cell approach to solos. Coltrane also made ingenious use of a four-note *ostinato* keyed to the lyric "a love supreme." Moved by Coltrane's fervor and intensity, audiences received the recording as a profound, courageous statement of a man seeking musical and spiritual truth. *A Love Supreme* is a suite in four movements: "Acknowledgement," "Resolution," "Pursuance," and "Psalm."

A **pedal point**, also called *pedal tone*, is a sustained or repeated bass note or drone played to accompany a melody.

An **ostinato** is a repeated melodic or harmonic idea that forms the basis for a section or an entire composition.

LISTENING GUIDE

"Acknowledgement"
CD **2**   Track **6**

John Coltrane: "Acknowledgement," from *A Love Supreme* (Coltrane), from the album of the same name. Impulse A-77. Englewood Cliffs, New Jersey, December 9, 1964. Coltrane, tenor saxophone; McCoy Tyner, piano; Jimmy Garrison, bass; Elvin Jones, drums.

The following schema illustrates the sections of "Acknowledgement."

Intro	**I**	**II**	**III**	**IV**	**V**
Cadenza	Add bass	Tenor solo	Transposed	Vocal	Drop vocals
	Add drums		motives		Drop piano
	Add piano				Drop drums
					Bass solo ending

Introduction

0:00   The piece begins with a sparsely accompanied, out-of-tempo cadenza.

I—Layered background texture

0:32   Garrison on bass begins a four-note ostinato that establishes the tempo, beat, and modal center F Dorian on the motive, F–A♭–F–B♭. This ostinato provides the thematic material, that is, its motivic cell.

Jones on drums joins the bass, playing a relatively simple beat that grows more complex and insistent as the piece intensifies.

Tyner on piano follows with chords that reinforce the modal center. The rhythmic backdrop is complete.

II—Coltrane tenor saxophone solo

1:04   This solo is an immediate improvisation rather than a head statement. It centers on a few notes in F Dorian but begins to veer off the mode, which is perceived as a point of harmonic stability to which Coltrane returns.

1:44   The solo gradually becomes more elaborate and intense as he varies and explores the numerous rhythms and patterns he can make with the first few notes.

3:52   Here the solo achieves its greatest intensity, highlighting Coltrane's preference for the high notes of the tenor, as if he were reaching for unplayable notes to express the ineffable.

II continued—Piano and bass

4:14   Coltrane develops a three-note idea here. Tyner and Garrison sometimes follow Coltrane's harmonic excursions but just as often react freely to them, as if to illuminate rather than track his musical path.

III—Transposed motives

4:56 Coltrane transposes the motive to all twelve keys before returning to state it in unison with the bass—as shown here:

IV—Vocal

6:07 Coltrane chants "a love supreme" along with the bass motive in a reprise of the four-note ostinato with added lyric. (According to recent research by Lewis Porter, the added voice you hear is Coltrane overdubbing himself.) The transposing-motives section followed by the vocal provides a recapitulation of this minimal but cogent thematic material.

V—Instruments drop out; motive transposed to E♭

6:37 In the midst of the vocal section, the motive and the general modal center abruptly drops down a whole step to E♭. One by one the vocals, the piano, and the drums drop out, disassembling the background texture erected at the beginning of the piece, to leave the bass to finish alone.

As the next movement, "Resolution," begins, the bass continues to solo in E♭ Dorian. Thus the shift to E♭ Dorian provides a connecting link between the two movements and underscores Coltrane's conception of the album as an extended work rather than a collection of separate pieces.

Each part of the suite is equally compelling. (See the Listening Guide for more on "Acknowledgement.") "Resolution" proceeds with an eight-measure theme over a single harmony. Tyner's piano solo is a powerful statement that demonstrates his ability to create a sense of harmonic evolution over a single modal center. The third movement, "Pursuance," is a 12-bar blues in B♭ minor, played over a blisteringly fast tempo. "Psalm" returns to the out-of-tempo playing of the opening, with Jones doubling on timpani. Coltrane biographer Lewis Porter has shown that the saxophone melody is in fact a wordless recitation to Coltrane's poem included in the liner notes to the album.[18]

The following points summarize Coltrane's mature modal jazz style:

▶ Free melody, usually not formed into square phrases

▶ Melodic connections based on development of motivic cells rather than voice leading, which was more prominent in his bop-oriented work

▶ Widely varying melodic rhythm, from long emotion-charged pitches to fast sheets of sound

▶ Concentration on upper range and extreme upper range of instrument

▶ Passionate expression

▶ Full, rich tone with raspy edge

▶ *Outside* playing, often featuring free chord-scale relationships

A Love Supreme, possibly Coltrane's most popular record, exemplifies his deeply felt spiritual commitment and confirms his intense religious faith.

COLTRANE AND THE AVANT-GARDE

Despite his musical advances and the great success of *A Love Supreme*, Coltrane was still interested in exploring new worlds. He had been supportive of the avant-garde players and took a strong interest in their expansion of musical resources. One of Coltrane's influences was tenor saxophonist Albert Ayler; another was Sun Ra's saxophonist John Gilmore, who provided a model for Coltrane's use of motivic cells. Among Coltrane's newly developing musical gestures were sounds that imitated human cries, an increased use of *multiphonics,* and an ability to create a "dialogue" within his solos by alternating different registers of the horn.

Coltrane's 1965 album *Ascension* unveiled a strong move to the jazz avant-garde. This was not completely surprising: the loose modal improvisation in *A Love Supreme* and other albums had foreshadowed Coltrane's evolution into free jazz. Although Ornette Coleman had been advocating jazz without tonal centers since the late 1950s, Coltrane had not rushed to embrace the controversial new style but had instead progressed naturally to it.

In addition to his regular quartet, Coltrane's group on *Ascension* was augmented by a second bassist (Art Davis, who during this time was working frequently with Coltrane's quartet), two trumpeters (Dewey Johnson and Freddie Hubbard), two alto saxophonists (Marion Brown and John Tchicai), and two other tenor saxophonists (Farrell "Pharoah" Sanders and Archie Shepp). The group recorded two takes of the composition "Ascension." In its use of collective group improvisation, it bore a superficial resemblance to Ornette Coleman's 1960 double quartet recording *Free Jazz,* but *Ascension* was much denser and more dissonant. For example, the relative transparency of Coleman's *Free Jazz* arose from a looser exchange of motivic ideas passed around among the soloists, whereas Coltrane's *Ascension* often relied on dense

Jazz musicians are said to be playing *inside* when their melodic lines favor the principal notes of the harmonies. The more players depart from the notes of the harmonies, the more they are said to be playing *outside*. These terms are most commonly associated with modern jazz. (Listen to Track 8 of the ⏺ Audio Primer CD to hear examples of inside and outside playing.)

Multiphonics is a technique of producing more than one note at a time on a wind instrument. Using nonstandard fingering and appropriate embouchure, the player produces a multinote "chordal" effect. The technique is difficult to control, may be strident, and is generally associated with avant-garde playing.

Sound fields result when coinciding melodic lines fuse into an indistinguishable web or mass of sound with irregular accentuation within each line.

blocks of sound created by the seven horn players, generating what writer Ekkehard Jost called *sound fields*.[19]

Ascension used both group improvisation and individual solos. Despite its freedom and spontaneity, it contained some predetermined material, which helped provide overall direction. Throughout the eight collective improvisational sections, the group loosely invoked different modes. Additionally, the melodic idea in the first collective improvisation section—stated by Coltrane—was a motive comprising the same intervals as the motivic cell of "Acknowledgement" had.

Coltrane continued to align himself with the avant-garde. Saxophonist Pharoah Sanders joined the group in the fall of 1965, as did a second drummer, Rashied Ali. Coltrane's 1965 recordings *Om* and *Kulu se Mama* moved closer to totally free improvisation and away from the modal improvisations of previous years. Unhappy with the group's new directions, both Jones and Tyner left the band by the end of 1965. Coltrane's wife, harpist and pianist Alice Coltrane, replaced Tyner. Among Coltrane's final recordings were *Interstellar Space* (a duet with drummer Rashied Ali) and *Expression*. Coltrane died of liver cancer on July 17, 1967, at the age of forty.

Since 1950 only Miles Davis has exerted a more powerful influence on jazz than John Coltrane has. Coltrane's intensity, technical skill, spirituality, and continual search for new sounds remain an inspiration to all jazz musicians. His legendary status was enhanced by his unfortunate early death, probably brought on by the effects of his heroin addiction and excessive drinking. Uniting non-Western musical models and modal jazz with his original mastery of bebop, John Coltrane created some of the most personal, powerful, and exciting jazz of the 1950s and 1960s.

ERIC DOLPHY

Perhaps no saxophonist has managed the borderline between hard bop and free jazz as convincingly as Eric Dolphy has. In parlance that was new at the time, Dolphy was equally convincing at playing both inside and outside; that is, he could move outside the harmonic progressions—with pitches not part of the given chord or mode—then deftly return inside to take up the harmonies. Dolphy's album titles *Outward Bound* and *Out to Lunch* punned on the notion of outside playing.

Born in Los Angeles, Eric Dolphy (1928–1964) performed on alto saxophone, flute, and bass clarinet. On alto he developed an original sound, characterized by wide intervallic leaps, unusual phrasing that often floated untethered from the beat, and the use of glissandi, smears, and nontempered intonation. In contrast to more-conventional players, Dolphy's rhythmic conception tended to be freer, that is, less tied to the beat. His influences ranged from Ornette Coleman to African and Indian music. He even attempted, he said, to imitate the music of birds.[20] His flute playing was more traditional; Dolphy often turned to the more pastoral instrument for jazz standards, as he did in his recording of "You Don't Know What Love Is" from *Last Date* (1964).

As his work with John Coltrane on "India" (from *Impressions*) and with Ornette Coleman on *Free Jazz* revealed, Dolphy was an outstanding virtuoso on bass clarinet, helping generate interest in an instrument fairly new to jazz settings. In addition to these recordings and his own, Dolphy appeared on several other significant albums with bassist Charles Mingus, trumpeter Booker Little, and arranger Oliver Nelson.

Dolphy made his first important musical alliance when he joined the quartet of Chico Hamilton in 1958. He recorded *Gongs East* with Hamilton, a West Coast drummer (discussed in Chapter 8), whose ensemble was notable for including a cellist.

Eric Dolphy and Booker Little

Dolphy's album *Far Cry* featured Booker Little, a trumpeter who maintained a close musical relationship with Dolphy until Little's tragic death in 1961 at the age of twenty-three. A hard bop player from Memphis, Little began his career as a devotee of Clifford Brown. He recorded his first albums with the Max Roach Quintet before he was twenty years old. Roach even recorded some of Little's compositions with a pianoless quintet that included Ray Draper on tuba. Little's "Larry LaRue," from Roach's *Words, Not Deeds,* was harmonically complex, with the melody—scored for trumpet, tenor saxophone, and tuba—frequently moving in parallel motion, a compositional technique that Little often brought to his writing. Little's playing was technically polished, lyrical, and creative.

Dolphy took part in Little's own recording for Candid Records, *Out Front.* The two also collaborated on a gig at the Five Spot, which was recorded and released in a series of albums that included Mal Waldron on piano, Richard Davis on bass, and Ed Blackwell on drums. On the Five Spot recordings, Dolphy's influence on Little is clear, as Little often adopted Dolphy's flurry-of-notes approach. Little's compositions employed complex and unusual forms.

After moving to New York in 1959, Dolphy began to work with Charles Mingus, an association that lasted until Dolphy's untimely death in 1964. Together Dolphy and Mingus recorded an astounding duet, "What Love," in which the two players floated in and out of tempo, creating a conversation between Mingus's bass and Dolphy's bass clarinet that mimicked human speech. Dolphy's alto solo on Mingus's "Hora Decubitis" bordered on free jazz (see Chapter 8 and CD 2, Track 3): the solo at times ignored and at other times projected the harmonic progression of the 12-bar blues.

Dolphy's work on Ornette Coleman's trailblazing *Free Jazz* solidified his reputation as a major presence in the jazz avant-garde; even so he never abandoned more-traditional settings. Amazingly, on the same day that he recorded *Free Jazz*—December 21, 1960—Dolphy also recorded his own album *Far Cry,* with a standard rhythm section consisting of Ron Carter on bass, Jaki Byard on piano, and Roy Haynes on drums. Several of the compositions paid tribute to Parker, such as Byard's "Ode to Charlie Parker" and the 12-bar blues "Mrs. Parker of K.C." On "Mrs. Parker" the rhythm section experimented with breaking up the time for the first chorus of each solo, creating rhythmic and harmonic conflicts before moving into a 4/4 swing. Dolphy's unaccompanied alto solo on the popular standard "Tenderly" showed his ability to underscore and outline the harmonies of the tune. (See the box "Eric Dolphy and Booker Little.")

An invitation to Dolphy to join the John Coltrane Quartet between 1961 and 1962 led to controversy, eliciting the negative label of "anti-jazz" from critics who thought the solos too long, anarchistic, and unswinging. Of course Coltrane had a more positive view: he insisted that Dolphy's inclusion in the group "had a broadening effect on us. There are a lot of things we try now that we never tried before. We're playing things that are freer than before."[21] Dolphy recorded *Live at the Village Vanguard* and *Impressions* with Coltrane and toured Europe with the group at the end of 1961.

Dolphy was also involved in third-stream and twentieth-century concert music; for example, he performed on Gunther Schuller's 1960 recording *Abstractions.* His interest in the European avant-garde led to a performance of Edgard Varèse's *Density*

21.5 for unaccompanied flute at the Ojai Music Festival in California. After touring Europe with Mingus in 1964, Dolphy elected to remain abroad rather than return to the United States. Shortly after, he died in Berlin from a heart attack brought on by diabetes.

Although critics often focused on the radical elements in Dolphy's playing, Dolphy's musical collaborators considered his breadth enormous and maintained that he was in complete control of all the musical elements. Pianist Jaki Byard remembered:

> Eric's freedom in playing and writing is never chaos. He always makes sense, and those critics who call him disorganized should first have the chords and the overall forms of his tunes written out for them before they make that kind of accusation. Eric is very well organized, but it's not the kind of organization that is immediately apparent to people who are accustomed to more conventional ideas of form.[22]

Avant-garde Jazz and Black Activism

As the avant-garde jazz movement expanded during the 1960s, it became intimately connected to and nurtured by black nationalism and militant protest. As pointed out earlier, an increase in black ethnic pride has paralleled the history of jazz. This increase was rooted in the Harlem Renaissance and, before that, in the writings of W. E. B. Du Bois and others. Du Bois's concept of the "talented tenth"—the elite of the black population, whose achievements could inspire and "uplift" blacks as a whole—helped spur the growth of a black intelligentsia. The Harlem Renaissance

Voices of Discontent

In part as a result of blacks' frustrations in their attempt to gain equality with whites, much social and racial turbulence erupted in the 1960s. Black separatism became a significant force in the African American community as many intellectuals sought to distance themselves from what they considered to be the unyielding white power structure. These efforts were often accompanied by conscious attempts to incorporate Afrocentrism into art and everyday life: African names and clothing as well as Afro hairstyles became more common.

Despite the Supreme Court rulings of the 1950s and the 1964 Civil Rights Act, the 1960s did not see the expected improvement in the relationship between the races. In fact the separation of whites and blacks increased through the creation

of the black ghettos in U.S. inner cities during this time. The ghettos were created largely by "white flight" to the suburbs, which left blacks in decaying city centers without jobs or opportunity. Long frustrated at the ingrained racism of white society, black people grew angry at the crime, housing conditions, poverty, and lack of opportunity in the inner city. This anger fueled greater militancy on the part of many. The phrase "Black power" was coined by activist Stokely Carmichael in response to the intransigence of white society. At the same time, the Black Panther Party was formed to promote a volatile mix of race, sex, and Maoist revolution [that] coalesced in a new violent cultural figure—a photogenic caricature of black masculinity, which the New Left loved for its seditious outrageousness and "authenticity"

and which would haunt the public's understanding of young black males for the next 30 years.*

Given such tension, small events could trigger major explosions. Eventually, rioting erupted in such urban centers as Newark, the Watts section of Los Angeles, and Detroit.

Musicians aroused by political concerns also became involved in the general turbulence of the black population. Early on, in the 1940s and 1950s, jazz musicians had focused on the importance of black contributions to music. In the 1960s LeRoi Jones—who later changed his name to Amiri Baraka—made an influential contribution to American social history by writing *Blues People* (1963). In this book

* Charles Johnson, "A Soul's Jagged Arc," *New York Times Magazine,* January 3, 1999, 16.

was an early realization of Du Bois's vision (see Chapter 4). Later the bebop musicians of the 1940s upheld the importance of black achievement when they worked to separate themselves from what they perceived as the subservience of older black entertainers to the white mainstream.

In the 1950s growing activism among blacks, including the brilliant legal tactics of Thurgood Marshall, led to pivotal court victories in which societal barriers to equality were overturned. For example, the Supreme Court decision in *Brown v. Board of Education* struck a major blow against segregation in the South. Further protests against segregation, including the "freedom" demonstrations of the early 1960s, eventually led to the passage of the Civil Rights Act of 1964, which officially

Copyright © Bettmann/Corbis

The original New York City newspaper caption read: "Noted jazz trumpeter Miles Davis (left) is led into court for arraignment here, August 26th [1959]. Davis, thirty-two, was arrested for felonious assault and disorderly conduct after allegedly grappling with a policeman outside the Birdland Jazz Emporium on Broadway [where Davis was performing]. Police said that Davis suffered a head laceration when a detective hit him with a blackjack. The trouble reportedly happened when patrolman Gerald Kilduff ordered the trumpeter to clear the sidewalk. Police said that Davis refused to move and that the jazz musician wrested a nightstick from the patrolman when Kilduff took Davis by the arm to lead him to the police station."

he claimed that jazz and American popular music in general were essentially black. Baraka argued that the blues defined blacks as Americans—that is, it made them American Negroes rather than displaced Africans working in a new land. The blues, once matured, later defined jazz:

> When Negroes began to master more and more "European" instruments and began to think musically in terms of their timbres, as opposed to, or in conjunction with, the voice, blues began to change, and the era of jazz was at hand.[†]

† LeRoi Jones, *Blues People* (New York: William Morrow, 1963), 70.

In the 1960s the onset of black militancy and separatism espoused by Malcolm X and the Black Panthers was paralleled by angry claims that, although jazz was a form of black music, its economic rewards flowed to whites, its imitators. These views were forcefully argued in 1970 by Frank Kofsky in *Black Nationalism and the Revolution in Music*, in which he stated:

> Whites can learn to play jazz . . . but for most whites . . . this new accomplishment will ordinarily come later in life than if they had been raised in the traditions of the ethnic group that they now seek to emulate; and in most cases the "second language" thus acquired will always be a touch more stiff and stilted for the "outsider" than for the "insider."[‡]

Kofsky also claimed:

> The number of white musicians who have made a permanent contribution to the tradition of jazz . . . is astonishingly small. More than likely, one could count them on one's fingers. . . . It is probably safe to state that there have been more black innovators of consequence on any *two* instruments we might choose at random—trumpet and trombone, say—than there have been whites on all instruments put together.[§]

Kofsky also proclaimed his view of the essential economic injustice of jazz. He quoted tenor saxophonist Archie Shepp at length, including Shepp's succinct summary of their views: "You own the music and we make it."[‖]

‡ Frank Kofsky, *Black Nationalism and the Revolution in Music* (New York: Pathfinder Press, 1970), 17.
§ Ibid., 19.
‖ Ibid., 26.

outlawed discrimination. Leaders such as Martin Luther King Jr. were instrumental in these efforts. Unfortunately, the legal end to segregation and discrimination did not lead to immediate acceptance of blacks into the dominant society. Black militancy in the 1960s was a direct result of these developments.

This revolution in black activism anticipated a wider rebellion within middle-class society as well. Inspired by the Beat movement of the 1950s, many young people in the subsequent decade rebelled against what they considered unthinking conformity and social duty. This rebellion took particular aim at the war in Vietnam, which many people, young and old, considered pointless and unwinnable. The smaller but more visible group called "flower children" embraced the hippie lifestyle and derided their parents' sexual timidity as "uptight." *Do your own thing* became a catchphrase.

The 1960s have rightly been considered pivotal in the history of U.S. society and of the West as a whole. The civil rights movement and racial rebellion formed only one part of a general cultural upheaval. The decade witnessed increasing activism among feminists, whose roots reached back to the women's suffrage movement in the nineteenth century but whose demands now included equal access to jobs and careers and equal pay for equal work. The so-called sexual revolution together with the birth control pill challenged conventional sexual mores, leading to growing sexual activity among unmarried adults and increasingly graphic depictions of sex in novels, movies, and television.

This was paralleled by a dramatic upturn in violence and explicit language in virtually all media. The Stonewall Rebellion—the rioting incited by a 1969 police raid on a gay bar in New York—galvanized political activism for gay rights and led to a growing acceptance of what were called "alternative lifestyles." The increasing popularity of rock music and political activism by leading rock stars provided a focal point for social protest and the antiwar movement. This era of unprecedented social rebellion was reflected in jazz, in particular by musical substyles that were as uncompromising as the attitudes of its foremost musicians.

ARCHIE SHEPP

Archie Shepp (b. 1937) was one of the most vocal and articulate of the avant-garde musicians championing the cause of blacks. His album, *Fire Music* (1965), featured the piece "Malcolm, Malcolm, *Semper* Malcolm," a tribute to black leader Malcolm X. Shepp studied dramatic literature at Goddard College, where he earned his bachelor of arts degree in 1959. Originally an alto player, he switched to tenor through the inspiration of John Coltrane, with whom he eventually performed. He also worked with Cecil Taylor, Bill Dixon, Roswell Rudd, and others.

Shepp thought that free jazz ought to be a political medium. His calls for justice for blacks have not wavered through the years. In 1999 he pointed out that Jewish survivors of the Holocaust were seeking monetary compensation: "What if our people asked for compensation for all the years of slave labour?"[23]

Shepp performed on Coltrane's free jazz album, *Ascension* (1965). In addition to *Fire Music,* Shepp recorded several other important albums in the 1960s, including *Four for Trane* (1964). Eloquent in his defense of black nationalist principles, Shepp became an educator, teaching at the State University of New York at Buffalo and the University of Massachusetts at Amherst.

ALBERT AYLER

Another notable contributor to the scene, Albert Ayler (1936–1970), brought a fiercely independent style and a plethora of avant-garde techniques to the tenor saxophone. Like Shepp, Ayler worked with Cecil Taylor. *Ghosts* and *Spiritual Unity* (both 1964) were two of his most outstanding albums. His works encompassed shrieks, cries, wails, multiphonics, and other techniques that can be summed up as a "sound"-oriented approach to the instrument rather than anything one could notate easily. Unfortunately, the jazz world would lose this innovator all too soon. In 1970 Ayler disappeared for almost three weeks before his body was found in New York's East River. He most likely committed suicide, but the official verdict was death by drowning.

Ayler's "Ghosts" had followed the first wave of the avant-garde jazz recordings by artists Ornette Coleman and Cecil Taylor. Many of the avant-garde tenor saxophonists of the 1960s, such as Ayler, Archie Shepp, and Pharoah Sanders, drew much of their initial inspiration from John Coltrane. For his part Coltrane keenly supported these players, even helping Ayler, Shepp, and Sanders obtain record contracts from Impulse Records.

"Ghosts" is from Ayler's most productive period: he recorded four albums in 1964. Ayler uses the entire range of the tenor saxophone during his solo. Gary Peacock is on bass, Sunny Murray is on drums, and there is no piano, which is typical of many free jazz recordings of the 1960s.

L I S T E N I N G   G U I D E

"Ghosts: First Variation" (excerpt)
CD 2   Track 7

Albert Ayler Trio: "Ghosts: First Variation" (Ayler), from *Spiritual Unity*. ESP 1002. New York, July 10, 1964. Ayler, tenor saxophone; Gary Peacock, bass; Sunny Murray, drums.

Like many of the avant-garde recordings, the improvisation to "Ghosts" makes listening particularly challenging. What is unusual, however, is the simplicity of its melody. Drawn to this simplicity, Ayler recorded at least five different versions of "Ghosts." "I'd like to play something—like the beginning of 'Ghosts'—that people can hum," he acknowledged. "And I want to play songs that I used to sing when I was real small. Folk melodies that all people would understand."[24]

The group follows the traditional melody-solos-melody format; but following the statement of the melody, members engage in free collective improvisation. The players abandon a regular pulse, an underlying tonal center or harmonic progression, and a predetermined formal structure.

Ayler plays extremely freely, developing a repertory of extended tenor saxophone techniques, overblowing notes and distorting pitches. Peacock's solo displays his clean technique; his sound and facility on the instrument are reminiscent of bassist Scott LaFaro (heard with Bill Evans on "Autumn Leaves," CD 2, Track 8). Murray's earlier work with Cecil Taylor contributes to the "arhythmic" approach to the drums heard here. Murray often played with a stripped-down drum set, using only cymbal, snare drum, and bass drum.

Introduction—8 bars

0:00   Ayler plays an introductory melody alone, using both fixed and indeterminate pitches.

Melody—Three 8-bar phrases

0:11 Bass and drums enter, accompanying Ayler beneath the melody. The melody is shown in the transcription below. It is based on the pentatonic scale (in this case F pentatonic, consisting of F–G–A–C–D–F), a scale often used in folksongs. Note Ayler's use of slides up to pitches, as well as distorted or overblown pitches. The hummable melody is similar to Sonny Rollins's lyrical calypso melody "St. Thomas."

0:11

(Overblown pitch)

0:21 Two folklike eight-bar ideas closely related to the melody appear, setting up a clear tonal center.

Ayler tenor saxophone solo

0:44 In the first minute of the solo, Ayler vaguely recalls the melody: the pitches are often indeterminate, but the phrasing seems to echo the starting and stopping places of the melody. Careful listening reveals the use of some of the motives from the melody.

BLACK ACTIVISM AND THE AVANT-GARDE TODAY

The struggle for equality and recognition of black achievement continues today, as it probably will for some time. Among the influential younger musicians who have sought greater recognition and advocated multiculturalism is clarinetist Don Byron (b. 1958). Byron has gained a reputation for combining jazz with Jewish klezmer music in addition to other crossover experimentation. Recently, he confronted racial stereotypes with his album *Nu Blaxploitation* (1998). Byron leads a band called Existential Dred, a name that neatly evokes contemporary angst, the *Dred Scott* Supreme Court decision of 1857, and Byron's own dreadlocks hairstyle. His album *Music for Six Musicians* (1995) featured a piece called "Shelby Steele Would Be Mowing Your Lawn." (Steele is a black scholar who has written against affirmative action programs.)

Although social statement remains an important mission of the black avant-garde, its message seems less urgent forty years later. Nonetheless, the black nationalist movement continues to focus attention on the essential black contribution to jazz. Some feel, however, that this focus has gone too far, that a kind of reverse racism has resulted, with white contributions to the music undervalued and fine white players overlooked. For example, the argument of the essential blackness of jazz has been countered recently by Gene Lee's *Cats of Any Color* (1995) and Richard Sudhalter's *Lost Chords: White Musicians and Their Contributions to Jazz, 1915–1945* (1999). These books argue that jazz is an American music whose innovators have been largely black but to which whites have contributed significantly and that without whites and their input, jazz would not be the rich music it is.

In any case, the jazz avant-garde of the 1960s pioneered forceful political statements that heightened awareness of and emphasis on the African heritage of jazz.

Courtesy Morgan Collection

Cecil Taylor's dissonant, athletic pianism was and remains fiercely uncompromising.

The general atmosphere of the 1960s, in both the black community and society in general, provided a sympathetic backdrop for musical revolution.

Cecil Taylor

Because much of the free jazz of the 1960s—such as Ornette Coleman's seminal quartet and the music of Albert Ayler—did not include piano, it is interesting that one of the foremost proponents of free jazz, Cecil Taylor, is a pianist. Taylor's piano style is dissonant and athletic. His power, energy, and unlimited drive produce a fascinating and sometimes foreboding wall of dense sound blocks. Taylor's study of timpani as a youth may have influenced his rhythmic conception because his keyboard concept is as much rhythmic as melodic, with rapid-fire clusters of hands, fists, forearms, and elbows. Throughout his career Taylor has remained a controversial and fiercely uncompromising figure.

Taylor drew his wide-ranging musical ideas from both jazz and the European concert tradition. Among jazz pianists, he was initially attracted to the dense harmonies of Dave Brubeck and the linear clarity of Lennie Tristano before turning to Duke Ellington, Thelonious Monk, and Horace Silver. He was also inspired by European composers Igor Stravinsky and Béla Bartók. Thus much of Taylor's music invoked the aesthetic of the European avant-garde alongside that of traditional jazz.

Born in 1929, Taylor was raised in the Corona section of Queens, New York, and began studying piano at age five. In 1952 he moved to Boston to attend the New England Conservatory of Music, where he studied piano, popular music, and music theory. At the conservatory Taylor studied the music of European composers while exploring Ellington, Monk, Silver, and other jazz and popular stylists.

Only gradually did Taylor reject convention and arrive at his mature style: his recordings prior to 1960 are considerably closer to the jazz mainstream than his later ones are. His first album as a leader was *Jazz Advance,* a trio and quartet recording from December 1955 with Steve Lacy on soprano saxophone, Buell Niedlinger on bass, and Dennis Charles on drums. The quartet still adhered to chorus structures; for example, Duke Ellington's "Azure" was given a fairly conventional reading, although both Taylor and Niedlinger occasionally wandered outside the harmonic structure. In other pre-1960 recordings, Taylor's harmonic language was often dissonant, but he continued to explore standards—Cole Porter's "Love for Sale" and "I Love Paris," for example. As a pianist he maintained the usual technique of right-hand melody accompanied by left-hand chords.

In 1957 Taylor's engagement at the Five Spot and appearance at the Newport Jazz Festival enhanced his visibility. Unfortunately, commercial success was slow in coming, so Taylor had to work as a cook and a dishwasher to support himself.

On his two Candid albums from 1960 and 1961, *The World of Cecil Taylor* and *New York R&B* (later rereleased), Taylor's performances became decidedly less traditional. He clearly was redefining his overall approach and innovating a new conception of jazz piano. Joined by Shepp, Niedlinger, and Charles, Taylor performed passages in dynamic free rhythm. In part because of *The World of Cecil Taylor*, Taylor won the *Down Beat* "New Star" award for pianists. Ironically, at the time he was unemployed.

Because Taylor's evolving stylistic direction began to conflict with the traditional role of the drummer as timekeeper, Taylor replaced Dennis Charles with Sunny Mur-

Taylor's *Unit Structures*

The title track from *Unit Structures* was sectional and highly organized; it showed Taylor's independence from the jazz mainstream. The work was conceived in five large sections, entitled "Anacrusis," "Plain 1," "Area 1," "Plain 2," and "Area 2." Following "Anacrusis," which lasted less than a minute, "Plain 1" comprised fifteen differentiated "units"—brief sections lasting anywhere from five to forty seconds. Some of the material in these units was composed, with the instruments introduced in varying combinations. At times the horns played in a loose unison; at other times the instruments interacted polyphonically, with fluctuating tempos. Included in the work were primary and subsidiary themes that were later reprised.

The complex organization of *Unit Structures* showed Taylor's rejecting not only the traditional harmonic and rhythmic principles of the jazz mainstream but also its usual methods for generating form. It was a repudiation of both the repeating chorus structure of traditional jazz and the head-solos-head organization that long dominated the music. In place of traditional methods of determining form, in *Unit Structures* we find the following:

▶ Various "unit sections" providing an overall large-scale shape

▶ Predetermined motivic or textural ideas replacing conventional harmonic progressions

▶ A separation and independence of sections, which undermined traditional progression and development

Along with saxophonist Jimmy Lyons, who successfully translated some of Charlie Parker's bebop rhetoric into a free jazz context, *Unit Structures* also featured Ken McIntyre on bass clarinet and oboe. The inclusion of instruments not associated with the jazz mainstream was also typical of Taylor's approach.

ray (b. 1937). Murray, who remained with Taylor until 1964, tended to avoid steady meter, instead projecting a fluid and kinetic style that matched Taylor's free approach to the keyboard.

In 1966 Taylor recorded two albums for Blue Note, *Unit Structures* and *Conquistador*, with two bassists—Henry Grimes and Alan Silva—and drummer Andrew Cyrille, who worked with Taylor from 1965 to 1975. Like his predecessor Sunny Murray, Cyrille conformed readily to full-group improvisation while downplaying pulse and meter. (See the box "Taylor's *Unit Structures*.")

Taylor won increased recognition during the 1970s. He taught at the University of Wisconsin–Madison and at Antioch College in Ohio, where he recorded his solo piano album *Indent*. During the decade he was awarded a Guggenheim Fellowship and an honorary doctorate from his old school, the New England Conservatory of Music. Taylor also performed for Jimmy Carter's 1979 White House Jazz Day. His solo piano recording, *Silent Tongues*, won the 1974 *Down Beat* "Jazz Album of the Year" award in its international critics poll. In discussing his composition "Abyss" from *Silent Tongues*, Taylor pointed out the plan at work in his conception of the different registers of the piano:

> Just in the keyboard element I can, if I want to, have four or five bodies of sound existing in a duality of dimension. In other words, I might decide to have three or four different voices or choirs existing and moving with different weight propelling their ongoing motion . . . so that one can have—say that two or three octaves below middle C is the area of the abyss, and the middle range is the surface of the earth, the astral being the upper range—you have three constituted bodies also outlined by a specific range, a specific function of how the innards of these groups relate to themselves and then to each other. You have, therefore, what starts out as a linear voice becoming within itself like horizontal because of the plurality of exchange between the voices.[25]

Taylor has continued to record and perform with his ensemble, the Cecil Taylor Unit, whose membership has remained somewhat fluid. Alto saxophonist Jimmy Lyons, who began playing with Taylor in 1960, was still with the group in 1978 for their recording *Idut*, which also included trumpeter Raphé Malik, violinist Ramsey Ameen, bassist Sirone (born Norris Jones), and drummer Ronald Shannon Jackson.

Over the decades some audiences have found Taylor's music difficult or impenetrable. As one writer observed, an initial unprepared encounter with Taylor's music usually causes complete confusion.[26] Nevertheless, even the unprepared respond to the music's intensity and energy.

Sun Ra

A unique jazz personality, Sun Ra led a legendary big band called the Myth-Science Solar Arkestra—one among several of its varied but similar names. Established in the midfifties, the Arkestra played "intergalactic music" that painted "pictures of infinity." It also contained numerous musicians loyal to Sun Ra, the music, and its uniquely mystical ambience. With the players and audiences chanting "Space is the place," the band's performances were transcendental. As his reputation continued to grow, Sun Ra emerged as one of the most colorful and discussed pioneers of the avant-garde.

Sun Ra made wide-ranging contributions to the avant-garde. He was among the first jazz performers to use electric keyboards and synthesizers and was one of

Courtesy Morgan Collection

Shown here at an electric keyboard and clad in exotic garb, avant-garde bandleader Sun Ra was one of the few big-band leaders to allow free improvisation.

the few big-band leaders to encourage extensive free improvisation. The group was especially creative with percussion, exploring a large palette of sound colors with timpani, celesta, bells, chimes, and other instruments less often heard in jazz. The emphasis on unusual timbre extended to nonpercussive instruments as well: Sun Ra's saxophonists doubled on such instruments as piccolo, oboe, bassoon, and bass clarinet. As alto saxophonist Marion Brown noted, "Sun Ra plays the piano, but his real instrument is the orchestra."[27] A number of writers have suggested that, with his idiosyncratic arranging techniques and the long-term tenure of many of his players, Sun Ra was something of an avant-garde Duke Ellington.

Sun Ra, however, remained an underground phenomenon, never achieving the mainstream success that Ellington had. He was born Herman Blount in Birmingham, Alabama, in 1914 and moved to Chicago in the midforties, working as the arranger-pianist Le Sony'r Ra in a variety theater. Between 1946 and 1947, he played piano for bandleader Fletcher Henderson. He then formed his own band; among his musicians were tenor saxophonist John Gilmore, who became a long-standing associate and who would later influence John Coltrane. His first recordings from the midfifties with the Myth-Science Solar Arkestra (*Sun Song* and *Sound of Joy*) merged Ellington-like ensemble colors with an idiosyncratic hard bop orientation. They featured unusual sounds, such as the timpani solos in "A Street from Hell." The band also included timpani on "A Call for All Demons," which hilariously combined atonal improvising with a mambo beat.

The Arkestra relocated from Chicago to New York in 1960. Once settled, the group continued to rehearse prodigiously, with all of the band members becoming multi-instrumentalists, especially on percussion. As the band moved decisively toward free jazz, the players collectively improvised, often over a background of dense percussion. Indeed some compositions focused primarily on percussion.

In general, improvised solos in the Arkestra often used modal or tonal centers rather than standard harmonic progressions. On some of the recordings from the 1960s, such as *The Heliocentric Worlds of Sun Ra,* there seemed to be no prewritten music; only the general formal outline was predetermined, invoked by cues from Sun Ra.

In the 1970s the Arkestra relocated again—this time to Philadelphia—and began using the city as a base for concert performance. Their 1976 television appearance on *Saturday Night Live* increased the band's exposure. Around this time the group began performing works of Duke Ellington, Fletcher Henderson, and Thelonious Monk.

The use of microtonal melodies and electronic effects enhanced the space-age aura of Sun Ra's music, as did his flowing robes and headdresses. Sun Ra's live performances recalled the "happenings" of the 1960s, complete with the psychedelic paraphernalia. Sun Ra died in 1993.

Chicago: AACM, the Art Ensemble of Chicago, and Anthony Braxton

By the later 1920s, the so-called Second City of Chicago was eclipsed by New York as the country's jazz center. Nevertheless, Chicago's jazz scene has remained active and was especially influential during the 1950s. Tenor saxophonist Sonny Rollins took the first of his extended sabbaticals there in 1955. Saxophonist Johnny Griffin, pianist Ahmad Jamal, and Sun Ra's band were based in the city. Additionally, several young Memphis jazz players came to Chicago in the 1950s to study, including pianist Harold Mabern, saxophonist George Coleman, trumpeter Booker Little, and alto saxophonist Frank Strozier. Drummer Walter Perkins's group, MJT + 3, employed at different times many Chicago-based players, including pianist Muhal Richard Abrams. Abrams became instrumental in creating the Association for the Advancement of Creative Musicians (AACM), a school and cooperative on the South Side that became the center of Chicago's avant-garde jazz scene.

Although Abrams began as a hard bop pianist, he gradually turned his attention toward free jazz, forming the Experimental Band in 1961, a rehearsal group that met weekly. By 1965 the band evolved into the AACM, an organization that sponsored concerts and performances, and—most important—fostered self-determination for musicians. In allowing musicians to be independent of commercial promoters and agents, it promoted artistic and creative goals. Later the group also produced radio shows and brought jazz education to inner-city schools.

The liner notes to alto saxophonist Joseph Jarman's recording *As If It Were the Seasons* (1968) described the aims of the organization:

> The Association for the Advancement of Creative Musicians, a non-profit organization chartered by the State of Illinois, was formed . . . when a group of Musicians and Composers in the Chicago area saw an emergent need to expose and showcase original Music which, under the existing establishment (promoters, agents, etc.) was not receiving its just due. A prime direction of our Association has been to provide an atmosphere conducive to serious Music and the performance of new, unrecorded compositions. The Music presented by the various groups in our Association is jazz-oriented.[28]

The music was indeed jazz oriented. It was particularly indebted to the free jazz movement, as Jarman's tribute "Ornette" suggested, but it was also new in other ways. Jarman's own background in drama inspired him to add extramusical, theatrical elements to the performances. On Jarman's "Non-cognitive Aspects to the City" (from his recording *Song For*), he recited his own spoken poetry following a prelude consisting of fragmented melodic ideas and a drum solo.

Along with poetry and social statement, much of the music of the AACM explored timbre, tone color, nontempered intonation, collective improvisation, and the use of unusual instruments. It also relied on humor and surprise. Trumpeter Lester Bowie's earliest experiences were with R&B bands and the tent shows of an itinerant carnival troupe, experiences he brought to bear on his work with the AACM. His album *Numbers 1 and 2* used gongs, police sirens, and nonsense syllables sung in falsetto. In it, after someone yells "Ring the bell, man," a cowbell is played furiously. In search of freedom, the AACM players were clearly seeking a release from the conventions of traditional jazz. As Bowie noted in the liner notes to *Numbers 1 and 2:*

> Jazz, at first apart from this struggle for renewal in the western world, has come to face these "freedoms." But there is only one true freedom for us, and that is what this music seeks. The signs of the revolution permeate most of jazz today, and in Chicago there are young musicians who, desiring freedom, are beginning to know how it is created.[29]

Bowie's *Numbers 1 and 2* was made with saxophonists Jarman and Roscoe Mitchell and bassist Malachi Favors, who together became the four founders of the Art Ensemble of Chicago. Pursuing the path begun by the early AACM recordings, the Art Ensemble of Chicago relied heavily not only on free, collective improvisation but also on theater: they incorporated into their performances dramatic sketches, poetry, costumes and makeup, dance, pantomime, comedy, and parody. The group moved to Paris in 1969, recording albums for the French label BYG, including several film scores.

Rejecting specialists' roles as performers, the members of the Art Ensemble of Chicago each played several instruments. When the group moved to Europe, they took about five hundred instruments with them. On recordings such as *A Jackson in Your House,* the group mixed comical pastiche—mock Dixieland and swing—with sound explorations and free improvisations that were in part a rejection of the showy virtuosity of bebop. The recordings the group made during their eighteen months overseas revealed the varied instruments, many of them percussion, handled by the performers. A list of their instruments compiled by Ekkehard Jost shows this breadth:

- Lester Bowie: flugelhorn, trumpet, cow horn, and bass drum
- Roscoe Mitchell: soprano, alto, and bass saxophone; clarinet; flute; cymbals; gongs; conga drums; steel drum; logs; bells; siren; and whistles
- Joseph Jarman: soprano, alto, and tenor saxophones; clarinet; oboe; bassoon; flutes; marimba; vibraphone; guitar; conga drums; bells; gongs; whistles; and sirens
- Malachi Favors: double bass, Fender bass, banjo, zither, log drum, and other percussion instruments[30]

The group added drummer Don Moye, whose first recording with the band was on the soundtrack to *Les Stances à Sophie.* Moye increased the huge arsenal of percussion instruments and joined the others in wearing African hats, costumes, and makeup. The group continued to record after resettling in the United States in 1971, although the players also concentrated on their own projects. Their recordings for ECM Records included *Nice Guys* and *Urban Bushman,* the latter a double-LP live recording that showed the dramatic breadth of the group. The members of the Art Ensemble of Chicago continued to collaborate—involved in tours and projects that took them throughout the world—and stayed together for more than thirty years.

Whereas the Art Ensemble of Chicago celebrated African elements in its music and theater, the music of another Chicagoan tilted toward European formal organization. Alto saxophonist Anthony Braxton (b. 1945) joined the AACM in 1966.

Braxton's earliest influences were cool jazz altoists Paul Desmond and Lee Konitz, but after joining the AACM he began studying Ornette Coleman and John Coltrane, seeking in part to translate Coltrane's raw expressiveness to the alto. He also studied the techniques of avant-garde concert-music composers such as John Cage and Karlheinz Stockhausen.

Along with Leroy Jenkins and Leo Smith, Braxton formed the Creative Construction Company in 1967. The group explored free improvisational methods on Braxton's *Three Compositions,* recorded the following year. In 1968 Braxton made *For Alto,* his first unaccompanied alto saxophone recording. It was the first solo jazz saxophone album. Following in the footsteps of the Art Ensemble of Chicago, the Creative Construction Company traveled to Paris in 1969. The group was not particularly well received—in part, thought Braxton, because they lacked a rhythm section.

Braxton later teamed up with the stellar rhythm section of pianist Chick Corea, bassist Dave Holland, and drummer Barry Altschul. The new group, Circle, recorded a concert in Paris for ECM in February 1971. Braxton's improvisations were masterpieces of free interaction, weaving together multiphonics, unusual sonic and timbral resources, and pointillism. When Corea disbanded Circle in 1971, Braxton formed his own group, combining the bassist and the drummer of Circle with Kenny Wheeler on trumpet. Braxton's later recordings for Arista Records in the 1970s—*New York Fall 1974, Five Pieces 1975,* and *For Trio*—incorporated echoes of bebop, combined notated and improvised music, and brought together free collective improvisation, individual solos, and written ensemble passages.

As a result of his many activities, Braxton became one of the leading figures of the avant-garde. In addition to his jazz work, Braxton has written for band and large orchestra, sometimes with elements of theatricality that recall the early work of the AACM. His compositions often avoid conventional titles and use instead geometric designs, arrangements of numbers and letters, and human and animal figures. Braxton has served as a member of the faculty of Wesleyan University in Middletown, Connecticut, for many years.

Black Artists Group and the World Saxophone Quartet

Inspired by artistic independence, self-sufficiency, and many of the ideals of black nationalism—the same goals that helped launch the AACM—other cities formed creative arts organizations that embraced the avant-garde. A particularly successful group of free jazz players in St. Louis formed a cooperative organization in 1968, the Black Artists Group (BAG). Like the AACM, the BAG tutored young musicians, sponsored musical and multimedia performances, and received support from government and state grants. Although the BAG folded in 1972, three of its former members—alto saxophonists Oliver Lake and Julius Hemphill and baritone saxophonist Hamiet Bluiett—formed the World Saxophone Quartet (WSQ) in 1976. The fourth member was a Californian, tenor saxophonist David Murray.

The WSQ was unique—a versatile ensemble that turned the absence of a rhythm section to their advantage. Although the players were influenced by the free jazz of Ornette Coleman and Albert Ayler, they also relied heavily on both composed music and traditional styles of improvisation. The four saxophonists produced a remarkable cross section of twentieth-century music, incorporating elements of bebop, swing, and collective improvisation into an eclectic mix that ranged from the sound of the

Ellington saxophone section to that of Stravinsky-style ballet. Their album *Live in Zurich* demonstrated their diversity, combining swing and mambo in "Hattie Wall," bebop in "Funny Paper," and French classical saxophone quartet music in "Touchic." For improvisational sections, one or two saxophones would create an ostinato figure over which another improvised.

Bluiett's muscular, sometimes raucous baritone provided the underpinning for the group. Of the two alto saxophonists, Lake was initially influenced by bebop altoist Jackie McLean, but he later rejected the predictability of the style. Hemphill maintained a cleaner, purer alto sound. Murray was strongly eclectic, able to draw upon the entire history of tenor saxophone playing.

A long-lived group, the World Saxophone Quartet has continued to perform in recent years. They are highly effective in concert, with marked variety of programming and a lighthearted, engaging stage manner. Recent projects of the WSQ have included other musicians, especially drummers and African percussionists.

The jazz avant-garde of the 1960s, like the jazz styles of earlier eras, has inspired numerous artists and innovative approaches in our own day. After consideration of the more mainstream musical currents of the 1960s in Chapter 10 and the pop-fusion jazz of the late 1960s and 1970s in Chapter 11, we return to the avant-garde in Chapter 12 to examine its legacy.

Free Jazz Styles

TIMBRE
▶ Emphasis often on hard-edged sound
▶ Use of entire range of instrument, but upper range more prominent
▶ Wide variety of attacks and articulations
▶ Use of vocal sounds—cries, shrieks, etc.—played by instruments
▶ Extended techniques such as multiphonics on individual instruments emphasized

PHRASING
▶ Extremely irregular

RHYTHM
▶ Free use of extreme rhythms, from held notes to "sheets of sound" effects
▶ Syncopations
▶ Often lack of steady pulse

THEMATIC CONTINUITY
▶ Usually motivic

CHORD-SCALE RELATIONS
▶ Outside playing, if a tonal center exists at all

LARGE-SCALE COHERENCE
▶ Gestural, motivic, sometimes based on set-theoretical principles

Questions and Topics for Discussion

1. How did the 1960s avant-garde overturn traditional practices in jazz? Cite factors that include instruments, repertory, melody, harmony, and rhythm.

2. Who were the principal musicians of the jazz avant-garde? How did these musicians differ in terms of their level of political involvement? Was this evident in their music?

3. What were John Coltrane's three stylistic periods? In a brief biographical outline, show how his musical evolution paralleled his spiritual and professional life.

4. How did the social movements that called for integration and the greater acceptance of blacks into mainstream society affect avant-garde jazz works? Can the word *freedom* be applied to both musical and political relationships? How?

5. How did free jazz resemble the New Orleans and Chicago Dixieland jazz of the 1920s?

Additional Listening Downloads

Search for these classic jazz performances at your favorite online music store.

- John Coltrane: *The Complete 1961 Village Vanguard Recordings;* "India" (1961)

- John Coltrane: *A Love Supreme;* "Pursuance" (1964)

- Albert Ayler: *Spiritual Unity;* "Ghosts: Second Variation" (1964)

- Sun Ra: *Heliocentric Worlds, Vol. 1;* "The Cosmos" (1965)

- Archie Shepp: *Fire Music;* "Malcolm, Malcolm, *Semper* Malcolm" (1965)

- Cecil Taylor: *Unit Structures;* "Unit Structure/As of a Now/Section" (1966)

GLOSSARY

AABA song form A musical form that comprises an eight-bar theme (A) played twice. A contrasting melody (B) follows, also usually eight bars long, before the A theme returns. Quite often the second and third A sections will vary slightly.

ABAC song form A musical form in which each section is usually eight bars and has three themes (A, B, and C). Musicians often speak of the "first half" of the tune (AB) and the "second half" (AC).

acid jazz A fusion style that incorporates sampling of older jazz recordings, rap, and hip-hop grooves and techniques.

amplitude modulation Sound modulation in which the amplitude (the range of loud and soft) of the wave is modified by another wave, producing a sound vastly different from the original. *See also modulation* and *frequency modulation.*

antiphony The trading of melodic figures between two different sections of the band; the formal musical term for *call-and-response.* Listen to Track 47 of the Audio Primer CD: the trumpet and the saxophone, by trading twos, engage in a form of antiphony.

arpeggiated figure (arpeggio) A melodic fragment based on the notes of the chord harmony and played in succession. Listen to Track 2 of the Audio Primer CD to hear various arpeggios.

Arp synthesizers Among the first synthesizers made specifically for live performance.

arranger The person who plans the form of a band's performance and often notates the parts for the different instruments. *See also head arrangement.*

atonality A description of music that avoids the standard chords, scales, harmonies, and keys of tonality. It is sometimes associated with free jazz, which flourished in the 1960s.

avant-garde *See free jazz*

back-beat (change-step) A stride piano technique in which the performer breaks up the regular striding left hand with its normal alternation of bass note and mid-register chord—that is, 1-2-1-2 ("1" refers to a bass note and "2" refers to a chord). Instead, the left hand plays a more complex pattern such as 1-1-2-1/1-2-1-2 or 1-2-2-1/2-2-1-2/1-2-1-2, which is called a back-beat

(not to be confused with backbeats). Listen to Track 5 of the Audio Primer CD to hear a back-beat.

backbeats Heavy emphases on beats 2 and 4, as played by the drummer (usually) on the snare drum. (Other drums or the hi-hat can be used for quieter backbeats.) Backbeats can be added to a 4/4 swing rhythm as well. They increase danceability by clarifying the rhythm and adding to the excitement of the music.

back catalog All the recordings that a company holds in its vaults—or claims the rights to by having purchased other record labels. Many of these recordings are out of print or were never issued.

back phrasing A musical technique in which the singer momentarily delays the entry of a new phrase, in effect freeing the rhythm of a composition. Occurring most often in ballads, it generally conveys a loose feeling, as though the singer were delivering the song spontaneously.

balance The ability of a section to blend. In a well-balanced section, none of the players will be too soft or too loud relative to the others.

banjo A stringed, strummed instrument that often provided the chords in New Orleans and Chicago-style (Dixieland) jazz.

bass A low-pitched stringed instrument and one of the members of the rhythm section in a jazz band. Listen to Track 43 of the Audio Primer CD to hear an acoustic bass.

bebop A nervous, energetic style of jazz that developed in the 1940s. The term probably developed from the nonsense syllables used by scat singers to re-create the characteristic melodic phrases of the new style. Also called *bop.*

bent pitch A small glissando or slide from one frequency to (usually) a slightly higher one. On guitar it is achieved by pushing against the string on the fret board, thus "bending" it.

big band A large jazz ensemble typically including three to four trumpets, three to four trombones, four to five reeds (saxophones and doublings), and rhythm (typically piano, guitar, bass, and drums).

block-chord style *See locked-hands style*

blue note A bent, slurred, or "worried" note. Most often occurs on the third of the scale, but any note can be made "blue" by varying its intonation in a blues or jazz performance.

blues An African American folk music that appeared around 1900 and exerted influence on jazz and various forms of U.S. popular music.

blues form A basic 12-bar chord progression that may be varied depending on the blues or jazz style. The basic progression is shown in Music Example 1-7. Its fundamental harmonies are I (4 bars), IV (2 bars), I (2 bars), V (1 bar), IV (1 bar), I (2 bars). Listen to Track 11 of the Audio Primer CD to hear a modern version of blues form.

blues scale A form of scale that incorporates the principal notes used in the blues. Most often, 1–♭3–4–#4–5–♭7. Listen to the second scale played on Track 1 of the Audio Primer CD. See the box "The Character of Early African American Music" in Chapter 1 for a classic blues scale in music notation.

boogie-woogie A form of blues piano playing in which the performer maintains a driving eighth-note rhythm in the left hand while improvising blues figures in the right hand.

book *See library*

bop *See bebop*

bossa nova A Latin jazz style that developed from Brazilian music in the late 1950s and early 1960s. Stan Getz was prominent among jazz players with bossa nova hits.

break A short pause in a band's playing—usually one or two bars—to feature a soloist. Often a band will play in stop time while the soloist improvises breaks between the band's chords.

cadence The closing strain of a phrase, section, or movement. Also refers to a common closing chord progression.

cakewalk A dance involving an exaggerated walking step. In exhibitions of cakewalking, the most talented couple won a cake at the end of the evening. The cakewalk may have been an imitation of the way members of white "high society" comported themselves.

call-and-response A musical procedure in which a single voice or instrument states a melodic phrase—the *call*—and a group of voices or instruments follows with a responding or completing phrase—the *response*.

chair Each part of a section, as in first trumpet chair, first trombone chair, and so on.

change-step *See back-beat*

chart A common term for a jazz band arrangement.

Chicago jazz A type of New Orleans–style jazz created by Chicago musicians in the 1920s.

chorus Each time the performers execute or work through the form of a song, it is called a chorus—for example, once through a 12-bar blues or once through a 32-bar song.

chorus reverberation An electronic effect that guitarists use to "fatten," or fill out, sounds. The sound signal is enriched through the addition of reverb (echo) and a chorus effect (that is, added frequencies complement the sound, giving the effect of several voices or tones sounding at once).

chromatic scale A scale with all twelve notes of the Western musical system, for example, all the adjacent notes on the piano. There are twelve notes in an octave, which create a chromatic scale.

clarinet A single-reed woodwind instrument. Listen to Tracks 20 and 21 of the Audio Primer CD to hear examples of the clarinet.

collective improvisation The term often applied to the simultaneous improvising of the New Orleans (Dixieland) jazz ensemble.

comping The chordal accompaniment provided by pianists or guitarists in jazz bands. This accompaniment is often syncopated. The term *comp* is probably derived from a contraction of the word *accompany* or *complement*. Listen to Al Haig's syncopated comping behind Charlie Parker and Dizzy Gillespie on "Salt Peanuts" (CD 1, Track 24).

complete reissue The duplication of an artist's or a group's entire available body of recorded material—including errors, outtakes, and technical problems.

concerto A concert composition featuring a soloist accompanied by an orchestra or a larger ensemble.

contrafact The composition of a new melody to fit the harmonic and formal structure of a previously composed popular song.

cool jazz In part a reaction to bebop that involved more-complex compositions, slower tempos, and sometimes less overt emotional involvement.

cornet A medium-range brass instrument much like a trumpet but with a larger bore and hence a mellower sound. Heard mostly in New Orleans and Chicago jazz in the 1920s where, like the trumpet, it was a lead instrument.

countermelody A separate line that runs in counterpoint to the main melody. Like an obbligato, a countermelody is a secondary melody that accompanies the main melody. A countermelody, however, is generally heard on the trombone or in a lower voice, has fewer notes than the obbligato, and is often improvised. Another word for countermelody is *counterline*. Listen to Track 7 of the 🎵 Audio Primer CD; the piano enters in the middle register with a countermelody.

counterpoint The use of simultaneously sounding musical lines. *See also polyphony.*

Creoles of Color People of mixed black and white ancestry, often from New Orleans. Until the late nineteenth century, they enjoyed more freedom and were better educated than the general black population. Musicians from this group generally had classical training and could read musical scores.

crossover The practice of mixing musical styles and cultures. As first seen in the concert jazz of the 1920s and the third-stream practices of the 1950s, crossover can include different styles from a given culture—for example, bluegrass and classical music—or it can involve music from entirely different cultures, such as traditional Japanese music and bebop.

crossover music Music that combines jazz or jazz values with other styles and music of other cultures.

cross-rhythms The performance of simultaneous and contrasting rhythms, such as patterns with duple and triple groupings. Superimposing one rhythmic pattern on another causes a cross-rhythm to develop. Cross-rhythms are sometimes called *polyrhythms.*

cubop The mixing of Afro-Cuban music with bebop.

digital delay An electronic effect that creates an echo or a secondary sound so that a guitarist can, in effect, play several parts at once.

Dixieland The jazz style that originated in New Orleans and flourished in the late 1910s and 1920s. The Dixieland jazz band often had a front line (of trumpet or cornet, trombone, and clarinet) accompanied by a rhythm section (of piano, guitar or banjo, bass, and drums). Also called *New Orleans jazz.*

double-necked guitar A guitar that has two necks. Sometimes the second neck has twelve strings rather than the usual six.

dropping bombs A technique in which bebop drummers used the bass drum to make sharp, irregular accents in the rhythmic accompaniment.

drums The backbone of the jazz rhythm section. Usually a drum kit consists of snare drum, bass drum, several tom-toms, and various cymbals. Listen to Tracks 26–35 of the 🎵 Audio Primer CD to hear a range of drum sounds.

Echoplex A commercial electronic device that adds echo to a sound. The rate of speed of the echo can be altered to make the delay effect slight or more pronounced. This device was popular in the late 1960s and the 1970s.

elastic meter A rhythmic effect created when the soloist or rhythm section masks the strong metric downbeats so that the meter seems to be stretched. This illusion is often created when musicians play unusually long phrases that move the melodic emphasis off the expected downbeats that occur at the beginning of each measure.

extended chord tones Notes added to seventh chords to make the harmony richer and more pungent. These tones are usually ninths, elevenths, and thirteenths. Extended chord tones will usually resolve to more-stable pitches, such as roots, thirds, and fifths. Also called *tensions.*

false start An incorrect start of a performance—a musician begins playing a measure or two, then, realizing the mistake, stops abruptly.

feedback A distorted effect created when the sound coming from a speaker is picked up by an electronic sensing device such as a microphone and routed again back to the speaker. As this process multiplies, harsh electronic wails are created.

flat five *See tritone*

formula A worked-out melodic idea that fits a common chord progression. Most improvisers develop formulas especially for up-tempo improvisation because the rapid tempo does not allow time for total spontaneity. A formula is more popularly known as a *lick.*

free jazz The 1960s jazz substyle that overturned many of the traditional elements of the music. Also called *avant-garde* and the *New Thing.*

frequency modulation Sound modulation in which the frequency (the range of high and low) of the wave is modified by another wave, producing a sound vastly different from the original. *See also amplitude modulation* and *modulation.*

front line The lead (melody) instruments in early jazz bands. The front line usually included trumpet (or cornet), trombone, and clarinet. (Common use of saxophone was a later development.)

fugue A baroque form characterized by continuous counterpoint based on a principal melodic idea called the *subject.* At the beginning of a typical fugue, in a section known as the *exposition,* each voice (or part) enters by stating the subject.

full-chord style *See locked-hands style*

funky jazz A style that combines elements of gospel music and R&B with jazz. It began to emerge in the 1950s as an outgrowth of hard bop and became quite popular in the 1960s. Also called *soul jazz.*

fusion *See jazz-rock*

ghost bands Groups whose founding leaders have died but who continue to travel and work under new direction.

glissando A technique whereby notes are slurred directly from one to another, producing a continuous rise or fall in pitch.

guitar A string instrument played as either a lead instrument (through picking) or a rhythm instrument (through chord strumming). It can be acoustic or amplified. Listen to Tracks 36–42 of the 🅟 Audio Primer CD to hear examples of acoustic and electric guitars in different settings.

hard bop A jazz movement of the 1950s that drew on the speed, intensity, and power of bebop and sometimes married bop to gospel and blues-influenced music.

Harlem Renaissance A period—roughly 1921 to 1929—of outstanding artistic activity among African Americans. The movement was centered in Harlem in New York City.

harmolodics A theory of music devised by Ornette Coleman. Although its meaning is unclear, harmolodics has provided the theoretical motivation behind Coleman's work since the 1970s.

harmon mute A hollow metal mute that, when placed in the bell of the trumpet, gives its sound a distant, brooding quality. Miles Davis's use of the harmon mute from 1954 onward helped popularize its use. Listen to Track 14 of the 🅟 Audio Primer CD to hear an example of a harmon mute.

harmonic substitution The technique of replacing an expected chord with a more unusual one. Listen to Track 6 of the 🅟 Audio Primer CD to hear examples of harmonic substitution.

harmonic superimposition The technique of adding chords on top of the harmonies already present in a song, thereby creating further harmonic complexity.

head arrangement A musical plan and form worked up verbally by the players in rehearsal or on the bandstand.

hipster A young follower of jazz who affected the dress, speech, and manner of jazz musicians working in the new jazz styles of the late 1940s and early 1950s.

hot bands Jazz bands that featured fast tempos and dramatic solo and group performances, usually with more improvisation than sweet bands had. See also *sweet bands.*

inside playing The jazz technique of playing melodic lines that favor the principal notes of the harmonies. *See also outside playing.* Listen to Track 8 of the 🅟 Audio Primer CD to hear examples of inside and outside playing.

intonation The ability of a musician to reproduce a given pitch. Musicians with good intonation are said to be playing "in tune." That is, the players know how to make small adjustments in the pitch of their instruments as they play so that they match the pitches of the other players in the section.

jazz chair A player hired especially for improvisational fluency; spoken of as the jazz chair of a given section. For example, Bix Beiderbecke occupied the jazz trumpet chair in the Paul Whiteman band, as did Bubber Miley in the Ellington band.

jazz-funk *See jazz-rock*

jazz pedagogy The discipline that comprises the methods and the philosophies of teaching students how to perform jazz.

jazz repertory movement A movement since the 1980s in which ensembles devoted themselves to the re-creation and performance of the works of historically significant jazz artists. Just as classical music has an accepted repertory of great works, the jazz repertory movement is trying to establish an official canon for jazz.

jazz-rock A form of jazz that combines elements of rock (or R&B funk) and jazz. Also called *jazz-funk* or *fusion.*

lead player The player in a section who usually takes the melody or top part and occupies the first chair of the section. The lead player usually plays slightly more loudly than the other players in the section.

lead trumpet The lead chair or first trumpet player of the trumpet section. This player needs to be dominating and capable of precision, power, and control of the high register. A big band is particularly dependent on the lead trumpet.

legato The technique of playing notes smoothly in a connected manner. The opposite of legato is *staccato.*

library A band's collection of arrangements or pieces. These are usually songs but may also include larger-scale works. A library is necessary for big bands, but smaller groups may have one. Also called *book.*

lick *See formula*

locked-hands style A mode of performance in which the pianist plays a four-note chord in the right hand and doubles the top note with the left hand an octave below. The hands move together in a "locked" rhythmic pattern as they follow the same rhythm. This style is also called *block-chord* or *full-chord style*. Listen to Track 9 of the ⏺ Audio Primer CD to hear an example of locked-hands style.

LP A long-playing record that typically plays at 33⅓ rpm (revolutions per minute). LPs first became commercially available in 1948. LPs were made with polyvinyl chloride (hence the nickname "vinyl" for records) and allowed up to about twenty-five minutes of music per side.

Mellotron An electronic instrument used for string-ensemble effects in the 1970s. An early, analog sound module, the Mellotron produces notes by activating short tape recordings of a string ensemble playing each note of the scale. When a key is pressed, the tape recording of the chosen note plays.

meter A rhythmic pattern arising from regular groupings of two or three beats. These define, respectively, duple or triple meter. Most music has meter.

metric displacement A technique whereby the soloist implies or states in the melody a rhythm that seems to go against the underlying basic meter of the piece. It also can be achieved by placing melodic phrases irregularly against the underlying meter.

metronomic sense A steady rhythmic pulse, often associated with drums and with music from Africa.

microtones Pitches between the tempered notes of the chromatic scale. *See also* **nontempered intonation.**

MIDI An acronym for *Musical Instrument Digital Interface.* This standard language allows computers to control synthesizers or samplers.

minstrelsy A form of U.S. musical theater and variety show that flourished in the nineteenth century. Traveling troupes performed songs, dances, and skits based on caricatures of African Americans. Performed by both blacks and whites in blackface, minstrelsy is often considered the first distinctively U.S. musical genre.

modal jazz A body of music that makes use of one or more of the following characteristics: modal scales for improvising, slow harmonic rhythm, pedal points, and the absence or suppression of functional harmonic relationships. Significant early examples of modal jazz come from Miles Davis's recording *Kind of Blue* (1959) and the recordings of John Coltrane's classic quartet (1960–1964).

modulation Changing a sound by feeding one sound wave through another. *See also* **amplitude modulation** and **frequency modulation.**

moldy figs A term used by younger musicians and fans in the 1940s to describe older jazz fans who clung to the music of the 1920s and 1930s and derided the newer bebop style.

motive (motivic material) A short melodic fragment used as the basis for improvisation or development.

motivic cells Short melodic ideas subject to variation and development. Also called *thematic cells.*

multiphonics A technique of producing more than one note at a time on a wind instrument. Using nonstandard fingering and appropriate embouchure, the player splits the air stream into two or more parts, thus producing a multinote "chordal" effect. The technique is difficult to control, may be strident, and is generally associated with avant-garde playing.

multitracking *See* **overdubbing**

mute Device played in or over the bells of brass instruments to alter their tone. Different mutes create different kinds of effects, but a muted brass tone will usually be less brilliant than the "open" horn. Listen to Tracks 13, 14, 15, 23, and 24 of the ⏺ Audio Primer CD to hear examples of muted brass sounds.

neo-swing A popular movement in the 1990s that re-created the style of the 1930s and 1940s big bands.

New Orleans jazz *See* **Dixieland**

New Thing *See free jazz*

nontempered intonation The use of pitches unrestricted by the "equal-tempered," twelve-note chromatic scale. For example, a nontempered pitch might be a note between D and E♭. *See also* **microtones.**

obbligato A complementary melodic part, played at the same time as the main melody. In jazz the obbligato part is usually improvised. In early jazz obbligato parts were often florid, usually played by the clarinet, and sometimes improvised. To hear an obbligato-like clarinet melody, listen to Track 21 of the ⏺ Audio Primer CD.

ostinato A repeated melodic or harmonic idea that forms the basis for a section or an entire composition.

out-chorus The final chorus of a jazz performance. When exuberant, it may also be called a *shout chorus.*

outside playing The jazz technique of playing notes that depart from (or are "outside" of) the chords of a given piece. *See also* **inside playing.** Listen to Track 8 of the ⏺ Audio Primer CD to hear examples of inside and outside playing.

overdubbing A recording-studio technique that was generally available by the 1950s. The recording tape has several parallel tracks that enable musicians to record additional performance parts at later times. The added part is called an *overdub*. By wearing headphones, the players follow and "play to" the previously recorded tracks. Also called *multitracking*.

partial A series of higher notes that occurs when a note is sounded and that contributes to the timbre of the original pitch. These higher notes are based on mathematical relationships to the original note, known as the *fundamental*. *Partial* is also known as *overtone*.

pedal point A sustained or repeated bass note or drone played to accompany a melody. Also called *pedal tone*.

pedal tone *See pedal point*

pentatonic scale A five-note set that avoids the interval of a tritone and can be arranged as a series of perfect fourths or perfect fifths. The black notes of the keyboard form one such scale. Also called *pentatonic set*.

pentatonic set *See pentatonic scale*

phase shifter An electronic device that alters the sound of an instrument by altering the sound wave's shape. The resulting sound has a bubbling or slightly hard-edged quality.

piano The principal Western keyboard instrument. In jazz it functions as a solo instrument and as part of the rhythm section (usually with bass and drums and sometimes added guitar or banjo). The piano trio (with bass and drums or bass and guitar) is a common small jazz ensemble that features the piano.

piano rolls Cylinders of rolled paper punched with holes. When fed through a properly equipped player piano, the holes activate hammers that play the piano automatically.

plagal cadence A type of cadence that contains the harmonic progression IV–I (instead of the more common progression V–I). It is often used at the ends of hymns with the concluding "Amen." Plagal cadences were featured frequently in funky/soul jazz. Sometimes called *church cadence* or *Amen cadence*.

player piano A piano equipped with a mechanism that allows it to play piano rolls.

plunger A type of mute derived from a plumber's sink plunger. The rubber cup of the plunger is held against the bell of the instrument and manipulated with the left hand to alter the horn's tone quality.

polymeter The simultaneous juxtaposition of two or more musical lines in different meters.

polyphony Distinct, simultaneous musical parts. Another name for a polyphonic texture is *counterpoint*.

polyrhythms *See cross-rhythms*

portamento A smooth, uninterrupted slide from one tone to another, especially with the voice or a bowed stringed instrument.

postmodernism An attitude toward art and culture that has become common since the 1970s. It disavows some of the cerebral, audience-distancing tenets of modernism and replaces them with a freewheeling conception of culture. Some postmodernist practices blend styles and cultures; forgo structural unity as a necessity for art; incorporate older styles and genres; project an ironic, even cynical conception of art and expression; and break down barriers between popular and fine art.

race record An early recording, usually of jazz or blues and typically performed by and marketed to African Americans.

ragtime An African American musical genre that flourished from the late 1890s through the mid-1910s and is based on constant syncopation in the right hand often accompanied by a steady march bass in the left hand. Associated now primarily with piano music, ragtime was originally a method of performance that included syncopated songs, music for various ensembles, and arrangements of nonragtime music. Scott Joplin was ragtime's most famous composer.

reharmonization The bop practice of inserting different chords into the fundamental chord structure of a well-known song to freshen the interpretation and expand harmonic options for the soloist.

remastering The digital enhancement of an original recording's sound quality. It includes such techniques as filtering out extraneous noise and boosting certain frequencies.

rent party An informal gathering in the 1920s, held to help raise money to pay the rent or buy groceries. At such parties musicians would often gather and perform, sometimes in competition with one another.

rhythm changes The harmonies of the 1930 George and Ira Gershwin song "I Got Rhythm." (The final two-bar tag of the original song is omitted, so that a symmetrical 32-bar AABA plan results.) The bridge in rhythm changes consists of two-bar harmonies following a circle-of-fifths pattern that returns to the tonic. For example, if rhythm changes are performed in B♭, the harmonies of the eight-bar bridge are D7 (2 bars), G7 (2 bars), C7 (2 bars), and F7 (2 bars). The F7, as the dominant of the tonic B♭, leads back to the A section. Extremely popular since the 1930s, rhythm changes are still commonly used by jazz musicians for improvisation and composition. Listen to Track 10 of the 🎵 Audio Primer CD to hear an example of rhythm changes.

rhythm section A part of a jazz band that provides the rhythmic pulse, harmonies, and bass line. It may include any of the following: piano, guitar, bass, or drums. Early jazz bands sometimes included banjo and tuba in place of the guitar and bass. Listen to Tracks 44 and 45 of the 🎵 Audio Primer CD to hear a modern rhythm section; Track 44 has bass and drums; Track 45 adds the piano.

riff A short melodic idea, usually one to two bars long, that is repeated as the core idea of a musical passage. Sometimes different band sections trade riffs in a call-and-response format, often over changing harmonies. Usually rhythmic and simple, the riff also can provide an effective background for an improvising soloist. Listen to Track 49 of the 🎵 Audio Primer CD to hear a trumpet playing a background riff in a small-group context to back up the tenor soloist.

ring shout A rhythmic dance performed in a circle, originally derived from African religious practice. Worshipers moved in a counterclockwise direction while singing spirituals and accompanying themselves by clapping and stamping. Some historians describe the ring shout as contributing the essence of African song, dance, and spirit to African American music.

rubato The technique in which performers take liberties with a steady pulse by speeding up or slowing down the musical flow.

running the changes Improvising by maintaining mostly up-tempo eighth-note lines that articulate the chord changes in a virtuoso manner. The practice is particularly associated with bebop, where it became widespread.

samplers Electronic devices used both to sample and to play back sounds.

sampling The practice of recording sounds for musical use in playback. Any kind of sound can be sampled, from a note on an acoustic instrument, to natural sounds, to a passage of music already recorded. For playback the sound is usually activated by computer or by pressing a key on a keyboard. *See also samplers* and *sound modules.*

saxophone A single-reed instrument made of brass that is common in all jazz styles except New Orleans (Dixieland). The saxophone comes in many sizes and ranges. Listen to Tracks 16–19 of the 🎵 Audio Primer CD to hear the four most common saxophones.

scat singing A jazz vocal style in which the soloist improvises using made-up or "nonsense" syllables.

section A group of related instruments in a big band; three trumpets and three trombones might form the brass section.

sheets of sound An expression coined by jazz critic Ira Gitler to describe John Coltrane's method of playing that features extremely fast notes with irregular phrase groupings. Sometimes unusual harmonies are introduced over the given chord change.

shout chorus The climactic chorus of a jazz performance; it often occurs at the end of the piece, in which case it is also an out-chorus.

shuffle A 4/4 rhythmic pattern in which each beat is represented by the drummer playing a dotted-eighth and a sixteenth note, usually on the ride cymbal.

sideman A player who is not a lead player or featured soloist.

slap bass A technique in which the bass player percussively hits the low strings of the electric bass while picking melodies on the higher ones. This "slapping and popping" style was created by Larry Graham and subsequently imitated by jazz, funk, and pop bass players.

slash notation A method of showing the harmonies (or "chord changes") in jazz and popular music. Each slash in a measure denotes a beat. The arranger places chords over the slashes to show the beats on which the harmonies change. (See Music Examples 1-1 and 1-7 for examples.)

smooth jazz A popular form of fusion jazz that combines rock or funk grooves with an electronic ambience to create an "easy listening" feel. While improvisation may be present, the pleasant quality of the groove and the melody are its dominant features.

song plugger In the 1920s someone who performed a song, usually at a music store, to encourage people to buy the sheet music.

soul jazz *See funky jazz*

sound fields A musical effect created when coinciding melodic lines fuse into an indistinguishable web or mass of sound with irregular accentuation within each line.

sound modules Electronic devices that play back pre-recorded samples. *See also sampling.*

speakeasy A Prohibition-era nightclub in which liquor was sold illegally.

spirituals African American songs that arose in the nineteenth century and consisted of religious lyrics with folk melodies. They were often harmonized for vocal choir.

staccato The technique of playing short notes with distinct spaces between them. The opposite of staccato is *legato*.

standard A song that, unlike the vast majority of popular music, outlasts its contemporaries and enjoys a long-lasting place in current repertories. "I Got Rhythm," for example, is a standard written by George and Ira Gershwin in 1930.

step connection The principal means of stringing together the melodic and harmonic elements. The steps are often based on the scale determined by the key of the piece. This is a key element in voice leading.

stock arrangement (stock) An arrangement created and sold by a publishing company to bandleaders. Bands played stock arrangements to keep up with the latest hit songs.

stop time The punctuation of distinct beats, often to accommodate a soloist's improvisations between the band's chords.

stride piano A school of jazz piano playing based on a moving left-hand accompaniment alternating bass notes and chords with an appropriate right-hand figuration pulling or tugging at the left hand.

subject The principal melodic idea of a piece, such as a fugue.

suite A European classical musical work that has several sections, each with distinctive melodies and moods. The sections may be related thematically. Often composers will extract the most popular or most effective sections from extended works, such as operas and ballets, to create a suite for concert performance.

sweet bands Bands that played relatively less-syncopated, slower pieces, such as ballads and popular songs. *See also **hot bands**.*

swell The rapid change in volume that can be created by pushing down on or releasing the volume pedal of an electronic or conventional organ.

swing Generic term for the jazz and much popular music of the midthirties through the midforties.

swing-bass The stride-derived practice of alternating bass note and midrange chord on every beat.

syncopation The unexpected accenting of a "weaker" melody note or off-beat. Syncopation displaces the accent, or emphasis, from an expected to an unexpected position. For example, because the first and third beats are usually emphasized in each bar of a 4/4 piece, emphasizing the second beat would be syncopation. In general, syncopation involves unexpected accents occurring within a regular pulse stream. See Music Example 1-3, third measure, and listen to Track 4 of the ⓟ Audio Primer CD. The Joplin phrase is played first as it was written (with syncopation), then without.

tag A short, codalike section added to the end of a composition to give it closure.

tailgate trombone The New Orleans style of playing trombone with chromatic glissandos. The trombonist would play in the back—on the tailgate—of the New Orleans advertising wagons when the bands traveled during the day to advertise their upcoming dances. Listen to Track 25 of the ⓟ Audio Primer CD to hear an example of tailgate trombone.

tensions *See **extended chord tones***

terminal vibrato A vibrato added to the end of a sustained note.

territory band In the swing era, a band that played and toured a region around a major city that served as a home base.

texture The density of musical sound, as determined by the instruments (or voices) heard, the number of instruments, and the number of notes or sounds being played by them. Textures are often described as thick (many notes heard) or thin (few notes).

thematic cells *See **motivic cells***

third-stream music A blend of jazz and European concert music. In many instances, third-stream composers create concert works that allow for improvisation within larger-scale structures influenced by both jazz and concert music.

timbre The specific quality of a sound associated with an instrument.

Tin Pan Alley The collective name applied to the major New York City sheet music publishers. Tin Pan Alley flourished from the late 1800s until the midtwentieth century.

tonality A Western musical system in which pieces are organized according to harmony within some key or with respect to some central pitch.

trading twos, trading fours, or **trading eights** Improvisational jazz formats common since the swing era. In trading fours, for example, each soloist improvises for four bars before the next soloist takes over for four bars. Any number of soloists may participate, but most typically two to four do. Trading solos is often used to create climactic moments in performances. Listen to Track

47 of the 🎧 Audio Primer CD to hear an example of trading twos.

transcribe To write in standard, European music notation what the transcriber hears when listening to a piece of music. *See also* **transcription.**

transcription The notated version of a piece of music. Transcriptions of the same piece of music can vary widely, depending on the quality of the original sound source, the skill of the transcriber, and what the transcriber chooses to include in the notation.

tritone A diminished fifth or an augmented fourth—a popular interval in bebop melodies. Sometimes called a *flat five* by jazz musicians.

trombone A lower brass instrument that changes pitch by means of a slide. (There is also a less common valve trombone that works largely like a lower-pitched trumpet.) In New Orleans jazz, it typically provides countermelodies to the trumpet lead. Big bands often feature sections of three or four trombones. It is also an important jazz solo instrument. Listen to Tracks 22–25 of the 🎧 Audio Primer CD to hear examples of trombone playing.

tuba A low brass instrument that sometimes provided the bass part in New Orleans and Chicago-style (Dixieland) jazz. Uncommon in later jazz styles.

twelve-tone composition A twentieth-century procedure pioneered by Viennese composer Arnold Schoenberg in the 1920s. In twelve-tone composition, as it was originally conceived, all twelve pitches of the chromatic scale are arranged into an ordered *set,* also called a *tone row* or *series.*

vertical improvisation An improvisation based on the chord harmonies (stacked vertically) as opposed to the melodic contour (running horizontally).

vibrato A method of varying the pitch frequency of a note, producing a wavering sound. A vibrato brings a note to life. Heard mostly on wind instruments, strings, and vocals.

vocalese The technique of setting lyrics to existing jazz solos. Eddie Jefferson was probably the most notable pioneer of this technique, although the practice can be traced to the late 1920s.

voice leading A means of making logical melodic and harmonic sequences within an improvised solo. Step connection, a key element in voice leading, is the principal means of stringing together the melodic and harmonic elements. The steps are often based on the scale determined by the key of the piece.

wah-wah pedal A pitch-frequency filter, operated by the foot, that is usually used by guitarists or electric keyboardists. When the pedal is pressed, the note or chord being held makes a *wah* sound. (An acoustic *wah* sound can be achieved by brass players' using their left hands or mutes over the bells of their instruments.) The up-and-down movement of the pedal creates the repeated *wah-wah* effect. (Listen to Track 41 on the 🎧 Audio Primer CD to hear jazz-rock guitar with wah-wah pedal.)

walking bass A musical technique in which the bass player articulates all four beats in a 4/4 bar. The bass lines often follow scale patterns, avoiding too many disruptive leaps between notes. The walking bass is quite common in jazz, heard in all styles since becoming firmly established during the swing era. Listen to Track 43 of the 🎧 Audio Primer CD to hear a walking bass.

West Coast jazz A jazz style from the 1950s that embodied many of the principles of cool jazz as performed by a group of players centered in California.

whole-tone scale A scale with whole steps only and thus no dominant, making it impossible to form major or minor triads. There are only two whole-tone scales: C–D–E–F#–G#–B♭ and D♭–E♭–F–G–A–B. Notice that they share no notes. The scale is often associated with French twentieth-century composers such as Claude Debussy. Listen to Track 1 of the 🎧 Audio Primer CD; the whole-tone scale is the fifth scale played.

LISTENING GUIDE CD TRACKS

AUDIO PRIMER CD TRACKS

PART ONE — BASICS

1 **Scales.** Major, blues, acoustic (or melodic minor, ascending form), octatonic (or diminished), whole-tone.

2 **Arpeggios.** Various seventh chords.

3 **Melody without chords, then with chords.**

4 **Syncopation.** First four bars of Scott Joplin's "The Entertainer" as written (with syncopation), then the same four bars with the syncopation removed.

5 **Back-beat or change step.** A stride left-hand chord progression is played twice; the first time without a back-beat, the second time with a back-beat.

6 **Harmonic substitution.** A ii7–V7–I progression stated simply, then gradually embellished with extensions and tritone substitutions.

7 **Counterline/countermelody with guitar and piano.** Two blues choruses: the first chorus is performed without a counterline; the second chorus includes a counterline on the piano.

8 **Inside/outside melodic lines with guitar and piano.** A ii7–V7–I progression is played twice: first the guitarist plays inside over the chords, then he plays outside over the chords.

9 **Locked hands.** A brief demonstration of this technique.

10 **Rhythm changes with piano, bass, and drums.** A 32-bar chorus of rhythm changes.

11 **Blues changes with piano, bass, and drums.** Demonstration of blues chord changes.

PART TWO — JAZZ INSTRUMENTS AND PERFORMANCE EFFECTS

Trumpet

12 Open

13 Cup mute

14 Harmon mute without stem (Miles Davis sound)

15 Harmon mute with stem (wah-wah effect)

Saxophone Family

16 Soprano

17 Alto

18 Tenor

19 Baritone

Clarinet

20 Swing clarinet sound

21 Obbligato part in Dixieland setting

Trombone

22 Open

23 Cup mute

24 Growl effect

25 Glissando and tailgate effect

Drum Set

26 Snare

27 High tom

28 Low tom

29 Bass

30 Ride cymbal (swing beat)

31 Hi-hat with *chick* sound (foot pedal)

32 Hi-hat with swing beat; combine foot/hand

33 Sample crash cymbals

34 All drums/cymbals together in swing groove

35 All drums/cymbals with brushes in swing groove

Acoustic and Electric Guitar

36 Acoustic chords: comping

37 Acoustic melody

38 Acoustic bossa nova style

39 Early electric sound

40 Jazz-rock (fusion) sound

41 Jazz-rock with wah-wah pedal

42 Phasing, echo, and other effects

Acoustic Bass

43 Walking bass

PART THREE — BUILDING THE JAZZ BAND THROUGH SIX BLUES CHORUSES

Bass, Drums, Piano, Trumpet, and Tenor Saxophone

44 *First chorus:* Bass and drums playing alone in a swing walking style.

45 *Second chorus:* Add piano comping.

46 *Third chorus:* Trumpet solo breaks on bars 1–2, 5–6, and 9–10.

47 *Fourth chorus:* Trumpet and saxophone trade twos. Example of antiphony or call-and-response.

48 *Fifth chorus:* Tenor saxophone solo accompanied by three-quarter-note stop time.

49 *Sixth chorus:* Tenor saxophone solo accompanied by trumpet playing a background riff.

Musicians: Keith Waters (1, 2, 3, 6, 9, and all ensemble work), piano; Henry Martin (4 and 5), piano; Ron Miles, trumpet; Rich Chiaraluce, clarinet and soprano, alto, and tenor saxophones; Mark Harris, baritone saxophone; Joe Hall, trombone; Bill Kopper, guitar; Ken Walker, bass; and Todd Reid, drums.

Recorded February 12 and 13, 2001, at the Career Education Center, Denver, Colorado. Engineer: Joe Hall. Assistant engineers: Ty Blosser, Jerry Wright, and John Romero. Produced by Henry Martin and Keith Waters.